INTERMEDIARIES IN COMMERCIAL LAW

This book is the first to examine intermediaries in a holistic and systematic manner. The classical model of face-to-face contracting between two individuals is no longer dominant. Instead, deals frequently involve a number of parties, often acting through intermediaries. As a result, it is important to understand the role and power of intermediaries.

Intermediaries tend to be considered within discrete silos of the law. But by focusing upon a particular, narrow area of law, lessons are not learned from analogous situations. This book takes a broader approach, and looks across the traditional boundaries of private law in order to gain a proper assessment of the role played by intermediaries.

A wide range of jurisdictions and topical issues are discussed in order to illuminate the role intermediaries play in commercial law. For example, the continued growth of electronic commerce requires consideration of the role of websites and other platforms as intermediaries. And developments in artificial intelligence raise the prospect of intermediaries being non-human actors. All these issues are subject to rigorous analysis by the expert contributors to this book.

Intermediaries in Commercial Law

Edited by
Paul S Davies
and
Tan Cheng-Han SC

•HART•
OXFORD • LONDON • NEW YORK • NEW DELHI • SYDNEY

HART PUBLISHING
Bloomsbury Publishing Plc
Kemp House, Chawley Park, Cumnor Hill, Oxford, OX2 9PH, UK
1385 Broadway, New York, NY 10018, USA
29 Earlsfort Terrace, Dublin 2, Ireland

HART PUBLISHING, the Hart/Stag logo, BLOOMSBURY and the Diana logo are trademarks of Bloomsbury Publishing Plc

First published in Great Britain 2022

A catalogue record for this book is available from the British Library.

Library of Congress Cataloging-in-Publication data

Names: Bentham House Conference (2021 : Online) | Davies, Paul S. (Law teacher), editor. | Tan, Cheng-Han, editor. | University College, London. Faculty of Laws, sponsoring body.

Title: Intermediaries in commercial Law / edited by Paul S Davies and Tan Cheng-Han.

Description: Oxford ; New York : Hart, 2022. | "The papers in this book were presented at the UCL Bentham House Conference 2021 on 10 and 11 June 2021, which was held over Zoom. We are very grateful for the generous support of the Faculty of Laws, UCL, and to all those who participated in the conference for helping to improve the final product. That UCL conference was the first in a biennial series of conferences on different aspects of commercial law, organised in collaboration with City University of Hong Kong, Notre Dame Law School and the National University of Singapore ..." —ECIP preface. | Includes bibliographical references and index.

Identifiers: LCCN 2022022056 (print) | LCCN 2022022057 (ebook) | ISBN 9781509949090 (hardback) | ISBN 9781509949137 (paperback) | ISBN 9781509949113 (pdf) | ISBN 9781509949106 (Epub)

Subjects: LCSH: Commercial law—Congresses. | Agency (Law)—Congresses.

Classification: LCC K1004.8 .B46 2021 (print) | LCC K1004.8 (ebook) | DDC 346.07—dc23/eng/20220617

LC record available at https://lccn.loc.gov/2022022056

LC ebook record available at https://lccn.loc.gov/2022022057

ISBN: HB: 978-1-50994-909-0
ePDF: 978-1-50994-911-3
ePub: 978-1-50994-910-6

Typeset by Compuscript Ltd, Shannon

PREFACE

This project began when the editors met in London in autumn 2019, and its path to completion has been far bumpier than we could ever have predicted. As priorities have shifted, and we have all been confronted with the need to deal with various consequences of the COVID-19 pandemic, the shape of the book has continued to evolve. Understandably, some of those who originally intended to contribute to the book proved unable to do so, and we look forward to seeing their work appearing elsewhere. We hope that this book will provoke further attention to the role of intermediaries in many different contexts; there is much more to be written!

The papers in this book were presented at the UCL Bentham House Conference 2021 on 10 and 11 June 2021, which was held over Zoom. We are very grateful for the generous support of the Faculty of Laws, UCL, and to all those who participated in the conference for helping to improve the final product. That UCL conference was the first in a biennial series of conferences on different aspects of commercial law, organised in collaboration with City University of Hong Kong, Notre Dame Law School and the National University of Singapore, and we appreciate the support of colleagues from the four collaborating law schools.

We would like to thank Ben Cartwright and John Choi for excellent research assistance, Catherine Minahan for careful copy-editing, and everyone at Hart Publishing for supporting this project from an early stage. Paul would also like to acknowledge the generous support for his work from the Leverhulme Trust through a Philip Leverhulme Prize. We are very grateful to our families for their patience in allowing us to work on this book during a very difficult period.

Paul S Davies
Maidenhead
Tan Cheng-Han
Hong Kong
20 January 2022

CONTENTS

LIST OF CONTRIBUTORS

Roger Alford is Professor of Law at Notre Dame Law School and Concurrent Professor in the Keough School of Global Affairs; Former Deputy Assistant Attorney General, Antitrust Division, Department of Justice (2017–19).

Henry Chong is CEO, Fusang Corp.

Matthew Conaglen is Professor of Equity and Trusts at the University of Sydney Law School.

Paul S Davies is Professor of Commercial Law at University College London and a barrister at Essex Court Chambers.

William Day is a barrister at 3 Verulam Buildings and a Fellow of Downing College, Cambridge.

Deborah A DeMott is the David F Cavers Professor of Law at Duke University School of Law.

Jodi Gardner is a University Lecturer in Private Law at the University of Cambridge and a Fellow of St John's College, Cambridge.

Andrew Godwin is Principal Fellow at Melbourne Law School.

Louise Gullifer QC (hon) FBA is Rouse Ball Professor of English Law at the University of Cambridge, and a fellow of Gonville and Caius College, Cambridge.

Ying Hu is a Lecturer at the National University of Singapore and a JSD candidate at Yale Law School.

Rachel Leow is Assistant Professor at the National University of Singapore.

Hin Liu is Legal and Business Consultant, Fusang, and a Lecturer of Law and DPhil Candidate, University of Oxford.

Alexander Loke is Professor at the City University of Hong Kong School of Law, and Director of the Hong Kong Commercial & Maritime Law Centre.

Laura Macgregor is Professor of Scots Law at the Law School, University of Edinburgh.

Ben McFarlane is Professor of English Law at the University of Oxford and a Fellow of St John's College, Oxford.

Gerard McMeel QC is Professor of Commercial and Financial Law at the University of Reading and a barrister at Quadrant Chambers.

Sarah Paterson is Professor of Law at the London School of Economics and Political Science.

Tan Cheng-Han SC is Dean and Chair Professor of Commercial Law at the City University of Hong Kong.

Andreas Televantos is an Associate Professor at the University of Oxford and Hanbury Fellow in Law at Lincoln College.

Chee Ho Tham is Professor of Law at the Yong Pung How School of Law, Singapore Management University.

Hans Tjio is the CJ Koh Professor of Law at the Faculty of Law, National University of Singapore, and Director of the EW Barker Centre for Law and Business.

Christian Twigg-Flesner is Professor of International Commercial Law at Warwick University.

Wai Yee Wan is Associate Dean and Professor at City University of Hong Kong.

Qinzhe Yao is Counsel at Skandan Law LLC.

TABLE OF CASES

TABLE OF LEGISLATION

Australia

British Virgin Islands

Cayman Islands

China

European Union

Hong Kong

Malaysia

New Zealand

Singapore

United Kingdom

United States

1

Introduction

PAUL S DAVIES AND TAN CHENG-HAN

Commercial transactions often involve third parties. A classical model of face-to-face contracting between two individuals is no longer dominant. Instead, deals involve a number of parties, often acting through intermediaries. It is important to consider the role played by intermediaries in a range of commercial contexts. Yet beyond well-established intermediaries such as agents and trustees, the broader topic of intermediaries has received scant attention. This is a lacuna, but an understandable one given the wide range of intermediaries and the potential issues that can arise. Nevertheless, a greater awareness of intermediaries and the legal issues that are involved is of value. The chapters in this book analyse key concepts and themes, and it is to be hoped that they will provoke wider and further studies.

Situations involving intermediaries are often difficult. This is because the intermediary, Janus-like, faces two ways towards both sides of a transaction. Indeed, where any transaction concerns more than two parties, the obligations owed by intermediaries may similarly multiply. Careful analysis of different fact-patterns is therefore crucial to understand the rules that apply.

However, some general themes must be borne in mind. It is important to determine on whose behalf the intermediary acts. The intermediary may be able to act in an entirely self-serving and self-interested manner, and their only obligations may arise under contractual arrangements. In other situations, the intermediary will owe fiduciary duties to their principal, sometimes in the context of agency or a trust relationship.

Yet a blinkered view of an intermediary's duties to the party for whom they act should be avoided. The intermediary's conduct as regards the party, or parties, on the other side of the transaction must also be considered. This is an area that may drive forward developments regarding good faith in commercial law; it is invariably difficult for an intermediary to escape sanction when acting in bad faith. However, traditional private law enforcement mechanisms may prove ineffective in ensuring an appropriate balance is struck between competing interests, and there appears to be an increasingly significant role for regulation governing different types of intermediaries. The interest of regulators and legislators in the role played by intermediaries in financial contexts, for example, is both welcome and unsurprising. Similarly, there is now greater interest in and support for the regulation of internet platform intermediaries that stand at the intersection of much that is being consumed today, whether information or goods: as commercial structures increasingly employ intermediaries for reasons of efficiency and expertise, so must the law keep pace.

***

One well-established category of intermediary concerns agency. Expositions of the law of agency often draw a divide between the 'internal' and 'external' dimensions of the subject. The former focuses on the relationship between principal and agent, and the latter considers the rights of, and duties towards, third parties. In chapter 2, 'The Fiduciary Status of Agents', Matthew Conaglen concentrates upon the internal dimension and the question of whether all agents are fiduciaries. Neither the term 'agency' nor the term 'fiduciary' is free from controversy, but Conaglen's careful analysis of earlier case law concerning the accounting process in equity provides a stable foundation for some of the more recent discussion of this issue.

Determining whether a party is a fiduciary is inevitably a fact-sensitive exercise, and bold statements that all agents are fiduciaries appear too sweeping. This is perhaps reinforced by observing that the label 'agent' is often used by commercial parties to refer to a party who may not have the power to bind their principal to a contract with a third party. For example, it is increasingly common in complex commercial transactions for the parties to employ experienced negotiators to act as their 'agents' in drafting the terms of an agreement. Such negotiators have neither actual nor apparent authority to bind their principals. Yet even in those circumstances, they may well owe fiduciary obligations, albeit moulded by the terms of their relationship with their principal: it all depends on context. In any event, it seems unlikely that those branded 'agents' would be able to act in bad faith. Conaglen's thorough analysis provides support for recent decisions that conclude that some agents may be permitted to act in their own interest and therefore should not be subject to the standard fiduciary prohibitions on conflict and profit-making. This demands a very focused, fact-specific inquiry. Nevertheless, in the vast majority of situations where an agent can alter the position of their principal, the agent should owe a duty of loyalty to their principal and be considered a fiduciary – even though the scope of those fiduciary duties may be narrow.

An intermediary may also not owe fiduciary duties where they act 'ministerially'. As Rachel Leow observes in chapter 3, 'Ministerial Acts', someone appointed to undertake only 'ministerial' acts may owe relatively limited duties to their principal. The language of 'ministerial acts' is well entrenched in the law, but can mean different things in different contexts. This is problematic: using the same term to mean different things is a recipe for confusion. Leow usefully clarifies the different ways 'ministerial acts' are used in commercial law, and how the concept can be used both to explain why the intermediary does not owe extensive duties to their principal (the internal dimension) and why they should not be liable to third parties (the external dimension).

Leow concludes that it would be better if the language of 'ministerial acts' were used to refer only to acts that do not involve the intermediary's discretion, trust or confidence in performing them. This definition may assume greater importance as machines (automatically) carry out various 'ministerial' tasks. Narrowing the scope of 'ministerial acts' in this way could also help to clarify existing private law doctrine. So, for instance, there should be no need to talk of 'ministerial receipt' in the context of claims for knowing receipt. This would be welcome: the idea that a recipient who knowingly, or unconscionably, receives trust property should be permitted to escape liability simply because they are acting for a principal is a blunt and unsatisfactory tool to protect financial institutions from private law claims.

In chapter 4, 'Justifications for and Limitations on Interventions by Undisclosed Principals', William Day considers an important aspect of the 'external dimension' of agency and vexed questions surrounding undisclosed principals. In particular, Day considers whether the 'Intervention Rule' is justified, under which an undisclosed principal may sue the third party under the contract, and may in turn be sued if either the agent or principal fails to perform their side of the bargain. The latter has been said to afford the third party an 'unexpected godsend'[1] as soon as they learn about the undisclosed principal. The former may seem just as generous to the principal.

The Intervention Rule is well-entrenched, but Day gives fresh reasons to re-evaluate its basis and questions its continuing importance, arguing that the difficult decision in *Said v Butt*[2] should be sidelined. Day highlights that some recent decisions have been very willing to find that the rule has been excluded by implication. This raises tricky questions about how easy it should be to exclude the rule, balancing considerations such as the reasonable expectations of the parties and commercial certainty. Where the personality of the contracting parties is objectively immaterial, it may be an uphill struggle to argue that the Intervention Rule should be excluded. Interestingly, Day suggests that the effect of undisclosed agency is that the principal is subject to a *non*-contractual liability to the third party created by the exercise of the agent's authority and that, by authorising the agent so to act, the principal obtains a *non*-contractual power to enforce the agent's contractual rights against the third party. This would have an impact upon the remedies available against the undisclosed principal by the third party, for example: the orthodox view is that the remedies are contractual in nature, but again this would need to be revisited under Day's approach.

Day's chapter underscores the importance of party autonomy, and a desire to ensure that parties are not bound (through intermediaries) to other parties to whom they did not (expressly) agree to be bound. Gerard McMeel picks up the theoretical debate about the basis of important aspects of agency in chapter 5, 'Agency Theory Revisited and Practical Implications'. McMeel illustrates the importance of public policy in explaining commercially significant doctrines such as apparent authority, and that agency law is not solely explicable on the basis of the parties' consent. This is a further reason why agency law cannot readily be subsumed within other private law compartments and should be viewed as an independent subject, albeit under the broader umbrella of intermediaries. The law of agency has developed pragmatically in response to evolving commercial pressures, and continues to display the flexibility required to ensure it matches up to modern commercial structures.

One area on which McMeel focuses as an illustrative example is section 39(3) of the Financial Services and Markets Act 2000, which addresses some of the problems that arise where self-employed individuals or independent corporate intermediaries

[1] *Armstrong v Stokes* (1872) LR 7 QB 588, 604 (Blackburn J).
[2] *Said v Butt* [1920] 3 KB 497 (KBD).

are appointed representatives of either a product provider firm or a financial advisory network. Section 39(3) provides:

> The principal of an appointed representative is responsible, to the same extent as if he had expressly permitted it, for anything done or omitted by the representative in carrying on the business for which he has accepted responsibility.

This has given rise to difficult questions of interpretation, and McMeel is critical of decisions[3] that have not interpreted this provision to provide a safeguard to consumers who deal with appointed representatives, such that they are ultimately unable to seek redress from the party that granted permission to the appointed representative in the first place. The desire to ensure satisfactory redress for those who are wronged by intermediaries from those who cloak the intermediaries with authority is understandable. However, there is also the pragmatic consideration that Independent Financial Advisers (IFAs) increasingly find it difficult and expensive to obtain indemnity insurance: if IFAs were unable to afford proper insurance, that would lead to judgments that could not be enforced, and to a reduction in consumer choice, perhaps even leading them to unregulated 'introducers'. These are not easy considerations for a court to grapple with, and it is to be expected that, beyond the courts, regulators and legislators will continue to take a keen interest in this area.

***

Improvements to the infrastructure underpinning the Internet, most notably high-speed fibre-optic backbones and last-mile broadband access available at low cost, together with the rise of Internet-enabled mobile devices, have led to high Internet penetration rates, cloud computing and an 'always-on' culture, with far-reaching effects on human consciousness and social interaction. Online content and services have proliferated as a consequence, so that today many people socialise, obtain news and entertainment, and transact online. Businesses are also heavily reliant on the Internet today. In many industries, traditional intermediaries and gatekeepers, such as news agencies, broadcasters, and bricks and mortar retailers, have found themselves diminished by Internet platforms that have emerged as powerful intermediaries and gatekeepers.

While this has given rise to many benefits, it has also led to an upsurge in criminal activity and other socially undesirable activities online. Many of these activities are not new, but their effects are now capable of being magnified exponentially, thereby causing far greater regulatory concern. A good example relates to disinformation and misinformation. Where an individual's means of reaching out to large groups of people are limited, the capacity to spread false information is restricted. Broadcasters and news agencies have the means to do so but are bounded by the need to preserve their reputations for integrity and accuracy. Less reputable ones may not care about their reputations, but their stories have less credibility to begin with. In any event, many jurisdictions have laws that allow for some degree of regulation of broadcasters and news agencies, and can take action in serious cases of disinformation and misinformation. In the real world, the most pernicious spread of false information is likely

[3] Notably *Anderson v Sense Network* [2019] EWCA Civ 1395, [2020] Bus LR 1.

to be state-sponsored, but that can be mitigated in places where the press is relatively free. However, where every person has the means to disseminate information, and the ability for others to spread such information is virtually costless, the spread of false information is a much greater problem today.

Another example involves the dissemination of terrorism-related material and propaganda, often with a view to recruiting active participants to the cause. Online social media platforms have been frequently used to such ends, as outlined by Ying Hu in chapter 6, 'Platform Liability for Terrorist Activities'. They have many advantages, including anonymity, network effects and low cost. The social costs imposed by activity on online social media platforms are increasingly leading to calls for some form of gatekeeper liability to be imposed on such platforms. Sometimes these platforms are the lower-cost providers able to detect content that facilitates harmful terrorist activities, which the platforms can then remove. But they are also unlikely to have sufficient incentives on their own to take adequate steps to curb undesirable activities. Given these factors, there is a prima facie case for some degree of oversight or regulation, including imposing some degree of gatekeeper liability. Notwithstanding this, the chapter posits that imposing such liability can only be justified if the benefits of imposing such liability outweigh those costs. Such costs could include a less vibrant and competitive ecosystem if smaller and less established platforms do not have the financial or human resources to effectively detect unlawful use of their services. There are also concerns about over-removal of content and the deleterious effect on free speech, as well as potentially significant litigation costs that have to be borne by online platforms. Hu suggests that, taking these considerations into account, a platform should only be liable for content if it has knowledge that the content is likely to cause serious harm to others. At the same time, online platforms should be subject to rules that incentivise them to monitor harmful content on their platforms.

While few will argue with the latter, the former arguably sets the standard too high. Also, given the risk of terrorist activity today and the highly deleterious effect of it, the burden may be on online social media platforms to establish clearly that the costs of imposing oversight on them outweigh any benefits. This, it is suggested, will be a heavy burden.

Another undesirable outcome of the rise of Internet platforms has been the abuse or potential abuse of a dominant market position. This is well illustrated by Roger Alford in chapter 7, 'How Intermediaries Entrench Google's Position in the Advertising Display Market'. Focusing on Google and the online advertising display market, Alford explains that this market benefits from significant network effects that entrenches the market power of a dominant intermediary such as Google. It has monopoly power on the sell side, the buy side, and the exchange and adjacent markets. Despite the inherent conflicts of interest that this creates, Google uses its monopoly power throughout these different markets to advantage itself at the expense of its own clients. It leverages its power through its intermediaries, strategically located in different segments of the ad tech stack to exercise market power. In almost every case, the function of these intermediaries is to advantage Google rather than to enhance consumer welfare or promote competition.

To address Google's anticompetitive conduct, Alford outlines two possible responses. The first, unsurprisingly, is legislative, which features in a number of the other chapters dealing with online platforms. Indeed there are proposals in the United States (US)

House of Representatives to make it illegal for companies to give preferential treatment to their own products over the products of a competitor hosted on the same platform, thereby discouraging discriminatory treatment against business competitors. The other avenue is litigation, particularly actions that allege breach of competition law. There are existing cases underway, but one disadvantage of this response is that litigation is usually a long-drawn-out affair that can take many years to resolve. Accordingly, while the prospect of litigation can exercise a restraining effect on dominant platforms, the length of time taken to come to a conclusion could lead to a situation where the market has moved on, rendering the practical effect of the result moot save for a substantial financial penalty imposed on the platform.

Many Business-to-Consumer (B2C) e-commerce platforms exist, and some of the more established include Alibaba's TMall, Farfetch, Mercado Libre, Sea Limited's Shopee, and Shopify. But perhaps the best known and most established is Amazon.com. Focusing on Amazon.com in chapter 8, 'The Platform as Agent', Deborah DeMott discusses the unsettled US law around products liability when goods sold through transactions intermediated by online platforms lead to physical harm when a defect in a product causes personal injury. The uncertainty arises from how to characterise such a platform. Is it a seller, an agent on behalf of third-party sellers, a neutral provider of services or a conduit for information? Unsurprisingly, how a B2C platform is characterised will determine if it incurs any liability for defective products sold on the platform. In the case of Amazon.com, some uncertainty has arisen because retail sales via its platform take place in an environment characterised by its all-encompassing participation, in which it serves as the face of the sale rather than simply connecting buyers to external vendors. Related to this, it is the sole channel of communication for customers and third-party sellers on its website. Also, unlike many other e-commerce platforms, a significant portion of its sales are goods from inventory it owns.

The Amazon model has led to mixed results in products liability cases for defective goods purchased that have led to personal injury. Cases accepting Amazon.com's argument that its business model places it beyond the reach of products-liability law may emphasise, in relation to goods sold for third parties, that it does not hold title to goods sold via its platform, or that its capacity to control product quality is limited, or that it does not fit within definitions – in particular that of 'seller' – of actors who are subject to liability. Other courts were not so persuaded, for instance, that Amazon.com was only an 'interactive computer service provider' under a provision in the federal Communications Decency Act that grants immunity to providers for claims arising from their publication of information created by third parties, or that it was not a seller of goods that were shipped directly to the plaintiff by a third-party seller.

In DeMott's view, Amazon.com is not a tangential participant in the business of selling. Its omnipresence in the transactional environment its platform creates is integral to sales effected through the platform. In this regard, she suggests that introducing insights gleaned from agency doctrine can enrich and deepen the analytic framework. The doctrines and vocabulary of agency law that address the consequences of constructing an appearance are instructive in assessing responsibility for creating the widely-held perception that Amazon.com is the seller of goods on its platform subject to a seller's ordinary responsibilities for product liability. For instance, like an agent acting for an undisclosed principal, it may be a party to the contract just as its principal is. The more vexed question is whether its principal can disclaim liability if Amazon.com acted outside the scope of its authority. This brings us to the difficult case of *Watteau v Fenwick*,[4] where an undisclosed principal was liable for acts of its agent outside authority even though there could have been no manifestation of authority to the third party given that the latter did not know of the existence of any principal. However, it may be that in practice this will not be an issue, as the contractual terms between Amazon.com and its third-party sellers are likely to repose a great deal of authority in Amazon.com. Where it is clear to the purchaser that Amazon.com is merely an intermediary, the doctrines of apparent authority and apparent agency under US law may also constrain third-party sellers from denying the consequences of sales through the platform.

Moving beyond B2C platforms, particularly the less common Amazon.com variety, to platforms more generally, in chapter 9, 'Online Intermediary Platforms and English Contract Law', Christian Twigg-Flesner focuses on the question of whether contract law can sufficiently put limits on the ability of Online Intermediary Platforms (OIPs) to act without constraints vis-à-vis users, whether suppliers or consumers. Successful platforms can wield a substantial amount of market power though network effects as a result of the two-sided markets in which many operate. This leaves them with considerable ability to determine the terms of contracts entered into with users. Aside perhaps from the possible control over an OIP operator's exercise of discretionary powers under contracts entered into with its users, Twigg-Flesner expresses the view that the ability of contract law to constrain OIPs from fully utilising contract law in their favour is limited.

Given this, regulatory responses are in his view likely to grow in importance. One such response is the European Union's Regulation 2019/1150 on promoting fairness and transparency for business users of online intermediation services. This implements a specific regulatory objective aimed at limiting the unfettered freedom of an OIP operator by regulating aspects of the contract between said operator and its business users, rather than by imposing a set of obligations directed at the operator's conduct. Examples of this are that the contract must set out how access to the OIP might be suspended, terminated or otherwise restricted, and information provided about additional distribution or marketing channels through which the OIP operator might market the goods and services offered by business users. The objective is not to impose substantive obligations but to increase transparency on the part of the OIP. However, where the contract provides the OIP with certain powers, the exercise of such powers is controlled by the Regulation. For instance, prior to taking a decision to restrict or suspend a business user from the platform, a statement of reasons must be given no later than the moment when this decision becomes effective. If the decision is to terminate the contract, a minimum of 30 days' notice must be given together with reasons. Some requirements are also imposed to ensure that contractual relations are conducted in good faith and based on fair dealing, such as requiring that an OIP operator must not impose retroacting changes to the terms of the contract.

[4] *Watteau v Fenwick* [1893] 1 QB 346.

As Twigg-Flesner points out, how some provisions in the Regulation might co-exist with existing principles of contract law will have to be thought through, for example the exercise of an OIP operator's discretion with respect to restriction, suspension or termination with how the courts police the exercise of discretion under the common law, and the remedial consequences of a breach by an OIP operator of one or more of the obligations inserted into the terms and conditions by the Regulation or some other regulatory measure. Twigg-Flesner concludes that it is likely Parliament will ultimately have to step in to address more of the legal challenges of online platforms. The editors believe this is inevitable. We are in an era of significant and rapid technological change, and the typical development cycle of the common law as well as its present state may not be best placed to resolve many of the issues that have arisen and will emerge.

In chapter 10, 'Agency, Artificial Intelligence and Algorithmic Agreements', Tan Cheng-Han also considers the strain that technology can place on existing common law principles. Like chapter 9 on 'Online Intermediary Platforms and English Contract Law', he first considers the role of contract law, but in the context of agreements entered through a platform's use of artificial intelligence, where the algorithm used by the platform has operated in error and no human input was involved. In a decision of the Singapore Court of Appeal in *Quoine Pte Ltd v B2C2 Ltd*,[5] the majority held that there was no operable mistake that vitiated such contracts, as the trades were entered into pursuant to deterministic algorithmic programs that acted exactly as they had been programmed. In any event, even if there was an operative mistake, the respondent had no requisite knowledge of the mistake as the trades were executed in accordance with its algorithm without any human intervention. The evidence did not suggest that the respondent's algorithm had been designed to take advantage of mistakes of the kind that arose in *Quoine*. From a doctrinal perspective the decision fits into existing notions of unilateral mistake in common law, but it is difficult not to sympathise with the dissenting judgment of Mance IJ that the law must be adapted to the new world of algorithmic programmes and artificial intelligence in a way leading to results that reason and justice would lead one to expect. It is suggested that the final word on this is yet to be written, and future courts may prefer the more robust approach of Mance IJ.

The potential difficulties that the law may face in this new world of algorithms powered by artificial intelligence has led some commentators to suggest that platforms/algorithms/artificial intelligence (collectively 'platforms') should be equated as agents at law, so that agency principles can assist in determining the rights and obligations (if any) of the parties that are brought together through such intermediation. While it is possible that in some instances the entity that owns or licenses the platform may be an agent,[6] the argument goes further than this and equates the platform itself as an agent. Tan is sceptical of this for a variety of reasons, not least because the law as it stands requires a legal agent to have legal personality, and this will require legislative

[5] *Quoine Pte Ltd v B2C2 Ltd* [2020] SLR 20.
[6] See *Ruscoe v Cryptopia Ltd* [2020] 2 NZLR 809.

intervention as the common law has been reluctant to ascribe such personality to non-human entities.

***

Another area that seems likely soon to require regulation concerns crypto-assets, which are the subject of Hin Liu, Louise Gullifer and Henry Chong's chapter 11 on 'Client-Intermediary Relations in the Crypto-Asset World'. The spot-trading volume for crypto-assets is roughly equal to that of global equities, and is increasingly well-established in the commercial sphere. Most crypto-assets are held in ways involving intermediaries but, despite increasing litigation, there is little certainty as to the possible legal relationships that can arise between crypto-asset intermediaries on the one hand, and clients such as investors on the other. The authors rightly observe that the nature of the legal relationship will depend upon the intention of the parties, so in some situations there may be an outright transfer of title, or a mere contractual obligation, but in most circumstances the likely legal relationship will involve the venerable trust. The authors sensibly reject the idea that a bailment relationship could exist between a client and an intermediary of crypto-assets, since the common law does not allow a party to create a bailment of an intangible asset. Even less appealing is the idea of a 'quasi-bailment'; the unhappy history of 'quasi-contract' illustrates the problems that can arise when fictions are introduced into foundational areas of private law, and such a concept is simply unnecessary. If crypto-assets are a recognised form of property, they can be held on trust.

However, that premise has not yet been thoroughly tested. Cases seem to have simply accepted the proposition that, in principle, a crypto-currency *could* be held on trust without this being challenged.[7] Yet the public and private keys necessary for crypto-assets such as Bitcoin to function may be viewed as essentially forms of information, which is not (normally) thought of as proprietary. It was (and perhaps still is) a feature, rather than a bug, of Bitcoin that it is unregulated, and largely operates outside the legal system. Nevertheless, as a matter of commercial reality, the direction of travel is clearly shifting towards acceptance of a need to regulate digital asset intermediaries, as Liu, Gullifer and Chong point out. But it may require legislation, or at least suitable litigation where the point truly needs to be decided, to persuade some doubters that crypto-assets really are a form of property that can be held on trust.

The use of trusts and sub-trusts is of crucial importance in the context of intermediated securities.[8] The relevant intermediary may only have an equitable interest in the shares they hold on trust. In those circumstances, if the intermediary's equitable interest is transferred to a third party, can that third party avail itself of the defence of bona fide purchaser for value without notice? The instinctive response is 'No', since the third party does not acquire legal title. However, in chapter 12, 'As Complex as ABC? Bona Fide Purchasers of Equitable Interests', Ben McFarlane and Andreas Televantos,

[7] See recently *Zi Wang v Graham Darby* [2021] EWHC 3054 (Comm).
[8] See generally L Gullifer and J Payne (eds), *Intermediation and Beyond* (Oxford, Hart Publishing, 2019).

following a thorough review of the history of the bona fide purchaser defence, argue that the response should really be 'Yes'. This relatively modest extension of the rule would be commercially desirable given the prevalence of sub-trusts where securities are held by intermediaries.

It would, however, take a bold judge to adopt the authors' approach – at least below the level of the Supreme Court. The traditional requirement that the bona fide purchaser defence only protects those who acquire legal title is too well-engrained for it to be abandoned by puisne judges. But legislation in this area would be welcome. The importance of protecting third parties who deal with intermediaries is clear, and this small, incremental extension of the bona fide purchaser defence would be valuable.

The role of good faith is also important in the context of partnership, as recognised by Laura Macgregor in chapter 13, 'The Partner's Fiduciary and Good Faith Duties: More than Just an Agent?'. In a similar vein to Conaglen, Macgregor notes that it is too quick simply to assume that all partners owe fiduciary obligations. As active participants in their own business, partners are unlikely simply to sit back and trust the work of their fellow partners; nevertheless, as with agency more generally, in the vast majority of cases fiduciary obligations will probably arise. And even if the relationship is not fiduciary, it seems likely that obligations of good faith will arise. The development of good faith in the law of contract in both England and Scotland has reached an interesting juncture; in *Al Nehayan v Kent*,[9] Leggatt LJ was clear that even though a joint venture did not give rise to fiduciary obligations, meaningful duties of good faith could still bite under the contract. These principles of good faith could help to inform how new types of partnership, such as the Private Fund Limited Partnership, could operate.

Debt collectors are one type of intermediary that often does not seem to act in good faith as regards third parties. This is explored by Jodi Gardner and Chee Ho Tham in chapter 14, 'Debt Collection and Assignment of Debts: Navigating the Legal Maze'. Debt collection is a significant and fast-growing industry in the United Kingdom, dealing with £200 billion in loans. Debt collectors are an important intermediary in contracts between creditors and debtors. Generally, a debt-collecting firm 'purchases' the debt from the original creditor at a significant discount and then obtains a profit from collecting the original debt in full, often with additional fees and charges added.

The freedom of creditors to assign their debts is important. Receivables financing helps businesses to ensure necessary cash flow; engaging debt collectors as intermediaries can be a commercially efficient means of shifting the risk of non-payment on to the intermediary, whilst still ensuring some of the money owed by the debtor is received by the creditor. However, as the authors point out, this can have a deleterious effect upon individual debtors, particularly those already in financial distress, which may be exacerbated by the COVID-19 pandemic. It is unlikely that private law litigation will be able to take into account the wide range of policy factors in play here; moreover, the sums owed are typically small and unlikely to be the subject of appellate consideration. If individual debtors need further protection, and if there were to be restrictions on a creditor's ability to assign its debts, then legislation (or more stringent regulation) would be required.

[9] *Al Nehayan v Kent* [2018] EWHC 333 (Comm), [2018] 1 CLC 216.

Further regulation may also be required of those intermediaries providing financial advice to individual consumers. In chapter 15, 'Financial Wellbeing – the Missing Link in Financial Advice under Private Law and Statute', Andrew Godwin, Wai Yee Wan and Qinzhe Yao argue that current regulation is too focused on the process of giving advice, rather than on outcomes. The authors examine the challenges inherent in achieving good consumer outcomes in the area of financial advice, and how those challenges might be overcome through the adoption of a statutory duty to consider financial wellbeing. Using Australia as a case study, they argue that incorporating the concept of financial wellbeing into the regulatory framework would be advantageous for two reasons. First, it would give substance to, and assist to operationalise, the existing responsibilities and duties of financial advisers under private law and statute, such as the obligation to act in the client's 'best interests' and the obligation to provide advice that is appropriate to the client. This is because it would enable advice to be tailored to individuals and households by reference to their own financial wellbeing, and would therefore direct attention towards outcomes and beyond the traditional focus on conduct obligations and the process for complying with those obligations. Second, the inclusion of financial wellbeing as a factor in financial advice would enable consumers to make financial decisions on an informed basis and to assume an appropriate level of responsibility for the financial decisions they make since they would be in a better position to determine outcomes.

The concept of financial wellbeing would, accordingly, act as a yardstick against which the appropriateness of financial advice and the satisfaction of the 'best interests' obligation could be measured. Admittedly, it seems difficult to define 'financial wellbeing' with great precision, but given the difficulties consumers face in even formulating the 'correct' questions to ask their advisers, it is appropriate to go further than simply demanding that advisers adhere to their instructions. From a regulatory perspective, it would be desirable for financial institutions and advisers to disclose how they implement the financial wellbeing framework and satisfy continuous reporting requirements by reference to an agreed set of indices for financial wellbeing.

***

While commercial life benefits significantly from the use of intermediaries, it also brings about costs, including those that are borne by third parties when the acts of intermediaries are not binding on their principals. This arises not only in three-party situations but also in two-party cases involving the indoor management rule and rules of attribution. In chapter 16, 'Adjudicating Intermediary-Related Losses', Hans Tjio explores how informational costs on third parties can be reduced without unduly increasing the costs of adjudication. He rightly points out that much of the work today in resolving disputes over the acts of intermediaries is done through the doctrines of notice and burden of proof. This can often be onerous for third parties, and can increase overall transactional costs unless principals are in some way incentivised to control agency costs. He suggests that there needs to be more responsibility placed on principals to disclose information and greater use of technology for more notice-creating mechanisms to ease the informational burdens of third parties. An analogue to the latter suggestion can be found in other areas, such as from advocates of the use of technology to reduce harmful activity online. A further suggestion that also deserves consideration is that perhaps it is time to develop notions of proportionate liability, so that in certain cases a principal ought to bear some responsibility for the third party's belief even if the third party is to bear primary responsibility for their incorrect premise. This may incentivise principals to lower agency costs themselves *ex ante*.

While the focus on intermediaries is often targeted towards the facilitation of commercial enterprise, intermediaries perform other roles as well. In chapter 17, 'Intermediaries as "Gatekeepers" in International and Domestic Regulation' and chapter 18, 'A Fine Balance: Insolvency Practitioners and the Leveraging of Intermediary Power', Alexander Loke and Sarah Paterson explore the gatekeeping role of intermediaries in financial markets and the insolvency context respectively. As Paterson points out, core characteristics of any gatekeeping intermediary are independence and integrity. Yet, as both chapters highlight, actual and potential conflicts of interest are never far away and require measures to maintain a fine balance. In the case of capital markets gatekeepers such as auditors and credit-rating agencies, the risk of reputational loss has been found wanting because business considerations often trump reputational risk. This has led to legal reform, giving rise to more regulation and oversight, sometimes through new regulatory organisations such as the Public Company Accounting Oversight Board. To this the editors would add that clearer and stricter rules can also play an important role in providing gatekeepers such as auditors with a shield with which to resist pressure brought by clients. The relatively successful regulation of financial intermediaries in global anti-money laundering and counter-terrorism financing also illustrates the effectiveness of even soft norms where real consequences follow non-compliance. Loke's chapter is a sobering reminder of the limits of intermediary self-regulation.

Paterson points out that the way in which insolvency practitioners leverage their intermediary power to get more work is under-theorised. In recent years, there have been complaints that although the insolvency practitioner in legislation governing Company Voluntary Arrangements (CVAs) is conceived of as a gatekeeper intermediary between companies in financial distress and creditors, the objectivity of insolvency practitioners may be impacted by their role as advisers to companies that approach them for assistance in developing a viable proposal. Yet curiously, even if this amounts to gatekeeper failure, it does not appear that anyone has been harmed by it. In part this is because CVAs may be contested, and landlords can exercise rights to break the lease and re-enter. The courts have also held that CVAs cannot remove a landlord's right of forfeiture. It is argued that insolvency practitioners must take their statutory intermediary gatekeeper role seriously if they wish to retain their privileged status in the fight for insolvency work. If they do not, this will amount to a breach of duty and may lead to further calls for regulation or the involvement of others in the process. It is a timely reminder that exogenous calls for reform ever threaten the roles of gatekeeper intermediaries who do not discharge their functions adequately.

2

The Fiduciary Status of Agents

MATTHEW CONAGLEN*

This chapter is concerned with whether agents owe fiduciary duties to their principals. To many, that question will sound odd, as undergraduate law students are uniformly taught that the relationship between an agent and his or her principal is one of the settled categories of 'accepted fiduciary relationships'.[1] However, there are indications in the case law, stretching back well into the nineteenth century, that agents are not necessarily fiduciaries vis-à-vis their principals. The object of this chapter is to examine that material, with a view to understanding and explaining it. These cases reveal a number of important points about agents, fiduciaries and also accounting in equity; while agents are normally fiduciaries, instances can be identified where that is not so.

The rather cryptic discussions of non-fiduciary agents found in earlier case law were driven predominantly by the peculiarities of the accounting process in equity, but those dicta still require explanation. Further, while the more modern dicta are also somewhat enigmatic, it is suggested that, on closer inspection, they are the result of conventional principles of agency and fiduciary doctrine. Thus, one reason for agents' not always being fiduciaries is that the 'agency' label has been misapplied to the relationship between the parties, which is common in business, in part because of a misapprehension as to the meaning of the concept of agency and in part because it can be difficult to determine whether the circumstances of a given relationship did in fact create an agency relationship. A second reason involves the application of the recognised proposition in fiduciary doctrine that the scope of a fiduciary's duties is moulded to the circumstances of the relationship between the parties, and those circumstances may indicate that fiduciary duties were not appropriate (or not appropriate in their normal form) to the particular relationship at hand, notwithstanding that it involved agency.

* I am grateful, with the normal disclaimer, to Jamie Glister, Jeff Gordon, Jess Hudson, Joellen Riley and Andreas Televantos for helpful comments.

[1] *Hospital Products Ltd v United States Surgical Corp* (1984) 156 CLR 41, 96.

I. The Issue

There are, of course, countless instances over several centuries of case law of agents' being held liable for breach of fiduciary duty, particularly applying the core fiduciary prohibitions on making a profit from the fiduciary position[2] and on acting with a conflict between the fiduciary's personal interest and the duty owed to his or her principal.[3] Lord Thurlow explained the agent's fiduciary liability in *York Buildings Co v Mackenzie*:

> [I]t is exceedingly manifest that the common agent did take upon himself the employment of carrying on the sale to the utmost advantage for the benefit of the creditors … That being your situation, it is utterly impossible for you to maintain (perform?) that duty in such a manner as to derive an advantage to yourself. This seems to be a principle so exceedingly plain, that it is in its own nature indisputable, for there can be no confidence placed, unless men will do the duty they owe to their constituents, or be considered to be faithfully executing it, if you apply a contrary rule.[4]

The decision of the Court of Appeal in Chancery in *Parker v McKenna*[5] exemplifies this form of analysis. The plaintiff bank resolved to issue new shares and Mr Stock underwrote the issue. When a large number of the new shares were not taken up, Stock was left with a considerable liability, which he wanted to enlist the help of others to defray. The defendant directors personally agreed to take some of the shares from Stock, effectively sub-underwriting the issue to that extent, which shares they later sold at a profit. Lord Cairns LC explained that the underwriting agreement between Stock and the plaintiff bank was executory and long-running, and that the defendant directors were agents of the bank for the purpose of watching the interests of the bank in the enforcement of that agreement.[6] Once the defendant directors had personally agreed to buy some of the shares from Stock, their enforcement of Stock's underwriting agreement with the bank would in effect be enforcement of the underwriting agreement against themselves. The directors relaxed a number of Stock's obligations in the underwriting agreement.

[2] eg *York Buildings Co v Mackenzie* (1795) 3 Paton 378, 398–99 and 400–01; 1 Scots RR 717; *Earl of Lonsdale v Church* (1789) 3 Bro CC 41, 45; 29 ER 396; *East India Co v Henchman* (1791) 1 Ves Jun 287, 30 ER 347; *Massey v Davies* (1794) 2 Ves Jun 317, 30 ER 651; *York & North-Midland Railway Co v Hudson* (1845) 16 Beav 485, 51 ER 866; *Turnbull v Garden* (1869) 38 LJ Ch 331, 334 and 335; *Grant v Gold Exploration & Development Syndicate Ltd* [1900] 1 QB 233, 255; *Andrews v Ramsay & Co* [1903] 2 KB 635, 636; *Christoforides v Terry* [1924] AC 566, 571, 575 and 578; *Birtchnell v Equity Trustees, Executors & Agency Co Ltd* (1929) 42 CLR 384; *Regier v Campbell-Stuart* [1939] 1 Ch 766.

[3] eg *Oliver v Court* (1820) 8 Price 127, 161 and 164; 146 ER 1152; *Benson v Heathorn* (1842) 1 Y & CCC 326, 341; 62 ER 909; *Bentley v Craven* (1853) 18 Beav 75, 76–77; 52 ER 29; *Parker v McKenna* (1874) LR 10 Ch App 96, 118; *Armstrong v Jackson* [1917] 2 KB 823. Similarly where the agent owes conflicting duties to multiple principals: see discussion in M Conaglen, 'Fiduciary Regulation of Conflicts Between Duties' (2009) 125 *LQR* 111.

[4] *York Buildings v Mackenzie* (n 2) 393; see also ibid 398–99 per Lord Loughborough LC.

[5] *Parker v McKenna* (1874) LR 10 Ch App 96.

[6] ibid 116.

As Lord Cairns recognised, those decisions could potentially have been in the interests of the bank,[7] but the personal agreements between the defendants and Stock made it

> utterly impossible for the directors … to exercise an independent and unbiassed judgment upon the subject of these relaxations. … No man can in this Court, *acting as an agent*, be allowed to put himself into a position in which his interest and his duty will be in conflict.[8]

James LJ emphasised the same approach in his judgment, applying the profit principle:

> [N]o agent in the course of his agency, in the matter of his agency, can be allowed to make any profit without the knowledge and consent of his principal; [that] rule is an inflexible rule, and must be applied inexorably by this Court.[9]

The defendants' agency positions meant they were subject to fiduciary doctrine's prohibition on acting with a conflict between duty and interest and on profiting from the fiduciary position; the defendant directors had so acted, and so they were held liable to account for the profits that they had made on the share transactions.

However, the case law also contains important dicta, at the highest judicial levels, that call this approach into question, at least in some situations. In his speech in *Boardman v Phipps*, for example, Lord Upjohn observed that the question whether assumption of office as an agent would make someone accountable required detailed consideration:

> The facts and circumstances must be carefully examined to see whether in fact a purported agent and even a confidential agent is in a fiduciary relationship to his principal. It does not necessarily follow that he is in such a position (see *In re Coomber*).[10]

Lord Upjohn dissented in *Boardman v Phipps*, but his dissent has been said to be 'on the facts but not on the law',[11] and it has influenced other senior judges. For example, in *Hospital Products Ltd v United States Surgical Corp*, Gibbs CJ commented upon Finn's argument that a fiduciary is 'simply, someone who undertakes to act for or on behalf of another in some particular matter or matters'.[12] Relying on what Lord Upjohn had said, Gibbs CJ observed of Finn's statement that '[e]ven if it were meant that every agent is a fiduciary, the statement would be open to doubt'.[13] And suggestions of this sort are not a recent phenomenon: they can be traced back into the nineteenth century. In *Moxon v Bright*, for example, Lord Hatherley LC observed that 'It was not every agent who held a fiduciary position as between himself and his principal.'[14] The burden of this chapter is to seek to explain what is meant by such observations, and in particular what it means to say that an agent may not owe fiduciary duties.

[7] ibid 117.
[8] ibid 118 (emphasis added).
[9] ibid 124.
[10] *Boardman v Phipps* [1967] 2 AC 46, 127.
[11] *Queensland Mines Ltd v Hudson* (1978) 52 ALJR 399, 400 (PC).
[12] PD Finn, *Fiduciary Obligations* (Sydney, Law Book Co, 1977) [467].
[13] *Hospital Products* (n 1) 71. Gibbs CJ also cited *McKenzie v McDonald* [1927] VLR 134, 144 and FE Dowrick, 'The Relationship of Principal and Agent' (1954) 17 MLR 24, 31–32.
[14] *Moxon v Bright* (1869) LR 4 Ch App 292, 294.

II. Accounts in Equity

The early references to agents' not necessarily occupying a fiduciary position are found in cases about whether a court would order that an account be taken in equity. The equitable jurisdiction to take accounts was, as Lord Cottenham LC explained, 'concurrent with that of the Courts of law, and [was] adopted because, in certain cases, it has better means of ascertaining the rights of the parties'.[15] The difficulty addressed in the cases, and which matters to the present discussion, lies in identifying which 'certain cases' were appropriate for determination in equity rather than at law. The case law on this topic is rather confused, involving a number of inter-related strands of thought.

A. Doctrine

There were cases where the courts were prepared to order that an account be taken in equity on the basis that the defendant was an agent and was required to account as such.[16] Particularly where the defendant was a 'confidential agent and steward',[17] whose obligation was to receive rents and manage the estates owned by his principal, the obligation to account was clear.[18] Thus, in a beguilingly short judgment in *Mackenzie v Johnston*, Leach V-C states that 'The Defendants here were agents for the sale of the property of the Plaintiff, and wherever such a relation exists, a bill will lie [in equity] for an account.'[19] And five months later, during argument in *Massey v Banner*, Leach V-C reiterated that 'I have held that a principal may in all cases file a bill against an agent for an account.'[20] In *Smith v Pococke*, where a solicitor, Mr Dixon, acted as general agent for Miss Morris for many years, making various investments on her behalf, Kindersley V-C considered that the claim could be dealt with in equity (and was not subject to the Statute of Limitations) because that agency relationship meant that Miss Morris 'could have filed her bill against him to account to her for all the sums of money belonging to her that he had in his hands'.[21]

[15] *North-Eastern Railway Co v Martin* (1848) 2 Ph 758, 762; 41 ER 1136. Accounts were relatively rare at common law by this period, although not unknown (see, eg *Baxter v Hozier* (1839) 5 Bing 288, 132 ER 1115); but there were other common law remedies available to the parties if an equitable account was refused (see, eg, the cases discussed below in nn 32–34 and 44–45). On the concurrent and other jurisdictions of equity generally, see H Ballow, *A Treatise of Equity*, vol 1, ed J Fonblanque (London, Whieldon & Butterworth, 1793) 10–20 (note f); G Jeremy, *A Treatise on the Equity Jurisdiction of the High Court of Chancery* (London, J & WT Clarke, 1828) xxxiii; J Story, *Commentaries on Equity Jurisprudence*, 2nd edn (London, A Maxwell 1839) vol 1, 73–74; JD Heydon, MJ Leeming and PG Turner, *Meagher, Gummow & Lehane's Equity: Doctrines and Remedies*, 5th edn (Chatswood, LexisNexis, 2015) [1-090]–[1-110].

[16] See, eg, *Lord Hardwicke v Vernon* (1798) 4 Ves 411, 31 ER 209, (1808) 14 Ves 504, 33 ER 614.

[17] *Beaumont v Boultbee* (1800) 5 Ves 485, 492, 31 ER 695.

[18] Affirmed on re-hearing: (1802) 7 Ves 599, 32 ER 241.

[19] *Mackenzie v Johnston* (1819) 4 Madd 373, 375; 56 ER 742.

[20] *Massey v Banner* (1819) 4 Madd 413, 417; 56 ER 757.

[21] *Smith v Pococke* (1854) 2 Drew 197, 203; 61 ER 694. See also *Oddy v Secker* (1854) 2 Sm & G 193, 194; 65 ER 361.

However, this apparently simple position is complicated by indications elsewhere in the case law that a bill would not necessarily lie in equity merely because the case concerned an agency relationship. It is these contra-indications that generate the dicta regarding non-fiduciary agents.

In *Hirst v Peirse*, an agent was sued at law on a promissory note, and filed a bill in equity seeking to restrain the legal action and have an account taken in equity, arguing that he was owed a considerable sum for work he had done as agent. Richards CB rejected this bill on the basis that 'There must be monies paid or accounted for, both on one side and the other, to raise an account between parties. I never yet heard that agency merely was matter of account.'[22] This decision could potentially be explained on the basis that the account was sought in equity by the agent, rather than by the principal, and that the rights of the principal and agent are not correlative: as Turner V-C said in *Padwick v Stanley*, 'The right of the principal rests upon the trust and confidence reposed in the agent, but the agent reposes no such trust or confidence in the principal.'[23] However, less than four months earlier, in *Phillips v Phillips*,[24] Turner V-C had himself refused to allow an account to proceed in equity where the plaintiff argued, relying on *Mackenzie v Johnston*, that it was entitled to have an account taken in equity because it was the principal in an agency relationship. Turner V-C refused the account for reasons similar to those mentioned by Richards CB in *Hirst v Peirse*: the arrangements between the parties, in which the defendants had sold shares on the plaintiff's behalf, and had made and received payments on his account, did not involve a mutual account (one where *both* parties to the arrangement made and received payments on behalf of the other[25]).

Where an account was complicated, to the extent that it was inappropriate for it to be taken at law before a jury, courts of equity would take the account: as Lord Redesdale LC(I) put it, in a passage later approved by Lord Cottenham LC,[26] 'Courts of Equity constantly act by taking cognizance of matters, which, though cognizable at Law, are yet so involved with a complex account, that it cannot properly be taken at Law.'[27] That concurrent jurisdiction necessarily involved a considerable amount of discretion on the part of the equity judges to determine which cases were appropriate for equitable resolution, as Lord Cottenham LC pointed out elsewhere.[28] Where a case was relatively straightforward, such that the account could be taken adequately at law, a demurrer would be allowed against a bill seeking to have the account taken in equity, including in cases involving agency.[29] Indeed, Kindersley V-C indicated in *Fluker v Taylor*[30] that even a mutual account would not necessarily justify an account's being taken in equity if it was not complicated in nature; although in *Padwick v Hurst*, Romilly MR had treated

[22] *Hirst v Peirse* (1817) 4 Price 339, 345; 146 ER 483. Similarly, see *Dinwiddie v Bailey* (1801) 6 Ves 136, 31 ER 979.

[23] *Padwick v Stanley* (1852) 9 Hare 627, 628; 68 ER 664.

[24] *Phillips v Phillips* (1852) 9 Hare 471, 68 ER 596.

[25] *Padwick v Hurst* (1854) 18 Beav 575, 579–80; 52 ER 225.

[26] *Taff Vale Railway Co v Nixon* (1847) 1 HLC 111, 121–22; 9 ER 695.

[27] *O'Connor v Spaight* (1804) 1 Sch & Lef 305, 309.

[28] *North-Eastern Railway v Martin* (n 15) 762.

[29] See, eg, *Freitas v Dos Santos* (1827) 1 Y & J 574, 148 ER 800; *Mare v Lewis* (1869) 4 IR Eq 219, 239.

[30] *Fluker v Taylor* (1855) 3 Drew 183, 192; 61 ER 873.

mutual accounts as one basis for an equitable accounting, with complication being a justification for a one-sided account's being taken in equity, suggesting that the two were alternative bases for an equitable accounting.[31]

It is against this background that one finds the rather confused case law as to whether the fiduciary status of an agent could provide a basis for ordering that an account be taken in equity. The case law contains apparently inconsistent strands of authority on that question. One strand of authority is reflected in Alexander LCB's decision, sitting on the equity side of the Court of Exchequer, in *King v Rossett*.[32] The plaintiff filed a bill asking that an account be taken in equity against the defendant stockbrokers regarding their dealings as the plaintiff's agents with a substantial holding of Consols. The defendants had earlier produced an account of those dealings, pursuant to which the plaintiff appeared to owe them £625, and the plaintiff had agreed to pay that debt (and had paid £50 of it). However, the plaintiff alleged that he then discovered numerous inaccuracies in the defendants' account, and so filed a bill seeking to have an account taken in equity. The defendants (who had separately sued at law to recover the outstanding £575) filed a demurrer, arguing want of equity, relying on cases like *Hirst v Peirse*. In support of the bill, the plaintiff relied on the defendants' fiduciary status as agents: he argued that he was entitled to an account in equity because

> [t]his bill is filed by the principal against his agents, which distinguishes it from the cases cited, which were those of agents against their principal: in the one case, a confidence is reposed; in the other, all the circumstances must be within the knowledge of the party.[33]

Alexander LCB was explicit in his rejection of that argument:

> Undoubtedly, a principal is entitled to an account from his agent, and may apply to a Court of Equity for that purpose; but, as I conceive, before that Court will interfere, a ground for its interposition must be laid, by showing an account which cannot fairly be investigated by a Court of Law.[34]

That had not been done, and so the defendants' demurrer was allowed.

In *Padwick v Hurst*, Alexander LCB's view was challenged on the grounds it was decided in the Court of Exchequer, which was now abolished,[35] and did not accurately reflect the practice of the Court of Chancery. That argument was rejected by Romilly MR: Alexander LCB had practiced in Chancery for nearly 30 years, he had been a Master in Chancery for 15 years before being appointed Chief Baron,[36] and Romilly MR considered him to be 'a very eminent lawyer and a Judge perfectly acquainted with the principles of equity'.[37]

[31] *Padwick v Hurst* (n 25) 579. See also *Smith v Leveaux* (1863) 2 De GJ & S 1, 5; 46 ER 274.
[32] *King v Rossett* (1827) 2 Y & J 33, 148 ER 820.
[33] ibid 35.
[34] ibid.
[35] The Court of Exchequer's equity jurisdiction was abolished in 1841: WH Bryson, *The Equity Side of the Exchequer* (Cambridge, Cambridge University Press, 1975) 8.
[36] See J Hutchinson, *Notable Middle Templars* (London, Middle Temple, 1902) 2–3.
[37] *Padwick v Hurst* (n 25) 581.

There were, however, indications elsewhere that the fiduciary status of an agent would justify an account's being taken in equity. In *Foley v Hill*,[38] for example, in explaining that a customer is not entitled to an account in equity against his banker, Lord Cottenham LC referred to the fact that the banker

> does not hold [a] fiduciary character, and therefore there is no such original jurisdiction; and if there be no such original jurisdiction growing out of the relative situations of the parties, then, to see if the account is of such a nature that it cannot be taken at law, we are to look to the account itself … We find no complicated account at all here.[39]

The banker's relationship with his client was compared with that of an agent or factor,[40] suggesting that the fiduciary character of the relationship between those types of actors and their principals could justify an account's being taken in equity in its 'original' or exclusive jurisdiction. Similarly, in *Padwick v Hurst*, having referred to mutual and complicated accounts as bases for accounts being taken in equity, Romilly MR separated these from 'the fiduciary relation and the trust reposed by the principal in the agent' as different justifications for 'bills for an account by a principal against his agent'.[41]

However, notwithstanding these dicta, the cases continued contemporaneously to indicate that the mere fact of a relationship of agency was not necessarily sufficient justification for an account to be taken in equity. In *Navulshaw v Brownrigg*, for example, Lord Cranworth V-C – who was undoubtedly familiar with fiduciary doctrine[42] – rejected an argument to that effect:

> [I]n a case in which there is no fraud, not only all the authorities but all the text-books shew that this Court will not decree an agent to account to his principal, unless the case is one which is not capable of being conveniently inquired into in a Court of law.[43]

In *Barry v Stevens*, a publisher had agreed to publish a text written by Barry (concerned, somewhat ironically, with the statutory jurisdiction of the Court of Chancery), and had sued at law to recover its costs and commission when the book sold only 49 copies. Despite having viewed the unsold copies of the book, Barry was convinced that more copies must have been sold, and filed a bill seeking to force the publisher to account in equity. Romilly MR emphasised that a principal is entitled to an account of his agent's dealings, but he allowed a demurrer against Barry's bill (thereby refusing to have the account taken in equity) on the basis that it was a mere money account that could be dealt with perfectly well at law.[44] This seemed to suggest that the justification for an equitable account based on the account's being complicated also operated as some form of limitation or requirement that had to be satisfied even where an account was sought against a fiduciary agent, as had been argued in the case.[45] The decision in *Barry v Stevens*

[38] *Foley v Hill* (1848) 2 HLC 28, 9 ER 1002.
[39] ibid 39–40.
[40] ibid 35–36, 37 and 43.
[41] *Padwick v Hurst* (n 25) 579.
[42] See, eg, his famous speech in *Aberdeen Railway Co v Blaikie Bros* (1854) 1 Macq 461, 149 RR 32.
[43] *Navulshaw v Brownrigg* (1851) 1 Sim (NS) 573, 584–85; 61 ER 221. Affirmed on appeal: (1852) 2 De GM & G 441, 42 ER 943.
[44] *Barry v Stevens* (1862) 31 Beav 258, 268–69; 54 ER 1137.
[45] ibid 266.

is not completely clear in that regard, as Barry (who argued his case personally) did not make clear precisely why he considered the publishers to have been his agents; but Malins V-C later said that 'the principle has been acted on frequently, that the principal has no right to file a bill against the agent unless the account is of a complicated nature'.[46]

In other cases, decided at around the same time, the courts continued to recognise the fiduciary status of the agent as a separate basis for an account's being taken in equity, but did so in a way that suggested that agents are not always fiduciaries and so this would not always justify an equitable account against an agent. It is these cases that further embed the proposition that an agent was not necessarily a fiduciary. For example, in *Hemings v Pugh*,[47] the plaintiff filed a bill seeking an account of monies received by the defendant on behalf of the plaintiff. In support of the defendant's demurrer, Richard Malins as counsel relied on *Foley v Hill* and *Phillips v Phillips* to argue that a bill would not lie where there was no mutuality of account. Stuart V-C allowed the demurrer, but he emphasised that mutuality was not the only basis on which the court would exercise its jurisdiction to take an account:

> In the case of a steward or land agent the receipts and payments are almost necessarily on one side; that is, no mutual payments and receipts. Yet that is a case in which this Court from the most ancient times … has exercised this jurisdiction. That jurisdiction still remains, and *whenever an agency partakes of a fiduciary character this Court has jurisdiction*, and will direct an account, although the receipts and payments are all on one side, and there are no mutual payments between the parties. That rule has not been shaken by the decision in *Phillips v Phillips*.[48]

In the case at hand, the demurrer was allowed because Stuart V-C considered that 'there is no allegation of any mutual dealings, or of anything fiduciary in the relation of the parties, who on the bill are stated as mere principal and agent'.[49]

In *Makepeace v Rogers*,[50] Richard Malins again sought to deflect a bill for an equitable account, not long before he was appointed as a Vice-Chancellor alongside Stuart V-C, by arguing that the relevant accounting was neither mutual nor complicated. In the Court of Appeal in Chancery, Knight Bruce LJ explained that he did not think Turner V-C had intended in *Phillips v Phillips* to suggest that a bill for an account in equity could only lie where there were mutual accounts:

> The existence of a fiduciary relation between the parties, as, for example (as was the case here) that of principal and agent, was sufficient to confer jurisdiction on this Court, and allegations of fraud or special circumstances were unnecessary.[51]

Turner LJ himself said in *Makepeace v Rogers* that he had decided *Phillips v Phillips* as he did because 'the bill made no case of general agency, alleging only an isolated agency transaction connected with the sale by the Defendant of some railway shares belonging

[46] *Blyth v Whiffin* (1872) 27 LT 330, 334.
[47] *Hemings v Pugh* (1863) 4 Giff 456, 66 ER 785.
[48] ibid 459 (emphasis added).
[49] ibid.
[50] *Makepeace v Rogers* (1865) 4 De GJ & S 649, 46 ER 1070.
[51] ibid 653.

to the Plaintiff'.[52] This again indicates that the fiduciary nature of an agency relationship could justify an account's being taken in equity, apparently as a separate basis from the mutuality of accounts or their complicated nature, but at the same time these cases suggest that not all agencies involve a fiduciary relationship of the relevant kind.

B. Analysis

One possible analysis of the dicta that have been referred to in this section of the chapter is to alight upon one apparently unqualified dictum, such as that of Leach V-C in *Mackenzie v Johnston*, and treat all subsequent denials of that unalloyed position as having 'inexplicably reframed'[53] the law in a way that was 'misconceived in a train of unsupported assertion'[54] and wrought an unprincipled[55] distortion.[56]

An alternative approach is to acknowledge the expertise in nineteenth-century Chancery jurisprudence of people like Leach V-C – but also Turner LJ, Romilly MR, Stuart V-C, Malins V-C, Alexander LCB and Lord Cranworth LC[57] – and to seek to understand what they meant by what they said in these judgments. Once that is understood, one can consider the degree to which it remains relevant in modern jurisprudence; but it is a mistake to dismiss the thinking of these eminent judges, with deep expertise in Chancery practice, without first having done that.

It is suggested that although the dicta that have been surveyed in the preceding section are confusing, they are neither incomprehensible nor mere misconceived assertion. In understanding them, it is important to recall that 'vocabulary can stay the same over hundreds of years, even as its meaning changes'.[58] This is particularly the case for the legal concept represented by the descriptor 'fiduciary', which had a range of potential meanings, particularly in the Victorian period.[59] In the present context, one can discern from the cases at least two subtly different senses in which the word 'fiduciary' has been deployed, each of which links to different aspects of the equitable jurisdiction.

i. General Agency

First, the fiduciary label is used in some of these cases – as it was, for example, by Turner LJ in *Makepeace v Rogers* – as a convenient encapsulation of the concept

[52] ibid 654. Confusingly, he added that any misapprehension in this regard should have been dispelled by what he said in *Padwick v Stanley* (as to which, see n 23 above); but his comments there concerned the lack of correlation between the rights of principals and agents, rather than the difference between general and isolated agencies.

[53] R Flannigan, 'Fiduciary Agency Denied' [2021] *Journal of Business Law* 50, 51.

[54] ibid 51.

[55] ibid 60.

[56] ibid 56.

[57] Similarly, leading texts: eg, SE Williams, *Law of Account* (London, Stevens & Sons, 1899) 3–4 and 222–24; HW Seton, *Forms of Judgments and Orders*, 7th edn by AR Ingpen, FT Bloxam and HG Garrett (London, Stevens & Sons 1912) 1330–31.

[58] A Televantos, 'Losing the Fiduciary Requirement for Equitable Tracing Claims' (2017) 133 *LQR* 492, 492.

[59] LS Sealy, 'Fiduciary Relationships' [1962] *CLJ* 69, 70–72; LS Sealy, 'The Director as Trustee' [1967] *CLJ* 83, 85–86; Televantos (n 58) 493 and 513.

of a general agency, in contradistinction to a single or isolated agency transaction.[60] While the concept of general agency is not explained directly in these cases, it was a concept that was used in agency cases in the nineteenth century, particularly in identifying the extent of the implied authority of an agent. Reflecting general usage in the period,[61] Paley explained:

> By a general agent is understood, not merely a person substituted in the place of another for transacting all manner of business (since there are few instances in common use of an agency of that description), but a person whom a man puts in his place to transact all his business of a particular kind … [A] special agent [is] employed about one specific act, or certain specific acts only.[62]

The dicta under discussion here, regarding the circumstances in which an account would be taken in equity, reflected practices that were developed over many decades during which the Court of Chancery did not have a large judicial manpower.[63] It is understandable that the Court would restrict access to its accounting processes, at least in the concurrent jurisdiction, to those cases where it could offer advantages over the process available at common law. A general agency was normally complicated in a way that an agency in a single transaction was normally not,[64] and thus justified the account's being taken in equity. Thus, for example, in *White v Lady Lincoln*, Lord Eldon LC explained that the defendant was 'not to be looked at as a mere attorney … while he was general agent, auditor, land-steward, and manager'.[65]

ii. Trust-Like Arrangements

A second, and it is suggested more central, sense in which the fiduciary descriptor was used in these cases about equitable accounting referred to the defendant's management of property for the plaintiff. As Jeremy said, describing the circumstances in which an account would be taken in equity:

> The relation of principal and agent generally is one of great extent. It seems to comprise all cases in which one is authorized to act for another; but *with reference to the subject now before us, it is limited to those in which the control or management of property is so confided.*[66]

[60] See also *Mare v Lewis* (n 29) 240.

[61] See also, eg, J *Story, Law of Agency*, 5th edn (Boston, MA, Little Brown & Co 1857) 18, 146; JW Smith, *Mercantile Law*, 6th edn, ed GM Dowdeswell (London, V & R Stevens & GS Norton, H Sweet & W Maxwell, 1859) 134–35; CH Smith, *Master and Servant*, 2nd edn (London, H Sweet, 1860) 165, 168.

[62] W Paley, *The Law of Principal and Agent* (London, J Butterworth & J Cooke 1812) 139–40.

[63] Chancery only had adequate judges for its work from the middle of the 19th century: P Polden, 'The Court of Chancery, 1820–1875' in W Cornish et al, *The Oxford History of the Laws of England*, vol XI: *1820–1914: English Legal System* (Oxford, Oxford University Press, 2010) 646, 660. See also, regarding the early 19th century, A Televantos, *Capitalism Before Corporations* (Oxford, Oxford University Press, 2021) 27–28; JH Baker, *An Introduction to English Legal History* (5th ed, Oxford, Oxford University Press, 2019) 122.

[64] See also *Re Lee* (1869) LR 4 Ch App 43, 45–46; *Mare v Lewis* (n 29) 240.

[65] *White v Lady Lincoln* (1803) 8 Ves 363, 369; 32 ER 395.

[66] Jeremy (n 15) 513 (emphasis added). See also IP Cory, *A Practical Treatise on Accounts*, 2nd edn (London, W Pickering, 1839) 246–48.

The relevance of the defendant's management and control of the plaintiff's property seems to lie in the fact that it meant the defendant was operating in a way that bore similarities to the role of a trustee. It was clear that a trustee would be compelled to render an account in equity, in its exclusive jurisdiction, 'upon the mere fact of the relation which subsists between him and his *cestui que trust*'.[67] It is thus understandable that someone who controlled property of another could sensibly be subjected to a similar accounting regime, notwithstanding that the agency relationship meant that common law procedures could also be applied.

Thus, for example, in *Scott v Surman*, Willes LCJ explained that where A has given money to B to purchase property, and B does not do so, A could bring an action against B at law in money had and received *or* 'bring a bill against him considering him as a trustee [and] Courts of Equity always retain such bills when they are brought under a notion of a trust'.[68] As Televantos has explained, the words 'trust' and 'fiduciary' were much more fluid in their meanings in this period: this sort of fiduciary control of another's property was often conceived of as a trust.[69] Obviously that changed, as the trust concept came to bear a more precise meaning, and other similar relationships came to be referred to more commonly as fiduciary relationships. The point that matters for present purposes, again bearing in mind Chancery's need to control access to its limited judicial resources in this period, is that it made sense for the court to assert accounting control over relationships that were similar to those involved in trusts, while refusing to make those processes available in other agency cases where a remedy was available at law and where the facts were neither complicated nor similar to a trust arrangement. It is suggested that this is the core meaning of the observations made in the cases that suggested that an agent would not be held to account in equity if he were not a fiduciary.

In *Mackenzie v Johnston*, for example – the case in which Leach V-C said that the defendants' agency was what justified the account's being taken in equity – the plaintiff had consigned goods to the defendants to be shipped to India and sold, the proceeds (less expenses) to be paid to the plaintiff. It is notable that argument on both sides was focused on whether the defendant was in a position like that of a trustee.[70] Similarly in *Foley v Hill*, in explaining why an account would not be ordered in equity against a banker, Lord Cottenham LC differentiated the position of the banker from that of a factor or agent in the following way:

> [A]s between principal and factor, there is no question whatever that that description of case … has always been held to be within the jurisdiction of a Court of Equity, because the party *partakes of the character of a trustee*. … So it is with regard to *an agent dealing with any property*; … though he is not a trustee according to the strict technical meaning of the word, he is quasi a trustee for that particular transaction for which he is engaged; and therefore in these cases the Courts of Equity have assumed jurisdiction.[71]

[67] Jeremy (n 15) 523.

[68] *Scott v Surman* (1742) Willes 400, 405; 125 ER 1235. See also Paley (n 62) 51.

[69] Televantos (n 58) 497–98. See, eg *Burdett v Willett* (1708) 2 Vern 638, 23 ER 1017; *Charitable Corp v Sutton* (1742) 2 Atk 400, 405–06; 26 ER 642 and (1742) 9 Mod 349, 355; 88 ER 500.

[70] *Mackenzie v Johnston* (n 19) 375.

[71] *Foley v Hill* (n 38) 35–36 (emphasis added).

It is suggested this explains what Lord Hatherley LC said in *Moxon v Bright* when he observed that '[i]t was not every agent who held a fiduciary position':[72] immediately preceding that observation he had noted:

> There were numerous cases shewing that where the relation of principal and agent had imposed a trust upon the agent, the Court would entertain a bill for an account, and the only difficulty was in determining what constituted this species of trust. … *Foley v Hill* shewed that though a banker was the agent of the customer for many purposes, they were not such as would constitute a trust … [T]he sole point in this suit was whether there existed between them an agency in which a fiduciary position was created.[73]

Similarly, in *Hemings v Pugh* – in which Stuart V-C indicated that an account could be obtained against an agent in equity *if* the agent were a fiduciary, even if the payments and receipts were not mutual – he gave the instance of a steward or land agent as an example of 'an agency [that] partakes of a fiduciary character'.[74] And in *Makepeace v Rogers* – which both Knight Bruce and Turner LJJ considered a clear case of 'fiduciary relation between the parties',[75] justifying an account in equity – the defendant had for many years been employed as the plaintiff's 'agent and manager of his estates';[76] in other words, 'his steward'.[77]

As the example of a land steward demonstrates, this second sense in which the fiduciary concept was used in the cases could often overlap with the first: the sorts of agents who were in the core class of agents generally subject to accounting in equity – agents such as land stewards, factors, brokers – were often both general agents[78] and also held or controlled property belonging to the plaintiff. Thus, for example, in *Smith v Pococke*, the defendant solicitor was obliged to account in equity when he acted as a money scrivener for his client:

> He acted *under a general agency* to make investments for her … and she could have filed her bill against him to account to her for all the sums of money *belonging to her that he had in his hands*. … This is not, then, a mere legal demand for damages; it is a question of items in an account.[79]

C. Implications

It remains to comment on the implications of this analysis for understanding the modern law regarding the fiduciary duties of agents. It is suggested that the nineteenth-century

[72] *Moxon v Bright* (n 14) 294.

[73] ibid 294–95. Similarly, see *Massey v Banner* (1820) 1 Jac & W 241, 247; 37 ER 367; *Burdick v Garrick* (1870) LR 5 Ch App 233, 240 and 243; *Ex parte Cooke* (1876) 4 ChD 123, 128; *Marris v Ingram* (1879) 13 ChD 338, 344 and 345; *New Zealand and Australian Land Co v Watson* (1881) 7 QBD 374, 382 and 383–84; *Piddocke v Burt* [1894] 1 Ch 343, 346.

[74] *Hemings v Pugh* (n 47) 459.

[75] *Makepeace v Rogers* (n 50) 653.

[76] ibid 652.

[77] ibid 653.

[78] See, eg Story (n 61) 151; JH Watts, *Smith and Watts Compendium of Mercantile Law*, 12th edn (London, Stevens & Sons; Sweet & Maxwell, 1924) 180.

[79] *Smith v Pococke* (n 21) 203–04 (emphasis added).

dicta that refer to agents who are not necessarily fiduciary are best understood as reflecting the peculiarities of the availability of an accounting in equity in the Court of Chancery's concurrent jurisdiction. Relief would normally be available against an agent at law, but an account could be taken in equity if (i) this was necessary because the common law process was not sufficiently nuanced to the case, as where the accounts were mutual or otherwise unusually complicated; or (ii) the relationship between the principal and agent bore characteristics similar to those involved in a trust (in the form of control or management of the plaintiff's property). Absent a sufficient reason for the account to be taken in equity, the parties would be left to their remedies at law.

Understanding the case law in this way supports the undeveloped contention that these dicta are 'illustrations not so much of the character of an agent's obligation to the principal as of the technical requirements of a suit in equity for an account'.[80] They are concerned with the question when equity would make available its accounting procedures. While they are cryptic, particularly at this remove in time, it is suggested that they were not 'misconceived' 'distortions' of equitable principle but rather an attempt to describe the practices the Court of Chancery had been following in a rather technical area.[81] It is also important to recall, in this regard, that the distinction between common law and equitable accounting procedures essentially evaporated after the Judicature reforms, following which the equitable rules were applied.[82] It thus became irrelevant to seek to limit the availability of equitable accounting procedures to complicated or fiduciary property-holding situations, and so dicta of the sort considered here disappeared from the case law.

Importantly for present purposes, the nineteenth-century dicta considered here were not concerned with the question whether the defendant agents owed duties of the kind that would, in modern legal parlance, be referred to as fiduciary duties. These dicta are found in cases where the plaintiff had filed a bill seeking a general account of the defendant's conduct as agent; these were not cases where the plaintiff was seeking an account of profits of the sort ordered where a fiduciary has made an unauthorised profit from his or her fiduciary position.[83] There is thus nothing in these decisions to suggest that an agent would not be subject to the recognised fiduciary principles that require a fiduciary to avoid acting with conflicts and to eschew unauthorised profits. On the contrary, there were cases where those principles were applied to agents – including in relatively simple, single transaction cases – and the agents were required to disgorge profits.[84] Thus, despite these dicta, Story was still able to state as a rule of 'general application'[85] that agents could not bind their principals where they had an adverse interest,

[80] Heydon, Leeming and Turner (n 15) [5-215].

[81] Lord Cottenham LC acknowledged that 'pleading in equity is somewhat cumbrous, and not quite well reduced to principle': *Foley v Hill* (1838) 3 My & Cr 475, 482; 40 ER 1010.

[82] Judicature Act 1873, s 34(3); Rules of the Supreme Court 1875, Ord XV, r 1. See J Story, *Commentaries on Equity Jurisprudence*, 3rd English edn by AE Randall (London, Sweet & Maxwell, 1920) 184.

[83] Ellinger's suggestion that the plaintiff sought an account of profits in *Foley v Hill* (see EP Ellinger, E Lomnicka and CVM Hare, *Ellinger's Modern Banking Law*, 5th edn (Oxford, Oxford University Press, 2011) 120) misapprehends the pleadings in that case: see *Foley v Hill* (n 81) 477; *Foley v Hill* (1844) 1 Ph 399, 406; 41 ER 683.

[84] See, eg *Lord Hardwicke v Vernon* (n 16); *Beaumont v Boultbee* (1802) 7 Ves 599; 32 ER 241; *Benson v Heathorn* (n 3); *Parker v McKenna* (n 5); *De Bussche v Alt* (1878) 8 ChD 286.

[85] Story (n 61) 246.

and that this was so '*not only* in cases of persons, confidentially intrusted with the management of the property of others'.[86] He went on:

> Indeed, it may be laid down as a general principle, that, in all cases where a person is … an agent for other persons, all profits and advantages, made by him in the business, beyond his ordinary compensation, are to be for the benefit of his employers.[87]

The question of how those profits were held by the agent was more complicated,[88] but there was no doubt as to the obligation of the agent to account for unauthorised profits.

One case that requires brief mention in this regard is Kekewich J's decision in *Dooby v Watson*,[89] as its poor reasoning highlights the difference between equitable accounting processes and what would be regarded in modern terms as fiduciary duties. In this case, the plaintiff engaged her solicitor to sell her property and invest the proceeds. The proceeds were invested in a mortgage granted by one of the solicitor's other clients, which provided insufficient security. The plaintiff could have sued in negligence but was time-barred, and so she sought to argue that the solicitor was a trustee who should account on a wilful default footing. Kekewich J held that there was 'not the slightest impropriety in the transaction'[90] and refused to make that order. Consistently with his reputation for expeditious but inaccurate decisions,[91] *Dooby v Watson* was incorrect as to the fiduciary aspects of the case, but if that error is put to one side the remainder of the judgment could potentially be justified. The decision was incorrect in fiduciary terms because the solicitor had suggested the mortgage loan be made to a client who was indebted to the solicitor, and Kekewich J recognised that 'certainly there was an advantage which accrued to the firm by reason of this transaction'.[92] Unless the plaintiff were shown to have consented to that conflicted position, that ought to have been sufficient for equitable remedies to be available, and Kekewich J's suggestion to the contrary is inconsistent with much authority. But if that point is ignored, the refusal of an account on the footing of wilful default is otherwise understandable.[93] In order to have an account taken in that way, one must convince the court that the trustee failed in a duty to acquire more for the trust fund.[94] Kekewich J's view of the solicitor's instructions was that he was asked to advise on how the proceeds of sale should be invested (which advice was clearly conflicted, as discussed), but that once a mortgage had been settled upon, his only instructions – and so his only duty as trustee – were to make that (not any other more profitable) investment. In other words, he was not exercising

[86] ibid 248 (emphasis added).

[87] ibid 251–52.

[88] *Lister & Co v Stubbs* (1890) 45 ChD 1.

[89] *Dooby v Watson* (1888) 39 ChD 178.

[90] ibid 183–84.

[91] *The Times* (25 November 1907) 5.

[92] *Dooby v Watson* (1888) 57 LJ Ch 865, 868. The nature of the solicitor's conflict is strangely excised from the official report, and is only apparent in the Law Journal report. Also noted by Flannigan (n 53) 64 (fn 84).

[93] cf Flannigan, ibid 64.

[94] An account in common form would not have achieved what the plaintiff wished, because (except for the flaws generated by the conflicted nature of the solicitor's advice) the mortgage was authorised. For the difference between an account taken in common form and an account taken on the footing of wilful default, see M Conaglen, 'Equitable Compensation for Breach of Trust: Off *Target*' (2016) *Melbourne University Law Review* 126, 129–35.

a general power of investment (and probably had none), and so it could not be argued that he had failed as a trustee to acquire for the plaintiff something that he ought to have acquired. Thus, while the decision is badly flawed in terms of its application of fiduciary principles, it is an understandable decision in terms purely of the relevant trust accounting principles.

This again emphasises the importance of understanding what was said in the nineteenth-century cases about accounts in equity within the relevant context. It is suggested that the dicta in those cases do not mean that the courts were recognising agents who did not owe what would today be considered to be fiduciary duties.

III. Modern Observations

However, there are also statements in the more modern case law that warn against thinking that agents are necessarily fiduciaries. What remains is to explain these statements. It is suggested that these statements are reflections of two rather prosaic observations about agency and fiduciary doctrine respectively:

(a) The fact that someone is described as an agent does not necessarily mean that person is acting in a true agency capacity; if the person is not actually an agent, or at least not an agent for the plaintiff, it is easier to understand that he or she may not owe fiduciary duties.
(b) Fiduciary principles 'must be moulded according to the nature of the relationship'[95] and may be inappropriate in a particular agency relationship.[96]

While those points are easily expressed, it is suggested that there is value in expanding upon them and giving examples, as that approach illuminates the complexity in these cases that generates statements like those of Lord Upjohn in *Boardman v Phipps* and Gibbs CJ in *Hospital Products*.

A. Non-Agency 'Agents'

The first key category of case where one finds agents who do not owe fiduciary duties is a consequence of a point famously observed upon by Lord Herschell in *Kennedy v De Trafford*:

> No word is more commonly and constantly abused than the word 'agent'. A person may be spoken of as an 'agent', and no doubt in the popular sense of the word may properly be said to be an 'agent', although when it is attempted to suggest that he is an 'agent' under such circumstances as create the legal obligations attaching to agency that use of the word is only misleading.[97]

[95] *New Zealand Netherlands Society 'Oranje' Inc v Kuys* [1973] 1 WLR 1126, 1130 (PC).

[96] A similar view is suggested by P Watts and FMB Reynolds, *Bowstead & Reynolds on Agency*, 21st edn (London, Sweet & Maxwell, 2018) [6-037].

[97] *Kennedy v De Trafford* [1897] AC 180, 188. See also *Jones v Bouffier* (1911) 12 CLR 579, 587 and 611; *McKenzie v McDonald* (n 13) 144; *Colonial Mutual Life Assurance Society Ltd v Producers & Citizens*

In other words, like the word 'fiduciary' (particularly in the Victorian period), the words 'agent' and 'agency' have different meanings when used in different contexts. In the legal context, those words have a reasonably (if not completely) well defined meaning; but, as Lord Herschell observed, the words are not used in that precise way in all contexts. As Gleeson CJ put it in *Scott v Davis*, 'the protean nature of the concept of agency … bedevils this area of discourse'.[98] Thus, perhaps even more so than in other areas of law, the mere application of the word by the parties does not necessarily mean that is the legal effect of the arrangement the parties have created (nor their failure to so describe it, and nor indeed their denial of that).[99] Given 'the word "agent" [can be] used simply in its primary dictionary sense of one who acts',[100] it necessarily 'has a potentially wide and varying meaning in life and business and …, on some occasions, the business description will be given to someone who is not a fiduciary'.[101]

i. Labels and Authority to Act

In *Kennedy v De Trafford*, for example, two tenants in common had mortgaged their property. When the debt was not repaid, the mortgagee exercised its power of sale, and sold to one of the co-owners, Dodson. The other co-owner, Carswell, sought to argue (inter alia) that Dodson had acted as agent for Carswell (and then for the mortgagee) in collecting rents and managing the property, and that his fiduciary position prevented him from buying the property for himself. This was rejected, essentially because Dodson collected the rents in his capacity as a co-owner of the property: 'He did not need agency or the appointment of agent to justify him in collecting those rents.'[102] Having made the observation quoted above, Lord Herschell explained:

> [W]hatever expressions Dodson may have used calling himself an agent, and however true or applicable they may have been in a popular sense, in point of law and in their legal sense they are meaningless. Dodson was not the agent of [Carswell's trustee in bankruptcy], and he was not the agent of the mortgagees. If that be so, there is an end of the fiduciary relationship which is supposed to prevent his being a purchaser.[103]

Co-operative Assurance Co of Australia Ltd (1931) 46 CLR 41, 50; *Potter v Customs & Excise Commissioners* [1985] STC 45, 51 and 54 (CA); *Scott v Davis* [2000] HCA 52, (2000) 204 CLR 333 [299].

[98] *Scott v Davis* (n 97) [4]. The phrase 'fiduciary relationship' has also been described as a protean term: *Wood v Commercial First Business Ltd* [2021] EWCA Civ 471, [2021] 3 WLR 395 [36].

[99] *UBS AG (London Branch) v Kommunale Wasserwerke Leipzig GmbH* [2017] EWCA Civ 1567, [2017] 2 Lloyd's Rep 621 [87]; *South Sydney District Rugby League Football Club Ltd v News Ltd* [2000] FCA 1541, (2000) 177 ALR 611 [161]; *Tonto Home Loans Australia Pty Ltd v Tavares* [2011] NSWCA 389 [95], [143] and [182]; (2011) 15 BPR 26, 699; *Pengelly v Business Mortgage Finance 4 plc* [2020] EWHC 2002 (Ch), [2020] PNLR 29 [33]. For the same point in other legal contexts, see, eg, *Street v Mountford* [1985] 1 AC 809, 819; *Agnew v Commissioner of Inland Revenue* [2001] UKPC 28, [2001] 2 AC 710 [32]; *Re Spectrum Plus Ltd (in liq)* [2005] UKHL 41, [2005] 2 AC 680 [141].

[100] *Potter v Customs* (n 97) 53.

[101] *Tonto Home Loans* (n 99) [177].

[102] *Kennedy v De Trafford* (n 97) 187. Dodson had to account to Carswell for his share of the rents under an agreement (see ibid), but that did not mean he was a fiduciary to Carswell. This further emphasises the lack of identity between fiduciary principles and accounting principles; see also JA Watson, *The Duty to Account* (Sydney, Federation Press, 2016) [416] and [462].

[103] *Kennedy v De Trafford* (n 97) 188.

In other words, the label applied to the defendant in his or her business dealings is not necessarily determinative of the question whether that person was actually an agent in what he or she did. As James LJ had said earlier in *Great Western Insurance Co v Cunliffe*, 'Whether [the defendants] are called insurance brokers, or insurance agents, or merchants doing brokerage business or insurance business, the mere name is a matter of not the slightest consequence whatever.'[104]

Other cases illustrate this point in ways that usefully emphasise the wide range of circumstances to which the label 'agent' is applied in general speech without any legal relationship of agency. In *WT Lamb & Sons v Goring Brick Co Ltd*,[105] the defendant brickmaker had appointed the plaintiff builders' merchant as 'sole selling agents' of its bricks. The defendant sought to sell bricks directly to purchasers, rather than through the plaintiff's agency, and the plaintiff complained. The defendant sought to justify its actions by reference to the position of real estate agents, who would earn no commission if the vendor arranged a sale directly with a purchaser, even if the agent had been appointed as exclusive agent by the vendor. The court held that this was not an agency of that sort. In the Court of Appeal, Scrutton LJ observed:

> [I]t is well known that in certain trades the word 'agent' is often used without any reference to the law of principal and agent. The motor trade offers an obvious example, where persons described as 'agents' are not agents in respect of any principal, but are purchasers who buy from manufacturers and sell independently of them; and many difficulties have arisen from this habit of describing a purchaser … as an agent.[106]

Indeed, Greer LJ appeared rather annoyed by the failure to notice this distinction:

> It is somewhat remarkable that, notwithstanding the numerous cases in which the difference between a buyer and an agent has been pointed out, there are still innumerable persons engaged in business who do not understand the simple and logical distinction between a buyer and an agent for sale, but are content to treat the two words as synonymous.[107]

The words 'sole selling agents' were construed as meaning that the defendant had contracted only to sell its bricks to the plaintiff, but the plaintiff purchased the bricks in its own right and then sold them to builders – the description of the plaintiff as 'agents' was incorrect.[108]

The High Court of Australia's decision in *International Harvester Co of Australia Pty Ltd v Carrigan's Hazeldene Pastoral Co*[109] also illustrates the point made in *WT Lamb*. The plaintiffs bought an automatic hay baler, manufactured by the defendant, through a company – Hassan & Kensell – that carried on business as 'machinery and general agents' in rural New South Wales. The plaintiffs had first seen the baler at the defendant's stand at an agricultural show, and had been told there to see the defendant's agents, Hassan & Kensell. When the baler proved faulty, the plaintiffs sued the defendant,

[104] *Great Western Insurance Co v Cunliffe* (1874) LR 9 Ch App 525, 536.
[105] *WT Lamb & Sons v Goring Brick Co Ltd* [1932] 1 KB 710 (CA).
[106] ibid 717. On car dealers, see also the comments in *Potter v Customs* (n 97) 50.
[107] *WT Lamb v Goring* (n 105) 720.
[108] ibid 721 and 722.
[109] *International Harvester Co of Australia Pty Ltd v Carrigan's Hazeldene Pastoral Co* (1958) 100 CLR 644.

arguing that they had contracted with the defendant through Hassan & Kensell (which was now in liquidation). The High Court rejected that argument. The documentation by which the baler was bought indicated that the plaintiffs had bought the baler from Hassan & Kensell, and that documentation did not mention the defendant:

> There is nothing to indicate that the defendant company ever authorised Hassan & Kensell Pty Ltd to contract on the former's behalf and nothing to indicate that Hassan & Kensell Pty Ltd purported to do so. The employment of the word 'agents' in the description of their business supplies no reason for making any contrary assumption.[110]

Citing what was said in *WT Lamb*, and also *Kennedy v De Trafford*, the court noted:

> For almost a century cases have appeared from time to time in the law reports illustrating the fact that the word 'agent' is often used in business as meaning one who has no principal but who on his own account offers for sale some particular article having a special name … Agency is a word used in the law to connote an authority or capacity in one person to create legal relations between a person occupying the position of principal and third parties. But in the business world its significance is by no means thus restricted.[111]

And speaking specifically about the sort of role carried on by the 'agents' in the case:

> No one supposes that the 'distributing agent' or 'exclusive agent' in a particular 'territory' for a proprietary commodity or specific kind of article or machine is there to put a 'consumer' into contractual relations with the manufacturer. In the case of any wide geographical distribution there is a general understanding of the practices of allotting territories, of zoning, of providing some regional superintendence of dealers or distributing 'agents' as well as of the maintenance, and sometimes of the proper use, of the machine or article. None of this implies that the manufacturer or the head supplier contracts with the ultimate buyer or 'consumer' as vendor.[112]

These quotations are somewhat lengthy, but they are useful in their identification of circumstances in which an 'agent' might not be a true agent in legal terms, and so might not owe fiduciary duties. Ultimately, of course, the fact that someone is not a legal agent is not itself determinative of whether that person owes fiduciary duties,[113] but the point that matters for present purposes is that the mere fact that someone is described as an agent – particularly in business – is also not determinative of whether that person owes fiduciary duties because he or she might not actually be an agent in a legal sense. Thus, someone could easily be described as an 'agent' without owing fiduciary duties.

ii. Other Agency Roles

Further, even in the legal sense, agency is not always limited to situations where the agent has authority to enter into binding legal relations on behalf of his or her principal. Given the context of the case, that was the focus of the court's attention in *International Harvester*, but agents can also represent clients in ways that do not necessarily involve

[110] ibid 650.
[111] ibid 652.
[112] ibid 653.
[113] *Tigris International NV v China Southern Airlines Co Ltd* [2014] EWCA Civ 1649 [155].

that kind of authority.[114] For example, an estate agent has a limited agency,[115] in the sense that he or she does not normally enter into a contract of sale on the client's behalf, although he or she does make representations to potential purchasers that can bind the client.[116] Further, 'introducing agents', who seek out clients and assist them in making proposals to enter into business transactions with another party (such as an insurer, or a financial lender), *can* sometimes act as agents of that other party, notwithstanding their lack of ability to conclude a binding contract on their behalf,[117] *but* they do not always do so (even where they hold a stock of application forms, or have access to computer-based application forms, complete those forms and forward them to the lender).[118]

'The notion of being an "agent" is in some ways an imprecise one. … [O]ne needs to consider the *purpose for which* one is enquiring whether A is P's agent.'[119] Where the purpose is to determine whether someone owes fiduciary duties, the imprecision in the agency concept is compounded by the lack of a clear definition or test in the case law for determining when someone will be considered to be a fiduciary vis-à-vis another. 'The enquiry is inevitably extremely fact sensitive.'[120] Circumstances that appear to involve some form of agency, and thus fiduciary duties, are not always found to be so. As *International Harvester* shows, the mere fact that someone occupies a position where he or she stands between two other parties in some way does not identify for which of the two parties – if either – that person is acting,[121] and so does not necessarily mean that the person occupies a fiduciary position vis-à-vis one or the other, or possibly even both, of those other parties. The mere fact that one party has acted in a way that is in the interests of another party or for that other party's benefit – and even has done so at the request of that party, in a way that performs an important function for that party, and which is remunerated by that party[122] – is not itself necessarily sufficient to establish an agency or fiduciary relationship between those two parties: 'the expressions "for", "on behalf of", and "in the interests of" signify that the fiduciary acts in a "representative" character'.[123] Thus, '[n]ot every independent contractor doing work for or for the benefit of someone will be that person's agent',[124] as it depends on whether he or she is acting in a representative capacity.[125]

[114] *Tonto Home Loans* (n 99) [174] and [183]; *Serventy v Commonwealth Bank of Australia (No 2)* [2016] WASCA 223 [35].
[115] *Regier v Campbell-Stuart* (n 2).
[116] *Kirkpatrick v Kotis* [2004] NSWSC 1265, [87]; (2004) 62 NSWLR 567.
[117] See, eg, *Colonial Mutual* (n 97) 47 and 48–49; *Norwich Fire Insurance Society Ltd v Brennans (Horsham) Pty Ltd* [1981] VR 981 (FC); *Premium Real Estate Ltd v Stevens* [2009] NZSC 15, [2009] 2 NZLR 384 [23] and [68]; *Tonto Home Loans* (n 99) [178].
[118] See, eg, *Plevin v Paragon Personal Finance Ltd* [2014] UKSC 61, [2014] 1 WLR 4222 [33]; *Wombat Nominees Pty Ltd v De Tullio* (1990) 98 ALR 307, 315 and 316–17; *NMFM Property Pty Ltd v Citibank Ltd* [2000] FCA 1558, [551]–[552], [557] and [562]; (2000) 107 FCR 270; *Tonto Home Loans* (n 99) [194]–[195] and [257]; *Serventy v CBA* (n 114) [35]–[37] and [59].
[119] *Kirkpatrick v Kotis* (n 116) [83] and [86].
[120] *Eze v Conway* [2019] EWCA Civ 88 [38]. See also *Wood v Commercial First* (n 98) [26].
[121] See *Norwich Fire Insurance v Brennans* (n 117) 985.
[122] See, eg, cases cited in n 118.
[123] *Hospital Products* (n 1) 97. See also *Plevin* (n 118) [33].
[124] *Alliance Craton Explorer Pty Ltd v Quasar Resources Pty Ltd* [2013] FCAFC 29, [72]; (2013) 296 ALR 465. See also *Tonto Home Loans* (n 99) [177].
[125] See *Colonial Mutual* (n 97) 49 and 50; *Tonto Home Loans* (n 99) [175].

Other cases illustrate that it can be difficult to determine whether that is the case in a given set of circumstances. The High Court of Australia's decisions in *Jones v Bouffier*[126] and *Dowsett v Reid*[127] illustrate the point, as does the more recent English decision in *Eze v Conway*.[128] In *Jones v Bouffier*, the defendant was a non-practising solicitor who assisted the plaintiffs with recovery of some property that had been bought in breach of the fiduciary self-dealing rule, in return for a 25 per cent share in that property. Various efforts were then made to sell the property, particularly by the defendant. The defendant was not legal owner of that property, and so could not sell the property directly, but he arranged a deal with a company that would purchase the property, along with some other adjacent land the defendant had acquired. In order to give effect to that deal, the defendant bought the property from the plaintiffs, and he then sold it to the company. When the plaintiffs realised that he had done so at a profit, they sued on the basis the profit had been generated in a fiduciary capacity as their agent. The defendant had advised the plaintiffs to join with him in acquiring the adjacent land, on the basis the company would require it for the purchase to proceed, and had offered to act as their agent in negotiating the sale, but that offer had been rebuffed by the plaintiffs. As Griffith CJ said, when the defendant was negotiating with the company he was in a sense acting as agent for the plaintiffs,[129] and he spoke casually in those terms (including describing one of the plaintiffs as his partner), but the majority of the court considered that those casual expressions were not determinative:[130] although he was negotiating a sale of the plaintiffs' property, he was doing so as an equitable co-tenant and so was negotiating as a principal rather than as agent for the plaintiffs.[131] The majority of the court considered there was no agency, and no fiduciary relationship, which made it unnecessary to determine whether there had been full disclosure of all material facts.[132]

In *Dowsett v Reid*, Reid was 'an auctioneer and commission agent'.[133] The defendant wanted to sell or let his property, and asked Reid whether he could find a purchaser. Reid made some inquiries, but to no avail, and later asked whether he could lease it himself, to which the defendant agreed. Reid sought specific performance of the lease, and the defendant countered by seeking rescission on the grounds of the fiduciary relationship between the two parties. This was rejected, on the basis that what the defendant had done did not establish a relationship of trust and confidence with Reid,[134] although that decision was more easily reached than it might otherwise have been because the defendant's case had involved a denial of any agency relationship.[135] Even if that had not been the case, any agency that might have existed appeared to have come to an end when the

[126] *Jones v Bouffier* (1911) 12 CLR 579.
[127] *Dowsett v Reid* (1912) 15 CLR 695.
[128] *Conway v Eze* [2018] EWHC 29 (Ch); *Eze v Conway* [2019] EWCA Civ 88.
[129] *Jones v Bouffier* (n 126) 594.
[130] ibid 599.
[131] ibid 591, 595, 600 and 604–05.
[132] ibid 600.
[133] *Dowsett v Reid* (n 127) 696.
[134] ibid 705 and 708.
[135] ibid 702.

parties began negotiations over the terms of the proposed lease to Reid, and Reid had no superior information regarding the property of which he could take advantage.[136]

While it is not necessary, at least within the settled categories of fiduciary relationship, for someone subjectively to repose trust in another in order for a fiduciary relationship to arise,[137] where the parties to a relationship are each acting in their own interests, and known by the other to be doing so, it will be very difficult to establish that one had undertaken to act in the interests of the other to the exclusion of his or her own several interests.[138] Without that, there is no relationship of trust and confidence,[139] which is to say the same thing as that there is no fiduciary relationship.[140] This is what is meant when judges say that the parties were dealing at arm's length,[141] as in both *Jones v Bouffier*[142] and *Dowsett v Reid*.[143]

A similar view of the facts in the case seems to be what underpins the Court of Appeal's decision in *Eze v Conway*.[144] In this case, Prince Eze entered into a contract to buy a property from the Conways, but failed to complete and sought to avoid liability on the basis the Conways had paid a commission to his agent in the transaction. The purchase price for the property had been negotiated with the Conways by Obahor, who described himself as an 'acquisition agent'.[145] In negotiating the price, Obahor had pretended to be representing a client when in fact he had none at that stage; having secured an agreement regarding the price, Obahor then approached Eze (with whom he had had no previous contact), suggesting that he buy the property. In a very brief conversation, Obahor advised Eze that he considered the purchase to be a good deal;[146] Eze agreed to proceed, telling Obahor to contact Eze's financial adviser in the United Kingdom to progress the transaction. Obahor convinced both Eze and the Conways to pay him a commission on the transaction, and the payment by the Conways would undoubtedly have constituted an unauthorised commission if Obahor had been in a fiduciary relationship with Eze.[147] But both the first instance judge and the Court of Appeal considered that the relationship between Obahor and Eze was not a fiduciary one.

Analysing the facts is complicated by the fact that Eze granted Obahor authority to instruct solicitors to exchange contracts with the Conways (Eze having previously

[136] ibid 705.

[137] *Hospital Products* (n 1) 69 and 147.

[138] ibid 96-97; *Bristol & West Building Society v Mothew* [1998] Ch 1, 18 (CA); *Arklow Investments Ltd v Maclean* [2000] 1 WLR 594, 598–600 (PC); *Brandeis (Brokers) Ltd v Black* [2001] 2 All ER (Comm) 980, [36]–[37] (QBD); *Galambos v Perez* [2009] SCC 48, [2009] 3 SCR 247, [66] and [75]–[79]; *Grimaldi v Chameleon Mining NL (No 2)* [2012] FCAFC 6, (2012) 200 FCR 296, [177]; *FHR European Ventures LLP v Cedar Capital Partners LLC* [2014] UKSC 45, [2015] AC 250, [5]. For discussion, see M Conaglen, 'Mason's Fiduciary Principles' in B McDonald, B Chen and J Gordon (eds), *Dynamic and Principled* (Sydney, Federation Press, forthcoming 2022) 296.

[139] *Gibson Motorsport Merchandise Pty Ltd v Forbes* [2006] FCAFC 44, [12]; (2006) 149 FCR 569.

[140] It is also possible for the fiduciary status of a relationship to change, where it becomes clear that the undertaking to act in the interests of the other party is no longer being relied upon: see, eg, *Tigris v China Southern Airlines* (n 113) [159]. See also *Kirkpatrick v Kotis* (n 116) [88]–[89].

[141] BH McPherson, 'Fiduciaries: Who are they?' (1998) 72 *Australian Law Journal* 288, 290.

[142] *Jones v Bouffier* (n 126) 607.

[143] *Dowsett v Reid* (n 127) 705.

[144] *Eze v Conway* (n 120).

[145] *Conway v Eze* [2018] EWHC 29 (Ch) [8].

[146] ibid [27].

[147] ibid [116].

signed the contract), but Obahor did not have authority to negotiate or change any terms in the contract.[148] While that authority made it natural for Eze to argue that an agency relationship was in place, the courts rejected that view of the facts. This was a difficult case, and the facts are close to the line, particularly given the implicit advice that Obahor had given to Eze that the price was competitive,[149] and the authority (albeit limited) that Eze had given Obahor to convey instructions to solicitors on his behalf. But limited actions that could potentially be characterised as involving agency will not identify an agency arrangement if the other elements of the relationship are not consistent with that characterisation.[150] Obahor also lied freely in arranging the transaction, particularly in extracting his commission from the Conways,[151] but fraud is not itself a justification for finding that the parties were in a fiduciary relationship.[152] The Court of Appeal noted that agents do not necessarily owe fiduciary duties, and that fiduciary duties can be owed by people who are not agents,[153] but the fundamental reason for Eze's loss lies in the Court's view that Obahor was not acting as Eze's agent. Rather, he was seen as a salesman who had a product (the deal that he had negotiated with the Conways) that he was seeking to sell to Eze: 'he was in substance a salesman acting on his own behalf and for his own commercial interest'.[154] Obahor had not been acting on behalf of Eze when the contract price was negotiated, and Eze's reliance on his UK financial adviser meant that his relationship with Obahor did not develop into one where he was a trusted adviser.[155] When his role in the transaction is seen in that way, there was no basis for Eze to consider that Obahor had undertaken to act in Eze's interests to the exclusion of Obahor's own personal interest.

A different set of facts produced a similar conclusion in *CH Offshore Ltd v Internaves Consorcio Naviero SA*.[156] In this case, a Venezuelan company invited tenders for charterparties. The invitation was sent to numerous potentially interested parties, including the defendant shipbrokers, who sent it to another shipbroker (Seascope) that forwarded it to the claimant shipowner. The claimant tendered and was informed by Seascope that an increased commission was required, for division among other brokers. The defendant brokers then negotiated with Seascope to reduce the claimant's daily rate in the tender, with a view to the defendants' being able to retain the difference. The claimant's tender was accepted, and it entered into commission agreements with the defendant brokers and signed the charterparties. When the ships were not needed, a claim against

[148] ibid [115]; *Eze v Conway* (n 120) [18].

[149] In *Medsted v Canaccord*, delivered on the same day and by the same judges that decided *Eze v Conway*, a representation of that sort (in the context of a different relationship) was considered important in establishing a fiduciary relationship: *Medsted Associates Ltd v Canaccord Genuity Wealth (International) Ltd* [2019] EWCA Civ 83, [2019] 1 WLR 4481 [32]. On the relevance of advice in identifying fiduciary relationships, see also *McKenzie v McDonald* (n 13) 145; *Tufton v Sperni* [1952] 2 TLR 516, 525, 531–32 and 533 (CA); *McWilliam v Norton Finance (UK) Ltd* [2015] EWCA Civ 186, [2015] 1 All ER (Comm) 1026 [39] and [44].

[150] *Marme Inversiones 2007 SL v Natwest Markets plc* [2019] EWHC 366 (Comm) [415], applying *UBS v KWL* (n 99).

[151] *Conway v Eze* (n 145) [9], [38] and [41]; *Eze v Conway* (n 120) [11].

[152] *Hospital Products* (n 1) 73–74 and 149.

[153] *Eze v Conway* (n 120) [39]–[40].

[154] *Conway v Eze* (n 145) [112].

[155] *Eze v Conway* (n 120) [46]–[53].

[156] *CH Offshore Ltd v Internaves Consorcio Naviero SA* [2020] EWHC 1710 (Comm).

the Venezuelan company was settled, but the defendant brokers successfully brought arbitration proceedings for their unpaid commissions. On appeal to the High Court, Moulder J considered that the brokers were intermediaries between the claimant and the Venezuelan company, but they had not acted as agents for either of those parties: while the brokers had a duty to communicate messages honestly between the parties,[157] that did not extend to a duty to disclose the bargaining position of the other party.[158] Somewhat like *Eze v Conway*, the claimant had its own agent, Seascope, and the defendants did not owe any duty to avoid conflicts:

> [T]o impose such a fiduciary duty would result in the commercial absurdity that he would be unable to act and perform the role inherent in that of an intermediary as someone who stands between two parties to facilitate the relationship.[159]

iii. Partial Agency

A final point that deserves mention in the present context is to note the possibility of a person's being an agent in respect of *part only* of his or her activities, and not in respect of other activities. In *Brandeis (Brokers) Ltd v Black*,[160] for example, a broker operating on the London Metal Exchange was held to owe fiduciary duties when clients placed orders with it to buy or sell on the market, but it was recognised that fiduciary duties would probably not be relevant where the client sold to or bought from the broker directly. The broker's role in buying on the market was an agency role,[161] and so subject to fiduciary duties, but 'a person may be a fiduciary in some but not all aspects of his relationship with another'.[162] For reasons that have already been discussed, this can be the case even where those other activities are for the benefit of the other person. Thus, for example, it is well known that banks do not owe fiduciary duties in respect of client deposits: 'the sum in question is forthwith regarded as being lent by the customer to the bank'[163] and 'is then the banker's money; he is known to deal with it as his own; he makes what profit of it he can, which profit he retains to himself'.[164] But the debtor–creditor relationship between bank and customer is only part of the story.[165] As Lord Brougham recognised in *Foley v Hill*, there are 'certain acts that are often performed by a banker [that] may, in addition to his position of banker, make himself an agent or a trustee'.[166] As Lord Atkinson put it in *Westminster Bank Ltd v Hilton*:

> It is well established that the normal relation between a banker and his customer is that of debtor and creditor, but it is equally well established that *quoad* the drawing and payment of

[157] ibid [68]–[69].
[158] ibid [83]–[84].
[159] ibid [74]; see also [67] and [81].
[160] *Brandeis v Black* (n 138).
[161] A broker in that situation is expected to sell to a third party, rather than taking the property for itself: *Brookman v Rothschild* (1829) 3 Sim 153, 214–15; 57 ER 957; affirmed in (1831) 2 Dow & Cl 188, 195; 6 ER 699 (HL).
[162] *Brandeis v Black* (n 138) [37].
[163] Ellinger (n 83) 223. See also *N Joachimson v Swiss Bank Corp* [1921] 3 KB 110, 127 (CA); M Brindle and R Cox, *Law of Bank Payments*, 2nd edn (London, Sweet & Maxwell, 1999) [7-116].
[164] *Foley v Hill* (n 38) 36.
[165] R Cranston, *Principles of Banking Law*, 2nd edn (Oxford, Oxford University Press, 2002) 131–32.
[166] *Foley v Hill* (n 38) 44. See also Cranston (n 165) 132; Ellinger (n 83) 123–24.

> the customer's cheques as against money of the customer's in the banker's hands the relation is that of principal and agent.[167]

Fiduciary duties could, therefore, be owed in respect of the agency aspects of the banker's role,[168] notwithstanding the lack of fiduciary liability in respect of the banker's other activities.

It is important, therefore, to be precise as to the agency role that is said to found fiduciary duties. In *Nordisk Insulinlaboratorium v Gorgate Products Ltd*,[169] for example, the defendant had been the 'selling agent' in England for one of the plaintiff's insulin products before the Second World War broke out. Shortly before the war broke out, the plaintiff deposited stocks of a different form of insulin (the raw material for the product the defendant had been selling) at branches of a bank in England, with assistance from the defendant. As a Danish corporation, the plaintiff became an enemy when Germany invaded Denmark, and the raw insulin became vested in the Custodian of Enemy Property. The defendant persuaded the Custodian to sell the raw insulin to it, relying on a special or moral claim based on its prior association with the plaintiff, and then subsold it to Boots Pure Drug Co Ltd at a profit. The plaintiff's claim to recover that profit, as having been made in breach of fiduciary duty, failed on the basis that the defendant had not benefited from any special or confidential knowledge regarding the raw insulin, and the agency agreement was limited to the defendant's selling of the refined insulin product: the defendant had no agency relationship with the plaintiff regarding the stocks of raw insulin. A person 'may be in a fiduciary position quoad a part of his activities and not quoad other parts: each transaction, or group of transactions, must be looked at'.[170]

B. Non-Fiduciary Agents

The discussion at this juncture points towards part of the difficulty in discussing whether agents necessarily owe fiduciary duties, in the sense that it emphasises the overlap between the two concepts and that key indicators of one concept are often used to determine whether the other concept is applicable for the purposes of deciding a case. Thus, for example, one finds cases in which the question whether a person was acting in a representative character – one of the central aspects of agency[171] – is used to identify whether that person owed fiduciary duties;[172] and similarly there are cases where an ability to profit personally from the arrangement – inconsistent with fiduciary doctrine's central prohibition on unauthorised profit-taking – is used as a reason to conclude that the person was not acting as an agent.[173] The difficulty then lies in disentangling the

[167] *Westminster Bank Ltd v Hilton* (1926) 43 TLR 124, 126 (HL). See also *Re Farrow's Bank Ltd* [1923] 1 Ch 41, 50–51 (ChD) and 53–54 (CA); *London Joint Stock Bank Ltd v Macmillan* [1918] AC 777, 789 and 814; Brindle and Cox (n 163) [3-146], [7-102] and [7-114]; Ellinger (n 83) 224, 488 and 687.

[168] *Nimmo v Westpac Banking Corp* [1993] 3 NZLR 218, 237 (HC).

[169] *Nordisk Insulinlaboratorium v Gorgate Products Ltd* [1953] Ch 430 (CA).

[170] *NZ Netherlands Society* (n 95) 1130.

[171] *Tonto Home Loans* (n 99) [177].

[172] *Hospital Products* (n 1) 97.

[173] See, eg *Potter v Customs* (n 97) 52; *Tonto Home Loans* (n 99) [185]–[[195].

concepts in the cases. It is suggested that this can be done by focusing attention on these central indicators of the two concepts: there are cases that indicate that there can be circumstances where one person is acting in a representative capacity for another, including in the sense of having power to bind that other person, and is thus acting as agent for that other person, but the circumstances are such that the 'agent' is permitted to exercise that power in his or her own interests, and so the person is not in a fiduciary position vis-à-vis the other (at least regarding the exercise of that power; possibly for all purposes).

In *Halton International Inc (Holding) SARL v Guernroy Ltd*,[174] for example, the parties were founding investors in an airline. At various points in time, financial pressures prompted consideration of capital structure revision. The company's chairman also sought to negotiate a franchise agreement with British Airways (BA), but that failed when the necessary funds were not raised. Facing renewed pressure to find a way to avoid liquidation, the shareholders signed a voting agreement that gave the defendant shareholder 'a power of attorney enabling it to act as the agent of and to vote the shares of the other shareholders for the purposes set out in the agreement'.[175] The purpose of the agreement was to enable the defendant to negotiate a new deal with BA, and the agreement stated that the defendant could seek to raise the funds needed for such an agreement in any manner the defendant saw fit. The defendant succeeded in securing a new BA franchise offer. At that point, the defendant provided the company with short-term finance, and was given security for that debt as well as a right to subscribe for the entire issue of shares needed to secure the finance for the franchise agreement. An extraordinary general meeting was then held, at which the defendant exercised its voting power under the agreement to confirm the issue of these new shares to itself and three other subscribers, who the plaintiffs alleged were close friends and associates of the defendant's owner.

In deciding whether the defendant's power to exercise the voting rights of the plaintiffs' shares was held in a fiduciary capacity, Patten J emphasised the importance of understanding the context in which that power had been granted. The defendant had been asked to try to raise finance for a new BA franchise in circumstances where it was clear (from the failure of the first franchise attempt) that current shareholders were unlikely to provide that finance, and so the defendant was in effect being asked to underwrite the share issue itself in order to be able to guarantee to BA that the necessary funds would be raised; it was 'hardly surprising that [the defendant] was only prepared to do that on terms that [it] was given complete control'.[176] The defendant's power of attorney could only be used for the purpose for which it was granted – to attempt to procure the funding needed for the BA franchise[177] – but that limitation is not peculiar to powers held in a fiduciary capacity.[178] It was clear that the defendant had not treated the interests of the plaintiffs as its primary concern when it exercised its power to vote their shares,[179] but Patten J considered this was permissible under the

[174] *Halton International Inc (Holding) SARL v Guernroy Ltd* [2005] EWHC 1968 (Ch).
[175] ibid [25].
[176] ibid [90]; see also [94], [96] and [150].
[177] ibid [149]–[150].
[178] M Conaglen, *Fiduciary Loyalty* (Oxford, Hart Publishing, 2010) 44–50.
[179] *Halton v Guernroy* (n 174) [152].

voting agreement: the 'commercial realities' were such that the defendant owed no fiduciary duty to refrain from issuing shares to itself or associates of the defendant's owner, and to 'superimpose on this a radically different set of [fiduciary] obligations would be quite inconsistent with the relevant circumstances in which the voting agreement came to be made'.[180]

An appeal considered (and failed on) a limitation point only, leave to appeal having been limited to that issue. This is unfortunate, as Chadwick LJ had indicated that 'there were realistic prospects of success'[181] on some of the substantive grounds of appeal, but it is not clear what those were. That perhaps weakens the authority of Patten J's decision, but the point that matters for present purposes is that Patten J's decision is understandable in orthodox fiduciary terms, notwithstanding its effect that an agent holding a power of attorney was not subject to fiduciary duties in the exercise of that power. Where the circumstances of an appointment are such that it is clear that the agent is permitted to act in its own interests, or in those of persons other than the principal, the agent has not 'undertaken to act for or on behalf of another in a particular matter in circumstances which give rise to a relationship of trust and confidence';[182] there is no fiduciary relationship.

It is important in understanding such cases firmly to bear in mind the well-established tenet of fiduciary doctrine that a 'fiduciary relationship, *if it is to exist at all*, must accommodate itself to the terms of the contract so that it is consistent with, and conforms to, them'.[183] As Lord Wilberforce put it, 'the precise scope of it must be moulded according to the nature of the relationship'.[184] If one person has given to another the power to bind him or her, and it is made clear in their agreement, or it is clear from the circumstances in which that agreement is made that the power can be used in the interests of the donee, it is not a misuse of either the English or the legal lexicon to describe that donee as an agent, but one who is not bound by fiduciary duties in the exercise of that power. That is relatively unusual, of course, because an agent is normally appointed in circumstances where it is clear that he or she is expected to represent, and act in the interests of, his or her principal, to the exclusion of his or her own several interests; and so fiduciary duties are normally owed. But *Halton v Guernroy* is an example that shows that is not always the case. The relative rarity of such cases explains the view that the general rule is that agents owe fiduciary duties: cases like *Halton v Guernroy* are the exception that prove the (existence of the general) rule.

As is clear from the discussion above, the decision in *Halton v Guernroy* was heavily dependent on the factual circumstances in which the power had been granted to the defendant. But other kinds of agents act in contexts in which their fiduciary duties are modified in response to that context in a more general way. An auctioneer, for example,

[180] ibid [150].
[181] *Halton International Inc v Guernroy Ltd* [2006] EWCA Civ 801 [7].
[182] *Mothew* (n 138) 18. See also text accompanying nn 137–141.
[183] *Hospital Products* (n 1) 97 (emphasis added). See also *Kelly v Cooper* [1993] AC 205, 215 (PC); *Henderson v Merrett Syndicates Ltd* [1995] 2 AC 145, 206; *Breen v Williams* (1996) 186 CLR 71, 109 and 132–33; *John Alexander's Clubs Pty Ltd v White City Tennis Club Ltd* [2010] HCA 19 [91], (2010) 241 CLR 1; *Australian Competition and Consumer Commission v Flight Centre Travel Group Ltd* [2016] HCA 49 [78]; (2016) 261 CLR 203.
[184] *NZ Netherlands Society* (n 95) 1130.

'is agent for *both* seller and buyer, so as to bind them by his signature'.[185] But this is 'due to the exigencies of a sale by auction',[186] so the agency for the seller is limited to the time of the sale,[187] the auctioneer 'is not his agent for all purposes',[188] and it does not mean that the auctioneer owes no fiduciary duties to the seller.[189] Similarly, '[i]t is plain that residential estate agents could not sensibly carry out their function if the normal conflict rule applied, and any person instructing an estate agent must appreciate that fact',[190] so an estate agent is permitted to act for multiple vendors simultaneously, notwithstanding the conflict of duties inherent in that role.[191] Likewise, where an agent's authority is granted to secure an interest of the agent: 'Where the parties agree that [an] agent is to have a personal financial interest in the performance of his agency, over and above the receipt of his remuneration, his duty of loyalty is to that extent compromised.'[192]

Another situation where this is common across a category of actors is the appointment of receivers out of court by mortgagees and other debenture holders.[193] Such receivers are invariably appointed as agents of the company in receivership, '[b]ut … it is quite plain that a person appointed as receiver and manager is concerned, not for the benefit of the company but for the benefit of the mortgagee bank, to realize the security: that is the whole purpose of his appointment'.[194] The receiver is, thus, 'no ordinary agent'.[195] The receiver's agency is

> primarily a device to protect the mortgagee or debenture holder. Thus, the receiver acts as agent for the mortgagor in that he has power to affect the mortgagor's position by acts which, though done for the benefit of the debenture holder, are treated as if they were the acts of the mortgagor.[196]

Therefore, despite the agency, the circumstances are such that it is clear that the receiver need not act in the interests of the company: the agency exists for the benefit of the receiver and mortgagee, rather than for the mortgagor.[197] As Tipping J put it:

> It does not seem to me to be necessary or consistent with principle to hold the view that a receiver also stands in a general fiduciary relationship with the company in receivership. It is one thing to impose upon a receiver a duty of care, it is quite another to hold that his duties

[185] *Mews v Carr* (1856) 1 H & N 484, 488; 156 ER 1292 (emphasis added). See also *Chaney v Maclow* [1929] 1 Ch 461 (CA).
[186] *Chaney v Maclow* (n 185) 477.
[187] *Bell v Balls* [1897] 1 Ch 663.
[188] *Flint v Woodin* (1852) 9 Hare 618, 622; 68 ER 660.
[189] See, eg, *Oliver v Court* (n 3).
[190] *Rossetti Marketing Ltd v Diamond Sofa Co Ltd* [2012] EWCA Civ 1021 [25], [2013] 1 All ER (Comm) 308.
[191] *Kelly v Cooper* (n 183).
[192] *Angove's Pty Ltd v Bailey* [2016] UKSC 47 [8], [2016] 1 WLR 3179; see also ibid at [9].
[193] The position differs where the receiver is appointed by the court: see *Re Newdigate Colliery Ltd* [1912] 1 Ch 468, 477–78 (CA); G Lightman et al, *Lightman & Moss on the Law of Administrators and Receivers of Companies*, 6th edn (London, Sweet & Maxwell, 2017) [29-020]; PW Young, C Croft and ML Smith, *On Equity* (Sydney, Lawbook Co, 2009) [16.620].
[194] *Re B Johnson & Co (Builders) Ltd* [1955] Ch 634, 644–45 (CA).
[195] *Gomba Holdings UK Ltd v Homan* [1986] 1 WLR 1301, 1305 (ChD). See also *Visbord v Federal Commissioner of Taxation* (1943) 68 CLR 354, 382; *Silven Properties Ltd v Royal Bank of Scotland plc* [2003] EWCA Civ 1409, [2004] 1 WLR 997 [24].
[196] *Gomba Holdings UK Ltd v Minories Finance Ltd* [1988] 1 WLR 1231, 1233 (CA).
[197] *Sheahan v Carrier Air Conditioning Pty Ltd* (1997) 189 CLR 407, 433.

3

Ministerial Acts

RACHEL LEOW*

I. Introduction

References to merely ministerial acts occur surprisingly frequently. There is no shortage of synonyms; the same idea is conveyed by references to persons' being 'conduits',[1] 'mere messengers',[2] an 'instrument',[3] 'mediums of communication',[4] acting equivalent to 'a postman'[5] or doing 'mechanical' acts.[6] Specialised terms may be preferred in specific contexts. 'Amanuensis' is typically used in connection with the production of written documents: text may be dictated to an amanuensis who transcribes it;[7] an amanuensis may take meeting minutes[8] or affix engravings of the principal's signature onto documents.[9] The language of 'messenger', on the other hand, is most apt when referring to the conveyance of messages or documents between one person and another.[10] While statements might pass through a 'conduit', equally, so can money: in *Agip (Africa) Ltd v Jackson*, Millett J described an agent who receives a mistaken payment on behalf of the principal as 'a mere conduit pipe'.[11]

* I am very grateful to Michael Bridge, Paul Davies, Jason Neyers, Andreas Televantos and Francis Reynolds for very helpful comments on an earlier draft.

[1] *Charles Russell Speechlys LLP v Pieres* [2018] 7 WLUK 476; *R v Varley* [2020] 4 WLUK 554.

[2] *Dunhill v Burgin* [2014] UKSC 18, [2014] 1 WLR 933.

[3] *Lord v Hall* (1848) 2 Carr & K 698, 175 ER 292.

[4] *Hollins v Fowler* (1874-75) LR 7 HL 757 (HL), 800.

[5] *Solomon Lew v Kaikhushru Shiavax Nargolwala* [2021] SGCA(I) 1.

[6] *Parkin v Williams* [1985] NZCA 112, [1986] 1 NZLR 294.

[7] eg *Lord St John v Boughton* (1838) 9 Sim 219, 59 ER 342; *Reed v Columbia Fur Dressers & Dyers Ltd* [1965] 1 WLR 13 (QB) (hospital records entered on behalf of doctors); *Shuck v Loveridge* [2005] EWHC 72 (Ch) (will). In Scotland see, eg, *Joseph Evans & Sons v John G Stein & Company* (1904) 12 SLT 462 (Ct of Session, Inner House) (amanuensis writing letters on business), 464–65; *Moffat v Hunter* (1972) SLT (Sh Ct) 42 (statements typed up by amanuensis).

[8] *Lee Panavision Ltd v Lee Lighting Ltd* [1991] BCC 620 (CA) 627 (company secretary).

[9] *Jenkins v Gaisford and Thring* (1863) 3 S & T 93, 164 ER 1208.

[10] *Lake v Simmons* [1927] AC 487 (HL), 489; *Coldunell Ltd v Gallon* [1986] QB 1184 (CA), 1206; *FM Capital Partners Ltd v Marino* [2018] EWHC 1768 (Comm) [321]. Though it can also be used in different circumstances, eg *Whittaker v Forshaw* [1919] 2 KB 419 (KB), 423 (farmer's daughter delivered pints of milk to customers); *Patel v Willis* [1951] 2 KB 78 (Div Ct), 81 (if goods delivered to messenger to collect, possibly no 'supply' of goods to messenger under statute).

[11] *Agip (Africa) Ltd v Jackson* [1990] Ch 265 (Ch).

References to ministerial acts are scattered widely across the leading work on agency law, *Bowstead & Reynolds on Agency*. They appear in discussing whether a person who simply follows specific instructions falls within a classic definition of agency.[12] They also appear as an exception to the *delegatus non potest delegare* rule (an agent cannot delegate discretions).[13] Someone appointed to do only 'ministerial' acts may owe relatively limited duties to his principal.[14] The 'ministerial' nature of acts arguably appears to play the most significant role in the relationship between agents and third parties. It is suggested that an agent who receives payments for his principal may have a defence of 'ministerial receipt' to restitutionary claims brought by the payor;[15] an agent who does only 'ministerial acts' to property may escape liability for conversion[16] and, possibly, knowing receipt.[17] Agents of trustees may avoid liability for 'inconsistent dealing' where they follow the instructions of their principals honestly.[18]

The idea of ministerial acts is itself of considerable antiquity. In the past, it might have been necessary to use an amanuensis when a person was uneducated and unable to write even his name;[19] secretaries or clerks had to deliver share certificates.[20] Illiteracy is, happily, greatly reduced today. The move towards share dematerialisation obviates the need to send messengers around with physical share certificates. But other reasons for the use of ministerial actors still hold. Illness or infirmity is one: in *Lord St John v Boughton*, an attack of gout in the hand led an amanuensis to be employed, but poor health was also the reason for using an amanunesis in *Shuck v Loveridge*, where the testator of a will had been admitted to a hospital psychiatric ward.[21] Increasing use of bank transfers means that payments will frequently be made through banks, and cross-border transactions may require intermediaries for communication where the parties do not speak the same language.[22]

The idea of ministerial acts is thus unlikely to disappear; it may even increase in importance. In the future, increasing numbers of ministerial acts will also be done by machines. A relatively primitive example is a 'signature writing machine' with the trademark of 'Ghostwriter'[23] in *Ramsay v Love*, used to produce the signature of the celebrity chef Gordon Ramsay on legal documents.[24] (A different 'Ghostwriter' was used to sign autographs on books and photographs.)[25] Machines may sign documents,

[12] P Watts and F Reynolds (eds), *Bowstead & Reynolds on Agency*, 22nd edn (London, Sweet & Maxwell, 2020) paras 1-005, 1-047 (hereinafter *Bowstead & Reynolds*).

[13] ibid paras 5-001–5-003.

[14] ibid para 6-037.

[15] ibid paras 8-174, 8-214. Compare also ibid para 9-106.

[16] ibid paras 9-127, 9-129.

[17] ibid para 9-139.

[18] L Tucker, N Le Poidevin QC and J Brightwell, *Lewin on Trusts*, 20th edn (London, Sweet & Maxwell, 2020) para 42-117.

[19] *King v John Morris* (1814) 2 Lea 1096, 168 ER 644.

[20] *Ruben v Great Fingall Consolidated* [1906] AC 439 (HL), 444.

[21] *Shuck v Loveridge* [2005] EWHC 72 (Ch). See also *Barrett v Bem* [2012] EWCA Civ 52 (testator unable to sign will himself when given pen due to his hand's shaking); *Fulton v Kee* [1961] NI 1 (testator suffered from severe disseminated sclerosis, which made movement difficult).

[22] eg, *Amoutzas v Tattersalls* [2010] EWHC 1696 (QB), where the principal spoke virtually no English and was heavily reliant on agents to interpret, speak and write on his behalf.

[23] *Ramsay v Love* [2015] EWHC 65 (Ch) [74].

[24] ibid [77].

[25] ibid.

make or receive payments via automated payment systems;[26] algorithmic trading software may automatically execute trades following pre-set parameters.[27]

The wide range of situations in which the idea of 'ministerial' acts is relied on raises some interrelated questions. What is a ministerial act? Is there a single, uniform conception of ministerial acts across these different areas? If not, should we be more precise in our usage of the term?

This chapter tackles these questions. After considering six different areas where ministerial acts appear relevant, it shows that there are at least four different conceptions of ministerial acts. For example, ministerial acts in conversion are not the same as ministerial acts in sub-agency; both differ from ministerial acts in knowing receipt. These four conceptions differ from one another in multiple ways: they may be used for different purposes, some are questions of degree while others adopt a bright-line approach, and some require special justification while others do not.

In principle, two options are available. The first is to retain the different meanings of a 'ministerial act', simply taking care not to use them interchangeably. Plurality in meaning is not a problem if we are not deceived into thinking that the same word bears the same meaning. A second, more reformative option is to limit the use of the label 'ministerial acts'. In this chapter it is suggested that the second approach ought to be preferred. Three reasons are given in its favour: it is likely to be less productive of error and mistake, it enables accurate labelling of distinct concepts and, perhaps most importantly, it helps identify aspects of the law in need of further investigation. In particular, it suggests that the label of 'ministerial act' has concealed difficulties with when and why the actor performing 'ministerial acts' can avoid liability to third parties in conversion, knowing receipt, restitutionary claims and inconsistent dealing.

Sections II, III and IV examine areas where references to 'ministerial acts' are frequently seen. Section II examines 'ministerial acts' that are treated as the principal's own. Section III examines 'ministerial acts' involving little or no exercise of discretion, trust and confidence in their performance, and section IV examines the wide range of cases where the actor incurs no personal liability to third parties for his 'ministerial acts'. Section V concludes that there is no single conception of ministerial acts but at least four different ones. Section VI explores possible ways forward, concluding that it is best to limit the term 'ministerial act' to acts that do not require discretion, trust or confidence for their performance.

II. Ministerial Acts as Instances of Agency

First, a 'ministerial act' may simply refer to one that can be treated as the principal's own. This is just the standard outcome of agency: *qui facit per alium, facit per se* (he who acts through another, acts himself). The agent acts for the principal; his acts are treated as the principal's own. This sense of 'ministerial act' is no different from any other authorised

[26] See the Australian Royal Commission, *Royal Commission into Misconduct in the Banking, Superannuation and Financial Services Industry*, vol 1, Final Report (February 2019) 150–51.

[27] *Quoine Pte Ltd v B2C2 Ltd* [2020] SGCA(I) 2, [2020] 2 SLR 20.

act done by an agent for his principal.[28] Examples include some standard agency cases, and the 'ministerial receipt' doctrine in unjust enrichment and in sub-agency.

A. Ministerial Acts as the Principal's Own

Ministerial acts are frequently seen when they are treated as the principal's own. This is just the standard outcome of agency. Some examples illustrate. An insurance agent who fills out insurance forms for proposed insureds, acts as the insureds' amanuensis or agent, so the statements he makes in the forms are the insureds' own.[29] In the classic case of *Winter v Irish Life Assurance plc*,[30] the proposed insureds, a married couple, had cystic fibrosis. They were advised by their insurance agent to leave questions about their medical condition unanswered. He told them that he would fill in the blank questions. The agent was aware of the insureds' medical condition but did not disclose it on the forms. When the husband tried to enforce the policy, it was held that the agent's statements in filling out the forms were the insured's. Thus, the insurer could set aside the policy for non-disclosure.

This use of ministerial acts may also occur in a wide range of cases, as cases on statement-making show. In *R v Kishor Derodra*, a criminal case, the accused had been the victim of a burglary. He subsequently took out insurance and then made a claim for the losses of the burgled items, for which he was charged under the Theft Act 1968. The issue was whether a police record of the burglary could be admitted into evidence even if the police officer could not be found. This turned on whether the statement-maker could give evidence. It was concluded that when information had been provided to a police officer who wrote it up in a report, the maker of the document was the officer but the maker of the statement was the information-supplier.[31] The police officer had acted only as 'a mere conduit pipe or amanuensis for the recording of information given by another'.[32] Thus, the record could be admitted, since the accused was present. Similar reasoning can be found in the earlier Scottish case, *Moffat v Hunter*.[33] Again the case concerned the admissibility of written statements made to an investigating insurance company. A statement had been written by a Mr Stewart, who took it to the insurance company's secretary to be typed. He then signed the typed copy. Some months later he died. It was recognised that '[t]he words are wholly those of Mr Stewart though passed, as I say, through an amanuensis'.[34] No conflict of interest arose by the insurance secretary's typing of the statements, and the evidence could thus be admitted.

A 'ministerial act' for this purpose includes both acts where the agent has little discretion and those where it had great discretion. The former includes cases where the

[28] See, eg, *Bowstead & Reynolds* (n 12) para 1-005.

[29] See also *Newsholme Bros v Road and Transport and General Insurance Co* [1929] 2 KB 356 (CA); *Zurich General Accident and Liability Insurance Co v Leven* (1940) SC 406 (Ct of Session, Inner House).

[30] *Winter v Irish Life Assurance plc* [1995] CLC 722 (QB).

[31] *R v Kishor Derodra* [2000] 1 Cr App R 41 (CA), 47–48.

[32] ibid 45.

[33] *Moffat v Hunter* 1974 SLR (Sh Ct) 42.

[34] ibid 43.

principal specifically directs an amanuensis to sign for him[35] or endorse his name to a bill of exchange.[36] The latter includes cases such as *Charles Russell Speechlys LLP v Pieres*, where a wife entrusted proceedings to her husband to be taken in her name.[37] In the latter case, we seem to be squarely in the realm of standard cases of agency. Indeed, some cases stress this point. In *Pieres*, it was said:

> The conduit for providing instructions to Speechlys was Mr Pieres … One textbook definition of agency is 'a body of general rules under which one person, the agent, has the power to change the legal relations of another, the principal.' This is clearly the power demonstrated by Mr Pieres.[38]

Here, ministerial acts seem to mean nothing more than acts, done by another, that can be regarded as the principal's. It involves nothing but the standard result of agency.

B. Ministerial Receipt in Unjust Enrichment

Similar is one version of the doctrine of 'ministerial receipt' in unjust enrichment. Well-known but surprisingly complicated, 'ministerial receipt' may be used for two distinct purposes. Sometimes it is used to explain why a claim lies against the principal. Other times it explains why no claim lies against the agent. The former concerns the principal–third party relationship, explaining how the ministerial agent's acts are the principal's own, while the latter concerns the agent–third party relationship. Here we consider only the former; the latter is considered later.

An instance of 'ministerial receipt' used to establish the payor's right to restitution against the principal can be seen in *Agip (Africa) Ltd v Jackson*, where Millett J explained:

> Money paid by mistake to [an agent who has accounted to his principal] cannot afterwards be recovered from the agent but only from the principal … In such a case the agent is treated as a mere conduit pipe and the money is taken as having been paid to the principal rather than the agent.[39]

Later, in *Portman Building Society v Hamlyn Taylor Neck (a firm)*, Millett LJ (as he had then become) reiterated:

> The general rule is that money paid (eg by mistake) to an agent who has accounted to his principal without notice of the claim cannot be recovered from the agent but only from the principal … At common law the agent recipient is regarded as a mere conduit for the money, which is treated as paid to the principal, not to the agent. The doctrine is therefore not so much a defence as a means of identifying the proper party to be sued.[40]

Similar statements of more ancient origin can be found. A classic case is *Sadler v Evans*, where sums were paid to the agent of Lady Windsor in the mistaken belief that those

[35] *Jenkins v Gaisford* (1863) 3 Sw & Tr 93, 164 ER 1208 (HC of Admiralty).
[36] *Lord v Hall* (1848) 2 Car & K 698, 175 ER 292 (Assizes).
[37] *Charles Russell Speechlys LLP v Pieres* [2018] 7 WLUK 476 (Senior Courts Costs Office).
[38] ibid [30].
[39] *Agip* (n 11) 288, not addressed on appeal: [1991] Ch 547 (CA).
[40] *Portman Building Society v Hamlyn Taylor Neck (a firm)* [1998] PNLR 664 (CA), 669.

sums were due.[41] In an action to recover them from the agent, Lord Mansfield held that 'the plaintiff ought not to recover against the defendant, in this action; and that the action ought to have been brought against Lady Windsor herself, and not against her agent'.[42] Similarly, in *Edgell v Day*, Erle CJ concluded that '[t]he general principle of law is, that a payment of money to an agent is payment to the principal'.[43]

The modern explanation is that while the agent physically receives the sums, it is the principal who has been enriched at the payor's expense. In a unanimous judgment in *Investment Trust Companies v HMRC*, the Supreme Court emphasised the general requirement that enrichment of the defendant at the claimant's expense requires a direct provision of a benefit by claimant to defendant. Lord Reed, delivering the sole reasoned speech, explained that

> where the agent of one of the parties is interposed between them … the agent is the proxy of his principal, by virtue of the law of agency. The series of transactions between the claimant and the agent, and between the agent and the defendant, is therefore legally equivalent to a transaction directly between the claimant and defendant.[44]

In this sense, 'ministerial receipt' only means that the agent's acts will be treated as the principal's own; the principal is then obliged to make restitution of the sums. The underlying principle is the same as that in the earlier category.

C. Sub-Agency

In a third area, sub-agency, ministerial acts again refer to acts that can be treated as the principal's own. Here, the question is: When can agents delegate their authority to act for the principal to another agent (a sub-agent)?[45] The general rule, *delegatus non potest delegare*, prohibits agents from delegating their authority to act for the principal except with the principal's express or implied authority to do so. But this rule does not apply to 'purely ministerial acts'.[46] An agent may thus appoint another to perform purely ministerial acts even without the principal's authority to do so.

In sub-agency, a ministerial act is one where performance requires no exercise of trust, confidence or discretion. The general rule applies because there is trust, confidence or discretion reposed in the agent.[47] Where trust, confidence or discretion is absent, the justification for the general rule does not apply.[48]

Examples of such ministerial acts include a daughter's endorsing a signature to a bill of exchange on her mother's instructions in *Lord v Hall*,[49] a real estate agent's executing a memorandum in writing as a mere formality when all terms of the contract had

[41] *Sadler v Evans* (1766) 4 Burr 1984, 98 ER 34.
[42] ibid 1986.
[43] *Edgell v Day* (1865) LR 1 CP 80, 84.
[44] *Investment Trust Companies v HMRC* [2017] UKSC 29, [2017] 2 WLR 1200 [48].
[45] On distinguishing between co-agency and sub-agency, see *Bowstead & Reynolds* (n 12) paras 5-008–5-011.
[46] H Beale (ed), *Chitty on Contracts*, 33rd edn (London, Sweet & Maxwell, 2018) vol 2, para 31-041.
[47] *De Bussche v Alt* (1878) 8 Ch D 286 (CA), 310.
[48] eg *Allam & Co Ltd v Europa Poster Services Ltd* [1968] 1 WLR 638 (Ch), 642.
[49] *Lord v Hall* (1848) 2 Car & K 698, 175 ER 292 (Williams J).

been agreed,[50] signing a bill of lading,[51] giving notice to licensees to terminate their licences,[52] giving instructions to dispose of funds,[53] clerks' receiving money and doing other acts for an attorney,[54] and a secretary's bidding at an auction pursuant to her boss's instructions.[55]

In these cases, the performance of the act requires no exercise of trust, confidence or discretion. The *delegatus* rule is not triggered. The agent can thus procure another to do these ministerial acts without the principal's express or implied authority to do so. The ministerial acts are treated as the agent's acts, which in turn are the principal's.[56] Again, *qui facit per alium, facit per se.*

III. Ministerial Acts as Acts Not Requiring Trust, Confidence or Discretion

'Ministerial acts' might also refer to acts that can be performed without requiring the exercise of trust, confidence or discretion. This meaning is found in sub-agency and when assessing the duties an actor owes, particularly fiduciary duties.

A. Sub-Agency

As seen earlier, 'ministerial acts' in sub-agency are important because their performance can be delegated by an agent without the principal's express or implied authority. The *effect* of a ministerial act's being done is that the ministerial act is treated as the agent's own, which can then be treated as the principal's own where it falls within the agent's scope of authority. However, the *test* used for a ministerial act in that context is that the act is one that does not require trust, confidence or discretion. As Buckley J explained in *Allam & Co Ltd v Europa Poster Services Ltd*:

> Where the principal reposes no personal confidence in the agent the maxim has no application, but where the principal does place confidence in the agent, that in respect of which the principal does so must be done by the agent personally, unless, either expressly or inferentially, he is authorised to employ a sub-agent or to delegate the function to another.[57]

Similarly, in the New Zealand case of *Parkin v Williams*, it was said:

> Certainly if there is an element of discretion or confidence involved the signing will not be a mechanical or ministerial act and other considerations will apply. But if the skill

[50] *Parkin v Williams* [1985] NZCA 112, [1986] 1 NZLR 294.
[51] *The Berkshire* [1974] 1 Lloyd's Rep 185 (QB), 188.
[52] *Allam* (n 48).
[53] *Amoutzas v Tattersalls* [2010] EWHC 1696 (QB).
[54] *Hemming v Hale* (1859) 7 CB NS 487, 141 ER 905.
[55] *Bremner v Sinclair* [1998] NSWSC 552. But here it could not be shown that the secretary was so acting and that the ultimate bid was the product of the boss's personal judgement, so the act was not merely ministerial.
[56] See, eg, the reasoning in *Ex parte Sutton* (1788) 2 Cox 84, 30 ER 39.
[57] *Allam* (n 48) 642.

> and discretion reposed in the agent has been exercised it is immaterial who performs the necessary mechanical acts needed to implement the agent's decision.[58]

Examples of ministerial acts for purposes of sub-agency have already been discussed earlier. They are generally acts the ministerial actor has been specifically directed to do, in narrow and precise terms that leave little room for the actor to exercise any independent judgement.

B. Agents' Fiduciary Duties to the Principal

A similar meaning of ministerial acts is adopted in discussions of when agents owe duties to their principals, especially fiduciary duties. It is generally accepted that most, even if not all, agents owe fiduciary duties to their principals.[59] In discussing fiduciary duties, *Bowstead & Reynolds* suggests that a person who is an agent but 'is authorised to carry out an exactly specified act, may … act in no more than a ministerial capacity, even if in so doing the principal's legal position is altered'.[60] The implication: the agent may owe only limited duties to the principal. This restates the general rule that the precise duties owed in any given agency relationship will depend on factors such as the extent of authority given to the agent, and any agreements between principal and agent.[61] The Singaporean case of *Tonny Permana v One Tree Capital Management Pte Ltd* provides an excellent statement of the principles:

> The legal term 'agent' is not homogeneous or monolithic … Simply using the terms 'agent', 'relationship of agency' or 'duties as agent', however, sheds little to no light on the nuances of the relationship between a specific agent and his or her principal … agents and agency relationships exist across a spectrum. This must be borne in mind. It is therefore unsurprising that each unique agency relationship will be accompanied by distinct sets of rights and obligations. It is not the case that every agent will owe, for example, fiduciary duties … In general, it may be said that the more extensive the agency relationship, ie, the greater an agent's authority or ability to affect the principal's interests, the more onerous the duties imposed upon the agent will be.[62]

An individual authorised to carry out a precisely specified act will still owe some duties, including to carry out the task instructed, to act with due care and skill, and, possibly, to inform the principal if the agent no longer wants to do the act.[63] But there will likely be little scope for other duties, such as fiduciary ones. Much ink has been spilt on fiduciary law, with most accounts focusing in some way on the fiduciary's powers to be exercised

[58] *Parkin* (n 50).

[59] See in this volume, ch 2 by Matthew Conaglen on 'The Fiduciary Status of Agents'.

[60] *Bowstead & Reynolds* (n 12) para 6-037.

[61] See, eg, *Kelly v Cooper* [1993] AC 205 (PC). In relation to fiduciary duties, see also *Re Coomber* [1911] 1 Ch 723 (CA).

[62] *Tonny Permana v One Tree Capital Management Pte Ltd* [2021] SGHC 37 [91]–[94] (Chan Seng Onn J), appealed on other grounds: [2021] SGHC(A) 8.

[63] *Volkers & Midland Doherty* (1985) 17 DLR (4th) 343 (British Columbia CA) [12] (salesman of stockbroker agreed to purchase shares at market price first thing in the morning but chose not to because he was concerned about the wisdom of the order).

for other-regarding purposes[64] and the special vulnerability of the principal to misuse of these powers.[65] It seems uncontroversial that the more limited the ministerial agent's powers, the less scope for fiduciary duties to bite. Again, as explained by Chan Seng Onn J in *Tonny Permana*:

> Where an agent is able to unilaterally and significantly influence his/her principal's position or interests and has been conferred such powers in trust and confidence, extensive fiduciary duties may arise. On the other hand, where the agent has limited authority and discretion, the agent will owe few, if any, fiduciary duties.[66]

IV. Ministerial Acts as Explaining why Agents are Not Personally Liable to Third Parties

Perhaps the most frequent references to 'ministerial acts' occur where the agent's personal liability to third parties is considered. Although it is sometimes said that agents 'drop out', this is only clearly true in a limited range of situations such as the formation of contracts by agents who objectively undertake no personal responsibility under the contract.[67] An agent who makes fraudulent misrepresentations for his principal is still personally liable for deceit; he does not drop out.[68]

But sometimes references are made to the ministerial nature of acts to indicate that the agent is not personally liable to third parties. Four examples are considered: conversion, ministerial receipt in unjust enrichment claims, the beneficial receipt requirement in knowing receipt, and inconsistent dealing.

A. Conversion

We first consider conversion, 'by a very considerable margin the most important of the property torts'.[69] Conversion is concerned with the protection of superior possessory rights in personal property.[70] Although a conversion is difficult to define, it has been described as covering acts done with 'an intention on the part of the defendant … to

[64] eg L Smith, 'Fiduciary Relationships: Ensuring the Loyal Exercise of Judgement on Behalf of Another' (2014) 130 *LQR* 608; P Miller, 'The Fiduciary Relationship', in AS Gold and P Miller (eds), *Philosophical Foundations of Fiduciary Law* (Oxford, Oxford University Press 2014).

[65] eg PB Miller, 'Justifying Fiduciary Duties' (2013) 58 *McGill Law Journal* 969; *Hospital Products Ltd v United States Surgical Corporation* (1984) 156 CLR 41329 (Mason J). This feature is typically relied on by deterrence-based accounts of fiduciary law: see, eg, R Flannigan, 'The Boundaries of Fiduciary Accountability' (2004) 83 *Canadian Bar Review* 35; M Conaglen, *Fiduciary Loyalty: Protecting the Due Performance of Non-Fiduciary Duties* (Oxford, Hart Publishing, 2010). For a useful discussion of different types of theories of fiduciary duties, see L Smith, 'Parenthood is a Fiduciary Relationship' (2020) 70 *University of Toronto Law Journal* 395, 401–18.

[66] *Tonny Permana* (n 62) [99].

[67] See generally R Stevens, 'Why Do Agents "Drop Out"?' [2005] LMCLQ 101, 101.

[68] *Standard Chartered Bank v Pakistan National Shipping Corporation* [2002] UKHL 43, [2003] 1 AC 959.

[69] M Bridge et al, *The Law of Personal Property*, 2nd edn (London, Sweet & Maxwell, 2018) para 32-013.

[70] S Green and J Randell, *The Tort of Conversion* (Oxford, Hart Publishing, 2019) 46.

deny the owner's right or to assert a right which is inconsistent with the owner's right'.[71] Similarly, in the leading case of *Hollins v Fowler*, a conversion was said to be 'acts done with the intention of transferring or interfering with the title to or ownership of [goods], or which are done as acts of ownership of them'.[72]

But ministerial acts are not conversions. There exists 'a long line of authority' showing that 'possession of goods by an agent on the instructions of their apparent owner for the purpose of carrying out what have been described as ministerial acts such as storage of carriage does not amount to conversion'.[73] This principle was stated by Blackburn J in the Divisional Court in *Hollins v Fowler*:

> I cannot find it anywhere distinctly laid down, but I submit to your Lordships that on principle, one who deals with goods at the request of the person who has the actual custody of them, in the bona fide belief that the custodier is the true owner, or has the authority of the true owner, should be excused for what he does if the act is of such a nature as would be excused if done by the authority of the person in possession, if he was a finder of the goods, or intrusted with their custody.[74]

Blackburn J continued to give some examples of ministerial acts:

> Thus a warehouseman with whom goods had been deposited is guilty of no conversion by keeping them, or restoring them to the person who deposited them with him, though that person turns out to have had no authority from the true owner … And the same principle would apply to … persons 'acting in a subsidiary character, like that of a person who has the goods of a person employing him to carry them, or a caretaker, such as a wharfinger'.[75]

Here, a person doing only 'ministerial' acts does not commit the wrong of conversion; he is thus not personally liable. Ministerial acts, for conversion's purposes, are those done without intention to act inconsistently with the rights of the person with the superior possessory right (for ease of reference, the 'true owner').

One common ministerial act, suggested in *Hollins v Fowler*, is the moving of goods.[76] In *Re Samuel*, a solicitor who handed jewellery to another of the principal's servants on the instructions of his (bankrupt) principal did not commit conversion; he 'merely transferred the possession of it from one agent of the bankrupt to another agent of the bankrupt'.[77] Similarly, in the Singaporean Court of Appeal decision of *Tat Seng Machine Movers Pte Ltd v Orix Leasing Singapore Ltd*,[78] Tat Seng was found not to have committed conversion when it moved a machine, the 'Heidelberg 4C', from its original premises to a new location on the instructions of movers who had been hired by the apparent owners of the machine. The apparent owners had in fact obtained the machine on hire-purchase.[79] Nor was there any conversion where Tat Seng eventually redelivered the

[71] *Lancashire and Yorkshire Railway Co v MacNicoll* (1918) 88 LJ KB 601, 605.
[72] *Hollins v Fowler* (n 4) 785.
[73] *Marcq v Christie Manson and Woods Ltd (t/a Christies)* [2003] EWCA Civ 731, [2004] QB 286 [14].
[74] *Hollins v Fowler* (n 472) 766–67.
[75] ibid 767.
[76] ibid.
[77] *Re Samuel* [1945] Ch 408 (CA) 415.
[78] *Tat Seng Machine Movers Pte Ltd v Orix Leasing Singapore Ltd* [2009] SGCA 42, [2009] 4 SLR(R) 1101.
[79] ibid [68].

machine to those who entrusted it with the goods.[80] Again, Tat Seng's involvement was described as only 'ministerial':[81] it did not intend to act inconsistently with the owner's rights.

Likewise, merely storing goods is ministerial if the storer does not demonstrate an intention to act inconsistently with the rights of the true owner.[82] Where the intermediary has no knowledge of the true owner, he commits no conversion. Thus, a warehouseman who keeps goods or returns them to the depositor without knowledge of any competing claims to the goods commits no conversion,[83] and a carrier who stores goods temporarily because the intended new warehouseman refuses to accept the goods also commits no conversion.[84]

Another intermediary generating much attention in the cases is the auctioneer. Despite some early authorities to the contrary,[85] an auctioneer who sells goods and delivers them to a purchaser converts them, whether he sells under the hammer[86] or following a provisional bid.[87] By delivering to complete the sale to a new buyer, his acts demonstrate an intention to act inconsistently with the rights of the true owner. But he does not convert goods he is unable to sell and that he returns to the prospective seller.[88]

It should already be evident that the sense in which an act here is 'ministerial' certainly diverges in some respects from the earlier categories. While a 'ministerial' act is one where there is some act done to personal property without an intention to act inconsistently with the rights of the true owner, the earlier instances of 'ministerial' we saw bear no such property focus.

B. Ministerial Receipt

The next example concerns 'ministerial receipt' in unjust enrichment claims. As explained earlier, 'ministerial receipt' might be used either to explain why a claim for restitution lies against the principal of an agent who receives a mistaken payment for the principal, or to explain why no such claim lies against the agent. We now turn to the latter.

Two immediate difficulties arise. First, it is far from clear whether 'ministerial receipt' applies uniformly to all restitutionary claims in the latter use. There is some suggestion that it does not.[89] This difficulty can be put to one side for now as we focus on the core

[80] ibid.
[81] ibid [84].
[82] *Clayton v Le Roy* [1911] 2 KB 1031 (CA).
[83] *Hollins v Fowler* (n 4) 767.
[84] *Tat Seng* (n 78) [68].
[85] *National Mercantile Bank v Rymill* (1881) 44 LT 767; *Turner v Hockey* (1887) 56 LJ QB 301. For criticism, see *Barker v Furlong* [1891] 2 Ch 172 (Ch), 183–84; *RH Willis & Sons v British Car Auctions Ltd* [1978] 1 WLR 438 (CA), 443–44.
[86] *Consolidated Co v Curtis & Son* [1892] 1 QB 495 (QB); *Cochrane v Rymill* (1879) 40 LT 744.
[87] *RH Willis* (n 85).
[88] *Marcq* (n 73).
[89] See Stevens (n 67) 116–18 (failure of consideration).

case of a mistaken payment received by an agent for his principal, where the existence of 'ministerial receipt' is most widely accepted.

The second difficulty is that there appear to be two versions of 'ministerial receipt'. On the first, narrower formulation, no claim will lie against the agent only where he has paid away the sum to the principal or otherwise dealt with it irreversibly in good faith without notice of the claimant's claim to the money.[90] Sometimes described as 'agent payment over', it might be regarded as an early predecessor of the change of position defence.[91] The wider, more controversial formulation is that no claim will lie against any disclosed agent who receives sums for his principals, even if the agent still retains those sums in his hands.

All accept that no claim for restitution lies against the agent where payment over without notice has occurred.[92] But the correctness of the wider formulation remains difficult. Cases supporting it date back to at least *Sadler v Evans*.[93] For Lord Mansfield, the key was simply whether the agent received for another, not whether he still had the sums. As he said, 'The money was paid to the known agent of Lady W. He is liable to her for it; whether he has actually paid it over to her, or not: he received it for her'.[94] But nearly as old is *Buller v Harrison*, which goes the other way.[95] The agent was thus ordered to make restitution where he received sums, kept them, but gave the principal credit against sums the principal owed him. The modern cases are no different: some say the agent can be ordered to make restitution unless he has paid over without notice;[96] others say that he cannot be so ordered even if he still has the sums, as long as he received as agent.[97]

The latest word on ministerial receipt prefers the wider formulation, indicating that payment over is unnecessary. In *Skandinaviska Enskilda Banken AB (Publ) v Conway*, the Privy Council concluded that 'Agents may or may not act as trustees of moneys held for their principals, but they are not in either event enriched by payments made to them

[90] On irreversibility, see, eg *Jones v Churcher* [2009] EWHC 722 (QB), [2009] 2 Lloyd's Rep 94 [66]. In cases like *Buller v Harrison* (1777) 2 Cowp 565, 98 ER 1243 and *Colonial Bank v Exchange Bank of Yarmouth* (1885) 11 App Cas 84 (PC), the agent did not deal with the sums irreversibly.

[91] Established in *Lipkin Gorman (a firm) v Karpnale Ltd* [1991] 2 AC 548 (HL). See, eg, E Bant, *The Change of Position Defence* (Oxford, Hart Publishing, 2009). Rejecting the view that the two are the same, see *Portman BS* (n 40) 207; *Jones v Churcher* [2009] EWHC 722 (QB) [67], but see also [78].

[92] eg *Holland v Russell* (1863) 4 B&S 14, 122 ER 365.

[93] *Sadler v Evans* (1766) 4 Burr 1984, 98 ER 34.

[94] ibid 35.

[95] *Buller v Harrison* (1777) 2 Cowp 565, 98 ER 1243. See also *Cox v Prentice* (1815) 3 M & S 344, 348.

[96] *Agip* (n 11) 288 (suggesting that a claim would lie against an agent who accounts after notice of the claimant's claim); further developed in *Portman BS* (n 40) 669 ('If the agent still retains the money, however, the plaintiff may elect to sue either the principal or the agent, and the agent remains liable if he pays the money over to his principal after notice of the claim.'); *Jones v Churcher* (n 90) [67] (assuming payment over or irreversible change was required); *High Commissioner for Pakistan v the 8th Nizam of Hyderabad* [2016] EWHC 1465 (Ch) [140]–[150] (striking out application, suggesting that the claim against the agent could not be dismissed as unarguable without any real prospect of success) and after trial, *High Commissioner for Pakistan in the United Kingdom v Prince Muffakham Jah* [2019] EWHC 2551 (Ch), [2020] Ch 421 [286]–[290].

[97] *Jeremy D Stone Consultants Ltd v National Westminster Bank plc* [2013] EWHC 208 (Ch), [240]–[243]; *Sixteenth Ocean GmbH & Co KG v Société Générale* [2018] EWHC 1731 (Comm), (2018) 2 Lloyd's Rep 465 [109]. Criticising *Jeremy Stone*, see *Bowstead & Reynolds* (n 12) para 9-106, describing it as *per incuriam*; P Watts, '"Unjust Enrichment" – the Potion that Induces Well-meaning Sloppiness of Thought' [2016] *Current Legal Problems* 289, 315.

for the account of their principals.'[98] This suggests that the reason why no claim lies against the agent is that a necessary element of the claim is missing: enrichment (at the claimant's expense). Therefore, no right to restitution arises.[99]

C. Knowing Receipt

If a recipient receives trust property or its traceable proceeds in breach of trust with sufficient knowledge of the breach, he is subject to a personal claim in knowing receipt for the value of that received.[100] Many aspects of the doctrine raise persistent difficulties: its doctrinal basis,[101] the precise level of knowledge required[102] and available remedies.[103] These concerns need not detain us. Our interest is in one requirement: beneficial receipt. It requires the recipient to have received the trust property for his own use and benefit for him to incur knowing receipt liability. Its flipside: merely ministerial acts of receipt are excluded.

The leading case is *Agip (Africa) Ltd v Jackson.*[104] Setting out the general principle, Millett J explained:

> The essential feature [of knowing receipt] … is that the recipient must have received the property for his own use and benefit. This is why neither the paying nor the collecting bank can normally be brought within it. In paying or collecting money for a customer the bank acts only as his agent. It is otherwise, however, if the collecting bank uses the money to reduce or discharge the customer's overdraft. In doing so it receives the money for its own benefit.[105]

The requirement is generally accepted. Some Court of Appeal support exists,[106] though its force may be slightly blunted by Millett J's being the first instance judge in both

[98] *Skandinaviska Enskilda Banken AB (Publ) v Conway* [2019] UKPC 36 [87].

[99] A different enrichment-based explanation was suggested by C Mitchell, P Mitchell and S Watterson (eds), *Goff & Jones: The Law of Unjust Enrichment*, 9th edn (London, Sweet & Maxwell, 2017) para 28-04, which argues that the agent is not enriched because, although it receives the sums, it comes under an equivalent obligation to account for those sums to the principal. This was adopted in *Jeremy Stone* (n 97); *Sixteenth Ocean* (n 97). However, it has rightly been pointed out that this argument cannot explain ministerial receipt. An obligation to pay is less valuable than the sums themselves, so the agent would still be enriched by the difference: see A Burrows, *The Law of Restitution* (Oxford, Oxford University Press, 2011) 566–67.

[100] *El Ajou v Dollar Land Holdings plc* [1994] BCC 143 (CA); *BCCI v Akindele* [2001] Ch 437 (CA), 448.

[101] Lord Nicholls, 'Knowing Receipt: The Need for a New Landmark' in WR Cornish et al (eds), *Restitution: Past, Present and Future* (Oxford, Hart Publishing, 1998) 247; L Smith, 'Unjust Enrichment, Property, and the Structure of Trusts' (2000) 116 *LQR* 412; P Birks, 'Receipt' in P Birks and A Pretto (eds), *Breach of Trust* (Oxford, Hart Publishing, 2002) 213; C Mitchell and S Watterson, 'Remedies for Knowing Receipt' in C Mitchell (ed), *Constructive and Resulting Trusts* (Oxford, Hart Publishing, 2010) 115; R Chambers, 'The End of Knowing Receipt' (2016) 2 *Canadian Journal of Comparative and Contemporary Law* 1; W Swadling, 'The Nature of 'Knowing Receipt' in PS Davies and J Penner (eds), *Equity, Trusts and Commerce* (Oxford, Hart Publishing, 2017) 304. See most recently *Byers v Samba Financial Group* [2021] EWHC 60 (Ch) [107]–[110]; *Byers v Saudi National Bank* [2022] EWCA Civ 43, especially [69]–[79].

[102] *Belmont Finance Corporation Ltd v Williams Furniture Ltd* [1979] Ch 250 (CA); *In re Montagu's Settlement Trusts* [1987] Ch 264 (Ch); *Cowan de Groot Properties Ltd v Eagle Trust plc* [1992] 4 All ER 700 (Ch); *Eagle Trust plc v SBC Securities Ltd* [1993] 1 WLR 484 (Ch); *BCCI v Akindele* [2001] Ch 437 (CA).

[103] Closely linked to knowing receipt's doctrinal basis, see the references in n 101.

[104] *Agip* (n 11).

[105] ibid 292.

[106] eg *Polly Peck International plc v Nadir (No 2)* [1992] 4 All ER 769 (CA), 777; *El Ajou* (n 100) 154.

cases. The leading practitioner text *Lewin on Trusts* concludes that 'in a case where trust property is received in breach of trust by an agent in a ministerial capacity for onward transmission to his principal, while the principal will be exposed to liability for knowing receipt, the agent will escape liability under this head'.[107]

Here, the relevant ministerial acts seem to consist of receiving for the use and benefit of another. The most likely beneficiaries of this rule are collecting banks acting for customers whose accounts are in credit.[108] The bank receives payment, but only for the customer's account.[109] But its application is wider, encompassing all agents who receive payments for others. Consider *Agip* itself. Agip's chief accountant defrauded Agip by amending payment orders, substituting those of his choosing for the intended recipients. One such payee was Baker Oil. Acting on the payment order, Agip's bank, the Banque du Sud, paid out to Baker Oil's account with Lloyds Bank. The payment was then transferred to an accountancy firm's Lloyds Bank account, and thereafter dissipated. The funds being lost, Agip sought unsuccessfully to recover the payments from the partners of the accountancy firm, Jackson and Bowers, and its employee, Mr Griffin, in knowing receipt. As Millett J explained:

> [Mr Bowers] was a partner in Jackson & Co but he played no active part in the movement of the funds. He did not deal with the money or give instructions in regard to it. He did not take it for his own benefit. He neither misapplied nor misappropriated it. It would not be just to hold him directly liable merely because Mr Jackson and Mr Griffin, who controlled the movement of the money from the moment it reached Baker Oil, chose on this occasion to pass it through his firm's bank account instead of through [another company's] account as previously. Mr Griffin did not receive the money at all, and Mr Jackson and Mr Bowers did not receive or apply it for their own use or benefit. In my judgment, none of them can be made liable to account as a constructive trustee on the basis of knowing receipt.[110]

There is some evidence that, in England, this requirement excludes not just agents from liability, but also trustees.[111] In *El Ajou v Dollar Land Holdings*, no beneficial receipt was found when the recipient received it on trust to apply for a specific purpose.[112]

There are reasonable grounds for thinking that the beneficial receipt requirement in knowing receipt is simply misplaced.[113] The requirement might be justified if knowing receipt liability were a species of unjust enrichment, which Lord Millett (as he later became) appeared to support,[114] as a parallel doctrine of 'ministerial receipt' applies to such claims. But the unjust enrichment analysis of knowing receipt was doubted in *BCCI v Akindele*[115] and might be criticised on other grounds.[116] A second justification

[107] *Lewin on Trusts* (n 18) para 42-059.

[108] For criticism of the different treatment between accounts in credit and those in overdraft, see M Bryan, 'When Does a Bank Receive Money?' [1996] *Journal of Business Law* 165.

[109] See similar reasoning in *Polly Peck* (n 106) 777.

[110] *Agip* (HC) (n 11) 292.

[111] Supported also by Swadling (n 101) 314. Cf in New Zealand and Australia, *Gathergood v Blundell & Brown Ltd* [1992] 3 NZLR 643; *Springfield Acres Ltd v Abacus (Hong Kong) Ltd* [1994] 3 NZLR 502; *Port of Brisbane Corporation v ANZ Securities Ltd (No 2)* [2001] QSC 466, [2002] QCA 158; *Quince v Varga* [2008] QCA 376.

[112] *El Ajou* (n 100) 155.

[113] Describing it as 'bizarre', see Swadling (n 101) 314.

[114] eg *Twinsectra Ltd v Yardley* [2002] UKHL 12, [2002] 2 AC 164 (HL) [105].

[115] *BCCI v Akindele* (n 100) 448.

[116] eg L Smith, 'Unjust Enrichment, Property and the Structure of Trusts' (2000) 116 *LQR* 412.

for the requirement is the protection of banks from liability. But that objection is already met by the knowledge requirement. The real question then is whether we have good reason to protect banks from knowing receipt liability where they receive money with knowledge that it was acquired in breach of trust. We probably do not. If so, then the best move may be to abolish the beneficial receipt requirement.

D. Inconsistent Dealing

A final area to consider is 'inconsistent dealing', a doctrine closely related to knowing receipt. Just how closely related they are is an open question we will return to later. The leading case is *Lee v Sankey*.[117] A firm of solicitors was employed by trustees to receive proceeds of the testator's real estate, which had been compulsorily acquired by a railway company. They paid over the money to one of the trustees without the authority of the other. The recipient trustee later became bankrupt and died; the money was lost. The surviving trustee and beneficiaries sued the solicitors. Bacon VC held that they were personally liable for the monies received. He explained:

> It is well established by many decisions, that a mere agent of trustees is answerable only to his principal and not to *cestuis que trust* in respect of trust moneys coming to his hands merely in his character of agent. But it is also not less clearly established that a person who receives into his hands trust moneys, and who deals with them in a manner inconsistent with the performance of trusts of which he is cognizant, is personally liable for the consequences which may ensue upon his so dealing.[118]

Buried for some time in obscurity, inconsistent dealing made a reappearance in *Agip*, where Millett J distinguished it from knowing receipt:

> The second, and in my judgment, distinct class of case is that of the person, usually an agent of the trustees, who receives the trust property lawfully *and not for his own benefit* but who then either misappropriates it or otherwise deals with it in a manner which is inconsistent with the trust. He is liable to account as a constructive trustee if he received the property knowing it to be such, though he will not necessarily be required in all circumstances to have known the exact terms of the trust.[119]

This statement emphasises a similar requirement to that in knowing receipt: for the recipient to escape liability, he must receive the trust property for the benefit of another. Sometimes this requirement is framed as explaining that the recipient must be an agent.[120] Although the language of ministerial agency is not used here, it could well be used in just the same way as knowing receipt: the agent who receives not for his own benefit but for another's receives ministerially, not beneficially.

Thus, an agent who lawfully receives trust property and follows his principal's instructions will not incur liability for inconsistent dealing. In *Mara v Browne*, a solicitor proposed investments on mortgage to the trustees, who accepted.[121] They drew

[117] *Lee v Sankey* (1873) LR 15 Eq 204 (Ch).
[118] ibid 211.
[119] *Agip* (n 11) 291.
[120] eg *Lewin on Trusts* (n 18) para 42-114.
[121] *Mara v Browne* [1896] 1 Ch 199 (CA).

cheques on the trust funds, which were received by the solicitor and then paid over to the intended mortgagors. The 'speculative and risky'[122] investments were a breach of trust. Though the trustees might be liable, the solicitor was not; he purported to act throughout as solicitor and was understood to be doing so.[123] The agent's acts must be 'in strict conformity with his duty as agent'.[124] Where the agent must be 'merely carrying out the directions of their principal in the matter', no inconsistent dealing was found,[125] but if there were multiple principals and only one directed the act done by the agent, as in *Lee v Sankey*, the agent was found to have dealt with the property inconsistently.[126] These cases potentially provide another illustration of acting 'ministerially', explaining how the agent escapes liability.

V. Four Different Conceptions of a 'Ministerial Act'

Despite sharing the same name, ministerial acts have different meanings in different contexts. At least four possible meanings can be identified. These four different conceptions of ministerial acts also differ in other ways: the purposes for which they are used, whether they are a question of degree, and whether special justification is required for the concept.

A. Different Meanings

First, as section II shows, a ministerial act may just mean an act that can be treated as the principal's own. In this meaning, a ministerial act is no different from other acts done by agents for their principals. References to 'ministerial' here are otiose; 'ministerial act' is merely another way of saying 'act done as agent'.

Second, as in section III, a ministerial act may refer to acts where trust, confidence or discretion is not required for their performance. This meaning is adopted in sub-agency and in assessing the duties the actor owes. Standard examples are cases where the actor was given very specific instructions to do particular acts. Examples include signing a document where the decision to enter the transaction has been made by another,[127] transcribing or recording another's statement,[128] handing another documents,[129]

[122] ibid 209.

[123] ibid 207.

[124] *Morgan v Stephens* (1861) 3 Giff 226, 66 ER 392; *Williams-Ashman v Price and Williams* [1942] Ch 219 (Ch).

[125] *Brinsden v Williams* [1894] 3 Ch 185 (Ch).

[126] *Lee v Sankey* (n 117) 210–11.

[127] eg *Lord v Hall* (n 36); *Town Investments Ltd v Department of the Environment* [1976] 1 WLR 1126 (CA) (Secretary of State for the Environment executing document on behalf of the Queen).

[128] eg *R v Solihull Metropolitan Borough Council Housing Benefit Review Board* (1994) 26 HLR 370 (QB) (chairman of Board under personal obligation to record the necessary elements of reasoned decision which the Board came to, but can dictate to amanuensis); and the statement-making cases in section II.

[129] eg *Ruben v Great Fingall Consolidated and ors* [1906] AC 439 (HL) (secretary delivering share certificates to the owners of shares); *R v Varley* [2020] 4 WLUK 554 (dossier handed to accountant).

conveying messages,[130] drawing[131] or accepting bills of exchange,[132] or purchasing a set number of shares at a fixed price on the principal's instructions.[133]

Two further meanings of a ministerial act can be found in section IV, where the agent's personal liability to third parties is examined.

A third meaning is that a ministerial act is an act done for the benefit of another. This meaning is adopted in knowing receipt. The use of the term here might plausibly have derived from the verb 'to minister', that is, to attend to the needs of another. While superficially similar to the first meaning, this third meaning is broader. It includes both agents acting for their principals' benefit and trustees who act for their beneficiaries' benefit. The first includes only the former – trustees, although acting for the benefit of others, act as principals.[134] This definition is thus the broadest of the four.

Conversely, the fourth, and most narrow, is the meaning adopted in conversion. This unique meaning is adopted nowhere else. It refers to acts done to chattels without intending to act inconsistently with the true owner's rights or to assert the actor's own rights. As mentioned earlier, this is quite clearly distinct from the others, bearing a property focus.

B. Different Purposes, Different Relationships

Implicit in these four different meanings is that an act might be called ministerial for different purposes and in establishing different legal relationships. Some meanings are adopted in explaining the legal relations between principal and third party, some concern the principal–agent relationship and some are used in the agent–third party relationship.

Acts may be called 'ministerial' in treating them as the principal's own, as in section II. Here, describing an act as 'ministerial' is used to establish the principal's rights and duties against a third party with whom the ministerial actor has been dealing. The relevant relationship is that between principal and third party.

By contrast, other acts are described as ministerial when they determine the rights and duties between principal and agent. This use, seen in the discussion of fiduciary duties, is used when assessing the agent's fiduciary and other duties owed to the principal.

The third possibility, seen in section IV, is that acts are described as ministerial as short-hand for saying that the actor doing the ministerial act does not incur personal liability to third parties. This may be for different reasons: no wrong is committed (conversion), no duty to make restitution arises (ministerial receipt), or some other explanation.

[130] eg *Solomon Lew* (n 5) [45] ('mere intermediary or agent for each party in conveying their messages to the other – in the manner of a postman – coupled at best perhaps with an understanding on each side that he might seek to persuade the other of the good sense of a deal – in the manner of a mediator, without any authority to bind'.).

[131] *Ex parte Sutton* (1788) 2 Cox 84, 30 ER 39.

[132] *Re London and Mediterranean Bank, ex parte Birmingham Banking Co* (1868) LR 3 Ch App 651 (CA).

[133] *Volkers* (n 63).

[134] eg *Skandinaviska* (n 98) [89].

C. Bright-Line Classification or a Question of Degree?

The four meanings may also differ as to whether the ministerial nature of an act is a bright-line classification or a question of degree.

In the first, third and fourth meanings of ministerial acts, an act is either ministerial or not. In the first, one's act can be treated either as the principal's own or not. In the third, one acts for another's benefit or not. In the fourth, acts are done with the intention of interfering with the true owner's rights or not. In these meanings, a bright-line classification is adopted. There is no halfway house.

But in the second meaning, whether an act is ministerial is a question of degree. An act can be more ministerial or less ministerial. The less discretion, trust and confidence the actor has, the more ministerial his acts are. The converse is also true. A stockbroker specifically instructed to 'buy 100 shares in ABC Ltd at $10 only, and if no such shares are available, do not buy' is doing acts that are certainly ministerial under this meaning. But a stockbroker instructed to 'buy 100 shares in ABC Ltd at between $9.90 and $10 per share, and if no such shares are available, do not buy' clearly has more discretion. The latter might still be described as performing ministerial acts, though less ministerial than in the first example. In this meaning, there is a spectrum of ministerial acts.

D. Justifications

The meanings of 'ministerial acts' also differ on whether 'ministerial acts' are simply cases where a general rule does not apply, or whether special public policy-based justifications are required for the concept.

Where the 'ministerial act' is being treated as the principal's own, no special justification is necessary. A ministerial act is treated as the principal's own for the same reasons that other acts done by agents are so treated. The general rule is that through the agent's acts, the principal himself acts. Ministerial acts require no exception to this rule; they merely illustrate it. This is also true where ministerial receipt is used to explain why the principal owes a duty to make restitution of mistaken payments received by his agent. Through the agent's receipt, the principal is enriched at the payor's expense. Again, no special rule is required: the principal is bound through a combination of the standard requirements for restitutionary claims and agency rules.

Similarly, no exceptions to the general rule are required where 'ministerial acts' refer to acts where little trust, confidence or discretion is reposed in the actor. In sub-agency, the general rule is that delegation to a sub-agent requires the principal's authority. The justification is that as the principal's legal relations can be affected by acts over which the sub-agent has discretion, the principal's consent should be required. But where the acts do not involve the exercise of discretion, the justification for requiring the principal's authority is absent. Ministerial acts here reinforce the general rule. Likewise, onerous fiduciary duties are justified by the discretion, trust and confidence being reposed in the actor, which make the principal especially vulnerable to misbehaviour by the actor. Where discretion, trust and confidence are absent or present in only an attenuated form, that justification has less bite and either no or more limited fiduciary duties are owed.

While no special justification is necessary for ministerial acts in establishing the principal's rights and duties to third parties or principal–agent legal relations, special justifications do seem to be at least implicitly relied on in considering when the agent comes under duties, breaches them or is liable to third parties.

There is some evidence for this in conversion, where the development of 'ministerial acts' seems motivated by the protection of innocent intermediaries acting in good faith. *Hollins* singled out for protection those commercial intermediaries who deal with goods in carrying out a business or profession, such as warehousemen and carriers. In *Tat Seng*, the Singapore Court of Appeal expressly recognised concerns about those intermediaries' being held liable, saying that

> wise judicial minds in due course came to recognise that the rigorous and unthinking application of such a rule of strict liability could lead to injustice, and perhaps even constrict the growth and flow of commercial dealings; especially amongst those involved in the transportation and storage of goods industries … [I]f the tort is not sensibly circumscribed in the context of present day commerce, it could end up raising business costs by necessitating increased insurance coverage and premiums and perhaps, even stultifying trade flow.[135]

Recognising 'ministerial acts' that did not constitute conversions seems aimed at protecting innocent agents, protecting against the consequences identified by the Singapore Court of Appeal.

Similar trends might be observed in knowing receipt and ministerial receipt. As discussed earlier, it is plausible that Millett J introduced the beneficial receipt requirement to protect banks, who frequently receive payments. The modern explanation for ministerial receipt's operation does not rely on special justification for the doctrine, only on the agent's lack of enrichment at the principal's expense, but there have long been arguments justifying it on public policy grounds.[136] *Goff & Jones* suggests that the justification for ministerial receipt is that 'it is desirable to protect agents from being caught in the middle of disputes between their principals and third parties'.[137] An agent may face competing claims from both the principal and the payor for the benefit he has received. The agent may thus be faced with an 'impossible dilemma': should he account for it to his principal or return it to the payor?[138] Enabling agents to 'drop out' against third parties addresses this dilemma, indicating that the agent should account for the benefit to the principal and the payor should seek recovery of the benefit from the principal. Thus, the ministerial receipt doctrine is thought to enhance the ability of agents to act as intermediaries, make the law simpler and reduce the multiplicity of suits.[139]

[135] *Tat Seng* (n 78) [43].

[136] eg in the context of banks, see J Moore, *Restitution from Banks* (unpublished DPhil thesis, University of Oxford, 2000).

[137] *Goff & Jones* (n 99) para 28-04.

[138] ibid.

[139] ibid.

VI. Reserving 'Ministerial Act' for One Meaning

Despite use of a single label, there is considerable diversity in what constitutes a 'ministerial act'. At least four conceptions of ministerial acts can be identified. They differ further as to whether they concern the legal relationships between principal–third party, principal–agent or agent–third party. The ministerial nature of an act may be a question of degree or a bright-line classification. Whether special justification is required for 'ministerial acts' again depends on which meaning is adopted, with special justifications being invoked most where 'ministerial acts' are used to indicate that the ministerial agent should 'drop out'.

The greatest problem that this plurality of meanings poses is potential confusion. Using a single label may wrongly suggest that 'ministerial acts' consist only of one concept with one meaning, when the phrase conceals several distinct meanings used for different purposes. The risk is that the conception of ministerial act in one context may then be inappropriately applied to another.

In response to this problem, there are two main options. The first is to say that there is no difficulty with a plurality of meanings under the same label so long as no one is confused or misled. On this view, the solution is education. Judges, commentators and practitioners should be regularly reminded that there are different meanings of ministerial acts that must be kept separate. This solution is a moderate one, not seeking to change uses in existing language or law but merely striving to avoid associated problems. This approach is not entirely unknown. For example, we still use a single label of 'agents' to refer to a wide range of intermediaries, not all of whom exhibit the same features.[140] The second approach is to reserve the term 'ministerial act' for one meaning only. The advantage of this suggestion is greater precision. Different labels can be used to capture different concepts, with the use of different words already signifying that the concepts are not interchangeable. There is less risk of confusion and error. This solution is bolder, more reformative in character.

Of the two, the second appears to be the better route forward. First, it is doubtful whether education, however well-implemented, will be enough to avoid the risks of mistakes and inappropriate borrowing from one context to another. Accuracy is itself a good thing: reserving distinct concepts their own name promotes accurate labelling. But perhaps the most important reason for reserving the label 'ministerial act' to one specific meaning is that it enables us to see problems in the present law that are currently hidden from view. The greatest problem is that the label of 'ministerial act' has sometimes been used as a substitute for legal reasoning. This problem is most pronounced in the examples discussed in section IV, where 'ministerial acts' are used to signify when the agent is not liable to the third party. Calling an act 'ministerial' may sometimes be used as a substitute for reasoned justification when there is either no or insufficient explanation for why this act is one that should not trigger liability.

[140] See *Bowstead & Reynolds* (n 12) para 1-001, and compare R Leow, 'Understanding Agency: A Proxy Power Definition' (2019) 78 *CLJ* 99; F Reynolds and CH Tan, 'Agency Reasoning – A Formula or a Tool?' [2018] *Singapore Journal of Legal Studies* 43.

Recall Millett J's invocation of a beneficial receipt requirement in knowing receipt. No reasons were given for the requirement. As explained earlier, there are reasons to doubt its continued existence. It is difficult to justify why a bank receiving payments it knows are proceeds of fraud should not incur knowing receipt liability simply because it receives for another. The concern that banks may be put in a difficult position is more apparent than real. When faced with competing claims, the bank can always interplead, as Millett LJ himself pointed out later in *Portman BS v Hamlyn Taylor Neck*.[141]

Similar difficulties exist with conversion, inconsistent dealing and restitutionary claims. All involve causes of action that are somewhat controversial. Conversion arguably lacks a satisfactory definition, inconsistent dealing's independent identity is doubted, and the scope and justification for different restitutionary claims is controversial. The concern again is that the phrase 'ministerial act' papers over existing difficulties by conveying a veneer of doctrinal respectability.

In conversion, there are occasional hints that 'ministerial acts' are not conversions so as to protect innocent commercial intermediaries who deal with goods as part of their business. If this is the justification, it should be addressed more openly. After open discussion, it might be criticised and hence rejected. Conversely, it might be endorsed, in which case reform of the present law is probably necessary. Not all innocent commercial intermediaries are currently protected, with the most obvious example being the auctioneer who successfully sells auctioned goods and delivers them to the purchaser.

Likewise, the scope of 'ministerial receipt' faces its own difficulties. Does 'ministerial receipt' establish that the agent is not enriched, or is it a public policy-based defence? If the former, then 'ministerial receipt' is really tied to the concept of enrichment at the claimant's expense, a more difficult concept than it initially appears.[142] If the latter, it seems plausible that this reasoning should be extended from mistake to other reasons for restitution (ie unjust factors), though this has been doubted by Stevens.[143]

Inconsistent dealing too appears motivated by a desire to protect agents (typically solicitors) who carry out their principals' instructions in dealing with trust property, but it suffers from a larger identity crisis. It is not clear whether inconsistent dealing is an independent doctrine or part of knowing receipt. *Lewin on Trusts* takes the former view, saying that the difference between inconsistent dealing and knowing receipt is that in the former the recipient receives the trust property 'lawfully',[144] that is the transfer 'involves no breach of trust or other wrongful act'.[145] This assumes that in knowing receipt, the transfer to the recipient does involve a breach of trust or other wrongful act. This assumption appears incorrect. Consider the following scenario: in breach of trust, trustee transfers the trust property to A1, who then transfers to A2, who still has it. All the transfers are gifts, so that the recipients are not bona fide purchasers. A1 did not know of the breach of trust when he received and transferred the property to A2.

[141] *Portman BS* (n 40) 669–70.

[142] See, eg, the problems discussed in A Burrows, '"At the Expense of the Claimant": A Fresh Look' [2017] *Restitution Law Review* 167; S Watterson, 'At the Claimant's Expense' in E Bant, K Barker and S Degeling (eds), *Research Handbook on Unjust Enrichment and Restitution* (Northampton, Edward Elgar, 2020) 262.

[143] Stevens (n 67) 116–18.

[144] *Lewin on Trusts* (n 18) para 42-111.

[145] ibid para 42-112.

Assume also that A2 did not know of the breach of trust when he received the property, but that he has now acquired knowledge. In principle, A2 is liable for knowing receipt, but it is difficult to say that A1's transfer to A2 involved a breach of trust or wrongful act. A1 arguably owed no duties as trustee when he lacked knowledge,[146] so his transfer to the innocent A2 was not in breach of trust or wrongful. This casts doubt on *Lewin's* distinction between the two. More work is needed here. It may be that inconsistent dealing and knowing receipt are not so separate after all.[147]

These problems cannot be meaningfully worked out if they are hidden under the blanket of apparent doctrinal respectability. Once we remove the label of 'ministerial act', we can then see more clearly that the key question is why these 'ministerial' acts have the effects that they do. This is not controversial in working out the principal's legal relations with the third party and the duties owed by agent to the principal, but it is in the agent's legal relations with the third party.

If ministerial act is limited to one specific meaning then there is a secondary question that follows: Which? It is suggested that 'ministerial acts' should be used to refer only to acts that do not involve the actor's discretion, trust or confidence in performing them. These will typically be acts that are specifically dictated or prescribed by another. Some support can be drawn from comparative law. The United States' Legal Information Institute's legal encyclopaedia defines a ministerial act as 'an act performed in a prescribed manner and in obedience to a legal authority, without regard to one's own judgment or discretion'.[148] The Legal Information Institute cites examples such as the collection of taxes, the recording of documents and filing of papers, and the preparation of ballots as examples of ministerial acts, which it describes from the US *Restatement Second of Torts*.[149] This meaning also seems to be adopted by *Bowstead & Reynolds*, when describing cases where agents simply have specific instructions to do one thing as involving ministerial functions.[150] Furthermore, this seems to be the most distinctive but general sense of 'ministerial act'.

What, then, of the other meanings of 'ministerial act'? The broadest meaning can be found in knowing receipt, referring to acting for another's benefit. It can simply be referred to as such. In ministerial receipt and the principal's being bound by the agent's acts, 'ministerial act' seems to be used interchangeably with 'act done as agent'. Here the language of 'ministerial' can be replaced with 'agency' with no loss in meaning, as suggested in the *Pieres* case discussed at the start of the chapter. In the last and most specific meaning of 'ministerial act', in conversion, it might be most helpful to think of these acts as 'acts not interfering with ownership'. Each can be given its own label, clearly demarcating one from the others.

[146] *Westdeutsche Landesbank Girozentrale v Islington LBC* [1996] AC 669 (HL), 705.
[147] For a similar conclusion, see Swadling (n 101).
[148] Cornell Law School, Legal Information Institute, at www.law.cornell.edu/wex/ministerial_act/.
[149] ibid.
[150] *Bowstead & Reynolds* (n 12) para 1-005.

VII. Conclusion

This chapter is aimed as a corrective to the undiscerning use of the phrase 'ministerial act' and its many synonyms. Vivid metaphors of 'conduits' and 'postboxes' add colour but do little to improve understanding. Even where the core phrase, 'ministerial act', is used, examination shows that at least four conceptions of 'ministerial acts' are in play. These conceptions differ again according to which legal relationship is being considered, whether a ministerial act is a matter of degree or an absolute, and their justifications.

The problem is that using the same phrase to capture different meanings is a trap for the unwary. It risks unnecessary errors. While this problem might be managed with education, it has been argued that a better way forward is to limit 'ministerial act' to acts that do not require discretion, trust or confidence in their performance. The most important reason for taking this bolder step is that it means that the label of 'ministerial act' cannot be used in place of justifications when explaining when and why the actor (agent) does not owe duties, breach them or incur liability to third parties in respect of the act. Using the right labels enables us to see more clearly where the current law requires further work.

4

Justifications for and Limitations on Interventions by Undisclosed Principals

WILLIAM DAY*

I. Introduction

The basic conditions for when undisclosed principals 'intervene' on contracts entered into by their agents are reasonably well settled. First, the agent must enter into a valid contract with the third party; second, the agent must have acted within the scope of actual authority conferred by the principal; and, third, when so acting, the agent must have intended to exercise that actual authority. If those three conditions are satisfied, a principal may sue the third party under the contract and may be sued if either the agent or principal fails to perform their side of the bargain (the 'Intervention Rule' or the 'Rule').[1]

The reasons for having the Intervention Rule are less well settled. Writing in 1887, Pollock said that the 'plain truth ought never to be forgotten that the whole law as to the rights and liabilities of an undisclosed principal is inconsistent with elementary doctrines of the law of contract'.[2] That sentiment still holds true today. The best explanation the UK Supreme Court could provide on the last occasion it turned its attention to the Rule was to attribute its survival solely to 'its antiquity'.[3] Similarly, *Bowstead & Reynolds on Agency* states that the Rule is 'surprising' and 'difficult to accommodate within standard theories of contract, which emphasise, even though under objective criteria, the consent of the parties'.[4] Intervention by an undisclosed principal appears to allow an outsider to impose themselves on the contract against

* I am grateful for comments on a draft from the editors, Rachel Leow, Magda Raczynska and Timothy Pilkington. All remaining errors are my own.

[1] *Siu Yin Kwan v Eastern Insurance Co Ltd (The Ospery)* [1994] 2 AC 199 (PC), 207 (Lord Lloyd). Intervention is never possible on deeds.

[2] F Pollock, 'Note' (1887) 3 *LQR* 359.

[3] *Playboy Club London Ltd v Banca Nazionale del Lavoro SpA* [2018] UKSC 43, [2018] 1 WLR 4041 [12] (Lord Sumption).

[4] P Watts (ed), *Bowstead & Reynolds on Agency*, 22nd edn (London, Sweet & Maxwell, 2020) para 8.069 (hereinafter *Bowstead*).

the will of the third party, unsupported by the terms of the contract, and contrary to orthodox principles of objectivity, privity and consideration.

The limitations placed on the Intervention Rule are likewise not free from doubt; they remain 'ill-defined' and 'extremely difficult to formulate'.[5] This problem follows from the last. In principle, the Rule and its exceptions ought to have some coherence, with the rationales for the exceptions not undermining the rationale for the rule itself. But, in practice, limitations to intervention appear to have been imposed enthusiastically by the courts because of judicial wariness as to whether the Rule is justified at all.[6] This is not an unusual phenomenon in judge-made law, when courts are faced with a general rule that they cannot simply disregard but also do not want to follow. A willingness to allow a rule to be circumvented or qualified is often 'indicative of uncertainty as to the soundness of the basic rule itself' and 'uncertainty about the policy that underlies the basic rule, and/or its normative weight'.[7]

This chapter argues that the best way of understanding the Intervention Rule is to start from the proposition that the contract only ever lies between agent and third party.[8] The effect of undisclosed agency is that the principal is subject to a *non*-contractual liability to the third party created by the exercise of the agent's authority, and the principal obtains, by authorising the agent so to act, a *non*-contractual power to enforce the agent's contractual rights against the third party.

As to the Rule's limitations, it is suggested in this chapter that where the three preconditions for intervention are satisfied, only the terms of the contract itself should be capable of preventing that intervention. The proposition that there are *also* non-contractual bars to the Rule loosely based around notions of 'good faith'[9] or 'personality'[10] is, on analysis, not supported by authority and should be jettisoned. In particular, the authority commonly cited for the existence of this further type of limitation, *Said v Butt*,[11] which recently marked its centenary, should be recognised for what it is: an entertaining case on the facts but ultimately a red herring in respect of the relevant principles.[12]

II. Reasons for the Existence of the Intervention Rule

A vast amount of ink has been spilled by judges and academics seeking to explain the Rule. The principal justifications for its existence fall into three broad schools of thought.

[5] F Reynolds, 'Agency' in A Burrows (ed) *Principles of English Commercial Law* (Oxford, Oxford University Press, 2015) 1, para 1.78.

[6] F Reynolds, 'Agency: Theory and Practice' (1978) 94 *LQR* 224, 225; L Goodhart and CJ Hamson, 'Undisclosed Principals in Contract' (1932) 4 *CLJ* 320, 325–26.

[7] P Craig, 'The Legal Effect of Directives: Policy, Rules and Exceptions' (2009) 34 *EL Rev* 349, 350. The observation is being made in an entirely different legal context but is of wider applicability.

[8] And, in that sense, the word 'intervention' on a contract is something of a misnomer.

[9] Reynolds (n 5) para 1.80.

[10] Text to n 115 below.

[11] *Said v Butt* [1920] 3 KB 497 (KBD).

[12] There was a second principle arising from the case (decided in *obiter dicta*), that when a corporate agent acting 'bona fide within the scope of his authority' causes the corporate principal to commit a wrong, the agent cannot be sued as an accessory to that wrong: see ibid 506 (McCardie J). I have criticised that rule

A. Commercial Convenience

The first school of thought, and probably the dominant one, is that the Rule is 'justified on grounds of commercial convenience'.[13] On this view, it is an example of contract principle yielding to commercial practicality. As Lord Goff once put it, 'the objective of the judges … [is] to help businessmen, not to hinder them: we are there to give effect to their transactions, not to frustrate them: we are there to oil the wheels of commerce, not to put a spanner in the works, or even grit in the oil'.[14]

In modern scholarship, the most detailed exposition of the apparent commercial benefits of permitting intervention is provided by Tan. He argues that that the Intervention Rule encourages the use of specialist middleman in commerce. Professional intermediaries prefer to act on an undisclosed basis to protect their distribution networks.[15] Principals want to remain undisclosed where it will enable them to obtain a better price or improved terms, or because there is some other reason for wanting to conceal their activity from the market and their competitors. To take an example provided by *Restatement of the Law Third, Agency*, the Rule enables a principal to acquire an outstanding plot of land to complete a wider property development without paying a 'ransom' price for the final piece of the property jigsaw.[16] The Rule also encourages the use of intermediaries by principals without fear of credit risk, because if the intermediary does become insolvent, the principal can then intervene and deal with the third party directly. For these reasons and others, Tan reaches an 'incontrovertible' conclusion that 'the economic and commercial merits of the undisclosed principal doctrine are beyond dispute'.[17]

These commercial justifications for the Intervention Rule are not convincing for three reasons. First, there is no historical evidence that there was a real commercial problem solved by the creation of the Rule.[18] While the Rule can be traced back to *Schrimshire v Alderton* in 1743, the law report of that case actually indicates that the Rule was imposed by judicial will over the objections of the special mercantile jury

elsewhere: W Day, 'Skirting Around the Issue: the Corporate Veil after *Prest v Petrodel*' [2014] *Lloyd's Maritime and Commercial Law Quarterly* 269, 292–95. Regrettably, it remains in rude health: see, most recently, *Antuzis v DJ Houghton Catching Services Ltd* [2019] EWHC 843 (QB), [2019] Bus LR 1532 [108]–[133] (Lane J).

[13] *Siu Yin Kwan* (n 1) 207. See, eg, H Bennett, *Principles of the Law of Agency* (Oxford, Hart Publishing, 2013) 144–45; GE Dal Pont, *The Law of Agency*, 4th edn (Chatswood, LexisNexis Australia, 2020) para 19.33; GHL Fridman, 'Undisclosed Principals and the Sale of Goods' in D Busch, L Macgregor and P Watts (eds), *Agency Law in Commercial Practice* (Oxford, Oxford University Press, 2016) 69, 71–72; R Munday, *Agency: Law and Principles*, 3rd edn (Oxford, Oxford University Press, 2016) para 10.29; E Peel (ed), *Treitel: The Law of Contract*, 15th edn (London, Sweet & Maxwell, 2020) para 16.065; Reynolds (n 6) 225.

[14] R Goff, 'Commercial Contracts and the Commercial Court' [1984] *Lloyd's Maritime and Commercial Law Quarterly* 382, 391, discussing the law of common mistake and frustration.

[15] This is also the point emphasised by *Restatement of the Law Third, Agency* (St Paul, MN, American Law Institute, 2007) vol 2, 41 (hereinafter *Restatement, Third*).

[16] ibid 48. See also RE Barnett, 'Squaring Undisclosed Agency Law with Contract Theory' (1987) 75 *California Law Review* 1969, 1976–77; Bennett (n 13) 144–45.

[17] Tan CH, 'Undisclosed Principals and Contract' (2004) 120 *LQR* 480, 481–85.

[18] Indeed, the historical record is described as 'painfully meagre': OW Holmes Jr, 'The History of Agency' in Association of American Law Schools (eds), *Select Essays in Anglo-American Legal History: Vol III* (Boston, MA, Little, Brown & Co, 1909) 369, 390.

selected to resolve the issue.[19] Second, there are also no empirical studies to back up claims as to the Rule's continuing relevance to modern commercial life. Indeed, the relative scarcity of modern case law on undisclosed agency – despite its nebulous scope and limitations, which naturally invite litigation – suggests that it is not a regular feature of modern commercial practice. Third, by overriding the third party's ability to choose their counterparties, the Rule is contrary to party autonomy and to the instincts of a market economy, where choice of counterparty often matters just as much as price and other terms. Many, if not most, commercial parties would not be enthusiastic about the proposition that, when they enter into a contract with one counterparty, they may in fact be told later on that it was in truth a contract with someone else. Even if the Rule delivered the commercial advantages identified by Tan, that would have to be balanced against its detrimental impact on the certainty of counterparty otherwise provided by the objective principle. Certainty and autonomy are more important priorities for commercial parties than the ability to surprise (and be surprised by) as to the identity of a contractual counterparty through the use of undisclosed agency.[20]

Nor it is obviously correct that the Rule is required to deliver its perceived commercial advantages. It is commonly said that undisclosed agency was developed by judges in the eighteenth century to avoid a perceived prejudice caused to the principal by the risk of the agent's insolvency.[21] But as Ames pointed out in 1909, as a fiduciary for the principal, the agent would hold the benefit of any contract (such as money paid over by the third party) on trust anyway, and that trust would ringfence those benefits for the principal in the event of the agent's insolvency.[22] This is actually a more orthodox approach to the issue of insolvency risk, since the insolvency outcome is then simply conditioned by pre-insolvency proprietary entitlements rather by than any special doctrine.[23] As for the protection of networks, professional intermediaries do this by dealing on an unnamed rather than an undisclosed basis: they do not need to go as far as to pretend that they are themselves the principal.[24] Further, the potential negotiating advantages conferred on principals are doubtful given the limitations placed on the Intervention Rule, as elaborated below,[25] but in any event those advantages come at a cost to the third party. In the property development example given above, for example,[26] the use of undisclosed agency deprives the seller of the opportunity to demand a higher price for the outstanding plot of land. There is no good reason why the law should be structured to advance the position of one side over the other in a commercial negotiation in this way.

[19] *Schrimshire v Alderton* (1742) 2 Stra 1182, 93 ER 1114.

[20] See, eg, *Vallejo v Wheeler* (1774) 1 Cowp 143, 153; 98 ER 1012, 1017 (Lord Mansfield); *Printing and Numerical Registering Co v Sampson* (1874–75) LR 19 Eq 462, 465 (Sir George Jessel MR).

[21] See, eg, *Bowstead* (n 4) para 8.069; Goodhart and Hamson (n 6) 352; Fridman (n 13) para 5.05.

[22] JB Ames, 'Undisclosed Principal: His Rights and Liabilities' (1909) 18 *The Yale Law Journal* 443, 448.

[23] See, eg, K van Zwieten, *Goode on the Principles of Corporate Insolvency*, 5th edn (London, Sweet & Maxwell, 2018) para 3.03.

[24] As specialist agents, they might not be believed even if they were to make that claim anyway: the third party would expect them to be dealing for another client, even if unnamed.

[25] See section III.

[26] Text to n 16.

B. Principal's Contract Theory

A second explanation for the Intervention Rule is that, 'in truth, although not in form', the contract should be regarded as always having been between principal and third party.[27] This is what Holmes famously characterised as the 'technical fiction' or 'formula of identification',[28] whereby the principal and agent are deemed one and the same. On this 'fiction' or 'formula', when the agent enters into a contract, by definition the principal also enters that contract.

i. Doctrinal Support for the Principal's Contract Theory

The identification theory was probably the dominant approach in late nineteenth- and early twentieth-century case law. An example is *Watteau v Fenwick*.[29] The defendants, a brewery firm, owned the Victoria Hotel in Stockton-on-Tees, but it was operated by the manager in his own name. The brewery required the manager to use their supply of cigars and Bovril, who consequently did not have authority to buy those products from third parties. In breach of that authority, the manager bought them from the claimant, and the claimant was held to be entitled to sue the brewery, as undisclosed principal, for the price. Wills J's short judgment is difficult to understand but implicitly proceeds on the basis that there was an identity between undisclosed principal and agent, from which the principal could not escape: 'once it is established that the defendant was the real principal, the ordinary doctrine as to principal and agent applies'.[30]

Said v Butt is also best understood as exemplifying contemporary judicial enthusiasm for the identification theory. The case concerned a ticket holder who had been refused entry on the opening night of a revue called *The Whiligig* at the Palace Theatre in London because he had publicly accused the managing director and its staff of defrauding him over the previous production at the Palace, *Monsieur Beaucaire*, in which he had co-invested. The complication in the case was that the claimant, Boris Said, had not bought the ticket himself, but instead had asked a friend, Captain Edmund Pollock, secretly to buy it for him. The court proceeded on an assumption that the contract was between third party and undisclosed principal not between third party and agent, and concluded that there was no contract on the facts upon which an intervention could be made:

> Before the plaintiff can succeed he must establish that there was a valid and subsisting contract between *the Palace Theatre and himself* ... In my opinion, the defendant can rightly say, upon the special circumstances of this case, that no contract existed on December 23, 1919 upon which the plaintiff could have sued the Palace Theatre.[31]

[27] *Keighley, Maxsted & Co v Durant* [1901] AC 240 (HL), 261 (Lord Lindley).
[28] OW Holmes Jr, 'Agency II' (1891-1892) 5 *Harvard Law Review* 1, 5.
[29] *Watteau v Fenwick* [1893] 1 QB 346 (QBD).
[30] ibid 348.
[31] *Said v Butt* (n 11) 500 and 503 (McCardie J) (emphasis added).

In coming to this conclusion, the judge placed weight on section 19 of *Traité des Obligations*, where Pothier posited that an 'error in regard to the person with whom I contract' will, if the identity of the counterparty is significant to the contract, 'destroy my consent and consequently annuls the contract'; conversely, if identity of the counterparty is not significant to the contract, 'the contract ought to stand'.[32] The judge also cited numerous cases on mistaken identity.[33] All of these authorities are about the effect of such a mistake on whether a valid contract has been formed in circumstances where one party to it is mistaken as to the other's identity, and their relevance is therefore premised on the idea that the contract was always truly between the theatre company and Said or did not exist at all.

Even if the principal's contract theory were to be accepted, McCardie J's application of it in *Said v Butt* is problematic. There was no 'error' in the theatre company's belief that it was entering into a contract with Captain Pollock. Undisclosed agents do not 'drop out' of a contract. As Lord Lloyd confirmed in *Siu Yin Kwan*, after intervention, the 'agent of an undisclosed principal may also sue and be sued on the contract'.[34] The effect of undisclosed agency was thus not to *substitute* Pollock for Said as the counterparty but rather to create *additional* rights and liabilities for Said.[35] The relevant error (if any) by the Palace Theatre company can only have been that Pollock was the sole beneficiary of the rights conferred by the ticket for the opening night. It is doubtful that a mistake of that nature is sufficiently fundamental to mean that no contract can have been formed in the first place.[36]

In any event, and despite its endorsement in *Said v Butt*, this second explanation for the Intervention Rule is even less satisfactory than the first. A contract is formed by an agreement between two parties, objectively ascertained, involving some reciprocity (ie consideration) between those parties in the substance of what has been agreed. The doctrine of privity demands that only those parties to the contract who have provided the consideration can sue and be sued on it.[37] Treating the contract as always being between principal and third party drives a coach and horses through these basic principles of contract formation. The principal's contract theory also does not fit the Intervention Rule itself particularly well. If accepted, it would call into question why the agent can also be sued and sue on the contract, and why the principal's intervention is subject to defences the third party can raise against the agent, such as set-off.[38] It also begs the question as to why there are any limitations on the Rule at all – still less why, as we will see, those limitations are so robust.[39]

[32] ibid 501 (McCardie J), quoting *Smith v Wheatcroft* (1878) 9 Ch D 223 (Ch), 230 (Fry J) and *Gordon v Street* [1899] 2 QB 641 (CA), 647 (AL Smith LJ).

[33] See, eg, *Boulton v Stone* (1857) 2 H&N 564, 157 ER 232; *Archer v Stone* (1898) 78 LT 34 (Ch); *Phillips v Brooks* [1919] 2 KB 243 (KBD). For a detailed dissection of the authorities relied upon by McCardie J, see Goodhart and Hamson (n 6) 350–51.

[34] *Siu Yin Kwan* (n 1) 207 (Lord Lloyd).

[35] See also, eg, *Bowstead* (n 4) para 9.012.

[36] cf GL Williams, 'Mistake as to Party in the Law of Contract (Part II)' (1945) 23 *Canadian Bar Review* 380, 405.

[37] Substantial inroads were, of course, made into this doctrine by the Contract (Rights of Third Parties) Act 1999, but that is beyond the scope of this chapter.

[38] *Bowstead* (n 4) para 8.109; cf CH Tan, 'Implied Terms in Undisclosed Agency' (2021) 84 *MLR* 532, 544.

[39] See section III.

ii. Academic Support for the Principal's Contract Theory

Unconvincing attempts have been made by academics to save the principal's contract theory by suggesting ways of reconciling the Rule with orthodox requirements of contract formation.

Müller-Freinfels, for example, grounds the Rule in the doctrine of consideration; for him, consideration provides the 'essential link' because it is the undisclosed principal who 'ultimately bears the burden of the detriment, which is the consideration moving to the third parties', and the agent is 'the stranger to the contract, a mere conduit pipe'.[40] But this justification proves both too much and too little. If the ability to sue and be sued on contracts was measured by who bore the ultimate economic cost of providing consideration, many more parties could intervene on the contract than just the undisclosed principal who has conferred actual authority on the contracting party. At the same time, it does not explain why the objectively ascertainable agreement should be disregarded; at best the argument advanced by Müller-Freinfels removes the consideration objection to the Intervention Rule, without explaining how the other conditions for contractual formation can be satisfied.

More recently, Tan has resuscitated the principal's contract theory by reference to Diplock LJ's judgment in *Teheran-Europe Co Ltd ST Belton (Tractors) Ltd*.[41] There, Diplock LJ said that, so long as the third party is 'willing or leads the agent to believe that he is willing to treat as a party to the contract anyone on whose behalf the agent may have been authorised to contract', a contract arises between principal and third party. For good measure, Diplock LJ added that in a case of an 'ordinary commercial contract' such willingness could be presumed.[42] Tan takes this to mean that the 'third party therefore impliedly contracts with the agent as well as the agent's undisclosed principal from the outset'.[43]

The problems with this approach are threefold. First, Diplock LJ's presumption as to commercial attitudes is not sound: commercial parties *do* normally care about who their counterparty is; the market exists to enable parties to choose their counterparties. Indeed, as we have seen, the perceived commercial advantage of intervention is to enable the principal to choose to contract with the third party, while disabling the third party from choosing *not* to contract with the principal in return.[44] Second, this argument boils down to a claim that the third party intended to contract with anyone for whom the agent happened secretly to be acting.[45] But as the third party has no knowledge that the agent was an agent at all, and instead contracted with agent as principal, it is difficult to see how there could have been such an intention; all the third party can have intended (on an objective basis) is to deal with the agent *qua* principal. Put another way, a contract requires an agreement between objectively ascertained parties;

[40] W Müller-Freinfels, 'The Undisclosed Principal' (1953) 16 *MLR* 299, 306. Holmes also hints at this: OW Holmes Jr, 'Agency I' (1890-1891) 4 *Harvard Law Review* 345, 349; also (n 28) 4.

[41] *Teheran-Europe Co Ltd ST Belton (Tractors) Ltd* [1968] 2 QB 545 (CA).

[42] ibid 555 (Diplock LJ).

[43] Tan (n 17) 502.

[44] Text to n 16.

[45] Tan (n 17) 502.

on that test, the agreement can only have been between principal and agent. Third, since the identity of the parties to a contract is a term of the contract,[46] if it is to extend by implied term in fact to the undisclosed principal, it must satisfy either the officious bystander or the business efficacy test.[47] It is difficult to see either test satisfied in the ordinary run of cases. It lacks credibility to suggest that if a typical commercial party were asked, before contracting, 'Do you mind who your counterparty to this contract is?', it would reply 'Of course I don't!'. As for business efficacy, the contract should usually work perfectly well as between third party and undisclosed agent; it would be an odd bargain that only worked if a principal undisclosed to the third party at the time of contracting could later intervene.

Tan himself has recognised the difficulties of contending that a contract is implied in fact between the parties.[48] He has recently clarified that, on this theory for the Intervention Rule, the implied contract between principal and third party is instead one implied *in law*: the implied term arises because the law recognises the 'commercial utility' of undisclosed agency in 'facilitating economic relationships' and so wishes to give effect to it as a matter of policy.[49] This is not convincing for two reasons. First, and most importantly, the commercial utility of the Rule is questionable for the reasons already given.[50] In those circumstances, it is doubtful that the law should impose a contract between principal and third party for policy reasons. Second, the consequence of Tan's argument is that a new implied contract arises between principal and third party. But that is not how implication in law works: the implication in law does not create a contract where otherwise none exists; instead, it 'gap fills' within a contract *after* a contractual relationship between the parties has first been identified and categorised (eg as a contract for the sale of goods, of insurance, of employment).[51] On Tan's theory the implication by law goes beyond orthodox 'gap filling' and constitutes an entirely new contract.

C. Agent's Contract Theory

The better starting point for understanding the Rule is to regard the contract as always only being between agent and third party. So, applying this theory to the facts of *Said v Butt*, the contract must have been between Captain Pollock and the Palace Theatre. That is unobjectionable by reference to orthodox principles of contract law and reflects the

[46] See, eg, *Homburg Houtimport BV v Agrosin Private Ltd (The Starsin)* [2003] UKHL 12, [2004] 1 AC 715.

[47] *Marks & Spencer plc v BNP Paribas Securities Services Trust Co (Jersey) Ltd* [2015] EWHC 72, [2016] AC 742.

[48] Tan (n 38) 538.

[49] ibid 539.

[50] Text to n 18.

[51] See, eg, *Liverpool City Council v Irwin* [1977] AC 239 (HL), 257 (Lord Cross); *Scally v Southern Health and Social Services Board* [1992] 1 AC 294 (HL), 306–307 (Lord Bridge); *Société Générale, London Branch v Geys* [2012] UKSC 63, [2013] 1 AC 523 [55] (Lady Hale). That is not to say that sometimes the implied term is necessary to ensure sufficient *completeness* of agreement for it to constitute a contract; indeed, that is when the gap-filling function of implied terms in law becomes particularly important: see *Devani v Wells* [2019] UKSC 4, [2020] AC 129.

reinterpretation of *Said v Butt* subsequently suggested by both the Court of Appeal and the House of Lords.[52] The question then becomes what justifies the claim brought by, or against, the undisclosed principal in respect of the rights under a contract to which it is not a party at the time of contracting. Here, agent's contract theorists divide into two camps.

First, some argue that there is some form of 'transfer' of the contract from the agent to the principal, so that the principal can sue and be sued on it. This was the approach taken by Goodhart and Hanson, writing in vigorous opposition to McCardie J's adoption of the principal's contract theory in *Said v Butt*:

> [T]he theory … that the contract is a contract between the principal and the third party (i) is contrary to the express decision of several cases in which undisclosed principals were involved; (ii) is not taken as the ratio decidendi of any case in which there was an undisclosed principal except *Said v Butt* … The doctrine of the undisclosed principal is perhaps best considered as a primitive and highly restricted form of assignment.[53]

The problem is that Goodhart and Hansom simply asserted their analogy with assignment without explaining it. The only attempt to unpack it came some years later, when Barnett rooted it in the 'consensual agreement between agent and principal' whereby 'the agent is consensually committed (to the principal) to transfer to the principal the rights … he receives from a third party', so that 'these rights pass immediately to the principal without any further assent or act by the agent'.[54] This transfer argument is deeply problematic, because it cannot explain the agent's own rights and liability under the contract alongside those of the principal. For this reason, it was ultimately rejected by the Privy Council in *Siu Yin Kwan*, where it was unsuccessfully claimed that, if a contract was non-assignable, it must also be immune from any intervention by undisclosed principals. Lord Lloyd noted 'the dangers of proceeding by analogy' because of the 'many differences' between the two doctrines.[55] This echoed what Williams had pointed out many years earlier:

> [S]urely there are great differences between the two. An undisclosed principal is liable on the contract; an assignee is not. Assignment is an act subsequent to the contract; the status of an undisclosed results from the giving of authority before the contract. Assignment is subject to special requirements of form or (possibly) consideration, to which undisclosed principals are not subject. In the face of these differences the analogy between undisclosed principals and assignees is surely a very risky one …[56]

The second, and preferable, explanation for the Rule is that the contract is only ever between agent and third party, and does not extend to the principal by transfer (or otherwise). The rights and liabilities of the undisclosed principal are *not* contractual in nature, albeit they are built on foundations provided by the contract between agent and third party.[57] In particular, it is suggested that the legal effect of the agreement

[52] *Welsh Development Agency v Export Finance Co Ltd* [1992] BCC 270 (CA), 288 (Dillon LJ); *Shogun Finance Ltd v Hudson* [2003] UKHL 62, [2004] 1 AC 919 [88] (Lord Millett).
[53] Goodhart and Hamson (n 6) 347 and 352.
[54] Barnett (n 16) 1982–83.
[55] *Siu Yin Kwan* (n 1) 210.
[56] Williams (n 36) 408.
[57] *Welsh Development Agency* (n 52) 290 (Dillon LJ).

between agent and principal is to (i) confer a power on the principal against the agent's contractual rights against the third party, allowing the principal to enforce and take the benefit of those rights, and (ii) impose a reciprocal liability on the principal to that third party, replicating the contractual liability of the agent to the third party. Since the third party is not privy to the agency agreement itself, these rights and liabilities cannot be characterised 'in any relevant sense voluntary or consensual';[58] but it is nonetheless derivative on the contract that the third party has consensually entered into with the undisclosed agent. Without that underlying contract, there are no rights against which the principal can assert its power, nor any basis for imposing a reciprocal lability. As Weinrib puts it, 'the legal position of the undisclosed principal is derived from the [third party]–[agent] bargain even if … [not] clothed with the jural status of contract'.[59]

The underlying justification for the Intervention Rule, characterised in this way, is rooted in the relationship between agent and principal. An analogy has been drawn with trust law on the basis that an agent is (typically)[60] a fiduciary of the principal, and so holds the benefit of a contract made in the course of agency on trust for the principal.[61] While this is a much better analogy to make than to assignment,[62] there are perhaps dangers in placing too much weight on it.[63] The pitfalls can be seen in the way Higgins expresses the point:

> An undisclosed principal can sue the third party in the same way that a *cestui que trust*, who is *sui juris* and absolutely entitled to the trust property, can bring the trust to an end and then take action in his own name. The right of the third party to sue the undisclosed principal … may be possible … by making available to the other party the rights of the trustee against the *cestui que trust* … to indemnify his trustee. … [T]he only objection to suing him directly is purely procedural.[64]

Higgins' difficulty arises because he seeks to explain the Rule *entirely* by reference to trust law; something he cannot do, which leads him, unconvincingly, to dismiss what he cannot explain as not worth explanation.[65]

[58] *Playboy* (n 3) [14] (Lord Sumption). However, in the same paragraph, Lord Sumption said that they had still a 'contractual relationship', which might be viewed as a *non sequitur*.

[59] EJ Weinrib, 'The Undisclosed Principle of Undisclosed Principals' (1975) 21 *McGill Law Journal* 298, 306.

[60] Cf ch 2 of this volume by Matthew Conaglen, 'The Fiduciary Status of Agents'.

[61] *Bowstead* (n 4) paras 6.040–6.041.

[62] At least to the 'transfer' model of assignment, which is the model Goodhart and Hamson (n 6) appear to adopt. Cf J Edelman and S Elliott, 'Two Conceptions of Equitable Assignment' (2015) 131 *LQR* 228.

[63] As the rejection of complete identity between the two concepts in the *res judicata* context demonstrates: see, eg, *Pople v Evans* [1969] 2 Ch 255 (ChD), 264 (Ungoed-Thomas J).

[64] PFP Higgins 'The Equity of the Undisclosed Principal' (1965) 28 *MLR* 167, 170–71; cf Ames (n 22) 444–48.

[65] See also WA Seavey, 'The Rationale of Agency' (1920) 29 *The Yale Law Journal* 859, 876–77: 'the only abnormality is the informality of allowing a direct action at law … there should be no objection simply on the ground that a short cut has been taken'. Others have tried to deal with the conferral of a right of direct action by reference to a policy against circuity of action: see JL Montrose, 'The Basis of the Power of an Agent in Cases of Actual and Apparent Authority' (1938) 16 *Canadian Bar Review* 757, 770–71. But this essentially then becomes, again, an argument based on commercial convenience.

The better approach is to accept that the Intervention Rule is a 'distinctive'[66] or 'autonomous'[67] power, unique to agency, that goes *beyond* what is available to a beneficiary under a trust. This *sui generis* agency power is created by the unique triple helix of (i) the conferral of actual authority to enter into contracts on an undisclosed basis, (ii) the duty of the agent to hold the benefit of the contract for the principal, and (iii) the corresponding rights of control by the principal over the agent in respect of that contract throughout its existence. It is that combination of authority, control and fiduciary duty that comprises the defining characteristics of an agency agreement,[68] and it is that trilogy that justifies the principal's being able to sue and be sued by reference to the contractual terms agreed between agent and third party.

Of course, a trustee must also hold the benefit of a contract for a beneficiary, so it must be authority and control – features not inherent to trusts – that justify the greater rights a principal enjoys in respect of an agent's contract under the Rule. The principal is bound to be liable to the third party on intervention because an agent by definition has the authority to bind the principal and has acted with the intention of exercising that authority.[69] Conversely, a mere trustee has no such authority and so the beneficiary is not so bound. Control explains the third party's liability to the principal on the agent's contractual rights. As Seavey pointed out, the 'great difference' from a mere beneficiary is that the principal is 'a *cestui*, but he is also more. He is a master. A *cestui* receives profits; a principal receives profits and controls the manner of making them … [l]iability follows control …'[70] Crucially, control by a principal extends beyond the moment of entry into the contract on an undisclosed basis through its enforcement on breach: the principal can instruct the agent to sue, and then to account for the proceeds.[71] In that context, it would be incoherent if the principal's power against the agent's right also did not allow the principal to sue in the principal's own name. Conversely, beneficiaries do not have the same control rights over contracts entered into by their trustee. Their rights against the trustee's contractual rights are more limited,[72] and they cannot enforce them alone; they must instead join the trustee by the *Vandepitte* procedure.[73] That difference in outcome – that in cases of agency, the third party may well find itself in proceedings against the principal alone, whereas in trust cases the trustee will necessarily be party to the proceedings too – provides a further (albeit second-order) reason as to why the law demands in agency cases the *quid pro quo* that the third party be entitled to sue the principal as though they were the contractual counterparty.[74]

[66] Seavey (n 65) 877.
[67] Weinrib (n 59) 299.
[68] *Restatement, Third* (n 15) vol 1, § 1.01; cf *Bowstead* (n 4) para 1.018.
[69] Text to n 1.
[70] Seavey (n 65) 879.
[71] *Freeman & Lockyer (A Firm) v Buckhurst Park Properties (Mangal) Ltd* [1964] 2 QB 480 (CA), 503 (Diplock LJ). Also Montrose (n 65) 770.
[72] Indeed, they do not have a power against the right at all, but merely a right against the right.
[73] After *Vandepitte v Preferred Accident Insurance Corporation of New York* [1933] AC 70 (PC), 79 (Lord Wright).
[74] Cf Weinrib (n 59) 298, who appears to argue that the *quid pro quo* is the other way around, ie that the law permits the third party to sue the principal as the controller and beneficiary of the agent's actions, and as the *quid pro quo* the principal is given a reciprocal right of action.

III. Limitations on the Intervention Rule

A. Contractual Exclusion of the Rule

It is uncontroversial that the Rule can be excluded by the terms of the contract between agent and third party. As Lord Lloyd explained in *Siu Yin Kwan*:

> The terms of the contract may, expressly or by implication, exclude the principal's right to sue, and his liability to be sued. The contract itself, or the circumstances surrounding the contract, may show that the agent is the true and only principal.[75]

As framed in this passage in *Siu Yin Kwan*, this is the *only* bar to intervention by an undisclosed principal. Article 76(4) of *Bowstead & Reynolds* is in identical terms.[76] Similarly, *Restatement, Third* states that an 'undisclosed principal does not become a party to a contract if the contract excludes the principal',[77] and identifies no other category of limitation. As explained in the next section of this chapter,[78] that is in fact the correct characterisation of the common law. However, before making that point good, it is worth unpacking this contractual limitation to the Intervention Rule.

The capacity of the contractual terms to exclude intervention by undisclosed principals is uncontroversial. Commercial contract law is best conceptualised as providing in large part a series of default rules, out of which parties can contract where they consider it in their commercial interest to do so. This limitation on the Rule thus simply identifies it as one of commercial law's default, not mandatory, rules.[79] It is difficult to argue against it having that lesser status. Whether in disclosed or undisclosed cases, the third party cannot legitimately complain about not being able to sue the principal, because that is what they have agreed. Nor can the principal complain about not being able to sue the agent, since it authorised the agent to enter into a contract on those terms.[80] Indeed, this limitation is not even confined to undisclosed agency; it can also apply in disclosed agency cases where the principal does not appear on the face of the written agreement.[81]

In principle, the Intervention Rule is a 'sticky' default rule, which the parties have to work hard to avoid. The law is meant to assume that an ordinary commercial party is 'willing to treat as a party to the contract anyone on whose behalf the agent may have been authorised to contract'.[82] For this reason, Lord Lloyd cautioned against too liberal an approach to the interpretation and implication of contract terms to exclude

[75] *Siu Yin Kwan* (n 1) 207 (Lord Lloyd).

[76] *Bowstead* (n 4) para 8.068.

[77] *Restatement, Third* (n 15) vol 2, 43.

[78] Text to n 113.

[79] See, eg, J Morgan, *Contract Law Minimalism: A Formalist Restatement of Commercial Contract Law* (Cambridge, Cambridge University Press, 2013) 91.

[80] See also Dal Pont (n 13) para 19.7.

[81] See, eg, *Filatona Trading Ltd v Navigator Equities Ltd* [2020] EWCA Civ 109, [2020] 1 CLC 285, where both parties knew that the agent was acting for a Russian oligarch, but the oligarch's name was kept off the contractual documentation because at the time he was Deputy Minister of Finance and Chairman of a prominent financial institution.

[82] *Teheran-Europe* (n 41) 555 (Diplock LJ).

intervention in *Siu Yin Kwan*, since 'it would go far to destroy the beneficial assumption in commercial cases'.[83] But the beneficial assumption (if it is a good one)[84] is vindicated by its being the default rule; there is no need to take the additional step of making it difficult to exclude. In any event, the courts increasingly appear only to pay lip-service, making this a sticky default rule. It is *not* the case, despite the claims of one commentator, that the undisclosed principal's intervention should be held to be inconsistent with the terms of the contract only in 'exceptional cases'.[85]

In fact, it is not uncommon for a contract expressly to exclude undisclosed agency. Whether it does so is a question of construction. The mere fact that the contract is in the name of the agent obviously does not work as an express exclusion, since if that were sufficient then undisclosed agency would never be available. The terms must instead show that the undisclosed agent 'has contracted in such terms to show that he was the real and only principal'.[86] So, for example, the express terms will exclude the Rule where they provide that the parties must have certain attributes that the undisclosed principal lacks, like membership of a particular organisation.[87] Boilerplate provisions and standard form contracts often include a provision that the agreement is between the parties acting as principals and can only be enforced by them.[88] These provisions are drafted with undisclosed agency in mind.

But the courts have not stopped there. One decision suggesting a judicial willingness to find a contractual term precluding the Intervention Rule, even absent such express terms, is *Humble v Hunter*.[89] The undisclosed agent signed a charterparty as 'owner'; that was held to be sufficient to exclude the principal's intervention as the true owner of the ship. That decision, which has the potential to exclude the Rule from most sale of goods contracts,[90] was followed in *Formby Bros v Formby*,[91] where the agent was identified as the 'proprietor', and *Redebiaktiebolaget Argonaut v Hani*,[92] where the agent contracted 'as charterer'. In *The Astaynax*,[93] the agent was described as the 'disponent owner', which, while considered neutral in itself, when combined with the factual matrix, made it clear that he was contracting as principal. Despite that line of cases, since the decision of the House of Lords in *Fred Drughorn Ltd v Rederiaktiebolaget Transatlantic*, it is said that judicial willingness to use party descriptions to exclude intervention has been reduced.[94] In *Drughorn*, the agent was again

[83] *Siu Yin Kwan* (n 1) 207 (Lord Lloyd).
[84] Text to n 44.
[85] D Fox et al (eds), *Sealy and Hooley's Commercial Law: Text, Cases, and Materials*, 6th edn (Oxford, Oxford University Press, 2020) 193.
[86] *Finzel v Berry & Co v Eastcheap Dried Fruit Company* [1962] 1 Lloyd's Rep 370 (Com Ct), 375 (McNair J).
[87] *The United Kingdom Mutual Steamship Assurance Association Limited v Nevill* (1887) 19 QBD 110 (CA).
[88] Some examples are set out in *Filatona* (n 81) [90] (Simon LJ). See also, eg, *JH Rayner (Mincing Lane) Ltd v Department of Trade and Industry* [1990] 2 AC 418 (HL), 516 (Lord Oliver) and *Taylor v Van Dutch Marine Holding Ltd* [2019] EWHC 1951 (Ch), [2019] Bus LR 2610 [277] (Julia Dias QC sitting as a Judge of the High Court).
[89] *Humble v Hunter* (1848) 12 QB 310.
[90] Fridman (n 13) 80–81.
[91] *Formby Bros v Formby* (1919) 102 LT 116 (CA).
[92] *Redebiaktiebolaget Argonaut v Hani* [1918] 2 KB 247 (Com Ct).
[93] *Asty Maritime Co Ltd v Rocco Giueseppe & Figli SNC (The Astaynax)* [1985] 2 Lloyd's Rep 109 (CA).
[94] Munday (n 13) para 10.45; Tan CH, *The Law of Agency*, 2nd edn (Singapore, Academy Publishing, 2017) 328.

described as 'charterer'. Viscount Haldane distinguished *Humble v Hunter*, on the basis that the description as 'charterer' did not involve an assertion of a title to property inconsistent with the basis of the principal's proposed intervention.[95] Yet Viscount Haldane did not suggest the decision in *Humble v Hunter* was wrong. The alleged chilling effect of *Drughorn* may have been due to Lord Shaw's short concurring speech, in which he went further and questioned the correctness of *Humble v Hunter* itself.[96]

Although *Said v Butt* itself was determined on the erroneous basis that there was no contract,[97] it might be reconceptualised as a case involving an implied term excluding intervention for two reasons. First, Mr Said's undisclosed agent, Captain Pollock, gave evidence in cross-examination that, when he called for tickets, he chose to give his own name as the purchaser.[98] On the basis of this evidence, McCardie J could perhaps therefore have applied the *Humble v Hunter* line of case law. The second basis on which the Rule might have been impliedly excluded by the terms of the contract arose from the nature of the opening night. The managing director of the theatre, Sir Alfred Butt, gave evidence that 'he had a first night list of people who were invited, and he had a second list of people who had a preference to buy seats on the first night. All other applications were submitted to him personally.'[99] McCardie J accepted this evidence:

> A first night at the Palace Theatre is, as with other theatres, an event of great importance. The result of a first night may make or mar a play. If the play be good, then word of its success may be spread, not only by the critics, but by the members of the audience. The nature and social position and influence of the audience are of obvious importance. First nights have become to a large extent a species of private entertainment given by the theatrical proprietors and management to their friends and acquaintances, and to influential persons, whether critics or otherwise. The boxes, stalls and dress circle are regarded as parts of the theatre which are subject to special allocation by the management. Many tickets for those parts may be given away. The remaining tickets are usually sold by favour only. A first night, therefore, is a special event, with special characteristics.[100]

Lord Millett endorsed this reconceptualisation of *Said v Butt* in *Shogun Finance Ltd v Hudson*, where he said:

> The evidence showed that tickets for a first night are not transferable, from which it follows that they are incapable of being bought for an undisclosed principal; so that *even on its own terms* the contract could not be enforced by the plaintiff.[101]

This suggests that there should be a relative amount of latitude to find a term excluding intervention. Two recent decisions of the Court of Appeal – *Bell v Ivy Technology Ltd* and *Kaefer Aislamientos SA de CV v AMS Drilling Mexico SA de CV* – confirm this to be the case.[102]

[95] *Fred Drughorn Ltd v Rederiaktiebolaget Transatlantic* [1919] AC 203 (HL), 205–09 (Viscount Haldane).

[96] *Fred Drughorn* (n 95) 209 (Lord Shaw).

[97] Text to n 31.

[98] 'King's Bench Division: Charges Against Theatre Officials: Producer Denied Admission' *Daily Telegraph* (London, 12 June 1920) 3 (hereinafter *Daily Telegraph Day 1*). When asked why he had done this, it prompted a judicial witticism from the bench: 'Oh, a name might make all the difference. If a voice merely asks for three stalls the box-office might be busy but supposing the voice said, "I am the Right Hon Lloyd George" I think you would find there was an immediate scarcity of tickets for other people. (Laughter)'.

[99] 'King's Bench Division: Charges Against Theatre Officials: Evidence of Sir Alfred Butt' *Daily Telegraph* (London, 15 June 1920) 5 (hereinafter *Daily Telegraph Day 2*).

[100] *Said v Butt* (n 11) 501–02 (McCardie J).

[101] *Shogun Finance* (n 52) [88] (Lord Millett) (emphasis added).

[102] *Bell v Ivy Technology Ltd* [2020] EWCA Civ 1563; *Kaefer Aislamientos SA de CV v AMS Drilling Mexico SA de CV* [2019] EWCA Civ 10, [2019] 1 WLR 3514.

Starting with the former, while it has long been the case that a standard non-assignment clause is not enough to stop intervention,[103] the position now appears to be different for standard clauses adopted since the Contracts (Rights of Third Parties) Act 1999, so as to prevent that statute enabling third parties who benefit from performance of the contract being able to enforce its terms. In *Bell v Ivy Technology Ltd*, an appeal on an interlocutory application, the clause was in familiar terms:

> Nothing in this Agreement, express or implied, is intended to confer upon any third parties other than the Parties hereto or their respective successors and assigns any rights, remedies, obligations or liabilities under or by reason of this Agreement, except as expressly provided in this Agreement.[104]

Arnold LJ held that there was a 'very cogent' case that such a clause would preclude the Intervention Rule, albeit not so strong as to prevent the matter going to trial.[105] Given the ubiquity of such clauses, if this approach were adopted, a great number of contracts would be immune to intervention.

A more difficult decision is *Kaefer Aislamientos SA de CV v AMS Drilling Mexico SA de CV*. There, Green LJ held that a garden variety entire agreement clause showed 'that the named contractual parties were to treat each other, and no one else, as the parties with liabilities and rights under the agreement and hence the persons to sue or be sued thereunder'.[106] That seems dubious: entire agreement clauses are adopted to limit the scope for arguments about misrepresentation or collateral contracts. The Court was at pains to emphasise that an entire agreement clause was a 'cogent indication' rather than determinative.[107] That presumably means it could be counterbalanced by another term of the contract positively contemplating undisclosed agency; but where the contract is otherwise neutral, the conclusion will be that there can be no intervention. The willingness to read the entire agreement clause in this way again underlines the enthusiasm of judges to limit the operation of a Rule seen as anomalous.

One leading commentator suggests this liberal approach to the use of express and implied terms of the contract to preclude the Intervention Rule should go even further:

> It is likely that the doctrine is not as far-reaching, even in contract, as … assume[d]. In particular, while the doctrine can spring a surprise on a third party as to the existence of a counter-party, it is strongly arguable that the doctrine normally applies only where it makes little difference to the scope and weight of the obligations of the promisor who is being sued on the contract.[108]

[103] *Browning v Provincial Insurance Co of Canada* (1873) LR 5 PC 263 (PC). See too *Siu Yin Kwan* (n 1) 210 (Lord Lloyd). Cf P Watts, 'Agency' in W Day and S Worthington (eds), *Challenging Private Law: Lord Sumption on the Supreme Court* (Oxford, Hart Publishing, 2020) 257, 269: '[I]t is reasonably clear from the insurance examples that Lord Lloyd discussed that he also perceived that sometimes, perhaps often, the correct conclusion on the facts will be that assignability and the undisclosed principals doctrine will stand and fall together. In other words, Lord Lloyd was far from saying that the reasons that a contract has been made non-assignable can have no bearing on whether an undisclosed principal can intervene.'

[104] *Bell* (n 102) [16] (Arnold LJ).

[105] ibid [28] (Arnold LJ).

[106] *Kaefer* (n 102) [112] (Green LJ).

[107] ibid [114]. See also *Filatona* (n 81) [84]–[89] (Simon LJ).

[108] Watts (n 103) 268–69. Cf *Williams v Bulat* [1992] 2 Qd R 556 and *Alrich Development Pte Ltd v Rafiq Jumabhoy* [2008] 3 SLR(R) 340, discussed in Tan (n 94) 334–36.

There is much to commend this approach. It reflects how a reasonable person in the position of the parties would usually reply when asked by the officious bystander, 'Would you extend these terms to the undisclosed principal?'[109] *Siu Yin Kwan* itself, where intervention was permitted, was an unusual case where for the third party, the insurer, 'the actual identity of the employer was a matter of indifference. It was not material to the risk.'[110] That was perhaps an unusual set of facts. In many other transactions, the identity of the counterparty does matter. The *Restatement, Third* argues, for example, that an undisclosed principal should be precluded from intervening on a letter of credit because it would 'violate the principle of separation that protects [the] issuer of [the] letter from responsibility to police the underlying transaction that the letter is intended to finance'.[111] Another example is a standard credit relationship: a lender ought normally to be able to resist the intervention of the undisclosed principal because the lender has accepted the credit risk of the stated borrower rather than anyone else.[112]

B. 'Good Faith' or 'Personality' Limitations on the Rule?

Notwithstanding the terms of Article 76(4) of *Bowstead & Reynolds*, and the relevant part of *Restatement, Third*,[113] there appears to be a considerable support for the view that there is also a *non*-contractual bar on intervention. Reynolds characterises this as 'one of the comparatively few areas in common law where a principle of good faith might provide reasoning not otherwise available'.[114] But good faith is a notoriously amorphous concept, and the specifics of this further limitation on the Intervention Rule are disputed.

So, for example, Fridman states that 'the personality of the principal' must be 'a matter of indifference to the third party' before the Rule can operate.[115] Munday puts it the other way around: personality must be of 'particular importance' for the exception to the Rule to be engaged. He argues that this should apply to both ostensible principal (ie the undisclosed agent) and the true principal: the Rule should thus be barred where 'the personality of the agent is a matter of importance to the third party',[116] or where 'the personality of the undisclosed principal is of particular importance to the third party'.[117] In the commentary to Article 76(4), *Bowstead & Reynolds* tentatively endorses only the latter point – 'an undisclosed principal cannot intervene when the principal knew or should have known at the time of the contract that the third party would not have dealt with him' – and suggests this is to ensure that the Rule does not 'overly favour

[109] Cf text to n 47.
[110] *Siu Yin Kwan* (n 1) 210 (Lord Lloyd).
[111] *Restatement, Third* (n 15) vol 2, 50–51.
[112] Dal Pont (n 13) para 19.39.
[113] Text to n 76.
[114] Reynolds (n 5) para 1.80.
[115] GHL Fridman, *Canadian Agency Law*, 3rd edn (Toronto, LexisNexis Canada, 2017) 186.
[116] Munday (n 13) 282.
[117] ibid 284.

the principal'.[118] Tan arrives at the polar opposite conclusion: '[I]t does not appear that any personal reason for not wishing to deal with the undisclosed principal will prevent the latter from intervening. The personal considerations in question must relate to a positive reason for any wishing to deal with this agent.'[119]

We can only resolve this controversy in the commentary by looking at the underlying cases themselves. It is suggested below that, on examination, the cases are either (i) not about undisclosed agency at all, or (ii) better explained by reference to express and implied exclusions of the Rule within the terms of the contract.

i. Third Party's Personal Reasons for Dealing Only with the Undisclosed Agent

In some cases, the factual matrix shows that the third party has a particular reason for dealing with the undisclosed agent as principal. The agent may possess a particular skill that motivated the transaction.[120] So, for example, where 'the contracts in question were for the unique services of a musician' that 'would not have been capable of being performed vicariously by an undisclosed principal'.[121] But in such contracts, a prohibition on the Rule would be implied as a matter of obviousness and business efficacy. There is no need to rely on non-contractual bars to the Rule.

Boulton v Jones is sometimes cited as an authority in support of the agent's 'personality' barring the Rule,[122] and indeed was cited by McCardie J in *Said v Butt* itself.[123] *Boulton v Jones* was a case where Mr Jones had habitually bought leather from a business run by Mr Brocklehurst. Mr Boulton bought Brocklehurst's business, and the very same day a further order was received from Mr Jones. Mr Boulton fulfilled the order and, when Mr Jones did not pay, sued for the price. The Court of Exchequer held that there was no contract, essentially because the offer had been to Mr Brocklehurst not Mr Boulton.[124] This was a case of mistaken identity, not a case of undisclosed agency; indeed, the relationship between Mr Brocklehurst and Mr Boulton was one of buyer and seller of the business, not of principal and agent.[125]

In *Greer v Downs Supply Co*,[126] the third party agreed to buy timber from the undisclosed agent because the agent personally owed the third party a debt from a previous contract. The Court of Appeal held that the undisclosed principal could not sue for the price. Scrutton LJ's judgment is typically cited by those arguing for a 'personality' bar to the Rule:

> When a plaintiff claims as an undisclosed principal the question sometimes arises whether the contract was made with the agent for reasons personal to the agent which induced the other party to contract with the agent to the exclusion of his principal or any one else. When

[118] *Bowstead* (n 4) para 8.079.
[119] Tan (n 94) 337. See also, more recently, Tan (n 38) 541–42.
[120] Bennett (n 13) 146; Munday (n 13) 282.
[121] *Barrett v Universal-Island Records Ltd* [2006] EWHC 1009 (Ch), [2006] EMLR 21 [233] (Lewison J).
[122] *Boulton v Jones* (n 33). Tan (n 94) 331.
[123] *Said v Butt* (n 11) 503 (McCardie J).
[124] *Boulton v Jones* (n 33).
[125] Goodhart and Hamson (n 6) 350.
[126] *Greer v Downs Supply Co* [1927] 2 KB 28 (CA).

> the learned judge at the trial found that the respondent knew nothing about the appellant and honestly believed he was contracting with Godwin and when it was proved that he was contracting with Godwin because Godwin was his debtor, there was an end of the case for the appellant at the trial.[127]

Greer does not turn on the recognition of some non-contractual bar to the Rule. As the Court of Appeal noted, 'one of the terms' of the contract was that the third party 'should be allowed to set off 17l. against the contract price'.[128] The set-off clause thus excluded intervention in exactly the same way as other express terms considered in the last section.[129]

This understanding of *Greer* was confirmed by the Ontario Court of Appeal on similar facts in *Campbellville Gravel Supply Ltd v Cook Paving Co.*[130] The defendant had been used to dealing with Mr Harris on behalf of his business, Western. Western ceased trading, owing the defendant a substantial sum. A year later, Mr Harris approached the defendant, offering to sell its stone on a commission basis. Believing Mr Harris still to be acting for Western, the defendant agreed, on the basis that the commission would be paid by way of set off against the debt already owed. In fact Mr Harris was being employed by the claimant. But when the claimant sought to intervene, the set-off agreement precluded it from doing so. Having cited *Greer* with approval, Laskin JA added:

> The situation in the present case is within the following principle expressed in the *Restatement of the Law, Second, Agency* … 'A person with whom an agent makes a contract on account of an undisclosed principal is not liable in an action at law brought upon the contract by such principal … if the terms of the contract exclude liability to any undisclosed principal or to the particular principal'.[131]

Lastly, there is the case of *Collins v Associated Greyhound Racecourses Ltd.*[132] A prospectus was issued to attract underwriters of shares in a new company. Mr Collins instructed two intermediaries, Mr Mason and Captain Ovington, to subscribe for him initially in their own names and, after acceptance, register the shares in his own name. The prospectus contained a misrepresentation, and Mr Collins sought to rescind the transaction. The Court of Appeal refused to allow him to do so. Russell LJ did so on the basis of an orthodox application of the law of misrepresentation and the agent's contract theory:

> [R]escission of that contract between the company and Mason and Ovington could only be obtained at the suit of Mason and Ovington, and upon proof of an allegation that Mason and Ovington had been misled by the prospectus. Both those elements are absent in the present action.[133]

The Master of Rolls went further:

> In the present case it appears to me that the contract between the company and Mason and Ovington was one in which importance attached to the personality of the persons

[127] ibid 35 (Scrutton LJ).
[128] ibid 37 (Scrutton LJ).
[129] Text to n 103.
[130] *Campbellville Gravel Supply Ltd v Cook Paving Co* [1968] 2 OR 679 (Ont CA).
[131] ibid 682 (Laskin JA).
[132] *Collins v Associated Greyhound Racecourses Ltd* [1930] 1 Ch 1 (Ch and CA).
[133] ibid 37 (Russell LJ).

> with whom the company were contracting. In such a case it is not right to treat the agents as necessarily interchangeable with their principal so as to enable the principal to come forward and seek to disaffirm the contract on the ground of a misrepresentation on which he alone had relied.[134]

Taken out of context, there is a risk of overreading this as amounting to recognition of a 'personality' bar to the Rule. But in fact Lord Hanworth MR began his judgment by saying he was entirely satisfied that the first instance judge, Luxmoore J, had been right.[135] And Luxmoore J had referred to the terms of the application for the shares and concluded that

> the company is from the very nature of the transaction entitled to consider the personality of the applicant before deciding to accept the application, and on both these grounds I think the application itself imports that it is made by Mr Mason and Captain Spencer Ovington as the real and only principals.[136]

This must be understood as a decision that the Intervention Rule had been contractually excluded.[137] To put the matter beyond doubt, in the Court of Appeal, Lawrence LJ added:

> I agree with the learned judge that Messrs Mason and Ovington *contracted in such terms as to imply that they were the real and only principals*. The directors of a company owe a duty to their fellow members and to the company to see that an applicant for shares is a responsible and fit person to become a member: none the less so because the applicant may in fact turn out to be an underwriter or sub-underwriter and may have applied for the shares on behalf of a client of his. The directors are not bound to accept as the applicant for shares an unknown person because he happens to be a client of an underwriter or other agent and thus be deprived of the opportunity of seeing whether the applicant is a fit and proper person to become a member of the company. A contract to become a member of a company is, in my opinion, one of that class of contracts in which an undisclosed principal cannot insist on taking the place of a party apparently contracting on his own account.[138]

For these reasons, it is submitted that none of the cases relied upon in support the existence of a non-contractual bar to the Rule based on the agent's personality are actually authority for that proposition.

ii. Third Party's Personal Reasons for Dealing Only with the Undisclosed Principal

The same is true for the cases relied upon in support the existence of a non-contractual bar to the Intervention Rule based on the principal's personality. The case normally relied on for this proposition is *Said v Butt* itself. For example, in *Rolls-Royce Power Engineering plc v Ricardo Consulting Engineers Ltd*,[139] the issue was whether the contract

[134] ibid 33 (Lord Hanworth MR).
[135] ibid 28 (Lord Hanworth MR).
[136] ibid 19 (Luxmoore J).
[137] cf Tan (n 48) 546–47.
[138] *Collins* (n 132) 35–36 (Lawrence LJ) (emphasis added).
[139] *Rolls-Royce Power Engineering plc v Ricardo Consulting Engineers Ltd* [2003] EWHC 2871 (TCC), [2004] 2 All ER (Comm) 129.

was entered into by Rolls-Royce's subsidiary for itself as principal or as undisclosed agent for Rolls-Royce. The Court accepted the submission that the *Said v Butt* limitation on intervention 'did not postulate that unwillingness to treat as a party to the contract anyone on whose behalf the agent may have been authorised to act had to be manifested by means of a term of the contract'.[140]

This understanding of *Said v Butt* appears to arise because of the following passage in McCardie J's judgment:

> In my opinion the defendant can rightly say, upon the special circumstances of this case, that no contract existed on December 23, 1919, upon which the plaintiff could have sued the Palace Theatre. The personal element was here strikingly present. The plaintiff knew that the Palace Theatre would not contract with him for the sale of a seat for December 23. They had expressly refused to do so. He was well aware of their reasons. I hold that by the mere device of utilizing the name and services of Mr Pollock, the plaintiff could not constitute himself a contractor with the Palace Theatre against their knowledge, and contrary to their express refusal. He is disabled from asserting that he was the undisclosed principal of Mr Pollock.[141]

The law report itself is light on the nature of the animosity between the parties, but the two-day trial was set out in some detail in *The Times*, *Daily Telegraph* and *Daily Mail*, so posterity nonetheless has the benefit of a record of the evidence and submissions.[142]

The defendant, Sir Alfred Butt, was something of a celebrity West End figure. He joined the Palace as a secretary aged 19, was the manager by the time he was 25 and became managing director of the theatre company two years later. He used his base at the Palace as a springboard to build a business across a number of theatres in London and elsewhere in the country.[143] The claimant, Boris Said, was also in showbusiness. A short time before the litigation, the weekly 'Theatrical Notes' column in the *Daily Telegraph* reported that he was a:

> Russian gentleman who [was] attracted first and chiefly by the artistic side of the side of the drama [but] has for some little time past taken also a financial interest in certain theatrical enterprises, although up to now preferring that his name should not be publicly mentioned in connection with any.[144]

[140] ibid [56] (HHJ Seymour QC).

[141] *Said v Butt* (n 11) 503 (McCardie J).

[142] *Daily Telegraph Day 1* (n 98); *Daily Telegraph Day 2* (n 99); 'Theatre First Nights: Right to Refuse Seats: Claim against Sir Alfred Butt' *The Times* (London, 12 June 1920) 5 (hereinafter *The Times Day 1*); 'Theatre First Nights: Sir Alfred Butt's Evidence' *The Times* (London, 15 June 1920) 5; 'Barred From A First Night: Action against Sir A Butt' *Daily Mail* (London, 12 June 1920) 8; 'First-Night Audiences: Sir A Butt's "First and Second Lists"' *Daily Mail* (London, 15 June 1920) 4.

[143] A Crowhurst, 'Butt, Sir Alfred (1878–1962)' in *Oxford Dictionary of National Biography* (2004). Butt was knighted in 1919 for his services as director of rationing at the Ministry of Food during the First World War. He then sold the Palace at the end of run for *The Whirligig* in 1920 to focus on a political career. Butt spent 14 years in the House of Commons, until he had to resign in disgrace having allegedly traded on inside information about confidential budget proposals in 1936. He spent his last years as a racecourse owner, again with some apparent success.

[144] M Watson, 'Theatrical Notes' *Daily Telegraph* (London, 10 July 1919) 14. In his evidence at trial, Said said he was an engineer by background, who came to England in 1915 as an agent of the Imperial Russian War Office, and he decided to make his home in London when the Russian Revolution began in 1917.

Shortly after the First World War, Said partnered with American theatre producer Gilbert Miller to finance *Monsieur Beaucaire* at the Princes Theatre in London. Said and Miller then agreed with Butt to transfer the play to the Palace in the summer of 1919, although they quickly and very publicly fell out with Butt.

In particular, in July 1919, Said and Miller sought an injunction against Butt, who had started to market *Monsieur Beaucaire* without giving the appropriate credit to Miller. Butt conceded the point and gave an undertaking in the form of the injunction sought. However, he then gave notice to terminate the run of *Monsieur Beaucaire* for early October 1919, on the basis that the receipts had fallen below the £2,500 minimum level agreed by the parties at the outset. Butt and Miller alleged that the Palace Theatre had engineered the situation, artificially driving down receipts by telling theatre-goers that there were 'no seats available' when in fact there were 'a good many seats available'.[145]

It was when *Monsieur Beaucaire*'s run came to an end on 6 October 1919 that *The Whirligig* was put into pre-production, and its opening night was held on 23 December 1919. Mr Said's evidence as to basis on which he had obtained a ticket for the opening night, as recorded in *The Times*, was somewhat incredible:[146]

> Mr Hastings.[147] – You know that if you had asked Sir Alfred Butt to sell you a ticket for the first night he would have refused? – No, I think he would have sold me one.
>
> Yet you had charged him with dishonesty? – Yes.
>
> You know that first-night tickets are retained for friends of the management. Did you try to get them from the box-office? – Yes, I did, and was told that if I wanted the best seats I must see the manager. …
>
> Was not the whole object of getting the tickets in the way you did [through Captain Pollock] that the management should not know that the person coming was yourself – a person who was charging the management with fraud? – That is not so.

All of this is rather entertaining, as commercial disputes go. But it is ultimately a red herring. As we have seen, *Said v Butt* was in fact determined (albeit erroneously) on the basis that there was no contract,[148] and if it has to be reinterpreted, it should be along the lines proposed by Lord Millett in *Shogun Finance*, that is, as turning on an implied contractual exclusion of intervention based on the nature of an opening night.[149] After all, if McCardie J had meant to determine the case by reference to the animosity over *Monsieur Beaucaire*, one would have expected the evidence to that effect – rather than the personal nature of opening night – to have featured at greater length in his judgment.[150]

This is confirmed by the treatment of *Said v Butt* in *Dyster v Randall & Sons*.[151] The case concerned an agreement to sell two plots of land. The principal used an undisclosed agent because, like Mr Said in the earlier case, he knew that the third party would

[145] *The Times Day 1* (n 142).
[146] ibid.
[147] Counsel for Sir Alfred Butt. Later Attorney-General.
[148] Text to n 31.
[149] Text to n 101
[150] A point also made by Tan (n 94) 332.
[151] *Dyster v Randall & Sons* [1925] Ch 932 (Ch).

refuse to deal with him directly or through a disclosed agent. The third party later tried to cancel the contract and the principal sued for specific performance. If *Said v Butt* had stood for the proposition that intervention is barred where the principal's personality is of particular importance, one would have expected the principal's intervention in *Dyster* to similarly be barred. But Lawrence J allowed the claim for specific performance. He held that a contract for the sale of land, unlike a ticket for an opening night, was not a contract where 'some personal consideration formed a material agreement'.[152] While the reasoning is brief, that distinction drawn by Lawrence J supports the view that *Said v Butt* turns on an implied contractual exclusion of intervention arising from the peculiar considerations of opening-night performances.

IV. The Future of *Said v Butt*

This chapter is written as *Said v Butt* passes its centenary. *The Whirligig* ran for almost a year, until 27 November 1920, when it was 'played for the last time amid scenes of great enthusiasm'.[153] *Said v Butt* has had a much longer run, but the time has come for the curtain to fall on it too. Its *ratio decidendi* was that there was no contract between the undisclosed principal and the third party by reason of mistaken identity: a decision based on the discredited principal's contract theory and the misapplication of the principles for fundamental mistake. It does not stand for the proposition that, outside of the terms of the contract, a principal may be barred from intervening due to issues of personality or good faith. *Said v Butt* can be reinterpreted on the basis that opening-night tickets contain an implied term excluding intervention, but it would be no loss to English law if it were simply put to one side as an anomalous case of no wider application.

[152] ibid 939 (Lawrence J).
[153] 'The Theatres: A Varied Week' *The Times* (London, 29 November 1920) 12.

5

Agency Theory Revisited and Practical Implications

GERARD McMEEL QC

I. Introduction

The law of agency, whereby one person represents another person as a matter of law, remains for me a topic of scintillating theoretical interest. In law schools across the common law world it is generally encountered as a relatively minor topic in courses and texts on corporate law or commercial law. In the real world it functions so efficiently and seamlessly more than 99 per cent of the time that we do not even pause to consider that most of our dealings are with individuals acting on behalf of another, usually corporate, person. Indeed for the preponderant part of us at work, we are daily acting on behalf of another, again usually corporate, person. In my first significant lecturing role I was asked to act as legal adviser to the university's student union, and eventually ceased to be surprised by how blithely undergraduates booked substantial venues in the name of the university – and purported to pledge the university's credit – for balls and student society parties that never materialised. In contrast, I did not have the power to place an order to replenish the stationery cupboard. On such occasions we do stop and examine the authority or power we do have in our roles to act on behalf of others. I incorporated agency as a 'foundation' topic in my course on commercial law, and dutifully taught the two rival accounts explaining the basis of agency law, the 'consent' theory and the 'power-liability' theory. I was pressed by the keen undergraduates to say what I thought, and my attempt at an answer eventually crystallised into a journal article in which I attempted to rekindle academic lawyers' interest in this subject.[1]

Over two decades after that (comparatively) juvenile effort, I was tempted by this academic conference (and eventual volume) to revisit the topic for two reasons. First, I was aware that there had been some very interesting explorations of this topic in the common law world, and in particular I was concerned about a reductionist tendency

[1] G McMeel, 'Philosophical Foundations of the Law of Agency' (2000) 116 *LQR* 387.

in some domestic scholarship. Second, my experience in practice, focused on the intermediary-ridden context of financial services, gave me cause for concern that judges were not as situation-sensitive to the difficult issues and policies concerning responsibility for agents as they could be.

So first in this chapter I wish to revisit the philosophical foundations of the law of agency (section II). I will then attempt to consider those theoretical underpinnings in discussing the controversial, but central, agency concept of apparent or ostensible authority (section III). In section IV I will consider subsequent theoretical work on the topic, and in particular address those scholars who express scepticism about the very existence of an autonomous topic of agency. In section V I shall say more about agency's proper characterisation as a key element of the law of persons. Lastly, in section VI I address the public policy concerns and implication of recent financial services cases, including significant appellate discussion of statutory vicarious responsibility and of the consequences of dealings by or through unregulated intermediaries. These remain practically highly significant topics neglected in agency law scholarship.[2]

II. Philosophical Foundations of Agency Revisited

I was sufficiently intrigued by legal theory at university that I went so far as to undertake the perilous option (at least one derided by my peers) of taking a paper outside the law school on moral and political philosophy, and then a postgraduate course designed to explore the philosophical foundations of the common law. Like many embarking from a law school background onto these less familiar tides, I always experienced a nagging fear that I might not be very good at these more theoretical speculations, and nervousness that no contention was ultimately authoritative. On reading the examiners' reports by way of preparation, one saw scathing comments about law undergraduates' treating the pronouncements of philosophers as though they were those of High Court judges. The reassuring thing I have learnt in the intervening years is that there is a well-established tradition of lawyers' accepting or assuming they were not very good at more theoretical study.[3] Until the appointment of Herbert Hart to the Oxford chair of jurisprudence in the early 1950s, that seat had never been occupied by any philosophical heavyweight.[4] Neil Duxbury has approached legal theory through the prism of intellectual history, first providing a sympathetic and holistic account of the subject in United States (US) law schools in *Patterns of American Jurisprudence*.[5] However, when Duxbury turned his

[2] On reviewing the earlier scholarship I rediscovered that Professor Reynolds had pre-empted the title and concern of my paper in F Reynolds, 'Agency: Theory and Practice' (1978) 94 *LQR* 224.

[3] Lord Burrows has wryly observed that his philosopher friends 'seem to think that almost everything that any lawyer says in so-called legal reasoning is hopelessly superficial': 'Professor Sir Guenter Treitel (1928–2019)' (Talk at a workshop on Scholars of Contract Law, 7 May 2021) 17 at www.supremecourt.uk/docs/lord-burrows-speech-professor-sir-guenter-treitel.pdf (accessed 18 January 2022).

[4] For the definitive biography of the first great modern English legal philosopher, see N Lacey, *A Life of HLA Hart: The Nightmare and the Noble Dream* (Oxford, Oxford University Press, 2006). Since then, of course, the chair has been graced by Ronald Dworkin and John Gardner.

[5] N Duxbury, *Patterns of American Jurisprudence* (Oxford, Oxford University Press, 1995). The introductory chapter is entitled 'Jurisprudence as Intellectual History'.

gaze homeward he soon realised there would be 'no grand work' because of the scale and diffuseness of the topic, and that the work would have to be done in smaller chunks. The first instalment of his intellectual history of English jurisprudence, *Frederick Pollock and the English Juristic Tradition*, became a study in failure.[6] Although if I were half the failure that Pollock was, I would count myself lucky. So too Duxbury bluntly points put that Arthur Lehman Goodhart's volume of *Essays on Jurisprudence and Common Law* was no such thing, with only one essay dedicated to the former topic.[7] More recently, the most influential jurist in Commonwealth private law, Peter Birks, was himself extremely modest about his theoretical learning, despite having had an enormous impact on how a generation of scholars thought, taught and wrote about the subject.[8]

Nevertheless, Pollock was responsible for the exercise in codification that resulted in the still extant Partnership Act 1890 (copied around the common law world), and in this context one of the most popular quotes on the nature of agency: '[B]y agency the individual's legal personality is multiplied in space.'[9] The comparatist Muller-Freienfels added 'time' to the mix.[10] I think we can all appreciate the Gallifreyan dimensions that conjures. Those of us who work in universities or for companies appreciate being bit-part players in a story lasting decades, or in some cases a century or more. Complex organisations are able to multiply their legal personality through time and space through cohorts of human and other representatives. From the point of view of a transactional lawyer, agency is one of the tools that gets deals done. It is only from the, possibly warped, perspective of the litigation lawyer or judge that the focus is on the much less usual case of an organisation disclaiming responsibility for the acts or omissions of those who have acted in its name.

As stated in section I, when I first taught agency as part of commercial law courses, the standard texts told me there were two rival theories, namely, the consent theory and the 'power-liability' analysis.[11] As a matter of everyday business, the consent theory had obvious explanatory force in that in the vast majority cases a principal had entrusted responsibility for (aspects of) its business to one or more human or other agents, and consented, or perhaps one might say at least assented, to the consequences. The consent theory was usually bolstered by reliance on the Anglo-American commitment

[6] N Duxbury, *Frederick Pollock and the English Juristic Tradition* (Oxford, Oxford University Press, 2006). See 'Acknowledgement', ibid xi. AWB Simpson really puts the boot in in the 'General Editor's Preface' (as part of the Oxford Studies in Modern Legal History series), remarking that Pollock was 'a somewhat second rate collaborator with Maitland' and 'not quite in the same class as great figures as Maine or Maitland or Dicey'. Working with Maitland on legal history had not been Pollock's best career move from a reputational perspective. Contrast the more sympathetic account of Pollock by GH Jones in AWB Simpson (ed), *Biographical Dictionary of the Common Law* (London, Butterworths, 1984) 421. See also N Duxbury, 'English Jurisprudence between Austin and Hart' (2005) 91 *Virginia Law Review* 1.

[7] Duxbury, *Frederick Pollock and the English Juristic Tradition* (n 6) 139. Contrast the more rounded account of Goodhart by RFV Heuston in Simpson (ed), *Biographical Dictionary of the Common Law* (n 6) 211.

[8] P Birks, 'Mistakes of Law' (2000) 53 *CLP* 53. And see G McMeel, 'What Kind of Jurist was Peter Birks?' [2011] *Restitution Law Review* 15; and L Smith, 'Peter Birks and Comparative Law' (2013) 43 *Revue de Droit de l'Université de Sherbrooke* 143.

[9] F Pollock and P Winfield (eds), *Pollock's Principles on Contract*, 13th edn (London, Stevens & Sons, 1950) 45. See McMeel (n 1) 394. More recently R Leow, 'Understanding Agency: A Proxy Power Definition' [2019] *CLJ* 99, 114.

[10] W Muller-Freienfels, 'Law of Agency' (1957) 6 *American Journal of Comparative Law* 165.

[11] See the first edition of LS Sealy and RJA Hooley, *Commercial Law: Text, Cases and Materials* (London, Butterworths, 1994) ch 3.

to an objective approach to intention in the context of commerce.[12] The consent theory might also be pressed into service in explaining doctrines lying beyond the central case example of actual authority, such as ratification and undisclosed agency, or at least some elements of those related rules. It was more controversial whether consent could explain apparent or ostensible authority, of which much more later. It had no explanatory force with regard to miscellaneous statutory or common law instances of responsibility, such as agency of necessity, which were manifestly grounded in public policy.

We were then led to believe that modern thinking favoured the rival theory based on Hohfeld's schematic 'power-liability' analysis, especially as adopted by Dowrick:

> The essential characteristic of an agent is that he is invested with a legal power to alter his principal's legal relations with third persons: the principal is under a correlative liability to have his legal relations altered. It is submitted that this power-liability relation is the essence of the relationship of principal and agent.[13]

Note 'essential' and, in case we missed it, 'essence'. We have here an early instance of the dominant 'monistic' theme in recent private law scholarship: to identify and reduce a legal concept to one core idea. The apparent benefits of the power-liability theory were many. First, it emphasised that the existence of agency was a matter of law, not fact. Second, it accommodated much more easily non-central case instances of agency, such as apparent authority and agency of necessity. Third, it emphasised the triangular nature of agency, involving principal, agent and third party. Most significantly, Dowrick, and other externalised theories, insisted that, at bottom, the recognition of any instance of agency was grounded on public policy.

The intellectual hinterland to Dowrick's 'power-liability' model was provided by US scholar Wesley Newcomb Hohfeld,[14] based at Stanford then Yale, who died prematurely in 1918. Hohfeld represents a late flowering of formalist legal scholarship in American law schools. As Duxbury notes, 'He is best remembered for his quasi-scientific theory of "jural correlatives" and "jural opposites" which, he argued, constitute the lowest common denominators of the law.'[15] The seminal account of Hohfeld is usually taken from his posthumously published *Fundamental Legal Conceptions as Applied in Legal Reasoning*.[16] Hohfeld is still a name that even those with limited enthusiasm for jurisprudence tend to recall, and his legacy extends, unlike other writers in analytical jurisprudence, to citation in law reports,[17] most usually for his 'claim-rights' and for

[12] For discussion of the scope and limits of the consent theory and consideration of the 'objective principle' in English private law in this context, see McMeel (n 1) 388–92.

[13] FE Dowrick, 'The Relationship of Principal and Agent' (1954) 17 *MLR* 24, 36.

[14] 1879–1918.

[15] Duxbury (n 5) 87.

[16] WN Hohfeld, *Fundamental Legal Conceptions as Applied in Legal Reasoning* (Yale University Press, New Haven, CT, 1919). Originally published as (1913) 23 *Yale Law Journal* 16 and (1917) 26 *Yale Law Journal* 710. The publishing history is described in the Preface to a modern UK edition edited by David Campbell and Philip Thomas: D Campbell and P Thomas (eds), *Fundamental Legal Conceptions as Applied in Legal Reasoning by Wesley Newcomb Hohfeld* (Aldershot, Ashgate, 2001) vii.

[17] For an English example referring to the power-liability relation, see *Bromilow & Edwards Ltd v Inland Revenue Commissioners* [1969] 1 WLR 1180, 1190, where Megarry J rejected an argument that the word 'liability' meant a present liability and held it could extend to a contingent liability: 'I say this without discussing the meaning that the word bears in the celebrated classification in Hohfeld's Fundamental Legal Conceptions (1923), where it is the correlative of "power" and the opposite of "immunity".'

what is now called the 'bundle of rights' theory of property.[18] I was conscious when first discussing this topic that a subject whose theoretical foundations were still discussed in Hohfeldian terms was in danger of being perceived as old-fashioned, if not archaic, in modern academic circles. This concern was compounded by the cul-de-sac I entered when I pursued a suggestion I might also look at Albert Kocourek's attempts to develop Hohfeld's ideas further in his *Jural Relations*.[19] Here the waspish verdict of Brian Simpson is probably fair: '[O]nce fashionable, this strange work, which includes a lengthy glossary of invented terms, is now in oblivion.'[20]

More promising as a further development of Hohfeld's thinking is a discussion by distinguished legal philosopher John Finnis in 'Some Professorial Fallacies about Rights'.[21] Whilst claiming to say 'nothing new', Finnis's thesis is that Hohfeldian analysis is routinely misapplied, or not sufficiently rigorously undertaken. For example, Finnis noted that the privilege to walk in my own garden is not merely a liberty but rather 'a liberty surrounded by a perimeter of supporting claim-rights of the land-owner against attempted interference with him in the exercise of his liberty', a description he later acknowledged to be indebted to Hart.[22] Therefore Hohfeld was the progenitor of the 'bundle of rights' property theory, which emphasises the network of legal relationships between persons and entails that property rights are not rights against things.[23] Such accounts are labelled 'bundle of rights' theories of property in North American jurisprudence and case law, and by Penner, who defends the lay person's view that a property right is a right against a thing.[24] Edelman J, in the High Court of Australia in *Hocking v Director-General of the National Archives of Australia*, having subjected the 'bundle of rights' approach to the notion of property to critical analysis,[25] endorsed the

[18] For a very recent instance in an intellectual property case in the English Court of Appeal, see *Thaler v Comptroller General of Patents Trade Marks and Designs* [2021] EWCA Civ 1374 [133], where Arnold LJ observed *en passant*, 'This might be regarded as an instance of the more general proposition that intellectual property fits much more readily within Hohfeld's conception of property than it does within Blackstone's.' See also *Privacy International v Secretary of State for Foreign and Commonwealth Affairs* [2021] EWCA Civ 330, [2021] 2 WLR 1333 [73] and [75] (Hohfeld's powers and immunities in the context of whether real-life James Bonds could have a licence to kill or otherwise break the law).

[19] A Kocourek, *Jural Relations* (Indianapolis, IN, The Bobbs-Merrill Co, 1927). On the limits of logical analysis and invented terminology, see the response to Koucourek's earlier journal articles by Hohfeld's equally distinguished colleague AL Corbin, 'Jural Relations and their Classification' (1920-21) 30 *Yale Law Journal* 226.

[20] Entry on Koucourek by AWB Simpson in Simpson (ed), *Biographical Dictionary of the Common Law* (n 6) 298.

[21] J Finnis, 'Some Professorial Fallacies about Rights' (1972) 4 *Adelaide Law Review* 377; reproduced as J Finnis, 'Rights: Their Logic Restated' in J Finnis, *Philosophy of Law: Collected Essays* (Oxford, Oxford University Press, 2011) vol IV. See also J Finnis, *Natural Law and Natural Rights*, 2nd edn (Oxford, Oxford University Press, 2011) 199–205.

[22] Finnis, 'Some Professorial Fallacies about Rights' (n 21) 378–79; Finnis, 'Rights: Their Logic Restated' (n 21) 377 where a new footnote (ibid 388) acknowledges that the 'perimeter of supporting claim-rights' was 'a metaphor and conception' derived from Finnis's attendance at HLA Hart's lectures on Hohfeld in 1963.

[23] AM Honore, 'Ownership' in AG Guest (ed), *Oxford Essays in Jurisprudence: First Series* (Oxford, Oxford University Press, 1961) 106.

[24] J Penner, 'The 'Bundle of Rights' Picture of Property' (1996) 43 *UCLA Law Review* 711. See also J Penner, *The Idea of Property in Law* (Oxford, Clarendon Press, 1997) 23–31; T Merrill, 'Property and the Right to Exclude' (1998) 77 *Nebraska Law Review* 730; H Smith, 'Property is Not Just a 'Bundle of Rights'' (2011) 8 *Econ Journal Watch* 279; S Douglas and B Macfarlane, 'Defining Property Rights' in J Penner and H Smith (eds), *Philosophical Foundations of Property Law* (Oxford, Oxford University Press, 2014) 219.

[25] *Hocking v Director-General of the National Archives of Australia* [2020] HCA 19, (2020) 94 ALJR 569 [203]–[206].

view that the right to exclude was 'the essence of property right to, or "property" in, a chattel'.[26] This is another instance of the reductionist tendency in private law scholarship (and here in an appellate judgment) to attempt to reduce a private law phenomenon to a lowest common denominator. The better view is probably that excludability is one aspect, albeit an important aspect, of property rights. Indeed both the relationships between the person and the thing, and the person entitled to the thing and other persons, are significant.[27]

Returning to agency, I adopted the same approach as Finnis in trying to do Hohfeldian analysis more rigorously in my discussion of Dowrick's abbreviated account of agency in 'power-liability' terms. Returning to the source, I contrasted Hohfeld's brief, but more complex, analysis:

> The creation of the agency relation involves, inter alia, the grant of legal powers to the so-called agent, and the creation of correlative liabilities in the principal. That is to say, one party P has the power to create agency powers in another party A, – for example, … the power to impose (so-called) contractual obligations on P, the power to 'receive' title to property so that it shall vest in P, and so forth.[28]

It can be seen that Dowrick has elided Hohfeld's analysis by focusing on the power of the agent, whereas the seminal discussion had emphasised the *power of the principal* to invest the agent with power. Accordingly, the power to imbue agents with authority lines up with the power to enter into contracts, or dispose of property, as one of the facilities conferred on persons in private law. They are instances of the power-conferring rules that Hart[29] identified as constituting much of the detail of mature legal systems.[30] To overlook the principal's power overlooks Hohfeld's insight.

The next step in my argument was that standard discussions of the theoretical foundations of agency law are misconceived in seeking to oppose two supposedly competing explanations of the subject. There was simply nothing incompatible between the consensual theory and the power-liability analysis. The consent theory is one reason why we recognise that certain agents bind their principals: it is a justificatory or normative theory. It is not adequate to explain all cases of representation, beyond actual authority and ratification, and arguably apparent authority. In contrast, the power-liability or Hohfeldian analysis is concerned with illuminating how agency reasoning works, and is a descriptive or conceptual or ontological analysis. The two theories operate on different planes.[31]

In so arguing I was, at least sub-consciously,[32] utilising the insights of Atiyah on contract theory, in a mature work of his, 'Judicial Techniques in the Law of Contract',

[26] ibid [206].
[27] Compare Professor Gray: 'the law of property is concerned with entire networks of legal relationships existing between individuals in respect of things' in K Gray, *Elements of Land Law*, 1st edn (London, Butterworths, 1987) 8; K Gray and S Gray, *Elements of Land Law*, 5th edn (Oxford, Oxford University Press, 2008) 6: 'a network of jural relationships between individuals in respect of valued resources'.
[28] Hohfeld, *Fundamental Legal Conceptions* (n 16) 51–52.
[29] HLA Hart, *The Concept of Law* (2nd edn, Oxford University Press, 1994).
[30] For the detailed critique of the 'reductionist' approach to Hohfeldian reasoning in Dowrick and other agency literature, see McMeel (n 1) 392–96.
[31] ibid 396–99.
[32] By which I mean without appropriate citation!

to which I have returned many times and always with profit. Addressing academic controversy and judicial anxiety about the 'true' basis of contractual doctrines, such as discharge for frustration as a result of supervening events, Atiyah stated 'these controversies now appear to me to be largely, though not necessarily exclusively, about the use of techniques: they tell us nothing about the actual solution of the problems from which they sprang.'[33] Atiyah addressed what he regarded as the three main theories for frustration of contracts: construction or implied term, the 'just solution' and the 'change in the fundamental obligation' theories. He noted his own earlier view that it was right to reject the construction or implied term basis for frustration, but he now considered such objections 'largely misconceived'.[34] He concluded:

> [I]t is surely clear that they are all in part correct. There is no inconsistency between them because they do not purport to answer the same question …
>
> There are clearly several distinct questions involved in attempting to analyse the 'basis' of a doctrine. One such question might be, *what is the general justification for the doctrine*, what goal is the court trying to achieve when it uses the doctrine? Another question might be, *what technique do the courts use* when deciding these cases? A third such question might be, *when will the court find a contract to be frustrated*, what are the circumstances regarded as sufficient to justify invocation of the doctrine? *These questions are not on the same plane*. The 'construction' theory is not a theory at all, but a technique … The 'just solution' theory is likewise not a theory at all, but it is also not a technique. It is simply the end purpose – or anyhow one of the end purposes – of all legal techniques. And finally the 'change in the fundamental obligation' theory is not a theory either, nor again is it a technique. It is merely a statement of the conditions …[35]

I have recently discussed the frustration of contracts (which, ironically, I did not foresee at the time of writing even a couple of years ago would become a very fashionable topic), and on this occasion made proper acknowledgement of Atiyah's influence.[36] The point is that this approach is readily transferable to agency, with the truly competing 'general justifications' being either consent or public policy. But it can then be readily acknowledged that we give effect to consensual representation because public policy favours it. One ends up with a justificatory explanation with consent at its core, supplemented by pockets of policy-motivated agency. At the same time a thorough, Hohfeldian analysis, based on the power to confer power on others, supplies the conceptual analysis or description of the technique illuminating how the legal rules work.[37] Properly undertaken, such analysis highlights that agency is a triangular legal relationship of principal, agent and third party. Its mechanics or plumbing can then be illuminated by rigorous Hohfeldian analysis of the cluster of rules on all sides of the triangle. There remains room for debate about how far 'consent', even supplemented by an objective principle, or by a wider aim of protection of the reasonable expectations or of mitigating misplaced reliance, can explain aspects of agency law. In commerce and finance the usual reason

[33] PS Atiyah, 'Judicial Techniques in the Law of Contract' in PS Atiyah, *Essays on Contract* (Oxford, Clarendon Press 1986) 244.
[34] ibid 272.
[35] ibid 273 (emphasis added). We need to overlook some of the hyperbole about what constitutes a theory.
[36] G McMeel, 'The juridical basis of frustration revisited' [2020] *LMCLQ* 297.
[37] McMeel (n 1) 410–11.

why agency arises is the consent of the principal. Beyond consent, and it is debatable whether apparent authority lies beyond consent, each instance of common law and statutory agency is ultimately determined by public policy reasons or, as I suggested in my earlier discussion, the rationale is consent 'supplemented by a number of pockets of policy-motivated recognitions of agency in particular contexts'.[38] Let us therefore look more closely at the controversial doctrine of apparent authority

III. Explaining Apparent or Ostensible Authority

Very few discussions of apparent authority or ostensible authority – they are synonymous – go further back than Diplock LJ's seminal judgment in *Freeman & Lockyer (a firm) v Buckhurst Park Properties Ltd*[39] based on estoppel. The case concerned a small property company, which was unmeritoriously refusing to pay architects' fees that one of its directors had incurred, on the ground of lack of authority. Whilst the company's articles permitted the appointment of a managing director, that formal step had not been taken. The county court judge found that the director had carried on the company's business with the knowledge and approval of the other directors, and was in effect its managing director.

The importance of apparent authority – over actual authority – in commercial practice was stressed by Diplock LJ, bookending his analysis of the species of authority. Indeed, prior to disclosure of each side's documents in the course of litigation, one could rarely be sure of the state of the internal processes of a potential defendant acting through intermediaries:

> Actual authority and apparent authority are quite independent of one another. Generally they co-exist and coincide, but either may exist without the other and their respective scopes may be different. As I shall endeavour to show, it is upon the apparent authority of the agent that the contractor normally relies in the ordinary course of business when entering into contracts.
>
> An 'actual' authority is a legal relationship between principal and agent created by a consensual agreement to which they alone are parties. Its scope is to be ascertained by applying ordinary principles of construction of contracts, including any proper implications from the express words used, the usages of the trade, or the course of business between the parties. To this agreement the contractor is a stranger …
>
> An 'apparent' or 'ostensible' authority, on the other hand, is a legal relationship between the principal and the contractor created by a representation, made by the principal to the contractor, intended to be and in fact acted upon by the contractor, that the agent has authority to enter on behalf of the principal into a contract of a kind within the scope of the 'apparent' authority, so as to render the principal liable to perform any obligations imposed upon him by such contract. To the relationship so created the agent is a stranger. He … must not purport to make the agreement as principal himself. The representation, when acted upon by the contractor by entering into a contract with the agent, operates as an estoppel, preventing the principal from asserting that he is not bound by the contract. It is irrelevant whether the agent had actual authority to enter into the contract.

[38] ibid 410.
[39] *Freeman & Lockyer (a firm) v Buckhurst Park Properties Ltd* [1964] 2 QB 480.

> In ordinary business dealings the contractor at the time of entering into the contract can in the nature of things hardly ever rely on the 'actual' authority of the agent. His information as to the authority must be derived either from the principal or from the agent or from both, for they alone know what the agent's actual authority is. All that the contractor can know is what they tell him, which may or may not be true. In the ultimate analysis he relies either upon the representation of the principal, that is, apparent authority, or upon the representation of the agent, that is, warranty of authority.[40]

This passage gives some clue as to why attempts to merge or blur the distinction between actual and apparent authority, whether by reference to contractual construction or the objective principle, are misconceived. Whilst Diplock LJ describes the process of determining whether there is actual authority as one using the ordinary principles of contractual construction, that requires two qualifications. First, whilst commonly contractual, it is sufficient for agency to be consensual, in that no consideration is required, and he is careful to speak of 'legal relationship' and 'consensual agreement'. Second, it follows that the rules on the construction of contracts should be applied, at least by analogy. However, it is arguable that they should be modified dependent on the context. If there is a document embodying the consensual arrangement, it will ordinarily be sufficient to use standard construction principles. If it is not, and one is having to plug gaps by implication or usage, or one is looking even more broadly, including as to the whole 'course of business' between principal and agent, it cannot be argued that we are in the realm of standard principles on admissible background, or exclusions of prior negotiations or subsequent conduct.

That broader approach to admissible evidence is *a fortiori* in respect of the distinct estoppel-based relationship between principal and third party or contractor.[41] That is demonstrated by the next case in the sequence, featuring one of the most formidable judicial teams of four in a commercial case not to reach the highest level: *Hely-Hutchinson v Brayhead Ltd.*[42] In the context of an inchoate plan by R, the Chairman of B Ltd, to take over a smaller firm P Ltd, also engaged in electronic manufacture, he encouraged H-H, the managing director of P Ltd, to continue propping up that firm, and eventually provided an indemnity in the name of B Ltd to H-H.

Roskill J's ex tempore judgment, on the eve of the Christmas break, was a tour de force on complex facts. He ranged over the whole course of dealing between the various players and concluded, applying the *Freeman & Lockyer* estoppel test, that R was apparently authorised by B Ltd to provide the indemnity to H-H. He was upheld by a formidable Court of Appeal, comprising Lord Denning MR, Lord Pearson and Lord Wilberforce, which went a step further and found that the same factual findings equally supported a finding of implied actual authority, in addition to actual authority. Here two sides of the triangle, namely principal–agent actual authority, and principal–third party apparent authority did coincide. What is important is that there was no limit as to the evidence admissible to both enquiries. There was careful examination in each context

[40] ibid 502–03.

[41] G McMeel, 'Prior Negotiations and Subsequent Conduct – The Next Step Forward for Contractual Interpretation?' (2003) 119 *LQR* 272, 287–88.

[42] *Hely-Hutchinson v Brayhead Ltd* [1968] 1 QB 549.

as to what communications and related activities – in language that is now routinely used – crossed the line between specific parties, and as to what the third person knew about such exchanges. But this is a long way from an orthodox construction of an integrated written agreement. Indeed it could be said that *Freeman & Lockyer* itself might easily have been decided by the first instance judge on the basis of implied actual authority on its facts, as noted in passing by Diplock LJ,[43] although he was not prepared to take that additional step on appeal on the exiguous evidence.

The behemoth of the subject is *Armagas Ltd v Mundogas SA, The Ocean Frost*,[44] which reached the conclusion, surprising on its face, that a 'Vice-President (Transportation) and Chartering Manager' (V-P) of a shipping company had no authority to conclude a three-year charter of a vessel. It stands for the nutshell proposition that there can be no holding out, or self-authorising, by the agent itself (so-called 'bootstraps' agency[45]). On its particular facts, the decision looks defensible. Buyers had purchased the eponymous vessel in the context of a sale-and-charter back to the sellers, presumably with the charter's being intended to ensure an income stream to pay the financing of acquisition costs. It was the seller's agent with the cumbersome job title who colluded with shipbrokers acting for the buyers, which resulted not just in the ship sale and a one-year charter back, but also in the contested three-year charter of which senior management of the seller was wholly unaware. Crucially, on the evidence the buyers knew that the V-P had no actual authority to conclude the deal without the approval of his superiors. Staughton J suggested, and then held, that nevertheless the V-P did have apparent authority to notify that senior management approval had been obtained. This finding received short shrift from Robert Goff LJ on appeal, and at the hands of the House of Lords.[46] As a matter of principle, it is surely right that an agent might have apparent authority to communicate such approval, as was made clear in the contemporaneous reasoning of Browne-Wilkinson LJ in *Egyptian International Foreign Trade Co v Soplex Wholesale Supplies Ltd*.[47] The message from the appellate courts in *Armagas* was that whilst it could not be said this was never the case, it would be hardly ever be so.

In stark contrast came the philosophy and reasoning of the subsequent decision of the Court of Appeal in *First Energy (UK) Ltd v Hungarian International Bank Ltd*.[48] The Manchester branch manager of an overseas bank (with apparently only two UK offices) was known by its customer to have no authority to unilaterally approve a credit facility, as was the fact that generally two signatures were required. Nevertheless, the Court of Appeal held he had general ostensible authority to communicate approval from his senior management team. It is one of those handful of cases where Steyn LJ reached for his 'reasonable expectations of honest men' motto, which was probably his euphemism

[43] *Freeman & Lockyer* (n 39) 501: 'The county court judge did not hold (although he might have done) that actual authority had been conferred upon Kapoor by the board to employ agents.'

[44] *Armagas Ltd v Mundogas SA, The Ocean Frost* [1986] AC 717.

[45] *United Bank of Kuwait v Hammoud* [1988] 1 WLR 1051, 1066 (Lord Donaldson MR): 'He cannot pull himself up by his shoe laces.'

[46] See the discussion in McMeel (n 1) 403–04.

[47] *Egyptian International Foreign Trade Co v Soplex Wholesale Supplies Ltd* [1985] 2 Lloyd's Rep 36, 43.

[48] *First Energy (UK) Ltd v Hungarian International Bank Ltd* [1993] 1 Lloyd's Rep 194.

for standards of good faith and fair dealing.[49] The decision has always seemed to me to be clearly right, especially if one views the enquiry into apparent authority as a pragmatic and contextual exercise, considering all the evidence. Here the relevant factors include the style and title of the intermediary, level of seniority, the respective sizes of the businesses, the degree of reliance and realistic verification options. I may have over-emphasised the usefulness of the objective principle and the down-played the usefulness of the three-stage estoppel structure in my earlier discussion.[50] But I would emphasise situation-sense and commercial pragmatism, as the leading judicial guidance from Lord Diplock to Lord Steyn suggests. It was certainly my purpose to defend and explain *First Energy*, and to argue it represented the more usual approach to apparent authority, over the unnecessarily narrow statements of the appellate judges in *Armagas*. It was somewhat disheartening in subsequent years to discover I was an isolated academic champion of *First Energy*.

So by way of contrast, Cheng-Han Tan, surveying 'Unauthorised Agency in English Law' in a comparative law volume, said that *First Energy* 'appears to have gone too far'.[51] He considered that 'the correctness of *First Energy* is debatable' and 'it should perhaps be limited to the banking context'.[52] In the banking context it is invariably the case that both corporate and individual customers, borrowers and guarantors deal with a specially-trained, client-facing 'relationship manager'. The 'credit sanctioning' people are presumably kept in a darkened bunker for regulatory or other reasons, and direct communications with outsiders curtailed or strictly controlled. But lack of direct access to ultimate decision-makers is not a peculiar feature of the banking context. So too Howard Bennett, after careful discussion, concluded that the Court of Appeal in *First Energy* had departed from the statement of principle in *The Ocean Frost* in the very way 'prohibited' by the higher court's reasoning.[53] Similarly Roderick Munday discusses *First Energy* under the heading 'Departure from orthodox doctrine'.[54] So too in the admirable chapters on agency in *Sealy & Hooley's Commercial Law*, it is concluded that it is 'premature to herald *First Energy* as the harbinger of a new approach to apparent authority'.[55] Amongst agency lawyers in academe I seemed to be in a minority of one.

[49] The other examples include *G Percy Trentham Ltd v Archital Luxfer Ltd* [1993] 1 Lloyd's Rep 25, 27 and *Darlington Borough Council v Wiltshier Northern Ltd* [1995] 3 All ER 895, 903–04. See also J Steyn, 'Contract Law: Fulfilling the Reasonable Expectations of Honest Men' (1997) 113 *LQR* 433.

[50] See McMeel (n 1) 404–07.

[51] C-H Tan, 'Unauthorised Agency in English Law' in D Busch and L Macgregor (eds), *The Unauthorised Agent: Perspectives from European and Comparative Law* (Cambridge, Cambridge University Press, 2009) 185, 190.

[52] ibid 190–91. See also the discussion by L Macgregor, 'Unauthorised Agency in Scots Law' in Busch and Macgregor (eds) (n 51) 261, 272.

[53] H Bennett, *Principles of the Law of Agency* (London, Bloomsbury Publishing, 2013), paras 4.23–4.31.

[54] R Munday, *Agency: Law and Principles*, 2nd edn (Oxford, Oxford University Press, 2013) paras 4.27–4.35. (In the Preface, ibid v, *First Energy* is described as 'caliginous', which had me reaching for the dictionary, but the *Compact Oxford English Dictionary* was not up to the task.)

[55] D Fox et al, *Sealy & Hooley's Commercial Law: Text, Cases and Materials*, 6th edn (Oxford, Oxford University Press, 2020) 133. The following discussion of *Kelly v Fraser* states the facts so comprehensively against the appellant that one would wonder why Lord Sumption needed to engage so skilfully with the alleged tension between *The Ocean Frost* and *First Energy* (ibid 133–35).

Relief came from a source I might not have foreseen, when *First Energy* and its pragmatic approach subsequently received decisive endorsement in a brisk and meticulously reasoned judgment of Lord Sumption in *Kelly v Fraser*.[56] Mr Fraser was a top executive, becoming President and Chief Executive of the Island Life Insurance Company in Jamaica, having previously been engaged by another life office. He sought to transfer his accrued pension benefits from his former employer's scheme. The Vice-President (V-P) of employee benefits at his new employer had no actual authority to approve a pension transfer, which was naturally the responsibility of the trustees of the pension scheme. The V-P wrote to Mr Fraser confirming the transfer. The striking fact is that the moneys had been received by the new scheme. Subsequent statements suggested the transfer had taken place, and the V-P had been delegated power to conduct day-to-day administration of the scheme. Nevertheless the trustees were unaware of the transfer. Despite that, the V-P was held to have apparent authority to communicate that the necessary steps to complete the transfer had been performed.

Lord Sumption distinguished the decision in *The Ocean Frost* as one on 'complex and extraordinary facts', where the agent was holding himself out as having authority to do a specific act the third party knew he had no general authority to do. Significantly, Lord Sumption referred with approval to the statements of principle of both Browne-Wilkinson LJ in *Egyptian International Foreign Trade Co v Soplex Wholesale Supplies Ltd*[57] and Steyn LJ in *First Energy*. His Lordship stated:

> Like [Robert] Goff LJ, Lord Keith thought that while it was conceptually possible to have a case of 'ostensible specific authority to enter into a particular transaction', such cases were bound to be rare (p 777). It is clear that the whole of this analysis is dependent on the fact that in the *Ocean Frost* the agent was in reality holding out himself as having authority to do a specific thing that the third party knew that he had no general authority to do. Such cases are necessarily fact-sensitive. The *Ocean Frost* is not authority for the broader proposition that a person without authority of any kind to enter into a transaction cannot as a matter of law occupy a position in which he has ostensible authority to tell a third party that the proper person has authorised it.
>
> To take an obvious example, the company secretary does not have the actual authority which the board of directors has, but he is likely to have its ostensible authority by virtue of his functions to communicate what the board has decided or to authenticate documents which record what it has decided. The ordinary authority to communicate a company's authorisation of a transaction will generally be more widely distributed than that, especially in a bureaucratically complex organisation and in the case of routine transactions. It is not at all uncommon for the authority to approve transactions to be limited to a handful of very senior officers, but for their approval to be communicated in the ordinary course of the company's administration by others whose function it is to do that.[58]

As Lord Sumption noted, pension scheme trustees rarely communicate directly with members and beneficiaries, and communications are invariably with human resources or benefits personnel at the sponsoring employer. The denial of apparent authority

[56] *Kelly v Fraser* [2012] UKPC 25, [2013] 1 AC 450. See also G McMeel, 'Agency and the Retail Distribution of Financial Products' in D Busch, L Macgregor and P Watts (eds), *Agency Law in Commercial Practice* (Oxford, Oxford University Press, 2016) 177, 189–91, supportive of *Kelly*.

[57] *Egyptian International Foreign Trade Co v Soplex Wholesale Supplies Ltd* (n 47) 42–43.

[58] *Kelly v Fraser* (n 55) [12]–[13].

was as unmeritorious here as it had been in *First Energy*. Even so, *Armagas* continues to hold a grip on commentators, with Peter Watts, in a recent discussion largely supportive of all aspects of *Armagas*, grumbling that *Kelly v Fraser* 'has the potential to diminish the status of *Armagas*'.[59] To that I say *First Energy* and *Kelly v Fraser* are both superior statements of principle, and manifestly correct, commercial conclusions on their respective facts. Overall I consider it now probably safer to recognise that apparent authority is a public policy-motivated extension of agency reasoning, intended to promote the needs of commerce and finance, and to protect justified reliance on how enterprises conduct their businesses through others. The rationale is similar to the deployment of objective tests for both contract formation and the construction of contracts, but each is doctrinally distinct.

IV. Recent Agency Theory: Reductionism and Scepticism

Rachel Leow, in 'Understanding Agency: A Proxy Power Definition',[60] argues that existing definitions of agency are inadequate and proposes a 'proxy power' definition. The core of agency is that it permits a person to act 'through' another person as a matter of law.[61] She rejects sceptical accounts of the subject (which I deal with further below) and is fearful of agency's being split up into 'separate pockets of law'.[62] Leow notes most theories involve some combination of four elements: consent; a Hohfeldian power-liability relationship; that the principal's legal relations can be affected by the agent's acts; and a fiduciary relationship. *Bowstead & Reynolds*' definition embraces all four.[63] Leow rejects a Hohfeldian power-liability relationship on the unconvincing ground that it is too wide, embracing relationships outside of the law of agency. This is surprising, as Hohfeld clearly intended his conceptual schema to have explanatory force for many areas of law. Leow instances non-consensual examples of agency, including agency of necessity and statutory examples, citing section 5 of the Mental Capacity Act 2005. Leow's definition is 'A relationship is one of agency if the agent A has a proxy power: a power to exercise at least one of principal P's own powers.'[64] In terms of justifying when agency relationships arise, Leow states that most result from a unilateral manifestation of the principal's will. In addition, agency is also recognised where a principal is unable to effectively exercise his powers and it is necessary to protect the principal's interests, such as in the agency of necessity cases. This is an attractive and well-argued paper, but overall, despite Leow's protests, it would appear to be in the tradition of earlier externalised theories, and arguably much closer to Dowrick, with the focus on the agent's power as the lowest common denominator, than to Hohfeld.

[59] P Watts, 'Some wear and tear on *Armagas v Mundogas*: the tension between wanting and having in the law of agency' [2015] *LMCLQ* 36, 39–45.
[60] Leow (n 9).
[61] ibid 100, 114–15.
[62] ibid 102, 122.
[63] ibid 103, citing P Watts (ed), *Bowstead & Reynolds on Agency*, 21st edn (London, Sweet & Maxwell, 2018) para 1-001 (hereinafter *Bowstead & Reynolds*).
[64] Leow (n 9) 107.

It is surprising that a prominent trend of recent agency scholarship is its scepticism about the autonomous existence of the principles of the law of agency, that is, autonomous from subjects such as contract, tort or unjust enrichment, or company law. As in other areas of private law scholarship, some of our bolder essayists seem happy to asset-strip agency of its supposed basic concepts and re-allocate them to other topics like contract law.

This necessitates some consideration of what a legal topic or subject is. The usual starting point is Birks' distinction between conceptual categories of law and contextual categories of law.[65] The former include contract (or more broadly obligations arising from consent), tort (or more broadly wrongs), unjust enrichment and property. The latter comprise convenient groupings in the real world such as shipping law and banking law, and, as I have recently argued, commercial law.[66]

It also merits consideration of what we really mean when we talk about legal topics or sub-topics. Whilst the perspective of the university law school may often involve a survey of the whole map of the law, an image dating back at least to Blackstone, the practitioner's focus is, more usually, almost at a microscopic level. This is a contract. In the sub-category of sale of goods. The first steps in this reasoning may be entirely reflexive. The goods have been lost so we are in the realm of risk or possibly frustration (assuming neither seller nor buyer is responsible for the loss). Here we should note Lord Hoffmann's brief and allusive description of the nature of legal concepts such as an equitable charge as comprising clusters of rules. This may be the best we have done so far at capturing what the principles, rules and exceptions in a legal topic, or sub-topic, distilled principally from case law, consists of in a common law system. How dense the cluster of rules and exceptions may be depends on how litigated the topic is, and how much money has traditionally been at stake. So some fields are heavily encrusted with over-elaborate distinctions. Commercial landlord and tenant springs to mind. Other topics are bemoaned by scholars to be conceptually under-developed. One thinks of aspects of personal property law away from the specialist niches of intellectual property and trusts.

Lord Hoffmann's observations in *Re BCCI No 8* are more usually cited for the first two pragmatic propositions, but in my view the third proposition about the nature of legal concepts deserves equal billing:

> In a case in which there is no threat to the consistency of the law or objection of public policy, I think that the courts should be very slow to declare a practice of the commercial community to be conceptually impossible. Rules of law must obviously be consistent and not self-contradictory … But the law is fashioned to suit the practicalities of life and legal concepts like 'proprietary interest' and 'charge' are no more than labels given to clusters of related and self-consistent rules of law. Such concepts do not have a life of their own from which the rules are inexorably derived.[67]

[65] P Birks, *An Introduction to the Law of Restitution* (Oxford, Clarendon Press, 1989) 73–74.

[66] G McMeel, 'Are there Any General Principles of Commercial Law?' in C Mitchell and S Watterson (eds), *The World of Maritime and Commercial Law: Essays in Honour of Francis Rose* (Oxford, Hart Publishing, 2020) 181.

[67] *Re Bank of Credit and Commerce International SA (No 8)* [1998] AC 214, 228.

This echoes Robert Goff LJ in *Clough Mill v Martin*,[68] where in determining the proprietary consequences of a retention of title clause in a commercial sale, Robert Goff LJ cautioned 'In performing this task, concepts such as bailment and fiduciary duty must not be allowed to be our masters, but must rather be regarded as the tools of our trade.'[69]

Agency, with its central preoccupation with when one person is held in law to represent another person, conforms to this clusters-of-rules analysis as we work through actual authority, apparent authority, ratification and what seem like outliers, such as agency of necessity and breach of warranty of authority. Some of the more ambitious, and usually reductionist, efforts of recent private law scholarship overlook the reality of imperfect groupings of related rules. So too in mathematics, the lack of any structure or pattern to the sequence of prime numbers is said to have

> mystified human beings since early antiquity. Prime numbers are the essential elements in number theory, and the lack of an easily-seen structure tends to make number theory seem un-unified as a field, and its problems isolated, and difficult to solve, and without clear implications to other fields of mathematics.[70]

Many legal debates also tend to require close work on isolated clusters of authorities and rules, and agency law is replete with such examples. The implications for the wider picture may be limited or non-existent. We bring our general legal skills to such issues as best we can. Yet there is an over-arching unity to the law of agency. It is the groupings of legal rules that answer the question of when in law one person represents someone else. Inevitably such questions are linked to, and overlap with, issues of liability in contract, tort and unjust enrichment.

The general rule in cases where contract intersects with agency is that that an agent acting within the scope of his actual authority on behalf of a disclosed principal 'drops out' of the resulting contractual picture. In contrast, in the law of tort there is generally 'no get out of jail' card for persons who do acts that meet the ingredients of a particular tort by saying they were doing so on behalf of another. Indeed, the liability of a principal for its agent's tort (even if not engaged on a common design) is a paradigm instance of joint tortfeasorship.[71] So take two apex appellate decisions. First, *Williams v Natural Life Health Foods Ltd*,[72] where the issue was whether the managing director and principal shareholder of a small company was personally responsible for negligent misrepresentations in the firm's brochure and prospectus. In the absence of a personal assumption of responsibility for the statements, he was not. Whether there was a personal duty of care was a question for the law of tort, but equally the question whether the individual was liable as a principal, or was an agent of the company, making it liable for the tort,

[68] *Clough Mill Ltd v Martin* [1985] 1 WLR 111.

[69] ibid 116.

[70] A Aczel, *Fermat's Last Theorem: Unlocking the Secret of an Ancient Mathematical Problem* (New York, Basic Books, 1997) 8.

[71] A Tettenborn (gen ed), *Clerk and Lindsell on Torts*, 23rd edn (London, Sweet & Maxwell, 2021), para 4-004; *Fish & Fish Ltd v Sea Shepherd UK (The Steve Irwin)* [2015] UKSC 10, [2015] AC 1229; noted [2016] *LMCLQ* 29; *Bowstead & Reynolds* (n 63) para 9-120.

[72] *Williams v Natural Life Health Foods Ltd* [1998] 1 WLR 830; *Bowstead & Reynolds* (n 63) para 9-117. Contrast *Merrett v Babb* [2001] EWCA Civ 214, [2001] QB 1174.

is a question of representation or agency. In contrast, in *Standard Chartered Bank v Pakistan National Shipping Line Corp*[73] a director was sued in deceit for issuing a false bill of lading on behalf of a company. Here the commission of the ingredients of the tort of deceit by the individual entailed the liability of both company and director for intentional wrongdoing. In this context the state of mind of the director is appropriately attributed to the company on agency principles, but there is no corresponding exoneration in the law of tort. As Lord Hoffmann stated, 'No one can escape liability for his fraud by saying "I wish to make it clear that I am committing this fraud on behalf of someone else and I am not personally liable".'[74] These two cases, like many others, can profitably be examined from the perspectives both of the law of tort and of the law of agency.

The opposite view is favoured by two Oxford private lawyers. So Robert Stevens, in 'Why Do Agents "Drop Out"?',[75] addresses the rule that an agent who makes a contract purporting to act solely on behalf of a disclosed principal is not a party to it, and cannot sue or be sued on it.[76] Stevens poses the question: 'Does this principle follow from the application of a rule specific to the law of agency?' His answer is 'No'. It is simply an application of the objective principle and ordinary rules for the construction of contracts. Stevens cites *Shogun Finance Ltd v Hudson*[77] as authority for the proposition that identifying the correct parties to the contract is as much a question of construction as any other term. But that can be contrasted with *The Starsin.*[78] Lord Millett stated 'The identity of the parties to a contract is fundamental. It is not simply a term or condition of the contract. It goes to the very existence of the contract itself. If it is uncertain, there is no contract.'[79] The inquiry is factual, and the better view is that all relevant evidence is admissible. In *The Starsin*, Lord Millett continued 'it is a question of fact and may be established by evidence. Such evidence is admissible even where the contract is in writing, at least so long as it does not contradict its express terms and possibly even where it does.'[80] That refers to a disagreement in the earlier authorities about the admissibility of evidence to contradict a written agreement, which Stevens appears to assume is resolved by the majority reasoning in *Shogun*. This issue cannot be resolved here, but it remains arguable that a document may not represent the entire agreement of the parties (although an appropriate clause may negate that argument),

[73] *Standard Chartered Bank v Pakistan National Shipping Line Corp* [2002] UKHL 43, [2003] 1 AC 959.

[74] ibid [22].

[75] R Stevens, 'Why Do Agents "Drop Out"?' [2005] *LMCLQ* 101.

[76] Citing what is now Article 97 of *Bowstead & Reynolds* (n 63) para 9-001.

[77] *Shogun Finance Ltd v Hudson* [2003] UKHL 62, [2004] 1 AC 919. For discussion see DW McLauchlan, 'Parol Evidence and Contract Formation' (2005) 121 *LQR* 9; DW McLauchlan, 'Mistake of Identity and Contract Formation' (2005) 21 *Journal of Contract Law* 1; G McMeel, 'Interpretation and Mistake in Contract Law: "The Fox Knows Many Things …"' [2006] *LMCLQ* 49. Contrast R Stevens, 'Objectivity, Mistake and the Parol Evidence Rule' in A Burrows and E Peel (eds), *Contract Terms* (Oxford, Oxford University Press, 2007) 101.

[78] *Hombourg Houtimport BV v Agrosin Private Ltd, The Starsin* [2003] UKHL 12, [2004] 1 AC 715.

[79] ibid [175]. In addition see Lord Millett's statement ibid [187]. See also K Lewison, *The Interpretation of Contracts*, 7th edn (London, Sweet & Maxwell, 2020), paras 10.09–10.21.

[80] *The Starsin* (n 78) [175], citing *Young v Schuler* (1883) 11 QBD 651. See H Beale (ed), *Chitty on Contracts*, 33rd edn (London, Sweet & Maxwell, 2018) paras 13-127–13-128 (on the uncertainty as to whether evidence is admissible to contradict a written contract in the agency cases); and *Bowstead & Reynolds* (n 63) Arts 99 and 100.

and in such cases factual evidence is admissible. The concept of agency is critical to the appreciation that it can even be argued that the person negotiating the contract may not be personally liable on it.

More comprehensively, Thomas Krebs, in 'Agency Law for Muggles',[81] considers that the debate between consent and power-liability theories is irrelevant. Focusing on contract law, he argues that agency is not properly to be seen as an exception to privity of contract.[82] Building on Oliver Wendell Holmes,[83] he argues that agency is simply an application of the ordinary contractual rules of offer and acceptance (although it is necessary to leave undisclosed agency out of the analysis). He boldly asserts that 'there is in fact no agency law properly so-called, but simply a set of concepts which are used to express what are essentially straightforward contractual rules in three-party scenarios'.[84] He considers that proper emphasis on the objective principle of contract formation causes the distinction between actual authority and apparent authority to fall away, with estoppel not the basis for the latter. Krebs considers that most contractual issues in agency law are matters of interpretation. He concludes, invoking Birks' famous causative event analysis of the law of obligations – consent, wrongs, unjust enrichment, miscellaneous other events – that agency does not belong in the miscellany. The answer to the last point is 'of course not': in the wider picture of private law, agency is not within the law of things – obligations and property – at all, but in the anterior law of persons, as will be developed in section V.

Interestingly, Krebs mentions in passing the '"non-agency" law of contract', but if that means two individuals negotiating with full capacity on their own behalf, and no intermediaries engaged, this probably comprises less than 1 per cent of transactions, perhaps mainly domestic sales of secondhand cars. Even sales of residential property will probably involve others, such as estate agents and solicitors having some authority in respect of some aspects of the transaction.

This phenomenon of agency scepticism or denial was noted by Rachel Leow in her recent discussion, and she also points the finger at the leading practitioner text, *Bowstead & Reynolds*.[85] My response to the scepticism of Stevens, Krebs and others is, first, that their arguments belong to that school of modern private law theory that seeks, like Dowrick before them, the essence, or best explanation, or perhaps the lowest common denominator of private law concepts.[86] This approach is, in my view, too reductionist, and of little interest to practitioners and judges who navigate the law's untidy richness and complexity. Second, pushed too far this reasoning would denude agency law of content, and would appear to overlook centuries of European legal tradition. Third, such interpretive theories overstate the explanatory power of contractual construction, when what is going on in the factual enquiries undertaken to ascertain whether

[81] T Krebs, 'Agency Law for Muggles: Why There is No Magic in Agency' in A Burrows and E Peel (eds), *Contract Formation and Parties* (Oxford, Oxford University Press, 2010) 205.

[82] Contrast the historical discussion in J Baker, *An Introduction to English Legal History*, 5th edn Oxford, Oxford University Press, 2019) 375–78.

[83] OW Holmes, 'Agency' (1890-91) 4 *Harvard Law Review* 345.

[84] Krebs, 'Agency Law for Muggles' (n 81) 205, 210.

[85] Citing *Bowstead & Reynolds* (n 63) para 1-027. She also discusses various articles by Professor Watts, the general editor, to like effect.

[86] See McMeel (n 8) 32–33.

there is apparent authority, or implied actual authority, whilst related, is not the same as largely textual analysis of integrated instruments.

V. At Home in the Law of Persons

To my mind the distinction between the law of persons and the law of things – comprising interests arising out of obligations and interests in property – is hard-wired. First-year Roman law tutorials with the late Peter Birks, coupled with his then recent translation of *Justinian's Institutes*,[87] may be responsible. But more than two decades of subsequent reading have not shifted my understanding that this is one of the basic facts of Western legal civilization. In most instances it will be uncontroversial who is claiming the benefit of obligations or an entitlement to an asset. In legal practice a distinction is drawn between corporate and commercial work. The former focused on the appropriate vehicle for trade. The latter on the transactions between individuals and other legal persons. Whilst not a specialist in the former, I have encountered in practice all forms of commercial vehicle, partnerships,[88] limited liability partnerships,[89] the (perhaps less well-known) limited partnerships[90] and companies, whether limited by shares or guarantee.[91] On the more human side, sensitive issues arise around mental capacity, powers of attorney and the work of the Court of Protection. So in my original discussion I considered it sufficiently obvious that the law of agency comprised part of the law of persons that I confined that assertion to a footnote.[92]

As a matter of history, agency's roots may ultimately lie in the powers of the King, and the 'legal deadness of monks',[93] later in the activities of brokers and factors in commerce and the affairs of the early corporations.[94] Sir William Blackstone located his very abbreviated account of agency ('stewards, factors and bailiffs') in the law of persons (in a chapter on master and servant) and thus in volume I of his four-volume *Commentaries*.[95] This was typical of his cursory treatment of contract and commercial law generally, which is curious given that his work was contemporaneous with Lord Mansfield's gracing the King's Bench as Chief Justice, and providing the foundations

[87] P Birks and G McLeod, *Justinian's Institutes: Translated with An Introduction* (London, Duckworth, 1987).

[88] Under Sir Frederick Pollock's Partnership Act 1890.

[89] Under the Limited Liability Partnerships Act 2000, now the principal vehicle for professional firms, such as solicitors and accountants.

[90] Under the Limited Partnerships Act 1907. In my experience these are principally used as vehicles for unregulated collective investment schemes.

[91] Corporations as distinct legal persons have a long history in English law, but the principal modern vehicle for trade has proliferated since the second legal concession (in addition to personhood) of limited liability in the 1840s. The modern detailed statutory framework is the Companies Act 2006.

[92] McMeel (n 1) 387 and fn 4.

[93] F Pollock and FW Maitland, *The History of English Law before the Time of Edward I* (Cambridge, Cambridge University Press, 1898) vol II, 225–26 and fn 177.

[94] WS Holdsworth, *A History of English Law* (London, Sweet & Maxwell, 1937) vol 8, 223–29. See also Baker (n 82) 375–78, on agency as a principal device used to try to circumvent privity of contract reasoning over the centuries.

[95] Sir William Blackstone, *Commentaries on the Laws of England*, 1st edn (1765–69; Chicago, IL, University of Chicago, repr edn 1979) vol I, 415.

of those subjects for burgeoning trade and commerce.[96] Very recent scholarship has traced the development of the topic through the crucial nineteenth century,[97] and Televantos has suggested the first judicial usage of ostensible authority can be traced to 1859.[98] Looking more widely, it is difficult to accept that a couple of thousand years of Western legal tradition is unsound:[99] the concept of agency or representation is a feature of non-primitive societies and legal systems, and reflects the reality that some individuals lack capacity, or at times lack capacity, and artificial persons must act through human actors. Then mercantile practice creates pressure for the recognition of intermediaries. Without agency there can be no artificial legal persons, such as companies. Agency is a central component of the law of persons, and is not subservient to contract, tort or unjust enrichment reasoning.

VI. Statutory Vicarious Responsibility

It is an obvious point that statutory extensions of agency reasoning should be construed with their purpose and the context to the fore. Problems arose in the routine triangular relationship where individuals acquired vehicles from car dealers but also entered into the finance contract with another entity, negotiated through the same salesperson who had steered their choice to that car. In that context, in his insightful dissenting speech in *Branwhite v Worcester Work*,[100] Lord Wilberforce stated:

> It may be that some wider concept of vicarious responsibility other than that of agency, as normally understood, may have to be recognised in order to accommodate some of the more elaborate cases which now arise when there are two persons who become mutually involved or associated in one side of a transaction.

That was a clear recognition that public policy may require statutory or other extensions of common law agency. The consequence of the decision of the majority in *Branwhite* was introduction of statutory protections, including by way of deemed statutory agency, for the customer in triangular cases in the credit and hire context in sections 56 and 75 of the Consumer Credit Act 1974. It is my understanding that, where they apply, those measures have worked well in practice. Less successful have been similar statutory interventions in financial services and markets.

In teaching agency law, one important point we try to get across is for students to distinguish the proper legal analysis of different sides of the triangle. So the principal–agent side, or the internal relationship, is the dimension concerned with

[96] N Poser, *Lord Mansfield:] Justice in the Age of Reason* (Montreal, McGill-Queen's University Press, 2013) ch 13. See also Sir John Baker (n 82), 374–75; and G McMeel, 'Pillans v Van Mierop (1765)' in C Mitchell and P Mitchell (eds), *Landmark Cases in the Law of Contract* (Oxford, Hart Publishing, 2008) 23.

[97] See A Televantos, *Capitalism before Corporations: The Morality of Business Associations and the Roots of Commercial Equity and Law* (Oxford, Oxford University Press, 2020) chs 3 and 4; and Sir Ross Cranston, *Making Commercial Law through Practice 1830–1970* (Cambridge, Cambridge University Press, 2021) ch 3.

[98] Televantos (n 97) 71–72. I am grateful to Dr Televantos for this reference.

[99] R Zimmermann, *The Law of Obligations: Roman Foundations of the Civilian Tradition* (Oxford, Clarendon Press, 1990) 43–58; K Zweigert and H Kotz, *An Introduction to Comparative Law*, 3rd edn, tr T Weir (Oxford, Oxford University Press, 1998) ch 32.

[100] *Branwhite v Worcester Works Finance Ltd* [1969] 1 AC 552, 587.

actual authority, whether express or implied. Any restrictions on the agent's power to act, which would ordinarily be explicit, should be found here. Contrast the principal–third party side (usually the hypotenuse on my diagrams), or the external dimension, which is where the facts and evidence going to apparent or ostensible authority should be found, such as conduct amounting to a holding out of the agent by the principal to the third party, and any consequential reliance by the third party on the principal. The real presence of the agent always muddies the picture, and we have to concede that conduct and statements by the agent in which the principal acquiesces are all part of this inquiry into the existence of apparent authority, if any. In a well-organised relationship the actual and the apparent authority of the agent, such as the agent's having all the legal powers of the principal, should coincide exactly. In less tidy situations the apparent authority of the agent may be greater than his actual authority, either there being no actual authority (sometimes termed agency by estoppel) or there being some actual authority but the appearance of authority being greater (perhaps originally termed apparent authority).

In the leading case of *Hely-Hutchinson v Brayhead Ltd*,[101] Lord Denning MR stated:

> Actual authority, express or implied, is binding as between the company and the agent, and also as between the company and others, whether they are within the company or outside it.
>
> Ostensible or apparent authority is the authority of an agent as it *appears* to others. It often coincides with actual authority. Thus, when the board appoint one of their number to be managing director, they invest him not only with implied authority, but also with ostensible authority to do all such things as fall within the usual scope of that office. Other people who see him acting as managing director are entitled to assume that he has the usual authority of a managing director. But sometimes ostensible authority exceeds actual authority. For instance, when the board appoint the managing director, they may expressly limit his authority by saying he is not to order goods worth more than £500 without the sanction of the board. In that case his actual authority is subject to the £500 limitation, but his *ostensible* authority includes all the usual authority of a managing director. The company is bound by his ostensible authority in his dealings with those who do not know of the limitation.[102]

This should be uncontroversial. So why mention it in the context of statutory examples of deemed agency? From the perspective of a litigator or a student doing a problem question, agency issues often present themselves as a series of alternatives. Is there express actual authority? If not, are there grounds to argue implied actual authority? Further or alternatively, is there apparent or ostensible authority? If not, is there some other basis to make the principal liable, such as evidence of ratification? If all else fails, the last ditch is a claim for breach of warranty of authority against the agent personally. Save for the last, each doctrine, or cluster of rules, increases the situations in which a principal may be held responsible for the actions of others. So where Parliament has legislated on the grounds of public policy to deem principals responsible for others in certain circumstances, it would follow that it is doing so in territory where it would otherwise be the case, or at least arguable, that the alleged agent had acted outside the scope of both actual and apparent authority, and was liable on no other basis.

[101] *Hely-Hutchinson v Brayhead Ltd* (n 42).
[102] ibid 583.

Statutory agency must have been intended to increase the scope of a principal's responsibility for others, otherwise Parliament would have legislated in vain.

So how in 2019 could a unanimous Court of Appeal in *Anderson v Sense Network*,[103] faced with a statutory measure for the protection of persons dealing with financial intermediaries, construe it so that it conferred no greater protection than the doctrine of actual authority (or perhaps express actual authority)? How could it be that an internal limitation in the confidential business arrangements between principal and agent curtails a statutory extension of agency? It is directly akin to Lord Denning's £500 limitation trumping broader apparent authority.

We may all have probably encountered intermediaries when dealing with ordinary retail financial services, in respect of mortgages, general insurance or investments, whose business cards or website contain (as mandated by the regulator) the circumlocution that 'Agent Limited is an appointed representative of Principal Limited, which is authorised and regulated by the Financial Conduct Authority'.[104]

The concept of the statutory appointed representative has been embedded in UK financial services legislation since 1986, and the extent of the principal's statutory responsibility has been controversial from the outset. The easy answer ought to be that where a customer has dealt with Agent Ltd, and is concerned about bad advice or product mis-selling, she ought to complain to Principal Ltd, the directly authorised firm. Indeed complaints are ordinarily handled by Principal Ltd, and any further complaint to the statutory Financial Ombudsman Service is against Principal Ltd as respondent. Principal Ltd is directly bound by the regulatory rules of the Financial Conduct Authority (FCA), including as to complaints-handling and maintaining professional indemnity cover. Litigation is invariably brought against Principal Ltd alone. However, the clunkiness of the statutory language of vicarious responsibility has opened up room for argument at odds with the obvious investor and consumer protection motivation behind the measure.

Section 39(3) of the Financial Services and Markets Act 2000 (FSMA) (and previously section 44(6) of the Financial Services Act 1986 (FSA)) addressed the problem of self-employed individuals or independent corporate intermediaries who were appointed representatives of either a product provider firm or a financial advisory network:

> The principal of an appointed representative is responsible, to the same extent as if he had expressly permitted it, for anything done or omitted by the representative in carrying on the business for which he has accepted responsibility.

As with many central provisions of financial services law, the roots of this lie in Professor Jim Gower's seminal 1980s report into investor protection. Addressing the widespread use of self-employed agents by life insurance companies and others, he concluded:

> Hence, I suggest that if the tied salesmen are to continue to be self-employed it should be specifically enacted that the company to which they are tied is fully responsible for their acts to the same extent as if they were its employees with full authority to act on its behalf.[105]

[103] *Anderson v Sense Network* [2019] EWCA Civ 1395, [2020] Bus LR 1.
[104] See the importance of business cards in *Martin v Britannia Life Ltd* [2000] Lloyd's Rep PN 412.
[105] Gower Report, *Review of Investor Protection* (Cmnd 9125, 1984) para 8.50. Gower added 'This should apply even if, in any particular case, the salesman sold the product of another company.' See further Recommendation 58: 'The Act should provide that life offices and managers of unit trusts and mutual funds are fully responsible for the activities of their tied intermediaries whether they are employed or self-employed.'

The recommendation was akin to imposing vicarious liability on firms as if for employees. The White Paper of that dangerously progressive Conservative Government headed by Mrs Thatcher concurred that authorised businesses should be required 'to take total responsibility for sales by tied agents as well as their employees'.[106] The clear purpose of section 39(3) and its predecessor is to create a form of statutory agency – or, in Lord Wilberforce's prescient phrase in *Branwhite*, 'vicarious responsibility'.

Under the FSMA, the structure of the legislation is that appointed representatives are independent businesses responsible in the first instance for their own acts and omissions. Traditionally they were self-employed salespersons ('the man from the Pru'), but nowadays they are more typically companies. Section 39 of the FSMA has at least two functions. If a business does not want to be directly authorised by the FCA, which can be onerous and expensive, it can obtain exemption from the general prohibition on carrying out investment business in the UK in section 19 through becoming an appointed representative

If a firm meets the conditions in section 39(1) of the FSMA and is an appointed representative under the legislation, its principal, the authorised person, is made vicariously responsible under section 39(3) for its acts and omissions in conducting the investment business for which it has accepted responsibility. Section 39(4) makes the directly authorised firm similarly responsible to the FCA for its representative's conduct for disciplinary and enforcement purposes. This second aspect of section 39 is plainly aimed at investor protection. The responsibility of the principal is strictly secondary to, and in addition to, the primary responsibility of the principal for its advice to its customers. Purists might say this is not therefore agency, because the intermediary does not drop out. But that is true of many agency doctrines away from the central case of actual authority. In *Page v Champion Financial Management Ltd*, Simon Picken QC, sitting as a Deputy Judge, stated:

> Responsibility under Section 39(3), which covers both civil and criminal liability, means that a claimant has the ability to pursue both the authorised [*recte* appointed] representative and the principal – in this case, both the First Defendant and the Fifth Defendant. As Mr Burroughs [counsel] neatly put it, Section 39(3) prevents an authorised representative from 'falling through the net', so that there is no regulation of his activities by the FCA, achieving this by making the principal responsible for the authorised representative's actions and enabling the principal to be sanctioned if its authorised representative fails to meet the requirements only indirectly imposed on the authorised representative.[107]

The reference to criminal liability requires treating with caution, because section 39(6) provides for a more restricted rule about the attribution of knowledge for the commission of offence, but in civil cases an investor claimant can sue both principal firm and appointed representative, although they tend to sue the former because of the rule about professional indemnity cover. Similarly in *Goldstone v Becque Wayman Investments Ltd*, HHJ Hodge QC stated that the purpose of section 39(3) 'is to provide an *additional*

[106] Department for Trade and Industry, *Financial Services in the United Kingdom: A new framework for investor protection* (Cmnd 9432, 1985) para 10.6.

[107] *Page v Champion Financial Management Ltd* [2014] EWHC 1778 (QB) [10].

layer of protection for customers and investors'.[108] The question can arise whether any contract for services is with the principal firm or the appointed representative. It depends of course on the contractual terms. In my experience, larger 'brand name' advisory networks tend to contract with the underlying customer, but *Goldstone* suggests the default position is that any contract for services is with the appointed representative. If the parties wished to make it clear that any contract for services was with the principal, the contract would need to say so expressly. Of course, any resulting contract with a product provider firm, whether mortgage lender, insurer or investment firm, is with that provider, and both authorised principal and appointed representative drop out of that relationship.

The predecessor measure, section 44 of the FSA 1986, had provided:

> The principal of an appointed representative shall be responsible, to the same extent as if he had expressly authorised it, for anything said or done or omitted by the representative in carrying on the investment business for which he has accepted responsibility.

It was considered in three cases. First, in *J Rothschild Insurance plc v Collyear*,[109] the significance of section 44(6) of the FSA 1986 was identified in the context of a claim by a life insurance company against a professional indemnity insurer arising from pension mis-selling. Rix J observed:

> The pensions in question were sold through JRA's sales force of 'appointed representatives' who have self-employed status but who enter into contracts for services to act as agents for JRA. JRA are responsible under s44(6) of the Act for everything that their appointed representatives do in carrying on JRA's investment business.[110]

Second, in *Emmanuel v DBS Management plc*,[111] a case on unusual facts, where Jonathan Sumption QC, sitting as a Deputy Judge (as he then was), held the statute could not stretch to an investment directly into a financial advisory practice. To the extent that that case decides that statutory vicarious responsibility extends only to business for which the principal had accepted responsibility and in the capacity of carrying on the business of that principal, it is probably correctly decided. Third, *Martin v Britannia Life Ltd*,[112] where Jonathan Parker J adopted a broad and purposive approach to section 44 and held that whilst a mortgage was not an 'investment' for the purposes of the 1986 Act, the concept of 'investment advice' was broad enough to encapsulate an 'associated or ancillary transaction'. This is an early instance of what is now described as 'blended advice', which includes both a regulated product and an unregulated product bundled together. Jonathan Parker J accepted that the source of the adviser's actual authority must derive from the appointed representative agreement, which could and did contain express limitations on the scope of the adviser's actual authority, but that 'such limitations take effect subject to the statutory agency imposed by section 44(6) of the 1986 Act'.

[108] *Goldstone v Becque Wayman Investments Ltd* [2012] EWHC 3549 (Ch) [45].
[109] *J Rothschild Insurance plc v Collyear* [1998] CLC 1697, [1998] CLC 1697.
[110] ibid 1700.
[111] *Emmanuel v DBS Management plc* [1999] Lloyd's Rep PN 593.
[112] *Martin v Britannia Life Ltd* (n 104); see also J Powell and R Stuart (gen eds), *Jackson & Powell on Professional Liability*, 8th edn (London, Sweet & Maxwell, 2017) para 15-027. See also *Emptage v Financial Services Compensation Scheme Ltd* [2013] EWCA Civ 729.

those parties, and no customer could know whether or not the products recommended were on the list. Obviously the list did not include the Ponzi scheme. The Court of Appeal, in a highly literal reading of the FSMA, held that section 39(1) permitted the authorised firm to limit the scope of responsibility to retail customers under section 39(3) by its contract with the appointed representatives to particular categories of business, even though (like Lord Denning's internal company restriction on the powers of the managing director) there was no way the counterparty could know of these restrictions.

This was a disastrous decision, frustrating the clear intention of the legislative policy. Almost immediately the UK Government proposed reversing the effect of *Anderson v Sense* by amendments to the primary legislation, to ensure the gap in consumer protection would be eliminated and that those who deal with appointed representatives will have full recourse to statutory dispute resolution, whatever the restrictions in the appointed representatives agreements.[124] For the present the law appears to be that the principal is responsible under the statute for mis-selling by an appointed representative of any financial product on its contractual list (even though the appointed representative did not comply with its principal's rules for doing business) under *Ovcharenko*, but not if an appointed representative mis-sells, arranges or advises on any financial product not on the principal's approved list or the product of a provider who is not on the list under its private contract with the appointed representative (the contract is not a public document and usually subject to commercial confidentiality), as a result of *Anderson*. It is hard to see how the statutory language mandates this difficult distinction. In any event, it is difficult to see how the purpose of the statute to provide investor protection is given effect. To complicate the picture, *Tenetconnect* would suggest that where there is 'blended advice', such as to sell an interest in a regulated product and invest the proceeds in an unregulated one (even a Ponzi scheme), the statutory responsibility does apply.

The blended-advice approach of *Tenetconnect* has since been followed in a subsequent decision of the Court of Appeal in *Adams v Options SIPP*,[125] dealing with a separate provision of the FSMA intended to protect investors who have dealt with

[124] Since the conference and writing the original version of this chapter, consultations have been launched by both HM Treasury and the FCA concerning the future and reform of the appointed representative system. The Treasury acknowledges the gap in consumer protection caused by role of the agreement in s 39 FSMA and the decision in *Anderson v Sense*: HM Treasury, *The Appointed Representatives Regime: Call for Evidence* (December 2021). See especially paras 2.1–2.5, 3.6–3.8, 3.18, 3.26–3.34, 3.42–3.43, 4.6, and the reform proposal at paras 4.32–4.34, effectively proposing to reverse *Anderson v Sense* by amendment to the primary legislation, at least so far as access to the Financial Ombudsman Service is concerned. The Financial Ombudsman Service jurisdiction now extends to all consumers and most small and medium-sized enterprises, and can make binding awards up to £350,000. See also Financial Conduct Authority, *Improving the Appointed Representatives Regime* (Consulation Paper CP 21/34; December 2021), paras 2.7, 3.26–3.27 and 4.23–4.28. The impetus for these consultations was to a large extent the House of Commons Treasury Committee Sixth Report of Session 2021–22, *Lessons from Greensill Capital* (July 2021), paras 45–51.

[125] *Adams v Options SIPP UK LLP (formerly Carey Pensions LLP)* [2021] EWCA Civ 474, [2021] Bus LR 1568, [2021] EWCA Civ 1188. On 30 March 2022 the Supreme Court refused permission to appeal.

unregulated intermediaries. The context was a paradigm pension scam. Mr Adams, a road haulage driver, was persuaded by an offshore and unregulated intermediary (CLP) to transfer his personal pension with Friends Life to a self-invested personal pension (SIPP) with the respondent, Options, formerly known as Carey. CLP also recommended he invest the cash proceeds of the transfer in an unregulated, commercial property 'store pods' scheme, consisting of a number of disused shipping containers on an industrial park in Blackburn, Lancashire. Some 580 of Carey's clients were in the same boat, having made the same investments, nearly all introduced by CLP.

The principal basis of claim was that Mr Adams was entitled to reverse his investments under the statutory mechanism in sections 27 and 28 of the FSMA. Whilst the judge had rejected this claim, the Court of Appeal considered it was plainly made out. Section 27 put the risk of entering into agreements with investors introduced by unregulated firms squarely on Carey as an authorised person under the FSMA. If the intermediary engaged in FSMA-regulated activities such as advising on or arranging investments, the resulting agreement was presumptively unenforceable. On the facts CLP had made three recommendations: (i) sell the Friends Life pension; (ii) buy the Carey SIPP; and (iii) buy store pods. Whilst the third was an unregulated product, it was inextricably linked with the first two elements of the advice. Newey and Andrews LJJ both specifically approved *TenetConnect*, where Ouseley J spoke of a 'single braided stream of advice' being given about regulated and unregulated investments, with the former being part and parcel of the latter, and therefore the advice on unregulated investments becoming part of the regulated advice.[126] Andrews LJ stressed the need for realism in such assessments. *Adams* represents greater judicial willingness to adopt a contextual and purposive approach and give teeth to statutory measures for consumer protection, and it sits alongside *First Tower Trustees Ltd v CDS (Superstores International) Ltd*.[127] Like in that case, but in contrast to *Anderson*, the Court of Appeal treated contractual restrictions as subsidiary to issues of public policy embodied in the statute. In *Adams*, Newey LJ dutifully recorded Carey's boilerplate disclaimers and warnings, the emphasis being very much on giving effect to investor protection measures. Indeed Andrews LJ cautioned that 'the basis on which [firms] contract with their clients will only go so far to protect them from liability'.[128]

To conclude, in the particular context of financial intermediation it is still essential for judges and practitioners to have a firm grasp of the complications posed by the armies of agents that proliferate in this field, and to engage properly with the purpose and context of statutory rules. Agency law remains a challenging topic, as a matter both of theory and of practice.

[126] *R (TenetConnect Services Ltd) v Financial Ombudsman* [2018] EWHC 459 (Admin), [2018] 1 BCLC 726 [53].
[127] *First Tower Trustees Ltd v CDS (Superstores International) Ltd* [2018] EWCA Civ 1396, [2019] 1 WLR 637.
[128] *Adams* (n 125) [131].

6

Platform Liability for Terrorist Activities

YING HU*

I. Introduction

In recent years, there have been growing concerns that online platforms, such as Twitter and YouTube, are being used to facilitate terrorist activities.[1] Regulators worldwide have pressured online platforms to take more proactive measures against extremist content.[2] Victims of terrorist attacks brought a series of claims against online platforms to seek compensation for their loss.[3] In response, platforms have taken various steps to remove extremist content and to suspend accounts linked to terrorism. For example, in 2017, Facebook, Microsoft, Twitter and YouTube founded the Global Internet Forum to Counter Terrorism (GIFCT), a non-governmental organisation (NGO) to prevent extremists from misusing digital platforms.[4] On 15 March 2019, after terrorist attacks against two mosques in Christchurch, New Zealand, a group of world leaders and tech companies adopted the Christchurch Call to Action, which is a series of voluntary commitments to prevent the upload and dissemination of extremist content online.[5]

This chapter considers whether and, if so, to what extent it is appropriate to impose legal duties on online platforms to detect and prevent terrorist-related content. It proceeds as follows. Section II explains the various ways in which terrorists and their

* I would like to thank Professors Tan Cheng-Han, Paul Davies, Yip Man, Alvin See, James Penner, Rebecca Lee and Roger Alford for their helpful comments. All mistakes are mine.

[1] See, eg, R Cohen-Almagor, 'The Role of Internet Intermediaries in Tackling Terrorism Online' (2017) 86 *Fordham Law Review* 425; D Citron, 'Extremist Speech, Compelled Conformity, and Censorship Creep' (2018) 93 *Notre Dame Law Review* 1035; M Lavi, 'Do Platforms Kill?' (2020) 43 *Harvard Journal of Law & Public Policy* 477. For the purpose of this chapter, terrorism is defined as 'violence by non-state actors intended to terrorise or frighten a target audience'.

[2] For a summary of the regulatory pressure facing technology companies, see Citron (n 1) 1040–49.

[3] See, eg, *Force v Facebook* 934 F 3d 53 (2nd Cir 2019); *Fields v Twitter* 881 F 3d 739 (9th Cir 2018); *Crosby v Twitter* 303 F Supp 3d 564 (ED Mich 2018); *Gonzalez v Google* 282 F Supp 3d 1150 (ND Cal 2017); *Pennie v Twitter* 281 F Supp 3d 874 (ND Cal 2017). However, these claims have largely failed in the United States because online platforms are often immune from liability under the Communications Decency Act of 1996, s 230.

[4] GIFCT, 'About GIFCT' a gifct.org/about/ (accessed 27 July 2021).

[5] Christchurch Call, 'About Christchurch Call' at www.christchurchcall.com/call.html (accessed 27 July 2021).

supporters use online platforms to facilitate terrorist activities. Section III sets out both the benefits and costs of imposing gatekeeper liability on online platforms to combat terrorism. Section IV critically examines two approaches to platform liability for terrorist-related content.

II. How Platforms Facilitate Terrorist Activities

A. Terrorist Use of Online Platforms

Terrorists are active on social media.[6] Take Twitter as an example. According to a 2015 report published by Brookings Institute (hereinafter referred to as 'Berger and Morgan's study'), from October to November 2014, at least 46,000 Twitter accounts were used by ISIS supporters.[7] Moreover, while Twitter users grew by approximately 30 per cent in 2013, ISIS users nearly doubled.[8] ISIS supporters on Twitter were not only far more active than ordinary users,[9] they also had a greater number of followers than ordinary users: the estimated median number of followers among ISIS supporters was 177, compared to 61 for average active Twitter users.[10]

Online platforms can play various roles in facilitating terrorist activities.

i. To Incite Violence and Recruit Members

First of all, online platforms provide a venue for terrorists and their supporters to publish promotional videos to incite violence, praise past terrorist attacks and recruit new members.[11] ISIS operatives have relied on both bots and active human users known as *mujtahidun* to disseminate terrorist content to the general public.[12] Much online propaganda is 'flashy, hi-tech, and interactive', enabling terrorists to deliver their messages in ways that appeal to a young audience.[13] In a 2019 study, Bloom, Tiflati and Horgan explain how ISIS members used Telegram, a messaging app, to further their cause: semi-official Telegram channels mainly disseminated photos, recruitment and beheading videos, audio files and other links; at the same time, Telegram chatrooms provided members with a virtual support group where they engaged with one another.[14]

[6] See, eg, AEJ Goodman, 'When You Give a Terrorist a Twitter: Holding Social Media Companies Liable for Their Support of Terrorism' (2018) 46 *Pepperdine Law Review* 147; Lavi (n 1).

[7] JM Berger and J Morgan, 'The ISIS Twitter Census: Defining and Describing the Population of ISIS Supporters on Twitter' (*Brookings*, March 2015) at www.brookings.edu/wp-content/uploads/2016/06/isis_twitter_census_berger_morgan.pdf (accessed 23 March 2021).

[8] ibid 17.

[9] ibid 18, 28.

[10] ibid 30.

[11] See, eg, *Cohen v Facebook* 252 F Supp 3d 140 (EDNY 2017) 146, where the plaintiffs alleged that Palestinian terrorist groups and associated individuals used their Facebook pages for 'general and specific incitements to violence and to praise past terrorist attacks'.

[12] Berger and Morgan (n 7) 23–25.

[13] See J Lieberman and S Collins, 'Violent Islamist Extremism, the Internet, and the Homegrown Terrorist Threat' (Senate Committee on Homeland Security and Government Affairs, 110th Cong, 1st sess, 2008).

[14] M Bloom, H Tiflati and J Horgan, 'Navigating ISIS's Preferred Platform: Telegram' (2019) 31 *Terrorism and Political Violence* 1242, 1244–48.

Propagandists also distributed 'limited time giveaways', ranging from news and videos, to ISIS-specific emojis to keep chatroom users constantly online for fear of missing out.[15] These researchers suggest that excessive exposure to ISIS channels and chatrooms can cause users to be less sensitive to violence and hence more likely to be exploited.

Research further indicates that a significant number of individuals who carried out terrorist attacks consumed extremist content online. According to MI5, the United Kingdom's domestic intelligence agency, Al-Qaeda in the Arabian Peninsula's (AQAP's) *Inspire* magazine was 'read by those involved in at last seven out of the ten attacks planned within the UK since its first issue in [2010]'.[16] In a 2017 empirical study of 223 convicted UK-based terrorists (hereinafter referred to as 'Gill and others'), Gill and others found that at least 30 per cent of the offenders accessed extremist materials online, and 14 per cent chose to engage in violence after witnessing some extremist materials online.[17] For example, Roshonara Choudhry, who caused serious bodily injury to a UK Member of Parliament, referred in her police interview to a specific YouTube video of Sheikh Abdullah Azzam that made her realise that she was obligated to fight.[18] The Tsarnaev brothers, who planted explosives at the Boston Marathon, were reportedly influenced by online sermons of Anwar al-Awlaqi.[19]

Moreover, online platforms likely increase the pool of potential candidates for terrorists to recruit and radicalise. They also make it easier for terrorists to maintain relationships with their followers, especially those overseas. Experts suggest that chat apps such as WhatsApp and Telegram further act as 'key filters' for terrorists to '[funnel] people further into its recruitment pipeline'.[20] Previously, terrorists often had to rely on existing acquaintances to identify potential recruits. By contrast, online platforms enable terrorist sympathisers to actively seek out virtual terrorist groups. Terrorist organisations' violent propaganda also appeals to individuals who are predisposed to violence, which enables strategies to encourage 'lone wolf' attacks by people who are not fully committed to the terrorist ideology.[21] Nevertheless, the effectiveness of online propaganda in facilitating terrorist recruitment should not be exaggerated. Commentators point out that terrorists are rarely radicalised solely online.[22] Rather, they engage in both online learning and off-line interactions with other terrorists (while engaging in online learning is strongly correlated with face-to-face interactions with other terrorists).[23]

[15] ibid 1250.

[16] M Conway, 'Determining the Role of the Internet in Violent Extremism and Terrorism: Six Suggestions for Progressing Research' (2017) 40 *Studies in Conflict & Terrorism* 77, 81.

[17] P Gill and others, 'Terrorist Use of the Internet by the Numbers' (2017) 16 *Criminology & Public Policy* 99, 107.

[18] ibid 108.

[19] S Horwitz, 'Investigators Sharpen Focus on Wife of Dead Boston Bombing Suspect' *Washington Post* (3 May 2013) at washingtonpost.com/world/national-security/investigators-sharpen-focus-on-boston-bombing-suspects-widow/2013/05/03/a2cd9d28-b413-11e2-baf7-5bc2a9dc6f44_story.html (accessed 13 October 2021).

[20] S Meichtry and S Schechner, 'How Islamic State Weaponized the Chat App to Direct Attacks on the West' *Wall Street Journal* (21 October 2016) at wsj.com/articles/how-islamic-state-weaponized-the-chat-app-to-direct-attacks-on-the-west-1476955802 (accessed 2 August 2021).

[21] Berger and Morgan (n 7) 58–59 (providing examples of ISIS' 'lone wolf' strategy).

[22] Conway (n 16) 80.

[23] Gill and others (n 17) 110.

ii. To Prepare and Carry Out Attacks

Planning and carrying out terrorist attacks sometimes require skills that people without military training do not normally possess, such as constructing bombs and infiltrating buildings. Terrorist organisations have sought to disseminate such information through online platforms. For example, AQAP's *Inspire* magazine contained detailed instructional manuals and images to teach readers how to carry out attacks, including information about bomb-making, enemy targeting, gun training, car destruction, building destruction and so on.[24] For example, issue 13 of *Inspire* contained a 15-page guide on 'Making the Hidden Bomb'; issues 14 and 15 included a step-by-step guide on planning and executing an assassination.[25] Some security experts went so far as to comment that 'the virtual jihadist network has replaced al Qaeda training camps'.[26]

It is possible that online instructional materials replace part of the need for new recruits to travel to remote terrorist compounds to train and acquire the skills to kill, which is the intended purpose for magazines such as *Inspire*.[27] Many analysts believe that the perpetrators of the 2013 Boston bombing used instructions in a piece entitled 'How to Make a Bomb in the Kitchen of your Mom' in that magazine.[28] *Inspire* itself claims credit for motivating not only the Boston attack, but also various attacks in New York and Paris.[29] Gill and others reveal that terrorists accessed a wide range of online resources to prepare for their attacks, including bomb-making videos, poison manuals, terrorist training manuals and *Inspire* magazines, as well as information about assassination, torture techniques, suicide-vest production and body disposal.[30] Moreover, 10 per cent of the offenders in that study used online resources to overcome obstacles in their preparation for attacks.[31] The researchers also found that certain types of terrorists were more likely to use online resources: those who planned to use an improvised explosive device (IED) and lone-actors were 3.34 times and 2.64 times more likely to have learned online respectively.[32] Nevertheless, some commentators question the effectiveness of online materials in equipping potential terrorists with the necessary skills.[33] They claim that certain skills, such as bomb-making, cannot be adequately acquired without in-person training.[34] David Benson, for example, has sought to demonstrate empirically that the al Qaeda transnational attacks have been less deadly since they began to rely heavily on the Internet for those attacks.[35]

[24] M Conway, J Parker and S Looney, 'Online Jihadi Instructional Content: The Role of Magazines' in M Conway et al (eds), *Terrorists' Use of the Internet* (Amsterdam, IOS Press, 2017) 182 at ebooks.iospress.nl/volumearticle/46554 (accessed 2 August 2021).

[25] ibid 186.

[26] DC Benson, 'Why the Internet Is Not Increasing Terrorism' (2014) 23 *Security Studies* 293, 299 and fn 24.

[27] Conway, Parker and Looney (n 24) 191 (noting that the *Inspire* magazine included statements such as 'my Muslim brother: we are conveying to you our military training right into your kitchen to relieve you of the difficulty of travelling to us' and 'we give our readers suggestions on how to wage their individual jihad').

[28] ibid 191.

[29] ibid.

[30] Gill and others (n 17) 107.

[31] ibid 108.

[32] ibid 110.

[33] Benson (n 26) 306–07.

[34] Conway, Parker and Looney (n 24) 183.

[35] Benson (n 26) 315.

Moreover, unlike local terrorists, transnational terrorists often cannot rely on local support for recruitment, surveillance or carrying out operations.[36] As such, long-distance communication is critical for them. Messaging tools enable terrorists to communicate with multiple parties from different locations almost instantaneously, which facilitates the planning and execution of attacks.[37] For example, Rachid Kassim, a French member of the Islamic State, reportedly exchanged encrypted Telegram messages with a number of perpetrators of fatal attacks in Paris.[38] Not only did Kassim publish a 'Guide for Loan Lions', which included names of individuals to murder and explanations of various attack methods, he also advised his followers on how to avoid drawing suspicion and getting caught by the police.[39]

iii. To Finance Terrorist Activities

Terrorist organisations and sympathisers have also used online platforms, such as social media websites, to conduct fundraising campaigns.[40] For example, in 2013, one of the users in a Facebook group called for donations to support a fighter in Syria who needed 'equipment, food and pharmaceuticals'.[41] Individuals and organisations have also used crowdfunding websites under the guise of charitable donations to raise funds for terrorism.[42] More recently, a group called al Sadaqah sought anonymous donations in the form of cryptocurrency to improve conditions for jihad fighters in Syria.[43]

Certain platforms, such as YouTube, also allow users to profit from the content they publish. It is conceivable that a terrorist might receive revenue from YouTube every time someone views an advertisement accompanying the videos uploaded by the terrorist. For example, in *Gonzalez v Google*, the plaintiffs argued that Google directly contributed to ISIS' unlawful activities by sharing advertising revenue with ISIS.[44] However, they did not prove that any revenue was actually shared with the user who posted an ISIS video, nor that the user was an ISIS member.[45] Advertisers such as AT&T, after discovering that their advertisements appeared alongside content promoting terrorism and hate, pulled advertisements from YouTube.[46] Since then, YouTube has taken a tougher stance against offensive content, removing thousands of videos containing extreme views.[47]

[36] ibid 297.

[37] S Feldstein and S Gordon, 'Are Telegram and Signal Havens for Right-Wing Extremists?' (*Foreign Policy*, 13 March 2021) <foreignpolicy.com/2021/03/13/telegram-signal-apps-right-wing-extremism-islamic-state-terrorism-violence-europol-encrypted/> accessed 20 May 2021.

[38] Meichtry and Schechner (n 20).

[39] ibid.

[40] See, eg, 'Emerging Terrorist Finance Risks,' (*FATF*, October 2015) <fatf-gafi.org/media/fatf/documents/reports/Emerging-Terrorist-Financing-Risks.pdf> accessed 18 September 2021.

[41] ibid 31.

[42] ibid 31–32.

[43] B Forrest and J Scheck, 'Jihadists See a Funding Boon in Bitcoin' *Wall Street Journal* (20 February 2018) at wsj.com/articles/jihadists-see-a-funding-boon-in-bitcoin-1519131601 (accessed 13 October 2021).

[44] *Gonzalez* (n 3) 1169–70.

[45] ibid 1170.

[46] O Solon, 'Google's Bad Week: YouTube Loses Millions as Advertising Row Reaches US' *The Observer* (25 March 2017) at theguardian.com/technology/2017/mar/25/google-youtube-advertising-extremist-content-att-verizon (accessed 13 October 2021).

[47] K Roose and K Conger, 'YouTube to Remove Thousands of Videos Pushing Extreme Views' *New York Times* (5 June 2019) at nytimes.com/2019/06/05/business/youtube-remove-extremist-videos.html (accessed 13 October 2021).

iv. To Terrorise the Public

Lastly, terrorists have used online platforms to upload graphic depictions of terrorist activities to instill fear into the public directly. The Islamic State, for example, has posted content to social media that 'feature[s] punishment based on radical Islamic tenets', including images and videos about 'executions, beheadings, the cutting off of hands, people set on fire and women stoned to death'.[48]

Terrorists have also used social media to broadcast their attacks in real time. In 2013, al-Shabaab live-tweeted throughout their attack at the Westgate shopping mall in Nairobi, Kenya.[49] In 2015, a terrorist who gunned down four people at a kosher grocery in eastern Paris reportedly recorded the attack on a GoPro camera and tried to email the video out.[50] More recently, perpetrators of the attack at Christchurch, New Zealand, during which dozens people were killed, live-streamed the event on Facebook and even posted a message prior to the attack on an anonymous online forum, 8chan, directing users to the relevant Facebook page.[51]

B. Unique Features of Online Platforms

Several unique features of online platforms make them particularly attractive to terrorists.

i. Anonymity

First of all, as George J Tenet, former Director of the CIA, has pointed out, the Internet enables terrorists to 'work anonymously and remotely to inflict enormous damage at little cost or risk to themselves'.[52] For example, many online platforms, such as Facebook, Twitter and YouTube, allow users to sign up for an account with as little information as an account name (which may not be real) and a phone number or email address. Terrorists can also use various tools, such as virtual private networks (VPN) or The Onion Router (TOR), to avoid being traced online. Certain platforms have gained increasing popularity among terrorist supporters because they offer more security features: unlike WhatsApp, which keeps logs of user chats, Telegram provides users

[48] A Chang and P Dave, 'Social Networks Crack down on Terror Posts' *Los Angeles Times* (21 August 2014) at latimes.com/business/la-fi-social-media-beheading-20140821-story.html (accessed 13 October 2021).

[49] D Mair, '#Westgate: A Case Study: How al-Shabaab Used Twitter during an Ongoing Attack' (2017) 40 *Studies in Conflict & Terrorism* 24.

[50] P Cruickshank, J Sciutto and S Almasy, 'Official: Gunman Recorded Terror Attack on Kosher Grocery' *CNN* (31 January 2015) at cnn.com/2015/01/30/europe/coulibaly-kosher-grocery-attack/index.html (accessed 13 October 2021).

[51] J Marsh and T Mulholland, 'How the Christchurch Terrorist Attack Was Made for Social Media' *CNN* (16 March 2019) at cnn.com/2019/03/15/tech/christchurch-internet-radicalization-intl/index.html (accessed 13 October 2021).

[52] T Zeller Jr, 'On the Open Internet, a Web of Dark Alleys' *The New York Times* (20 December 2004) at nytimes.com/2004/12/20/business/technology/on-the-open-internet-a-web-of-dark-alleys.html (accessed 28 July 2021).

with the 'self-destruct option', which deletes messages immediately after they are viewed by the intended recipient.[53] As a result, law enforcement may not be able to obtain user chats from Telegram.[54]

ii. Network Effect

Moreover, online platforms are particularly effective at publicising terrorist content for three reasons. First, people share messages that capture their interest with their friends and family through social media, thereby contributing to the wider dissemination of those messages.

Second, many online platforms use proprietary algorithms that match content with people, making it easier for terrorist messages to reach their target audience. For example, Facebook's algorithms analyse a user's past activities in order to display posts that will most likely interest that user in his personalised 'newsfeed' page.[55] An individual who has actively searched terrorist-related phrases is likely to receive a greater number of inciting messages. In addition to posts, platforms such as Facebook also make recommendations about new friends, groups, products and local events based on the vast amount of data they have collected about the user. Studies also reveal that Twitter's 'who to follow' recommendations accurately suggested ISIS supporters to follow to users who started following even one or two jihadist supporters.[56] Repeated exposure to terrorist social messages and events might result in an echo chamber, which reinforces an individual's disposition towards radical beliefs.

Third, Facebook's advertising algorithms also enable advertisers to target advertisements based on recipients' characteristics, such as race, religion and recent activities, which makes it easier for terrorists to proactively reach out to recipients who are most likely to be sympathetic to their cause.

iii. Low Cost

Further, online platforms considerably lower the cost of disseminating terrorist propaganda and recruitment. Instead of sending mass mails, terrorists can upload materials to online platforms and message their followers online at little to zero cost. As noted earlier, they can also take advantage of algorithms used by online platforms to target their audience more accurately. The prevalence of terrorist content online also increases the likelihood of self-radicalisation, further reducing terrorists' cost of recruitment.

[53] Bloom, Tiflati and Horgan (n 14) 1242–43.

[54] ibid 1243.

[55] In *Force v Facebook* (n 3), the plaintiffs alleged that Facebook directed content generated by Hamas leaders and their associates to users who were most interested in Hamas and its terrorist activities, including individuals who harmed the plaintiffs.

[56] JM Berger, 'Zero Degrees of al Qaeda' (*Foreign Policy*, 14 August 2013) at foreignpolicy.com/2013/08/14/zero-degrees-of-al-qaeda/ (accessed 29 July 2021). Berger and Morgan's study suggests that Twitter's email recommendations, as opposed to the 'who to follow' recommendations, lead to similar result. Berger and Morgan (n 7) 37.

Additionally, online communication tools, such as WhatsApp and Telegram, are generally free, which lowers the cost of mobilising supporters and planning attacks, especially those overseas. For example, in *Pennie v Twitter*, the plaintiffs argued that Hamas' ability to radicalise and influence individuals to conduct terrorist operations outside the Middle East would not have been possible without platforms such as Twitter, Facebook and Google.[57]

III. Online Platforms as Gatekeepers against Terrorist Activities

A. Rationale for Imposing Gatekeeper Liability on Online Platforms

The framework proposed by Reinier H Kraakman for analysing gatekeeper regimes provides a useful tool to determine whether, and to what extent, online platforms should be liable for publishing content that facilitates terrorist activities. In his seminal article, *Gatekeepers: The Anatomy of a Third-Party Enforcement Strategy*, Kraakman argues that successful gatekeeping requires (i) serious misconduct, which cannot be effectively deterred through direct enforcement against the primary wrongdoers; (ii) inadequate private gatekeeping incentives; (iii) the ability of gatekeepers to detect misconduct at reasonable cost; and (iv) the ability of gatekeepers to reliably prevent misconduct.[58] This chapter will examine each of these requirements and propose that it is sometimes appropriate to impose liability on online platforms to incentivise them to facilitate the detection and prevention of terrorist activities. The threat of liability can provide ex-ante incentives for platforms to dissociate themselves from wrongdoers and to serve as gatekeepers to prevent misconduct.

i. Ineffective Direct Deterrence

Direct deterrence is less likely to be effective against terrorists who intentionally use online platforms for unlawful purposes. As noted previously, online platforms provide their users with a level of anonymity, making it more difficult for prosecutors and victims of misconduct to track down their identities in real life. Moreover, terrorists, even if they can be located, might reside out of the jurisdiction. As a result, additional hurdles must be overcome to bring criminal or civil actions against them. As the court noted in *Boim v Holy Land Foundation for Relief & Development*, collecting damages against terrorist organisations, let alone terrorists (even assuming that they can be identified), is 'well-nigh impossible': they operate overseas, often act covertly and are impecunious.[59]

[57] *Pennie v Twitter* (n 3) 876.

[58] *RH Kraakman, 'Gatekeepers: The Anatomy of a Third-Party Enforcement Strategy' (1986) 2 Journal of Law, Economics, & Organization* 53, 61.

[59] *Boim v Holy Land Foundation for Relief & Development* 549 F 3d 685, 691 (7th Cir 2008).

By contrast, monetary judgments against online platforms that facilitate terrorist activities are likely to achieve better deterrent effects.

ii. *Online Platforms' Ability to Detect Misconduct*

Compared to the state or victims of terrorist activities, online platforms are sometimes the likely lower-cost providers to detect content that facilitates harmful terrorist activities on their platforms (including dissemination of terrorist propaganda, communications between terrorists and their supporters, and fundraising for terrorist activities). To begin with, many online platforms already engage in some content moderation to provide a hospitable environment for its users. It might be consistent with their business objectives to take additional steps to identify misuse of their platforms by terrorists and their supporters. Second, since each online platform is more familiar with its own design and the behaviour of its users, it is more likely able to implement cost-effective measures to identify errant users/content. For example, online platforms may be able to monitor and analyse their users' behaviour to identify suspicious activities: some activities may be obviously suspicious, while others might be suspicious because they represent a sharp departure from a user's ordinary behaviour.[60] This advantage is magnified by the fact that many online platforms possess proprietary data about their users, which may not be available to outsiders such as the police. Finally, given the sheer number of online platforms and the amount of user activity facilitated by each platform, it is impractical for victims or law enforcement to monitor them all.

Online platforms also have a variety of tools at their disposal to identify content that facilitates terrorist activities.[61] For example, they can periodically search for high-risk keywords, such as 'mujahideen' and 'beheading', on their platforms. For images and videos, platforms can sometimes rely on hash-based identification. A hash is a unique numerical representation of a file. GIFCT has created a database of 'hashes' of terrorist images and videos that have been removed by a GIFCT member. Each member can use these hashes to identify visually similar content and decide whether to remove such content from their platforms.[62] Platforms can also rely on their users to report suspicious content. YouTube, for instance, has a Trusted Flagger program, which provides tools for eligible individuals, government agencies and NGOs to notify YouTube of content that violates its Community Guidelines.[63] More recently, platforms have also experimented with using artificial intelligence to identify problematic content or users.[64] For example, Facebook has analysed texts that it has removed for praising or supporting terrorist organisations to develop algorithms that can detect similar posts.[65] It has also used

[60] D Lichtman and EA Posner, 'Holding Internet Service Providers Accountable' (2006) 14 *Supreme Court Economic Review* 221, 237.

[61] See, eg, Cohen-Almagor (n 1).

[62] GIFCT, 'Tech Innovation' at gifct.org/tech-innovation/ (accessed 27 July 2021).

[63] Google, 'YouTube Trusted Flagger Program – YouTube Help' at support.google.com/youtube/answer/7554338?hl=en (accessed 15 October 2021).

[64] See D Keller, 'Facebook Filters, Fundamental Rights, and the CJEU's Glawischnig-Piesczek Ruling' (2020) 69 *GRUR International* 616, 619.

[65] 'Hard Questions: How We Counter Terrorism' (*About Facebook*, 15 June 2017) at about.fb.com/news/2017/06/how-we-counter-terrorism/ (accessed 15 October 2021).

algorithms to try to identify terrorist accounts based on factors such as whether an account is friends with a large number of accounts disabled for terrorism and whether the account shares the same attributes as those accounts.[66]

iii. Online Platforms' Ability to Prevent Misconduct

Once an online platform has identified content that facilitates terrorist activities, it can remove that content or suspend the account that has uploaded that content. Removing such content is likely to cripple terrorists' ability to terrorise the public or to prepare for attacks. For example, removing gruesome images or videos depicting terrorist activities protects the public from any emotional harm that they might suffer from seeing such content. Removing terrorist propaganda helps reduce their ability to incite violence or recruit new members. Content removal also diverts terrorist resources to rebuilding their networks: Berger and Morgan's study suggests that more than 8 per cent of online activity by ISIS supporters was dedicated to rebuilding the network.[67]

However, even if one platform succeeds in deleting all terrorist-related content from its platform, it does not necessarily reduce the overall amount of such content in society. Terrorists and their supporters might simply turn to other platforms: for example, when Twitter started to suspend a large number of ISIS-supporting accounts, ISIS supporters moved to platforms such as Telegram to build their 'virtual caliphate'.[68] While this replacement effect represents a valid concern, it does not altogether preclude the effectiveness of enlisting online platforms as gatekeepers. If the majority of the largest online platforms collectively take measures to prevent unlawful terrorist content, they are likely to make a significant positive impact. They are likely to drive wrongdoers to use smaller and less mainstream platforms, which has a dual benefit: it prevents the less tech-savvy terrorists and their supporters, who are unaware of those platforms, from posting harmful content; moreover, content posted on those smaller platforms is likely to receive less exposure, which in turn reaches (and adversely affects) fewer viewers. Further, those smaller platforms may not contain the same features that terrorists find particularly attractive: for example, public online platforms such as Twitter are arguably more effective for distributing terrorist propaganda and recruiting new members than more private platforms such as Telegram. One Telegram post reportedly wrote:

> Telegram is not a media platform for dawa [proselytising] to all Muslims and the west. No one will enter your channel except the Ansar [ISIS supporters] who already know the truth. Or your enemies to report you. Rarely would you find someone from general public following you. That's why our main platform is [w]here the General Public is found. Like on Twitter and Facebook.[69]

[66] ibid.

[67] Berger and Morgan (n 7) 55.

[68] Bloom, Tiflati and Horgan (n 14).

[69] JM Berger and H Perez, 'The Islamic State's Diminishing Returns on Twitter: How suspensions are limiting the social networks of English-speaking ISIS supporters' (2016) *George Washington University Occasional Paper*, February 2016, 19, at extremism.gwu.edu/sites/g/files/zaxdzs2191/f/downloads/JMB%20Diminishing%20Returns.pdf (accessed 25 October 2021).

Removing content that facilitates terrorist activities, however, may not always be the most effective way to prevent such activities. For example, terrorists sometimes use WhatsApp to communicate with other members and to plan terrorist attacks. While WhatsApp might be able to use algorithms to identify and remove terrorist-related accounts, whether such efforts can effectively prevent or reduce the number of terrorist attacks in real life is far from clear. As noted earlier, it might cause terrorists to migrate to platforms that are less amenable to regulation. Worse still, it might tip off terrorists that their accounts are being monitored, and interfere with ongoing investigations by law-enforcement agencies. Removing suspicious content might also make it more difficult for law-enforcement agencies to collect evidence that may be used in legal actions against terrorists. In such cases, it might be more appropriate to require online platforms to report suspicious content/accounts to the relevant agency.

iv. High Transaction Costs for Private Contracting

Imposing gatekeeper liability on online platforms would not be necessary if those platforms already had an adequate incentive to serve as gatekeepers, or if individuals could effectively contract with those platforms for gatekeeping services. Neither is likely to be the case.

An online platform only has an incentive to engage in gatekeeping where its expected benefits of doing so exceed the expected costs. Assuming that online platforms are not held liable for user-generated content, the expected benefit of gatekeeping mainly derives from the increase in profit-generating users (calculated as the increase in users/user engagement multiplied by the average value of each user/user engagement to the platform) as a result of content moderation measures. By contrast, the expected costs of gatekeeping mainly consist of (i) the costs of detecting and preventing content that facilitates terrorist activities, and (ii) a decrease in profit-generating users (if any). If a platform's expected cost of gatekeeping exceeds the expected benefit, it will not have an adequate incentive to serve as a gatekeeper, even if doing so would be welfare-enhancing from society's perspective. This may be the case, for example, where, despite the presence of content that facilitates terrorist activities, very few platform users choose to leave the platform (eg, where the platform's recommendation algorithm accurately tailors content to users' personal tastes).

Even if an online platform does not have an adequate incentive to act as a gatekeeper, one might argue that third parties, such as platform users, might contract with the platform for gatekeeping services. However, such private contracting is unlikely to occur for several reasons. First, terrorists and terrorist supporters are unlikely to pressure online platforms to remove terrorist-related content. On the contrary, they are likely to persuade the platform to take measures to facilitate their unlawful activities. Second, victims of a terrorist attack may not be using the same online platforms that terrorists used to plan the attack or to recruit members to carry out that attack. Victims may not even be aware of the role played by a particular platform in causing their harm. They are therefore unlikely to be able to negotiate with that platform ex-ante to take measures to prevent terrorist activities.

B. Costs of Imposing Gatekeeper Liability on Online Platforms

Nevertheless, imposing gatekeeper liability on online platforms can impose costs on both the platforms and society at large. It can only be justified if the benefits of imposing such liability outweigh those costs, which are outlined below.

i. Costs of Detecting Terrorist Activities

To begin with, platforms must incur costs in detecting unlawful use of their services. A platform can employ its own agents to do so, rely on the user community to report suspicious behaviour, or develop algorithms to identify such content or users. In practice, each of these detection measures can impose significant costs on the platform. First of all, human content moderators are limited by their reading speed and the number of hours they can work each day. Depending on the amount of user-generated content hosted by a platform, the platform may have to hire a large number of human moderators to sift through that content to distinguish unlawful materials from lawful ones. For example, Facebook reportedly employed 15,000 content moderators in 2020, while researchers recommended that it double that number.[70] Second, while an online platform can save some monitoring costs by relying on its users to report unlawful content, it still has to incur labour costs reviewing the reports made by those users and deciding what actions to take in response. Third, employing automated filters requires a platform to invest significant upfront costs to develop and train algorithms to distinguish unlawful and lawful content: for example, training an algorithm to identify anomalies in user behaviour often requires the platform to code a significant amount of existing user data to train the algorithm. Moreover, the platform also has to incur on-going costs to ensure that the algorithm remains accurate and efficient. This is compounded by the fact that algorithms trained to detect one type of unlawful content may be ill-equipped to detect other types of illegal materials.[71] While giant platforms such as Facebook, Twitter and YouTube can afford to invest in the development of automated tools and employ tens of thousands of moderators to remove potentially unlawful content, smaller and less established platforms may not have the financial or human resources to do so.

ii. Over-Removal of Terrorist-Related Content

Imposing liability on online platforms can sometimes have a significant chilling effect on free speech. As Assaf Hamdani has pointed out, there is a divergence of incentives between online platforms, which do not fully capture the value of the content they host, and their users.[72] Platforms have a greater incentive to remove potentially unlawful

[70] G Edelman, 'Stop Saying Facebook Is "Too Big to Moderate"' (*Wired*, 28 July 2020) at wired.com/story/stop-saying-facebook-too-big-to-moderate/ (accessed 27 September 2021).

[71] Even Facebook only recently started experimenting with more generalised algorithms to moderate content. See S Condon, 'Facebook Shares AI Advancements Improving Content Moderation' (*ZDNet*, 18 August 2021) at zdnet.com/article/facebook-shares-ai-advancements-improving-content-moderation/ (accessed 27 September 2021).

[72] A Hamdani, 'Who's Liable for Cyberwrongs' (2001) 87 *Cornell Law Review* 901, 917.

content, because their decisions do not adequately take into account the cost of wrongful removal to their users.[73] In a similar vein, Felix Wu and Seth Kreimer claimed that this mismatch in incentives can lead to significant collateral censorship problems, which is objectionable on First Amendment grounds.[74] From a platform's perspective, instead of investing considerable time and costs in assessing its exposure to legal claims, it is arguably more cost-effective to take down most, if not all, questionable content to avoid potential lawsuits.[75]

The risk of over-removal of terrorist-related content is further exacerbated by three factors. First, the line between terrorist and acceptable speech is sometimes blurred. To begin with, different countries have different lists of officially designated terrorist organisations.[76] Moreover, as one commentator has noted, certain extremist groups 'purposely use humour and irony in their messaging to mask violent intentions'.[77] Second, platforms increasingly resort to automated filters to remove questionable content. While automated filters are better at deleting duplicates of specific content previously found to be unlawful, they are often unable to recognise the contexts in which an expression is used and therefore cannot reliably detect unlawful content in novel situations.[78] Filters are also known to produce false positives (eg, deleting human rights videos in an attempt to remove terrorist content) and false negatives (ie, a failure to flag terrorist content) due to various technical reasons.[79] Third, third parties and possibly the government might abuse a platform's monitoring system and request removal of lawful content to further their own objectives (eg, to stifle competition or political dissent).[80]

More importantly, even if a piece of content facilitates terrorist activities, removing that content may not be the best course of action.[81] Allowing terrorists and their supporters to publish certain content carries several benefits. First, it provides an opportunity for them to interact with people from different backgrounds and to see different responses to their views. This reduces the likelihood that people with extremist views would retreat to a corner of the Internet with like-minded people, where their views are reinforced in an echo chamber.[82] There is some evidence of this echo

[73] ibid 919–20.

[74] SF Kreimer, 'Censorship by Proxy: The First Amendment, Internet Intermediaries, and the Problem of the Weakest Link' (2006) 155 *University of Pennsylvania Law Review* 11. FT Wu, 'Collateral Censorship and the Limits of Intermediary Immunity' (2011) 87 *Notre Dame Law Review* 293.

[75] D Keller, 'Empirical Evidence of "Over-Removal" by Internet Companies under Intermediary Liability Laws' (*Center for Internet and Society*, 12 October 2015) at cyberlaw.stanford.edu/blog/2015/10/empirical-evidence-over-removal-internet-companies-under-intermediary-liability-laws (accessed 21 January 2021).

[76] See, eg, B Freedman, 'Officially Blacklisted Extremist/Terrorist (Support) Organizations: A Comparison of Lists from Six Countries and Two International Organizations' (2010) 4 *Perspectives on Terrorism* 46.

[77] C Wallner, 'Against the Clock: Can the EU's New Strategy for Terrorist Content Removal Work?' (*RUSI*, 26 January 2021) at rusi.org/commentary/against-clock-can-eu-new-strategy-terrorist-content-removal-work (accessed 24 April 2021).

[78] D Keller, 'Internet Platforms: Observations on Speech, Danger, and Money' (Hoover Institution, 2018) at hoover.org/sites/default/files/research/docs/keller_webreadypdf_final.pdf (accessed 12 April 2019) 6–7.

[79] See, eg, E Engstrom and N Feamster, 'The Limits of Filtering: A Look at the Functionality & Shortcomings of Content Detection Tools' (Engine, 2017) at engine.is/the-limits-of-filtering (accessed 25 January 2021).

[80] Citron (n 1) 1057.

[81] For a discussion of various problems with content removal, see E Goldman, 'Content Moderation Remedies' (2021) 28 *Michigan Technology Law Review* 1, 21–23.

[82] For a detailed examination of the echo chamber effect, see E Pariser, *The Filter Bubble: How the New Personalized Web is Changing What We Read and How We Think* (London, Penguin Books, 2011).

chamber effect: Berger and Morgan's study found that while ISIS-supporting social networks had been substantially reduced by Twitter's suspension campaign, the remaining ISIS supporters became 'more internally focused over time'; for example, they were 'increasingly following other ISIS supporters rather than a broader selection of accounts'.[83] This may in turn enhance ISIS' ability to selectively present information to its adherents, facilitating its indoctrination and radicalisation process. Related to this, public discussion in an open forum also provides an opportunity for counter-speech to persuade potential, and possibly existing, terrorists to adopt more peaceful measures to express their ideology and beliefs. Members of a more internally focused terrorist organisation would have less opportunity to be exposed to such deradicalising influences. Additionally, allowing people an opportunity to express extremist views gives them a chance to vent; as a result, they might be less likely to resort to violence in real life. Finally, it might also provide law-enforcement agencies with an important source of information to monitor and thwart terrorist activities.[84] Law-enforcement agencies may be able to locate terrorists through the information they post on online platforms: some ISIS supporters on Twitter revealed reliable GPS coordinates in ISIS territories.[85] Gill and others also show that 5 per cent of the offenders they studied signalled their plans to engage in terrorist attacks online prior to their attacks.[86] Law enforcement might also be able to subpoena information about terrorist suspects from the platform they use, or infiltrate online terrorist groups to carry out sting operations.

iii. Litigation Costs

Imposing liability on online platforms for user-generated content also exposes them to potentially significant litigation costs. Any person aggrieved by a piece of content might bring an action against the platform hosting that content. Even assuming that most of those claims are unmeritorious, the legal costs involved in reviewing and defending such claims can potentially render a platform insolvent. As the Ninth Circuit noted in *Fair Housing Council of San Fernando Valley v Roommates.com*, websites could be forced to 'face death by ten thousand duck-bites, fighting off claims that they promoted or encourage – or at least tacitly assented to – the illegality of third parties'.[87] The court therefore concluded that section 230 of the Communications Decency Act (CDA), which provides online platforms with wide immunity for user-generated content in the

[83] Berger and Morgan (n 7) 37. See also Berger and Perez (n 69) 4 ('ISIS English-language social networks are extremely insular').

[84] E Ottolenghi, 'Social Media is an Intel Gold Mine. Why Aren't Governments Using It?' (*Foreign Policy*, 26 March 2021) at foreignpolicy.com/2021/03/26/social-media-big-tech-facebook-twitter-intelligence-sharing-law-enforcement/ (accessed 8 June 2021).

[85] Berger and Morgan (n 7) 54–55. Interestingly, anecdotal observation from Berger and Morgan's study indicates that seemingly less influential Twitter accounts with very small numbers of followers tend to provide the most valuable intelligence.

[86] Gill and others (n 17) 109. See also J Mueller (ed), *Terrorism Since 9/11: The American Cases* (Mershon Center, Ohio State University, 2020) 1 at politicalscience.osu.edu/faculty/jmueller/SINCE.pdf (accessed 28 July 2021) (revealing that a significant number of them were arrested after voicing support for terrorism or plans to carry out attacks on Facebook).

[87] *Fair Housing Council of San Fernando Valley v Roommates.com* 521 F 3d 1157 (9th Cir 2008) 1173.

United States, must be interpreted to protect websites from 'having to fight costly and protracted legal battles'.[88] Similarly, Eric Goldman pointed out that an important benefit of section 230 of the CDA is allowing unmeritorious claims to be dismissed at an early stage, thereby reducing a defendant's out-of-pocket costs to defeating such claims.[89]

iv. Disrupt Valuable Services and Market Competition

Another concern is that imposing gatekeeper liability on online platforms might force them to reduce their activity level, which could result in a net loss to society. Since online platforms do not internalise all the positive externalities of their activities, requiring them to internalise a disproportionate proportion of the negative externalities they generate is likely to put them in a difficult position: a platform might be driven out of business either because it cannot afford the costs of detecting or preventing user misconduct, or because it cannot afford the legal costs of defending its actions. To shield itself from potential liability from user misconduct, the platform may choose to discontinue part or all of its business. For example, Craigslist closed down its personals section after the passing of the Allow States and Victims to Fight Online Sex Trafficking Act of 2017, which created an exception to the broad immunity provided by section 230 of the CDA.[90] Nevertheless, those discontinued services might sometimes be on balance beneficial for society.

Worse still, new and potentially welfare-enhancing online platforms might never appear in the market if the costs of gatekeeping were prohibitively high. While established tech companies such as Google and Facebook can afford to invest millions or billions of dollars to comply with regulatory requirements, newly launched startups might lack the money or manpower to do so. Imposing overly burdensome gatekeeping obligations on those new market entrants might in turn make it more difficult for them to compete with existing dominant players, which further entrenches the latter's market power and reduces the amount of competition in the market.[91]

IV. Platform Liability for Publication of Unlawful Terrorist Content

Section III has set out both the benefits and the costs of imposing gatekeeper liability on online platforms to combat terrorism. The difficulty lies in designing a carefully calibrated liability regime where its cost can be justified by its benefit. There are two main

[88] ibid 1175.

[89] E Goldman, 'Why Section 230 is Better Than the First Amendment' (2019) 95 *Notre Dame Law Review Reflections* 33, 40–41.

[90] M Kennedy, 'Craigslist Shuts Down Personals Section After Congress Passes Bill On Trafficking' (*NPR*, 23 March 2018) at npr.org/sections/thetwo-way/2018/03/23/596460672/craigslist-shuts-down-personals-section-after-congress-passes-bill-on-traffickin (accessed 29 September 2021).

[91] E Goldman, 'An Overview of the United States' Section 230 Internet Immunity' in G Frosio (ed), *The Oxford Handbook of Online Intermediary Liability* (Oxford, Oxford University Press, 2020) 155, 163.

approaches to imposing liability on online platforms for publishing unlawful terrorist content generated by its users. This section will take a closer look at the advantages and disadvantages of both approaches.

A. Secondary Liability for Assisting Users in Publishing Unlawful Terrorist Content

The first approach imposes liability on an online platform for assisting its users in publishing unlawful terrorist content.[92] There are two potential problems with this approach.

The first problem relates to over-removal of terrorist-related content. As explained more fully in section III, online platforms have a greater incentive than their users to remove potentially unlawful content because their decisions do not adequately take into account the cost of wrongful removal for their users.[93] Moreover, online platforms are likely to prefer removing potentially unlawful content from their platforms over less drastic measures, such as restricting access to such content or facilitating counter-speech against terrorism. The latter measures are not only more costly to implement, but also have a greater chance of exposing platforms to liability for user-generated content. However, as noted earlier, removing terrorist-related content may not always produce the most socially beneficial result.

The second problem is that imposing liability on online platforms does not ensure that platforms will implement the socially optimal monitoring measures. In theory, monitoring is optimal when a platform invests in any monitoring measure for which the social cost of monitoring (ie the platform's costs of monitoring) is less than or equal to the social benefit of monitoring (ie reduction in harmful terrorist content).[94] However, as explained in section III.B, online platforms do not always have adequate incentives to invest in monitoring, even where it is socially beneficial to do so.

These two concerns can be alleviated in several ways.

i. Narrowly Define 'Unlawful Terrorist Content'

To begin with, to reduce the risk of over-removal, we can define 'unlawful terrorist content' narrowly to include only content that is likely to cause serious harm to people.

[92] If an online platform knows that one of its users is a terrorist, who uses its platform to facilitate terrorist activities, then the platform can potentially be liable for aiding, abetting or conspiring with a person who commits an act of terrorism. However, in practice, it is often difficult for a platform to know for certain whether a user belongs to a terrorist organisation. See Z Bedell and B Wittes, 'Tweeting Terrorists, Part I: Don't Look Now But a Lot of Terrorist Groups Are Using Twitter' (*Lawfare*, 14 February 2016) at lawfareblog.com/tweeting-terrorists-part-i-dont-look-now-lot-terrorist-groups-are-using-twitter (accessed 22 April 2021).

[93] Hamdani (n 72) 919–20.

[94] Follows J Arlen, 'Corporate Criminal Liability: Theory and Evidence' in A Harel and KN Hylton (eds), *Research Handbook on the Economics of Criminal Law* (Cheltenham, Edward Elgar Publishing, 2013) 144, 173 ('Corporate policing is optimal when firms invest in any policing measure for which the direct social cost of policing (as measure by the cost to the firm of the investment in policing) is less than or equal to the social benefit of policing, as measured by the social benefit of the crimes deterred.').

Examples of such content include images and videos of violent terrorist activities and instructional manuals on how to carry out terrorist attacks. By contrast, holding a platform liable for any 'opinion or belief that is supportive of a [terrorist] organisation' might be casting the net too wide.[95] For example, comments that seek to explain the role of religion in a terrorist event might sometimes be interpreted as supporting that terrorist organisation.

Narrowly defining unlawful terrorist content has several benefits. First, it ensures that the social benefit of removing such content is high, which increases the likelihood that the benefit of imposing gatekeeper liability on online platforms outweighs the cost. Moreover, since unlawful terrorist content (narrowly defined) likely violates vital community values, members of society, including platform owners, users and the general public, all have an interest in detecting and removing such content. It is therefore less objectionable to require them to bear some of the costs associated with the imposition of gatekeeper liability. Further, online platforms will have an incentive to remove only terrorist content that is likely to cause serious harm. This in turn enables platforms to experiment with less drastic content moderation measures for less harmful content. In addition, providing clearer guidance on what type of terrorist content is likely to cause serious harm will help reduce a platform's compliance costs considerably.[96]

ii. Knowledge-Based Liability

The risk of over-removal of terrorist-related content can be further reduced by holding online platforms liable only if they know the relevant content amounts to unlawful terrorist content.[97] This knowledge requirement has several implications.[98] First, a platform cannot be liable if it only has general knowledge that its service can and probably

[95] The UK Terrorism Act 2000, s 12(1A), provides that 'A person commits an offence if the person (a) expresses an opinion or belief that is supportive of a proscribed organisation, and (b) in doing so is reckless as to whether a person to whom the expression is directed will be encouraged to support a proscribed organisation.'

[96] For example, the United Kingdom has provided additional guidance in the *Interim Code of Practice on Terrorist Content and Activity Online* (Home Office, 2020) at assets.publishing.service.gov.uk/government/uploads/system/uploads/attachment_data/file/944036/1704b_ICOP__online_terrorist_content_v.2_11-12-20.pdf (accessed 25 October 2021).

[97] Here, knowledge should include actual knowledge, so-called 'blind-eye knowledge' and possibly reckless indifference. For a more detailed discussion of the knowledge requirement for accessory liability, see P Davies, 'The Mental Element of Accessory Liability' (2022) 138 *LQR* 32.

[98] The proposed knowledge requirement appears consistent with the US courts' interpretation of the Digital Millennium Copyright Act, which provides that a platform will lose protection under its 'safe harbor' provisions if it (a) has actual knowledge of the infringing material/activity; (b) is aware of facts or circumstances from which infringing activity is apparent; or (c) after acquiring such knowledge or awareness, does not remove the infringing material expeditiously. For example, in *Viacom International v YouTube* 676 F 3d 19 (2nd Cir 2012) 30–33, the court emphasised that the relevant knowledge or awareness must relate to the specific infringing material in question. Proving that YouTube was aware that a significant proportion of the material on its platform was infringing (eg, YouTube's survey estimated that 75–80% of its streams contained copyright material) was held to be insufficient. Moreover, according to *Capitol Records, LLC v Vimeo, LLC* 826 F 3d 78 (2nd Cir 2016) 95–97, the mere fact that a website's employee has viewed an infringing video, and that the video contains nearly all of a copyrighted song that is 'recognizable,' would be insufficient to satisfy the knowledge requirement. This is because the employee might have viewed the video only briefly or for a purpose that '[has] nothing to do with recognition of infringing music'.

has been used to publish unlawful terrorist content. The platform's knowledge must relate to the specific piece of unlawful content in question. Second, before a platform can be held liable for a piece of content, at least one person acting on behalf of the platform (eg one of its employees) must have had a reasonable opportunity to review that content for the purpose of determining whether it is unlawful. For example, the mere fact that a platform has used an algorithm to check the content on its platform for spelling errors is probably not sufficient proof that the platform has knowledge of any unlawful terrorist content. Third, if the person acting on behalf of the platform genuinely, though mistakenly, believes that the relevant content is lawful, the platform generally should not be liable for publishing it. The proposed knowledge-based liability provides online platforms with greater certainty as to the scope of their liability, thereby reducing their incentive to remove most, if not all, terrorist-related content.

One problem with the knowledge requirement is that it sometimes provides an additional incentive for a platform to scale back its monitoring measures to detect unlawful content. From a platform's perspective, there are two ways to avoid potential liability for user-generated content: (i) avoid acquiring information about its users or the content they generate; and (ii) remove or refuse to publish any content that it deems to be unlawful terrorist content. It is possible that some platforms might find it more cost-effective to adopt the first strategy, since it also reduces their monitoring costs. Therefore, knowledge-based liability for user-generated content should be supplemented with measures to incentivise platforms to invest in monitoring.

iii. Duty to Monitor Terrorist Content

There are two ways to incentivise online platforms to invest in optimal monitoring measures to detect unlawful terrorist content. The first option is to impose liability on platforms that fail to discharge their monitoring duties (the 'stick' approach). As such, a platform will be separately liable for (i) assisting in publishing unlawful terrorist content and (ii) failing to take adequate monitoring measures. The second option is to reward platforms that discharge their requisite monitoring duties (the 'carrot' approach). The reward may be financial (eg a tax break), or may take the form of immunity from secondary liability for publishing unlawful terrorist content.

For the stick approach to succeed, the benefits of monitoring must, from a platform's perspective, outweigh its costs. The main benefit of monitoring is avoiding the sanctions for failing to do so. In other words, the sanctions imposed on a platform for its failure to monitor multiplied by the probability of enforcement should generally exceed a platform's costs of monitoring. One problem with the stick approach is that some platforms do not internalise many of the positive externalities generated by their activities. As a result, the amount of profit they generate might be lower than the cost of optimal monitoring. However, it would on balance be socially beneficial for these platforms to continue operating if they generate sufficient amounts of positive externalities. Adopting the stick approach might sometimes put these platforms in a difficult situation: they do not have sufficient resources to either adequately discharge their monitoring duties or pay the fines for failing to do so; as such, they have no choice but to cease business.

There are two possible responses to this problem. The first is to adopt the stick approach only for low-cost monitoring measures that most platforms are able to undertake. This may include, for example, using search functions to locate accounts that self-identify as terrorists/terrorist organisations, recording certain user information and cooperating with police investigations (if any). When the cost of a particular monitoring measure is sufficiently high (eg, designing algorithms to identify terrorist accounts), the government can either subsidise the measure or take the carrot approach instead.[99] The second response is to impose different monitoring requirements for online platforms depending on their size and profitability: bigger and more profitable platforms would be subject to stricter monitoring duties. For example, the new Digital Service Act proposed by the European Commission imposes more stringent regulatory requirements for very large platforms.[100]

B. Liability for Failing to Implement Appropriate Compliance System

The second approach imposes liability for failure to implement an appropriate compliance system to minimise the risk of harm caused by user-generated content. An example of this approach can be found in UK's draft Online Safety Bill 2021, which imposes a duty to 'operate a service using proportionate systems and processes' designed to minimise or prevent access to various types of unlawful content.[101] This approach focuses less on a platform's failure to remove a specific piece of content and more on whether the platform has an adequate system of rules to address unlawful content, which carries several benefits. First, since the presence of unlawful terrorist content does not necessarily lead to liability, platforms have less incentive to remove all potentially unlawful content. Second, this approach is sufficiently flexible to facilitate the development of different content moderation rules, depending on the nature and severity of the harm posed by the content in question as well as the size and capability of the relevant platform. Content removal is but one of the tools available to a platform.

Nevertheless, there are two potential problems with this approach. First, this approach relies on the lawmaker to set the appropriate monitoring and preventive duties for each online platform. It therefore imposes significant costs on the court and/or the regulator to determine the magnitude of the harm caused by various types of terrorist content, as well as the costs associated with different measures for detecting and preventing such content. Moreover, since a platform is liable only when it fails to meet the standard of care set by the lawmakers, the effectiveness of this approach depends largely on the ability of the relevant lawmaker to accurately ascertain the optimal standard of care.

[99] This is consistent with Geest and Dari-Mattiacci's theory. They argue that the carrot approach should be preferred in two cases. First, when the lawmaker does not know what to expect from each individual citizen, in which case 'sticks are likely to punish citizens who are unable to comply with the norm and likely to cause wasteful transaction costs, risks, and undesirable wealth changes'. Second, when the lawmaker needs to require significantly greater efforts from some citizens than from others. G De Geest and G Dari-Mattiacci, 'The Rise of Carrots and the Decline of Sticks' (2013) 80 *University of Chicago Law Review* 341.

[100] European Commission, 'Europe Fit for the Digital Age: New Online Rules for Platforms' at ec.europa.eu/info/strategy/priorities-2019-2024/europe-fit-digital-age/digital-services-act-ensuring-safe-and-accountable-online-environment/europe-fit-digital-age-new-online-rules-platforms_en (accessed 18 October 2021).

[101] See, eg, UK draft Online Safety Bill 2021, cls 9(3) and 10(3).

A key question, which is outside the scope of this chapter, is which institution is best positioned to perform this task.

The second problem relates to enforcement. Platform users are likely to encounter significant informational hurdles to observe the actual content moderation rules implemented by an online platform and to demonstrate that those rules fall below the standard imposed by the lawmaker. For example, since users do not have access to a platform's internal records, they may have to spend costly time and effort to document content moderation decisions made by the platform over an extended period of time. By contrast, regulators are better positioned to require platforms to provide information to assess their compliance with their duties.[102] Nevertheless, an important drawback to relying on regulators for enforcement is that they usually have limited financial and human resources, and can only carry out a limited number of investigations each year.

V. Conclusion

This chapter argues that it is sometimes appropriate to impose gatekeeper liability on online platforms for publishing certain terrorist-related content generated by their users. However, a platform should only be liable for a piece of content if it has knowledge that the content is likely to cause serious harm to others. At the same time, online platforms should be subject to rules that incentivise them to monitor harmful content on their platforms. Further, the two approaches to platform liability examined in this chapter are not mutually exclusive: a successful gatekeeper liability regime will likely need to incorporate both approaches.

[102] See, eg, UK's draft Online Safety Bill 2021, which confers various powers to require information and to investigate on Ofcom, the United Kingdom's communications regulator.

7

How Intermediaries Entrench Google's Position in the Advertising Display Market

ROGER P ALFORD*

I. Introduction

The United States is the largest advertising market in the world. In previous decades, most advertising was via traditional ads in print, television and radio. Consumers accessed these media outlets for free or for subsidised rates. These ads were not targeted to specific users but rather reflected the demographics of the average audience member for the particular media outlet. Today the majority of ad spending is digital, with digital ad spending in the United States making up approximately 54 per cent of total ad spend in 2019.[1] According to industry analysts, 'It is projected that digital advertising expenditures in the United States will increase by more than a 100 per cent between 2019 and 2024. In that five year period US digital ad spend will grow from 132.46 to 278.53 billion dollars.'[2]

Online display advertising differs from traditional advertising in two important respects. Most display ad inventory is bought and sold through real-time auctions and centralised trading venues called 'ad exchanges'. Traditional advertising agreements, by contrast, are negotiated in person between publisher and advertiser executives. Second, unlike traditional ads, which appear the same to everyone, online display ads target specific users, and those real-time sales occur each time you visit a website or mobile app. Almost every time you load a page, the ad space targeted specifically to you is auctioned. The old saying in the traditional advertising industry is that 'half my

* The author is an expert consultant for the Texas Office of Attorney General in *Texas v Google*, Civil Action No: 4:20-CV-957-SDJ. Consistent with that role, portions of this article mirror allegations in the Amended Complaint in *Texas v Google*. See complaint available at www.texasattorneygeneral.gov/news/releases/filings-related-google.

[1] R Sentance, 'Thirteen Stats that Show How Advertising is Changing' (*Econsultancy*, 22 September 2020) at econsultancy.com/13-stats-that-show-how-advertising-is-changing (accessed 28 November 2021).

[2] Statista Research Department, 'Digital advertising spending in the United States from 2019 to 2024' (*Statista*, 21 May 2021) at statista.com/statistics/242552/digital-advertising-spending-in-the-us/ (accessed 28 November 2021).

advertising spend is wasted; the trouble is I don't know which half'. That is not the case with online targeted ads. Instead of targeting broad audience segments with content that represents the demographics of a broad audience, digital advertisers are able to target specific users and serve ads in real time, taking into account factors such as an individual user's interests, browsing history, time and location.

Search ads and display ads are in different but related markets. A key difference between search and display advertising is that search ads help satisfy demand while display advertising helps create demand. Search advertising is a form of paid advertising that promotes a particular product on a search engine result page. Displays are dramatically different, allowing ads to be displayed across different websites that users are browsing across the Web. Display ads place ads directly in front of customers without waiting for them to search for a particular product.[3] In this sense, display and search advertising are complementary tools, not competing ones.

We take for granted that the Internet is free and open. Hiding information behind a paywall is the exception, and the primary mechanism for monetising online content is through programmatic advertising. Google's take rate (or buy–sell spread) between what the advertiser pays and what the publisher receives is exorbitant – between 30 and 50 per cent per transaction.[4] This far exceeds the commodity pricing one would expect with exchange markets. The result is inefficient spending by advertisers and lost revenue for publishers. The ripple effects of this lost revenue are spread across the economy: 'Since 2004, this sector in the US has shed 47% of newsroom jobs, paywalls and subscription prices have increased, and 20% of newspapers have closed.'[5]

Publishers' and advertisers' inability to secure a reasonable return on their investments from online advertising threatens the sustainability of the free Internet. Google's dominant role across the ad tech marketplace threatens to transform much of the Internet into a closed system controlled by Google intermediaries that each charge a toll at billions of daily online transactions. Without meaningful remedies to thwart Google's monopoly behaviour, a Google tax of our online activity will become a permanent feature of our daily lives.

This chapter discusses the anticompetitive market for online display advertising. It discusses how Google has established numerous intermediaries to advantage itself, exclude competition and harm consumers. It summarises the nature of a display advertising market in which Google intermediaries preference one another across the ad tech stack in order to acquire, maintain and solidify Google's monopoly positions. As a result of Google's monopolies, the take rates of Google intermediaries reflect monopoly

[3] C Hatch, 'Display Ads vs Search Ads: Everything You Need to Know, Disruptive Advertising' (*Disruptive Advertising*, 1 April 2020) at disruptiveadvertising.com/ppc/display-vs-search-ads/ (accessed 28 November 2021).

[4] See A Barker, 'Half of Online Ad Spending Goes to Industry Middlemen' *Financial Times* (London, 5 May 2020) at ft.com/content/9ee0ebd3-346f-45b1-8b92-aa5c597d4389 (accessed 28 November 2021); and R Benes, 'Why Tech Firms Obtain Most of the Money in Programmatic Ad Buys' (*eMarketer*, 16 April 2018) at emarketer.com/content/why-tech-firms-obtain-most-of-the-money-in-programmatic-purchases (accessed 28 November 2021) (industry analysts from Warc estimating intermediaries collectively charge 55% of programmatic spend worldwide, based on data shared by advertising agency Magna Global).

[5] D Srinivasan, 'Why Google Dominates Advertising Markets: Competition Policy Could Lean on the Principles of Financial Market Regulation' (2020) 24 *Stanford Technology Law Review* 55.

pricing behaviour, leaving publishers with far less revenue than they deserve, and advertising spending far less than they should. It suggests that the relationship between Google intermediaries is the key to understanding how the display advertising market is fundamentally broken.

II. Industry Background

Online display advertising is the market for users' time and attention. The average American spends several hours every day on the Internet.[6] When an Internet user freely accesses a website that employs advertising, they are not a consumer, they are the product. Their time and attention are for sale to the highest bidder. The website is the 'publisher' offering its online real estate to advertisers that will target individual users. As the website is loading, an instantaneous advertising auction occurs for the users' time. The publisher has hired a Google intermediary – called a publisher ad server – to identify the users who are visiting the publishers' webpage, tag each individual user with a unique ID, and then leverage information provided by another Google intermediary to sell to a third Google intermediary, an ad broker that represents advertisers that want to provide targeted advertising on the publishers' website. The advertisement is user-specific – targeted to the particular individual based on information Google has gathered about that user. This auction can occur on a number of different exchanges, but Google users its power to steer the transactions toward the Google-owned and Google-operated exchange.

This complex process of serving display ads to users happens billions of times a day to millions of Internet users. Every time every consumer accesses every ad-supported website, a remarkable transaction occurs of pricing, clearing, executing and settling a display ad. Effective control of the online display market is equivalent to controlling the currency of Internet.

Display ads are targeted to each individual user. Google CEO Sundar Pichai represents that Google will never sell personal information to anyone.[7] But Google leverages intimate user data and personal information to broker billions of daily online ad impressions between publishers and advertisers that target individual users based almost entirely on their personal information. The amount of information Google has obtained about each individual user is staggering. Based on Google's default settings of Google products alone, it includes everything you have ever searched on Google or on Chrome, every email you have sent or read on Gmail, everywhere and every time you have ever travelled on Google Maps, everything you have ever done on every Android app, every

[6] See, eg, G Deyan, 'How Much Time Does the Average American Spend on Their Phone in 2021?' (*TechJury*, 1 November 2021) at techjury.net/blog/how-much-time-does-the-average-american-spend-on-their-phone/#gref (accessed 28 November 2021) (average of 6 hours per day); H Lebo et al, 'The 2017 Digital Future Report: Surveying the Digital Future' (Los Angeles, CA, Center for the Digital Future, 2017) at digitalcenter.org/wp-content/uploads/2013/10/2017-Digital-Future-Report.pdf (accessed 28 November 2021) (average of 24 hours per week).

[7] S Pichai, 'Privacy Should Not Be a Luxury Good' *New York Times* (New York, 7 May 2019) at nytimes.com/2019/05/07/opinion/google-sundar-pichai-privacy.html (accessed 28 November 2021).

video you have ever watched on YouTube, every meeting you have ever attended on Google Calendar and everyone you know in your Google Contacts. It also includes a massive amount of third-party data, including information from sites and apps that use Google services and that every online publisher and advertiser using Google ad products has about the user. Google uses that information to sell targeted ads to every Google user. It also wields that information as a weapon to force publishers and advertisers to use Google intermediaries when buying and selling display ads.

The original vision of Google was to make the world a better place. At one time its corporate vision was to 'organize the world's information and make it universally accessible and useful'.[8] Google's motto became famous: 'Don't be evil.' For the old Google, this motto meant creating a company that 'does good things for the world even if we forego some short term gains'.[9] The halcyon days of Google's youth are a distant memory. Today, Google has dropped the 'don't be evil' motto, and its business practices reflect that change. Again and again we see that Google's goal is to eliminate competition and destroy consumer choice. And it uses a network of intermediaries to accomplish the goal of monopolising the markets it controls.

To the general public, Google presents itself as a company that 'connects people and information all around the world for free'.[10] Which begs the question: how can a company that provides its services for free become one of the wealthiest companies in the history of the world with annual revenue exceeding $182 billion? The answer is that in terms of its business model, Google is not a search company, or an information company, or a content company. It is an advertising company. Any time anyone uses Google for free they are not the consumer, they are the product. Google leverages private, intimate, personal information of its users to create the largest advertising company in the history of the world.

Google is able to maintain its monopoly by establishing its presence in almost every sector of online display advertising markets. This allows Google to influence behaviour in multiple complementary and related markets and generate conglomerate effects.

Google is a super monopoly that has a monopoly position in numerous markets. Google has monopoly power in the various online advertising display markets. In essence, publishers sell their display advertising space to advertisers through ad exchanges. The structure of this market is complicated, but in most respects it is similar to other exchange markets such as financial markets. There are sellers on one side of the market, buyers on the other side of the market, exchanges or auctions where buyers and sellers transact with one another, and ancillary markets that provide services – such as information – to buyers and/or sellers.

The online display advertising market benefits from significant network effects, with the substantial adoption and usage of exchange platforms by publishers on the one side and advertisers on the other side, which increases the value of the exchanges for everyone. Generally speaking, publishers and advertisers prefer to multi-home across

[8] L Page and S Brin, '2004 Founders' IPO Letter' (*Alphabet Investor Relations*, 2004) at abc.xyz/investor/founders-letters/2004-ipo-letter/ (accessed 28 November 2021).

[9] ibid.

[10] ibid.

multiple exchanges to promote exchange competition, which reduces exchange fees, enhances quality and increases output. This assumes that there is sufficient ad inventory and publisher supply to generate network effects on multiple exchanges to justify multi-homing. Significant multi-homing through multiple exchanges results in market-wide benefits, including increased volume and commoditised pricing behaviour.[11]

By contrast, Google prefers that publishers and advertisers avoid multi-homing and buy and sell ads through Google's exchange. Preventing multi-homing across exchanges allows Google to increase its exchange take rate, so Google applies leverage power through supply-side or buy-side brokers to force publishers and advertisers to use Google's exchange. If Google is able to significantly impede multi-homing, network effects on other exchanges will collapse, and the market will tip toward a winner-take-all or winner-take-most result. Barriers to entry will increase, rivals will exit the market and new competition will be dissuaded from entering.

In mature and efficient markets – such as the financial markets – there is vigorous competition such that the markets have become commoditised: there is competition among seller brokers to service sellers, competition among buyer brokers to service buyers, competition among exchanges for transactions, and competition in ancillary markets to provide services to buyer brokers and seller brokers.

Because of Google's abuse of its monopoly power, that is not how the different markets within online display advertising function. Google has monopoly power on the sell-side, the buy-side, the exchange and adjacent markets. Despite the inherent conflicts of interest that this creates, Google uses its monopoly power throughout these different markets to advantage itself at the expense of its *own* clients. It leverages its power through its intermediaries strategically located in different segments of the ad tech stack to exercise market power. In almost every case, the function of these intermediaries is to advantage Google rather than to enhance consumer welfare or promote competition.

If one thinks of an intermediary as an entity that acts as a broker facilitating transactions between two sides of an exchange, then Google has strategically placed its own intermediaries in positions to serve both publishers and advertisers in order to control the flow of information and corner the online display advertising markets. In so doing, it has undermined the central tenet of the Internet, which is to promote decentralisation and preclude any one company from becoming the controlling node and central authority for online advertising, which serves as the primary currency enabling a free and open Internet.

In a competitive market, intermediaries pursue the goals of their advertiser and publisher clients. Advertiser intermediaries facilitate access to the best media outlets and target the right consumers, allow advertisers to effectively analyse and measure the quality and reach of ad campaigns based on industry standards, and conduct audits to reduce or eliminate low-quality or inappropriate ad placements. Demand-side platforms should compete with one another to accomplish these and similar advertiser goals.

[11] The New York Stock Exchange, for example, charges $0.0005 per share as a transaction fee for traded securities. See NYSE, 'American Equities Price List' (as at 16 November 2021) at nyse.com/publicdocs/nyse/markets/nyse-american/NYSE_America_Equities_Price_List.pdf (accessed 28 November 2021).

Likewise, publisher intermediaries facilitate access to a large, diverse and high-value inventory of ads at competitive prices, and provide detailed user information to enhance the value of targeted ads. Supply-side publisher ad servers should compete with one another to accomplish these and similar publisher goals.

Note the multiple roles that Google intermediaries play in these transactions. They include sell-side ad servers representing publishers, buy-side ad brokers representing advertisers, information brokers to facilitate the targeting of ads to particular users, and the exchange itself where the transactions take place. At each point in the transaction flow Google charges a fee – a sell-side brokerage fee, a buy-side brokerage fee, an information brokerage fee and an exchange fee. This real-time auction happens every minute of every day for millions of Americans browsing the Internet, which explains how Google earns billions by selling our time and attention.

III. Anticompetitive Conduct

The online display advertisement is highly concentrated, allowing Google to leverage its power in different segments to control the market, increase prices, eliminate competitors and reduce consumer choice. This section briefly outlines Google's power in the different markets and Google's anticompetitive conduct to maintain that power.

A. The Online Display Advertisement Ecosystem

The online display advertising market is not one giant market. Rather, it represents a series of related market segments that interact with each other. To the extent Google has market power in one market segment, it can use that power to leverage its products and services in an adjacent market. It can then expand its power in that segment to leverage its power in other market segments. Successfully leveraging of these various intermediaries allows Google to control and monopolise the entire ad tech stack.

There is the market to serve the needs of publishers, known as the publisher ad server market. That market helps publishers manage their online display advertising inventory, including forecasting what inventory will be available to sell, managing sales channels, reporting on ad performance, determining which ads will be served and providing yield management technology. Google has market power in the publisher ad server market, as evidenced by the fact that 90 per cent of large publishers use Google's ad server, known as Google Ad Manager (GAM). This power is also reflected by the fact that Google charges supra-competitive fees.

On the other side is the market to serve the needs of advertisers, known as demand-side platforms for the ad-buying market. That market helps advertisers effectively bid for ad space that publishers make available on exchanges. Large and sophisticated advertisers use trading desks to fulfil their ad needs through Google's large ad-buying tool, DV360. Small and unsophisticated advertisers interface directly with Google's ad-buying tool, known as Google Ads. Google has market power in the demand-side advertiser ad market, as evidenced by the fact that it charges supra-competitive fees and has a dominant market share in the advertiser market, particularly the small advertiser market.

In the middle is the exchange market that matches and facilitates the transaction for the sale and purchase of display ads. Exchanges have the ability to offer auctions in real time on an impression-by-impression basis as web pages are loading. Exchanges interface with publishers through their brokers – the publisher ad servers, and with advertisers through their brokers – demand-side ad-buying tools. Google has market power in the exchange market, as evidenced by the fact that it charges supra-competitive fees and has a dominant market share in the exchange market. Even when competitors vigorously compete on price, Google does not lose market share.

In addition to exchange markets, display ads are also offered in other ways. These include direct sales, in which publishers and advertisers deal directly with one another on a one-to-one basis. Such deals are typically large investments, with ad managers interfacing to book ads without recourse to real-time auctions. In addition, smaller advertisers use networks instead of exchanges, which are not offered in real time, do not provide the same features as exchanges and charge different prices. But both of these avenues for publishers and advertisers to interface with one another are sufficiently different that they are not substitutes for ad exchanges.

Google also collects enormous amounts of data about its users and leverages that data to promote targeted advertising. Google claims that it never sells personal information to anyone, but it leverages the power of data to foreclose competitors' access to Google data. Google's access to intimate user data and personal information allows it to broker billions of daily online ad impressions between publishers and advertisers that target individual users. Google seeks to increase the information asymmetry it already has with its competitors by eliminating cookie-based tracking, the primary mechanism available to such competitors to gather information necessary to offer targeted advertising.

In addition to Google's influence in these markets, it also influences the market for display advertising through its ownership of YouTube. Video advertising on YouTube is a major source of revenue for advertisers, and YouTube's substantial reach among US consumers makes it essential for advertisers offering online instream video inventory. In other words, Google is not only the most significant broker for advertisers, it also owns some of the most important real estate for advertisers wanting to sell video ads to publishers.

Finally, Google has a monopoly for search as well as search advertising. The US Department of Justice estimates that Google has an 88 per cent market share of the general search advertising market and a 70 per cent market share of the search advertising market.[12] With Google's market power in search advertising, Google can force advertisers to use Google intermediaries for search ads, and then leverage its relationship with advertisers in search advertising to enhance and maintain its power in display advertising.

[12] *United States v Google*, Case 1:20-CV-03010 (20 October 2020) 29–35.

B. Leveraging Intermediaries

The central concern regarding Google's dominance in the ad tech market is its ability to leverage its power in one segment of the market to enhance its power in other segments of the market. To the extent Google intermediaries have market power, Google will use those intermediaries as choke points to force publishers and advertisers to use other Google products. With enough choke points along the ad tech supply chain, Google can dominate the entire display advertising marketplace, and foreclose competition, raise barriers to entry, reduce quality, degrade innovation and charge monopolistic prices.

The fundamental change for Google dates back to its 2008 acquisition of DoubleClick, the leading provider of the ad server tools that online publishers, including newspapers and other media companies, use to sell their graphical display advertising inventory on exchanges. As the new middleman between publishers and exchanges, Google quickly began to use its new position to exert leverage. Immediately after acquiring a publisher ad server and launching its exchange in 2009, Google made it so the small advertisers bidding through Google Ads had to transact in both Google's ad network and Google's ad exchange. Google also made it so that the large publishers wanting to receive bids from the many advertisers who used Google's ad-buying tool had to trade in Google's exchange and license Google's ad server. By requiring publishers to license Google's ad server and transact through Google's exchange in order to do business with the one million plus advertisers who used Google as their middleman for buying inventory, Google was able to leverage power of one of its intermediaries to enhance the power of its other intermediaries.

In essence, Google was able to demand that it represent the buy-side, where it extracted one fee, as well as the sell-side, where it extracted a second fee, and it was also able to force transactions to clear in its exchange, where it extracted a third, even larger fee. In doing so, Google acted against the best interests of the small advertisers bidding through Google Ads by not routing their bids to the exchanges that offered the lowest prices.

In addition to foreclosing exchange competition by forcing publishers to transact in Google's exchange, Google used its control over publishers' inventory and its status as publishers' agent to foreclose exchange competition through a pattern of anticompetitive conduct. Google restricted publishers from selling their inventory in more than one exchange at a time, started routing publishers' inventory to Google's exchange, and blocked publishers from accessing and sharing information about their heterogeneous inventory with exchanges. In doing so, Google foreclosed exchange competition and dramatically increased the cost of transacting on ad exchanges, enabling Google's exchange to charge high fees.

Publishers recognised that Google's efforts to force them to trade in Google's exchange were anticompetitive and would lead to higher prices and less quality. In response, in 2014, publishers adopted a new innovation called 'header bidding' that permitted them to route inventory to multiple exchanges. Header bidding was a creative piece of code that publishers could insert into the header section of their webpages to facilitate competition between exchanges. When a user visited a page, the code enabled publishers to direct a user's browser to solicit real-time bids from multiple exchanges, before Google's ad server could prevent them from doing so. Instead of being subject to the whims of Google's ad server, header bidding shifted routing from the ad server to the browser. Publishers then sent the highest exchange bid in header bidding into their Google ad server. In short, header bidding created a technical workaround for publishers to circumvent Google's efforts to foreclose competition in the exchange market.

With header bidding, publishers saw their ad revenue jump overnight simply because exchanges could compete with one another. Header bidding was also a positive development for advertisers and consumers. Google tried to eliminate competition from exchanges in header bidding by creating a header bidding alternative that secretly stacked the deck in Google's favour. Google devised exchange bidding to exclude competition from exchanges in multiple ways. The purpose of header bidding was to liberate publishers from the obligation to trade through Google's exchange simply because they were using another Google intermediary as publisher ad server.

Such an innovation was a fundamental threat to Google's business model because it drastically reduced its exchange margins, and threatened its publisher ad server monopoly. In an effort to undermine header bidding, Google relied on its power as a publisher intermediary to undermine the publishers' effort to promote exchange competition.

It did so in several ways. First, Google diminished the ability of non-Google exchanges to return competitive bids by further lowering their ability to identify users associated with publishers' ad space in auctions. Header bidding let each exchange access a cookie on the user's page, which permitted each exchange to recapture some information about the user's identity. Google's new program prohibited exchanges from directly accessing the user's page. As a result, they identified users in auctions even less often, causing them to bid and win less often. This practice of blocking publishers from accessing and sharing information about their heterogeneous inventory with other exchanges made trading on those exchanges less competitive.

Second, Google foreclosed exchange competition by charging publishers an additional 5 to 10 per cent penalty fee for selling inventory in a non-Google exchange. The fee made advertisers' bids through rival exchanges less competitive than advertisers' bids through Google's exchange because Google's exchange did not pay the additional fee.

Third, when publishers chose to route their ad space from their Google ad server directly to multiple exchanges at the same time, Google's new program required them to route their space through Google's exchange, even if publishers did not want to do so. Thus, Google's publisher ad server forced publishers to trade in Google's own exchange.

Fourth, Google designed open bidding to provide Google's exchange a special 'prioritisation', which Google kept secret. Google made it so Google's exchange won publishers' inventory even over another exchange's much higher bid.

These tactics were only possible because of Google's monopoly power in the publisher ad server market. Using the power of its supply-side intermediary, Google sought to foreclose competition in the exchange market by reducing the competitive threat of other exchanges.

Google further leverages intermediaries and forecloses competition by blocking publishers' ability to access information about their heterogenous inventory and share that information with exchanges. Publishers, and the exchanges that sell inventory on their behalf, need to know the identity of users associated with publishers' impressions in order to sell those impressions for competitive prices. User IDs permit publishers and their exchanges to understand the value of inventory, cap the number of times that users see the same ad, and effectively target and track online advertising campaigns.

While Google blocked publishers from accessing and sharing the user IDs with exchanges and networks, Google shared the same raw IDs with Google's network and exchange, as well as Google's buy-side middlemen. Google encrypts the user IDs differently for each publisher using Google's ad server (eg, John Connor = user QWERT12345) and each advertiser bidding through Google's ad buying tools (eg, John Connor = user YUIOP67890). As a result, publishers and advertisers could not easily know that two different user IDs actually belonged to the same user. However, for Google's network exchange, and ad-buying tools, John Connor is always HJKLM54321. In other words, publishers and advertisers could not easily know that two different user IDs actually belonged to the same user, unless they used Google's ad-buying tools and exchange.

By blocking publishers' ability to access and share their ad server user IDs, Google's exchange always has better information about publishers' heterogeneous inventory. Google also uses its exclusive access to publishers' raw ad server user IDs to develop a number of internal non-transparent auction programs designed to exclude competition in both the exchange and ad-buying tool markets. The programs ensure that publishers' impressions, especially the high-value ones, transact through Google. At a high level, the programs exclude competition by manipulating advertisers' bids and auction price floors. All of these complex programs are designed by Google's quantitative analysts to serve a simple purpose: use Google's information and access advantage in ways that no other exchange can replicate. The programs create inefficiencies in the allocation of impressions and reduce competitors' ability to compete on price.

Finally, Google leverages its power as the owner of YouTube to prevent advertisers from using non-Google ad-buying tools when advertising on YouTube. Google uses its power in the online instream video inventory market to force advertisers to use Google ad-buying tools when advertising on YouTube. Advertisers prefer to minimise the number of ad-buying tools they use, so forcing them to use Google ad-buying tools for video ads increases the likelihood that they will use those intermediaries for all of their advertising needs. Cutting off access to YouTube foreclosed competition in the ad-buying tool markets and protected Google's market power in these markets.

Similar to leveraging its power with YouTube, Google also leverages its market power in search advertising. Google is able to force publishers and advertisers to trade in Google's exchange, and force publishers to use Google's publisher ad server, because of Google's market power for ad-buying tools for small advertisers. Google requires advertisers to use Google intermediaries to purchase search ads on Google search. Google then uses its pre-existing relationship with advertisers from search ads, and leverages that relationship when advertisers purchase display ads. Cutting off access to Google search advertising foreclosed competition in the ad-buying tool markets for display advertising and protected Google's market power.

To summarise, Google intermediaries use leverage to force publishers and advertisers to do things they would not otherwise do if given the opportunity. The combined effect of these different leverage points is an ad tech market that is overwhelmingly dominated by Google.

C. Conflicts of Interest

These multiple intermediate roles create inherent conflicts of interest. As the United Kingdom's Competition and Markets Authority (CMA) has concluded, 'While vertical integration can allow intermediaries to realise technical efficiencies, it can also give rise to conflicts of interest.'[13] Google has the ability and incentive to favour its own sources of supply-side and demand-side intermediaries, and its market power gives it the ability to exploit these conflicts.

As the intermediary for publishers, Google has an obligation to secure from advertisers the highest price it can negotiate for ads on the publishers' websites. As the intermediary for advertisers, Google has an obligation to do the exact opposite, to negotiate the lowest price it can secure for ads on publishers' websites. As the intermediary for both publishers and advertisers it has the duty to place the ad transaction on the ad exchange that has the lowest price, including auctions that are not owned and operated by Google. But because Google serves as an intermediary for both publishers and advertisers, as well as operating its own exchange, Google has different incentives that are not aligned, and Google steers publishers and advertisers to its own exchange where it can extract high transaction fees that are not in the best interest of its clients – publishers and advertisers.

The conflicts of interest do not end there. Google also acts as its own publisher by owning and operating YouTube. When advertisers want to offer ads on YouTube, Google forces them to use Google as the intermediary. And acting as the advertiser intermediary, Google should be attempting to secure the lowest prices for ads placed on YouTube. But because it owns YouTube, it has an interest in charging as much as possible for ads on its own property. Google has the market power from its owned-and-operated products, such as YouTube, to force advertisers to use its intermediaries, undermining the ability of third-party intermediaries to compete.

Google also engages in insider trading by collecting information from publishers and then using that information against them. A publisher may route its inventory to multiple exchanges, then route the winning exchange bid to Google's publisher ad server. Google then uses its ad server to let Google's exchange displace the other exchange bid by paying one penny more. Google trades on inside information in other ways. Google's ad server shares competing bids on publishers' inventory with Google's advertiser intermediary. This permits Google's ad-buying intermediary to use that information to optimise its own bidding strategy. This form of insider trading gives Google the unique position of being the only bidder that returns a bid knowing what others are simultaneously bidding. In both instances, Google is sharing inside publisher information with other Google intermediaries in other parts of the ad tech markets to harm publishers.

[13] CMA, *Online platforms and digital advertising: Market study final report* (1 July 2020) 19 at www.gov.uk/cma-cases/online-platforms-and-digital-advertising-market-study.

D. Lack of Transparency

Google's lack of transparency in how it operates the ad tech market facilitates these conflicts of interest. The conflicts of interest inherent in Google's operating at multiple levels of the intermediation chain on both the buy-side and sell-side are exacerbated by the fact that advertisers and publishers are unable to scrutinise Google's behaviour.

Google structures almost every aspect of the online display advertising markets that is within its control to minimise transparency. In so doing, Google ensures that its competitors are unable to compete effectively and its clients have minimal understanding of its anticompetitive behaviour. This lack of transparency poses a fundamental challenge for Google's clients to understand how the online display markets work or create new competitors or innovations that would result in increased consumer welfare. Google's lack of transparency and market structure are designed to harm the competitive process and prevent effective market competition.

Google's consumers, particularly advertisers on the buy-side and publishers on the sell-side, suffer from a lack of pre-trade and post-trade transparency over key aspects of market functionality, including the effectiveness of advertising, the way auctions are carried out and prices determined, and the take rate of Google intermediaries. Google's advertisers know how much they spend on an advertisement, but do not know the take rate of Google intermediaries nor the revenue a publisher receives for an advertisement. Conversely, Google's publishers know how much they receive in revenue for the placement of an advertisement, but do not know the take rate of Google intermediaries nor the spend of advertisers. This lack of transparency prevents either side from knowing the buy-sell spread, and allows Google to charge anticompetitive fees to its advertiser consumers on the buy-side and its publisher consumers on the sell-side.

In furtherance of this scheme, Google blocks advertisers and publishers from circumventing Google to determine the true market value of the commodity exchanged. Google assigns a unique code to both sides of the commodity. Publishers who sell the commodity see one unique scrambled code, while advertisers who buy that same commodity see a different unique scrambled code. As such, Google deliberately keeps advertisers and publishers from synching up each commodity sold, to ensure that only Google is aware of the true market value of each individual commodity, allowing it to extract monopoly rents.

The lack of transparency makes it difficult to determine the take rate by intermediaries at various levels of the online display advertising supply chain. According to advertiser submissions made to the Australian Competition & Consumer Commission (ACCC), publishers receive 25 per cent of ad spend, while intermediaries in the ad tech supply chain share 75 per cent of spend.[14] Another advertising organisation estimates that publishers receive 40 per cent of ad spend, while intermediaries collect 60 per cent.[15] According to the United Kingdom's CMA, publishers receive around 65 per cent of initial advertising revenue that advertisers paid, meaning that the buy-sell

[14] ACCC, 'Digital platforms inquiry – final report' (2019) section 3.5.1 at www.accc.gov.au/publications/digital-platforms-inquiry-final-report.

[15] ibid.

spread (ie the intermediary take rate) is approximately 35 per cent.[16] According to Google, publishers receive around 68 per cent of revenue that advertisers paid, and Google's take rate is 32 per cent.[17] These widely divergent conclusions underscore the uncertainty of Google's true take rate, an uncertainty created by Google's opaqueness.

The trading costs of online display advertising are orders of magnitude greater than other auction markets that feature transparency, such as securities, bonds, currencies, cryptocurrencies, art, automobiles and real estate. Without a mechanism – similar to an open electronic order book in the securities markets – to publish buy and sell orders, the online display advertising market lacks sufficient transparency to effectively promote competition and reduce intermediary take rates. Publishers have proposed to enforcement authorities the creation of a transparent system of programmatic receipting, such as the creation of a complete, reconcilable record for every ad transaction.[18] Thus far, no authority has imposed such a requirement.

The lack of transparency enhances Google's ability to arbitrage its intermediate fees, charging lower intermediate fees at points in the supply chain where there is actual competition in the market and higher intermediate fees at points in the supply chain where there is little or no competition. The lack of transparency decreases competitive pressure at different points in the supply chain and increases opportunities for rent-seeking and arbitrage.

The lack of transparency on Google's take rate means that its publishing and advertising clients are unable to audit and verify the fees that Google charges for its intermediary services. Without an ability to audit or verify fees, there is too much uncertainty to induce innovation or promote effective competition, as Google deliberately shields its take rate from the public and its clients. This lack of transparency depresses competition, discourages new entrants and acts as a barrier to innovation. Most significantly, the lack of transparency prevents Google's own clients – the publishers and advertisers – from establishing the true market value of the commodities they exchange between themselves.

Google's lack of transparency prevents advertisers and publishers from knowing the quality and effectiveness of online display advertisement campaigns. Because auctions occur in fractions of seconds and depend on a combination of quality and price, advertisers and publishers do not have sufficient transparency on how a winning bid is determined. This degrades the bidding process and impedes advertisers' ability to effectively bid and publishers' ability to effectively offer ad space. As a result, Google benefits from these competitive harms, because only Google is aware of the delta between the auction buy and sell prices. In so doing, Google obtains monopoly rents from these information asymmetries, while output is reduced, prices are inflated and competitors are excluded.

[16] CMA (n 13) [2.70].

[17] Google Answer to Amended Complaint, *Texas v Google*, Civil Action No: 4:20-CV-957-SDJ, [55] ('Google admits … that its AdSense for Content service typically retains a 32% revenue share (paying 68% to the publishers)'); [97] ('Google admits that publishers receive 68% of the gross revenue from sales made via the ad network AdSense for Content.').

[18] ACCC (n 14) section 3.5.1.

The lack of transparency in online display advertisers also makes it difficult for publishers and advertisers to engage directly with one another in order to bypass intermediaries and sign direct deals. By preventing publishers from accessing information on potential advertisers interested in direct sales of their inventory, Google impedes competition through direct sales. Google uses its market power to prevent disintermediation.

The lack of transparency also means that Google's potential and actual competitors have difficulty assessing the possible competitive fees they might charge and the possible return on investment that they might obtain if they enter the market and compete with Google as an intermediary. Lack of transparency prevents more efficient competition that would drive greater innovation, increase the quality of intermediary services, increase output and create downward pricing pressure on intermediary fees.

Finally, Google's lack of transparency imposes substantial costs on the display market through a lack of trust that it engenders:

> Buyers and sellers are more likely to participate in markets, including advertising markets, if they have a strong expectation that they 'get what they pay for' or are 'getting value for the money they spend.' … The more transparent the terms and conditions that sellers offer buyers, the more likely it is that competition will reward those sellers who offer the more attractive terms and conditions.[19]

If advertisers and publishers cannot trust the Google intermediaries that they enlist to buy and sell ads, they lack confidence that the display ad market is a fair one that provides the best possible returns for their investment. Opaqueness risks market failure.

IV. Responses

There are two possible responses to address Google's anticompetitive conduct in using its intermediaries to monopolise the display advertising markets.[20] The first are legislative responses that seek to address Google's conduct through new rules against self-preferencing. Proposals in the US House of Representatives and the US Senate would make it illegal for companies to give preferential treatment to their own products over the products of a competitor hosted on the same platform.[21] The key objective of this legislation is to prohibit discriminatory conduct by dominant platforms, including preferencing their own services or disadvantaging the services of rivals. The Senate version prohibits a covered platform from engaging in conduct that would:

> (1) unfairly preference the covered platform's own products, services, or lines of business over those of another business user on the covered platform in a manner that would material harm competition on the covered platform; (2) unfairly limit the ability of another business user's products, services, or lines of business to compete on the covered platform relative

[19] ibid section 3.3.2.

[20] See generally, RP Alford, 'The Bipartisan Consensus on Big Tech' (2022) 71(5) *Emory Law Journal* 893.

[21] American Choice and Innovation Online Act, HR 3816, 117th Congress (2021); Anticompetitive Exclusionary Conduct Prevention Act of 2020, S 3426, 116th Congress (2019–20); American Innovation and Choice Online Act, S 2992, 117th Cong (2021).

> to the covered platform operator's own products, services, or lines of business in a manner that would materially harm competition on the covered platform; or (3) discriminate in the application or enforcement of the covered platform's terms of service among similarly situated business users in a manner that may materially harm competition on the covered platform.[22]

The European Commission's Digital Market Act likewise addresses concerns about self-preferencing in the context of gatekeeper platforms.[23] The Digital Market Act recommends that

> the gatekeeper should not engage in any form of differentiated or preferential treatment in ranking on the core platform service, whether through legal, commercial or technical means, in favour of products or services it offers itself or through a business user which it controls.[24]

In a similar fashion the United Kingdom's CMA has suggested new regulation that goes further and provides the CMA with the authority to 'implement ownership separation and operational separation and to oblige parties to provide access to inventory on reasonable terms'.[25] The CMA specifically argues that the use of separation powers may be necessary to address Google's vertical integration and conflicts of interest in open display.[26] The types of separation suggested included ownership separation (ie divestiture), operational separation (ie management separation and firewalls) and restrictions directly targeting conflicts of interest.[27]

All of these regulations attempt to fashion rules that would address the abuse of power that occurs in contexts such as Google's market power in the display advertising market. None of these proposals have yet been adopted, and it remains unclear whether there is political will to adopt them.

The other avenue is litigation. Attorneys General from 17 US States have sued Google for monopolising the display advertising market.[28] That litigation has been consolidated with over a dozen cases filed by private parties that address similar claims.[29] The remedies sought in those cases include structural relief, such as divestiture or operational separation, as well as behavioural remedies that would impose restrictions on anticompetitive behaviour.

In addition, the US Department of Justice is reportedly investigating the online display advertising market, and may file suit against Google in the near future.[30] Assuming the cases raise similar concerns about Google's use of buy-side and sell-side intermediaries to maintain its monopoly position in online display advertising markets, one can anticipate that the Department of Justice would likewise request all equitable

[22] American Innovation and Choice Online Act (n 21) § 2(a).

[23] European Commission, 'Proposal for a Regulation on contestable and fair markets in the digital sector' COM (2020) 842 final.

[24] ibid at 26.

[25] CMA (n 13) 28.

[26] ibid 354.

[27] ibid 404.

[28] *Texas v Google*, Civil Action No: 4:20-CV-957-SDJ.

[29] *In re Google Digital Advertising Antitrust Litigation*, Civil Action No: 1:21-md-03010-PKC. The latest version of the complaint is available at www.texasattorneygeneral.gov/news/releases/filings-related-google.

[30] C Kang, 'Justice Dept Is Said to Accelerate Google Advertising Inquiry' *New York Times* (New York, 1 September 2021) at www.nytimes.com/2021/09/01/technology/google-antitrust-advertising-doj.html.

relief that is appropriate in the circumstances, including structural and behavioural remedies.[31]

Such litigation will take years to resolve, and will face headwinds, as Google will deploy all available resources to challenge litigation that goes to the core of its business model. But the combined impact of proposed regulation and protracted litigation may eventually address Google's abusive conduct with respect to its use of intermediaries to monopolise the display advertising market.

V. Conclusion

Google has the scale and power to dominate the currency of the Internet. It has positioned Google intermediaries at key positions within the online display advertisings market to stifle competition and limit freedom of consumer choice. Publishers and advertisers buying and selling online ads have little choice but to use Google products and services. Integration across business lines allows Google to compete directly with other companies that depend on Google to access publishers, advertisers, exchanges and information. The fundamental thrust of Google's operation is to dominate several markets at once in order to advantage itself in other lines of business, thereby increasing prices and reducing innovation. Google intermediaries are the means for achieving its anticompetitive ends.

[31] Compare *United States v Google*, Case No: 1:20-cv-03010-APM (Google Complaint requesting structural and injunctive relief against Google for anticompetitive conduct in search and search advertising).

8

The Platform as Agent

DEBORAH A DEMOTT*

I. Introduction

Goods sold through transactions intermediated by online platforms lead to physical harm in the real world when a defect in a product causes personal injury – whether to the purchaser, another user of the product or a bystander – or damages property other than the product itself.[1] Notwithstanding the volume of on-line retail transactions effected via platforms and the inevitability of injury caused by product defects, the legal consequences for the platform itself (more precisely, for the business firm that owns and operates it) remain unsettled. This is especially so when a third-party seller retains title to the goods in question but the platform controls the transactional process, potentially up through delivery to the purchaser, and the third-party seller proves to be insolvent or not even amenable to suit in the buyer's jurisdiction. Much turns on an underlying issue: How should the law characterise transactional platforms? And how broadly or narrowly should the inquiry be conducted? Cases from courts in the United States stemming from transactions conducted via the platform of Amazon.com, Inc, reach disparate outcomes that mostly – but not entirely – turn on characterising the platform: as a seller, an agent on behalf of third-party sellers, a neutral provider of services or a conduit for information? Along the same lines, as one court formulated the question, is Amazon.com 'like a virtual big-box store' or 'more akin to an online flea market'?[2] In its 2020 Annual Report, Amazon itself characterises as 'currently unsettled' the law 'relating to the liability of online service providers', also noting that governmental regulation could require changes in how it conducts business.[3]

* Many thanks to Tianyi Yang (Duke Law JD 2022 (anticipated)) for helpful information about e-commerce in China. For comments on an earlier draft, I thank Tan Cheng-Han and conference participants.

[1] Losses stemming from harm to the defective product are generally not recoverable in tort. American Law Institute, *Restatement (Third) of Torts: Products Liability* (St Paul, MN, American Law Institute Publications, 1998) § 21, comment d. Even when a defect makes the product unreasonably dangerous (and not 'merely ineffectual'), most courts limit plaintiffs to claims and remedies as provided in the Uniform Commercial Code: ibid.

[2] *McMillan v Amazon.com, Inc*, 983 F 3d 194, 196 (5th Cir 2020) (certifying to Texas Supreme Court question whether under Texas product-liability law Amazon acts as a 'seller' of third-party products sold on its website) (certified question accepted 8 January 2021).

[3] See Amazon.com, Inc, 'Annual Report 2020' (2020) 8 at s2.q4cdn.com/299287126/files/doc_financials/2021/ar/Amazon-2020-Annual-Report.pdf (accessed 31 October 2021) (hereinafter *2020 Annual Report*).

Given retail consumers' shift to online shopping, the stakes are significant if the law tolerates the operation of transactional platforms that control and serve as the 'face' for a sale while also occupying a liability-free zone when a defect in the product causes injury.[4] This undoes a principal consequence of well-settled tort law in the United States, which operates to assure that (with some exceptions and limitations) a victim injured by a defective product has access to at least one defendant from among the actors within the product's chain of actors through commerce, from manufacturing to marketing and distribution. Crucially underpinning this web of assurance when a product proves defective, actors within the distribution/marketing components of the chain are subject to liability on a strict or no-fault basis in almost every State, either categorically or when the product's manufacturer is insolvent or beyond the reach of civil litigation in the jurisdiction.[5] Statutes in many States provide that non-manufacturing defendants are not subject to strict liability when the manufacturer is subject to the jurisdiction of a court of the plaintiff's domicile and is not or is not likely to become insolvent.[6] Otherwise, a non-manufacturing defendant who is not independently at fault has an indemnity claim against the manufacturer.[7] Underscoring the stakes is the sad parade of injury left by defective products sold via Amazon, especially products sourced from third-party sellers not subject to jurisdiction in the United States. As detailed in section II, a business model in which a platform's profitability heavily depends on maximising the number of transactions to generate per-transaction fees can be conducive to turning a blind eye to problematic third-party sellers and products.[8]

To be sure, Amazon's increased presence in retail transactions may have lowered prices paid by consumers by flattening distribution and marketing chains. However, large-scale disintermediation also carries costs, suggested by the fact that Amazon's increased dominance in e-commerce was followed by a 'proliferation of dangerous and counterfeit products' offered for sale via its platform, in the recent assessment of a Congressional committee report.[9] Large-scale disintermediation may eliminate discrete steps at which goods must pass inspection as well as middlemen who may bar judgment-proof manufacturers and sellers from access to markets in the United States.[10] Shifting away from a multi-step distribution chain reduces 'friction',[11] but that fact does

[4] Nor is the question of platform liability resolved under EU law. See C Busch, 'When Product Liability Meets the Platform Economy: A European Perspective on *Oberdorf v Amazon*' (2019) 8 *Journal of European Consumer and Market Law* 173, 174 (editorial) (questionable whether platform would be considered an 'importer', a 'producer' or a 'supplier' under the Product Liability Directive, which 'harks back to the pre-Internet era when supply chains where [*sic*] organized as "pipelines" involving importers, wholesalers and retailers').

[5] *Restatement (Third) of Torts* (n 1) § 1.

[6] ibid comment e.

[7] American Law Institute, *Restatement (Third) of Torts: Apportionment of Liability* (St Paul, MN, American Law Institute Publications, 2000) § 22(a)(2)(ii).

[8] US House of Representatives Subcommittee on Antitrust, Commercial and Administrative Law of the Committee on the Judiciary, *Investigation on Competition in Digital Markets* (2020) 292 (hereinafter *Competition in Digital Markets*) (noting 'proliferation of dangerous and counterfeit products' in the wake of Amazon's increased dominance in online markets).

[9] ibid.

[10] *Erie Insurance Co v Amazon.com, Inc*, 925 F 3d 135, 144 (4th Cir 2019) (Motz J concurring).

[11] For this usage, see CM Sharkey, 'Holding Amazon Liable as a Seller of Defective Goods: A Convergence of Cultural and Economic Perspectives' (2020) 115 *Northwestern University Law Review* 1, 16, quoting Motz J in *Erie* (n 10) 144.

not entail that the costs associated with a defective product should remain with those injured by the product. By fixing those costs on manufacturers, sellers and other actors subject to liability, tort law serves dual objectives: it provides a mechanism to compensate injured parties as well as creating incentives to improve product safety. Distinct from tort law – but an integral component of the wider landscape – the availability of insurance to cover product liability[12] can address the risk of slippage in inspecting and handling manufactured products.[13] Although Amazon.com, Inc maintains liability insurance, its 2020 Annual Report discloses that 'we cannot be certain that our coverage will be adequate … or that insurance will continue to be available to us on commercially reasonable terms, or at all'.[14]

Missing so far from scholarly inquiry in this context are the distinct insights that the vocabulary and doctrines of common law agency can contribute. To the extent that Amazon and any counterparts create the appearance that they operate as sellers and are responsible for goods purchased via their websites, they resemble parties to agency relationships who, on the one hand, construct an appearance that reasonably invites reliance from third parties while, on the other hand, reserving the prospect of revealing that the relationship was other than it appeared. Agency law is alert, as George Cohen writes, to the many ways in which 'a principal can collude with its agent to the detriment of third parties', whether implicitly or explicitly.[15] Agency law reflects this alertness through robust doctrines of apparent authority and apparent agency, as well as rules applicable to undisclosed principals. Overall, this portion of agency law functions to protect third parties against the risk that a constructed appearance – whether of agency, an agent's scope of authority, or even the absence of an agency relationship – will later be disavowed by the principal responsible for the appearance.[16] As prior scholarship notes,

[12] Product liability coverage can be structured as a component of a general liability policy or as a separate or standalone policy.

[13] Reportedly, Amazon's increased commitment to 'HOTW' (Hands Off The Wheel) – a press to use automated systems across the board – inhibited its capacity to detect counterfeit products offered through its platform. *Competition in Digital Markets* (n 8) 272. Automated systems may also suffer limitations when the focus is detecting products made unreasonably unsafe due to defects. Amazon's quality-control mechanisms appear to be triggered by customer complaints and third-party sources, including press reports. See, eg, *State Farm Fire & Casualty Co v Amazon.com, Inc*, 2021 WL 1124787 *2 (WD Ky 24 March 2021) (after becoming aware of press reports of hoverboard fires, 'Amazon's products safety team identified 17' instances of damage allegedly caused by hoverboards sold through its platform, leading to 'deep dive' investigation by the head of team, culminating in removal of hoverboard listings from the platform); *Bolger v Amazon.com, Inc*, 53 Cal App 5th 431, 609–10 (2020) (plaintiff's lawsuit was 'the first safety report Amazon received' for replacement laptop battery, leading it to 'suppress' listing for the product and 'purge' inventory in its possession).

[14] *2020 Annual Report* (n 3) 14.

[15] GM Cohen, 'Law and Economics of Agency and Partnership' in F Parisi (ed), *Oxford Handbook of Law and Economics*, vol 2 (Oxford, Oxford University Press, 2017) 399, 403.

[16] On the basic rationale for apparent authority, see American Law Institute, *Restatement (Third) of Agency* (2006) § 2.01, comment c ('A principal may not choose to act through agents whom it has clothed with the trappings of authority and then determine at a later time whether the consequences of their actions offer an advantage'). For the counterpart doctrine in French law, see S Saintier, 'Unauthorised agency in French law' in D Busch and L Macgregor (eds), *The Unauthorised Agent* (Cambridge, Cambridge University Press, 2009) 17, 21 (stating doctrine of *mandat apparent* as 'if in good faith, a third party mistakenly believes that the person he contracted with had authority to bind his principal, the latter can be bound by this appearance of authority providing that certain conditions are complied with'). Since 1962, *mandat apparent* has been an independent doctrine, decoupled from tort doctrine, that does not require establishing fault on the part of the principal, just proof from the third party 'that he legitimately believed that the agent had authority to bind his principal': ibid 25–26.

some courts create in effect an 'Amazon' exception to products liability law through reasoning that does not delve into the specifics of Amazon's control over transactions and its relationships with buyers.[17] One dimension of the latter relationship is the carefully constructed appearance – through site design, branding, the Amazon Prime program, branded packaging and much more – that by buying on Amazon's platform, a purchaser buys from Amazon. Put differently, Amazon does more than 'mask' the underlying reality of its relationships with third-party vendors or 'hide' its true role.[18] It affirmatively constructs the appearance of itself as a seller or the party responsible for a product, while not prominently dissuading its customers from believing it stands behind the safety of goods sold via its platform. By introducing insights gleaned from agency doctrine, this chapter enriches and deepens the analytic framework.

The chapter opens with a brief introduction to the range of business models that typify e-commerce as a prelude to identifying the elements that make Amazon's business model distinctive. The next section briefly surveys the history of products liability law in the United States and then details the recent run of cases in which the issue is Amazon's liability under settled law. These cases reach disparate outcomes. Courts differ on the applicable analytic framework, reflecting among other things the novelty of Amazon's business model relative to the age of the case precedents and statutes. The chapter next articulates the distinctive analytic insights that agency law can contribute through its attentiveness to the implications of constructed appearances and distinguishes among potentially salient doctrines.[19] A brief conclusion sums up, situating issues surrounding Amazon within the long history of tort law in the United States. This history reflects both doctrinal stability over time, as well as responsiveness to changes in underlying circumstances.

II. Platform Business Models and Structures

Nothing intrinsic to e-commerce dictates using any particular business model. Amazon's model is distinctive in ways that are striking against the backdrop of other models. In China, the world's largest e-commerce market, the two dominant platforms have similar models. Neither resembles Amazon's.[20] Both Tmall.com and JD.com use hybrid models suitable for both business-to-consumer and consumer-to-consumer transactions. Sales by the platforms themselves amount to only a small portion of total sales. On both platforms, buyers usually purchase directly from third-party sellers, who handle storage, packaging and shipping.[21] Many buyers communicate directly with potential

[17] EJ Janger and AD Twerski, 'The Heavy Hand of Amazon: A Seller Not a Neutral Platform' (2020) 14 *Brookyn Journal of Corporate, Financial & Commmercial Law* 259, 262.

[18] For this terminology, see ibid 259 and 263.

[19] Potential implications for regulatory responses are beyond the scope of this chapter, including whether Amazon's business model or practices constitute 'unfair or deceptive acts or practices affecting commerce' for purposes of the Federal Trade Commission Act (1914).

[20] In 2019, the Chinese e-commerce market accounted for USD $1.94 trillion, or about 35% of total retail sales, which is over three times the size of the e-commerce market in the United States.

[21] Under Chinese law, an e-commerce platform is not subject to strict liability for injuries caused by defective products. E-commerce Law of the People's Republic of China (2018), Art 38 adopts a negligence standard.

sellers to ask questions and bargain, with no intervention from the platform. Tmall.com and JD.com charge small service fees for advertising and technical and administrative support; they do not charge commission fees to sellers. Nor is Amazon's business model distinctive only in comparison to e-commerce platforms in other countries. Based in the United States, eBay – on which millions of small business and individuals sell goods of all sorts – does not compete against third-party sellers. eBay primarily generates revenue through fees on successful transactions and its classified advertising.[22] eBay sellers are free to customise their listings; eBay itself emphasises that customers are not trading with it.[23]

The novelty of Amazon's business model has several dimensions, disaggregated in part in this section. But overall, in one judicial assessment, retail sales via Amazon's platform take place in an environment characterised by its 'all-encompassing participation', in which it serves as the 'face' of the sale.[24] In more technical terms, Amazon's business model owes its distinctiveness to characteristics of the relationships that connect it to third-party sellers and, separately but relatedly, to its relationships with retail customers. For starters, and unlike the dominant Chinese e-commerce firms (and eBay), Amazon itself sells goods from inventory it owns via its website (and for those sales it is incontestably a 'seller' for products liability purposes).[25] Amazon's website offers shoppers a choice among products responsive to the shopper's search terms, which may be sourced from Amazon itself or from a third-party seller. But using a proprietary algorithm, Amazon alone determines the single seller from among all vendors of the same product (including itself) to feature in the Buy Box, a white box on the right-hand side of the page. Most Amazon shoppers – about 80 per cent – next proceed to click 'Add to Cart'.[26]

The Amazon Services Business Solutions Agreement (the 'BSA'), a document running to forty-nine pages in length, articulates the terms of Amazon's relationship with third-party sellers.[27] Sellers pay fees to Amazon, including a monthly subscription fee plus a referral fee for each item sold, which is set at a percentage that varies across categories of goods and other items offered for sale.[28] The BSA gives each seller a choice between two basic options: (i) apply for and be accepted into the program, 'Fulfillment by Amazon' (FBA), in which Amazon will provide storage and order fulfilment services, plus customer service, for additional fees charged to the seller; or (ii) 'Fulfillment by Seller' (FBS), which saves the fees associated with FBA but may pose logistical challenges for smaller sellers.

[22] See C Dunne, 'eBay vs Amazon – The Complete Comparison Guide (2021)' (*RepricerExpress*, 2021) at repricerexpress.com/ebay-vs-amazon/ (accessed 31 October 2021).

[23] ibid. See also *Inman v Technicolor USA, Inc*, 2011 WL 5829024 *6 (WD Pa 18 November 2011) (facts alleged in complaint insufficient to raise inference that eBay may be liable under Pennsylvania law as a 'seller' of allegedly defective vacuum tubes or had anything more than a 'fleeting connection' with them).

[24] *Steiner v Amazon.com, Inc*, 164 NE 3d 394, 402 (Ohio 2020) (Donnelly J, concurring).

[25] As Amazon describes this portion of its business, 'we design our stores to enable hundred millions of unique products to be sold by us and by third parties': *2020 Annual Report* (n 3) 3.

[26] *Competition in Digital Markets* (n 8) 249.

[27] For the BSA, see Amazon, 'Amazon Services Business Solutions Agreement' (updated 2021) at sellercentral.amazon.com/gp/help/external/G1791?language=en_US (accessed 31 October 2021).

[28] For fee information, see Amazon, 'Selling on Amazon Fee Schedule' (updated 2021) at sellercentral.amazon.com/gp/help/external/200336920 (accessed 31 October 2021).

Sellers who use FBA may market their goods to members of Amazon's Prime program. Prime members pay $12.99/month or $119.99/year in exchange for benefits that most notably include free shipping. Prime members, who now number 200 million (147 million in the United States), outspend other Amazon customers by a factor of more than two.[29] Access to them is a significant draw for third-party sellers, in significant part because membership in Amazon Prime functions as pre-payment for shipping.[30] Prime functions to 'lock consumers into the Amazon ecosystem, on the logic a consumer who pays upfront for shipping is likely to aggregate purchases on the platform in preference to using other retail options'.[31] But Prime also appears to be a loss leader for Amazon, albeit a good deal for consumers, who receive an estimated $860 in value in exchange for the $199 annual fee.[32]

The environment for third-party sellers on Amazon's platform as defined by the BSA confers rights on Amazon that empower it to exercise substantial control over sellers. For example, although FBA sellers retain title to their goods, Amazon holds the inventory and reserves the right to 'ship Units together with products purchased from other merchants, including any of our Affiliates'.[33] Amazon's default storage method is product-by-product, not seller-by-seller. A seller may opt out from commingling its merchandise with that of other sellers, but at the risk of increased shipping time and lower ratings on Amazon's internal metrics; as noted above, which seller's product appears on the buyer's screen in the 'Buy Box' is Amazon's decision.[34]

Additionally, for all sellers (whether proceeding FBM or FBA), Amazon may require that a seller maintain liability insurance when the gross proceeds from its sales over three months exceed a defined 'Insurance Threshold' or 'if otherwise requested by us'.[35] The insurance policy must name Amazon and its assignees as insureds. The BSA also empowers Amazon in its sole discretion to withhold payment to sellers 'for so long as we determine any related risks to Amazon or third parties persist'.[36] Interestingly, the BSA expressly disclaims the creation of 'any partnership, joint venture, agency … relationship between us',[37] but in collecting, holding and disbursing monies due sellers, Amazon acts in an agency capacity under well-settled law.[38] And Amazon has discretion under

[29] R Bullard, 'Out-Teching Products Liability: Reviving Strict Products Liability in an Age of Amazon' (2019) 20 *North Carolina Journal of Law and Technology* 181, 194.

[30] A Doyer, 'Who Sells? Testing Amazon.com for Product Defect Liability in Pennsylvania and Beyond' (2020) 28 *Journal of Law and Policy* 719, 729 (direct access to Prime members can increase sales 'significantly by increasing visibility and attractiveness' of a seller's products). FBM sellers can have access to Prime members, but only by paying a premium and submitting to demanding guidelines governing shipping and product quality: ibid.

[31] *Competition in Digital Markets* (n 8) 259–60.

[32] ibid 298 (noting estimate made by JP Morgan & Co).

[33] BSA (n 27) F-5 Fulfillment.

[34] Janger and Twerski (n 17) 269.

[35] BSA (n 27) 9 Insurance. The 'Insurance Threshold' for the United States is $10,000. BSA Definitions. The policy must satisfy the 'Insurance Limits' per occurrence and in aggregate. For the United States, these are $1 million.

[36] BSA (n 27) 2 Service Fee Payments; Receipt of Sales Proceeds.

[37] BSA (n 27) 13 Relationship of Parties.

[38] How parties label their relationship is not dispositive of its legal status. *Restatement (Third) of Agency* (n 16) § 1.02 and comment b (when an agreement between parties negatively characterises it as not one of agency, although the statement may be relevant to determining whether the parties consent to an agency relationship, the statement is not determinative 'and does not preclude the relevance of other indicia of consent').

the BSA to terminate its relationship with a seller if it determines that the seller's use of its services 'has harmed, or our controls identify that it might harm, other sellers, customers, or Amazon's legitimate interests'.[39]

The power to expel a seller makes Amazon, in Rory Van Loo's terminology, a potential 'enforcer firm'. This is because Amazon is positioned to 'police' its third-party sellers through its data-informed capacity to cease doing business with them[40] as a dominant force in retail markets.[41] Additionally, Amazon has power to set the terms of entry (or re-entry) onto its platform by imposing requirements, such as the contingent insurance requirement discussed above. Just as establishing an e-commerce platform does not require using a particular business model, it does not proscribe the use of otherwise-legal selection criteria for eligibility to sell through the site. One straightforward possibility is credible evidence that a seller is amenable to civil process in a jurisdiction and is solvent. It is feasible for Amazon to require such evidence from sellers; in response to the attractiveness of its site to sellers of stolen merchandise, Amazon now conducts interviews to verify sellers' identities for almost all prospective sellers, also requiring government-issued identification, taxpayer information and bank-account details.[42] Separately – and distinct from the law – Amazon's shift toward more fully exercising its gatekeeping powers to bar its site to sellers of stolen merchandise illustrates the power of optics in shaping business conduct. Aware of its status as a focal point for law-enforcement authorities and investigations conducted by retailers victimised by shoplifting, Amazon responded.

Finally, and in sharp contrast to the experience of shoppers and sellers on Chinese e-commerce platforms – who may communicate directly and bargain with each other – Amazon is the sole channel of communication for customers and third-party sellers on its website. This prohibition limits the capacity of third-party sellers to move off Amazon by proscribing an obvious route for marketing themselves and the products they sell.[43] In short, Amazon's 'all-encompassing participation' defines a transactional environment in which it is the ever-present face of a transaction that defines the experience, and brands it, for retail shoppers and third-party sellers, beginning when a shopper initiates a search on Amazon's website and concluding when the goods arrive in packaging that often bears Amazon's name and logo.

[39] BSA (n 27) 3 Term and Termination.

[40] R Van Loo, 'The New Gatekeepers: Private Firms as Public Enforcers' (2020) 106 *Virginia Law Review* 467, 471. See also A Martin, 'A Gatekeeper Approach to Product Liability for Amazon' (2021) 89 *George Washington Law Review* 768 (applying gatekeeper theory and proposing legislation imposing liability to consumers injured by defective products sold through site premised on analogy to vicarious copyright infringement).

[41] If anything, this understates Amazon's power over third-party sellers given that it now accounts for around 50% of online retail markets in the United States: *Competition in Digital Markets* (n 8) 15. As of 2020, the platform had 2.3 million active third-party sellers; 70% relied on sales through Amazon as their sole source of income: ibid.

[42] See R Ballhaus and S Ramachandran, 'Inside a $45 Billion Retail Crime Spree' *Wall Street Journal* (2 September 2021) A1 and A8 (reporting that Amazon 'is one of the biggest outlets for criminal networks, given its huge pool of potential customers and, in investigators' view, insufficient vetting of sellers or their identities').

[43] *Competition in Digital Markets* (n 8) 250.

III. The Development of Products Liability Law and the Amazon Discontinuity

The ongoing history of tort law in the United States evidences stability over time as well as innovation in response to changes in the external circumstances that define the situations to which this body of law applies.[44] For starters, from the early days of the twentieth century onward, the widespread popularity of automobiles plus the crashes and law suits that followed generated profound changes in tort law and its administration.[45] It is not surprising that this ongoing legacy includes the 1916 case generally understood as the starting point for products liability as a distinctive portion of tort law, *MacPherson v Buick Motor Co.*[46]

This section begins with a brief sketch of the history of products liability law and the tenets of doctrine that are well-settled in most States.[47] An exploration of the cases in which Amazon is a defendant follows.

A. The Distinctiveness of Products Liability Law

Early steps in the development of product defect law rely on negligence as a theory of liability and differentiate claims in tort from contractual claims for breach of warranty. The plaintiff in *MacPherson* was injured in a single car crash while driving his recently purchased Buick when one of the car's wheels suddenly collapsed.[48] Buick sourced the wheel, 'made of defective wood', from another manufacturer; the defect could have been revealed by careful inspection, which Buick omitted. The plaintiff did not buy his car directly from Buick but from a dealer, which had purchased the car from Buick. The court held that the car's manufacturer owed a duty of reasonable care, encompassing a duty to inspect the car's components, to persons who would use it 'without new tests'.[49] *MacPherson* built on three precedents that imposed duties of care in the absence of contractual privity: on the manufacturer of a poison, mislabelled as a medicinal herb and dispensed to the plaintiff by a retail pharmacist;[50] a contractor who constructed a scaffold and sold it to a painter, leading to injury to the painter's employees when

[44] For a leading historical account emphasising links between tort doctrine and broader intellectual currents, see GE White, *Tort Law in America: An Intellectual History*, expanded edn (New York, Oxford University Press, 2003). On the philosophical backdrop in particular, see JR Hackney, Jr, 'The Intellectual Origins of American Strict Products Liability: A Case Study in American Pragmatic Instrumentalism' (1995) 39 *American Journal of Legal History* 443.

[45] N Freeman Engstrom, 'When Cars Collide: The Automobile's Tort Law Legacy' (2018) 53 *Wake Forest Law Review* 293.

[46] *MacPherson v Buick Motor Co*, 111 NE 1050 (NY 1916), discussed in Engstrom (n 45) 315.

[47] A few (five) States do not follow the doctrinal approach outlined in this section. Defective-products claims are litigated as claims for breach of warranty and as negligence claims. See GC Christie and others, *Cases and Materials on the Law of Torts*, 6th edn (St Paul, MN, West Publishing, 2019) 891.

[48] *MacPherson* (n 46) 1051.

[49] ibid 1053.

[50] *Thomas v Winchester*, 6 NY 397 (1852).

the scaffold collapsed;[51] and the manufacturer of a coffee urn that exploded, injuring a customer of the restaurant that purchased the urn.[52]

MacPherson, rooted in negligence precedents, also exemplifies the evident focus in subsequent cases on the particular product and its type. As the court reasoned, although a car, unlike a poison, is not within the set of 'things which in their normal operation are instruments of destruction', if negligently made it becomes a 'thing of danger'.[53] And the manufacturer's duty of care does not end with the 'immediate purchaser', the dealer to whom the manufacturer sold the car. The dealer purchased to resell, and in any event the size of the three-seated car made it apparent that 'persons other than the buyer' would use it.[54] The facts did not require that the court comprehensively address relationships between tort theories of liability and contract; in *MacPherson*, neither the manufacturer nor the dealer appears to have disclaimed or otherwise attempted to limit warranties, whether express or implied, that accompanied the sale of the car. Later cases expanded the scope of tort liability beyond 'users' of a product to foreseeable third-party victims of a product defect.[55]

In 1960, *Henningsen v Bloomfield Motors*[56] resolved two issues of foundational significance for the ongoing development of products liability law and commercial law. The plaintiff, driving a new car bought by her husband, was injured in a one-car accident allegedly caused by a mechanical failure or defect in the car's steering mechanism. The court held that a warranty runs to a foreseeable third party, consistent with the scope of the duty of care articulated in *MacPherson*. Additionally, warranties of merchantability and of fitness for a particular purpose ran from both manufacturer and dealer. Buried as they were in fine print on the back of the sales contract, the dealer's and manufacturer's attempts to limit the warranty to disclaim liability for personal injury were ineffective.[57] And as stated in the sales article of the Uniform Commercial Code, statutory commercial law now explicitly makes ineffective any provision that limits the recovery of consequential damages for personal injury in a consumer sale.[58]

Henningsen's legacy in product defect law was soon muted by the rapid acceptance of tort theories of liability. These focused on defects in the product itself and de-emphasised alleged negligence by the manufacturer and other actors responsible for the product's sale, including dealers in distribution chains for motor vehicles. Pre-dating *Henningsen*, strict-liability concepts entered the products liability realm via an influential Concurring Opinion in *Escola v Coca Cola Bottling Co* from the California Supreme Court in 1944.[59] Employed as a waitress in a restaurant, the plaintiff was injured when

[51] *Devlin v Smith*, 89 NY 470 (1882).

[52] *Statler v Ray Manufacturing Co*, 195 NY 478 (1909).

[53] *MacPherson* (n 46) 1053.

[54] ibid.

[55] eg, *Codling v Paglia*, 32 NY 330 (1973) (manufacturer subject to liability without proof of negligence when defective product causes injury; plaintiff injured when car in which she was a passenger was suddenly hit head-on by another driver's car when its power steering locked). In general, '[o]ne engaged in the business of selling or otherwise distributing products who sells or distributes a defective product is subject to liability for harm to persons or property caused by the defect'. *Restatement (Third) of Torts: Products Liability* (n 1) § 1.

[56] *Henningsen v Bloomfield Motors*, 161 A 2d 69 (NJ 1960).

[57] ibid 95–97.

[58] Uniform Law Commission, *Uniform Commercial Code* (UCC) § 2-719(3).

[59] *Escola v Coca Cola Bottling Co*, 150 P 2d 436 (Cal 1944).

a glass bottle of Coca Cola exploded in her hand. A majority of the Court upheld a jury verdict for the plaintiff, holding that the facts satisfied the requisites for *res ipsa loquitur*, which permits an inference of negligence.[60] Although the defendant submitted evidence that it exercised precaution in visually inspecting for defects in bottles and checking the pressure when it filled them, it was a question of fact for the jury to determine whether the defendant succeeded in dispelling the inference of negligence permitted by *res ipsa loquitur*.

The legacy of *Escola* stems from the Concurring Opinion of Justice Roger Traynor, which urges a shift to 'absolute' or strict liability for manufacturers (like the Coke bottler) for 'an article placed on the market, knowing that it is to be used without inspection' when it 'proves to have a defect that causes injury to human beings', citing *MacPherson*.[61] The Opinion emphasises asymmetries in knowledge and capacity as between manufacturers and consumers; the manufacturer, responsible for the product reaching the market, is better able to take precautions and to insure against risk. It can 'distribute [the costs] among the public as a cost of doing business'.[62] Relatedly, even when not equipped to test a product, a retailer gives an 'absolute warranty' of fitness and merchantability to its customer that encompasses product safety, which it can in turn recoup from the manufacturer.[63] Two decades later, a unanimous majority of the court held in *Greenman v Yuba Power Co* (1963) that the manufacturer of a power tool (sold through a retailer) was subject to liability on a strict-liability theory – without proof of negligence – when the tool's 'defective design and construction' led to a malfunction that resulted in serious injuries to the plaintiff.[64] Two years later, the *Restatement (Second) of Torts* formalised the principle in Section 402A, imposing liability on 'one who sells any product in a defective condition unreasonably dangerous to the user or consumer or to his property'.[65] Liability extended to persons 'engaged in the business of selling' goods that are 'expected to and do reach the user or consumer without substantial change in the condition in which' they are sold.[66]

To be sure, products liability law continued to evolve after 1965. In several States, products liability law became statutory, often in terminology drawn from Section 402A.[67] By 1998 and the completion of the portion of *Restatement (Third) of Torts* focused on products liability, the law differentiated among types of defects: products that departed from their intended design contained manufacturing defects, to which a strict-liability regime applied; in contrast, products were defective in design only when foreseeable risks of harm could have been avoided or reduced by using a reasonable

[60] These are: (i) the defendant's exclusive control of the instrumentality causing the injury; and (ii) 'the accident is of such a nature that it would not occur in the absence of negligence by the defendant', ibid 438.

[61] ibid 440.

[62] ibid 441.

[63] ibid 441–42.

[64] *Greenman v Yuba Power Co*, 377 P 2d 897, 899 (Cal 1963).

[65] American Law Institute, *Restatement (Second) of Torts* (1979) § 402A.

[66] ibid § 402A(1).

[67] In South Carolina, the legislature adopting the statute – SC Code §15-73-30 – identified the comments to Section 402A as legislative intent. See *Branham v Ford Motor Co*, 701 SE 2d 5, 14 (2010) (explaining that by adopting the statute in 1974, the legislature 'expressed no intention to foreclose court consideration of developments in products liability law', including *Restatement (Third) of Torts: Products Liability* (n 1), which separately defines design defect).

alternative design.[68] This focus, present in the cases on which the *Restatement* drew, looks backwards from the product itself to the process and decisions that generated the product, in light of design alternatives then available. In G Edward White's assessment, it represents an instance of the persistence of negligence theory working to limit liability.[69] As will soon be evident, distinctions among types of product defect are not salient in the cases stemming from injuries caused by products sold via Amazon's platform. But negligence theory and strict products liability are both potentially relevant to determining liability.

B. The Amazon Discontinuity

Within the mine-run of product defect cases, those involving Amazon are distinctive in several respects. For starters, unlike the plaintiff in *Escola*, the Amazon plaintiffs were not injured as employees in the course of employment, with the consequence that a workers compensation claim against an employer is not an available source of compensation.[70] Additionally, the Amazon cases do not raise issues about either the presence of a product defect or proving a type of defect. Distinctively, apart from Amazon.com, Inc, no other actor in the manufacturing/marketing/distribution chain is available as a defendant in these cases. Finally, with a few exceptions, the courts deciding Amazon cases are federal courts, which arguably has had substantive consequences for tort law. Although product defect cases (like tort cases generally) are governed by the application of State law, Amazon's consistent litigation strategy has been to exercise its right to remove cases filed in State court to federal court on the basis of the parties' diversity of citizenship.[71] In a federal forum on this basis, the court's mandate is to apply State law as discerned from State-law authorities, in particular statutes and cases decided by the State's supreme court.[72] Given the novelty of Amazon's business model and the issues it raises, federal courts – charged to apply State law – may strain to discern how the State's supreme court would respond to the facts, confined as the federal court necessarily is to State-court precedents. In two Amazon cases to date, federal appellate courts have submitted certified questions about State law on given facts to State supreme courts. The certification route fits federal-court cases in which questions

[68] *Restatement (Third) of Torts: Products Liability* (n 1) § 2 (a) and (b). Likewise, proving a product defect on the basis of inadequate instructions or warnings required proving that foreseeable risks of harm could have been reduced or avoided by the provision of reasonable instructions or warnings, and their omission made the product not reasonably safe: ibid § 2 (c).

[69] White (n 44) 249.

[70] Many products liability cases originate in the workplace. But workers compensation statutes limit recoverable damages, creating an incentive for injured employees to sue the manufacturer (or seller) of machinery or other products that injured them. Christie and others (n 47) 946–47. When an employee's injury stems from a defect in a product chosen by the employer over alternatives alleged to be safer, the manufacturer does not bear responsibility for the employer's choice. See *Riley v Becton Dickson Vascular Access, Inc*, 913 F Supp 879, 891 (ED Pa 1995).

[71] *Erie Insurance Co* (n 10) 145 (counsel represented to court that sole instance in which Amazon did not remove to federal court was due to absence of diverse citizenship). Under the relevant statute, 28 USC §1446, Amazon is a citizen of both its State of incorporation (Delaware) and its principal place of business (the State of Washington). Removal also requires that the amount in controversy in the case exceed $75,000.

[72] *Erie Railroad Co v Tompkins*, 304 US 64 (1938).

of State law are both determinative and unresolved by State-law precedents. Amazon settled one case (discussed below), after the Supreme Court of Pennsylvania agreed to answer the question.[73] The Texas Supreme Court decided the second certified-question case in Amazon's favour.[74]

The trajectory of outcomes in Amazon cases shifts over time. Amazon succeeded in the initial run of cases, then encountered more mixed results. Generalising in the midst of a still-ongoing saga is perilous, but overall cases in which judicial inquiry delves more deeply into the operation of Amazon's business model may either reject its claim that it lies beyond the reach of tort law or express regret that settled law requires this result and invite legislative intervention.[75] Cases accepting Amazon's argument that its business model places it beyond the reach of products liability law may emphasise that it does not hold title to goods sold via its platform,[76] or that its capacity to control product quality is limited,[77] or that it does not fit within definitions – in particular of 'seller' – of actors who are subject to liability.[78] Most recently, in *Amazon.com, Inc v McMillan*, the Texas Supreme Court, applying the State's statutory definition of 'seller', held that Amazon was not subject to liability for injuries caused by defects in products manufactured and owned by others.[79] Distinct from products liability law, Amazon's initial defence strategy relied on its status as an 'interactive computer service provider' under a provision in the federal Communications Decency Act (CDA) that grants immunity to providers for claims arising from their publication of information created by third parties.[80] Some courts were persuaded that CDA immunity covered all products liability claims,[81] whether or not grounded in Amazon's status as an online publisher of content authored by others. But other courts were unpersuaded,[82] except for claims

[73] See *Oberdorf v Amazon.com, Inc*, 930 F 3d 136, vacated by 936 F 3d 182 (3rd Cir 2019). See also 818 Fed Appx 138 (3rd Cir 2020) (certifying question to Pennsylvania Supreme Court). On the settlement, see Sharkey (n 11) 4.

[74] *Amazon.com, Inc v McMillan*, 625 SW 3d 101 (Tex 2021), discussed below. See also *McMillan* (n 2) 202 (noting that the possibility of certification was raised by neither party but in an amicus curiae brief, to be met by pushback by counsel for Amazon).

[75] See *Stiner v Amazon.com, Inc*, 164 NE 3d 394 (Ohio 2020) 404 (Donnelly J concurring: 'Closing the obligation gap in the Ohio Products Liability Act for actors like Amazon would ensure the utmost protection that Ohio consumers deserve. But as the majority says, such concerns are for the General Assembly …').

[76] See, eg, *Erie Insurance Co* (n 10) 142 (applying Maryland law); *Eberhart v Amazon.com, Inc*, 325 F Supp 3d 393, 397 (SDNY 2018) (applying New York law).

[77] See, eg, *Fox v Amazon.com, Inc*, 930 F 3d 415, 425 (6th Cir 2019) (applying Tennessee law); *Great Northern Insurance Co v Amazon.com, Inc*, 2021 WL 872949 (ND Ill 9 March 2021) (applying Illinois law).

[78] See, eg, *State Farm Fire & Casualty Co v Amazon.com, Inc*, 835 Fed Appx 213, 216 (9th Cir 2020) (applying Arizona law); *Allstate New Jersey Insurance Co. v Amazon.com, Inc*, 2018 WL 3546197 **7–8 (DNJ 24 July 2018) (applying New Jersey law); *Stiner v Amazon.com, Inc*, 164 NE 3d 394, 399–400 (Ohio 2020).

[79] *Amazon.com, Inc v McMillan*, 625 SW 3d 101 (2021).

[80] Communications Decency Act 1996, 47 USC § 230.

[81] See, eg, *Great Northern Insurance Co v Amazon.com, Inc*, 2021 WL 872949 (ND Ill 9 March 2021) (CDCA bars negligent misrepresentation claim based on statements made by third-party seller on platform); *Erie Insurance Co v Amazon.com, Inc*, 2018 WL 3046243 (D Md, 22 January 2018), reversed in part, 925 F 3d 135 (4th Cir 2019); *Oberdorf v Amazon.com, Inc*, 295 F Supp 2d 496 (MD Pa 2017), reversed in part by 930 F 3d 136 (3rd Cir 2019), vacated by 818 Fed Appx 138 (3rd Cir 2020).

[82] *State Farm Fire & Casualty Co v Amazon.com, Inc*, 390 F Supp 2d 964, 973–74 (WD Wis 2019) (product liability claim does not implicate CDA immunity because it does not require consideration of whether Amazon was negligent in publishing product listing or responsible for publishing it).

alleging that Amazon failed to add warnings to a seller's product detail page.[83] In some cases, Amazon conceded that CDA immunity did not apply to tort law claims grounded in its alleged assumption of a duty to warn about defective products.[84] Separately, in a series of cases stemming from defective batteries in hoverboards, negligence became an available theory of liability once Amazon sent emails to hoverboard purchasers notifying them of reported safety problems but not of risks of fire and explosion or Amazon's internal response, which culminated in its worldwide cessation of hoverboard sales.[85] By choosing to send the email, Amazon assumed a duty to act with reasonable care to warn of the dangers associated with defective hoverboards; if the email recipients acted in reliance on the email, which Amazon internally intended to be 'non-alarmist', it is subject to liability for physical harm caused as a consequence.[86]

On the basic products liability question, by 2021 the overall trajectory of cases was less receptive to Amazon's stance that it bore no responsibility for the safety of goods sold via its platform. For some commentators, a turning point came in *Oberdorf v Amazon.com, Inc* (2019), in which a majority of the court held that under Pennsylvania law Amazon was subject to liability as a 'seller' although it never held title to the goods, which were shipped directly to the plaintiff by the third-party seller.[87] *Oberdorf*'s impact stemmed in part from its facts, which are both mundane and memorable. The plaintiff bought a dog collar via Amazon's platform, shipped directly by a third-party seller, 'The Furry Gang'. One month later, after the plaintiff attached a retractable leash to the collar to take her dog for a walk, the collar's D-ring broke when the dog lunged. This caused the leash to retract and strike plaintiff's eyeglasses, leading to permanent blindness in one eye. The plaintiff's suit named both The Furry Gang and Amazon as defendants; neither the plaintiff nor Amazon was able to locate a representative for The Furry Gang, which no longer had an active vendor account on Amazon's platform.

Crucially, the majority's opinion relies on the usage of 'seller' in earlier Pennsylvania cases and in the commentary to *Restatement (Second)*, Section 402A. The Pennsylvania precedents hold that exclusive sales agents,[88] as well as bailors and lessors, fit within the 'seller' category;[89] financial lessors do not, because their tangential participation in the transaction disables them from effecting or overseeing product safety.[90]

[83] See, eg, *Erie Insurance Co* (n 10) 139–40; *Oberdorf v Amazon.com, Inc*, 930 F 3d 136, 153 (3rd Cir 2019); *McMillan v Amazon.com, Inc*, 433 F Supp 2d 1034, 1044–45 (SD Tex 2020) (CDCA immunity applicable only to claim that Amazon failed to provide warnings on web page, not to other product defect claims).

[84] See *Fox v Amazon.com, Inc*, 930 F 3d 415, 428 fn 8 (6th Cir 2019) (material issues of fact precluded granting summary judgment on tort law claim premised on Amazon's assumption of a duty to warn plaintiff of dangers posed by hoverboard via individual email).

[85] eg, *Fox v Amazon.com, Inc*, 930 F 3d 415, 420 (6th Cir 2019) (applying Tennessee law); accord, *State Farm Fire & Casualty Co v Amazon.com, Inc*, 2021 WL 1124787 (WD Ky 24 March 24) (applying Kentucky law). But see *Garber v Amazon.com, Inc*, 380 F Supp 2d 766, 782 (ND Ill 2019) (no evidence Amazon voluntarily undertook duty to warn).

[86] American Law Institute, *Restatement (Third) of Torts: Liability for Physical and Emotional Harm* (2012) § 42; *Restatement (Second) of Torts* (n 65) §§ 323 and 324A.

[87] *Oberdorf* (n 83). On the significance of *Oberdorf*, see Busch (n 4) 173 ('could have a seismic effect for online marketplaces'); Janger and Twerski (n 17) 26 (characterising case as 'an outlier'); Sharkey (n 11) 3 ('we may have reached a possible inflection point').

[88] *Oberdorf* (n 83) 148, citing *Hoffman v Loos & Dilworth, Inc*, 452 A 2d 1349 (Pa Super 1982).

[89] *Oberdorf* (n 83) 149, citing *Francioni v Gibsonia Truck Corp*, 392 A 2d 736 (Pa Super 1977).

[90] *Oberdorf* (n 83) 149, citing *Nath v National Equip Leasing Corp*, 439 A 2d 633 (Pa 1981).

Moreover, the business of financial lessors is 'circulating funds', not 'the business of selling or marketing merchandise'.[91] Amazon's argument, persuasive to some other courts, that dictionary or commercial law definitions of 'seller' should govern, was unsuccessful. The *Oberdorf* majority responded by citing the commentary to Section 402A, which 'makes clear that the term "seller" is not limited by its dictionary definition'.[92] In short, for the *Oberdorf* majority, as for the courts that shaped the earlier history of products liability law, the issues are governed by tort law.[93]

Likewise, two post-*Oberdorf* opinions from the California Court of Appeal unanimously hold that Amazon is subject to liability on products liability grounds when product defects cause personal injury to purchasers.[94] In neither case did the third-party seller appear after suit was initiated. Both opinions situate Amazon within the category of actors at least potentially subject to liability when a defective product causes injury, under the reasoning of the (ample) California precedents, finding it to be a direct link in the vertical chain of distribution for the product,[95] an active participant in marketing instrumental to sale and the creator of the environment that enabled the sale.[96] And, as in *Oberdorf*, in the more recent of the two cases the third-party vendor shipped the product (a hoverboard that caught fire) directly to the consumer.[97]

In short, Amazon is not a tangential participant in 'the business of selling', comparable to the common carrier that brings its packages to customers' doorsteps or an auctioneer who 'sells' as a consignor's agent.[98] Instead, its omnipresence in the transactional environment its platform creates is integral to sales effected through the platform. And through that constructed environment it has ample capacity to exercise control over third-party sellers, to 'police' them through its power to expel them from the platform and to impose requirements for entry or continued presence in the platform's environment. To consumers, it is the 'face' of the transaction, likely to be a frequently-seen face by Amazon Prime customers who have pre-purchased shipping at a bargain price.

[91] *Oberdorf* (n 83) 149, quoting *Nath* (n 90) 636.

[92] *Oberdorf* (n 83)150–51, citing *Restatement (Second) of Torts* (n 65) § 402A, comment f ('The rule stated in this section applies to any person engaged in the business of selling products for use or consumption. It therefore applies to any manufacturer … any wholesale or retail dealer or distributor … It is not necessary that the seller be engaged solely in the business of selling such products.'). Subsequent language excepts 'occasional sellers', not engaged in 'the business of selling', including a neighbour's sale of a pot of jam to another neighbour.

[93] The Dissenting Opinion in *Oberdorf* reads the Pennsylvania precedents more narrowly and ascribes more significance to Amazon's choices in structuring its business model.

[94] *Loomis v Amazon.com, Inc*, 63 Cal App 5th 466 (2021) (hoverboard caught fire, causing burns to purchaser's hand and foot); *Bolger v Amazon.com, Inc*, 53 Cal App 5th 431 (2020), review denied (Cal, 18 November 2020) (laptop battery exploded, causing severe burns to customer).

[95] *Loomis* (n 94) 772.

[96] *Bolger* (n 94) 616.

[97] *Loomis* (n 94) 780.

[98] Although Amazon has argued that these comparisons are apt. See *McMillan* (n 2) 200 and fn 29 (noting that Amazon also argued it resembled a food-delivery service). Auctioneers, who act as agents for consignors and purchasers at auction, are not treated as sellers for products liability purposes. *Restatement (Third) of Torts: Products Liability* (n 1) § 20, comment g.

IV. Agency Law and the Consequences of Constructed Appearance

The lawyer who represented the plaintiff in *Oberdorf* urged courts to 'catch up to consumers' perception that Amazon is responsible for the goods it sells'.[99] The doctrines and vocabulary of agency law that address the consequences of constructing an appearance (and later denying its consequences) are instructive on assessing responsibility for creating that widely-held 'perception', doing so in one judge's assessment through actions that provide 'the face of a retail sale … all without ever owning, possessing, or even seeing the product that was sold'.[100] As two seasoned scholars write, Amazon holds 'all of the apparent attributes of ownership'[101] from which a consumer might reasonably infer it is the seller, comparable to a bricks-and-mortar merchant, subject to a seller's ordinary responsibilities with no warning to the contrary.[102] How effective such a warning might be is open to question; recall that contemporary sales law does not enforce limitations on recovery for consequential damages for personal injury.[103] And products liability law itself invalidates disclaimers and limitations on remedies when interjected to bar recovery for personal injury caused by defects in new products.[104]

Consider first agency law's doctrinal response when a party who appears to be a principal – buying or selling on her own account – is instead acting as an agent for an undisclosed principal whose existence and identity are unknown to the third party with whom the agent deals. The agent is a party to any contract made with the third party,[105] but might a principal be tempted to deal through a prospectively insolvent agent? The principal, like the agent, is a party to the contract and thus subject to liability to the third party, unless the contract itself excludes liability of parties other than those named.[106] But might an undisclosed principal be tempted to deny that the agent acted within the scope of her actual authority in making the particular contract when its price or other terms are unwelcome to the principal? The robust doctrine of apparent authority (as elaborated more fully below) constrains this temptation when an agent acts on behalf of a disclosed principal, but by definition apparent authority does not fit when the principal is undisclosed.

[99] P Boykoff and C Sebastian, 'Who's Responsible for What You Buy on Amazon? A Court is About to Decide' *CNN* (19 February 2020), quoted in Sharkey (n 11) 5.

[100] *Stiner* (n 75) 164 NE 3d 394, 402 (Donnelly J concurring). To another judge, it is 'surely no accident' that Amazon does not hold title to goods sold via its platform notwithstanding the 'outsized' role it plays in transactions effected through the platform. *Erie Insurance Co* (n 10) 144–45 (Motz J concurring).

[101] Janger and Twerski (n 17) 267.

[102] A platform designed to be easy and quick to use does not prompt most consumers to read closely and with a sceptical frame of mind about transactional basics. Relatedly, a 'consumer would have to be a Philadelphia lawyer to understand the difference in legal regime caused by three seemingly identical transactions', in which Amazon itself sells and ships a product, Amazon fulfils a sale from a third-party seller, or the third-party seller fulfils the order: ibid 268.

[103] UCC § 2-719 (3).

[104] *Restatement (Third) of Torts: Products Liability* (n 1) § 18.

[105] *Restatement (Third) of Agency* (n 16) § 6.03 (2).

[106] ibid § 6.03 (1).

One of the best-known cases in the classical agency canon, *Watteau v Fenwick* (1893),[107] remains a controversial instance of liability for an undisclosed principal who argued that his agent acted beyond the scope of actual authority.[108] The agent, who had owned a pub that operated under an established trade name (the Victoria Hotel), sold the pub to defendants but stayed on as their manager while the fact of new ownership remained undisclosed. When their agent purchased items routine for a pub and did not pay the vendor, the vendor sued the defendants, who argued that the manager had acted beyond the scope of his authority. The court held the defendants liable in a brief (but obscure) judgment.[109] As recently suggested by Tan Cheng-Han, the outcome fits within established paradigms of apparent authority if the principal is recharacterised as unnamed (or unidentified)[110] on the reasoning that the third-party seller believed he sold to the Victoria Hotel and whomever its owners might be.[111] Or perhaps the owners represented that the business and the agent who managed it 'were one and the same person',[112] not through an express representation but by creating a situation in which a third party would not be likely to investigate further, especially for routine transactions conducted consistently with prior transactions.

Likewise, the doctrine of apparent authority, created by a principal's manifestation that an agent has authority of a particular type or scope, denies a principal the prospect of '[choosing] to act through agents whom it has clothed with the trappings of authority and then [determining] at a later time whether the consequences of their acts offer an advantage'.[113] At least in cases from the United States, apparent authority frequently figures as the basis on which a principal is subject to liability, perhaps because its existence can be proved without access to the internal communications and other records of interactions between principal and agent requisite to showing actual authority.[114] Agency law in the United States has long grounded apparent authority in a manifestation made by the principal that a third party reasonably understands to mean that an actor has authority to act as an agent on the principal's behalf.[115] This rationale is

[107] *Watteau v Fenwick* [1893] 1 QB 346.

[108] See Cohen (n 15) 411–12 (noting although that court's imposition of liability on the undisclosed principal 'does in some sense excuse a third party's negligent failure to investigate the agent's creditworthiness', it also deters principal–agent collusion through a strategy that 'deliberately increases the costs to the third party of determining the true ownership' of business assets).

[109] On the obscurity of *Watteau*'s rationale, see Tan C-H, 'Estoppel in the Law of Agency' (2020) 136 *LQR* 315, 330–32.

[110] See *Restatement (Third) of Agency* (n 16) § 1.04(2)(c) ('A principal is unidentified if, when an agent and a third party interact, the third party has notice that the agent is acting for a principal but does not have notice of the principal's identity.'). 'Unidentified principal', 'unnamed principal' and 'partially disclosed principal' are synonymous. When a third party knows a principal's identity but not the principal's name, the principal is disclosed, not unidentified: ibid § 6.01, comment c. It is a question of fact whether any principal's existence and identity have been disclosed: ibid.

[111] To be sure, the court's judgment states that the seller gave credit to the manager 'and to him alone'. *Watteau* (n 107) 348.

[112] Tan (n 109) 332.

[113] *Restatement (Third) of Agency* (n 16) § 2.03, comment c.

[114] Actual authority, in contrast, turns on proving the agent's reasonable belief at the time the agent takes action with legal consequences for the principal that the principal wishes the agent so to act: ibid § 2.01.

[115] ibid § 2.03 and comment c ('Apparent authority holds a principal accountable for the results of third-party beliefs about an actor's authority to act as an agent when the belief is reasonable and is traceable to a manifestation of the principal.').

distinct from estoppel, which at most occupies a secondary and marginal role in US agency law.[116]

The rationale for apparent authority also encompasses the somewhat separate doctrine of apparent agency, in which the principal's manifestations lead a third party reasonably to believe that an actor is an agent. The belief, stemming from appearances created by the apparent principal, that a particular actor is an agent may shape the third party's own conduct and decisions. In recent cases, the doctrine of apparent agency holds hospitals to vicarious liability due to acts of malpractice committed by non-employee apparent agents, when it is reasonable for a patient to believe an apparent agent acts on the hospital's behalf in providing medical services that hospital employees might furnish.[117]

In short, agency law responds to the risk that, through a constructed appearance later disavowed by the principal, third parties will suffer detriment. Amazon's creation of the 'perception' that it sells the goods available through its platform should carry operative significance for its responsibility when defects in goods cause injury, just as agency law holds a principal to the consequences of a constructed appearance when a third party reasonably believes what the appearance depicts.

V. Conclusion

In a much earlier episode in the long history of tort law in the United States, the New York Court of Appeals declined to follow the then-recent precedent, *Rylands v Fletcher.*[118] In *Losee v Buchanan*, in which the defendant's newly installed steam boiler exploded and then 'projected' like a rocket onto plaintiff's premises, the court held that the defendant was not subject to liability without proof of negligence.[119] Reasoned the court, 'we must have factories, machinery, dams … [t]hey are demanded by the manifold wants of mankind and lay at the base of all our civilization'.[120] And having them requires holding one's own property 'subject to the risk that it may be unavoidably or accidentally injured by those who live near me'.[121] Later 'confined to its special facts' by *MacPherson*,[122] *Losee*'s broad rationale of social necessity for leaving losses – however created or imposed – with those who suffer them is inconsistent with broad swathes of later developments in the law and regulation. Even assuming 'we must' have on-line

[116] ibid § 2.05.

[117] *Cefaratti v Aranow*, 141 A 3d 593 (Conn 2016); *Jones v Healthsouth Treasure Valley Hospital*, 206 P 3d 473 (Mont 2009).

[118] *Rylands v Fletcher* (1865–66) LR 1 Ex 265.

[119] *Losee v Buchanan*, 51 NY 476 (1873). Nor did the plaintiff succeed in a separate suit against the boiler's manufacturer. See *Losee v Clute*, 51 NY 494 (1873) (risk of injury too remote). By 1916, *Clute* was 'confined to its special facts' when the court held that a car manufacturer owed a duty of reasonable care to the plaintiff, who bought the car from a retail dealer. *MacPherson* (n 46) 386. *MacPherson* notes that the manufacturer in *Clute* 'knew that his own test was not the final one'; the boiler exploded when first deployed by its purchaser, the property-owner defendant in *Buchanan*: ibid.

[120] *Losee v Clute*, 51 NY 494, 485.

[121] ibid.

[122] *MacPherson* (n 46) 386.

shopping via platforms, and that it lies 'at the base of all our civilization', wide-scale externalisation of the predictable injuries caused by defective products is unjustified.

Agency law's doctrines and rationales are responsive to intentionally constructed appearances linked to injuries or other losses inflicted on third parties. When a platform's owner constructs a transactional environment that leads consumers to believe it is responsible for the goods sold via the platform, it differentiates itself from platform intermediaries – such as eBay and JD.com – and strengthens the case for its responsibility.

9

Online Intermediary Platforms and English Contract Law

CHRISTIAN TWIGG-FLESNER

I. Introduction

This chapter focuses on one particular form of intermediary that has emerged as a core component of the digital economy: platforms. Platforms are the beating heart of the digital world, bringing together those who provide and those who acquire: on social media, people share their lives with their followers; content creators use photo- or video-sharing platforms to distribute their output to viewers; service providers can offer their services as and when they wish to do so; and businesses can offer their goods to trade and consumer customers. Online platforms take a variety of forms.[1] This chapter excludes from its scope social media and content-sharing platforms,[2] and focuses on platforms facilitating contracts for the supply of goods, services and digital products. Such platforms are referred to as online intermediary platforms ('OIPs'). They are commonly described as marketplace platforms, or 'market makers', because they create a digital version of a marketplace that brings together suppliers of goods, services and digital products with prospective customers.

The digital environment means that the number of suppliers and customers is not limited by space or capacity (unlike bricks and mortar shops). To bring both groups together, OIPs often seek to present themselves as pure intermediaries, confined to creating the digital environment that enables suppliers of goods and services and interested customers to be brought together and to conclude contracts with each other. The reality, however, is that most platforms do more than act as a passive operator of a digital space for suppliers and customers to conclude contracts. OIPs constitute a market ecosystem, with the OIP operator serving as both market *creator* and market *regulator*.[3]

[1] See European Commission, 'Staff Working Document – Online Platforms' SWD (2016) 172 final, for an overview.

[2] Some social media platforms have started to venture into the e-commerce/marketplace platform arena, but for present purposes this need not be considered further.

[3] See, eg, M Cantero Gamito, 'Regulation.com. Self-Regulation and Contract Governance in the Platform Economy: A Research Agenda' (2017) 9 *European Journal of Legal Studies* 54; JK Winn, 'The Secession of the Successful: The rise of Amazon as a Private Global Consumer Protection Regulator' (2016) 58 *Arizona Law Review* 193.

In its role as regulator, the operator can control access of suppliers to the platform, determine the conditions on which contracts are concluded and performed, require the use of payment service and/or fulfilment services offered by or through the platform, allow customers to leave feedback and ratings on their experience and use these to sanction suppliers. Furthermore, many OIPs provide a dispute resolution mechanism in respect of disputes between customers and suppliers as an alternative to court-based dispute resolution. The design of such mechanisms varies from acting as an intermediary to ensure that complaints are received and responded to, to actively intervening by, for example, withholding payments collected through the OIP from a customer and to be transferred to the supplier.

The architecture of OIPs is based on contracts. The core contractual structure of any OIP comprises three contractual relationships:[4] (i) the contract between the OIP and the supplier, setting out the conditions on which the supplier can offer its products via the platform; (ii) the contract between OIP and customer, which enables the customer to place orders; and (iii) the main supply contract between supplier and customer. There can be additional contractual relationships collateral to this triangle of contracts that might concern the provision of payment facilities, warehousing and distribution services for suppliers, or guarantees given by the platform to customers in respect of supply contracts concluded via the platform.

An important feature of the contracts between the OIP operator and the platform's suppliers and customers (ie the platform users) is that these are not transactional, unlike the contracts concluded between suppliers and customers. Rather, the contracts between the OIP operator and platform users govern the relationship between the operator of the OIP and the users of the OIP for as long as they are using the platform. As such, these contracts constitute the governance structure for an online platform.

There are several aspects about the role of contracts and contract law in the context of online platforms that merit exploration. This chapter first considers the fact that online platforms are an instance of 'governance by contract',[5] which leads to questions over the suitability of contracts and of English contract law for this purpose. Second, the OIP operator has a significant role in managing participation of, and in the resolution of disputes between, platform users, but does contract law ensure that the OIP operator cannot act in this role in an unfettered manner? Third, the contracts comprising the platform architecture might not only serve to regulate platform users, but themselves become the target of regulation. Finally, with regulation of online platforms a priority for both national and supranational legislators,[6] the contractual architecture of an online platform and the wider regulatory context have to interact. The overarching purpose is to question whether a predominantly contract-focused approach to platforms

[4] C Twigg-Flesner, 'Legal and Policy Responses to Online Platforms – A UK Perspective' in U Blaurock, M Schmidt-Kessel and K Erler (eds), *Plattformen – Geschäftsmodelle und Veträge* (Baden-Baden, Nomos, 2018) 139.

[5] Cf L Bygrave, *Internet Governance by Contract* (Oxford, Oxford University Press, 2015).

[6] In particular, the European Union's recent proposals for a Digital Services Act (Commission, 'Proposal for a Regulation on a Single Market for Digital Services (Digital Services Act)' COM (2020) 825 final) and a Digital Markets Act (Commission, 'Proposal for a Regulation on contestable and fair markets in the digital sector' COM (2020) 842 final).

is sufficient, and therefore whether any specific regulatory objectives can be pursued effectively through the regulation of the platform contracts. The academic literature on platforms discusses a variety of regulatory approaches alternative to contract law, ranging from the direct regulation of the activities of OIP operators[7] to treating OIPs as a new organisational form to be regulated analogously with companies.[8] However, direct regulatory intervention in pursuit of specific policy objectives is not a new phenomenon in contract law,[9] for example through the implications of particular terms into contracts between business and consumers.[10] However, the fact that contracts are used in the context of OIPs to construct the governance architecture rather than for transactions might pose challenges for contract law, for example by taking into account the interdependencies between the various OIP contracts or the relational nature of each contract.

II. Law and New Digital Business Models

A preliminary step is to locate the present discussion in the wider contextual debate about adapting law to the legal issues associated with new business models in the digital economy (of which OIPs are one instance) and the wider challenge of keeping the law in step with technological development.

Broadly speaking, this debate is characterised by the tension between seeking to apply existing laws to new developments, and a focus on developing targeted laws in response to novel legal issues raised by new business models. The former approach essentially starts from the perspective of existing laws (such as contract law) and seeks to establish how a new development would slot into established legal rules. One example of this approach are attempts to analyse how contract law might deal with so-called 'smart contracts'.[11] The latter prioritises the identification of whatever novel legal or regulatory questions a new business model has raised, and the development of targeted legal solutions to tackle these. Brownsword has described these respective approaches as reflecting, on the one hand, a 'coherentist' mindset and, on the other hand, a 'regulatory-instrumentalist' mindset.[12] However, these are not necessarily mutually exclusive approaches. Rather, having identified the specific issues of a new development, it might first be considered whether existing contract law can do the job of addressing these and whether contract law could evolve as necessary. This does not mean that statutory

[7] See, eg, T Rodrigues de las Heras Ballell, 'The Legal Anatomy of Electronic Platforms: A prior study to assess the need of a law of platforms in the EU' (2017) 3 *Italian Law Journal* 149.

[8] IHY Chiu, 'The platform economy and the law of organisations and governance' in RM Barker and IHY Chiu (eds), *The Law and Governance of Decentralised Business Models* (Abingdon, Routledge, 2020) 189.

[9] Many contract types have been the subject of direct regulation, eg, to protect the interests of parties in contracts regarded as inherently imbalanced, such as consumer or employment contracts, or because a contract is of a particularly complex nature (eg, financial services). Furthermore, other areas of law interact with contracts and contract law, such as intellectual property law, competition law or tax law.

[10] Under the Consumer Rights Act 2015.

[11] See Law Commission, *Smart Legal Contracts – Advice to Government* (2021); also M Durovic and A Janssen, 'The Formation of Blockchain-based Smart Contracts in the Light of Contract Law' (2018) 26 *European Review of Private Law* 753; for critique, see, eg, K Lowe and E Mik, 'Pause the Blockchain Legal Revolution' (2020) 69 *ICLQ* 135.

[12] See, eg, R Brownsword, *Law, Technology and Society* (Abingdon, Routledge, 2019).

intervention in pursuit of regulatory objectives would not be needed, but it might only become necessary where a contract-focused approach does not provide the answers. In this regard, Eliza Mik recently wrote:

> The revolution in how people conduct business need not result in a revolution in Contract Law. Contract Law can absorb technological change. The question is not do traditional principles apply? But how do they apply?[13]

When it comes to OIPs, the capacity of contract law to deal with the particular features of platforms needs to be examined first, before effort is expended on developing new legal and regulatory provisions specifically for OIPs. To the extent that the application of contract law does not provide a solution to an identified issue, a different route for addressing it would have to be taken. Indeed, scholars have mooted whether alternative approaches focusing on the market-making and market-controlling role of an OIP operator could be a basis for developing a regulatory strategy instead;[14] there have been suggestions in that direction, for example by focusing on the market-creating role of OIP providers[15] or by introducing some form of accountability of the OIP operator towards platform users collectively.[16] However, the task for this chapter is to explore whether contract law can absorb the changes brought about by OIPs.

III. The Contractual Architecture of Platforms

A platform is set up by the operator through contracts with both suppliers and users. Although these are all discrete contracts, they are standard-form contracts, and so the contractual architecture of a platform consists of a very large number of contracts to which the OIP operator is one party and the many suppliers and customers are, individually, the other party. One can divide this almost infinite number of contracts into three types: first, the contract between an OIP operator and the suppliers seeking to offer their goods or services through the platform. This contract sets out the conditions for the admission of a supplier to the platform, and it can cover matters such as a supplier's obligations when dealing with platform customers, the requirement to use the platform for receiving orders and communicating with customers, conditions for suspension or permanent removal of access, as well as the process for varying the terms of the contract. Second, there is the contract between customers and the OIP operator, usually created by a customer's registering on the platform, which allows the customer to browse and place orders. Many platforms do not require customers to pay to register, although they will seek consent to collect data from customers. Some platforms will offer paid-for membership, which provides additional benefits to paying customers.

[13] Cf E Mik, 'The resilience of contract law in light of technological change' in M Furmston (ed), *The Future of the Law of Contract* (Abingdon, Routledge 2020) 112, 139.

[14] C Twigg-Flesner, 'The EU's Proposals for Regulating B2B Relationships on online platforms – Transparency, Fairness and Beyond' (2018) 7 *Journal of European Consumer and Market Law* 222.

[15] T Rodriguez de las Heras Ballell, 'Refusal to deal, abuse of right and competition law in electronic markets and digital communities' (2014) 22 *European Review of Private Law* 685.

[16] Cf N Helberger, J Pierson and T Poell, 'Governing Online Platforms: from contested to cooperative responsibility' (2018) 34 *The Information Society* 1.

The third contract is the supply contract for goods, services or digital content concluded between suppliers and customers. The OIP operator is not a party to this. Indeed, most OIP operators go to great lengths to make it clear in their terms and conditions that they are only providing an intermediation service and that they are not involved in the supply contract. Even where an OIP operator is a stranger to the supply contract, it will have had some influence over the terms of that contract. For instance, an OIP may require that the supply contract is based on standard terms set by the platform, and it may also require that performance of some of the contractual obligations, such as payment, is made through facilities provided by the platform.

This simplified triangular analysis of the various contracts obscures several aspects, however. First, there may be more contractual relationships than just the three described above. Often, OIPs are themselves complex corporate groups, and both suppliers and customers may have multiple contracts with the various OIP companies. For example, payments may be processed by one OIP company, fulfilment services might be provided by another and the main digital platform might be operated by a third. Second, even the contractual relationship between the OIP operator and a supplier often consists of multiple contracts: there might be conditions of use of the digital facility, separate terms of service for each of the various services provided by the platform and so on. So instead of talking about the contract between an OIP and a platform user, the contractual relationship between both might be better understood as comprising a bundle of contracts.

A. Platforms Self-Designating as Intermediaries

One feature of the OIP contractual architecture is the way in which the OIP operator seeks to determine its relationship with suppliers and customers, particularly in respect of the main supply contract. The OIP operator usually defines its role as that of an intermediary, whether described as a hosting service or possibly as an 'agent'[17] acting on behalf of suppliers (irrespective of whether the relationship is truly one of agency). This is done by using specific labels to denote the role of the various parties, which are intended to limit the role of the OIP operator to that of an intermediary. There are two likely motivations for this: first, the OIP operator can benefit from liability exemptions for hosting services available to providers of information society services (ISS) under the Electronic Commerce Regulations (especially regulation 19).[18] Second, the OIP operator would avoid incurring any direct liability under the main supply contract between supplier and customer towards the customer.

However, several of the leading online platforms have been the subject of litigation at both the national and European level in order to test whether their claim to be a pure intermediary withstands scrutiny. In the United Kingdom, the Supreme Court

[17] See, eg, clause 4.1 of the Uber services agreement considered in *Uber BV v Aslam* [2021] UKSC 5, [2021] 4 All ER 209 [25]: 'Customer: (i) appoints Uber [BV] as Customer's limited payment collection agent solely for the purpose of accepting the Fare …'

[18] The Electronic Commerce (EC Directive) Regulations 2002 (SI 2002/2013), which implement Directive 2000/31/EC on E-Commerce. In addition, under the Directive, ISS providers established in one Member State cannot be made subject to regulation in another Member State.

indirectly touched on this issue most recently in its ruling in *Uber*.[19] The central question for the Court was whether Uber drivers were self-employed (as claimed by Uber) or workers (as argued by the claimants). The Employment Tribunal,[20] Employment Appeal Tribunal[21] and the Court of Appeal (by a majority)[22] had all concluded that drivers fell within the definition of worker. Uber had relied on the wording of its standard contracts, which sought to present its business model as intermediating between drivers and passengers, and as acting as 'booking agent' on behalf of the drivers. In the lower courts, the mismatch between the written contract and the reality of the situation in the way Uber operated its business was central to the determination, relying on the *Autoclenz* principles[23] to be applied in disregarding the terms of the agreement when determining the true nature of an employment relationship. In the Supreme Court, Lord Leggatt, who gave the only judgment, stressed that the *Autoclenz* approach was particular to employment contracts because the rights at issue were granted to workers under statute; that is, this was not a straightforward situation involving the construction of a contract.[24] The extent of Uber's influence over the way in which the drivers provided their services was consistent with their classification as workers.[25] However, Lord Leggatt also stressed that in situations not involving employment, ordinary principles of contract interpretation would apply. He gave the examples of accommodation-booking platforms, which are much more likely to be operating as intermediaries,[26] not least because accommodation providers offering their services are competing with one another[27] and can also be on multiple platforms at the same time.

Uber, however, has fared no better before the Court of Justice of the European Union (CJEU), which has considered whether both Uber and Airbnb, two of the leading platforms, qualify as ISS providers and fall within the scope of the E-Commerce Directive. The first was Case C-434/15 *Asociación Profesional Élite Taxi v Uber Systems Spain SL*.[28] The question considered by the CJEU described Uber as an 'intermediation service … the purpose of which is to connect, by means of a smartphone application and for remuneration, non-professional drivers using their own vehicle with persons who wish to make urban journeys'.[29] However, in the CJEU's assessment, Uber offered urban transport services that incorporated an intermediation service.[30] It held that

[19] *Uber v Aslam* (n 17).

[20] *Aslam v Uber BV* [2017] IRLR 4 (Employment Tribunal).

[21] *Uber BV v Aslam* [2018] RTR 14 (Employment Appeal Tribunal).

[22] *Uber BV v Aslam* [2019] EWCA Civ 2748, [2019] 3 All ER 489. Underhill LJ dissented on the basis that this was not a situation where the terms of the agreement could be disregarded as being inconsistent with the reality of the situation, and that the terms of the agreement should govern the classification of the drivers and of Uber's role.

[23] *Autoclenz Ltd v Belcher* [2011] UKSC 41, [2011] 4 All ER 745.

[24] *Uber v Aslam* (n 17) [68]–[70].

[25] ibid [93]–[101].

[26] ibid [103]–[104].

[27] See also *Secret Hotels2 Ltd v Her Majesty's Commissioners of Revenue and Customs* [2014] UKSC 16, [2014] 2 All ER 685, a VAT case, reaching a similar conclusion in the context of a hotel booking platform. Here, the statutory context of the VAT regime, which gives freedom to taxable persons to determine their organisational structure (ibis [107]).

[28] Case C-434/15 *Asociación Profesional Élite Taxi v Uber Systems Spain SL* ECLI:EU:C:2017:981, [2018] QB 854.

[29] ibid [33].

[30] ibid [38].

Uber organised the general operation of the transport services undertaken by individual drivers;[31] evidenced, for example, by the fact that prospective passengers use the services of drivers selected by Uber.[32] Most significantly, Uber exercised 'decisive influence' over the drivers' services, such as the fare to be charged, the quality of the vehicles that could be used and the conduct of the drivers.[33] Consequently, Uber's central business activity was the provision of transport services, with a subsidiary ISS element only.[34]

In contrast, when considering whether Airbnb provided an information society service or an accommodation service, the CJEU reached the opposite conclusion.[35] It described Airbnb as an online platform allowing professional and non-professional hosts to offer accommodation on a short-term basis to prospective guests via the platform. Airbnb offered additional services, such as a payment system that holds a guest's payment in escrow for 24 hours from guest check-in and from which Airbnb deducts a commission, a formatting tool for presenting the accommodation, a photography service, a guarantee and insurance scheme, and a tool for estimating the rental value of the accommodation (but, crucially, not for determining the price the host can charge).[36] In the CJEU's view, Airbnb's core activities involved the creation of lists of available accommodation based on criteria set by a prospective guest to then enable the guest to make a booking.[37] This service competed with other channels for advertising accommodation.[38] Crucially, Airbnb did not determine the rental price to be charged,[39] and the additional services offered by Airbnb were merely ancillary and did not 'constitute an end in itself'. The crucial distinction between Airbnb and Uber was that Uber had a decisive influence over the provision of the transport service, that is, the underlying supply transaction, whereas Airbnb did not have such influence.[40]

Despite the very different legal questions in issue, a common strand in these cases is that, when classifying the activities of an online platform, the OIP's active control over the provision of the main supply contract, particularly where this involves the provision of a service, and over the price to be paid by the customer can undermine the claim by an OIP operator that it is merely acting as an intermediary. This can be so despite the careful drafting of the relevant contracts with a view to limiting the OIP operator's role to that of an intermediary. This poses some limitations on the use of contracts for designing the architecture of a particular platform, with the effect of displacing the

[31] ibid.

[32] Ibid [39].

[33] ibid.

[34] One explanation for this ruling might be that to treat Uber as an ISS would mean Uber would not be subject to national regulations, such as licensing requirements, in respect of personal transport services and consequently create a regulatory vacuum. The CJEU confirmed its assessment in Case C-320/16 *Uber France SAS v Nabil Bensalem* ECLI:EU:C:2018:221 (GC, 10 April 2018), which involved a provision of French law imposing criminal penalties for organising a system to put customers in touch with drivers to transport them by road without having obtained authorisation for this.

[35] Case C-390/18 *Criminal proceedings against X (Airbnb Ireland)* ECLI:EU:C:2019:1112, [2020] 2 CMLR 22.

[36] ibid [39].

[37] ibid [53].

[38] ibid [55].

[39] ibid [56].

[40] ibid [65]–[68].

wording of the contracts themselves – something that clearly troubled Underhill LJ in the Court of Appeal in *Uber*. The statutory context relevant to the assessment in *Uber* can be distinguished in other situations where the main issue is one of construction of the contract. Here, careful design of the contract can ensure that the OIP operator's role is confined to that of an intermediary, although more will be required than the use of particular labels – what matters is the substance of the respective obligations of the parties towards one another.[41] However, even an OIP operator might discover that its desire to be a passive intermediary is not endorsed by a court.

B. Platform Contracts and OIP Governance

The triangular view of the contractual relationships within an OIP ecosystem makes it seem that a platform essentially is an infinite replication of discrete triangular relationships. This might be true in respect of the contracts between suppliers and customers. However, as far as the contracts between OIP operator and platform users are concerned, there is a high degree of interconnectedness between them because of the nature of online platforms. For a platform to succeed, it needs to attract a large number of platform users both on the supply side and on the customer side. The more customers there are, the more suppliers there will be and vice versa. This is known as a 'positive indirect network effect' of platforms,[42] which creates a continuous cycle of growth of both sides, facilitated by the platform. An OIP operator will gain financially by attracting and retaining large numbers of both suppliers and customers. The more transactions are concluded through the platform, the greater the immediate economic benefit will be to the platform operator, for example due to a percentage charged on the price of each transaction. Similarly, the economic benefit to suppliers will be access to a much wider number of potential customers and the potential for increased business. Customers, in turn, will have access to a wider range of suppliers of a particular item, with price competition between them.

However, a much more significant economic benefit to the OIP operator than the commission charged on each transaction concluded on the platform is the vast amount of data the OIP operator can collect from all its users and from the transactions they conclude. Such data has economic value as a commodity, but it can also be used by the OIP operator to target advertising for additional services at platform users based on the profiles created through data analysis. It is also crucial for recommender systems,[43] which encourage customers to buy products based on their transaction history.

[41] eg, *Stoneleigh Finance Ltd v Phillips* [1965] 2 QB 537; *PST Energy 7 Shipping LC v OW Bunker Malta Ltd* [2016] UKSC 23, [2016] AC 1034. See also *Agnew v Commissioner of Inland Revenue* [2001] UKPC 28, [2001] 2 AC 710 [32] (Lord Millett) in the context of classifying security interests over book debts (ruling approved in *Re Spectrum Plus Limited (in liq)* [2005] UKHL 41, [2005] 2 AC 680).

[42] OECD, *An introduction to online platforms and their role in the digital transformation* (Paris, OECD, 2019) 22.

[43] C Busch, 'Crowdsourcing Consumer Confidence. How to regulate online rating and review systems in the collaborative economy' in A de Fraceschi (ed), *European Contract Law and the Digital Single Market* (Cambridge, Intersentia, 2016) 223.

Once a platform has reached a critical mass of users at both ends of the supply transaction facilitated by the platform, the OIP operator will be in a position of great strength to exercise its regulatory functions. Based on this significantly stronger bargaining power vis-à-vis platform users,[44] an OIP operator can act without constraint in setting the terms on which all the platform users can be active on the platform. Moreover, the OIP operator will often have extensive discretionary powers on a range of matters under the terms of its contracts with platform users, for example in respect of unilateral changes to the terms of the contracts. The OIP operator therefore has a strong hierarchical position towards the other platform users.

Invariably, this raises concerns about the OIP operator's ability to utilise this power in a one-sided manner. In the case of the economically most powerful platforms, competition law might be deployed to ensure that an OIP operator does not abuse its dominant position; however, it has proved to be a challenge to apply competition law principles to the particular features of online platforms.[45]

Matters of concern include the fact that the OIP operator can determine the conditions of access and can remove suppliers from the platform. It can also change the conditions suppliers must follow when concluding contracts with customers. An OIP operator has the power under its contracts with other platform users to exercise a broad range of powers regarding the management and governance of the platform, with little or no opportunity for other platform users to influence the OIP operator. In addition, the OIP will often have an internal dispute resolution system in respect of contracts between customers and suppliers, which effectively allows it to resolve such disputes based on its platform rules, which may not necessarily reflect precisely the respective legal rights of suppliers and customers.

The powers of the OIP operator go beyond the immediate management of platform activities. An OIP operator can generate value not only from the many supply transactions it facilitates (through commission on each transaction), but also from the data the OIP operator is able to collect from each user and arising from every transaction.[46] It is able to create this additional value as a result of the platform's positive indirect network effects, with the value of this data increasing, the more participants are active on the platform. So, as well as exercising a direct governance function, the OIP operator gains substantial value from platform interactions. Often, this is not shared with platform participants directly; indeed, an individual supplier often will not have access to data that has been derived from contracts with that supplier's customer. All of these aspects invariably attract proposals for regulation to control the exercise by an OIP operator of its powers. For example, the role of certain platforms as 'gatekeepers' to the market has prompted the European Commission to propose its Digital Markets Act.[47]

[44] The bargaining strength of platform users will, of course, vary. Some suppliers may be in a stronger position than others if their presence on the platform is particularly important to the OIP operator and the platform's customers.

[45] A Ezrachi and ME Stucke, *Virtual Competition* (Cambridge, MA, Harvard University Press, 2016) chs 14 and 16; AC Hoyng and R van Mastrigt, 'Is the current debate about changing the competition law toolbox warranted? A perspective from a digital platform' (2020) 41 *European Competition Law Review* 327.

[46] Chiu (n 8).

[47] European Commission (n 6).

How the United Kingdom might follow suit remains to be seen; it consulted on reform ideas during 2021.

The task here is to examine the potential of contract law to put some limits on the ability of an OIP operator to act without constraints.

i. Implications for Contract Law

It has been shown that the contractual architecture of OIPs enables an OIP operator to move into a position whereby it has broad powers under its contracts with customers and suppliers to control continuing access of users to the platform, to determine the terms and conditions of such access, and to set the terms of the underlying supply contracts.

The OIP operator's powers can be treated as a particularly broad type of contractual discretion, for example when considering whether to suspend access to the platform or varying the terms of the contract with its users. English contract law has developed a mechanism for controlling the exercise of discretionary powers, albeit one that is not without controversy. In *Braganza v BP Shipping Ltd*,[48] Lady Hale noted how common terms conferring discretion on one contracting party are, and stressed that the courts should not interfere with such terms, let alone substitute their views for those of the party given the discretionary power to make a decision.[49] This reflects the generous attitude of English contract law to contractual freedom and that the 'parties are ordinarily free to contract on whatever terms they choose and the court's role is to enforce them'.[50]

Nevertheless, a line of cases preceding *Braganza* has developed principles for curtailing the extent of such a discretionary power. In *Paragon Finance plc v Nash*,[51] for example, the Court of Appeal held that term granting a lender a discretionary power to vary the interest rate to be paid by a borrower was not completely unfettered; rather, the parties reasonably expect that the discretion would not be exercised dishonestly, for an improper purpose, capriciously, arbitrarily or in a way no reasonable lender, acting reasonably, would act. In *Gan Insurance Co Ltd v Tai Ping Insurance Co Ltd (No 2)*,[52] in considering whether there were any restrictions on when a reinsurer might withhold approval, the Court of Appeal recognised as a limitation that such a decision 'should take place in good faith after consideration of and on the basis of the facts giving rise to the particular claim and not with reference to considerations wholly extraneous to the subject-matter of the particular reinsurance'.[53] In *British Telecommunications plc v Telefónica O2 UK Ltd*,[54] Lord Sumption said that

[48] *Braganza v BP Shipping Ltd* [2015] UKSC 17, [2015] 1 WLR 1661.

[49] ibid [18].

[50] Lord Toulson in *Prime Sight Ltd v Lavarello* [2013] UKPC 22, [2014] AC 436 [47].

[51] *Paragon Finance plc v Nash* [2002] 1 WLR 685. See also *Abu Dhabi National Tanker Co v Product Star Shipping Ltd, The Product Star (No 2)* [1993] 1 Lloyd's Rep 397.

[52] *Gan Insurance Co Ltd v Tai Ping Insurance Co Ltd (No 2)* [2001] EWCA Civ 1047.

[53] ibid [67]. See also *Equitable Life Assurance Society v Hyman* [2002] 1 AC 408 (HL) in the context of a discretionary power to pay bonuses to policy holders, which could not be exercised in a manner that would conflict with policy holders' contractual rights.

[54] *British Telecommunications plc v Telefónica O2 UK Ltd* [2014] UKSC 42, [2014] 4 All ER 907.

> as a general rule, the scope of a contractual discretion will depend on the nature of the discretion and the construction of the language conferring it. But it is well established that in the absence of very clear language to the contrary, a contractual discretion must be exercised in good faith and not arbitrarily or capriciously.[55]

In *Braganza*, Lady Hale explained the problem of discretionary contractual powers thus:

> [T]he party who is charged with making decisions which affect the rights of both parties to the contract has a clear conflict of interest. That conflict is heightened where there is a significant imbalance of power between the contracting parties … The courts have therefore sought to ensure that such contractual powers are not abused. They have done so by implying a term as to the manner in which such powers may be exercised, a term which may vary according to the terms of the contract and the context in which the decision-making power is given.[56]

The fact that such a term will vary depending on the terms of the contract may explain the different expressions in the case law; in some instances, overt reference is made to good faith as the controlling principle, whereas in others, the criterion is whether the exercise of the power would be so unreasonable that no reasonable person in the contracting party's position would act in this way. In *Braganza*, the Supreme Court held that the approach to determining whether a discretionary power under a contract has been exercised reasonably should comprise both the process by which the decision to exercise the discretion in a particular way was made (ie whether it is based on the correct matters) and whether the substantive result is reasonable (ie not 'so outrageous that no reasonable decision-maker could have reached it').[57] In short, the approach follows the one used in the context of judicial review under the *Wednesbury* principle.[58] Whether this is the right standard is open to debate, and this instance of borrowing from public law has been criticised.[59]

Although the recognition of a control mechanism over discretionary powers in contracts is welcome, there are questions about the approach emerging from the cases leading up to *Braganza*. First, the control is inserted into a contract as an implied term, and it is one implied in fact[60] on the basis of the particular contract. This means that a term restricting the exercise of contractual discretion might not be implied into every contract providing for this. Second, the improper exercise of discretion would be a breach of the implied term, for which a remedy would be damages for any provable losses but not a reversal of the decision made. This makes this a rather ineffective control mechanism in many cases.

Moreover, there is, at least theoretically, a possibility that this implied term might be excluded altogether by an appropriately worded term in the contract itself.[61] It is possible that such a term might be caught by section 3(2)(b)(i) of the Unfair Contract

[55] ibid [37].
[56] *Braganza* (n 48) [18].
[57] ibid, Lady Hale at [24]; Lord Hodge at [53]; and Lord Neuberger at [103].
[58] *Associated Provincial Pictures Houses Ltd v Wednesbury Corporation* [1948] 1 KB 223.
[59] M Bridge, 'The exercise of contractual discretion' (2019) 135 *LQR* 227, 230.
[60] *Mid Essex Hospital Services NHS Trust v Compass Group UK and Ireland Ltd (trading as Medirest)* [2013] EWCA Civ 200 [82]. Implication in fact is strictly controlled via the 'business efficacy' and 'officious bystander' tests: *Marks and Spencer plc v BNP Paribas Securities Services Trust Company (Jersey) Limited* [2015] UKSC 72, [2016] AC 742.
[61] Bridge (n 59) 228–32.

Terms Act 1977 if it is contained in the standard terms used by the party exercising the discretion (ie the OIP operator), because it could be read as giving that party the right to 'render a contractual performance substantially different from that which was reasonably expected of him', for example in exercising a discretion for an improper purpose. In that case, it would have to pass the reasonableness test. However, insofar as the exercise of the contractual discretion concerns the performance of the other party (ie platform users), such a term would not be caught by section 3 of the 1977 Act at all.

As noted, the alignment with the *Wednesbury* test has not passed without criticism. As an alternative, Davies has argued[62] that 'fraud on a power', or the 'proper purpose' rule, might be a better means of controlling the exercise of contractual discretion. Crucially, the doctrine requires the exercise of a power (whether contractual or otherwise) for a proper purpose, and this rule is of a mandatory, non-excludable character. Exercising a power for an improper purpose should therefore mean that the exercise is void and thus the prior status reassumed.[63] Sales, who dislikes the influence of *Wednesbury* in current case law, has argued[64] that controls over discretion should start with the interpretation of the contract to determine what purposes for the exercise of a discretionary power were in the contemplation of the parties, and that 'fraud on a power' should be set in that context. Although the parallel with 'fraud on a power' has yet to become established in the common law approach to controlling the exercise of contractual discretion, decisions such as *BT v Telefónica*,[65] where the Supreme Court noted that contractual discretion 'must be exercised consistently with its contractual purpose',[66] are steering the law in that direction.

There is a recognition that the exercise of contractual discretion should be subject to constraint, therefore – even if the precise way in which this happens has yet to be settled definitively. However, an OIP operator does not have unfettered discretion to act as it pleases.

C. The Common Interests of Platform Users

The three contractual relationships at the core of the OIP architecture are often portrayed as discrete relationships, with no connection between them other than the fact that the OIP operator is a party to two of the three relationships. This is helpful insofar as it provides an abstraction of the *formal* legal relationship of suppliers and customers with the OIP and with each other (where they are parties to a supply transaction concluded via the platform). However, this analysis fails to capture the complexity and interconnectedness between the many relationships within an OIP. As noted, the success of a platform relies on the presence of many customers and suppliers, and there may be a collective interest among all users as to how they conduct their activities on the platform

[62] PS Davies, 'Excluding good faith and restricting discretion' in PS Davies and M Raczynska (eds), *Contents of Commercial Contracts – Terms affecting freedoms* (Oxford, Hart Publishing, 2020) 89.
[63] ibid 104–11.
[64] P Sales, 'Use of powers for proper purposes in private law' (2020) 136 *LQR* 384.
[65] *British Telecommunications v Telefónica* (n 54).
[66] ibid [37].

(how individual conduct of suppliers might reflect on the platform community; how actions by OIP can harm reputations and create adverse economic effects, etc). The contracts between an OIP operator and platform users might include specific terms regarding the conduct of users,[67] but this does not mean that users that have suffered a loss due to the conduct of another user will have a direct right of action: only the OIP operator and each platform user will be in privity.[68]

A core feature of online platforms is that all the platform users have a contract with the OIP operator, as (business) suppliers or customers. A platform therefore operates as a hub-and-spoke set-up, with the OIP operator as the 'hub' element and each platform user as a separate spoke. Those platform users who enter into supply contracts via the platform will have a direct contractual relationship, but all the platform users who do not conclude any supply contracts with one another will not. If the terms of their platform-user contracts require them to act in a manner that does not harm the interests of other platform users, would this be enforceable only by the OIP operator, or could other platform users take action directly against that platform user? Privity would suggest that only the OIP operator could act. There have been instances where English law has recognised the possibility that contractual rights can be created as between participants in a common endeavour, as older cases on insurance funds show.[69] A closer, but far from perfect, analogy is the sports competition cases. In *The Santanita*,[70] yacht owners entering their yachts in a race organised by a yachting club had concluded a contract with the club's committee, undertaking to be bound by certain rules and to accept liability for all damages arising from failing to obey the rules. One yacht owner sued another after the former's yacht was sunk in a collision, and the House of Lords held, without discussion of the relevant principles, that a contract came into existence between competing yacht owners once they started sailing in the race.[71] It seemed to matter that the rules included an undertaking to compensate other competitors. In contrast, in *Earl of Ellesmere v Wallace*,[72] a horse owner's agreement with the Jockey Club to enter his horse in two races did not thereby conclude a contract with all the other owners of the horses also in that race.

The difference between these instances and online platforms is that it is difficult to treat online platforms as membership organisations and platform users as members, and even less as analogous to sporting competitions. In contrast to membership organisations, such as a stock exchange,[73] the main objective for platform users is to gain access to the market to either buy or sell a wide variety of products, making this a much more diffuse grouping than an organisation like the stock exchange. What these cases do suggest is that any terms in the contract between a platform user and OIP operator

[67] Social media platforms usually operate with 'Community Standards' or similar.

[68] E Peel, *Treitel on the Law of Contract*, 15th edn (London, Sweet & Maxwell, 2020) ch 14.

[69] *Gray v Pearson* (1869-70) LR 5 CP 568 (manager appointed by insurance fund members could not sue members for unpaid contributions as only members contractually bound); approved in *Evans v Hooper* (1875) 1 QBD 45.

[70] *Clarke v The Earl of Dunraven and Mount Earl, The Santanita* [1897] AC 59 (HL).

[71] Similarly, all three judges in the Court of Appeal thought a contract was formed between the competitors who had accepted the rules and started the race: [1895] P 248.

[72] *Earl of Ellesmere v Wallace* [1929] 2 Ch 1 (CA).

[73] See, eg, *Kowloon Stock Exchange v Inland Revenue Commissioners (Hong Kong)* [1985] 1 WLR 133 (PC).

that might require acting in a way that is not detrimental to the platform could create binding obligations between the various platform users, although this is far from clear.[74]

A recent development in English contract law might suggest another possibility. Although the paradigm contract underpinning much of contract law is a bilateral transaction-focused contract, many contracts are intended to be long-term and to underpin a lasting commercial relationship. There is extensive academic literature exploring 'relational' contracts, that is, contracts with a long-term and collaborative focus.[75] There are signs that English contract law will recognise relational contracts as a particular type of contract.[76] In *Bates v Post Office (No 3)*,[77] Fraser J reviewed recent authorities and concluded that 'the concept of relational contracts is an established one in English law'.[78] Importantly, Fraser J recognised that in relational contracts, there is a (presumed[79]) implied obligation of good faith or fair dealing, obliging the parties to refrain from commercially unreasonable conduct, determined objectively and in the relevant context.[80] Whether this will be a term implied in law (ie into all relational contracts), or implied in fact (ie dependent on the context in each contract) remains to be determined,[81] although Fraser J seemed to take the view that the term is implied into all contracts that qualify as relational contracts.[82]

This leads to the question of how one might identify a contract as 'relational'. In *Bates v Post Office (No 3)*, Fraser J set out in some detail the characteristics of a relational contract.[83] Although the long-term nature of the contract will be central to characterising it as 'relational', this is far from sufficient. A relational contract also typically involves collaboration between the parties, with mutual trust and confidence reposed in one another, a high degree of communication and cooperation, expectations of loyalty and others. Whilst many contracts between an OIP operator and platform users are likely to be long-term, they seem some distance away from being 'relational'. Although both parties typically have an interest in a long-term relationship, their reasons are quite different. The OIP operator needs a large volume of suppliers and customers to maximise the indirect network effects of the platform and the direct and indirect value it can generate from transactions concluded via the platform. Suppliers will seek access to the platform to broaden their customer-base, and will have a long-term interest in

[74] There is also the possibility that a more precisely worded term could be enforceable by virtue of the Contracts (Rights of Third Parties) Act 1999, s 1(1), although the Act can be, and often is, excluded.

[75] See D Campbell (ed), *The Relational Theory of Contract: Selected Works of Ian Macneil* (London, Sweet & Maxwell, 2001); also I McNeil, 'Reflections on Relational Contract Theory after a Neo-classical Seminar' in H Collins, D Campbell and J Wightman (eds), *The Implicit Dimensions of Contract* (Oxford, Hart Publishing, 2003) 207.

[76] *Yam Seng Pte Ltd v International Trade Corp* [2013] EWHC 111 (QB); *Bristol Groundschool Ltd v Intelligent Data Capture Ltd* [2014] EWHC 2145 (Ch); *Al Nehayan v Kent* [2018] EWHC 333 (Comm).

[77] *Bates v Post Office (No 3)* [2019] EWHC 606 (QB).

[78] ibid [705].

[79] Cf ibid [721].

[80] ibid [711].

[81] Soper argues that a good faith term is unnecessary: CH Soper, 'Occam's razor or Leggatt's multiblade – good faith or clean shave?' [2021] *JBL* 580.

[82] Cf Davies (n 62) 94–97.

[83] *Bates v Post Office (No 3)* (n 77) [725].

maintaining this. But this does not make it a common endeavour, nor does it involve a high level of cooperation; the relationship between OIP operator and suppliers is not intended to be collaborative, even if it is to be long-term. In any case, the economic imbalance between OIP operator and platform users would suggest that this is not a collaborative endeavour. So even if 'relational contracts' become firmly established as a distinct contract type in English contract law, this would not seem to have any immediate significance for online platform contracts.

The significance of this development might lie elsewhere: the emergence of relational contracts is a flicker of an indicator that English contract law could develop a distinct approach to long-term contracts, particularly those involving more than common repeat transactions, such as subscription contracts or instalment supply contracts. In a similar way, the contractual architecture of an online platform might eventually gain distinct recognition at some point in the future. In particular, the very strong position of the OIP operator compared to (most of) its business users, and customers, and the relative imbalance of economic strength and control, might lead to the strengthening of existing control mechanisms, such as those over discretionary powers, as well as to the recognition of specific obligations appropriate to online platforms implied into the relevant contracts. One might, for instance, expect an implied term requiring the OIP operator to ensure that the platform continues to operate smoothly and not prevent platform users from being able to use the platform fully, analogous to the principle that each party to a contract impliedly agrees not to thwart the other party's ability to perform the contract.[84]

The tension between contractual and organisational norms in the context of platforms could be the trigger: as a legal form, platforms are contractual constructs, but platforms can also be viewed as an ecosystem with organisational characteristics. Indeed, this has led some to call for recognising platforms as a distinct organisational form in law.[85] It might not be necessary to go quite as far; recognising a type of contract reflecting the particular way in which contracts are used for the architecture of online platforms might well be sufficient. Yet, despite all this, such a development is a long way off, and so relying on contract law alone to address at least some of the challenges associated with online platforms might not suffice.[86]

IV. Contracts as a Regulatory Target

The preceding section has shown that the ability of English contract law to offer sufficient controls over the contracts between an OIP operator and its platform users is limited, other than perhaps the possible control over exercise by an OIP operator of its discretionary powers. Concerns about online platforms have been in the eye of

[84] Cf *Mackay v Dick* (1876) 6 App Cas 251.

[85] Chiu (n 8).

[86] Cf R Brownsword, 'Three approaches to the governance of decentralised business models' in RM Barker and IHY Chiu (eds), *The Law and Governance of Decentralised Business Models* (Abingdon, Routledge, 2020) 51.

policymakers for over half a decade,[87] particularly the strong controlling role of an OIP operator over everything that happens on its platform. As explained in section III.B, the strong position of the OIP operator is enshrined in the terms and conditions with platform users, and these generally determine the OIP operator's right to change the terms and conditions unilaterally, to suspend or remove a platform user, control over personal data, the use of ancillary services and so on. The ability of an OIP operator to take all these decisions gives it a powerful role vis-à-vis all the platform users. This prompted the European Commission to investigate, with two studies identifying as the main areas of concern a number of unfair business-to-business (B2B) trading practices on online platforms,[88] as well as the potential unfairness of some terms and conditions in online platform contracts.[89] As will be explained in section IV.A, it chose to respond by proposing a Regulation that would directly intervene in the contracts between an OIP operator and its *business* platform users.[90] To an English lawyer, this is a familiar technique; legislation has been used to require that contracts provide for certain matters, or to insert terms into particular types of contract,[91] and the common law has, on occasion, implied terms into particular types of contract as a matter of law.[92] Indeed, as discussed earlier, the ability of an OIP operator to exercise its discretionary powers under the platform contract would be constrained by a requirement that this needs to be exercised reasonably and for a proper purpose.

A. The B2B Fairness and Transparency Regulation

The Commission's proposal was eventually adopted as Regulation 2019/1150 on promoting fairness and transparency for business users of online intermediation services.[93] It implements a specific regulatory objective – to limit the unfettered freedom of an OIP operator – by regulating the content of several of the terms and conditions in the contract between the OIP operator and its business users, rather than by imposing a set of obligations directed at the OIP operator's conduct. It focuses on the contracts

[87] European Commission, 'Communication on Online Platforms and the Digital Single Market – Opportunities and Challenges for Europe' COM (2016) 288 final; House of Lords Select Committee on European Union, *Online Platforms and the Digital Single Market* (HL 2015–16, 129–X).

[88] Ecorys, 'Business-to-Business Relations in the Online Platform Environment – Final Report' (European Commission, 2017) at https://publications.europa.eu/en/publication-detail/-/publication/04c75b09-4b2b-11e7-aea8-01aa75ed71a1/language-en (accessed 14 September 2021).

[89] EY, *Study on Contractual Relationships between online platforms and their professional users – Final Report* (European Commission, 2018) at https://publications.europa.eu/en/publication-detail/-/publication/b3d856d9-4885-11e8-be1d-01aa75ed71a1/language-en (accessed 14 September 2021).

[90] European Commission, 'Proposal for a Regulation on Promoting Fairness and Transparency for Business Users of Online Intermediation Services' COM (2018) 238 final. See C Twigg-Flesner, 'The EU's Proposals for Regulating B2B Relationships on online platforms – Transparency, Fairness and Beyond' (2018) 7 *Journal of European Consumer and Market Law* 222.

[91] eg, Sale of Goods Act 1979, ss 13(1), 14(2) and 14(3); or Consumer Rights Act 2015, ss 9–11.

[92] *Liverpool CC v Irwin* [1976] 2 All ER 563; *Scally v Southern Social Services Board* [1991] 4 All ER 563; or *Ali Shipping Corporation v Shipyard Trogyr* [1999] 1 WLR 314.

[93] Regulation (EU) 2019/1150 of the European Parliament and of the Council of 20 June 2019 on promoting fairness and transparency for business users of online intermediation services [2019] OJ L187/57. This is now saved 'direct EU legislation' under s 3(1) and (2) of the European Union (Withdrawal) Act 2018 and continues in effect.

between an OIP operator and 'business users', that is, any business offering goods or service via an OIP to *consumers*.[94] The Regulation therefore constitutes a rare intervention in commercial contracts, but its scope is limited to OIPs where goods or services are offered to consumers by businesses.[95] It is supplemented by domestic regulations dealing with aspects of enforcement.[96]

One of the key objectives of the Regulation is to enhance transparency of the terms and conditions that form the basis of the contractual relationship between the OIP operator and business users. For these purposes, the phrase 'terms and conditions' includes all terms and conditions, whatever they are called or whichever form they take, that govern the contractual relationship between the OIP operator and business users (hereinafter 'terms'). These must have been determined unilaterally by the OIP operator, although in practice this will usually be the case. Whether they were determined unilaterally is established on an overall assessment and the relative size of the parties, but allowing for the possibility of some negotiation. The fact that some provisions might be the result of such negotiations would not, on its own, mean that terms as a whole were not 'unilaterally determined'.[97] The challenge of working out when that line is crossed is familiar to English lawyers thanks to section 3(1) of the Unfair Contract Terms Act 1977.[98]

The Regulation then stipulates a number of things regarding the terms, with regard to both their presentation and content. Thus, terms must be drafted in plain and intelligible language[99] and available from the pre-contractual stage right through the duration of the contract.[100] In addition, Article 3(c)–(e) require that the contract sets out how access to the OIP might be suspended, terminated or otherwise restricted; information about additional distribution or marketing channels through which the OIP operator might market the goods or services offered by business users; and the effect of the contract on intellectual property rights owned or controlled by business users. Terms that fail to comply with these requirements, either as a whole or in respect of specific provisions, are deemed to be 'null and void'.[101] This seems a drastic consequence, because if the terms as a whole are 'null and void', then it would almost certainly mean that there is no contract between OIP operator and business platform users at all. This cannot be what the parties would want in respect of non-compliance with these requirements. In the absence of any domestic or CJEU case law on this, it is impossible to say how strictly this would apply to the terms as a whole rather than individual non-complying provisions. In addition, in domestic law, a failure to comply with these requirements is treated as a breach of duty, and a business user is entitled to compensation for loss or damage

[94] EU Regulation 2019/1150, Art 2(1).

[95] This therefore excludes platforms that offer only peer-to-peer (P2P) or B2B transactions but not business-to-consumer (B2C) ones.

[96] The Online Intermediation Services for Business Users (Enforcement) Regulations 2020 (SI 2020/609).

[97] EU Regulation 2019/1150, Art 2(10).

[98] Unfair Contract Terms Act 1977, s 3(1), refers to 'the other's written standard terms of business'. In *Salvage Association v CAP Services* [1995] FSR 654, it was noted that a degree of negotiated amendment to standard terms would not take the contract out of the scope of s 3(1), but this required case-by-case consideration.

[99] EU Regulation 2019/1150, Art 3(1)(a).

[100] ibid Art 3 (1)(b).

[101] ibid Art 3(3).

suffered as a result.[102] However, it is unclear whether this would extend to losses caused by the fact that the terms as a whole, and therefore potentially the whole contract, are deemed null and void.

Furthermore, the procedure for varying terms is specified in Article 3(2), and requires a notice period, which must be reasonable and proportionate to the extent of the changes but in any case no shorter than 15 days.[103] A business user can decide to terminate the contract during the notice period if it does not wish to continue to operate via the platform on the basis of the varied terms. A business user may waive the notice period, and can be deemed to have done so if new listings are added during the notice period.

A variation that fails to comply with these requirements will also be 'null and void', although here this consequence makes more sense. As before, this will also be a breach of duty attracting a right to seek compensation for losses under UK law.[104]

There are several further transparency obligations. Thus, terms must state whether business users are restricted from offering their goods or services through channels other than the OIP, including the grounds for such restrictions (available to the public) based on relevant economic, commercial or legal considerations.[105]

Article 5, which deals with the ranking of search results, requires that the terms set out the main parameters, and their relative importance compared to other parameters, that determine the way rankings are created.[106] Where an OIP allows business users to pay for a higher ranking, this must also be stated.[107] Terms only need to provide sufficient information to allow business users to gain an 'adequate' understanding of whether and how rankings are based on the characteristics of the goods or services offered to consumers and the relevance of those characteristics for those consumers; there is no obligation to disclose details of the underlying algorithm or other information that would enable business users to mislead consumers by gaming the ranking system.[108]

Furthermore, Article 6 requires that terms specify which ancillary goods or services are offered by the OIP operator, and whether a business user is able to offer its own ancillary goods or services through the platform. Another issue is that some OIP operators (eg, Amazon) also offer their own goods or services through the platform and might rank them in preference to those offered by business users. The terms have to state where this is the case and describe the 'main economic, commercial or legal considerations' for this differentiation. In particular, this has to include whether differentiation relates to the fact that the OIP operator has access to personal or non-personal data that platform users provide when using the platform; rankings or other settings applied by the OIP operator that influence consumer access to goods or services offered by business users; as well as any direct or indirect payment for using the OIP.[109]

[102] Reg 3 of the Online Intermediation Services for Business Users (Enforcement) Regulations 2020.

[103] Except where there are legal or safety/cybersecurity reasons for the change: EU Regulation 2019/1150, Art 3(4).

[104] Reg 3 of the Online Intermediation Services for Business Users (Enforcement) Regulations 2020.

[105] EU Regulation 2019/1150, Art10(1).

[106] ibid Art 5(1).

[107] ibid Art 5(3).

[108] ibid Art 5(5)–(6).

[109] ibid Art 7(3).

Indeed, with regard to personal and non-personal data provided by platform users, the terms must specify whether and how business users are entitled to access such data. In any case, information has to be given about the OIP operator's access to such data and whether this is shared with third parties; whether business users can access data they provide or generate, or which are generated by transactions between a business user and its customers; and whether business users can access aggregate data based on all platform users.[110]

This overview shows that the Regulation requires that certain matters are expressly stated in the contract, but it does not go so far as to require substantive obligations: an OIP operator is free to give preferential rankings, or restrict access to data – but needs to be transparent about this. However, there might be an incidental effect from such transparency in that an OIP operator might adjust its approach to some or all of these issues as a result.

In addition to requirements regarding the content of a contract, the exercise of certain powers under the contract is also controlled by the Regulation. Thus, prior to taking a decision to restrict or suspend a business user from the platform, a statement of reasons must be given no later than the moment when this decision becomes effective.[111] If the decision is to terminate the contract altogether, a minimum of 30 days' notice[112] must be given, together with a statement of reasons. In either situation, the statement of reasons must explain the facts (including third-party notifications) leading to the decision and the relevant grounds for the decision stated in the terms and conditions.[113] There are no specific sanctions provided under the Regulation for failing to comply with these requirements, but in UK law such failure is also treated as a breach of duty in respect of which compensation for loss can be claimed.[114]

A number of further requirements are imposed to ensure that 'contractual relations … are conducted in good faith and based on fair dealing':[115] an OIP operator must not impose retroactive changes to the terms;[116] and terms must state how business users can terminate the contractual relationship, and also whether and how there will be post-termination access to information provided or generated by the business user.[117] The opening sentence of Article 8, quoted above, is difficult: as worded, it falls short of requiring the parties to act in good faith and based on fair dealing, and instead mandates a number of specific requirements that are treated as being in accordance with a general good faith and fair dealing principle. However, it could equally be treated as an 'exhortation'[118] to act in accordance with good faith and fair dealing, coming perilously close to introducing such a duty into this type of contract. If it were treated as a specific duty, a failure to act in accordance with such a duty would attract

[110] ibid Art 9.

[111] ibid Art 4(1).

[112] Again, this does not apply where there are legal reasons for this, or where the business user has repeatedly infringed the terms of the contract: ibid Art 4(4).

[113] ibid Art 4(5).

[114] Reg 3 of the Online Intermediation Services for Business Users (Enforcement) Regulations 2020.

[115] EU Regulation 2019/1150, Art 8.

[116] ibid Art 8(a).

[117] ibid Art 8(b) and (c).

[118] C Busch, 'Towards Fairness and Transparency in the Platform Economy?' in A De Franceschi and R Schulze (eds), *Digital Revolution – New Challenges for Law* (Munich, Beck/Nomos, 2019) 57, 63.

the possibility of claiming compensation for loss or damage suffered as a result.[119] However, the significance of this effect would lie elsewhere: legislation would impose a legal duty on the parties to a contract between an OIP operator and business user to act in accordance with good faith and fair dealing, which would mean that such a duty would be imposed in an commercial contract that does not seem to have any particular features meriting such a duty. The scope of Article 8 might eventually be clarified in court,[120] but for now uncertainty remains about the extent of its good faith and fair dealing element.[121]

Finally, OIP operators must provide an internal complaint-handling system in respect of complaints by business users regarding the OIP operator's compliance with the obligations imposed by the Regulation, as well as about technical matters or the behaviour of the OIP operator,[122] and provide information about the access and functioning of this in their terms and conditions.[123]

B. Implications of Regulatory Intervention in Contracts

Regulating aspects of the contract between the OIP operator and business users operating via the platform reflects the contractual architecture of platforms. However, one might question what the implications of using contracts as regulatory vectors in this way might be. The effect of such intervention, as the B2B Fairness Regulation shows, is to oblige an OIP to act in a particular way and to make this a contractual obligation towards every business customer. This leads to the question as to how such intervention might interact with the application of general rules of contract law? For example, the Regulation controls the exercise of an OIP operator's discretion with regard to restriction, suspension or termination of a business user's access to the platform. The use of discretionary powers is policed generally at common law under the *Braganza* line of cases, as discussed in section III.B. The decision to sanction a business user under the Regulation needs to relate to grounds for action specified in the terms and conditions, and requires transparency about the facts that have led the OIP operator to its decision. In this particular instance, English law would provide for a remedy in regulation 3 of the Online Intermediation Services for Business Users (Enforcement) Regulations 2020, but there might be instances where statutory control over discretionary powers does not attract specific sanctions, and so there might still be room for the *Braganza* principles to operate in such circumstances.

[119] Reg 3 of the Online Intermediation Services for Business Users (Enforcement) Regulations 2020 applies simply to a breach of Arts 3, 4 and 8 of EU Regulation 2019/1150.

[120] Although one might expect this to come from the CJEU rather than the domestic courts, most EU national legal systems already have a good faith duty, so would not regard Art 8 as raising any particular issues.

[121] It is also possible that the planned review of 'retained EU legislation' announced by the UK Government might lead to a repeal of the Regulation, or modifications to it, although this area is not among those identified in a list published as Cabinet Office and Lord Frost, '*Brexit Opportunities: Regulatory Reform*' (*GOV.UK*, 16 September 2021) at www.gov.uk/government/publications/brexit-opportunities-regulatory-reforms (accessed 30 October 2021).

[122] EU Regulation 2019/1150, Art 11(1).

[123] ibid Art 11(3).

Second, what would be the remedial consequences if an OIP operator had acted in breach of one of the obligations inserted into the terms and conditions by the Regulation or some other regulatory measure? English contract law prioritises damages as the remedy for breach of a term, but this requires that a claimant can demonstrate that it has suffered a loss. In addition, regulation 3 of the Online Intermediation Services for Business Users (Enforcement) Regulations 2020 provides for a right to compensation for loss or damage. However, not every breach of a regulatory obligation might result in a quantifiable loss, so damages may not always be the most appropriate remedy.

For most business users, ensuring compliance would probably be the preferred outcome. Securing compliance would mean a remedy to prevent further breaches of the terms, which would make an injunction a more suitable remedy. Usually, injunctions are granted infrequently in respect of a breach of contract, but there have been instances where a court has granted an injunction to stop a party from breaching a contract in a situation when damages would not have been an appropriate remedy.[124] Indeed, the Regulation itself envisages this as a means of enforcing compliance by an OIP operator,[125] and this is given effect in domestic law through regulations 4 and 5 of the Online Intermediation Services for Business Users (Enforcement) Regulations 2020. Under the 2020 Regulations, this right is granted to 'qualifying organisations or associations',[126] which covers associations with a legitimate interest in representing business users or public bodies[127] but not business users acting individually. Interestingly, this power is not available in respect of a breach of Article 8, which contains the express good faith and fair dealing aspect. As this obligation is not made a term of the contract itself, an individual business user could not seek an equitable injunction in respect of this but, as noted, there is the statutory right to claim compensation for any loss caused by a breach of Article 8.

V. Interaction between Contracts and Possible Regulatory Action

Whilst legislative action specifically targeting online platforms has not been extensive thus far, there are further measures in the pipeline. The EU will in due course have its Digital Services Act and Digital Markets Act, and the UK Parliament examined a draft Online Safety Bill during the 2021/22 session. A central focus of these measures is on social media and audio-visual media content-sharing platforms, particularly the problem of harmful and illegal posts on such sites. In the context of commercial OIPs, there are fewer concerns of this kind, but this does not mean that these will escape future regulatory action. Indeed, draft Article14 in the Digital Services Act proposal (notice and action mechanism) requires an online platform provider to provide for the

[124] *Araci v Fallon* [2011] EWCA Civ 668; *AB v CD* [2014] EWCA Civ 229.

[125] See EU Regulation 2019/1150, Art 14.

[126] Regs 4(1) and (3)(b) of the Online Intermediation Services for Business Users (Enforcement) Regulations 2020.

[127] Cf EU Regulation 2019/1150, Art 14.

possibility that individuals can notify the platform of 'illegal content' posted thereon. The definition of 'illegal content'[128] is broad and understood to include content in breach of consumer protection law.[129] Notification would trigger the need to remove or disable such content swiftly so as to preserve the liability exemption under draft Article 5. Furthermore, draft Articles 5 and 6 in the Digital Markets Act proposal impose a number of obligations on 'gatekeeper' platforms, such as permitting platform users to offer their products through other platforms or websites at different prices, which might differ from obligations contained in the terms of the contract between OIP operator and platform users.

It is therefore possible, even likely, that there will be future regulatory measures that will alter the overall legal and regulatory context for platforms and the contracts on which platforms are based. Even where such measures do not directly regulate those contracts (such as Regulation 2019/1150, discussed earlier), they could still potentially affect the ability of an OIP operator to set the terms of those contracts and, more generally, the conduct of an OIP operator in respect of all matters related to running the platform.

The specific challenges of online platforms will eventually have to produce some kind of regulatory intervention, because contract law does not seem likely to respond to many of these challenges,[130] although whether this will seek to start from contract or from regulatory objectives that indirectly affect the operation of contracts remains to be seen.

VI. Conclusions

Prompted by the role of OIP operators as self-proclaimed intermediaries in facilitating transactions between suppliers and customers enrolled on an online platform, this chapter has sought to probe the capacity of contract law to deal with some of the particular features of online platforms. Although contract law offers some hooks on which the development of targeted principles could be hung, these are far from solid. Contract law would have to make significant leaps to recognise the interconnectedness between the many contractual relationships that are formed through a platform, in particular between the infinite spokes created by the contracts between an OIP operator and platform users. It is therefore likely that Parliament will have to step in and address at least some of the legal challenges of online platforms. The EU B2B Fairness and Transparency Regulation (2019/1150), which continues to apply in the United Kingdom, at least for the immediate future, offers a template for how regulatory objectives can be reconciled with the contractual nature of an online platform.

[128] European Commission (n 6) draft Art 2(g).
[129] ibid draft recital 12.
[130] Brownsword (n 85).

10

Agency, Artificial Intelligence and Algorithmic Agreements

TAN CHENG-HAN*

I. Introduction

Intermediaries are a necessary convenience in life. We frequently rely on others to get things done for us, often in relation to other persons. We may, for instance, rely on our co-workers to interact with other co-workers or persons outside the organisation for us; engage intermediaries to obtain information or bring our attention to business or investment opportunities; ask family members or friends to perform certain tasks; procure a person to enter into a contractual obligation on our behalf; and in today's connected world, use a virtual platform to engage in transactions. We do not have unlimited time and space, so being able to leverage off others expands a scarce resource.

The sheer breadth of intermediaries means that many different bodies of law apply, depending on the type of intermediary and/or the acts in question. Trustees, bailees, bankers and many professionals are specific types of intermediaries around whom particular rules have developed. They are also subject to general areas of law applicable to broader groups of people, such as criminal law, torts, contract, etc. It is difficult to conceive of a Law of Intermediaries that is self-contained and manageable in the way other areas are. Having said this, the law of agency is the closest thing to a general law relating to intermediaries, and the flexibility of its application has facilitated certain perceived positive outcomes that would otherwise not have been possible.[1] The concept of agency, in other words, by virtue of its malleable nature, has expanded the universe of legal outcomes that are considered desirable in relation to intermediaries.

Until relatively recently, any discussion of intermediaries would refer to human persons. However, advances in computing that have led to sophisticated computer

* I am grateful to Francis Reynolds and Paul Davies for their comments on an earlier draft. The usual caveat applies.

[1] A striking example of this are cases that have extended the notion of agency beyond its conventional scope to render 'principals' liable for unauthorised wrongs committed by 'agents', eg *Hewitt v Bonvin* [1940] 1 KB 188 (CA); *Colonial Mutual Life Assurance Co of Australia Ltd v Producers' and Citizens' Co-operative Assurance Co of Australia Ltd* (1931) 46 CLR 41 (HCA).

programs now enable parties to engage in many transactions without the need for human intermediaries. The processing power of computers has allowed computer programs to take over many roles that once depended on human intermediaries. A good example relates to the sale and purchase of shares on a stock market, which increasingly take place over an electronic platform without a broker. Accordingly, there have been suggestions that such platform intermediaries powered by sophisticated computer software should be treated as agents under the law. This chapter suggests that while there may be a role for the law of agency, any such role is limited, notwithstanding the flexibility of the agency concept.

II. Agents versus Intermediaries

It will be useful to begin by delineating the difference between the legal concept of an agent against the more general term 'intermediary'. In general, it can be said that all agents are intermediaries but not all intermediaries are agents, at least in the sense that agency is understood in law. True or paradigmatic agency arises where a principal and agent agree that the latter shall have power or authority to act on behalf of the former. Such agency is succinctly defined in *Restatement, Third* in the following manner:

> Agency is the fiduciary relationship that arises when one person (a 'principal') manifests assent to another person (an 'agent') that the agent shall act on the principal's behalf and subject to the principal's control, and the agent manifests assent or otherwise consents so to act.[2]

Restatement, Third goes on to state that an agency relationship arises only when these elements are present.[3] This definition is a narrow one that requires a relationship of mutual assent, with the agent subject to the principal's control where the agent acts on the principal's behalf.

To the above definition it may usefully be added that in respect 'of what the principal has assented to, the agent is said to have authority to act; and this authority constitutes a power to affect the principal's legal relations with third parties'.[4] This external dimension gives the law of agency much of its legal relevance; the law of agency does not apply to all intermediaries and is concerned only with intermediaries/agents who have the power to affect their principal's legal relations, usually in contract, vis-à-vis third parties.[5] Thus, the law of agency is engaged if a managing director with authority enters into an agreement to purchase an office building on behalf of her company, but is unlikely to be if a friend buys a carton of milk for me on my instructions. In the latter case, my friend is likely to have purchased the carton as a principal on the understanding that she will be reimbursed by me. Should she change her mind and decide that she wants the milk for

[2] American Law Institute, *Restatement of the Law Third, Agency* (St Paul, MN, American Law Institute Publishers, 2007) § 1.01.

[3] ibid § 1.02.

[4] P Watts and FMB Reynolds, *Bowstead and Reynolds on Agency*, 22nd edn (London, Sweet & Maxwell, 2021) [1-001].

[5] Such power may also be present in the absence of mutual consent between the principal and agent, and this is discussed in the following paragraph.

herself, I am unlikely to have any rights against her as no intention to enter into legal relations would usually have been contemplated.

Yet while the technical definition of agency in law is relatively narrow, agency has a sphere of application that goes beyond this. A person who has no consent or authority to bind a principal may nevertheless do so where such person has apparent authority. Such apparent authority arises where the principal has said or done something that amounts to a representation to the third party that such person was authorised to perform the act in question. Often, the representation will be by placing the agent in a position that would normally have such authority.[6] A third party who reasonably relies on such a representation to enter into a contract with the agent acting on behalf of a principal may enforce such contract notwithstanding the agent's lack of authority. Using the doctrine of estoppel, the courts say that the principal is estopped from denying the existence of such authority as it was by the principal's own act, the representation, that the third party changed its position.[7] While the 'internal' agency dimension of mutual assent is not present, the 'principal' is bound as if the 'agent' had authority, and to this extent such instances of estoppel have traditionally been regarded as within the province of the law of agency.

Another example of broader agency are intermediaries that are commonly referred to as 'canvassing' or 'introducing' agents.[8] The role of such intermediaries is to introduce parties, who then negotiate and conclude contracts as between themselves with minimal involvement, if any, from the introducing agent. They have no authority to contract on behalf of any party. Nevertheless, they are regarded as being on the fringe of agency law, as they often have authority to receive or communicate information on behalf of one of the parties and to this extent may alter the legal relations of such party.[9] In addition, they may also owe certain fiduciary obligations to the parties that engage them. In *Yuen Chow Hin v ERA Realty Network Pte Ltd*,[10] the Singapore High Court held that an estate agent was in breach of his fiduciary duty to the vendor when the agent did not inform the vendor that the wife of the agent's supervisor was the intended purchaser of the property. It is debatable if such a strict duty should be imposed on mere introducing agents who perform their engagements diligently. Significantly, it appeared that no advertisement for the sale of the property had been placed and the agent may only have informed his supervisor of it. This would also potentially amount to a breach of the express or implied terms of the agent's engagement.

As a result of this extended application of agency, in *UBS AG v Kommunale Wasserwerke Leipzig GmbH*[11] Lord Briggs and Hamblen LJ, after referring to the submission that 'a relationship could never be identified as one of agency if none of the main characteristics, namely authority to affect the principal's relationships with third parties, fiduciary duty or control by the principal, was present', said 'We would not be minded to

[6] *Freeman & Lockyer v Buckhurst Park Properties (Mangal) Ltd* [1964] 2 QB 480 (CA).

[7] ibid. On the other hand, in the United States, apparent authority is seen as an aspect of the objective interpretation of contracts, see *Restatement, Third* (n 2) § 2.03, comment c.

[8] Watts and Reynolds (n 4) [1-020].

[9] ibid.

[10] *Yuen Chow Hin v ERA Realty Network Pte Ltd* [2009] 2 SLR(R) 721.

[11] *UBS AG v Kommunale Wasserwerke Leipzig GmbH* [2017] EWCA Civ 1567, [2017] 2 Lloyd's Rep 621 [91].

go quite that far, but the absence of any of these main characteristics must nonetheless be a significant pointer away from the characterization of a particular relationship as one of agency, even though there may be rare exceptions.'

Notwithstanding its being well established that agency operates beyond its paradigm situation, it has nevertheless been applied in circumstances that are difficult to rationalise. A good example can be seen from an unusual line of cases involving use of a means of conveyance such as a motor car.[12] The proposition in those cases is that where a person drives a car for the benefit or purpose of the owner, the driver does so as agent for the owner who will be liable for any damage caused by the agent's negligent driving. The matter was one of agency and not employment.[13] Liability did not depend on ownership but on the delegation of a task or duty, and was an illustration of the maxim *qui facit per alium facit per se*.[14] In *Ormrod v Crosville Motor Services Ltd*,[15] a car was being driven to pick up the owner, after which the owner, the driver and his wife would vacation together. An accident occurred because of the driver's negligence, and it was held that the owner was liable for the negligence of his agent.

The use of agency is difficult to justify. First, many of the cases revolve around social settings, where the law should be loath to find any intention to establish an agency relationship. Second, the cases involve tortious acts, and agency liability for such acts typically arises where the principal has directed or procured the tortfeasor to commit the wrongful acts.[16] Nothing of the sort existed in these cases. Third, it is questionable if the three main characteristics of agency identified in *UBS v Kommunale Wasserwerke*[17] were present. There would not appear to be any fiduciary duty owed by the driver to the owner, and actual control by the owner is not possible if the owner is not in the car, though the owner can of course give instructions prior to its use.[18] For reasons to be discussed in the next paragraph, the characteristic of authority or power to affect the principal's relationships with third parties also does not truly exist. Fourth, the cases were not decided because of an employment relationship (or anything akin to it) and therefore the doctrine of vicarious liability relied upon by the court to make the owner liable for the negligence of the driver should not have been applicable. Notwithstanding this, as Lord Pearson put it:

> [T]he principle by virtue of which the owner of a car may be held vicariously liable for the negligent driving of the car by another person is the principle *qui facit per alium, facit per se*. If the car is being driven by a servant of the owner in the course of the employment or by an agent of the owner in the course of the agency, the owner is responsible for negligence in the driving.

[12] The rule may be of wider application to other types of chattels, see *Morgans v Launchbury* [1973] AC 127, 135, 144.

[13] *Hewitt v Bonvin* (n 1) 194–95.

[14] ibid 195.

[15] *Ormrod v Crosville Motor Services Ltd* [1953] 1 WLR 1120 (CA).

[16] *Parkes v Prescott* (1869) LR 4 Ex 169; *Gabriel Peter & Partners v Wee Chong Jin* [1997] 3 SLR(R) 649.

[17] *UBS* (n 11).

[18] In *Scott v Davis* (2000) 204 CLR 333, a case involving an aeroplane, the High Court of Australia expressed scepticism over the use of agency to impose liability where the user was not under the control of the owner at the time of the accident. The English cases construe direction and control more liberally. In *Hewitt* (n 1) 195–96, du Parcq LJ was of the view that 'having the control of a vehicle' may be established where the owner is not present, as in the example of a father's consent to his son's use of the father's car for the entertainment or convenience of a family guest.

> The making of the journey is a delegated duty or task undertaken by the servant or agent in pursuance of an order or instruction or request from the owner and for the purposes of the owner.[19]

What is remarkable about these cases is that the finding of agency flows from the courts' determination that liability should be imposed, rather than from liability as a consequence of an agency relationship. The reasoning, in other words, is somewhat backwards. Agency is typically about intermediaries who have the power to affect their principal's legal relations either because of a conferment of authority or because of the doctrine of estoppel. In the vehicle cases, the drivers did not have actual authority to drive negligently, nor did the doctrine of apparent authority apply as the plaintiffs were involuntary victims who had not relied on any representation by the owner. Given the absence of actual or apparent authority, it would appear that the drivers were agents only because the consequences of their tortious acts were visited on the owners who were deemed principals by virtue of this.[20]

The doctrinal weakness of this line of cases points strongly to its policy basis, as exemplified well by Lord Wilberforce's observation that 'agency' in such contexts 'is merely a concept, the meaning and purpose of which is to say "is vicariously liable," and that either expression reflects a judgment of value – respondeat superior is the law saying that the owner ought to pay'.[21] While the underlying basis may be one of policy, now rendered largely redundant because of standard third-party insurance for motor vehicles,[22] the importance of this line of cases is that they provide a powerful illustration of the flexible use of agency to bring about what was regarded as a socially desirable outcome. It is often the case that when a new issue arises, the law will try to find a solution within existing doctrines, often by adapting a doctrine beyond what was envisaged originally. In the case of intermediaries such as the drivers in the motor cases, where no liability towards the owner would have been imposed under orthodox theory, the solution was found in extending the idea of agency, its being the closest general body of law applicable to intermediaries. The strength of such an approach – turning a mere intermediary into an agent – is the ability to fit the solution within an existing framework, though this can lead to a lack of robustness in articulating the rationale behind the solution and may create ripples of doctrinal difficulty.

Similarly, as the courts may not always like the outcome of the distinction between employees and independent contractors, given that vicarious liability can only be imposed for the acts of the former and not the latter even when functionally they may be similar, the concept of agency has occasionally been invoked so that liability

[19] *Morgans* (n 12) 140; see also ibid 139–40 (Viscount Dilhorne), 148 (Lord Salmon).

[20] See also D Fletcher, 'Two meanings of "agent" in the Australian law of torts' (2015) 22 *Torts Law Journal* 197, 205–06, calling for agency to be excised from this narrow area of road accident compensation so that the proper reasons for imposing liability can be the focus; Watts and Reynolds (n 4) [8-187], expressing the view that these cases 'do not link to agency, at least in the central sense of the word' and further details should be sought in works on tort; GE Dal Pont, *Law of Agency*, 4th edn (Australia, LexisNexis, 2020) [22.41], describing the line of cases as introducing 'an artificially constructed agency'; BS Markesinis and RJC Munday, *An Outline of the Law of Agency*, 4th edn (London, Butterworths, 1998) 12; FMB Reynolds and Tan C-H, 'Agency Reasoning – A Formula or a Tool?' [2018] *Singapore Journal of Legal Studies* 43.

[21] *Morgans* (n 12) 135.

[22] Callinan J in *Scott v Davis* (n 18) [346] opined that the presence of an insurer, or the likelihood that usually the owner will better be able to pay than the driver, influenced the results and distorted the law.

arises from a wrong committed by an independent contractor within the scope of the supposed agency.[23] In *Colonial Mutual Life Assurance Co of Australia Ltd v Producers' and Citizens' Co-operative Assurance Co of Australia Ltd*,[24] a principal was found liable for defamatory statements made by a canvassing agent who had no authority to enter into any contracts and was prohibited expressly from making such statements. Two of the judges in the majority, Gavan Duffy CJ and Starke J, expressed the view that a person is liable for another person's act if it employs that other person as an agent and the act complained of is within the scope of the agent's authority. It was not necessary that the particular act should have been authorised as long as the agent was put in a position to do the class of acts that are the subject of the complaint.[25] Such analysis raises difficulty, as yet again actual and apparent authority were absent and agency was invoked simply to justify the imposition of vicarious liability on the principal.

The other two judges in the majority, Dixon and Rich JJ, took a slightly different approach. In their view, the principal was liable because it had asked the agent to stand in the principal's place and act for it. The agent was the principal's representative in certain aspects of the negotiation, even if the agent did not have authority to conclude contracts binding on the principal.[26] The principal must therefore be considered as itself conducting the negotiation. What the agent did fell within his actual authority and the slanders made by the agent arose from the erroneous manner in which the agent's actual authority was exercised. The undertaking contained in the contract not to disparage other institutions was not a limitation of authority but a promise as to the manner of its exercise. This analysis also does not sit well with orthodox principles of agency. If the principal has prohibited a specific mode of performance, it seems a stretch to say this can nevertheless fall within actual authority. Additionally, while vicarious liability was not invoked, the reasoning mirrored the then 'Salmond test' for vicarious liability.[27]

The 'artificially constructed' agency in the motor car cases[28] and the use of agency to impose vicarious liability on certain independent contractors illustrate powerfully how agency doctrine or reasoning has been used to transform persons who might be expected to be mere intermediaries into agents whose acts have resulted in legal consequences for their 'principals'. Policy considerations are the likely explanation for the conscription of agency to such end, as there will be instances where the courts believe that a person ought to be responsible for the acts of an intermediary even though said intermediary does not fall easily into a recognised category of actors to justify such an outcome. In the next sections, we explore the role of agency in relation to contracting through electronic intermediaries, including platforms. In some instances, agency can apply conventionally, but it is doubtful whether the courts will extend its flexibility to electronic processes per se.

[23] P Morgan, 'Recasting Vicarious Liability' (2012) 71 *CLJ* 615, 628.

[24] *Colonial Mutual Life Assurance Co* (n 1).

[25] ibid 46–47.

[26] In *Scott v Davis* (n 18) [19], [67]–[68] Gleeson CJ and McHugh J respectively explained *Colonial Mutual Life* on this basis, even though McHugh J acknowledged that Gavan Duffy CJ's and Starke J's judgment may support a wider proposition.

[27] Namely, that an employee's tort falls within the course of employment if, inter alia, it is a wrongful and unauthorised mode of doing some act authorised by the employer.

[28] Dal Pont (n 20).

III. Algorithmic Agreements

Before turning to the specific issue of whether agency law has any meaningful role to play in the context of algorithmic contracts facilitated by electronic intermediaries, some explanation of such agreements is necessary.

An algorithmic contract is one where an agreement that affects the rights and liabilities of parties has come about as a result of the operation of an algorithm, often functioning within a platform.[29] Unfortunately, this does not tell us much, because the term 'algorithm' can be understood broadly in a number of ways.[30] For the purpose of this chapter, a suitable starting point may be found in the Algorithmic Accountability Act introduced in the US Congress in 2019.[31] Section 2 of the Bill provides a definition of 'automated decision system' in the following terms:

> The term 'automated decision system' means a computational process, including one derived from machine learning, statistics, or other data processing or artificial intelligence techniques, that makes a decision or facilitates human decision making, that impacts consumers.

An algorithm, in other words, is in essence a piece of computer code of varying sophistication that, in the context of contracts, can provide a process by which parties may find themselves, sometimes without any overt action on their part, in a binding contractual relation. Algorithms are fundamentally composed of software and, although somewhat of a simplification, are 'sets of defined steps structured to process instructions/data to produce an output'.[32] In this age of information technology, algorithms permeate our lives, and examples include self-learning algorithms (such as those that determine the results of web searches and what news is pushed to us) and dynamic pricing algorithms that adjust prices automatically in online markets.[33]

The degree of inputs required by the putative parties and/or the degree of control they exercise in relation to algorithmic contracts can vary considerably, as can the contractual settings. A consumer purchasing a garment will usually be able to choose from a variety of options, such as colour, size and fit. On the other hand, there are algorithms that execute contracts based on prevailing market conditions without any direct human input for each specific contract, though the parties must agree in advance to the terms on which the platform operates. In such circumstances, the algorithm itself may have determined the terms of the agreement.[34] A good example is automated trading

[29] See also LH Scholz, 'Algorithmic Contracts' (2017) 20 *Stanford Technology Law Review* 128, 134, who describes algorithmic contracts as 'contracts in which one or more parties use an algorithm to determine whether to be bound or how to be bound'.

[30] K Lum and R Chowdhury, 'What is an 'algorithm'? It depends whom you ask' *MIT Technology Review* (26 February 2021) at www.technologyreview.com/2021/02/26/1020007/what-is-an-algorithm/ (accessed 26 May 2021).

[31] Algorithmic Accountability Act 2019, HR 2231, introduced on 10 April 2019.

[32] R Kitchin, 'Thinking Critically about and Researching Algorithms' (2017) 20(1) *Information, Communication and Society* 14, 16.

[33] M Ebers, 'Regulating AI and Robotics – Ethical and Legal Challenges' in M Ebers and S Navas (eds), *Algorithms and Law* (Cambridge, Cambridge University Press, 2020) 37, 37–40. See also S Chopra and L White, 'Artificial Agents and the Contracting Problem: A Solution via an Agency Analysis' [2009] *University of Illinois Journal of Law, Technology & Policy* 363, 364–65.

[34] See also LH Scholz, 'Algorithmic Contracts and Consumer Privacy' in L DiMatteo, M Cannarsa and C Poncibo (eds), *The Cambridge Handbook of Smart Contracts, Blockchain Technology and Digital Platforms* (Cambridge, Cambridge University Press, 2019) 251, 254–55.

systems/platforms that use algorithms responding to market information in real time to determine optimal execution. As has been observed, automated trading is a tool that may observe market parameters or other information in real time to automatically generate or carry out trading decisions without human intervention.[35]

These more sophisticated electronic intermediaries, which are sometimes referred to as 'intelligent software agents' or as exhibiting 'artificial intelligence', are composed of sets of algorithms

> capable of independent action rather than merely following instructions. They exhibit high levels of mobility, intelligence, and autonomy according to which their actions are not always completely anticipated, intended, or known by their users.[36]

Such 'agents'

> employ more sophisticated decision-making mechanisms using statistical or probabilistic machine learning algorithms [where] there may be no strictly binary rules which determine the outcome. It is the combination of relevant factors, and the relative weights the system accords them, that determines the outcome.[37]

IV. Electronic Intermediaries, Algorithmic Agreements and the Limits of Contract Law (and More Generally Legal Rules as We Understand Them Today)?

As contracting is increasingly becoming automated without the involvement of traditional human agents or other intermediaries, a number of issues may arise that can be challenging for legal principles as we understand them today. An illustrative case is the Singapore Court of Appeal decision of *Quoine Pte Ltd v B2C2 Ltd*.[38]

Quoine Pte Ltd was an operator of a cryptocurrency exchange platform and also operated as a market maker where it conducted trades through its 'Quoter Program'. The respondent, B2C2 Ltd, was a trader on Quoine's platform, and did so through its algorithmic trading software that was designed to function with minimal human intervention and was deterministic in the sense of producing the same output given the same input. The case concerned several trades of two cryptocurrencies, Bitcoin and Ethereum, between the respondent on the one hand and two margin traders on the other, where the respondent bought Bitcoin and sold Ethereum. In April 2017, Quoine implemented changes to some login passwords on its trading platform but failed to implement certain necessary changes to the Quoter Program. This led to the Quoter Program's not being able to generate new trading orders for market-making purposes, leading to an abnormally thin trading volume. This in turn affected the value of the

[35] P Gomber et al, 'High Frequency Trading' (2011) 14 at ssrn.com/abstract=1858626 or dx.doi.org/10.2139/ssrn.1858626 (accessed 26 May 2021).

[36] EAR Dahiyat, 'Law and software agents: Are they "Agents" by the way?' (2021) 29 *Artificial Intelligence and Law* 59, 60.

[37] Chopra and White (n 33) 369.

[38] *Quoine Pte Ltd v B2C2 Ltd* [2020] SLR 20.

two margin traders' positions and triggered margin calls on them, together with the force closure of their positions by the placement of market orders to buy Etherium at the best available price on the platform. As a result of the extremely thin volume and the respondent's trading algorithm, which had a built in fail-safe 'deep price' of 10 Bitcoin to 1 Ethereum, a number of trades were concluded between the respondent and the margin traders at a rate of either 9.99999 or 10 Bitcoin for 1 Ethereum, which was approximately 250 times the then prevailing rate in the market of 0.04 Bitcoin for 1 Ethereum. These trades were automatically settled by the platform, with 3092.517116 Bitcoin debited from the margin traders' accounts and credited into the respondent's account, while 309.2518 Ethereum went the other way. As the margin traders did not have a sufficient Bitcoin balance to meet the amount that was debited, this resulted in a negative Bitcoin balance in their accounts. When Quoine became aware of the trades the next day, it unilaterally proceeded to cancel the trades. The respondent brought action against Quoine for breach of contract, and its claim for damages succeeded at first instance before the Singapore International Commercial Court.[39]

A number of issues was canvassed before the Court of Appeal, but for the purposes of this chapter we need focus only on the issue of unilateral mistake.[40] A unilateral mistake arises where one party has entered into a contract under a mistake as to a fundamental term of such contract and the other party had either actual or constructive knowledge of the mistake. Under Singapore law, in the former instance the contract is void at common law and in the latter it is voidable in equity if the non-mistaken party engaged in some unconscionable conduct in relation to the mistake.[41] Singapore law (unlike English law[42]) recognises a doctrine of unilateral mistake in equity. The majority in *Quoine* held there was no operable mistake that vitiated the contracts, as the trades were entered into pursuant to deterministic algorithmic programs that acted exactly as they had been programmed. In any event, even if there were an operative mistake, the respondent had no requisite knowledge of the mistake as the trades were executed in accordance with its algorithm without any human intervention. The evidence did not suggest that the respondent's algorithm had been designed to take advantage of mistakes of the kind that arose in *Quoine*. The 'deep price' was to ensure that the respondent's trading software would function continuously and not lack price inputs, while at the same time insulating the respondent from any adverse consequences of unexpected events.

Mance IJ dissented on the basis that the approach adopted by the trial judge (and the majority) looked at the position in the abstract and in advance, without any regard for the actual transactions or the market circumstances surrounding them. This was a different approach from that when considering mistake in the context of transactions completed by human intervention. In such cases, the law would consider the actual state

[39] *B2C2 Ltd v Quoine Pte Ltd* [2019] 4 SLR 17.

[40] Another important issue was whether digital tokens such as bitcoin are 'property' as understood in law, though ultimately the Court of Appeal did not think it was necessary to come to a conclusion on this issue given its view on the contract point. In *Ruscoe v Cryptopia Ltd (in liq)* [2020] NZHC 728, [2020] 2 NZLR 809, the New Zealand High Court found that digital tokens could be property.

[41] *Chwee Kin Keong v Digilandmall.com Pte Ltd* [2005] 1 SLR(R) 502.

[42] E Peel, *Treitel: The Law of Contract*, 15th edn (London, Sweet & Maxwell, 2020) [8-059].

of mind of each party in the light of the surrounding circumstances. The position taken at first instance

> involves omitting a usually important element in any appraisal of such a situation, namely, (here) whether there was anything drastically unusual about the surrounding circumstances or the state of the market to explain on a rational basis why such abnormal prices could occur, or whether the only possible conclusion was that some fundamental error had taken place, giving rise to transactions which the other party could never rationally have contemplated or intended.[43]

Instead, the test should be 'what any reasonable trader would have thought, given knowledge of the particular circumstances … because any reasonable person, knowing of the relevant market circumstances, *would* have known that there was a fundamental mistake'.[44] The law must be adapted to the new world of algorithmic programs and artificial intelligence in a way leading to results that reason and justice would lead one to expect. In the present case, the mistake on the part of Quoine was obvious to the respondent, because as soon as the respondent inspected the computer printouts the following morning, it emailed Quoine to say 'Major Quoine database breakdown'.[45] Accordingly, while Mance IJ agreed that there was no unilateral mistake at common law, he was of the view that the more flexible equitable doctrine applied, given that the error could be rectified without any resulting detriment to the respondent or any third party.

With respect, the author prefers the dissenting view of Mance IJ. Errors in algorithmic agreements will no doubt continue to occur, and while the author has great sympathy for the perspective of the majority that the parties had chosen to transact in a certain way and the court should not rewrite what had been agreed,[46] and keeping in mind also that the law should not save sophisticated commercial actors from bad bargains,[47] it is suggested that it seems overly inflexible to limit relief for mistake to instances where the programmer wrote the program knowing that certain trades could only take place as a result of an operative mistake. Such an approach would leave the doctrine of mistake with only the barest minuscule window of application. Effectively, it immunises a party from virtually any mistake made by a counterparty through the superimposition of an algorithm.[48] The price differential in *Quoine* was of a much greater magnitude than in the earlier Singapore decision of *Digilandmall*,[49] with the only difference being that a human person accepted the offer in the latter case. On the assumption that the outcome in *Quoine* was unsatisfactory, as this chapter believes, the case illustrates that there may be limits to contract law's arrival at fair outcomes in relation to algorithmic agreements.

One final observation is that on the facts, it was found that the margin traders were operating under a relevant mistake, as they never contemplated that trades would be transacted at prices that deviated so substantially from the actual market prices.

[43] *Quoine* (n 38) [192].
[44] ibid [200].
[45] ibid [203].
[46] ibid [104].
[47] See PS Davies, 'Bad Bargains' (2019) 72 *Current Legal Problems* 253.
[48] See also SNG Kiat Peng, 'Contract Formation and Mistake in Cyberspace (Again) – The Story So Far and Where to Next?' (2021) 33 *Singaporean Academy of Law Journal* 692.
[49] *Digilandmall* (n 41).

While it was accepted that the respondent's programmer did not input the deep price with belief that such price would be achieved only because of a mistake, the trial judge also found that the programmer had not 'considered that there was a real possibility of the deep price orders being executed'.[50] The purpose was to protect the integrity of the system and the respondent from illiquidity. Seen in this light, any qualitative difference in perspective between the margin traders and the programmer was de minimis and mistake could arguably have been made out at common law.

V. Algorithmic Agreements and Agency

It is suggested that if contract law is not capable of giving rise to a fair and sensible outcome, the law of agency may play a role. This is not to say that agency law is a panacea for every possible issue that can arise, and it will be argued later that the law of agency as it stands will have only a limited role, but on the facts it could have led to a different outcome in *Quoine*.

Many electronic platforms exist to facilitate transactions between two or more parties much as a physical marketplace does. Actors on the platform can initiate or close transactions, and these are conscious acts on their part, with the platform merely a medium for participants to manifest their intentions. Such situations do not involve agency. Yet there may be circumstances where agency is involved. For instance, the parties may expressly or impliedly agree that the owner or operator of the platform will use the platform to enter into transactions on behalf of its users. This was the case in *Ruscoe v Cryptopia Ltd*,[51] where the cryptocurrency exchange provided in clause 7.3 of its terms and conditions that it was the user's 'agent for any transaction in Coins that you have entered into through your account on the platform'. Similarly, it is submitted that the circumstances in *Quoine* were such as to involve agency. Agency was potentially relevant because Quoine's platform was executing trades on behalf of the margin traders due to the force closure of their margin positions. These were not trades initiated by the two margin traders but were executed automatically by the platform based on its algorithm.[52] As platforms themselves are not legal entities with separate personality, either the trades were to be regarded as trades by the margin traders or they were trades initiated by the platform owner. One fact that may point to the former is where the contractual documents between the platform owner and its users stipulate that all transactions for the benefit of users are deemed to have been taken by them, regardless of whether they were initiated personally or by way of the platform's algorithm.

This was not the case in *Quoine*. Accordingly, it is suggested that when the platform executed the trades for the margin traders' benefit based on the platform's algorithm, such trades ought to be regarded as acts by Quoine in accordance with instructions written by Quoine into the platform's algorithm. Item 6 of Quoine's 'Risk Disclosure Statement' supports this view. It stated that in the case of margin transactions, should

[50] *B2C2* (n 39) [123].
[51] *Ruscoe* (n 40).
[52] *B2C2* (n 39) [17].

losses 'increase significantly if market prices are inconsistent with [the margin traders'] expectations', Quoine (not the margin traders) 'may execute a compulsory reversing trade of your entire position and settle the transaction using the Company's prescribed methods'. The objective was to protect the margin traders from 'escalating losses'. Force sales were for their benefit, and Quoine was entitled to initiate such trades without regard to their wishes.

Given the malfunction, and not because of losses caused by market prices, the circumstances in which Quoine would have been entitled to execute reversing trades were not met. Quoine could therefore not have had authority to enter into the trades in question (even accounting for a wide degree of latitude in what can be a fast-changing market), and its lack of authority was underscored by the fact that Quoine sought to reverse the trades after the mistake was discovered. As no detriment had been incurred by the respondent from the trades, the respondent's claim should have failed and the reversals been upheld, as unauthorised transactions are void.[53]

Agency was not fully considered by the first instance court. The only agency argument made appeared to be in support of the proposition that the knowledge and intention of the programmer should be considered.[54] The respondent also submitted that the relationship between the parties was one where Quoine was a party to a contract with the buyer and a party to a separate contract with the seller. This was rejected by Simon Thorley IJ on the basis that the parties themselves were responsible for determining the terms on which orders would be placed or filled, and therefore the relationship between buyer and seller was a direct one.[55] It is suggested that such rejection was correct, though for a different reason. The nature of the force sales bore no resemblance to Quoine's buying and selling on its own account. It is true that many platforms, including Quoine's, are intended to facilitate direct contracting between parties without the need for any other intermediary. Nevertheless, for the reasons mentioned in the preceding paragraph, the force closure of the margin traders' positions was different, as it is difficult to see how they determined the terms of the orders executed for them when these took place without the margin traders' knowledge. An agency relationship should therefore have been found, but the correct arguments were not canvassed.

Agency also did not appear to be fully canvassed before the Court of Appeal, although subsequent to the hearing of the appeal Quoine drew the Court's attention to an article contending that Quoine must have been acting as an agent for the users of the platform in general for the purposes of matching trades. The clause in the agreement that provided for irreversibility of trades should therefore be construed to mean that only the instructions given by the users to Quoine as agent were irreversible and not the trades themselves.[56] The Court of Appeal did not accept this, as the majority was of the view that the platform simply provided a means for parties to deal with each other

[53] Watts and Reynolds (n 4) [8-066].

[54] *B2C2* (n 39) [201].

[55] ibid [131].

[56] K Low and E Mik, 'Unpicking a Fin(e)tech Mess: Can Old Doctrines Cope in the 21st Century?' (*Oxford Business Law Blog*, 8 November 2019) at www.law.ox.ac.uk/business-law-blog/blog/2019/11/unpicking-finetech-mess-can-old-doctrines-cope-21st-century (accessed 17 August 2021).

directly in much the same way that a messaging platform operates. There was no suggestion that trading instructions were first passed to Quoine as a third party before they were uploaded on the platform.[57]

The agency argument that was rejected by the majority was a narrow one relating to a particular construction of how the 'irreversibility' term in the agreement should be construed. It should therefore not be regarded as any wider authority foreclosing the applicability of agency in appropriate circumstances. As pointed out, force closure cases represent a different fact pattern. Nothing in the agreement between Quoine and the users of its platform excluded the possibility of agency arising where the trades were initiated by the platform for its users. In the absence of a term to such effect, the more natural interpretation is that the intervention of Quoine in such circumstances must be as agent for its users.

That agency could plausibly have been deployed was acknowledged by Mance IJ. According to his Lordship:

> A collateral observation which it is convenient to interpose at this point is that it is, to my mind, odd that attention at trial should have been so focused on the margin traders, and not on Quoine. It was Quoine whose computer was programmed to instruct the trades. Moreover, most of the BTC sold did not exist as assets of Pulsar [one of the margin traders], and there must at least be a question whether Quoine could have had ostensible authority to bind Pulsar by a sale of non-existent assets which Quoine can have had no actual authority to sell on Pulsar's behalf.[58]

As the point had not been canvassed, Mance IJ said no more about it. It is clear, though, that Quoine could not have had actual authority to sell Bitcoin on behalf of the margin traders that they did not own. While ostensible authority may exist in relation to Bitcoin that the margin traders did not have, it is suggested that such authority, whether in relation to Bitcoin that the margin traders owned or not, could not have existed on the facts because it was obvious that the exchange price was ridiculously outside the market rate. It would not have been reasonable for the respondent to believe that such a transaction had been made within authority. The ignorance of the respondent as to whether the transaction was one with or without the intervention of agency is irrelevant. Parties frequently contract without knowing if the counterparty is acting personally or on behalf of another, without this affecting the validity of the agreement.[59]

In *Quoine*, a party to a trade would or should know that the counterparty could be Quoine as market maker (or trader), or another counterparty because of a trade initiated by such party or by Quoine with a view to protecting such user from further loss. If the trade was initiated by Quoine for a user, the normal principles of agency apply. The transaction records would only show the trade as between the two users without Quoine's involvement – and therefore there was no undisclosed agency but merely a time lag in being informed of the identity of the counterparty – but this should not preclude the introduction of evidence to establish that the trade was initiated by Quoine for one of the counterparties. There can be cases where at the time of contracting the

[57] *Quoine* (n 38) [76].
[58] ibid [188].
[59] *Teheran-Europe Co Ltd v S T Belton (Tractors) Ltd* [1968] 2 QB 545 (CA), 555.

third party did not know whether the other party was contracting as principal or agent, because such party sometimes contracted in one capacity and sometimes in the other. In some such circumstances, as in *Cooke & Sons v Eshelby*,[60] the courts may form the view that the case involved disclosed rather than undisclosed agency, even though the existence of the principal was not disclosed at the time of the contract. *Cooke v Eshelby* is a case that has often been criticised because two of the three judges based their decision on estoppel, which is not a good ground when the third party has no knowledge of any specific principal who can make a representation of authority. Another way of understanding the case, however, is that there will always be circumstances or situations where the facts are sufficiently ambiguous that the courts are called upon to determine whether there was an agency relationship and, if so, what the most appropriate agency relationship was to find between the parties. In *Cooke v Eshelby*, the third party's knowledge of and indifference to the fact that the other party had acted both as principal and broker in the past led the court to treat the case as it would a typical agency relationship once it was established that the counterparty was acting as agent. While it is certainly open to debate if this was correct, it is at least understandable that if a third party does not enter into a contract with another person with the positive belief that such person was acting as principal, the doctrine of undisclosed agency ought not to apply, and such third party will be regarded as having contracted with the counterparty in the capacity that such counterparty acted.

It is true that the facts in Quoine are different, in that the counterparty in *Cooke v Eshelby* contracted with the agent while in *Quoine* the transaction took place through the platform without any ostensible involvement by Quoine as agent. Furthermore, the records of the trades would only have shown the respondent and the margin traders as counterparties. Notwithstanding this, it is submitted that this is ultimately a matter of fact, which should not preclude the courts from finding that agency was involved if the facts are capable of supporting such a determination. If a principal can intervene on a contract even if the principal's existence was not known by the counterparty at the time the contract was entered into, with all the conceptual difficulties this raises with the doctrine of privity of contract,[61] there is no good reason why in principle it cannot be established that an agreement was made through an agent where this was not apparent on its face, at least where it is known to be one of several modes in which an agreement may come about and the contractual documents are not inconsistent with the existence of an agency relationship.[62] To determine otherwise would appear overly formalistic, as it would preclude agency's applicability simply because certain transactions, such as those that take place over platforms, may not be as transparent as face-to-face transactions.[63]

[60] *Isaac Cooke & Sons v Eshelby* (1887) 12 App Cas 271 (HL).

[61] Generally, see Tan C-H, 'Undisclosed Principals and Contract' (2004) 120 *LQR* 480.

[62] This was no such inconsistency in *Quoine*, as the printouts of the trades can be understood as merely purporting to show who the ultimate contracting parties were; see *B2C2* (n 39) 106–08 ('Annex 3: Copy of the printout forms').

[63] Such reasoning is consistent with Mance IJ's dictum in *Quoine* that Quoine did not have actual authority to sell non-existent assets on behalf of the margin traders, and this potentially raised the issue of whether Quoine could have had apparent authority to do so.

VI. Are Platforms and Algorithms Agents?

It can be seen thus far that the normal principles of agency are capable of being applied to platforms where the owners or managers of the platform initiate a transaction on behalf of one of the parties. However, is agency or agency reasoning sufficiently flexible to give rise to a similar result where a transaction has taken place without the involvement of the platform's owners or managers? For instance, would a trader be bound by a trade initiated by her but which, as a result of a malfunction in the platform's programming, caused a much lower price to be transmitted and such price was automatically accepted by the counterparty's trading algorithm? If the mistake had been made by a human broker, and the mistake was an obvious one, agency notions of authority would likely operate so as to avoid the transaction. The opposite is true if there was no agency and *Quoine* correctly decided the legal question of whether there was an operative mistake.

Some commentators have suggested that platforms using automated processes giving rise to contracts should be regarded as agents.[64] One argument is that platforms or algorithms should not be regarded as mere tools, as this would impose strict liability on their principals even if design flaws or software bugs caused the artificial 'agent' to malfunction.[65] It is also said that the objective theory of contractual formation cannot be properly applied in the case of contracts entered into by electronic agents because the principal will usually not have a specific intention referable to a particular contract.[66] An agency law approach to artificial agents would resolve such issues.[67]

In similar vein, it is said that in highly sophisticated algorithms the program can lead to behaviour that could not have been anticipated by a principal, potentially resulting in the unenforceability of a contract.[68] The argument is that certain algorithms are of a level of sophistication that what they will do is unknown to the contracting parties, because the algorithms can move far beyond the intents and capacities of their authorising entities. The parties will therefore lack the level of objectively manifested intent necessary to ground a contractual promise. The manifested intent of a party to use such an algorithm is not necessarily the same as objectively assenting to the actual contracts selected by the algorithm, because what the algorithm will agree upon cannot be determined at the time the party puts the algorithm into use.[69] Beyond offer and acceptance, there is also no consideration, as such algorithms only give rise to an agreement to agree rather than a true bargain.[70] Given these difficulties, the solution is to cast such algorithms as constructive agents. The 'constructive' qualification is used because algorithms are not human persons. Leaving aside the lack of personhood of algorithms, the law should treat the intent and knowledge level of companies or individuals who use algorithms for contracting in the same way as the law would treat the intent and knowledge of a principal in agency law. Algorithms can be agents without legal personality, or

[64] Chopra and White (n 33); Scholz (n 29).
[65] Chopra and White (n 33) 371.
[66] ibid 375.
[67] ibid 392–94.
[68] Scholz (n 29) 136.
[69] ibid 150–55
[70] ibid 156.

quasi-agents for the purpose of understanding the legal obligations of their principals.[71] In terms of how authority is to be conferred on algorithms as constructive agents, ratification is likely to be the predominant method given that the principals may not be able to predict how the algorithms will behave.[72] The agency approach would also allow relevant persons to pursue actions against principals for fraud, market manipulation and other wrongful acts.[73]

These are not unattractive arguments to this author. An additional ground of support is agency's inherent flexibility as outlined earlier, including cases of agency being 'constructed' notwithstanding seeming variance with orthodoxy.[74] Nevertheless, it will be difficult without legislative intervention for courts to regard a piece of code as a legal agent even with the protean nature of the term 'agent'. The law of agency is premised on the notion that agents are sentient human individuals, or at least entities having legal personality that can act through sentient individuals whose mind and will are attributed to the legal entity.[75] An agent must have the ability to exercise thought and will,[76] which software, however sophisticated, lacks. And insofar as sophisticated intelligent algorithms are capable of moving well beyond what their authorising entities are capable of predicting or perceiving, it is difficult to see how such limited human thought and will can be attributed to such algorithms.

In addition, agents generally owe fiduciary duties to their principals,[77] and it is difficult to see how software code can owe such duties or how such duties may be meaningfully exercised against software. Where an agent exceeds authority, the agent breaches its warranty of authority to the third party.[78] It is hard to see how a software program that malfunctions and therefore acts outside authority can make a contractual promise to another, or how such a promise, if it exists, can be enforced against the program. If such claims may be made against the principal on the basis that the principal is the owner of the software within which the algorithm is embedded, it would seemingly make the principal both agent and principal. If, on the other hand, the software is owned by a different party and the claim is brought against the developer, it would have the remarkable effect of making software developers effectively agents.[79] It is essential to agency law as it stands today that there is a *person*, whether a legal fiction or otherwise, who mediates between two or more parties. While it is true that capacity to contract is not essential for an agent to bind a principal,[80] the concept of legal personality is distinct from legal capacity, and without the former there is no person capable of being on the other end of a contract.[81]

[71] ibid 165.
[72] ibid 167.
[73] ibid 168–69.
[74] Dal Pont (n 20) [22.41].
[75] See also *Restatement, Third* (n 2) § 1.04(5).
[76] Watts and Reynolds (n 4) [2-013]; *Restatement, Third* (n 2) § 3.05.
[77] *UBS* (n 11) [91].
[78] Tan C-H, *The Law of Agency*, 2nd edn (Singapore, Academy Publishing, 2017) 281.
[79] For similar reasons, owners of platforms that depend on algorithms to facilitate contracting by others should not by virtue of this alone be regarded as agents.
[80] Chopra and White (n 33) 400.
[81] Cf ibid 399–400.

In addition, as the majority in *Quoine* put it,[82] the platform in that case (and this is true of many platforms) is similar to an Internet messaging application that allows users to communicate with one another. It is no more an intermediary than any other communication device is. In addition, if messages are for some reason garbled when communicated over a device, one would not think of using agency law to resolve any misunderstandings that arose. If the dispute is over whether a contract was formed or a term of the contract, the doctrine of mistake ought to determine the position of the parties. The same should generally apply to contracts formed electronically without direct inputs from the contracting parties. If the law of mistake is not applicable, the implicit policy considerations behind such doctrine should arguably not be circumvented by creative use of agency.

Furthermore, leaving aside the fact that contract doctrine may not be flexible enough to deal with such 'mistakes', there would usually be very little practical reason to treat platforms and algorithms as agents. The inherent flexibility of agency has been useful in relation to intermediaries as a means of filling gaps where the law has been found wanting. With algorithmic contracting that does not involve the intervention of the platform owner in instituting an action for a user, no recourse to agency is necessary for an enforceable agreement to arise between users of the platform.[83] The position is analogous to *Thornton v Shoe Lane Parking*,[84] where a contract was found to be made with the garage owner when the ticketing machine at the entrance of the garage dispensed the parking ticket to the plaintiff. Today, an automated parking system may dispense with the parking ticket. The vehicle registration may be scanned at the entrance to the garage and the appropriate amount deducted at the point of departure from a pre-paid token or card. Similarly, in *Digilandmall*,[85] a contract came about when the defendant's website automatically processed the plaintiffs' orders and dispatched confirmation email notes to the plaintiffs' email accounts within minutes of the orders, although the contracts were subsequently vitiated for unilateral mistake. These are examples of contracts formed through an electronic intermediary without any need to rely on agency.

In addition, it is suggested that the inability of users to anticipate how an algorithm may work is unlikely to be a serious problem for contract formation, as *Quoine* illustrates. It is open to users with full knowledge to choose to be bound by (i) agreements about which they have incomplete details and (ii) the process under which contracts may arise. Often the threshold questions relate to the agreement between the platform and its users rather than the contracts entered into between users over the platform. The reason for this is that the platform through its agreements with individual users acts as a clearing house of sorts to bring all users of the platform under the same contractual framework. An example can be seen in *The Satanita*,[86] where it was held that there was a contract between all the competitors of a yacht race because of a letter each participant signed addressed to the secretary of the club that organised the race.

[82] *Quoine* (n 38) [76].
[83] See also S Bayern, 'Algorithms, Agreements, and Agency' in W Barfield (ed), *The Cambridge Handbook of the Law of Algorithms* (Cambridge, Cambridge University Press, 2020) 153, 157–61.
[84] *Thornton v Shoe Lane Parking* [1971] 2 QB 163 (CA).
[85] *Digilandmall* (n 41).
[86] *Clarke v Earl of Dunraven (The Satanita)* [1895] P 248 (CA).

Other concerns that may necessitate an agency approach are also not likely to arise, such as the need to impose fiduciary obligations on the program. If the owner of the platform or a user abuses it to the prejudice of others, it is likely that there will be contractual or tortious claims against the abuser and, depending on the facts, a claim for breach of fiduciary duty could also lie. And should the program cause harm, the owner or developer of the program may be responsible for its own acts without the need to use principles of vicarious liability that are sometimes extended to agents.[87] For instance, unless the agreement between Quoine and the margin traders limited Quoine's liability, the margin traders could have brought a claim against Quoine for any loss suffered by them if the transactions had not been reversed. For the most part, therefore, there is little reason to stretch the concept of agency to electronic platforms that have replaced human agents who in the past would have been the bridge between contracting parties that did not transact 'face to face' with each other.

VII. Conclusion

As a matter of good legal policy, there must be a way to arrive at a better solution than to allow, in a case such as *Quoine*, what was clearly a mistake in fact to lead to a party's benefitting 'to the tune of perhaps millions of dollars by way of what some would call an uncovenanted windfall'.[88] The obvious injustice of the case can be contrasted with the earlier decision of *Digilandmall.com*,[89] where the acceptance of the mistaken offer made through a website was vitiated by mistake even though the scale of the pricing differential with the normal price of the item was much less extreme. While users of a platform may have agreed to its terms of use knowing full well that they do not understand how the platform's algorithm may work, and should generally bear principal responsibility for the results of the algorithm, not every unfortunate outcome based on such an informational gap should be allocated to the user on whom the outcome falls. Where there has been a malfunction of a platform resulting in an outcome beyond the contemplation of reasonable persons, the law should arguably be sufficiently nimble to arrive at more optimal results. Should the costs of mistakes on the part of electronic agents fall on the contracting parties, the law of agency may occasionally ameliorate the position of the party that has to bear the brunt of the mistake. This will depend on the owner or operator of the electronic agent being considered an agent properly speaking and acting beyond actual or apparent authority. Unfortunately, this only shifts the burden to the owner/operator, as a claim for breach of warranty of authority may be brought against such agent and could lead to contractual damages far in excess of damages in tort for negligence.

One final observation is that there is at least one material difference between a messaging application and platforms through which transactions take place. In the

[87] Cf MU Scherer, 'Of Wild Beasts and Digital Analogues: The Legal Status of Autonomous Systems' (2018) 19 *Nevada Law Journal* 259, 287; Scholz (n 29) 132.

[88] *Quoine* (n 38) [195] per Mance IJ.

[89] *Digilandmall* (n 41).

former, the participants have the ability to express their intentions directly to the other party, whether contemporaneously or not. A messaging platform also does not (at least at this time) randomly generate replies on its own *and* transmit them without more to the other party. Platforms with sophisticated algorithms can go beyond such rudimentary messaging applications. There can be less control by the users of the platform, and even if this was part of the bargain entered into, the question is whether there are limits to whether the law should recognise every outcome, however bizarre, for which the parties did not specifically contract. In the past, where parties were not able to deal directly with each other, they would do so through an agent or other intermediary, which left scope for the courts to arrive at fair outcomes through agency principles such as authority and attribution. With electronic platforms and algorithmic contracts that may displace human agents completely in the transacting process, a potentially important safeguard no longer exists. The law may therefore need to develop rules that compensate for this.

11

Client-Intermediary Relations in the Crypto-Asset World

HIN LIU, LOUISE GULLIFER AND HENRY CHONG

I. Introduction

In a world where financially valuable assets are increasingly being stored in digital form, questions arise as to the legal categorisation of such assets. The question of whether crypto-assets can constitute property has been the subject of some recent litigation in common law courts[1] and thus legal analysis. If the answer to such question is in the affirmative, as the cases cited suggest, this raises a plethora of further questions that need to be resolved by the courts before investors, regulators and accountants alike can approach digital assets with a sufficient degree of legal certainty. One such question, on which this chapter focuses, concerns the relationship between a crypto-asset intermediary (such as a crypto-asset exchange or custodian) and its clients, in relation to its storage of cryptocurrencies or cryptosecurities for those clients.

Cryptocurrencies and cryptosecurities are examples of crypto-assets. According to the United Kingdom (UK) Task Force, the characteristic features of crypto-assets are '(a) intangibility, (b) cryptographic authentication, (c) use of a distributed transaction ledger, (d) decentralisation, and (e) rule by consensus'.[2] The discussion in this chapter assumes that crypto-assets can constitute property.

The relationship between a crypto-asset intermediary and its clients is of practical importance because the vast majority of crypto-assets are kept by intermediaries, yet we simply do not know with any reasonable certainty the basis on which these assets are being held. Most agreements between clients and intermediaries are extremely vague, and are silent as to the legal relationship between the parties. Yet since common law courts will have to determine the legal category into which the agreement falls, they

[1] *B2C2 Ltd v Quoine Pte Ltd* [2019] SGHC(I) 3; *Quoine Pte Ltd v B2C2 Ltd* [2020] SGCA(I) 02 (collectively '*Quoine*'); *Ruscoe v Cryptopia Ltd* [2020] NZHC 728 ('*Cryptopia*'); *AA v Persons Unknown* [2019] EWHC 3556 (Comm). See also *Fetch.ai Ltd v Persons Unknown* [2021] EWHC 2254 (Comm).

[2] UK Jurisdiction Taskforce, 'Legal Statement on Cryptoassets and Smart Contracts' (November 2019) [31]. See ibid [24]–[34] for a more detailed discussion of crypto-assets generally.

should be guided by a consistent set of principles that allow them to characterise agreements with a degree of certainty and practical justice that is acceptable to commercial parties. This is essential for the determination of clients' entitlements on the intermediary's insolvency, a question of high public policy importance that has arisen frequently in recent litigation.[3] Moreover, the characterisation of the relationship will determine what (if any) are the baseline duties owed by the intermediary to its clients, and to what extent those duties can be excluded by express agreement.[4] In addition, as crypto-assets are (at least at present) not subject to extensive regulation, intermediaries of such assets will not be constrained by many regulatory requirements in relation to investor protection. The determination of the precise legal relationship between the parties therefore becomes of even greater public policy importance. This chapter addresses the situation where the law applicable to the question of the proprietary characterisation of the client-intermediary relationship is the common law.[5]

This chapter argues that the most likely relationship between a crypto-asset intermediary and a client is one of trustee and beneficiary, although there are also other possible legal characterisations, namely, outright title transfer, 'quasi-bailment' and mere obligations sounding in contract. Ultimately, in a particular case, the legal characterisation of the relationship, as well as the precise obligations undertaken by the intermediary, will depend on the client-intermediary agreement itself. The crucial question is one of boundaries: what are the outer limits of each legal category? *When* does it remain possible to say that an agreement creates legal effect *x* (eg trust), even if the precise terms agreed appear to deviate dramatically from the paradigm case of *x* (eg where a trustee has a very extensive right of use over the crypto-assets in question)?

II. Crypto-Asset Custody: The Possible Legal Relationships

A custodian is a (natural or legal) person who holds property for or on behalf of a client. *Black's Law Dictionary* defines 'custodian of property' as a person 'responsible for managing real or personal property'.[6] Thus, on the basis that crypto-assets can constitute property, a custodian of crypto-assets is a person holding such assets for or on behalf of clients.

What is meant by 'holding' a crypto-asset? It is important to outline the essential components of a crypto-asset. In short, a crypto-asset is simply an asset that is

[3] One example is the cases arising from the Mt Gox insolvency: eg Reference no 25541521 Case claiming the bitcoin transfer (Tokyo District Court, Heisei 26 (Year of 2014), (Wa)33320, Judgment of Civil Division 28 of 5 August 2015 (Year of Heisei 27)); Decision of the Moscow Arbitrazh Court (Case no A40-124668/17-71-160F, 5 March 2018).

[4] See sections II and III.

[5] For example the United Kingdom, Hong Kong, Singapore, New Zealand, Australia, the British Virgin Islands and the Cayman Islands. The regimes in Canada and the United States will not be explored, as they rely heavily on statute. See pt VI of the Ontario Securities Transfer Act 2006. Also see Art 8 of the Uniform Commercial Code (US), which governs the position in relation to securities: many crypto-assets held by intermediaries are crypto-securities.

[6] *Cryptopia* (n 1) [173], citing B Garner (ed), *Black's Law Dictionary*, 10th edn (St Paul, MN, Thomson Reuters, 2014).

cryptographically secured on a (theoretically) tamper-proof ledger, the blockchain. The asset is what is recorded on the blockchain. A user of the blockchain system is given a 'public' and 'private' key pair, which are two pieces of information (alphanumeric strings) that allow the user to interact with the system and transfer the asset. Having access to the private key will enable the user to transfer the crypto-asset by issuing an instruction on the blockchain and thereby changing the blockchain record.

Although the public and private keys are pieces of information, the fact that they are secured on a tamper-proof ledger means that the double-spending problem would not arise, and analogies can be drawn with physical items.[7] Specifically, the public key can be compared to the location of a physical 'vault' that denotes the (virtual) 'location' of the asset, and the private key can be compared to a code or password that allows the user to unlock the vault and transfer the asset to a different vault. Thus, an intermediary 'holds' a client's crypto-asset if it has access to the private key in relation to the public key where the crypto-asset is located, enabling it to transfer the asset and to prevent others from transferring it. This type of access is called 'factual control' in this chapter. It encompasses both positive and negative control in respect of the asset. Positive control denotes the (factual) ability to use, dispose of and transfer the asset, whereas negative control involves the (factual) ability to prevent others from using the asset. The emphasis is on these abilities as a matter of fact, rather than as a matter of law. The degree of factual control required is similar to that required for a person to have possession of a tangible object.[8]

According to *Black's Legal Dictionary*, the duties owed by a custodian of property to its client generally include 'securing, safeguarding and maintaining the property in the condition received and accounting for any changes in it'.[9] Ultimately, the precise duties owed in each individual client-custodian arrangement will depend on the terms of the contract. Such duties are determined, at least initially, by the legal categorisation of the arrangement (title transfer, trust, etc). It is to this issue we now turn.

A. Outright Title Transfer

The first possible legal relationship between client and intermediary is that of outright title transfer, that is, where title is vested absolutely in the intermediary. This is to be discerned from the intention of the parties to the client-intermediary agreement. If, upon construing the terms of the agreement, it is intended that full title in the asset be transferred to the intermediary, then that title will vest in the intermediary as long as the relevant formalities for transfer (if any) are complied with. This arrangement is found in a banker-customer relationship: it was held in *Foley v Hill*[10] that a customer who

[7] H Liu, 'The Legal Nature of Blockchain Securities' [2021] *LMCLQ* 476.

[8] The degree of control required to constitute possession of a physical asset is exclusive physical control: see, eg, *Powell v McFarlane* (1977) 38 P&CR 452 (Ch) 471; L Rostill, *Possession, Relative Title, and Ownership in English Law* (Oxford, Oxford University Press, 2021) 15–19.

[9] *Cryptopia* (n 1) [173], citing Garner (ed) (n 6).

[10] *Foley v Hill* (1847) 2 HLC 28.

deposits money in a bank account transfers outright title to his money. The bank is only under a personal (contractual) obligation to pay an equivalent sum, and otherwise has unencumbered title to the money. Crypto-assets held in accounts by exchanges could also be held to give rise to an outright title transfer.[11]

The effect of an outright title transfer is that the intermediary can freely dispose of the assets held in its custody: it is the absolute owner, and is not under a duty to use the asset for the benefit of the client. Indeed, the commercial motivation behind an outright title transfer lies in the intermediary's desire to use the assets obtained from customers for their own commercial purposes, which in many cases benefits the customer as well. For example, the fact that banks have absolute title to their depositors' money means that they can obtain further returns from the money by, for example, making loans, which would translate into lower charges and fees, or even earned interest,[12] for customers using the bank's services. By the same token, if a crypto-asset exchange has outright title to the crypto-assets deposited by its customers, it can engage in activities such as market making, futures trading and offering margin accounts.[13] This again translates into lower fees for customers.

An outright title transfer also carries consequences in terms of insolvency, tax and accounting treatment. If the intermediary becomes insolvent, the client would not have any entitlement to the asset. Also, it is the intermediary who will be subject to tax, meaning that (for example) capital gains tax would not be levied upon the client but rather on the intermediary. In addition, the asset must be included on the intermediary's balance sheet.[14] Nonetheless, there will be contractual obligations owed by the intermediary as a result of the client-intermediary agreement.

B. Trust

Rather than holding the asset absolutely, the intermediary could hold the asset on trust for the client. For this to be the case, the 'three certainties' for creating a trust need to be satisfied (certainty of intention, subject matter and object). Certainty of subject matter and object are relatively uncontroversial in the current context. The certainty of subject matter requirement is satisfied irrespective of whether the assets are held in a segregated or omnibus account.[15] In turn, the certainty of object requirement is clearly satisfied as the assets are held on trust for the clients/accountholders; neither evidential uncertainty in identifying the individuals who hold each account, nor the fact that the 'identity of

[11] *Quoine* SGCA (n 1) (see section II.B) is an example of this, although the decision has been the subject of criticism, see K Low, '*Quoines* in *Cryptopia*: When (if ever) are Cryptoasset Exchanges Trustees?' (2020) 84 *Conveyancer and Property Lawyer* 70, 75.

[12] Such as through an interest-bearing bank account or a certificate of deposit.

[13] See nn 25–26 and accompanying text.

[14] The fact that the asset appears on the intermediary's balance sheet is a strong indication of an intention to transfer title.

[15] See *Cryptopia* (n 1) [141]–[147] and [157]; *Pearson v Lehman Brothers Finance SA* [2010] EWHC 2914 (Ch); *Hunter v Moss* [1993] EWCA Civ 11; *Re Harvard Securities* [1997] EWHC 371; *White v Shortall* [2006] NSWSC 1379.

the beneficiaries is constantly changing' defeats the trust.[16] Thus, for current purposes, the crucial task is to determine whether the requisite intention to create a trust can be ascertained from the agreement. What must be intended is that the intermediary will not have free use of the asset.[17]

Indeed, from recent case law, it is clear that courts have been willing to recognise that a trust can be created over cryptocurrencies (and there is no particular reason to assume that the same conclusion does not apply to other types of crypto-assets). Two cases are particularly relevant: *Cryptopia* and *Quoine*.

In *Cryptopia*, a cryptocurrency exchange became insolvent, and investors in the exchange wished to establish the existence of a trust to gain priority over the exchange's general creditors. The New Zealand High Court held that a trust was found in respect of the cryptocurrencies. The three certainties were satisfied. Certainty of intention was established because the exchange never intended to (and never did) trade in the digital assets in its own right.[18] The computer database created by the exchange 'showed that the company was a custodian and trustee of the digital assets'.[19] Certainty of subject matter was found as cryptocurrencies were held to be property,[20] and certainty of objects was established because the beneficiaries were clearly identified as the accountholders with positive balances in the relevant cryptocurrencies.[21]

In *Quoine*, an unanticipated flaw in the trading system of a cryptocurrency-trading platform (Quoine) led to the execution of certain cryptocurrency trades with a market maker (B2C2) at 250 times the market rate. As a result, Quoine attempted to 'correct' the trades to the state they would have been in without the flaw. B2C2 claimed that the 'correction' was a breach of contract and a breach of trust. The breach of trust issue required establishing the existence of a trust, and the Singapore High Court held that a trust existed as the three certainties were satisfied. Certainty of intention was found despite the absence of express language, as there was segregation of Quoine's own trading assets from other users' assets: this was considered sufficient evidence of the requisite intention.[22] In turn, certainty of subject matter was found as cryptocurrencies were held to be property, and certainty of objects was established because the users of the platform could be identified by individual account numbers.[23] The Singapore Court of Appeal allowed Quoine's appeal on the breach of trust issue, but only on the basis that certainty of intention was not found on the *facts* (as opposed to falling short of any separate legal requirement). Specifically, the Court found that there was insufficient segregation of B2C2's assets from Quoine's own trading assets.[24] It is notable that the Court applied the *general* rules on certainty of intention (ie those that would apply to tangible assets and choses in action): thus, if there had been sufficient segregation of Quoine's own

[16] *Cryptopia* (n 1) [148]–[150] and [157].
[17] See, eg, *Lambe v Eames* (1871) 6 Ch App 597.
[18] *Cryptopia* (n 1) [154].
[19] ibid [153].
[20] ibid [50]–[133] and [141]–[147].
[21] ibid [148]–[150].
[22] *Quoine*, SGHC (n 1) [144]–[145].
[23] ibid[142]–[143].
[24] *Quoine*, SGCA (n 1) [144]–[149].

trading assets from B2C2's assets, the lower court's decision would probably have been left undisturbed.

It is noteworthy that the business model adopted by an exchange (or other intermediary) can provide a powerful indication as to the legal relationship it has with its clients, as this would directly affect whether there is the necessary certainty of intention to create a trust. In *Quoine*, Quoine was itself engaged in futures trading and market making, as well as offering margin trading, and the amount of assets held by Quoine at any time did not necessarily match the amount credited to its clients' accounts with it (if necessary, Quoine would purchase more assets to fulfil its clients' requirements).[25] As such, the necessary inference was that these activities required an outright title transfer.[26] In contrast, as Cryptopia did not engage in these activities, and did not use customer funds for its own purposes, the relationship was one of trustee and beneficiary.

Apart from satisfying the three certainties, the trust also has to be constituted, that is, the trustee must have legal title: this would be satisfied automatically if the asset were owned by the intermediary (trustee) itself. If not, there must be a transfer of title from a relevant third party, or from the client.

There are various consequences of the crypto-assets being held on trust for the client, the acknowledgement of which can also be an indication that a trust is intended. First, the assets would not be held on the intermediary's balance sheet. In *Cryptopia*, the fact that the intermediary 'did not assert any ownership in the cryptocurrency' in its 'internal financial accounts' was a factor in favour of the court's decision that a trust had been created.[27] Second, in the case of the intermediary's insolvency, its creditors would not be able to access the assets being held on trust, and the client would be able to obtain them. This provides a very strong form of protection to the client, in contrast with the position under outright title transfer, where the intermediary's creditors have full recourse to the assets being transferred and the client has no entitlement to the asset.[28] If the agreement warns the client of this risk, this is a strong indication that an outright transfer is intended: if there is no such warning the indication is that a trust is intended.[29]

Third, a trust relationship imposes a baseline set of obligations on the trustee.[30] The trustee is obliged to use the asset for the best interests of the beneficiary, which means that it cannot put itself into a position of conflict of interest, or use the asset to make a personal profit.[31] If the trust is a 'bare' trust, as was the case in *Cryptopia*,[32] the trustee is obliged to act upon the beneficiary's instructions.[33] The trustee is also subject to a duty of care, whereby it needs to take the 'precautions which an ordinary man of business

[25] ibid [147].

[26] *Cryptopia* (n 1) [165]; *Quoine* SCGA (n 1) [147].

[27] *Cryptopia* (n 1) [165].

[28] The risk to the client is so great that there is a strong case for regulatory intervention, such as requiring disclosure of the risk, imposing capital requirements on the intermediary or banning the creation of such relationships with consumers.

[29] *Cryptopia* (n 1) [165].

[30] The extent to which these obligations can be modified, or liability for breach excluded, is considered below in section III.C.

[31] *Bristol and West Building Society v Mothew* [1998] Ch 1.

[32] *Cryptopia* (n 1) [183] and [196].

[33] ibid [196].

would take in managing similar affairs of his own'.[34] If these duties are breached, the beneficiary may be entitled to an extensive set of remedies against the trustee and potentially third parties, such as compensation for loss, recovery of gains, the power to set aside certain transactions, proprietary remedies against the trustee and third parties (including tracing and following), as well as personal claims against third parties (in knowing receipt and dishonest assistance).[35]

In addition to the baseline set of common law obligations, 'professional trustees' such as custodians and/or exchanges are likely to fall within the regulatory remit in certain jurisdictions,[36] and be subject to a range of regulatory duties as specified by the conditions of the particular licence. These duties are likely to include segregating client assets from house assets,[37] safeguarding the value of the assets, and a prohibition on deploying the funds into speculative or spurious investments. There will also be requirements in relation to record-keeping and customer due diligence.[38]

C. Quasi-Bailment

A bailment relationship arises where there is a voluntary transfer of possession of a tangible asset, with the consent of the transferee. If a bailment relationship is created, the bailor is under a duty to take reasonable care of the goods. The negligence standard of care applies, and may be varied according to whether the bailee is acting gratuitously or for reward.[39] Where the bailment arises by contract, the terms of the contract govern the bailment relationship, and so there is an obligation not to deviate from the *terms* of the bailment.

The question arises whether a bailment relationship could exist between a client and an intermediary of crypto-assets. However, under the current common law, it is impossible to create a bailment of an intangible asset (including crypto-assets). The rationale is that since (according to the conventional view) it is impossible to have possession of intangible assets in common law jurisdictions, and since possession is required for a bailment, it is impossible to have a bailment of intangible assets.

It has been suggested that a crypto-asset can be 'possessed' on the footing that it is a 'concrete' object.[40] More specifically, it is argued that anything that does not

[34] *Speight v Gaunt* (1883) 9 App Cas 1, 19. This general law duty may, however, be displaced by the statutory duty of care: see Trustee Act 2000, s 1.

[35] See generally B McFarlane and C Mitchell, *Hayton and Mitchell on the Law of Trusts and Equitable Remedies*, 14th edn (London, Sweet & Maxwell, 2015), chs 10–13 and 18.

[36] See section VII. Note that in other jurisdictions, similar regulatory requirements are triggered by other criteria, based on defined function (eg, the CASS Rules in the United Kingdom apply to any firm carrying out certain activities: see CASS 6.1.1).

[37] Assets owned by the exchange for its own use and benefit.

[38] See, eg, Hong Kong Companies Registry, 'Guidelines on Licensing of Trust or Company Services Providers', 29.

[39] M Bridge et al (eds), *The Law of Personal Property*, 2nd edn (London, Sweet & Maxwell, 2017) [11-024]–[11-035].

[40] S Green and F Snagg, 'Intermediated Securities and Distributed Ledger Technology' in L Gullifer and J Payne (eds), *Intermediation and Beyond* (Oxford, Hart Publishing, 2019) 337. This argument is now reflected in a call for evidence on Digital Assets by the Law Commission of England and Wales (April 2021).

'depend on the existence of, or relationship between, individuals for its existence'[41] can meaningfully be possessed, if the characteristics of excludability and exhaustibility are satisfied. Therefore, as a crypto-asset is not destroyed upon the death of particular individuals,[42] it can be the subject of possession. This analysis, nonetheless, remains highly controversial,[43] and many jurisdictions adhere to the view that bailments are impossible in relation to intangible assets.[44]

While it could be argued that 'factual control', as explained above, denotes a degree of control over a crypto-asset that would amount to possession of a physical asset, it would be a very significant step (probably requiring legislation) to conclude that crypto-assets can be possessed. The only argument that can currently be made is that the analogy is so close that crypto-assets can be subject to a relationship analogous to bailment, which we have called 'quasi-bailment'. However, the conclusion reached in this chapter is that the concept of 'quasi-bailment' is redundant, for the reasons set out in section IV.

One potential obstacle to the creation of a (quasi-)bailment over crypto-assets arises from the argument that crypto-assets cannot be transferred, insofar as the movement of value through the blockchain happens through the creation and destruction of informational entities[45] instead of the movement of the same asset from place to place or from person to person. In this sense, it may be that crypto-assets are 'transmitted' instead of 'transferred'.[46] One of the constitutive elements of a bailment is that the bailor has title to the asset in the bailee's possession.[47] If there is transmission instead of transfer, the asset in the possession of the 'bailee' is not an asset to which the 'bailor' has title, because when the asset leaves the 'bailor' it is destroyed and a *new* asset is created in the hands of the 'bailee'.[48]

Nonetheless, the arguments as to 'transmission versus transfer' appear to be finely balanced. Against the 'transmission' view explained above, it could be argued that such a view erroneously equates the informational entities (that are destroyed and created) with the assets themselves. Instead, one can conceptualise the informational entities as part of a *process* by which the underlying crypto-asset (such as a bitcoin) is being

[41] Green and Snagg (n 40) 346.

[42] Crypto-assets are also transferable (from address to address) and excludable (through the use of a private key).

[43] For example, K Low argues that the concept of possession should be confined to tangible objects: see K Low, 'The Perils of Misusing Property Concepts in Contractual Analysis' (2014) 130 *LQR* 547, 549–51.

[44] eg Hong Kong, Singapore, Australia, Canada.

[45] JG Allen, 'Negotiability in digital environments' (2019) 7 *Butterworths Journal of International Banking and Financial Law* 459, 460–61, citing D Fox, 'Cryptocurrencies in the Common Law of Property' in D Fox and S Green (eds), *Cryptocurrencies in Public and Private Law* (Oxford, Oxford University Press, 2019) 139, paras 6.19 and 6.53.

[46] UK Jurisdiction Taskforce (n 2) [62].

[47] J Glister and J Lee (eds), *Hanbury and Martin, Modern Equity*, 21st edn (London, Sweet & Maxwell, 2018) [2-002]: bailment is 'where a chattel owned by X is, with X's permission, in the possession of Y'.

[48] The 'transmission' issue does not pose a problem in outright title transfer or trust (and by extension, mere contract). With a trust, instead of a transfer of the same property to the intermediary to hold on trust, there can be a destruction of property in the client and the creation of new property in the intermediary that is declared on trust. With an outright title transfer, the client parts with the asset and the intermediary obtains a new asset. Finally, with a mere contract, there is simply no need to deal with transmission because no property will have been transmitted in the first place.

transferred from address to address. Irrespective of how each blockchain organises its informational entities throughout the process of 'transfer', the end result is that an asset is transferred from person to person.[49] Alternatively, it can be argued that since the focus of bailment is the imposition of a particular set of duties on the bailee (most notably the duty of care), this can happen regardless of whether the thing held is exactly the same thing as that 'transferred'. Thus, even if the 'transmission' objection fails to be rebutted, this would not pose an insuperable obstacle to the creation of a quasi-bailment.[50]

D. Mere Contract

Where there is no outright title transfer or trust, and assuming that quasi-bailment is not a possibility, the legal relationship between the client and intermediary will only sound in contract (assuming that the requirements for contract formation are satisfied).

In addition to obligations expressly set out in the contract, there would also be terms implied by statute into the client-intermediary agreement. This is the case where the intermediary is performing a service (as in in the vast majority of cases), in which case there is an implied term to carry out the service with reasonable care and skill.[51] Alternatively, if the intermediary is supplying 'digital content', there will be an implied term of reasonable care and skill not to damage the client's digital content as long as the latter is a consumer.[52]

If the parties intend merely to create a contractual relationship, they need to be careful not to unintentionally create a custody relationship that would be characterised as a trust (or, if it were possible, a quasi-bailment). This could happen if the intermediary were to gain factual control of the asset and agree to hold it for the client.

It seems, however, that this characterisation would only occur if the intermediary were to gain exclusive factual control,[53] that is, it is the only entity with access to the private key. However, what if both the intermediary and the client have access to the private key from the outset?[54] In this case, it is unlikely that the arrangement would be characterised as a trust (since the trustee would probably not have legal title to the asset, and there would probably not be evidence of intention to create a trust) or, if possible, as a quasi-bailment.

[49] This would seem to be the case irrespective of whether the 'UTXO model' or the 'account model' is used, since in both cases we can identify where the asset is by reference to the blockchain record (even if we may need to trace the process of 'creation and destruction of informational entities' to locate where the asset is).

[50] But see the arguments made in section IV as to the redundancy of this concept.

[51] Supply of Goods and Services Act 1982, s 13. This is a UK statute, but there are similar statutes in other common law jurisdictions: see, eg, Supply of Services (Implied Terms) Ordinance (Cap 457, Laws of Hong Kong), s 5; Competition and Consumer Act 2010 (No 51 of 1974, Laws of Australia), s 60.

[52] eg Consumer Rights Act 2015, s 46(1).

[53] Exclusive possession is required for a bailment (*Yearworth v North Bristol NHS Trust* [2010] QB 1, [48](d)), and even if, as argued in this chapter, the likely analysis of a custody relationship is a trust, it would appear appropriate for exclusive factual control to be required for the trustee to have legal title to the asset.

[54] Or if the private key is 'split' into two parts (meaning that each person has a shorter alphanumeric string that constitutes only part of the original string) and the custodian and client each knows only one part of the full key?

Conversely, some intermediaries may claim that they are mere 'providers of technology' (instead of custodians) and are thus under no, or minimal, legal duties in relation to the asset.[55] Where a 'technology provider' offers its services to the client, there is, of course, a contract (eg a licensing agreement, or a sale relationship, depending on how the software is provided) under which some duties will be imposed expressly or impliedly. However, such a contract does not relate to the property rights of the client, because the technology provider, at least as a starting point, does not obtain any property rights to the underlying assets if it does not have factual control of the assets.

Scenarios where the technology provider does not have factual control are common, such as in cases where a software provider (eg AWS)[56] has the private keys stored on its database but cannot access the private keys, and thus cannot access the assets themselves. In such a case, there is no positive control and thus no 'factual control'. Nonetheless, there may be negative control, as the software provider could deny access to the private keys, whether accidentally or deliberately. An accidental denial of access would occur in cases involving a 'desktop wallet' where the private key sits with a laptop computer. If there is a bug in the software, this could lead to the loss of the private keys (most notably if the bug destroys all stored data), without this being deliberately intended. A deliberate denial of access would occur in a case where the software developer deletes the relevant application. Where a mobile application allows the user to type in and store private keys on a database, the developer of the application could still decide to delete it entirely. If this happens, all data contained on it (including the private keys) would be erased.

In such scenarios, the technology provider is likely to deny the existence of any relevant legal duties owed to the client, and so the client may have no available redress, even though the destruction of the private keys in practice means that the client would not be able to access their crypto-assets at all. Since the technology provider is not a trustee of the asset,[57] any duties would have to arise in tort or contract. It is likely that the relevant licence agreement will include an obligation (express or implied) not to deliberately and/or negligently destroy the asset.[58] Whether that obligation (or liability for breach) can be successfully excluded is considered in the next section.

III. Modification of the Baseline Position by Contract

The preceding analysis identifies obligations incumbent on the intermediary in relation to the crypto-asset(s) in the absence of contrary agreement of the parties. This section considers whether, and to what extent, these obligations can be varied by such agreement (initially or subsequently).

[55] Many intermediaries would like to disclaim as many duties and/or liabilities as possible vis-à-vis their clients. For example, Ledger's 'Live Terms of Use' deny the existence of a custodial relationship: 'Ledger operates non-custodial services, which means that we do not store, nor do we have access to your Crypto Assets nor your Private Keys. We do not send or receive Crypto Assets. Any Crypto Asset transfer occurs on blockchain networks and not on a network owned or controlled by Ledger.' (Ledger, 'Ledger Live Terms of Use | Ledger) (*Ledger*) at https://shop.ledger.com/pages/ledger-live-terms-of-use (accessed 27 May 2021).

[56] Amazon Web Services.

[57] Since it has no factual control, see section II.B.

[58] See nn 51–52.

A. Mere Contract

Where the relationship between the client and intermediary is one where there is a 'mere contract', the obligations between the parties are by definition governed by their contractual agreement. Thus, they can be varied, modified or excluded by the parties, subject to the relevant statutory controls: for example, the parties are free to include exemption and limitation clauses subject to the limits of the Unfair Contract Terms Act 1977 and the Consumer Rights Act 2015.[59]

In relation to the obligation on a technology provider not to destroy the asset, this can be excluded or modified by agreement, as long as the statutory controls (such as the 'reasonableness' test adopted in many jurisdictions) are not violated. It is therefore possible for negligence liability to be exempted.[60] This would mean that where there is an 'accidental denial of access' caused by a system bug, leading to loss of the client's private key (temporarily or permanently), there would be no contractual or tortious claim. In such circumstances, it may be thought unfair for the client to be left with no remedy, especially in relation to this new area of technology where there is likely to be a significant informational disparity between the parties and where the client lacks the ability to monitor the intermediary's conduct. Thus, it may be that crypto-asset services should be subject to a bespoke regulatory regime, in order for clients to have adequate avenues of legal redress and be sufficiently protected.

B. Outright Title Transfer

For an outright title transfer, the baseline position is that there is nothing to 'exclude': the asset is at the free disposal of the intermediary because it has absolute title. As such, anything agreed to in the contract will only serve to *increase* the obligations of the intermediary. The parties are free to choose what obligations are to be imposed, but this is again subject to any relevant statutory controls, for example when it comes to determining what liabilities can be excluded or modified. Parties wanting to create an outright title transfer transaction would need to be careful that their agreement would not be interpreted as creating a trust, which could happen if the agreement provided that the intermediary was not to have free use of the asset.[61]

C. Trust

The baseline obligations of the trustee are the duties of no conflict and no profit, the duty of care and the specific obligations in the trust instrument.[62] The extent to which

[59] Again, these are UK statutes, and there are similar statutes in other common law jurisdictions. See, eg, Unfair Contract Terms Act (Cap 396, Laws of Singapore); Control of Exemption Clauses Ordinance (Cap 71, Laws of Hong Kong).

[60] See the statutes cited in n 59.

[61] See section III.C.

[62] *Bristol and West Building Society v Mothew* [1998] EWCA Civ 533; *Youyang Pty Ltd v Minter Ellison Morris Fletcher* (2003) 212 CLR 484.

these duties can be excluded by a trustee is a subject of heated debate,[63] and in the crypto-asset context these debates are no less relevant. Crucially, if too many duties are being excluded (and/or too many rights are given to the trustee), the arrangement may not end up being a trust at all: instead, there would be a title transfer or, were it possible, quasi-bailment.

In the commercial context, the courts have been flexible in allowing commercial parties to exclude duties or confer rights on the trustee that prima facie appear inconsistent with a trust, yet hold that a trust exists.

In relation to duties, an instructive example is *Citibank v MBIA*.[64] Here, a trust was upheld despite considerable exclusions of duties: for example, the trustee was, in certain situations, bound to comply with the instructions of a third party (MBIA) and, in doing so, was 'not required to have regard to the interests of the [beneficiary] noteholders'.[65] Despite this, the Court of Appeal held that the obligations were not reduced below the 'irreducible core' identified in *Armitage v Nurse*[66] and the commercial arrangement was consistent with a trust.[67] Similarly, in the context of custodianship of digital assets, one may expect the court to adopt this expansive approach favouring party autonomy, although it is unlikely that basic duties, such as the duty not to make unauthorised disposals of the assets, could be excluded. It is likely that, in the future, the ambit of regulatory duties imposed on digital asset custodians will shape the kinds of duties that are seen as non-excludable in private law.

In relation to rights, the most pertinent issue concerns the trustee's right of use. This issue arises when determining whether an arrangement transferring legal title to the intermediary gives rise to a trust or an outright title transfer. The essence of a trust is that the trustee manages property for the benefit of the beneficiary. Thus, in general, the certainty of intention requirement for creating an express trust filters out arrangements where the trustee is intended to have *free use* of the asset. If an arrangement gives an intermediary a right of use amounting to free use of the asset, there would seem to be no trust.[68] Indeed, *Cryptopia* seems to distinguish between situations where the custodian engages in trading and cases where it just holds on to the asset.[69] Where the custodian is allowed to use the assets for its *own* commercial purposes (eg as a liquidity provider or lender),[70] this militates in favour of the arrangement's being a title transfer (and vice versa where the custodian merely 'holds on' to the asset for the client).

Nonetheless, it has been held in two cases that a right of use per se does not negate the existence of a trust.[71] The court's reasoning in both cases was that the disapplication of some duties did not preclude the relationship's being that of trust if other aspects

[63] See, eg, J Getzler, 'Ascribing and Limiting Fiduciary Obligations: Understanding the Operation of Consent' in A Gold and P Miller (eds), *Philosophical Foundations of Fiduciary Law* (Oxford, Oxford University Press, 2014) 39.

[64] *Citibank NA v MBIA Assurance SA* [2007] EWCA Civ 11.

[65] ibid [54].

[66] *Armitage v Nurse* [1998] Ch 248, per Millett LJ.

[67] For criticism, see A Trukhtanov, 'The Irreducible Core of Trust Obligations' (2007) 123 *LQR* 342.

[68] This is subject to the discussion of *Pearson v Lehman* (n 15), which follows shortly.

[69] See, eg, *Cryptopia* (n 1) [165]–[166].

[70] ibid [165].

[71] *Pearson* (n 15); *LBIE v RAB Market Cycles* [2009] EWHC 2545 (Ch).

pointed in favour of this conclusion.[72] The question arises as to when exactly the conferral of a right of use becomes inconsistent with the existence of a trust, resulting instead in creation of an outright title transfer.

In the *RAB* case, Briggs J held that a 'right to swap' (a right on the part of the trustee to sell or dispose of the relevant property, as long as an 'equivalent' substitute asset or right comes back in exchange)[73] was consistent with a trust,[74] since the asset or right[75] obtained in return for the original asset is held on trust for the beneficiary. This situation is distinguished from that where there is *nothing* coming back into the trust after the initial asset is disposed of (in which case there is no trust).[76] In essence, this means a trust can exist over a shifting class of assets. Typically, in the securities lending context, the substitute asset is the intermediary's right against its disposition counterparty (for money and/or for securities), and this will be held on trust for the client.

However, in *Pearson v Lehman*, it was held that one of the arrangements between the Lehman entities could not give rise to a trust.[77] This is because the intermediary (LBIE) had a right to dispose of the assets without a correlative obligation to hold any substitute assets on trust. For example, LBIE was permitted to use the assets to 'make good short positions both for other affiliates and for LBIE itself'.[78] As there was no substitute asset coming back in exchange that could form the subject matter of a trust, the intermediary's obligations (such as the obligation to get assets in at a future time) would only be personal: they did not relate to any specific asset. It was held that LBIE's permitted conduct 'much more closely resemble[d] that of a banker in relation to its customer's deposits'[79] as opposed to that of a trustee holding property for its beneficiary. Money deposited at a bank is transferred from the customer to the bank outright: the bank merely has an obligation in debt. There is no trust.[80]

Thus, the line between outright title transfer and trust would seem to be determined based on whether the 'trustee's' right of use comes with a correlative obligation to hold substitute property on trust.[81] If it does, the right becomes a 'right to swap'. If it does not, the right would make the position of the 'trustee' very similar to that of a banker in relation to his customer, meaning that the law would characterise the transaction as an outright title transfer.

This boundary makes logical and conceptual sense. A trust involves specific rights being held for the benefit of another.[82] Where there is a 'right to swap', there is a

[72] *Pearson* (n 15) [260]; *RAB* (n 71) [60]–[64].

[73] For the avoidance of doubt, the terminology of 'swap' used here does not denote 'swap derivative'.

[74] *RAB* (n 71) [61]–[62]; *Pearson* (n 15) [293].

[75] The right may be a personal right against the counterparty to have equivalent securities transferred back at a later date and/or assets obtained in exchange as collateral.

[76] See next two paragraphs.

[77] *Pearson* (n 15) [265]–[294].

[78] ibid [275]. If a trader makes good a short position, this 'closes out' the transaction, meaning that there is no further obligation on the counterparty.

[79] ibid [275].

[80] *Foley* (n 10).

[81] Thus, even a right conferred on the intermediary to keep profits from the use of the asset is consistent with a trust, as long as there is an asset (right) that the intermediary holds for the client. See, eg, *RAB* (n 71).

[82] See, eg, B McFarlane, 'Equity, Obligations and Third Parties' (2008) 2 *Singapore Journal of Legal Studies* 308, 318: '[T]he key feature of an equitable property right is that: (i) A is under a duty to B; and (ii) A's duty relates to a specific *right* held by A.'

substitute asset (right) held on trust for the beneficiary, despite the sale or disposition of the original property. A trust can exist because a right is being held for the benefit of another at all times. However, where there is no 'right to swap', all that exists is a personal obligation where the 'trustee' promises to pay the economic equivalent of the client's underlying entitlement.[83] A personal *obligation*, which is not a *right*, cannot be held on trust: thus, the absence of a right to swap is fatal to the existence of a trust, and this is explicable in conceptual terms.

D. Quasi-Bailment

As discussed previously and in the next section, it is unlikely that a quasi-bailment is possible, and therefore also unlikely that a relationship between a crypto-asset intermediary and a client would be characterised in this way. Were it possible, a duty of care in tort would arise (as well as duties in contract under the client-intermediary agreement). These duties could be modified subject to the relevant statutory controls.[84]

IV. The Redundancy of Bailment in the Crypto-Asset Context

As we have seen, the incidents of an English law trust can be heavily modified by the parties' agreement. Exclusions of trustee's duties remain compatible with the existence of a trust. Rights of use and disposal of the trust assets can also be conferred on the trustee without negating the existence of a trust. Furthermore, outside of the trust context, parties can agree on any set of legal rights and obligations by contractual agreement, subject only to the statutory and public policy limits on contractual freedom.

Thus, one might wonder whether the concept of 'quasi-bailment' is useful at all in the crypto-asset context,[85] if all (or almost all) the incidents of bailment can be replicated through a combination of trust and contract. The two most significant incidents of a bailment relationship are (i) the bailee's duty of care, and (ii) the bailee's right to sue third parties for deliberately or negligently interfering with the relevant property. First, as to the duty of care, this is a baseline incident of an express trust,[86] and in the context of the client-intermediary agreement there would be an implied term to carry out the relevant (custodial) service with reasonable care and skill. This duty can be excluded or modified by contract.[87]

Second, as to a bailee's right to sue third parties for interference, the same right exists where there is a trust or an outright title transfer: the custodian has the legal title and can thus sue third parties for interference. A *bailor* may also have a right to sue

[83] This is similar to a banker-customer relationship, which only imposes a personal obligation on the banker.
[84] Most notably the Unfair Contract Terms Act 1977 and the Consumer Rights Act 2015.
[85] See G McMeel, 'The Redundancy of Bailment' [2003] *LMCLQ* 169.
[86] *Speight v Gaunt* (n 34); Trustee Act 2000, s 1.
[87] *Armitage* (n 66) 253–54; Trustee Act 2000, sch 1, para 7; Supply of Goods and Services Act, s 16.

third parties for interference when it has a right to immediate possession (in relation to the property), allowing it to sue third parties in conversion.[88] A rough analogue for this right exists in the trust context, namely the *Vandepitte* procedure,[89] which allows a beneficiary to join the trustee and sue third-party wrongdoers, such as individuals who have converted the trustee's property.

Other features of a bailment relationship can be replicated by a trust as well. The duty of a bailee not to intentionally damage or destroy the property has an equivalent in the trust context: the duty to act in good faith in the beneficiaries' interests, which straightforwardly includes a duty not to intentionally damage or destroy the property. Finally, while it is settled that a trustee can have a right of use in relation to the trust property, it is not clear that a bailee can have such a right.

Since the incidents of bailment can be replicated through a mixture of trust and contract, any bailment analysis would be redundant in this context. Given that the trust has evolved throughout the centuries into such a dynamic and flexible doctrinal tool that can cater to many forms of property holding arrangements, one might argue that trusts can and should be the concept that does the heavy normative lifting. Contract is even more flexible: there are relatively few limits on contractual freedom. In contrast, the idea that bailments can only apply to tangible objects is firmly entrenched in English law.[90] To extend the concept of bailment to cover crypto-assets requires the development of a 'quasi-bailment', which requires a new conceptual structure to be created. For example, the issue of whether 'transmission' is sufficient to create a quasi-bailment would need to be tackled.[91] So would the difficult issue of whether the interest of the 'quasi-bailee' is sufficient to constitute an action in conversion and/or trespass. Furthermore, to claim that 'crypto-assets are like tangibles and thus there must be bailment' would be inconsistent with the trend in the common law world to treat crypto-assets as another type of intangible property other than choses in action.[92]

It would only be worth developing this new legal tool of 'quasi-bailment' if it were strictly necessary, and for the reasons mentioned above this is not the case, nor, given the existence of the trust, is the tool required as a 'gap filler' in relation to the holding of digital assets by an intermediary.

V. Drawing the Boundaries between Each Legal Characterisation: Further General Points

Having set out the different legal categories or 'buckets' into which the relevant client-intermediary arrangement may fall, it may seem that each category would be clearly delineated and that it would be easy to decide into which category a particular agreement falls.

[88] A Tettenborn (ed), *Clerk & Lindsell on Torts*, 23nd edn (London, Sweet & Maxwell, 2021) 16-60–16-61.

[89] *Vandepitte v Preferred Accident Insurance Co* [1933] AC 70.

[90] See, eg, *OBG v Allan* [2007] UKHL 21; *Your Response Ltd v Datateam Business Media Ltd* [2014] EWCA Civ 281. There are good reasons for restricting the concept of bailment to tangible assets: see, eg, Low (n 43) 549–51.

[91] See section II.C.

[92] See, eg, *Cryptopia* (n 1) [120]; UK Jurisdiction Taskforce (n 2) [35]–[85].

However, the reality is that there will be very difficult borderline cases, and the task of the court is to faithfully and accurately categorise the arrangement.

In this regard, there are three crucial points to note. First, labelling something as a particular legal arrangement (eg 'trust' or 'lease') cannot per se turn such an arrangement into a trust or lease, unless the substantive requirements of a trust or lease (or other legal category) are satisfied. As Lord Templeman noted in *Street v Mountford*, '[t]he manufacture of a five-pronged implement for manual digging results in a fork even if the manufacturer … insists that he intended to make and has made a spade'.[93] Similarly, Lord Millett in *Agnew v IRC* provides a useful starting point, by setting out a two-stage approach to categorisation.[94] The court must first ascertain what has been agreed between the parties, and *then* categorise such agreement in legal terms.[95]

Second, and despite the above, the label used by the parties could matter in a borderline case where the agreement seems to fall in between two legal categorisations (eg trust and outright title transfer). Take the example where there is a transfer of legal title to the intermediary, where the agreement provides that the intermediary has a right of use over the asset. Here, the agreement may give rise to an outright title transfer, but it could also give rise to a trust (as *Pearson v Lehman* makes clear that a right of use by the trustee can be consistent with the existence of a trust). Both categorisations are possible, and the task is to ascertain what the parties intended. In this context, the label chosen by the parties ('trust' or 'title transfer') would matter because it provides the court with information as to what the parties intended, which would ultimately be decisive as to how the arrangement is categorised. The label could also affect the interpretation of other terms in the agreement (ie influence how those terms are being read in context), which would again affect the legal outcome.

Third, if the parties attempt to create one kind of arrangement but ultimately fail to do so, the general approach is that the court will not recharacterise the arrangement into another 'bucket' unless the requirements of the alternative arrangement are satisfied.[96] Thus, cases have said that a court will not treat a failed gift (one type of title transfer) as a trust, unless the requirements for a trust are satisfied.[97] There have, however, been exceptions to this approach, where the courts have (at least ostensibly) appeared to 'rescue' an arrangement by recharacterising it, despite, arguably, the relaxation of the requirements of the alternative characterisation to accommodate the case in question.[98] Thus, it is worth keeping in mind this question: how easily will the court recharacterise the arrangement into another 'bucket' despite the significant difference between the arrangement and the paradigm case of that new 'bucket'?

[93] *Street v Mountford* [1985] AC 809, 819. If the requirements for creating a spade have not been satisfied, one has not created a spade.

[94] *Agnew v IRC* [2001] UKPC 28. The categorisation question in *Agnew* concerned the line between fixed and floating charges, but the general approach to categorisation set out in *Agnew* is applicable generally in English law.

[95] ibid [32].

[96] eg *Milroy v Lord* [1862] EWHC J78.

[97] ibid. See also *Richards v Delbridge* (1874) LR 18 Eq 11.

[98] eg *T Choithram International SA v Pagarani* [2000] UKPC 46; *Les Affréteurs Société Anonyme v Leopold Walford (London) Ltd* [1919] AC 801.

VI. The Most Likely Outcome

The preceding analysis has addressed the possible legal analyses of the relationship between a client and an intermediary, as well as how the court is to approach the question of distinguishing between different types of legal relationships. But this does not shed light on which legal relationship is in practice going to feature most frequently – the question we now address.

Which legal relationship is in practice going to feature most frequently depends on (i) what agreements are likely to be drafted, and (ii) the court's approach to the interpretation of contracts. We would expect to see that most client-intermediary agreements, where the intermediary has factual control of the crypto-asset, would give rise to a trust relationship.

Client-intermediary agreements in the crypto-asset context tend to be drafted in the form of 'give us the asset, and we will hold it on your behalf', but the vast majority of such agreements are silent as to the exact nature of the legal relationship between the parties. Nonetheless, this form makes outright title transfer an unlikely possibility, as the asset is expressed to be held on behalf of the client.[99] 'Mere contract' is also a very unlikely possibility, since the legal title and/or factual control is likely to be with the intermediary. Thus, the most likely possibility is a trust.

In the unlikely event that a quasi-bailment of digital assets were possible, is it likely that the parties would objectively intend such a relationship? First, the parties are likely to have intended an arrangement that would provide more commercial certainty, and the trust provides much more certainty. The English law trust has developed through centuries of case law, resulting in a concept that contains relatively well-defined boundaries yet is extremely flexible as applied to intangible property. This stands in stark contrast with bailment: the outer edges of that concept are far from settled, and whether it could apply to any sort of intangible property is, at best, extremely uncertain. Indeed, the trust has done a lot of heavy normative lifting over the centuries, and this creates a positive feedback loop through 'conceptual inertia'. The more case law there is on trusts, the more certainty there is as to how the trust operates, and so the more this causes parties to want to adopt the trust structure.

Second, to the extent that parties are likely to have intended a legal arrangement that would comply with regulatory requirements in the relevant jurisdiction, this provides a strong indication that a trust was (objectively) intended. This is because many regulators may require virtual asset providers (or at least providers of virtual securities) to hold assets on trust for their clients, and this is the case in Hong Kong.[100] This provides a further factor in favour of there being a trust.

Even if the intention of the parties in a particular case is to *avoid* being regulated in the first place (meaning that the second argument does not apply), the most likely

[99] See, eg, *Cryptopia* (n 1) [172]–[178]. But there would be an outright title transfer in specific circumstances, for example where the custodian has a right of rehypothecation over the assets and is not obliged to hold any substitute assets for the investor.

[100] Hong Kong Securities and Futures Commission, 'Position Paper – Regulation of virtual asset trading platforms' (6 November 2019) [46]–[47].

arrangement would still be a trust, since the parties are likely to have intended to create an arrangement that offers commercial certainty (ie the first argument does apply).

Thus, the most likely characterisation of the client-intermediary relationship is that of trustee and beneficiary. The two factors explored above create a strong presumption in favour of there being a trust.

VII. Practical Considerations

The conclusion that the most likely characterisation of the client-intermediary relationship is that of trustee and beneficiary is not, however, consistent with current market practice and expectations. As mentioned, most client-intermediary contracts are totally silent on the nature of the custodial relationship (or whether such a relationship exists at all). If intermediaries do address the nature of such a relationship, they attempt to argue that they have a mere contractual relationship (in which they will often disclaim any and all liability and duties to their client).

Intermediaries do not want to say that they are acting as trustees, as doing so would naturally imply certain duties (even if those duties can be reduced) and, of great practical significance, almost certainly trigger licensing requirements in many common law jurisdictions. With the important exception of the United Kingdom, which does not require licensing to (only) act as a professional trustee, many other jurisdictions, including Hong Kong,[101] Singapore,[102] Malaysia,[103] the Cayman Islands[104] and the British Virgin Islands (BVI)[105] (representing the vast majority of jurisdictions in which digital asset intermediaries are based outside of the United States), require intermediaries to be licensed to act as professional trustees.[106]

So far most digital asset intermediaries, and indeed most associated regulators, have not fully addressed the issue of how these digital asset intermediaries should be regulated or licensed, assuming that the underlying asset in which they deal is unregulated. For example, the Hong Kong Securities and Futures Commission (SFC) has decided that most digital asset intermediaries are outside its purview, as long as they deal in neither securities nor futures. The SFC has, however, introduced an 'opt-in' regulation for virtual asset exchanges, in which they can voluntarily come under the Commission's jurisdiction if those intermediaries *also* deal in at least one security or future.[107] Additionally, in those cases, the SFC has decided that those intermediaries must hold digital assets on trust, through a licensed trust company.[108] This, along with

[101] Anti-Money Laundering and Counter-Terrorist Financing (Financial Institutions) (Amendment) Ordinance (Cap 615), pt 5A.

[102] Trust Companies Act (Cap 336), s 3.

[103] Trust Companies Act 1949.

[104] Banks and Trust Companies Law (2020 Revision), s 5.

[105] Banks and Trust Companies Act 1990, s 3.

[106] That is, to provide trust services as an ongoing business for a profit, which would easily include holding assets for clients as a trustee-intermediary.

[107] Hong Kong Securities and Futures Commission (n 100) [8].

[108] ibid [47].

recent judgments in the *Quoine* and *Cryptopia* cases,[109] clearly shows a trend towards regulators and courts deciding that the proper and natural relationship between digital asset intermediaries and their clients is one of trust. Regulators and courts have, so far, stopped short of deciding that *all* digital asset intermediaries should hold those assets on trust. Given our analysis, and unless a digital asset intermediary can successfully argue that it should fall into a different category, this does mean that most digital asset intermediaries will immediately attract a requirement to be licensed as 'professional trustees'. This is separate from any other licensing requirements that they may trigger. This aligns with general public policy that looks to protect end investors, since licensing as 'professional trustees' would immediately bring into place 'know your customer' (KYC) and anti-money laundering (AML) rules, reporting requirements and regulatory oversight. Such licensing is 'no big deal' for the typical financial intermediary that deals in fiat money or securities, or indeed most other assets of value. This should likewise not be an issue for digital asset intermediaries, if they are genuinely operating in the best interests of their end investors.

Nonetheless, even if the client-intermediary relationship is one other than trust, this does not mean that the intermediary falls outside the regulatory remit. Certain jurisdictions have recently introduced regulatory requirements on crypto-asset service providers insofar as they engage in particular activities. For example, the UK Financial Conduct Authority (FCA) has imposed a registration requirement in respect of particular activities, such as crypto-asset exchange services and custodian wallet provider services.[110] The FCA has also announced an outright ban on the sale, marketing and distribution of certain crypto-asset products to retail investors.[111] Thus, it does not matter whether the client-intermediary relationship is one of trust: as long as the intermediary is conducting particular activities, it will fall under the FCA's regulatory remit.

This 'activity-based' approach to regulation can also be seen in other jurisdictions. In the Cayman Islands, for example, a licence is required before 'virtual asset services' can be provided.[112] These services include:

(a) exchange between virtual assets and fiat currencies;
(b) exchange between one or more other forms of convertible virtual assets;
(c) transfer of virtual assets;
(d) virtual asset custody service; or
(e) participation in, and provision of, financial services related to a virtual asset issuance or the sale of a virtual asset.[113]

[109] See n 1.

[110] The Money Laundering and Terrorist Financing (Amendment) Regulations 2019 (SI 2019/1511), in particular regs 3(1)(b), 4(1)(b) and 4(7); The Money Laundering, Terrorist Financing and Transfer of Funds (Information on the Payer) Regulations 2017 (SI 2017/692); The Financial Services and Markets Act 2000 (Regulated Activities) Order 2001 (SI 2001/544).

[111] UK Financial Conduct Authority, 'Prohibiting the sale to retail clients of investment products that reference cryptoassets' (Policy Statement PS20/10, October 2020).

[112] Virtual Asset (Service Providers) Law 2020, s 4. Virtual asset services can also be provided if the entity qualifies as a 'registered person': s 4(1)(a).

[113] ibid, s 2(1).

Thus, even if the relationship between the crypto-asset intermediary and the client is not one of trust, the intermediary would have to be licensed on the basis that it conducts one or more of the above activities.

The same approach can be seen with the European Union's proposed regulation, which regulates crypto-asset service providers.[114] Specifically, an intermediary falls within the regulatory ambit where a 'crypto-asset service' is provided, and such services are listed in Article 3(1)(9) of the proposed regulation:

> (a) the custody and administration of crypto-assets on behalf of third parties;
> (b) the operation of a trading platform for crypto-assets;
> (c) the exchange of crypto-assets for fiat currency that is legal tender;
> (d) the exchange of crypto-assets for other crypto-assets;
> (e) the execution of orders for crypto-assets on behalf of third parties;
> (f) placing of crypto-assets;
> (g) the reception and transmission of orders for crypto-assets on behalf of third parties
> (h) providing advice on crypto-assets …[115]

Again, an intermediary who conducts one or more of the above activities falls within the regulatory ambit, regardless of whether the relationship with its clients is one of trust.

With the BVI the law is more uncertain, insofar as there is no bespoke legislation for crypto-assets. Nonetheless, crypto-asset service providers may still be regulated under the traditional 'investment' regime.[116] There is no prohibition that specifically targets crypto-assets, but 'investments' is broadly defined: it includes shares, debentures, options and futures.[117] The BVI Financial Services Commission has issued guidance on how virtual assets are to be treated under existing BVI legislation. The guidance note states that '[w]here a virtual asset product or service provides a benefit or right beyond a medium of exchange, it may be captured under the Securities and Investment Business Act, 2010'.[118] Thus, apart from utility tokens and (perhaps) cryptocurrencies, other crypto-assets such as blockchain bonds and shares may constitute an 'investment', and (if so) would require a licence regardless of whether the relationship between the investor and the intermediary is one of trust.

VIII. Conclusion

This chapter has analysed the possible legal relationships between a client and an intermediary of crypto-assets, and has established that there are four types of legal relationships: namely, outright title transfer, trust, (quasi-)bailment and mere contract. In many cases it is difficult to determine whether a particular client-intermediary

[114] Proposal for a Regulation of the European Parliament and of the Council on Markets in Crypto-assets, and amending Directive (EU) 2019/1937 (COM/2020/593 final).

[115] ibid Art 3(1)(9). Also see definitions in Art 3(1)(10)–(17).

[116] Securities and Investment Business Act 2010, s 4.

[117] ibid, ss 2 and 3 and sch 1.

[118] British Virgin Islands Financial Services Commission, 'Guidance on the Regulation of Virtual Assets in the British Virgin Islands (BVI)' (10 July 2020) 3.

agreement gives rise to one type of legal relationship or another, but all turns on the interpretation of the agreement in accordance with settled principles of construction and characterisation. Furthermore, it is highly unlikely that the law will develop in a way such that a quasi-bailment analysis will be accepted in the context of crypto-assets. It is concluded that the most likely type of legal relationship that would appear in practice is the trust, because this accords with the objective intention of the parties, who wish to have commercial certainty and (possibly) wish to comply with regulatory requirements within the particular jurisdiction in question.

12

As Complex as ABC? Bona Fide Purchasers of Equitable Interests

BEN McFARLANE AND ANDREAS TELEVANTOS

I. Introduction

Where an intermediary, A, can exercise legal powers affecting the position of B, any legal system must take care to provide some protection not only to B, but also to C, a third party who deals with A in good faith and without notice of possible limits to A's powers. The best-known example in English law is the 'rules of equity for the protection of bona fide purchasers for value without notice'.[1] These rules provide that a bona fide purchaser of a legal title, for value and without notice of the pre-existing equitable interests, will take that legal title free of any pre-existing equitable interests affecting it. Any unqualified references in this chapter to the 'bona fide purchaser defence', or simply to 'the defence', are references to those specific rules.

In this chapter, we examine both the general nature of the defence[2] and a specific question about its requirements. As to its general nature, we compare the defence to the ostensibly similar rules that may protect C against a pre-existing legal interest of B, for example where C deals with a 'seller in possession' or 'buyer in possession'[3] of goods. It has been suggested that the defence equally operates to 'clear title', as an 'exception to *nemo dat*'.[4] We reject that view and argue that whilst the ultimate result of applying the defence resembles the effect of clearing title, the defence can only be understood as linked to the special nature of an equitable interest and the distinct means by which such a right may bind a third party.

[1] See, eg, *Westdeutsche Landesbank Girozentrale v Islington LBC* [1996] AC 669 (HL), 705 (Lord Browne-Wilkinson) and *Akers v Samba Financial Group* [2017] UKSC 6, [2017] AC 424 [82] (Lord Sumption). See too A Nair and I Samet, 'What Can "Equity's Darling" Tell Us About Equity?' in D Klimchuk et al (eds), *Philosophical Foundations of Equity* (Oxford, Oxford University Press, 2020) 264, 282.

[2] Note that our focus here is thus on the defence that applies against a 'full-blown' equitable interest of B, rather than against a 'mere equity' of B.

[3] Factors Act 1889, ss 8 and 9; Sale of Goods Act 1979, ss 24 and 25.

[4] See section II.A.

The specific question we examine is the defence's supposed requirement that, to take free from B's pre-existing equitable interest, C must acquire legal title: we refer to this as the 'legal title requirement'.[5] We use our analysis of the general nature of the defence to show that, conceptually, it is a mistake to restrict the defence to cases where C acquires legal title, as this creates an anomaly where the right in which B has an equitable interest is itself equitable. For example, consider a case where A has an equitable interest in shares, and A holds that interest on trust for B. A then transfers A's equitable interest in the shares to C, a bona fide purchaser for value without notice. It is clear that if A had instead been holding the shares themselves on trust for B, C, in acquiring the shares as a bona fide purchaser for value without notice, would take free from B's pre-existing equitable interest. In our view, exactly the same result should apply where A instead held an equitable interest on trust for B.

To support this conceptual claim, we examine the historical development of the legal title requirement of the defence. We agree with Adam Reilly's recent observation that in the eighteenth and nineteenth centuries, in decisions such as *Phillips v Phillips*, courts had to consider the relationship between two potentially overlapping sets of equitable rules: the first as to the availability of relief; the second as to the priority of interests.[6] This provides the context in which the legal title requirement arose in its current form. Departing from Reilly's analysis, we argue that neither set of rules operated to clear title, and that in *Phillips v Phillips* Lord Westbury was not attempting to preserve the distinction between the two sets of rules but rather to achieve the opposite, and to present a unified scheme capable of dealing with both relief and priority. Indeed, at least in the situation we focus on here, where B has a pre-existing equitable interest rather than a 'mere equity', that unification is accepted and there is no longer a need to distinguish between relief and priority. This, we argue, is a welcome advance, not least in avoiding undue complexity in the law; but the journey to that destination involved some judicial re-shaping of rules, and in that process the legal title requirement was used as a blunt instrument to narrow the scope of the defence. It is now possible, we argue, to provide a conceptually more accurate limit, one consistent with the special nature both of equitable interests and of the defence.

The limit, in our view, is that the defence should apply only if C acquires a right that is: (i) the very right of A in relation to which B has an equitable interest; or (ii) a right that otherwise does not depend on A's being under a duty to C, in respect of the same right in relation to which B has an equitable interest. So, for example, if A holds shares on trust for B and transfers those shares to C, the requirement is met, as the very right of A in relation to which B has an equitable interest has been acquired by C. Similarly, if A holds a freehold of land on trust for B and grants C a legal lease or easement, the requirement is met, as C's right does not depend for its existence on A's being under

[5] Of course, this is not a requirement of the form of bona fide purchaser defence that can apply where B's pre-existing interest is a mere equity, but, as noted at n 2, that particular defence is not examined here.

[6] A Reilly, 'What Were Lord Westbury's Intentions in Phillips v Phillips? Bona Fide Purchase of an Equitable Interest' (2021) 80 *CLJ* 156. See too A Reilly, 'Does Equity's Darling Need a Legal Title? Reassessing Pilcher v Rawlins' (2016) 10 *Journal of Equity* 89.

any duty to C in relation to A's freehold.[7] The important point in each case is that C's right has an existence *independent of* any duty owed by A to C in relation to A's right to the shares or to the land. The view developed by courts of equity was that if C has acquired such an independent right as a bona fide purchaser for value without notice of B's interest, then C's claim should have priority to that of B, as there are no grounds for depriving C of the benefit of C's right. In contrast, if A holds shares on trust for B, and then declares a conflicting trust of the shares in favour of C or grants C an equitable charge over the shares, then C's right lacks that element of independence from A's right: C is essentially in the same position as B, as C's right also depends on A's being under a duty to B in relation to A's right, and there is then no reason to prefer C's later acquired right to that of B.[8]

The difference between the legal title requirement and our suggested requirement may seem small: the two requirements lead to exactly the same outcomes in the three examples just given. Certainly, we are not arguing for a radical rethinking of the defence, or for its merging into a broader principle of third-party protection that would apply whether B's pre-existing interest is legal or equitable. Nor, as can be seen from the examples above, are we arguing for a return to the view that the plea of bona fide purchase should be a bar to relief in equity, irrespective of whether C acquired any right from A. Nonetheless, there is a difference between the effects of the legal title requirement and of our suggested requirement. The difference is a very important one in practice. For our requirement is consistent with the view, noted above, that C should be protected wherever C acquires, as a bona fide purchaser for value without notice, the very right of A in relation to which B has an equitable interest. This is significant in the case of sub-trusts, which are a key feature of commercial practices such as the intermediated holding of securities.[9] We agree with the view of the Financial Markets Law Committee in 2004 that there is a pressing contemporary need to extend the bona fide purchaser defence to at least some purchasers of equitable interests. We disagree, however, with the view that it is not possible for this extension to be made without legislation, although we accept that such legislation may be advisable given the unfortunate ubiquity of the legal title requirement in judicial and academic presentations of the defence.

[7] It is true of course that whenever C has a legal lease or easement, C will have a right that is prima facie binding on the rest of the world, including A, and so A will be under at least such a duty to C (note that C can have a legal lease without there being any further duties on A: as noted by Lewison LJ in *Procter v Procter* [2021] EWCA Civ 167, [2021] 2 WLR 1249 [52], it is possible to have a lease without enforceable covenants). However, C's legal interest of course goes beyond that duty owed by A, given the matching duty on the rest of the world, and does not depend on A's being under a duty to C specifically in relation to A's freehold.

[8] It can be said in such a case that C must take A's right as C finds it, ie subject to a duty to B. Note that the same reasoning need not apply where A incurs conflicting duties to B and C that do *not* relate to any specific right of A and so do not give rise to an equitable interest in either B or C: in deciding in such a case, for example, if specific performance should be granted in favour of B or of C, the timing of the contracts is just one factor a court may take into account in exercising its discretion.

[9] See, eg, Financial Markets Law Committee, 'Property Interests in Investment Securities: Analysis of the Need for and Nature of Legislation relating to Property Interests in Indirectly Held Investment Securities, with a Statement of Principles for an Investment Securities Statute' (July 2004) (Issue 3).

II. The Nature of the Defence

A. Distinguishing the Defence from Exceptions to *Nemo Dat*

The first distinction to be made is between two sets of rules: (i) where C can use the bona fide purchase defence to acquire a right free of B's pre-existing equitable interest; and (ii) where C can use one of the so-called '*nemo dat* exceptions', such as the seller or buyer in possession rules, to acquire a right free from B's pre-existing legal rights.

There has been a tendency in some scholarship to see any defence that protects C from B's claim as an exception to the *nemo dat* principle. Much American scholarship on priorities takes this for granted.[10] Some practitioner texts also take this approach.[11] Most recently, Hanoch Dagan and Irit Samet have argued that the bona fide purchase defence is not unique, as it operates in the same way as those defences that protect C from claims based on B's legal title: there is simply a line to be drawn, and in some cases B is preferred and in others C is protected.[12] Peter Birks too thought that the equitable bona fide purchaser claim was an exception to *nemo dat*, concerned with cases where intermediaries could not pass on good title, and on that basis argued it should have no place in a case where a claimant seeking restitution did have good title and argued that the transfer of that title to the defendant was flawed because, for example, of a mistake or the exercise of undue influence.[13] Certainly, we agree that in the standard two-party case where the defendant acquires a right directly from the claimant, the defendant's good faith acquisition of the right without notice of any flaw in the transfer does not in itself bar a restitutionary claim:[14] indeed, the acquisition of a right may be a pre-condition of liability,[15] and whilst the defendant's lack of awareness of any defect in the transfer may be relevant if there is a later change of position, it does not in itself prevent a claim.[16]

However, this does not mean we must accept the view that, when applied against B's equitable interest, the bona fide purchaser defence operates as an exception to *nemo dat*. That view is a consequence of a wider tendency to see an equitable and a legal property right as equivalent: it also led Birks, for example, to argue that a beneficiary of a trust should be able to make a strict liability restitutionary claim against an unauthorised

[10] See, eg, M Mautner, '"The Eternal Triangles of the Law": Toward a Theory of Priorities in Conflicts Involving Remote Parties' (1991) 90 *Michigan Law Review* 95; A Schwartz and R Scott, 'Rethinking the Laws of Good Faith Purchase' (2011) 111 *Columbia Law Review* 1332.

[11] See, eg, L Gullifer (ed), *Goode and Gullifer on Legal Problems of Credit and Security*, 6th edn (London, Sweet & Maxwell, 2017) ch 5.

[12] H Dagan and I Samet, 'Express Trust: The Dark Horse of the Liberal Property Regime Jigsaw' in S Degeling et al (eds), *Philosophical Foundation of the Law of Express Trusts* (Oxford, Oxford University Press, forthcoming 2022).

[13] P Birks, 'Notice and Onus in O'Brien' (1998) 12 *Trust Law International* 2 (discussing the Court of Appeal's decision in *Barclays Bank v Boulter*, later overturned by the House of Lords: [1999] 1 WLR 1919 (HL)).

[14] See, eg, W Swadling, 'Restitution and Bona Fide Purchase' in W Swadling (ed), *The Limits of Restitutionary Claims: A Comparative Analysis* (London, United Kingdom National Committee of Comparative Law, 1997) 79.

[15] See, eg, *Cressman v Coys of Kensington (Sales) Ltd* [2004] EWCA Civ 47, [2004] 1 WLR 2775 [24].

[16] See, eg, *Kelly v Solari* (1841) 9 M & W 54, 152 ER 24.

recipient of trust property, rather than having to rely on the existing rules as to knowing receipt.[17] However, that argument has not convinced the courts[18] and overlooks a key formal difference between an equitable interest and a legal property right.[19] The same problem undermines analyses of the bona fide purchaser defence as equivalent to defences to claims based on legal title. The point is that if A holds a right on trust for B and then (without authority under the terms of the trust) transfers that right to C, it is not true to say that A does not have good title so that C needs to invoke an exception to *nemo dat*. Rather, a crucial feature of the trust is that the trustee *does* have the right to the trust property[20] and, as an incident of that, has the power to transfer that right to C.[21] Of course, A does not have liberty, *as against B*, to make the unauthorised transfer and cannot, for example, bring that transfer into account if a claim is made by B; but that does not alter A's general power, as an incident of A's having the right, to transfer that right to a party such as C.[22] This can explain why B has no strict liability restitutionary claim against C: any enrichment of C comes at the expense of A, who held the right transferred to C, rather than at the expense of B.[23]

This analysis of the position where A holds a right on trust for B is consistent with the view of the Supreme Court in *Akers v Samba Financial Group* that, even if C is not bound by B's pre-existing equitable interest, A's transfer of the trust property to C is not a 'disposition' of B's property for the purposes of section 127 of the Insolvency Act 1986.[24] If C's use of a defence, such as the bona fide purchaser defence, in such a case were seen as an exception to *nemo dat*, allowing C to acquire B's title to the trust property, then surely a disposition of B's property *would* occur in such a case. The point is that in a case such as *Akers*, A did have title to the shares: the general question after a transfer in breach of trust is not whether C acquired such title but rather whether C's conscience is affected[25] in such a way that C comes under a duty, in relation to that title, to B. The role of the bona fide purchaser defence is to determine whether the circumstances of C's acquisition are such that, even if C later acquires notice of B's pre-existing interest, C's conscience cannot be said to be affected in such a way as to justify imposing a duty on C to B.

[17] See, eg, P Birks, 'Receipt' in P Birks and A Pretto (eds), *Breach of Trust* (Oxford, Hart Publishing, 2002) 213.

[18] See, eg. *BCCI v Akindele* [2001] Ch 437 (CA); *Farah Constructions Pty Ltd v Say-Dee Pty Ltd* (2007) 230 CLR 89.

[19] See, eg, L Smith, 'Unjust Enrichment, Property and the Structure of Trusts' (2000) 116 *LQR* 412.

[20] See further B McFarlane, 'Trusts, Property, and Rights' in S Degeling et al (eds), *Philosophical Foundations of the Law of Express Trusts* (Oxford, Oxford University Press, forthcoming 2022).

[21] See, eg, *Rolled Steel Products Ltd v British Steel Corp* [1986] Ch 246 (CA), 303 (Browne-Wilkinson LJ): 'If two trustees convey trust property in breach of trust, the conveyance is not void. As human beings they have the capacity to transfer the legal estate: their capacity to transfer flows from their status as human beings, not from the powers conferred on them as trustees. Even if their powers under the trust instrument did not authorise the conveyance, the legal estate will vest in the transferee.' See too Nair and Samet (n 1) 264, 276–84.

[22] On the difference between the general powers of a trustee and their powers as against the beneficiaries, see, eg, J Hudson, 'One Thicket in Fraud on a Power' (2019) 39 *OJLS* 577; J Hudson and C Mitchell, 'Trustee Recoupment: A Power Analysis' (2021) 35 *Trust Law International* 3, 8.

[23] See, eg, *Skandinaviska Enskilda Banken AB (Publ) v Conway* [2019] UKPC 36, [2020] AC 1111: the defendant's acquisition of a right in its capacity as trustee did not prevent the defendant's being liable to a restitutionary claim arising from its acquisition of the right.

[24] *Akers* (n 1). This analysis of the meaning of 'disposition' is also consistent with that of the House of Lords, in the context of s 53(1)(c) of the Law of Property Act 1925, in *Vandervell v IRC* [1967] 2 AC 291 (HL).

[25] See, eg, Lord Sumption in *Akers* (n 1) [89].

In our view, then, rules protecting C's good faith acquisition of a right from an intermediary may have a significantly different form according to whether B's pre-existing right is legal or equitable.[26] In relation to the former case, where sections 8 or 9 of the Factors Act 1889 apply, it is reasonable to see such rules as an exception to the *nemo dat* principle, as the statute makes clear that C is to be treated as though A had authority from B to transfer B's right to C. In contrast, where the bona fide purchaser defence applies to allow C to acquire trust property free from B's pre-existing equitable interest, there is no transfer of B's right to C. Rather, the circumstances of C's acquisition can be seen as giving C an immunity against B: B no longer has the power to make a claim against C, even if C later acquires knowledge that A held on trust and made the transfer without authority under that trust.[27]

B. Consequences for the Legal Title Requirement

To evaluate the legal title requirement of the bona fide purchaser defence, we need to consider the nature and purpose of that defence. On the analysis in section II.A, the defence does not operate to cure a defect in C's title, or to allow C to acquire a right that C would otherwise not acquire. Rather, it operates to deny B the opportunity to show that C's conscience was affected in a specific way: by C's holding of a right that depends on A's right, where C has knowledge that A was under a duty to B in relation to that right. The first point, then, is that the defence is not simply a more or less arbitrary means of resolving the perennially difficult disputes that may arise where parties make claims to the same resource. The defence, for example, focuses on the circumstances in which C acquired C's right, precisely because it is C's acquisition of a right that makes C potentially liable to the particular claim B wishes to make: this is because B's pre-existing equitable interest (unlike a legal property right) is not prima facie binding on the whole world. Rather, the 'proprietary' claim that B may bring against third parties is, as noted by Lord Sumption in *Akers*, limited to successors in title to A. In contrast, where C takes possession or otherwise deals as an owner of goods to which B has legal title, whether C acquires any right is irrelevant to B's claim. Similarly, C's conscience is irrelevant: as evidenced by the scope of torts such as conversion, C is prima facie strictly liable. Where B has a pre-existing legal interest, C's acquisition of a right can, however, make a difference if C can invoke an exception to *nemo dat* to show that the right acquired by C was in fact *B's* right, so that B did not have a right in the property when C interfered with it. That is not the role played by the bona fide purchaser defence.

[26] See too S Agnew and B McFarlane, 'The Paradox of the Equitable Proprietary Claim' in B McFarlane and S Agnew (eds), *Modern Studies in Property Law*, vol X (Oxford, Hart Publishing, 2019) 303, 311. Note too FW Maitland, *Equity* (Cambridge, Cambridge University Press, 1936) 142–43, noting the 'marked difference' between the *nemo dat* exceptions in the Factors Act 1889 and the bona fide purchaser defence in equity: whereas in the first cases, 'the buyer gets ownership, but we do not conceive that he gets it from the seller, for the seller never had ownership', in the latter cases 'the rule about the effect of a purchase in rendering equitable rights unenforceable is based on this[:] that the trustee has ownership, and transfers it to the purchaser, and that there is no reason for taking away from the purchaser the legal right which has thus been transferred to him'.

[27] See, eg, Agnew and McFarlane (n 26).

The second point is that our analysis of the nature of B's equitable interest, which sees it as founded on A's being under a duty to B in relation to a specific right held by A, also has consequences for C, in the case where the right later acquired by C is also an equitable interest. We can see this by returning to one of the examples in section I, where A holds shares on trust for B and then declares a conflicting trust of the shares in favour of C, or grants C an equitable charge over the shares. In such a case, even if C is a bona fide purchaser for value without notice of A's prior duties to B, C faces the difficulty that C is making essentially the same type of claim as B. C's claim, like that of B, depends on A's conscience being affected, and is rooted through A's performance of duties. Indeed, in arguing that C is bound by B's pre-existing equitable interest, B is most often arguing not that C has come under a duty to B (such as a duty to hold a particular right for B's benefit), but simply that A's pre-existing duties to B should be performed, and that A cannot escape or reduce those duties by pointing to C's position.[28]

C can of course avoid this difficulty where the right acquired by C is instead a legal title. In such a case, C's right, unlike that of B, has an existence independent of any duty of A in relation to a specific right. It is understandable that C's acquisition of such a right as a bona fide purchaser for value without notice should give C an immunity, allowing C to resist B's claim that, because of C's holding the right and later acquiring knowledge of B's position, C is now under a duty to B in relation to that right.

However, this argument should also avail C in any case where the right acquired by C as a bona fide purchaser for value without notice is not a legal interest but is nonetheless independent of any duty of A. That is true of one of the other examples discussed in section I: where there is a sub-trust. For example, consider the case where HT (the head trustee) holds shares on trust for A. There is a sub-trust and A holds A's equitable interest on trust for B. A then transfers that equitable interest to C. In such a case, C's claim is only to an equitable interest; but crucially, unlike B's equitable interest, C's claim does not depend on any duty of A in relation to A's equitable interest. Rather, the effect of the assignment of the equitable interest is that C's claim now depends on the duties owed to C by HT. In determining whether C is immune from a claim that C's conscience is affected by later acquiring knowledge of B's pre-existing equitable interest, the bona fide purchaser defence should potentially be available whenever C acquires the very right of A in relation to which B has an equitable interest, and that should be true whether A's right is legal or equitable.

III. The Legal Title Requirement: Setting the Stage

We have argued so far that whilst the current rules operate in a satisfactory way in many cases, there are both conceptual and practical reasons for rejecting a simple rule that allows C to have a defence to B's pre-existing equitable interest only where C acquires a legal, as opposed to an equitable, interest. We will now show how that simple rule

[28] See, eg, T Lewin, *A Practical Treatise on the Law of Trusts and Trustees* (London, A Maxwell, 1837) 686: 'The act of the trustee shall not alter the nature of the *cestui que trust's* estate' as a 'maxim for sustaining the trust estate against the laches or tort of the trustee'.

developed, tracing its formulation to Victorian concerns to unify two sets of initially distinct equitable rules: those governing equitable relief and those governing equitable priorities. In doing so, we will place the difficult case of *Phillips v Phillips*[29] in context.

A. An Initial Distinction: Claims to Relief and Priority Disputes

The first point is that, historically, there was no single doctrine of bona fide purchase.[30] For instance, Victorian treatise discussions of bona fide purchase simply list distinct instances where it might be advantageous for a defendant to set out that he is a bona fide purchaser.[31] In considering the development of the legal title requirement, two main sets of rules matter and need to be distinguished from each other: the general 'plea of bona fide purchase', which C might make as a means of resisting B's claim to equitable relief; and the specific question of the treatment of bona fide purchasers in priority disputes arising in equity. Courts had to wrestle with the often difficult interaction between these two sets of rules. In particular, as each set of rules was defined by the procedural context in which the claim arose, rather than conceptually, the same facts might fall within either set. In such a case, a decision therefore had to be made about which set of rules was to govern. The eventual outcome was that the requirements of the 'plea of bona fide purchase' were assimilated with the rules governing priority disputes. This outcome, we argue, was a sensible one, as the protection given to C by the general plea was too broad. We certainly do not, therefore, recommend a resurrection of the general plea. However, the legal title requirement, we argue, is an unfortunate legacy of the tussle between the two sets of rules.

B. Claims to Relief

It is to the general plea of bona fide purchase that Ames refers, in the first sentence of the first volume of the *Harvard Law Review*, when stating that 'It seems to have been a common opinion in early times that a court of equity would give no assistance against a purchaser for value without notice.'[32] The plea, which, as Ames points out,[33] did not require C to show that C had acquired a legal estate or interest, was a defence to a claim for equitable relief.[34] A David Fox puts it, from roots in the sixteenth century as 'an outworking of the old privity rules governing the law of uses and trusts', it 'developed a recognisable procedural shape as an equitable defence' delimiting the proper scope of

[29] *Phillips v Phillips* (1861) 4 De GF & J 208, 45 ER 1164.

[30] See too Reilly, 'Does Equity's Darling Need a Legal Title?' (n 6).

[31] See, eg, E Sugden, *Vendors and Purchasers*, 14th edn (London, Sweet, 1862) ch XXII, 'Of the Protection and Relief Afforded to Purchasers by Statutes'; ch XXIII, 'Of Equitable Relief and Protection'; and ch XXV, 'Of Pleading a Purchase'.

[32] JB Ames, 'Purchase for Value Without Notice' (1887) 1 *Harvard Law Review* 1, 1.

[33] ibid 3.

[34] See, eg, the analysis of Lord St Leonards LC in *Bowen v Evans* (1844) 1 Jo & Lat 178, 623–26, as reflected in his *Vendors and Purchasers* (n 31) 791–98.

equitable relief more generally.[35] If B brought a claim against C in Chancery, C could enter a 'plea' that she was a good faith purchaser for value, from a vendor with apparent title, without notice of B's title – a point affirmed by weighty authority.[36]

For example, imagine A were the freehold owner of Blackacre, over which A declared a trust in favour of B. Later, A sold the legal title to C, who was in good faith and had no notice of B's title. Were B to bring a bill in Chancery against C, seeking a conveyance of the legal title, and perhaps also an account of any rents or profits, then C would have been able to enter a plea of bona fide purchase in bar of B's claim. C would 'win' – Chancery would not help B, and C's rights would be enforced by a common law court. As Hackney points out,[37] referring to C as 'Equity's darling' is somewhat misleading, as it is common law, in such a case, that provides the rights and benefits to C, with equity simply refusing to intervene to limit C's enjoyment of such rights.

In such a case, however, the general plea did not depend on C's acquisition of *legal* title. Entering the plea did not depend on a purchaser's proving he had actually acquired *any* interest – and so a good faith purchaser could rely on the plea even if he had only an equitable interest,[38] or no title whatsoever, such as where the conveyance was forged.[39] Further, although the point was challenged in the eighteenth century, the weight of authority fell behind the view that it did not matter whether the claimant had either a prior legal or equitable title.[40] The general principle was that Chancery would not grant relief against a purchaser for value without notice.[41]

If C made out the plea then Chancery would enter immediate judgment for C, who did not therefore need to otherwise answer B's claim, and there was no need for a trial.[42] The defence was procedural in that it did not take effect until it was pleaded – it said nothing about the priority as between B and C's rights per se; it only said B could obtain no relief against C. The principle was simply one of non-interference – as Lord Loughborough LC ruled in *Jerrard v Saunders*, 'against a purchaser for value without notice this court will not take the least step imaginable'.[43]

C. Priority Disputes

A bona fide purchaser could also receive favourable treatment in a rather different context – the priorities dispute. In a case where Chancery was administering a

[35] D Fox, 'Purchase for Value Without Notice' in P Davies, S Douglas and J Goudkamp (eds), *Defences in Equity* (Oxford, Oxford University Press, 2017) 53, 65.

[36] See *Basset v Nosworthy* (1673) Rep Temp Finch 102, 23 ER 55 (Lord Nottingham LC); *White and Tudor's Leading Cases in Equity*, 1st edn (London, 1849–50) vol II, 1–5; *Jerrard v Saunders* (1794) 2 Ves Jun 454, 30 ER 721 (Lord Loughborough LC); *Maundrell v Maundrell* (1805) 10 Ves Jun 246, 32 ER 839 (Lord Eldon LC); *Joyce v De Moleyns* (1845) 2 Jones and La Touche 374 (Lord St Leonards LC). See also John Mitford, *A Treatise on the Pleading of Suits in the Court of Chancery*, 4th edn (London, 1827) 274–76.

[37] J Hackney, *Understanding Equity and Trusts* (New York, Fontana Press, 1987) ch 1.

[38] *Bassett* (n 36). See DEC Yale (1961–62) SS vol 79, 162–63; *Wallwyn v Lee* (1803) 9 Ves Jun 24, 32 ER 509.

[39] *Jones v Powles* (1834) 3 Myl & Kn 581, 40 ER 222.

[40] *Jerrard* (n 36); *Joyce* (n 36). For a full discussion, see *White and Tudor's Leading Cases in Equity* (n 36) 7–14.

[41] See the authorities cited in n 36.

[42] Mitford (n 36) 15.

[43] *Jerrard* (n 36) 458; 723. See also D O'Sullivan, 'The Rule in *Phillips v Phillips*' (2002) 118 *LQR* 296.

testamentary or bankrupt estate, for instance, it might well need to decide the order of priority of different claims to that estate.[44] In the alternative, B and C might both be equitable interest holders seeking to compel a third-party trustee to convey legal title to them.[45] Similarly, in a case where the same land had been mortgaged several times, the mortgagees themselves might seek a decree from the court as to what the priorities were.[46] In such cases the *plea* of bona fide purchase was irrelevant – in that a decree for priorities was not a form of relief, and each party sought Chancery's assistance. Neither party was barred from seeking a remedy, but the court would decide the priority of the rights.

The courts resolved such disputes by considering the relative fault of the parties – and within that, the fact that C was a bona fide purchaser for value without notice could involve C's being favoured over B. However, this would depend on (i) whether B or C was at fault in some way; and (ii) whether C had received a legal title. For example, imagine A had declared a trust in favour of B and then, without authority under the trust, A had given C a legal lease of the land. Again, C is a good faith purchaser for value without notice. A then dies, and Chancery as part of the administration of A's estate is making a decree as to priorities. Who would Chancery rule had priority? Again, the answer seems to be that if C had made all proper inquiries, had acted in good faith and paid value, the court would not take away the legal title that C had obtained by her diligence.[47]

Although many of the cases discussing the proposition concern fact patterns where C initially purchased an equitable title, and later acquired a legal title *that had priority over B*, the same principle applied where C took a legal estate subject to B's equitable interest at the time of the purchase.[48] B would have to show a 'superior equity' to have legal title taken away from C – the fact that B and C were equally blameless, and the fact that B was first in time, would not in combination be enough.[49] The reasoning here was identified with the rationale of the general plea of bona fide purchase – B and C were both equally deserving of protection as far as Chancery was concerned, and C would not be deprived of her legal title.[50] This explains why *White and Tudor's Leading Cases in Equity*,[51] published in 1849–50, discussed the priority of legal titles vis-à-vis equitable interests in their section on *Basset v Nosworthy*[52] – a case in fact decided by Lord Nottingham LC on the basis of the general plea of bona fide purchase entered by the defendant in bar of a claimant's bill for discovery.

[44] *Ex parte Knott* (1806) 11 Ves Jun 609, 32 ER 1225.

[45] *Mirfield v Morley* SS vol 79, p 672, discussed by Yale (n 38) fn 2.

[46] *Rooper v Harrison* (1855) 2 Kay & John 86, 69 ER 704.

[47] *Willoughby v Willoughby* (1787) 1 Term Rep 763, 99 ER 1366; *Attorney-General v Wilkins* (1853) 17 Beav 285, 51 ER 1043; *Jones v Powles* (n 39). On the diligence point, see *Maundrell* (n 36) and *Ex parte Knott* (n 44).

[48] See *Stanhope v Lord Verney* (1761) 2 Eden 81, 85; 28 ER 826, 828 ('a purchaser without notice for a valuable consideration, is a bar to the jurisdiction of this court, and it is of no consequence when the legal advantage was acquired, if the purchase was made, and the money paid without notice').

[49] *Rooper* (n 46). See also O'Sullivan (n 43).

[50] See text from n 36. For a clear example of the link's being recognised, see *Thorndike v Hunt* (1859) 3 De Gex & Jones 563, 44 ER 1386.

[51] *White and Tudor's Leading Cases in Equity* (n 36) vol II, 1–20.

[52] *Basset* (n 36).

Nonetheless, the general rule[53] was that if C was instead a bona fide purchaser of an equitable interest then, in the context of a decree for priorities, C would not have a defence – even if the availability of the general plea to C meant that Chancery would not have granted relief against C. Indeed, a justification for allowing a good faith purchaser of an equitable interest to enter the plea in bar of relief was that he might *later* be able to acquire priority – for instance by acquiring a legal title by paying off a first mortgagee with priority over all other incumbrances, and tacking all sums owed to the purchaser onto that mortgage.[54] In short, the protection given to C, a bona fide purchaser of an equitable interest, against relief was not equivalent to recognising that C's right had 'priority'; such 'priority' could only come later, if further steps were taken by C. So, where two equitable interest holders sought to claim legal title from trustees, or sought priority payment from a fund held by Chancery, the basic rule was that where the 'equities were equal', the interest that arose first in time would win, even if the later interest was acquired for value without notice of prior interests.[55]

In determining whether the 'equities were equal', the court would first ask which of the two interest holders was more to blame for the unauthorised transaction that caused the priority dispute to arise. Where C had the equity that arose later in time, if C could show that she had been a good faith purchaser for value without notice then she might be able to claim priority if she could show gross negligence or fraud on B's part.[56] However, if B had been just as blameless then B would have priority, B's interest having arisen first in time – the idea being that equitable interests were to be treated like legal rights, and so the default rule for priorities should be the order of their creation.[57]

Initially, then, the need for C to show acquisition of a legal estate or interest applied only in relation to priority disputes, and not where C instead sought to make out the general plea of bona fide purchase as a procedural bar to B's equitable claim against C. The key point arising from this is that the treatment of bona fide purchasers of equitable interests depended on the context of the litigation. This is clear from Lord St Leonards LC's judgment in *Bowen v Evans*.[58] X had an equitable interest in property, which she settled for value on C. Later X acquired the legal title, allegedly by fraud, from B. Lord St Leonards made clear that C would have been able to enter a plea of bona fide purchase in bar of claim for relief brought by B, but that did not mean that C had priority in the sense of the best claim to the legal title.

[53] There were some exceptions where C, as a bona fide purchaser of an equitable interest, could take priority: for example, as a result of a statutory rule (as discussed by eg Sugden: see n 31), or where C had had legal title conveyed to a trustee for his own benefit, and so was said to have the best right to call for the legal title.

[54] *Basset* (n 36); *Jerrard* (n 36).

[55] Views varied on whether first in time was the basic rule to be departed from only for very good reasons (*Cory v Eyre* (1863) 1 De GJ & S 149, 46 ER 58) or a longstop tie-breaker (*Rice v Rice* (1853) 2 Drew 73, 61 ER 646).

[56] *Cory* (n 55); *Rice* (n 55).

[57] For realty, see *Jones v Jones* (1838) 8 Simons 633, 59 ER 251; *Cory* (n 55). For personalty, see *Murray v Pinkett* (1846) 12 Cl & F 764, 8 ER 1612.

[58] *Bowen* (n 34).

IV. The Emergence of the Legal Title Requirement: The Assimilation of Two Sets of Rules

We have seen that the general plea of bona fide purchase and the priorities rules had different requirements and performed different functions. The former governed when Chancery would grant relief, and the latter determined when one right was subject to another. This meant that the protection given to a purchaser of an equitable interest depended to a large extent on whether another interest holder sought personal relief against the purchaser or simply sought a decree as to priorities. Judges, however, came to feel uncomfortable with the role the procedural context played in determining the outcome of disputes. For instance, in *Strode v Blackburn*,[59] Lord Loughborough LC refused to allow a defendant mortgagee without either possession of the land or priority to rely on the plea in bar of a claim for discovery. However, in *Wallwyn v Lee*,[60] Lord Eldon LC ruled that *Strode* was bad law. Matters came to a head later in the mid-nineteenth century. Whereas most earlier-century cases concerning the general plea of bona fide purchase, like *Strode* and *Wallwyn*, involved claims for discovery and delivery of deeds,[61] in the Victorian period defendants began to make the plea in bar of relief of other kinds – using the fact that discussion of the plea from Lord Nottingham's time onwards was in general terms. Judges came to be reluctant to deny personal relief to a claimant whose right had priority over a defendant bona fide purchaser. To address this anomaly, the scope of the plea of bona fide purchase was narrowed – a development that led to the modern rule that only a purchaser of legal title can ever rely on the bona fide purchase defence.

An early example is *Attorney-General v Flint*,[62] where a claim for rent and ejectment was met by a plea of bona fide purchase. Sir James Wigram V-C stated his view[63] that a purchaser could not rely on the plea of bona fide purchase where Chancery would not find in her favour had a decree for priorities been sought.[64] The same issue came before Chancery in *Finch v Shaw*,[65] later heard in the House of Lords as *Colyer v Finch*.[66] B, a legal mortgagee, brought a bill for foreclosure against C, a later bona fide purchaser of an equitable mortgage. As a matter of priorities, B's right had priority over C's. The defendant entered a plea of bona fide purchase for value without notice in bar of the relief sought. Sir John Romilly MR at first instance did not allow the plea – arguing that this would in substance deprive the legal mortgagee of the rights incident to his mortgage. The court would not allow a purchaser of a right *that did not have priority* to enter a plea of bona fide purchase to defeat a claim for relief sought by a party

[59] *Strode v Blackburn* (1796) 3 Ves Jun 222, 30 ER 979.

[60] *Wallwyn* (n 38).

[61] For example, most of the examples in Lord Nottingham's *Prolegomena of Chancery and Equity* concern discovery and delivery of deeds: see DEC Yale (ed), *Lord Nottingham's Manual of Chancery Practice and Prolegomena of Chancery and Equity* (Cambridge, Cambridge University Press, 1965) 204–12.

[62] *Attorney-General v Flint* (1844) 4 Hare 147, 67 ER 597.

[63] This was *obiter* as it was found on the facts that the defendants had notice.

[64] *Attorney-General v Flint* (n 62) 156; 601.

[65] *Finch v Shaw* (1854) 19 Beav 500, 52 ER 445.

[66] *Colyer v Finch* (1856) 5 HL Cas 905, 10 ER 1159.

with priority. The decision was upheld by the House of Lords on more limited grounds – Lord Cranworth LC ruled that a decree for foreclosure (like a bill seeking a decree as to priorities) was not really a form of 'relief'. The claimant bringing such a bill really asked the defendant to discharge the mortgage loan or give up his rights in the property – it did not therefore ask Chancery to intervene against the defendant. A plea of bona fide purchase would thus not bar the claim. The House of Lords' decision was more orthodox than that of the Master of the Rolls – in preserving the principle that a plea of good faith purchase for value without notice was a good defence to a claim for equitable relief. The difficulty is that the line drawn between foreclosure and relief was a thin one. As Lord St Leonards noted in his textbook on *Vendors and Purchasers*, 'no doubt the decree gave equitable relief against the purchaser', at least in substance.[67] Similar concerns about denying personal relief to a claimant with priority were expressed in *Stackhouse v Countess of Jersey*.[68]

A. *Phillips v Phillips*

The question of whether Chancery would grant relief against a good faith purchaser without priority came before the House of Lords again in *Phillips v Phillips*.[69] The claimant, B, held a rent charge over land. C, the defendant, had an interest in relation to that land under a marriage settlement – and so was a purchaser for value. C's interest in the land was equitable rather than legal, because the land had been mortgaged at law. B sought relief against C, in that he claimed payment from C by seeking to enforce the rent charge against him.

On the facts of the case, C had not properly pleaded bona fide purchase, and so B's claim succeeded. Lord Westbury nevertheless took the opportunity to set out when he thought a bona fide purchaser of an equitable interest could rely on the defence – limiting it to cases concerning (i) disclosure of deeds, (ii) *tabula in naufragio* and (iii) mere equities.

The judgment is well known to modern lawyers, but the rationale behind Lord Westbury's discussion is less well understood – in particular its failure to discuss the position of the bona fide purchaser for value who takes legal title from a trustee, despite his claims to set out when a plea of bona fide purchase could be relied upon. Things become clearer, however, when it is understood that Lord Westbury's concern was to limit the cases in which purchasers *of equitable interests* without priority – or purchasers who had received no interest at all – could rely on the general plea of bona fide purchase. In turn, this involved recasting the plea as a series of discrete doctrines rather than a *general* defence to claims for equitable relief. In our view, Lord Westbury's approach is consistent with a laudable desire to promote consistency between the general plea and the priorities rules by, in effect, subsuming the former within the latter.

[67] Sugden (n 31) 798.
[68] *Stackhouse v Countess of Jersey* (1861) 1 John & Hemm 721, 70 ER 933.
[69] *Phillips* (n 29).

As to his first category, Lord Westbury re-rationalised earlier cases that had discussed bona fide purchase in more expansive terms, as only concerning equity's auxiliary jurisdiction.[70] He ruled that a purchaser could *only* successfully plead the defence in bar of a bill for discovery or delivery of deeds sought in litigation ancillary to an action brought at law. Further, on slim authority,[71] he ruled that where a claimant with a prior legal title sought to rely on that title in litigation in Chancery, in a matter over which the common law courts and Chancery had concurrent jurisdiction,[72] a purchaser could not rely on a plea of bona fide purchase in bar of the claim.

Turning next to *tabula in naufragio*, the doctrine provided the following. Imagine X, over the same piece of land, successively granted A a legal mortgage, B an equitable mortgage and then C an equitable mortgage. Imagine also that C, at the time of advancing money to X, had no notice of B. *Even after acquiring notice of B*, C could acquire priority by paying off A, taking A's legal title (which had priority) and tacking on both the sum of C's initial advance and the sum paid to A. In such a case C had been a *bona fide purchaser of equitable title*, but had priority in that he was allowed to retain the paramount legal title acquired from A.[73] Allowing C in such a case to enter a plea of bona fide purchase, in bar of a claim brought by B, was simply a means of recognising C's priority.[74]

Finally, turning to mere equities, Lord Westbury's reasoning turns on the idea that 'mere equities' are entitlements to ask the court for proprietary relief that will not take effect until a court order is made[75] – an idea controversial even when *Phillips* was decided.[76] Where a claimant with a mere equity claimed such proprietary relief, a purchaser of an equitable interest in that same asset could enter a plea of bona fide purchase in bar of the claim. This involved giving effect to, rather than undermining, pre-existing priorities. On Lord Westbury's view, before litigation, the holder of the mere equity had no rights in the underlying asset, whereas the purchaser had an equitable interest – which had 'priority' in the sense at least of being the only equitable right in the asset. The purchaser could protect this 'priority' by entering a plea of bona fide purchase – in effect asking the court not to retrospectively *grant* the holder of the mere equity an equitable interest in the asset pre-dating the purchase, thereby robbing the purchaser of his priority claim.

[70] This was not uncontroversial – cf FO Haynes, *Outlines of Equity*, 5th edn (London, Maxwell, 1880) 392, fn (a).

[71] Lord Westbury generalised from special rules for dower and relied on a decision of Sir John Leach MR in *Collins v Archer* (1830) 1 Russ & M 284, 39 ER 109 inconsistent with higher authority, ie *Wallwyn* (n 38) (Lord Eldon LC). For a discussion, see Haynes, ibid, 403–15.

[72] That is, cases where a claim could be brought at law or in equity: see DEC Yale, 'A Trichotomy of Equity' (1985) 6 *Journal of Legal History* 194.

[73] See the discussion in *Macmillan Inc v Bishopsgate Investment Trust plc (No 3)* [1995] 1 WLR 978 (Ch) 1002–03; *The Serious Fraud Office v Litigation Capital Ltd* [2021] EWHC 1272 (Comm) [141].

[74] But see section IV.B.

[75] See Haynes (n 70) 339–452. See also Kitto J in *Latec Investments v Hotel Terrigal Pty Ltd* (1965) 113 CLR 265.

[76] The mere equity was treated as an equitable interest in the land *ab initio* in *Uppington v Bullen* (1842) 2 Dr & War 184; *Stump v Gaby* (1852) 2 De GM & G 623, 42 ER 1015; *Gresley v Mousley* (1859) 4 De G & J 78, 45 ER 31. See also Taylor J in *Latec Investments* (n 75) and Ames (n 32) 2 ('every equity attaching to property is an equitable estate').

We can see then that, contrary to Reilly's recent analysis,[77] Lord Westbury's motivation in *Phillips* was to prevent the rules about the availability of equitable relief undermining the priorities rules. Once this is appreciated, Lord Westbury's seemingly disparate list of instances when the plea would be available makes sense. Lord St Leonards' criticism of the judgment in his treatise on *Vendors and Purchasers* also becomes much easier to understand.[78] St Leonards rejected Westbury's assimilation of the plea of bona fide purchase with the priorities rules; while he accepted that B's rent charge had priority over C, he treated the issue of priorities as separate from the issue of whether B was entitled to relief against C. On that basis, C *should* have been able to enter a plea of bona fide purchase for value without notice to escape liability, although his interest did not have priority – as Lord St Leonards had himself ruled in *Bowen v Evans*.[79] On that view, Lord Westbury had confused the question of the proper scope of equitable relief with the separate question of priority. However, on our view, Westbury's objective was precisely to remove the troublesome distinction between those two sets of rules and to ensure that, where the priority rules protected B, C would not be able to escape this by making the general plea. A more limited contemporary analogy of the converse point is provided by *Byers v Samba*,[80] where Fancourt J held, and the Court of Appeal confirmed, that where the priority rules protected C, B would not be able to escape this by making a claim for equitable relief based on knowing receipt.

B. The Impact of *Phillips*

The reasoning in *Phillips* stuck, and lawyers came more and more to identify the priorities rules with those governing the availability of equitable relief against a purchaser. A very clear example is in the judgment of James LJ in *Pilcher v Rawlins*,[81] which specifically rejected the idea that there was a distinction between cases where a purchaser was able to plead bona fide purchase in bar of a claim for relief and cases of priorities.[82] It was held instead that the questions of whether a purchaser could enter the plea of bona fide purchase, or claim a right with priority, were identical.[83] James LJ emphasised the point again in his judgment in *Heath v Crealock*,[84] where he stated that a unitary rule governed purchasers, whether in the context of priorities or of relief being sought against them.[85]

[77] Reilly, 'What Were Lord Westbury's Intentions in Phillips v Phillips?' (n 6).

[78] Sugden (n 31) 796–98.

[79] *Bowen* (n 34).

[80] *Byers v Samba* [2021] EWHC 60 (Ch); [2022] EWCA Civ 43.

[81] *Pilcher v Rawlins* (1871–72) LR 7 Ch App 259.

[82] ibid 270–71.

[83] It is worth noting that *Pilcher v Rawlins* is actually a case about *tabula in naufragio* (see section IV.A). It is often cited today as authority for the proposition that a bona fide purchaser of legal title takes title free from the trust, and this is because it rejected as bad law some earlier suggestions (see, eg, *Attorney-General v Flint* (n 62) 156–57; 601 and *Carter v Carter* (1857) 3 Kay & Johnson 617, 69 ER 1256) that a bona fide purchaser of legal title from a trustee might be automatically fixed with notice of the trust, or was otherwise prevented from denying the trust's validity, if the trustee's own legal title was taken from the same instruments that created the trust itself.

[84] *Heath v Crealock* (1874–75) LR 10 Ch App 22.

[85] ibid 33.

The trend of assimilating relief and priorities is visible in contemporary treatise literature too.[86] Following *Phillips*, FO Haynes' *Outlines of Equity*[87] introduced a section on purchaser for value without notice. Although Haynes recognised a clear difference between a court's refusing relief to a claimant because of a plea of bona fide purchase and settling priorities, Haynes nevertheless took the view that *Phillips* itself was rightly decided in that 'the suit was virtually one to adjust the rights over the property in question'.[88] After *Phillips*, editions of *White and Tudor's Leading Cases in Equity* added discussion of priority rules as between equitable interests to the discussion following *Basset v Nosworthy*.[89] Further, the first edition of Edmund Snell's *Principles of Equity*,[90] published in 1868 after the decision in *Phillips*, discusses bona fide purchase purely in terms of priorities, as part of consideration of the maxims 'where there are equal equities the first in time shall prevail' and 'where there is equal equity the law must prevail'.[91] Snell adopted Lord Westbury's reasoning in *Phillips*, and argued that the plea of bona fide purchase

> assumes a conflict between a legal and an equitable estate; or between the holder of some estate equitable or legal, and some one who is trying to enforce an equity against him.[92] The conflict cannot exist between two legal estates if such were possible, for one must be legal, and the other not; nor can it exist between two purely equitable estates, for one must be prior in point of time.[93]

The passage here is significant because it shows that Snell, clearly influenced by the reasoning in *Phillips*, did not see any distinction between the plea of bona fide purchase and the priorities rules. He regarded it as conceptually impossible that a purchaser of one equitable interest should be able to enter the plea in bar of a claim brought by a prior equitable interest holder. The purchaser could only claim priority by proving, at trial, sufficient fault on the part of the holder of the prior interest – not by pre-emptively ending the litigation by entering a plea in bar of relief. Arthur Underhill's *A Concise Guide to Modern Equity* likewise identifies the plea with the priorities rules.[94] The formulations show the impact *Phillips* had in collapsing the distinction between bona fide purchase as a means of determining the proper scope of equitable relief and the priorities rules.

The trend for assimilating questions of priorities and the availability of equitable relief was encouraged by the other legal changes that further narrowed the circumstances in which a purchaser of an equitable interest could rely on the plea of bona fide purchase. Although there are instances post-*Phillips* of courts refusing to order a bona

[86] For a later treatment, see R Willoughby, *The Distinctions and Anomalies Arising Out of the Equitable Doctrine of the Legal Estate* (Cambridge, Cambridge University Press, 1912). Willoughby recognised the tendency after *Phillips* to assimilate the plea and the priorities rules but saw this as problematic.

[87] Haynes (n 70).

[88] ibid, 433–34, 444–52. The view was adopted in BL Cherry et al (eds), *Dart's Treatise on Vendors and Purchasers*, 7th edn (London, Stevens & Sons, 1905) vol II, 846.

[89] *White and Tudor's Leading Cases in Equity*, 3rd edn (London, 1866).

[90] EHT Snell, *The Principles of Equity* (London, Stevens & Haynes, 1868).

[91] ibid 16–27.

[92] Presumably a reference to mere equities.

[93] Snell (n 90) 19. See too the discussion further down that page.

[94] A Underhill, *A Concise Guide to Modern Equity* (London, 1885), Lecture VI.

fide purchaser to deliver over deeds,[95] in most cases the court would in substance grant the claimant relief.[96] Matters were brought to an end by *Ind Coope & Co v Emmerson*,[97] where the House of Lords ruled that defendants could no longer rely on a plea of bona fide purchase to escape discovery or delivery of deeds – for such a defence depended on Chancery's 'auxiliary' jurisdiction to courts of common law. It made no sense to think of such a jurisdiction following the procedural fusion of courts of law and equity. The doctrine of *tabula in naufragio* too was abolished in relation to mortgages of land by the Law of Property Act 1925, section 94,[98] though the extent to which the doctrine has been abolished in respect of mortgages of personal property remains controversial.[99]

In combination with *Phillips v Phillips*, this process of elimination has left us with the modern rule. A bona fide purchaser of legal title for value without notice takes his right free of prior equitable interests for the purposes of priority disputes, and free of claims for equitable relief against him by prior equitable interest holders. A later equitable interest holder, however, will generally be liable to claims by prior equitable interest holders for relief, and will generally rank behind them in a priorities dispute. It is this that has left us with the modern 'legal title' requirement for the bona fide purchaser defence.

V. Conclusion

Imagine a case where A holds legal title on trust for B and then grants C a *brand new* equitable interest over the same asset.[100] We argue that C should not be able to rely on the bona fide purchaser defence in such a case. Where B and C are equally blameless, their positions are equivalent – each benefits from a duty of A that relates to the same right held by A. There is no clear reason why C should be preferred over B in such a case – especially because B had a right capable of binding third parties that arose before C's right.

However, take a different case, where A holds equitable rights on trust for B and disposes of those rights to C, a bona fide purchaser for value. We argue that, in such a case, C should take free of B's pre-existing interest – despite not being a purchaser of legal title. What differentiates this latter case from the former, is that C has received the very right that A held on trust for B – and so C's position is very similar to that of a bona fide purchaser of legal title that A had held on trust.[101] As Ames put it, '[t]he analogy between the two cases would seem to be perfect'.[102]

[95] In *Heath* (n 84) and *Waldy v Gray* (1875) LR 20 Eq 238. In both cases other relief was allowed.

[96] *Newton v Newton* (1868–69) LR 4 Ch App 143; *Re Morgan* (1881) 18 Ch D 93; *Re Cooper* (1882) 20 Ch D 611 (delivery of deeds ordered); *Thorpe v Holdsworth* (1868–69) LR 7 Eq 139 (C ordered to produce deeds for inspection).

[97] *Ind Coope & Co v Emmerson* (1887) 12 App Cas 300.

[98] *Macmillan* (n 73) 1002.

[99] Gullifer (n 11) [5-17].

[100] For further consideration of this situation, see, eg, D Fox, 'Relativity of Title At Law and in Equity' (2006) 65(2) *CLJ* 330; *Litigation Capital Ltd* (n 73) [273]–[293].

[101] See too B McFarlane, *The Structure of Property Law* (Oxford, Hart Publishing, 2008) 245–47; and B McFarlane and R Stevens, 'Interests in Securities: Practical Problems and Conceptual Solutions' in L Gullifer and J Payne (eds), *Intermediated Securities: Legal Problems and Practical Issues* (Oxford, Hart Publishing, 2010) 33, 52–53.

[102] Ames (n 32) 11. See too Willoughby (n 86) 15.

Maitland attempted to justify the legal title requirement on the basis that legal rights were 'ownership', whereas equitable rights were not.[103] The view is difficult, though – Maitland does not explain what about the nature of ownership justifies treating it differently for priorities purposes. Further, as Willoughby argued, equating legal title with ownership does not make good sense – in that a bona fide purchaser of legal rights amounting to less than ownership, including those choses in action transferable at law, still attracts the application of the defence.[104] As we argued in sections I and II, the key conceptual distinction is between cases where C acquires a right that, like B's, depends on A's being under a duty to C in relation to a particular right of A, and those where, instead, C acquires an independent right that does not depend on such a duty of A. On our view, then, a purchaser of an equitable interest in intermediated securities, if acquiring that right as a bona fide purchaser for value without notice, must take free from other equitable encumbrances the seller had created over her interest.

In sections III and IV, we saw that the legal title requirement of the bona fide purchaser defence is an historical accident. It arose as an unfortunate side-effect of the medicine required to resolve a conflict between two sets of equitable rules, those as to the availability of relief and as to priority disputes. We agree that it was necessary to resolve that tension, as where the scope of rules is defined by the context of their operation, rather than their conceptual basis, inconsistency is inevitable. We argue, however, that the resolution can remain, and the side-effect be remedied, by close attention to the nature and effect of the bona fide purchaser defence. The resolution was, after all, motivated by a desire to avoid anomalies in the law, and one such anomaly is the apparent lack of protection for a bona fide purchaser of trust assets where those assets are themselves equitable interests. Curing that anomaly is necessary if the bona fide purchaser defence is to remain fit for its purpose in a world where hugely valuable commercial rights can take the form of an equitable interest under a sub-trust.

[103] Maitland (n 26).
[104] Willoughby (n 86) 11–13.

13

The Partner's Fiduciary and Good Faith Duties: More than Just an Agent?

LAURA MACGREGOR

I. Introduction

This chapter seeks to analyse the nature of fiduciary and good faith duties owed by partners in different types of UK partnerships. Partners are commonly described as owing fiduciary and good faith duties, these phrases often being used interchangeably.[1] It is possible, however, that the phrases are being used to refer to different types of duties. The question the author raises is whether the partner's good faith duty is a type of fiduciary duty,[2] or whether the good faith duty differs in nature and seeks to perform a different, non-fiduciary function.

The method used to answer this question involves the separation of the partner's fiduciary duties from the partner's good faith duties, the two being considered in two unequal halves of the chapter. In the first part the partner's fiduciary duties as a whole are analysed. Drawing on recent scholarship on fiduciary law, the author identifies characteristics thought to be common to fiduciaries (section II). She then examines the extent to which the partner displays these common fiduciary characteristics (section III). This helps us to understand the aims of fiduciary law in the specific context of partnership. The first part of the chapter thus provides a backdrop against which, in the second half, the partner's existing duty of good faith can be compared (section IV). Only if the partner's duty of good faith displays fiduciary characteristics can it be considered a type of fiduciary duty. The chapter therefore proceeds on the basis that it is not correct to consider all of the partner's duties as fiduciary in nature,[3] a view that some may find controversial.

[1] See, eg, R I'Anson Banks, *Lindley & Banks on Partnership*, 20th edn (London, Sweet & Maxwell, 2017) [16-06] (hereinafter *Lindley & Banks*).

[2] See in particular R Nolan and M Conaglen, 'Good Faith: What Does it Mean for Fiduciaries and What Does it Tell Us About Them?' in E Bant and M Harding (eds), *Exploring Private Law* (Cambridge, Cambridge University Press, 2010) 319; M Conaglen, 'Fiduciary Principles in Contemporary Common Law Systems' in EJ Criddle, PB Miller and RH Sitkoff (eds), *The Oxford Handbook of Fiduciary Law* (Oxford, Oxford University Press, 2019) 565, 571.

[3] *Bristol & West Building Society v Mothew* [1998] Ch 1, 16 (Millett LJ), *Hilton v Barker Booth and Eastwood* [2005] UKHL 8, [2005] 1 WLR 567 [29]. See also Conaglen, 'Fiduciary Principles' (n 2) 574–75 and 582.

Certain duties owed by the fiduciary are not fiduciary in nature, for example contractual or tortious duties.

Although partnership law benefits from many excellent treatises, little work has been carried out on a conceptual level. This chapter seeks to fill the gap in scholarship. It makes a contribution to scholarship by applying to partnership law the knowledge developed in recent times in the context of fiduciary law generally. The issues considered here are important both conceptually and practically: conceptually, because we need to know whether the partner's duty of good faith should be taken into account in a conceptual analysis of fiduciary law as a whole;[4] and practically, because we need to know whether the classic, stringent fiduciary remedies are available for breach of a partner's duty of good faith.

The partner's duties have been understood by reasoning by analogy with agency law. This analogical approach fails, however, to take into account the partner's important role as business owner. There is a need to consider this role when thinking about the partner's duties. In short, we need to recognise that the partner is much more than just an agent.

The primary focus of the chapter is Scots law, although reference is made throughout to English law. A key difference between these legal systems is the Scottish partnership's separate legal personality, an attribute not found in English partnerships (with the exception of the limited liability partnership, or LLP).[5] It is argued here that this difference is not significant in the fiduciary context: both legal systems can separate, on a conceptual level, duties owed by a partner to the firm (as a collectivity) from duties owed by one individual partner to another individual partner. Talking about both legal systems together is also helpful because of their shared legislative framework (the Partnership Act 1890, and indeed all legislation governing other types of partnerships, applies to the United Kingdom as a whole). Legislative change in this context would have to emanate from the UK Parliament and not the Scottish Parliament.[6] There is a need for caution, however – it should be stressed that Scots law did not experience the same separation between the courts of equity and common law as occurred in English law.[7] Although Scots lawyers use the expressions 'fiduciary' and 'fiduciary duties', and recognise a body of fiduciary law, they do not see this body of law as being connected to a wider notion of English equity. As a result, whilst the English lawyer may potentially look to wider equity for solutions in this and other contexts, this avenue is not open to the Scots lawyer.

II. How Do the Partner's Fiduciary Duties Arise?

This part of the chapter begins by exploring the current use of the partnership relationship or status to ascribe fiduciary duties, suggesting that the analogy with agency

[4] As observed by Conaglen in 'Fiduciary Principles' (n 2) 575 in relation to the fiduciary's duty of care and skill.

[5] For the LLP, see Limited Liability Partnerships Act 2000, s 1(2). For the legal personality of partnerships more generally, see LJ Macgregor, 'Partnerships and Legal Personality: Cautionary Tales from Scotland' (2020) 20 *Journal of Corporate Law Studies* 237.

[6] The 'creation, operation, regulation and dissolution of types of business association' are matters reserved for the UK Parliament: Scotland Act 1998, s 9 and sch 5, pt II C1.

[7] For the Scottish concept of equity, see D Carr, *Ideas of Equity* (Edinburgh, Edinburgh Legal Education Trust, 2017).

has acted as a red herring in this context. It then seeks, in section III, through discussion of recent scholarship on fiduciary law, to determine characteristics common to all fiduciaries. It can then be determined the extent to which the partner displays these characteristics.

The manner in which fiduciary duties arise has been a highly controversial question in fiduciary law generally. Finn famously suggested that 'It is not because a person is a "fiduciary" … that a rule applies to him. It is because a particular rule applies to him that he is a fiduciary … for its purposes.'[8] Thus the enquiry should begin with the duties themselves rather than characterisation of any party as a fiduciary. Contrary to Finn's approach, it has been common in the partnership context to identify, as a first step, the partnership relationship, and deduce from this relationship that the partner owes fiduciary duties. Partnership relationships are thus within the class of relationships in which fiduciary duties are thought to arise, 'partner-partner' being included in the list of relationships provided by Mason J in the leading case of *Hospital Products Ltd v United States Surgical Corporation*.[9] Status has been used as a preliminary step in a similar manner, although as illustrated in section II.B, status as *agent* rather than status as partner has often constituted this first step.[10]

A. The Fiduciary Duties

Before looking further at the way in which relationship and status have been used to impose fiduciary duties, it is useful to identify the exact nature of fiduciary duties in partnerships. In the United Kingdom, the partner's fiduciary duties developed within the common law before being codified in the Partnership Act 1890. The approach of the legislation is similar regardless of the type of partnership concerned (general, limited or limited liability).[11] The duties, which are default only, involve a duty to account (section 28), accountability of partners for private profits (section 29) and a duty not to compete with the firm (section 30). The exception to this general pattern is the Private Fund Limited Partnership, to which sections 28 and 30 do not apply.[12] The decision not to apply these duties, based, it seems, on the idea that limited partners routinely invest in a number of funds,[13] has drawn stringent academic criticism.[14]

[8] PD Finn, *Fiduciary Obligations* (Sydney, Law Book Company, 1977) [3].

[9] *Hospital Products Ltd v United States Surgical Corporation* (1984) 156 CLR 41, 96.

[10] Partnership Act 1890, s 5, although the partner's status as agent clearly pre-dates this Act.

[11] For the limited partnership, see Limited Partnership Act 1907, s 7, which applies the Partnership Act 1890 and the rules of 'equity and of common law applicable to partnerships' to limited partnerships, except as amended by the 1907 Act. For the limited liability partnership, see Limited Liability Partnerships Regulations 2001 (SI 2001/1090), pt VI, reg 7(8)–(10). See also J Hardman, 'Reconceptualising Scottish Limited Partnership Law' (2021) 21 *Journal of Corporate Law Studies* 179.

[12] Legislative Reform (Private Fund Limited Partnerships) Order 2017 (SI 2017/514).

[13] HM Treasury, 'Proposal on using a Legislative Reform Order to change partnership legislation for private equity investments: summary of consultation responses' (2016) [2.75].

[14] *Lindley & Banks* (n 1) Preface and paras [16-03] and [31-01], fn 10, where the decision is described as 'particularly perplexing'; E Berry, 'Limited partnership law and private equity: an instance of legislative capture?' (2019) 19 *Journal of Corporate Law Studies* 105, 123.

The nature of these statutory fiduciary duties is not explored here – that task has already been performed extremely well in the leading texts. Instead, in this part of the chapter we seek to ask *why* partners are fiduciaries, and to think about the purpose and aims of fiduciary law as it applies within the partnership context.

B. Agency – An Historical Red Herring?

It is clear from a review of partnership law that the partner's status as *agent* has, historically, performed a key function in explaining the partner's fiduciary duties. Whilst the historical development is examined here, the author does not seek to argue that we must adhere to the historical route as the only true route to understanding these duties. Legal history is not being used to 'freeze' doctrinal development.[15] Rather, the historical development of this area of law is useful because it can remind us of the reasons *why* specific actors have been treated as fiduciaries, an issue obscured by our reliance on relationship or status. What is it about the partnership relationship that leads to the types of abuses that have taken place? How are the actors placed vis-à-vis one another, and in what way have they harmed one another? These are the questions that we need to ask to truly understand the partner's duties.

Turning to that historical development, in cases decided close to the enactment of the Partnership Act 1890, the partner's status as agent is emphasised as the key issue in ascribing fiduciary duties. The approach of Lord Blackburn in the House of Lords case *Cassels v Stewart* is typical:

> These cases proceed upon the ground that a partner, being an agent *(for I think it is because he is an agent that the fiduciary character arises)* makes a profit out of the concerns of his principal and as acting for him, he must communicate it to his principal; he cannot make a profit out of his principal's business for himself. As I have said, a partner is an agent, and the principle applying to him is a branch of the general rule which applies to agents.[16]

Although this approach was followed in a further Scottish appeal to the House of Lords,[17] it conflicts with the historical development of partnership law in Scotland. Scottish partnership law developed from Roman law,[18] and specifically from the Roman consensual contract of *societas*. Partners in a contract of *societas* were not agents for the partnership and could not bind their fellow partners in contracts with third parties.[19] This was not because of the Roman attitude to partnership, but rather because of its attitude to agency.

[15] See M Conaglen, *Fiduciary Loyalty* (Oxford, Hart Publishing, 2010) 2.

[16] *Cassels v Stewart* (1881) 6 App Case 64, 69. See also *Dunne v English* (1874) LR 18 Eq 524 (emphasis added).

[17] *Hugh Stephenson & Sons v Cartonnagen Industrie AG* [1918] AC 239.

[18] English law too has been influenced by Roman law, see *Lindley & Banks* (n 1) [16-01], fn 2: 'This principle may be traced back to Roman law, where it was stated thus "*In societatis contractibus fides exuberet*": Cod. Iv, tit. 37, 1, 3' and Paul du Plessis, who describes the influence on English law as substantial, see P du Plessis, *Borkowski's Textbook on Roman Law*, 6th edn (Oxford, Oxford University Press, 2020) 293.

[19] JAC Thomas, *Textbook of Roman Law* (Oxford, North-Holland Publishing Company, 1976) 302; P Stein, 'The Mutual Agency of Partners in the Civil Law' (1958-1959) 33 *Tulane Law Review* 595, 595.

Roman law did not recognise agency, or direct representation,[20] using functional equivalents instead.[21] It was common to appoint a manager, but that manager did not need to be one of the partners.[22] For Scots law at least, agency could not explain the imposition of fiduciary duties in partnerships.

Instead, in Scots law it was the *nature* of the partnership contract that explained the duties the partner owed. In common with the other consensual contracts, in *societas* each party's obligations were determined by reference to good faith.[23] *Societas* was 'based on the mutual trust of the partners between whom it created a kind of brotherhood'.[24] The partnership imitated the community of natural brothers.[25] Good faith manifested itself in different ways, explaining, for example, the need for unanimity over the assumption of a new partner,[26] or requiring that the venture for which the partnership was constituted should not be incompatible with good faith.[27] Historically, the key idea underpinning partnership duties was the trust inherent in running a business together. Good faith informed the entire partnership venture, and did not arise because a partner was forming contracts for the partnership.

These key ideas of good faith and trust were carried through to the works of the Scottish institutional writers, writing from the late-seventeenth to the early-nineteenth centuries. Stair referred in this context to the 'fraternity amongst brothers'.[28] Erskine too derived a number of practical consequences from the existence within partnerships of an implied duty of good faith.[29]

The idea of a fiduciary or a fiduciary duty is, of course, a modern idea,[30] and one that has been fully embraced by Scots law. These words do not therefore appear in the Scottish historical sources. What we can say, nevertheless, is that behaviour that a modern lawyer would recognise as a breach of fiduciary duty is, in these Scottish historical sources, ascribed to a contractual, Roman-derived idea of good faith.[31] Statements in the modern law that the partner owes fiduciary duties *because* he is an agent seem,

[20] R Zimmermann, *The Law of Obligations Roman Foundations of the Civilian Tradition* (Oxford, Clarendon Press, 1996) 413–18.

[21] The head of an extended household or *paterfamilias* was able to operate business through his sons or slaves, for example. See WM Gordon, 'Agency and Roman Law' in WM Gordon (ed), *Roman Law, Scots Law and Legal History* (Edinburgh, Edinburgh University Press, 2007) 54, 55.

[22] du Plessis (n 18) 290.

[23] Zimmermann (n 20) 454; AGM Duncan (ed), *Trayner's Latin Maxims*, 4th edn (Edinburgh, W Green, 1993) 109, Contracts *bonae fidei, et stricti juris*.

[24] Thomas (n 19) 301, citing D.17.2.63pr; Zimmermann (n 20) 451 and 466.

[25] Zimmermann (n 20) 451 and 454.

[26] du Plessis (n 18) 290.

[27] ibid and A Watson, 'The Notion of Equivalence of Contractual Obligation and Classical Roman Partnership' (1981) 97 *LQR* 275.

[28] James Dalrymple, Viscount Stair, *Institutions of the Law of Scotland* (originally published in 1697, tercentenary edition by DM Walker) (Edinburgh, Edinburgh University Press, 1981) I.16.4 (hereinafter *Institutions*).

[29] J Erskine, *An Institute of the Law of Scotland* (originally pub 1773, 1st edn by KGC Reid) (Edinburgh, Edinburgh Legal Education Trust, 2014) III,3,20, citing *Inglis v Austine* [1624] Mor 14562.

[30] See Conaglen (n 15) 18–19; P Birks, 'The Content of Fiduciary Obligation' (2000) 34 *Israel Law Review* 3, 8.

[31] LJ Macgregor, 'An Agent's Fiduciary Duties: Modern Law Placed in Historical Context' (2010) 14 *Edinburgh Law Review* 121.

as a result, to be off the point. They fail to express the source and nature of the partner's duties. Fiduciary duties arise because of the trust inherent in the pooling of resources to run a business together.

Shifting our focus to English law, not every judge adopted Lord Blackburn's emphasis of agency as the key issue for understanding the partner's fiduciary duties. Bacon V-C stated:

> If fiduciary relation means anything I cannot conceive a stronger case of fiduciary relation than that which exists between partners. Their mutual confidence is the life blood of the concern. It is because they trust one another that they are partners in the first instance; it is because they continue to trust each other that the business goes on.[32]

This approach, not reliant on agency, reflects much more closely the nature of the Scottish partnership.

C. The Declining Importance of the Label 'Agent' in Ascribing Fiduciary Duties in Agency

In the immediately preceding section, it was concluded that the partner's status as agent has acted as a red herring historically in ascribing fiduciary duties in partnerships. Recent developments provide further pressing reasons suggesting that we should be slow to continue our understanding of partnerships by arguing by analogy with agency. Judging by recent English cases, the label 'agent' is declining in importance in ascribing fiduciary duties in the law of *agency*. The judiciary appear to be 'down-grading' the label of 'agent' and asking instead whether the relationship in question involves the type of trust that would be characteristic of a fiduciary relationship. If the label 'agent' is being down-graded in understanding fiduciary duties in agency, it should certainly not be used for this purpose in partnership law.

This phenomenon can be observed in, for example, *Prince Arthur Ikpechukwu Eze v Conway*.[33] In this case, Asplin LJ discussed the law of bribes and secret commissions, emphasising that for this to be engaged there must be a relationship of trust and confidence between the parties. Speaking of this type of relationship, she stated:

> Not all agents will be in such a position and the relationship may arise where there is no agency at all. It is not helpful, therefore, to consider what might be considered to be the paradigm of any particular type of agent … It all depends on the nature of the individual's duties and which of those duties is engaged in the precise circumstances under consideration. Although the relationship of principal and agent is a fiduciary one, not every person described as an 'agent' is the subject of fiduciary duties and a person described as an agent may owe fiduciary duties in relation to some of his activities and not others.[34]

[32] *Helmore v Smith* (1886) Ch D 436, 444.

[33] *Prince Arthur Ikpechukwu Eze v Conway* [2019] EWCA Civ 88.

[34] ibid [39]–[40]. In Scots law too, an agent's duties may be so limited as to indicate that she possesses no fiduciary duties, see LJ Macgregor, *The Law of Agency in Scotland* (Edinburgh, W Green, 2013) [6-55], relying inter alia on *Sao Paolo Alpargatas SA v Standard Chartered Bank* 1982 SLT 433.

Thus, the label 'agent' does not, in her view, play a significant role in ascribing fiduciary duties. This trend has continued,[35] visible in particular in joined cases *Wood v Commercial First Business Ltd* and *Business Mortgage Finance 4 plc v Pengelly*.[36]

Some might react to these observations by reminding us that the identification of a particular relationship or status is 'only the beginning of [fiduciary] analysis'.[37] Context has always been important as a second step in deriving the scope or *extent* of those duties. This is the case in both agency and partnership, the statutory fiduciary duties in partnership being default duties only. It can be countered that we do not see this classic two-step process in these cases. The court does *not* begin by identifying status and then move to allow the context to mould fiduciary duties. Rather, the first step, identification of a relevant status, has disappeared entirely.

These are relatively recent cases on agency, and the insights they provide have not yet 'fed through' into partnership case law. We can see from at least two partnership cases decided in the last 10 years or so that the label 'agent' continues to be used as a key factor in ascribing fiduciary duties in partnerships. In *F & C Alternative Investments (Holdings) Ltd v Barthelemy (No 2)*, a case concerning LLPs, Sales J read a good deal into the fact that 'there was nothing in the Act [ie the LLP Act 2000] to qualify the usual fiduciary obligations which an agent owes to his principal in relation to the transactions which the agent enters into on his principal's behalf'.[38] Although he then moved to consider whether the member in question had carried out any activities as an agent, the label of 'agent' was nevertheless given central importance in his reasoning. His approach was followed by Newey J five years later in *Hosking v Marathon Asset Management LLP*.[39]

Added to these conceptual problems are further, more practical problems. Put simply, some partners are not agents *stricto sensu*, and yet they can bear fiduciary duties. The limited partner has no agency powers,[40] and this has led some to suggest, contrary to the orthodox view, that her fiduciary duties toward a general partner may be limited.[41] In a general partnership, certain partners may lack agency powers. In large law firms, for example, management is often delegated to a small operational board. Some partners in the law firm will not be agents (although they could appear to third parties to have agency powers, potentially giving rise to apparent rather than actual authority). Non-agent partners may, nevertheless, indulge in conduct that could constitute acting in conflict of interest, or the taking of a secret profit or bribe. The partner

[35] *Medsted Associates Ltd v Canacord Genuity Wealth (International) Ltd* [2019] EWCA Civ 83 [29] (Longmore LJ); *Pengelly v Business Mortgage Finance 4 plc* [2020] EWHC 2002 (Ch) [33]–[34] (Marcus Smith J).

[36] Marcus Smith J suggested that the label cannot drive the consequences: *Pengelly* (n 35) [33]–[34]. His decision on a crucial aspect of the case, whether a fiduciary relationship was a pre-condition to access to remedies, was overturned; see *Wood v Commercial First Business Ltd* [2021] EWCA Civ 471, [2021] 3 WLR 395. His observations on the usage of the label 'agent' remain valuable, however.

[37] PB Miller, 'The Identification of Fiduciary Relationships' in Criddle, Miller and Sitkoff (eds) (n 2) 367, 370.

[38] *F & C Alternative Investments (Holdings) Ltd v Barthelemy (No 2)* [2011] EWHC 1731 (Ch), [2012] Ch 613, per Sales J at [219].

[39] *Hosking v Marathon Asset Management LLP* [2016] EWHC 2418 (Ch), per Newey J at [36]. For criticism of these LLP cases, see B Munro, 'Limited Liability Partnerships and Fiduciary Duties' (2017) 21 *Edinburgh Law Review* 417.

[40] Limited Partnership Act 1907, s 6(1).

[41] M Blackett-Ord and S Haren, *Partnership Law: The Modern Law of Firms, Limited Partnerships and Limited Liability Partnerships*, 6th edn (London, Bloomsbury Professional, 2020) [24-18].

could, for example, accept a bribe in exchange for agreeing to influence a major decision at a partnership meeting. That partner is not acting as an agent – she may not ultimately form any contract with a third party on behalf of the partnership. She may nevertheless be indulging in conduct that constitutes a breach of fiduciary duty.

Much depends ultimately on the way in which we define agency. The discussion in the immediately preceding paragraph proceeds on the basis that to act as an agent involves formation of a contract on the partnership's behalf. If we adopted a broader definition of agency, it could make sense to describe the types of conduct referred to above as 'agency' conduct. It is true that Scots law contains a relatively broad definition of agency, embracing simple actions such as delivering a letter or paying an invoice for a principal.[42] Nevertheless, the fact that we need to struggle to define agency before applying that definition to partnership suggests that it is not helping us to understand the partner's fiduciary duties. It adds an extra layer of complication to partnership law, an area not short of its own complications. The inevitable conclusion is that we should look beyond the partner's role purely as an agent to ascribe the partner's fiduciary duties.

To close this section, it is conceded that arguing by analogy with agency has led to certain (limited) benefits. Use of status in this way can act as a shortcut that allows us to avoid a close analysis of the nature of the relationship in order to ascribe fiduciary duties. It is the 'badge' or 'label', 'devised for the purposes of categorization, driven by considerations of ease and expediency'.[43] Should we therefore, as Miller has suggested, simply accept the limitations of this function?[44] Perhaps conscious of this, some justify the use of status only in modified form. To Edelman, for example, status may form part of the background material by informing the duties undertaken by particular persons.[45] Perhaps because it is located at the intersection of different areas of private law (contract, property, agency and organisational law), partnership law regularly draws on concepts from those other parts. It should do so only if to do so proves useful. Agency has, in this fiduciary contact, outlived its utility.

III. Measuring the Partner against Common Fiduciary Characteristics

A. Imbalance of Power and Vulnerability

At the beginning of this chapter it was stated that use of relationship or status has obscured the reasons why a partner owes fiduciary duties. In this section, the author draws on recent scholarship in fiduciary law that has identified core characteristics of

[42] Macgregor (n 34) [2-03].

[43] PB Miller, 'The Idea of Status in Fiduciary Law' in PB Miller and AS Gold (eds), *Contract, Status and Fiduciary Law* (Oxford, Oxford University Press, 2016) 25, 38.

[44] Miller (n 37) 367, 368.

[45] J Edelman, 'The Role of Status in the Law of Obligations: Common Callings, Implied Terms, and Lessons for Fiduciary Duties' in AS Gold and PB Miller (eds), *Philosophical Foundations of Fiduciary Law* (Oxford, Oxford University Press, 2014) 21. Miller too suggests its use in modified form, noting that it 'is most often invoked unreflectively', in 'The Idea of Status in Fiduciary Law' (n 43) 39.

fiduciaries, and compares the partner with these core characteristics. Although it is an analogical approach, the analogy drawn is not between partnership and another legal institution, such as agency or trust. The analogy is to characteristics common to fiduciaries. The approach draws on the work of authors searching for what it means to be a fiduciary. That 'essence' can then be applied to partnerships. Not only will this allow us to 'rank' the partner as a fiduciary amongst fiduciaries, but it also provides a backdrop against which we can later examine the partner's duty of good faith.

Constraints of space rule out the consideration of every common fiduciary characteristic. The analysis here is limited to the core ideas of imbalance or asymmetry of power, vulnerability or dependence, and loyalty. Consideration is also given to whether fiduciary duties are proscriptive only or can also be prescriptive in nature.

The analysis can begin with the idea that fiduciary duties tend to involve an imbalance or asymmetry of power,[46] which some have rendered as a presumption that parties to a fiduciary relationship are on an 'unequal footing due to the power that a fiduciary receives and holds on trust for the beneficiary'.[47] The fiduciary occupies a 'dominant position' relative to the beneficiary.[48] These ideas are probably connected to the idea of vulnerability, also identified as a key component of a fiduciary relationship.[49] Vulnerability has been described as the corollary of dependence.[50] This imbalance is said to be structural in nature.[51]

Applying these ideas to partnerships is not an easy task. Let us consider partner A relative to her fellow partners B, C and D. Are B, C and D vulnerable to A's actions? An affirmative response is counterintuitive: partners run the business from a starting position of equality, the equal sharing of profits and losses being the default rule under the Partnership Act 1890.[52] Generally, each partner will have a degree of business experience and a role in running the business (with the exception of the limited partner in a limited partnership).[53] Whilst imbalances in degrees of knowledge may indeed exist, these are likely to be less pronounced than the imbalance that exists, for example, between a solicitor and a client. The partner is also relatively well placed with regard to her access to financial information. Partners B, C and D have access to firm accounts. They may also routinely be in contact with contracting parties of the firm, which may help to protect them against A's activities.

[46] See, eg, PB Miller, 'The Fiduciary Relationship' in Gold and Miller (eds) (n 45) 63, 73, where he identifies three structural properties of the fiduciary relationship: inequality, dependence and vulnerability. See also G Klass, 'What if Fiduciary Obligations are like Contractual Ones?' in Miller and Gold (eds) (n 43) 93, 94 and 102.

[47] PB Miller and AS Gold, 'Introduction' in Miller and Gold (eds) (n 43) 13.

[48] Miller, 'The Fiduciary Relationship' (n 46) 73.

[49] ibid.

[50] ibid.

[51] ibid.

[52] Partnership Act 1890, s 24(1).

[53] This is because the limited partner's role is that of passive investor rather than active manager of the business. Indeed, a limited partner who takes part in the management of the limited partnership loses her status as a limited partner, becoming a general partner and thus liable jointly and severally for the debts of the limited partnership; see Partnership Act 1907, s 6(1). The recently created Private Fund Limited Partnership allows the limited partner to take part, to a greater degree, in the business of the partnership; see Limited Partnership Act 2017, s 6A.

The partner's true vulnerability, it is suggested, lies in the losses that can be caused to the firm by the secret, opportunistic behaviour of A.[54] Losses are experienced by B, C and D in the form of decreased shares of equity (the default rule under the Partnership Act 1890 being profit share for each partner rather than remuneration through salary).[55] The partner's vulnerability may be less than that which exists in many other fiduciary relationships.

Already it is possible to see that partners differ from the fiduciary norm. Nolan and Davies state that '[i]t is of the essence of a fiduciary relationship that the beneficiary is relieved of the need to watch over his own affairs and monitor the fiduciary'.[56] This comment, admittedly made outside the partnership context, fails to reflect the partner's role. As active participants in their own business, they are unlikely to sit back and trust to the work of their fellow partners as fiduciaries.

B. Loyalty

Conaglen suggests that there is 'a reasonably broad consensus that fiduciary doctrine is concerned with loyalty'.[57] There is, he observes, less clarity as to whether loyalty is a 'directly enforceable duty, or more an organizing or underpinning conceptualization of the reasons for (and consequences of) the duties which fiduciary doctrine enforces'.[58] There is a lack of agreement over the way in which non-legal ideas of loyalty relate to legal ideas, or whether the non-legal can shape the legal ideas.[59] It is difficult to measure partnerships against such a shifting backdrop of ideas.

When partners come together to form the firm, they hold a primary loyalty to that firm, and their interests as individuals come in second place. This pattern mirrors fiduciary loyalty generally: the fiduciary must place the beneficiary's interests above her own personal interests. The type of conduct proscribed by sections 28 to 30 of the Partnership Act is the type of loyalty to oneself that is penalised: secretly acting in competition with the firm or accepting secret profits, for example. Loyalty to the firm is necessary if the benefits the law provides to partnerships are to have any real meaning: Hansmann and Kraakman's entity shielding, so useful in the running of a business, would be meaningless if the partners transacted for themselves rather than for the business.[60]

[54] Gordon Smith suggests that opportunism is a particularly appropriate concern on which we ought to focus in the partnership context, see G Smith, 'Firms and Fiduciaries' in Miller and Gold (eds) (n 43) 293. For Smith, fiduciary law is a response to the risks of opportunism that arise when one party exercises discretion over the critical resources of another.

[55] Partnership Act 1890, s 24(6).

[56] D Nolan and J Davies, 'Torts and Equitable Wrongs' in A Burrows (ed), *English Private Law*, 3rd edn (Oxford, Oxford University Presss, 2013) 927, [17-202].

[57] Conaglen, 'Fiduciary Principles' (n 2) 566.

[58] ibid.

[59] Andrew S Gold is a proponent of accommodating extra-legal ideas in the legal concept of loyalty: AS Gold, 'Accommodating Loyalty' in Miller and Gold (eds) (n 43) 185. Stephen Smith disagrees: S Smith, 'The Deed, Not the Motive. Fiduciary Law Without Loyalty' in Miller and Gold (eds) (n 43) 211.

[60] H Hansmann and R Kraakman, 'The Essential Role of Organizational Law' in (2000) 110 *Yale Law Journal* 387; and H Hansmann, R Kraakman and R Squire, 'Law and the Rise of the Firm' (2006) 119 *Harvard Law Review* 1335. These ideas were applied to the Scottish partnership by the current author in L Macgregor, 'Partnerships and Legal Personality: Cautionary Tales from Scotland' (2020) 20 *Journal of Corporate Law Studies* 237.

In practice, partners are likely to feel an additional, non-legal loyalty to each other as individuals. This perhaps reflects the historical idea of brotherhood seen in the Roman sources and the Scottish institutional works. The Roman approach was closely linked to the concept of *delectus personae*: this phrase expressed the idea that partners choose one another for reasons of personal skill and talent. *Delectus personae* explained why the death of one partner terminated the partnership. Stair explained this idea in memorable terms: 'for it being one individual contract of the whole, and not as many contracts as partners, it is like a sheaf of arrows bound together with one tie, out of which, if one be pulled, the rest will fall out'.[61] *Delectus personae* (in addition to good faith) also explained the requirement for unanimity for the assumption of a new partner, a requirement that remains the default rule in the Partnership Act 1890.[62]

The partner is certainly required to show loyalty to the firm, placing the firm above her personal interests. This marks her out as a fiduciary. She is, of course, part of that firm, and so this necessarily involves being loyal to herself. To a certain extent, therefore, she can sometimes act in a self-interested manner.[63] She may also possess a different type of loyalty, and that is the loyalty to the individual partners with whom she has formed the firm. To echo Bacon V-C once more, 'their mutual trust is the life blood of the concern'.[64] This latter loyalty could be the type of non-legal idea that Gold in particular has argued could be relevant in a legal context.[65] Loyalty in partnerships therefore emerges as a complex amalgam of loyalty to the firm and to each other.

C. Prescriptive or Proscriptive?

An ongoing, and probably unresolved, debate in fiduciary law is whether fiduciary duties are essentially proscriptive in nature, or whether they may also extend to requiring prescriptive behaviour. Conaglen describes the traditional approach, which treats disclosure in the fiduciary context as a 'mechanism for avoiding fiduciary liability, rather than a positive obligation on the fiduciary'.[66] Claims that there are affirmative fiduciary duties requiring positive conduct from the fiduciary are, according to Getzler, 'controversial'.[67] Smith notes that although it has been stated that Canadian cases had revealed a tendency to view fiduciary obligations as both prescriptive and proscriptive, whereas Australian courts have only recognised proscriptive duties, this is to mischaracterise both.[68] In his view, fiduciary duties are indeed both proscriptive and prescriptive.[69]

Applying these ideas to partnership, we can consider the nature of the statutory fiduciary duties in sections 28–30 of the Partnership Act. Certain of these duties are

[61] *Institutions* (n 28) I.16.5.
[62] Partnership Act 1890, s 24(7).
[63] For the trustee's ability to act in a self-interested manner, see C Mitchell, 'Good Faith, Self-Denial and Mandatory Trustee Duties' (2018) 32 *Trust Law International* 92.
[64] See n 32.
[65] Gold (n 59).
[66] Conaglen, 'Fiduciary Principles' (n 2) 571.
[67] J Getzler, 'Ascribing Fiduciary Obligations' in Gold and Miller (eds) (n 45) 39, 42.
[68] L Smith, 'Can we be Obliged to be Selfless?' in Gold and Miller (eds) (n 45) 141, 145.
[69] ibid.

proscriptive in nature, including the section 30 duty not to compete with the firm. It is more difficult to characterise the general duty to account in section 28, and the duty to account for private profits where the partner has made use of the partnership 'property name or business connexion' within section 29. Whilst these duties are expressed in positive language, they simply express traditional ideas of disgorgement following conflict of interest. Few conclusions can be drawn here: partnerships perhaps differ little from other fiduciary contexts: certain conduct is proscribed subject to the proviso of a positive duty to account where profit is made in breach of fiduciary duty.

One further point should be made before drawing this section to a close. This relates to the way in which duties to account operate in the partnership context. Imagine that Partner B has made a secret profit. That profit is then disgorged to the firm. Partner B will, if she is a profit-sharing or equity partner,[70] share in that profit once it is disgorged to the firm.[71] Partner B, the partner in breach of fiduciary duty, therefore shares in her own 'ill-gotten gains'. This point is emphasised here because it illustrates that the analogy with agency in partnership is unhelpful. The ability of the non-performing partner to share in the disgorged proceeds reflects the presence of the partner at both levels of the agency relationship: the partner is both the agent and a part of the principal (the firm). Disgorgement, a relatively simple idea in agency, is more complex in partnerships. These arguments underline the need to consider the role of partner as business owner, and the trust and confidence inherent in that role, in understanding fiduciary duties.

D. Conclusions

This section has allowed us to reflect on the fact that, whilst certainly a fiduciary, the partner differs from other fiduciaries. Although vulnerable to losses as a result of opportunistic action by her fellow partners, the partner's expertise and access to information render her potentially less vulnerable than many other beneficiaries of fiduciary duties. Unlike other fiduciaries, her interest as business owner means that she may sometimes be entitled to act in a self-interested manner. She may possess multiple loyalties to different entities: to the firm; to her fellow partners; and even to herself as a business owner. This complex picture is aptly summed up by Getzler, who notes that '[c]ompanies, partnerships and looser joint ventures raise special problems since actors with multiple roles may mix self interest with multiple duties to intersecting entities'.[72]

The exercise has also facilitated reflection on the aims and nature of fiduciary law in the partnership context. Fiduciary duties aim to discourage self-interested behaviour and to protect the assets of the beneficiary from the abuse of managerial discretion. The firm is the beneficiary of those duties, and the duties protect the assets of that firm. That is the case whether we think of the firm as a separate legal person (as in Scots law), or as

[70] Not all partners are necessarily equity, or profit-sharing, partners. It is possible to agree in the partnership contract that certain partners will be salaried (or fixed-share) partners.

[71] *Hosking v Marathon Asset Management LLP* [2016] EWHC 2418 (Ch), per Newey J at [36], analysed by Munro (n 39).

[72] Getzler (n 67).

a collectivity of individuals (as in English law).[73] By definition, fiduciary duties do not protect a partner's individual and personal assets. Partner A has no duty to subordinate her personal interests to the personal interests of Partner C, or of Partner D. Fiduciary duties are, in fact, 'blind' to the existence of the partner as an individual. Subordination only occurs where the firm is the beneficiary of duties. These issues are worth bearing in mind as we proceed to consider the partner's duty of good faith in section IV.

IV. The Partner's Duty of Good Faith

Having explored the partner's fiduciary duties in the first part of this chapter, the partner's duty of good faith can be considered against that backdrop. This section begins by examining questions over the existence of the duty of good faith in certain types of partnerships, moves to examine the route to imposition of the duty of good faith and its nature, and ends by asking whether the duty displays fiduciary characteristics.

A. In Which Types of Partnership Does the Duty of Good Faith Arise?

Several of the leading texts state that each partner owes to the others a duty of good faith.[74] Statements like this sometimes fail to make clear to whom this duty is owed: 'to the others' could refer to the others collectively, as a firm, or to the others as individuals. Ribbens, in a comparative study of partnerships, used the terms 'vertical' and 'horizontal' to analyse partnership duties.[75] Partners owe, he suggested, vertical fiduciary-type duties to the firm, and lateral, horizontal duties towards one another as individuals. These terms are useful because they allow us to analyse the nature of partnership duties accurately, including identifying the correct beneficiary. Partnership scholarship in the United States similarly distinguishes duties that arise because of the role of partners as co-owners, and those that apply when they act as fiduciary managers.[76]

Duties of good faith clearly exist in UK general partnerships[77] and in limited partnerships.[78] Blackett-Ord and Haren suggest that, contrary to the orthodox view, the limited partner may not owe a duty of good faith to the general partner.[79] This, they explain, is because 'they [limited partners] are not agents for their fellow partners and

[73] Excepting again from this statement the LLP.

[74] See, eg, *Lindley & Banks* (n 1) [16-06], or Blackett-Ord and Haren (n 41) [11-1].

[75] DS Ribbens, *The Personal, Fiduciary Character of Members' Inter Se Relations in the Incorporated Partnership: A Historical and Comparative Analysis with Particular Reference to English, American, German, Scottish and South African Law* (Johannesburg, Lex Patria, 1988).

[76] M Manesh, 'Fiduciary Principles in Unincorporated Entity Law' in Criddle, Miller and Sitkoff (eds) (n 2) 79.

[77] *Lindley & Banks* (n 1) [16-06].

[78] *BBGP Managing General Partner Ltd v Babcock & Brown Global Partners* [2010] EWHC 2176 (Ch) [11]; *Lindley & Banks* (n 1) [31-01]. The totality of partnership law applies to the LP, except as amended by the 1907 Act.

[79] Blackett-Ord and Haren (n 41) 24.18.

have no authority to bind them'.[80] Thus the limited partner 'escapes' a duty of good faith because of her lack of agency powers. It is interesting to observe that Blackett-Ord and Haren are clearly thinking about duties both vertically and horizontally (although not using those terms).

Turning now to the LLP, although the possibility of applying a general duty of good faith was considered by the Government twice, no clear conclusion was reached and the legislation is silent.[81] Whittaker, Machell and Berry adopt an agency route: because members are agents for the LLP, they owe a duty of good faith to the LLP.[82] Because members are not agents *for one another*, they owe no duty of good faith to one another.[83] Blackett-Ord and Haren adopt a similar approach.[84] Young suggests that whilst no duty of good faith exists, it is open to the courts to develop one.[85] Only Berry suggests that a duty of good faith may, in some circumstances, be owed by one member of an LLP to another member.[86] Clearly the link with agency that dominated discussion of fiduciary duties, also dominates discussion of good faith duties (with the exception of Berry's work).

Nor is it clear whether a duty of good faith applies in the newest type of partnership, the Private Fund Limited Partnership (PFLP). Drawing on the decision to disapply two classic fiduciary duties to this type (sections 28 and 30), some have concluded that a duty of good faith does not exist. Only Berry again disagrees, concluding that the overriding duty of good faith applies in the PFLP.[87]

The uncertainty over the existence of duties of good faith has occurred in part because of an historical 'wrong-turn'. The original draft of the Partnership Bill preceding the 1890 Act, drafted by Sir Frederick Pollock, contained clause 45,[88] which provided that the partners must 'carry on the business of the partnership for the greatest common advantage' and 'be just and faithful to one another'. Despite the fact that this expressed the law at the time,[89] this clause did not survive the Bill's progression through the legislative process as the Bill became the Partnership Act 1890.

The absence of an express duty of good faith from the 1890 Act does not mean that it does not exist. The Act was a codifying statute, section 46 containing a saving for rules of equity and common law (which continue in force except so far as inconsistent with

[80] ibid.

[81] Once during the debate over the 2000 Act, and once in 2007 in the context of considering which rules of company law should be applied to LLPs. BERR, *Proposal for the Application of the Companies Act 2006 to Limited Liability Partnerships*, November 2007, 5.3–5.7 (URN 07/1476); G Morse et al (eds), *Palmer's Limited Liability Partnership Law*, 3rd edn (London, Sweet & Maxwell, 2017) A5-30.

[82] J Whittaker and J Machell, *The Law of Limited Liability Partnerships*, 5th edn (London, Bloomsbury Professional, 2021) [13.33]; E Berry, *Partnership and LLP Law*, 2nd edn (London, Wildy, Simmonds and Hill Publishing, 2018) [5.3.1].

[83] Whittaker and Machell (n 82) [13.33].

[84] Blackett-Ord and Haren (n 41) [25.64] and [25.72].

[85] S Young, *Limited Liability Partnerships Handbook*, 2nd edn (Haywards Heath, Tottel, 2007) [6.8] and [6.9].

[86] Berry (n 82) [5.3.1].

[87] ibid [5.2].

[88] In drafting the UK Partnership Bill, Pollock drew on his experience in drafting the Indian Contract Act. Clause 45 is very similar to s 257 of the Indian Contract Act 1872, which Pollock also drafted.

[89] *Const v Harris* (1824) Turn & R 496, 525, 37 ER 1191, 1202.

the 1890 Act). If the duty of good faith existed before the Act, it continues to exist after the Act.[90] This is why we know that it applies in the types of partnerships to which the totality of partnership law applies (the general partnership and the LP). What we do not know is whether it applies within LLPs and PFLPs (to which the totality of partnership law does not apply).

Notably, Pollock's clause 45 obliged the partners to be 'just and faithful to *one another*'[91] (echoing Lord Eldon's words in *Const v Harris*).[92] In the 1890 Act, the word 'firm' is used as a collective description for persons who have entered into partnership with one another.[93] Pollock did not use the word 'firm' to express the duty of good faith in clause 45: he used 'one another'. His drafting certainly appears to indicate that the duty of good faith is owed between partners *as individuals*. Here we see a contrast with the field of fiduciary duties, where no similar discussion of a partner-to-partner duty has taken place.

This subsection has painted a very complex picture. There is a lack of consensus on whether duties of good faith arise in the newer types of partnerships. Reasoning on this question displays the tendency to use agency as a point of reference. The historical development here clearly suggests that the common law that pre-dated the 1890 Act contained a horizontal, partner-to-partner duty of good faith.

B. Route to Imposition of the Duty

Whilst the partnership treatises refer to good faith, they do not explain why such a duty exists. What is its legal basis, and how does it arise? These are the questions considered in this subsection. There are several potential routes to the imposition of the duty of good faith. One is the treatment of partnership contracts as part of the family of contracts *uberrimae fidei* or of the utmost good faith. This category was transplanted from English into Scots law in case law in the late eighteenth century[94] and treated as binding by the leading Scottish texts.[95] Professor Sir Thomas Smith, a strong exponent of a general idea of good faith in contract, criticised this step, seeing no logic in 'varying standards of honesty'.[96] This type of good faith suffers from difficulties: although the

[90] There being nothing in the Act inconsistent with an idea of good faith.

[91] Emphasis added. The formulation of this idea in *Lindley & Banks* (n 1), that there is a duty of good faith imposed by the law on a partner 'towards his co-partners', is ambiguous. It could refer to a duty to partners as individuals or to the firm itself, see ibid [16-01].

[92] *Const v Harris* (n 89) 525; 1202.

[93] Partnership Act 1890, s 4(1).

[94] *Stewart v Morrison* (1779) Mor 7080, *Watt v Ritchie* (1782) Mor 7074, analysed by WM Gloag, *The Law of Contract*, 2nd edn (Edinburgh, W Green, 1929) 496–97.

[95] F Clark, *A Treatise on the Law of Partnership and Joint-Stock Companies According to the Law of Scotland* (1866) 182; G Brough (ed), *Miller on Partnership*, 2nd edn (Edinburgh, W Green, 1994) 156–58.

[96] TB Smith, *A Short Commentary on the Law of Scotland* (Edinburgh, W Green, 1962) 298, fn 68, quoting from MA Milner, 'Fraudulent Non-Disclosure' (1957) 74 *South African Law Journal* 177, 188. Smith believed, however, that *all* contracts in Scots law contained duties of good faith, a view that has not been borne out in the modern law. A later attempt to create a general contractual duty of good faith, this time by Lord Clyde in a Scottish appeal to the House of Lords, was unsuccessful: *Smith v Bank of Scotland* 1997 SC (HL) 111. This precedent has been applied only within its immediate factual context (the obligations of the lender to the cautioner (guarantor) where a debt is guaranteed by the cautioner).

duty clearly exists at the beginning and end of the contract, it is unclear whether it exists throughout the entire life of the contract.[97]

Another possible route is to see good faith as a term implied in law into partnership contracts.[98] The disadvantage of this route is the ease with which implied terms can be excluded by express drafting to the contrary. In the context of another contract *uberrimae fidei*, the insurance contract, it has recently been convincingly argued that good faith is much more than an implied term.[99]

Both of the above routes have inherent weaknesses. The former provides us with a duty of good faith engaged at key points in the partnership contract, and not throughout the whole life of the contract. The latter is a poor fit because good faith in partnerships seems to be much more than an implied term. It has the additional disadvantage of being an easily excludable duty. It is suggested instead that we should recognise the historic idea of good faith inherent in Scottish partnerships received from Roman law, which has shaped so much of partnership law. This strong and pervasive idea is much more than an implied term.

C. Nature of the Duty

It is true that the duty of good faith is particularly visible at specific points in the life of the partnership contract, and this explains the modern tendency to treat partnership as one of the contracts *uberrimae fidei*. In the pre-contractual stage,[100] where a misrepresentation is made that induces a party to enter into the partnership contract, breach of the duty allows the innocent party to reduce the contract.[101] The duty is also visible either where a partner is excluded by the other partners, or where the partnership is dissolved. Decisions to expel partners must be exercised in good faith and for the benefit of the partnership as a whole.[102] The editors of *Lindley & Banks* identify four situations in which the duty is engaged (numbered by the current author for ease of exposition):

(1) the partner who enters into an agreement with another partner at a time when he possesses information about the partnership accounts which is not disclosed;
(2) compliance with the partnership agreement;
(3) partners seeking to expel other partners from the firm; and
(4) (although this example is not beyond doubt) dissolving the firm by notice.[103]

[97] This problem is shared with another member of the class of contracts *uberrimae fidei* – insurance contracts.

[98] As noted by M Raczynska, 'Good Faiths and Contract Terms' in PS Davies and M Raczynska (eds) *Contents of Commercial Contracts: Terms Affecting Freedoms* (Oxford, Hart Publishing, 2020) 65, 81.

[99] H Bennett, 'The Three Ages of Utmost Good Faith' in C Mitchell and S Watterson (eds), *The World of Maritime and Commercial Law: Essays in Honour of Francis Rose* (Oxford, Hart Publishing, 2020) 63.

[100] *Ferguson v Wilson* (1904) 6F 779.

[101] ibid, per Lord Justice-Clerk Macdonald at 783.

[102] *Blisset v Daniel* (1853) 10 Hare 493; and see recently the Scottish case, *Rennie v Rennie* [2020] CSOH 49, and comment by the current author, LJ Macgregor '*Rennie v Rennie*: The Requirements of Natural Justice on Expulsion of a Partnership' (2020) 24 *Edinburgh Law Review* 416.

[103] *Lindley & Banks* (n 1) [16-01]–[16-02].

Notably, these are *not* limited to the beginning and end of the partnership. In situations (1) and (3), one individual partner has acted in an unfair manner towards another individual partner, causing harm to that individual partner. As such, this may involve breach of a horizontal duty (using Ribbens' terminology). In situations (2) and (4), a partner's conduct has harmed the firm as a whole, and may therefore involve breach of a vertical duty.

D. Is the Partner's Duty of Good Faith Fiduciary in Nature?

Having explored the way in which good faith arises and its nature, we can now apply the knowledge gained from the first part of this chapter and compare the duty of good faith against the fiduciary characteristics.

It may facilitate discussion to consider a classic example of the operation of good faith, namely, where partner A acts to unfairly exclude partner B from the firm. Good faith is clearly engaged in this situation in order to prevent A from acting in this way. We can consider issues such as vulnerability and loyalty within this factual scenario. Partner B may indeed be vulnerable, and suffer from an imbalance of power, the latter often being exacerbated by the withholding of key information from B, for example updated accounts. It is more difficult to identify A's loyalty. By unfairly excluding B, A is being potentially disloyal to several parties: to the firm, to the other partners and to B. This nicely illustrates Getzler's reference to partners' having 'multiple duties to intersecting entities'.[104] We might also look here for A's duty to subjugate her interests to those of a beneficiary (as would be characteristic of a fiduciary duty). In this scenario, A is not required to subjugate her interests to B's *personal* interests. A and B are both partners, and thus act towards one another on the basis of equality.

Staying with this example, we can look at the harm and determine to whom the harm is caused. B is the unhappy party, and the party who is likely to raise an action complaining about her unfair exclusion from the partnership. Ultimately, she seeks reduction of the decision to exclude her. Although the action will be raised against the partnership, the court will consider conduct on the part of partner A that has been unfair. Although it will consider whether the expulsion was in the best interests of the partnership as a whole,[105] harm to the firm itself is not the main focus. Harm to B is the main focus. Good faith is engaged to shape a duty owed by A to B in order to prevent sharp practices by A.

The final fiduciary characteristic considered in the first half of this chapter was the nature of the duty, whether proscriptive or prescriptive. It was concluded that there was a lack of consensus on this point, but that most fiduciary duties appear to be proscriptive. The duty of good faith in the partnership context is sometimes expressed as an active (and therefore prescriptive) duty. The editors of *Lindley & Banks* provide the example of a 'duty to speak, which will usually require a partner to disclose not only

[104] Getzler (n 67) 39, 60.
[105] *Blisset v Daniel* (1853) 10 Hare 493.

his own misconduct but that of any other partner or employee of the firm'.[106] This more active type of duty perhaps differs from the norm of proscriptive fiduciary duties.

Thus far, one could say that there seems to be a lack of fit between the duty of good faith in partnerships and fiduciary characteristics. Does the duty of good faith further the aims of fiduciary law in the partnership context? To recap, it was earlier suggested that fiduciary duties tend to protect the beneficiary's assets and prevent the abuse of managerial discretion. Let us consider another classic situation in which good faith operates: where A has acted dishonestly to induce B to join the partnership. The party protected by the duty of good faith appears to be B. It is B who has suffered because of a misrepresentation. Whether or not the partnership has suffered is largely irrelevant: B may or may not be good in her role in the partnership. Hoodwinking her into joining may in fact be a 'good thing' for the partnership. Good faith is not being engaged here to prevent the abusive use of managerial discretion or to protect the firm's assets; it is engaged to protect B against unfair conduct. This example also fails to fit the fiduciary mould of acting in conflict of interest. The fiduciary norm involves a fiduciary in benefitting herself rather than the beneficiary of the duty. In this partnership scenario, A's conduct benefits the partnership, benefitting A only indirectly, perhaps through increased profit share from B's assumption. In this respect good faith appears to have a wider scope, targeting more than simply acting in conflict of interest.

Turning now to remedies, where A has induced B to join the partnership through a misrepresentation, the court will reduce the assumption of B. Similarly, where A has acted unfairly to exclude B, B's exclusion will be reduced by the court. Damages may also be available for any additional losses that B is able to prove.

Do these remedies resemble fiduciary remedies? Certainly, fiduciary remedies may involve the reduction of contracts entered into in breach of fiduciary duty. In the scenarios discussed, there is rarely a profit made by A to be disgorged (although Berry notes the availability of profit-stripping remedies in this context in English law).[107] Given that there is rarely a profit in issue, other remedies such as the constructive trust are generally not engaged.

The author has, of course, only considered categories (1) and (3) from the examples given by *Lindley & Banks*. In (2) and (4) there might be a stronger argument that the firm is harmed by the conduct concerned, perhaps supporting the argument that good faith is engaged in a (vertical) fiduciary manner. It seems clear, however, that in the classic situations in which good faith is engaged, it is not performing a fiduciary function.

To conclude this part, the duty of good faith in partnership law seems to display important differences from a fiduciary duty. It does not always share the fiduciary aim of preventing the abuse of managerial conduct and protecting the beneficiary's (the firm's) assets. It often acts to protect an individual partner from conduct that is not necessarily 'managerial'. It does not involve the subjugation of the personal interests of a partner to those of a fellow partner, and it engages more than one type of loyalty. It may be broader than a fiduciary duty, preventing more than simply conflicts of interest.

[106] *Lindley & Banks* (n 1) [16-02].
[107] Berry (n 82) [5.1.3].

V. Conclusion

This chapter has sought to explore and map the duties that exist in Scottish partnerships. The exercise began by tracing the historic approach that treats partners as fiduciaries because of their relationship or status. The use of agency as an analogy for this purpose was described as a red herring. Taking a different approach, in this chapter the partner has been compared against common characteristics of other fiduciaries. Partners emerged from this exercise as slightly unusual fiduciaries. At the root of the difference is the partner's dual role as agent and co-owner of the business.

The comparison of the duty of good faith against this fiduciary backdrop disclosed sufficient difference to suggest that good faith is, in the partnership context, performing a non-fiduciary function. Most commonly it operates in a horizontal fashion, protecting one partner from the abusive conduct of her fellow partner. The duty is, it is suggested, a contractual duty, and is broader in scope than the partner's fiduciary duties. Essentially, it ensures that fairness is observed between partners as co-owners of a business.

The author does not purport to have resolved all outstanding issues in this highly complex area of law. Thus far she has stopped short of conclusively identifying the way in which good faith and fiduciary duties interrelate. A tentative answer can be given to the 'chicken and egg' question. Clearly, the story began with the good faith inherent in Roman *societas*. Fiduciary duties developed from this source. The development of fiduciary duties left, however, a 'residual rump' of good faith. We seem to have erroneously begun to consider that residual rump as fiduciary in nature. It is rather contractual, engaging, for example, contractual remedies.

Our collective memory lapse has already had unfortunate results, namely the view that duties of good faith do not exist between partners/members in LPs, LLPS and PFLPs. Although created to perform a corporate role, these types of partnerships share enough common ground with traditional partnerships to merit the imposition of duties of good faith between partners (as Berry seems to suggest). Further unfortunate results could follow. Good faith explains, for example, the requirement of unanimity over the assumption of a new partner.[108] Were we asked to analyse a dispute in this particular area, we would be unlikely to resolve it by thinking only of the partner as an agent. A partner-to-partner dispute would be resolved by the duty of good faith.

Another concern has recently appeared over the horizon. This is the incursion into the law of contract of public law ideas, for example *Braganza*-type implied terms.[109] A similar process may be taking place in partnership law: in a recent Scottish case, Lord Clark analysed the situation of unfair exclusion of a partner by reference to natural justice rather than good faith.[110] The author agrees with Davies that introducing public

[108] Partnership Act 1890, s 24(7), which reflects the position in Roman law; see du Plessis (n 18) 290.

[109] *Braganza v BP Shipping* [2015] UKSC 17, [2015] 1 WLR 1661; and see analysis by C Himsworth, 'Transplanting Irrationality from Public to Private Law' (2019) 23 *Edinburgh Law Review* 1.

[110] *Rennie v Rennie* [2020] CSOH 49; and see comment by the current author, above, n 102.

law ideas into contract law is 'unlikely to be helpful'[111] – we may be unable to predict how the public law concept will perform in its new home. To engage instead good faith would be to remain within the known universe, deploying a concept likely to fit well within the overall framework of Scottish private law. In short, we need not innovate because we already have the tools we need to hand.

[111] Paul S Davies has cautioned against this approach, stating that 'reliance on public law concepts and cases such as *Associated Provincial Picture Houses v Wednesbury Corporation* in the area of commercial contracts is unlikely to be helpful': PS Davies, 'Excluding Good Faith and Restricting Discretion' in Davies and Raczynska (eds) (n 98) 89, 104.

14

Debt Collection and Assignment of Debts: Navigating the Legal Maze

JODI GARDNER AND CHEE HO THAM*

I. Introduction

Debt collectors are an important intermediary in contracts between creditors and debtors, yet academic consideration of the legal issues arising from these relationships is limited. This chapter analyses debt collectors as intermediaries, focusing on the entitlements and obligations of a debt collector who has been assigned the benefit of a debt owed by a debtor to its creditor. Although the mechanisms by which debts incurred by businesses are assigned to debt-collecting agencies are the same, the assignment of consumer debt raises additional and distinct concerns. This chapter leaves aside analysis of the different legal issues and challenges posed by debt collection from businesses, focusing on debt collection in connection with consumer debt (ie debts incurred by individuals). But even so, considering the size of the market, and the profits obtained by debt collectors, the collection of consumer debt remains an important and significant market.

The debt collection process usually involves an assignment of a debt owed by a consumer[1] to a creditor (the assignor[2]) to the debt collector (the assignee[3]). For example: A, a commercial services provider (such as a telecommunications service provider like Vodaphone), provides services to B, a consumer, for a monthly fee. B then falls into arrears. A then 'transfers' the sums due and outstanding from B to a debt collector, C, typically at a deep discount to the sum due. We can surmise that the legal institution that is employed to effect this 'transfer' between A to C will be a form of equitable assignment that, oftentimes, happens also to satisfy the requirements of section 136(1) of the

* We would like to thank Devon Airey for her brilliant research assistance when preparing this chapter and Deborah Ferrett for her very helpful editing, both of which were made possible because of the financial support of St John's Returning Carer's Scheme. Thanks must also go to Paul Davies for his comments on an earlier version, and to the attendees of the UCL *Intermediaries in Commercial Law* conference for their comments.

[1] Referred to at times as 'B'.

[2] Referred to at times as 'A'.

[3] Referred to at times as 'C'.

Law of Property Act 1925 (in which case, the equitable assignment would be supplemented with additional statutorily-mandated features).

Since these assignments between A and C are for value, they are undoubtedly a form of commercial contract giving rise to associated advantages. For one, service providers may avoid the risk and practical burden of seeking repayment of outstanding amounts and of clearing balance sheets. However, there are many legal (and practical) challenges, particularly in the context of collecting outstanding money from individuals as opposed to businesses. Despite this, there is very little research on debt collectors as intermediaries in the consumer debt context. In addition, the specific mechanisms involved in assigning a debt, and what specific rights and liabilities may arise from such assignment, are not easy to understand, even from the perspective of seasoned legal practitioners, and there remains some academic debate as to the manner of their operation. This chapter addresses some of these questions, including how debts are assigned, what legal entitlements debt collectors have (especially regarding the collection of additional fees and charges from the debtor), and what statutory restrictions may be in place.

II. Debt Collection of Consumer Debt: Setting the Scene

The first section of this chapter outlines the process and environment of debt collection of consumer debt. It discusses the industry, entitlements and obligations of debt collectors, and how debts are assigned as a matter of English law.[4]

A. Debt Collection in the United Kingdom

Debt collection is a significant – and fast-growing – industry in the United Kingdom (UK), having a revenue of £2 billion and dealing with £200 billion in loans annually.[5] These processes have been utilised widely by the financial sector for consumer debts like those arising from contracts for telecoms and utilities services.[6] The industry has grown by a third in the last five years, and is likely to continue experiencing significant growth as a result of the economic ramifications of the global pandemic.

Given the significant commercial value of the industry, it has been analysed from a political-economy perspective. Montgomerie, in her discussion of debt collection and non-performing loans, commented:

> The debt collection industry exists because of a simple political loophole that treats debt differently from any other commodity bought and sold in markets. Imagine this scenario.

[4] Scots law on 'assignation' is distinct. Unlike equitable assignment, notice (termed 'intimation' in Scots law) to the debtor of the assignation is a constitutive requirement: see RG Anderson, *Assignation* (Edinburgh, Edinburgh Legal Education Trust, 2008) [6-01]. For present purposes, discussion of the Scots position is left aside, though much of the analysis in section III will also be relevant as the consumer protection legislation also applies to Scotland.

[5] Apex Insight, *UK Consumer Debt Collection and Debt Purchase* (2018) at www.credit-connect.co.uk/wp-content/uploads/2018/02/1259-Apex-Insight-UK-Consumer-debt-purchase-and-debt-collection-2018-summary-Credit-Connect.pdf (accessed 10 August 2021).

[6] ibid.

> You go shopping, buy a designer T-shirt on sale, originally £250, and pay £25 instead. The next day you return to the shop and demand a full-redemption rate refund of £250, on the grounds that this is the item's original retail price. No business would grant such a refund. Yet this is exactly what debt collection agencies do. Thanks to a political and regulatory exemption, debt collectors can buy discharged debt at a discount, from lenders, and turn around to borrowers and demand the full amount of the loan. These are the same borrowers identified as unable to repay (otherwise the debt would not be discharged).[7]

This analogy provides a useful insight into the economic process of debt collection. However, with all due respect to Montgomerie, it is insufficiently descriptive from a legal perspective. The authors suggest that a better metaphor would be a tool – say, a dragon-slaying sword. Thus: A owns the sword but does not have the skills or expertise to determine whether the sword is fully, partially or not working. A sells the sword to C at a fraction of the market price for a fully functioning sword (ie the amount of outstanding debt). C then utilises their expertise and puts the sword to work. C also does this with other swords from other hapless sword-owners. Sometimes the acquired sword works perfectly (ie the debt is repaid in full and C makes a good profit); sometimes it works partially (ie some of the debt is repaid and C breaks even or makes a slight profit); and sometimes it does not work at all (ie the debt is unpaid and C is out of pocket).

Viewing a debt *claim* as a tool granting the holder certain powers against the debtor allows clearer understanding of the debt collection process. It exposes the entirely rational basis by which debt collectors 'acquire' these assets at a seeming under-value, and shows how such discounted acquisition is in accord with efficient use of different skills and resources. What is missing, however, is the debtor – the rights or circumstances of the debtor are not mentioned.

It is important to remember that an individual lies behind these legal transactions, and that the entire debt collection industry is based around making profits by extracting payment from people who are often financially struggling. Even if a debt can, metaphorically, be viewed as a sword to be pressed against the debtor's throat, a debt also denotes a legally recognised relationship between the creditor (A) and the debtor (B). Though the law allows debts to be treated *like* assets, such assets arise out of relationships – which, in the present context, will be contractual. We cannot, therefore, ignore the circumstances of the legal persons to the debt relationship upon which the debt asset is predicated: we need to pay attention to B *as well* as to A and C.

B. What Are the Entitlements and Obligations of Debt Collectors?

The United Kingdom is one of a few countries in Europe with a regulatory regime for debt collection. The collection of consumer debts is a high-risk regulated activity[8] under the auspices of the Financial Conduct Authority (FCA), and there are specific restrictions

[7] J Montgomerie, *Should We Abolish Household Debts?* (Cambridge, Polity Press, 2019).

[8] Financial Services and Markets Act 2000 [FSMA] (Regulated Activities Order) 2001 (SI 2001/544) Art 39F.

on these practices in the FCA's Consumer Credit Sourcebook (CONC) and the FSMA (Regulated Activities Order) 2001. The first obligation is found under Principle 7 of the FCA's Principles for Businesses and requires all debt collectors to 'communicate information … in a way which is clear, fair and not misleading'. Coupled with this obligation is the requirement under CONC for firms not to misrepresent their legal position regarding the debt or debt-recovery process.[9] Firms therefore cannot undertake actions such as sending letters that look like court claims, use legalistic, threatening or unhelpful language, or contact individuals at unreasonable times.

Consumers who are in default or arrears have specific legal rights under CONC 7.3. This includes the requirement that firms, including debt collection firms, deal with them fairly[10] and with adequate forbearance and due consideration.[11] The firm must allow the customer reasonable time and opportunity to repay their debt,[12] and is even required to consider 'suspending, reducing, waiving or cancelling any further interest or charges' when a consumer is in financial difficulties.[13] The FCA has taken a number of regulatory actions to enforce these obligations, including a recent action against Barclays Bank for failing to show forbearance and due consideration to 1.5 million business and retail customers who fell into arrears or experienced financial difficulties, which resulted in a financial penalty of £26,000,000.

There are also restrictions on the fees and charges that can be levied against consumers (like B). Under CONC 7.7.2, debt collectors (like C) cannot claim any costs if there is no contractual right to do so. This includes situations such as claiming collection costs that were not outlined in the original agreement or adding unreasonable charges.[14] As will be discussed, very few contractual terms outline the costs that consumers are required to pay to debt collectors, which leaves this aspect of the collection process open to exploitation.

Despite these regulatory restrictions, there have been increased reports of exploitative and inappropriate debt collection activities in the United Kingdom, something that has been exacerbated by the COVID-19 pandemic.[15] The Financial Ombudsman Service (FOS), a consumer-friendly and free-to-use service that makes its decisions based on legal regulations and best practice guidance,[16] has jurisdiction over debt collection. The FOS's review of debt collection practices in 2019 revealed that in 2018, the Ombudsman received 3,300 enquiries about debt collection and took over 1,000 new complaints for investigation. Complaints included debt collectors asking consumers to repay incorrect amounts of money (21 per cent), consumer service issues (including being contacted

[9] CONC 7.11.1.
[10] CONC 7.3.2.
[11] CONC 7.3.2A.
[12] CONC 7.3.6.
[13] CONC 7.3.5(1).
[14] There are further restrictions on fees and charges and these are discussed in section III.B.i.
[15] See, eg, J Gardner and M Gray, 'Covid-19, Inequality and Council Tax: A Perfect Storm' (2020) *CHASM Briefing Paper BP8/2020* at www.birmingham.ac.uk/documents/college-social-sciences/social-policy/chasm/briefing-papers/covid19/chasm-bp8-2020.pdf (accessed 10 August 2021).
[16] E Kempson, S Collard and N Moore, *Fair and Reasonable: An assessment of the Financial Ombudsman Service*, University of Bristol, Personal Finance Research Centre Report, 2004.

excessively) (13 per cent) and people being chased for debts that did not belong to them (13 per cent). As a result of this review, the FOS called on all debt collecting firms to improve their practices, particularly in relation to dealing with vulnerable customers.[17] The situation has become so unacceptable that in January 2021, the FCA's Head of Retail and Authorisations wrote an Open Letter to the debt collection industry outlining poor practices and demanding improvements. For instance, it required debt collectors to allow customers to have sustainable repayment arrangements and signpost free debt advice.[18] These moves address difficulties arising after the debt collectors have come into the picture. But difficulties are present, even before this.

C. How Debts are Assigned

The business of debt collection often begins with the agreement between the service provider, A, and the consumer, B. There is, however, no standard usage or terminology in these agreements. We examined 28 different consumer contracts and found some service providers were empowered to deal with the debts incurred by their customers by way of outright grant, sale or transfer, or by way of a grant or transfer by way of security, or to novate the debt. Others empowered the appointment of agents or sub-contractors to collect outstanding debts on the service provider's behalf. And yet others merely alerted customers that the service provider might constitute a trust for itself over the customer's debts, or assign the benefit of such debts to another.

The lack of consistent terminology, and of generic terms such as 'sale' or 'transfer', obfuscates and confuses. Suppose A contracts to supply telecommunication services to B for a fixed monthly fee. If C desired to 'acquire' the benefit of B's indebtedness for value, A could 'sell' the debts accruing due from B to C in at least four distinct ways. In exchange for a mutually agreeable price, A could (i) appoint C to collect the debt on A's behalf, whilst simultaneously permitting C to retain such sums for C's own account;[19] (ii) constitute itself trustee over the benefit of such debt for C's benefit; (iii) assign the benefit of the debt to C; or (iv) novate the A–B contract such that B becomes duty-bound to C to make payment to C under a new C–B contract in place of the A–B one. Each of these structures has different effects.

For example, if technique (i) were employed, unless C were also invested with a proprietary interest in the collected sums,[20] C as a mere 'agent' would not be insulated against the effects of A's insolvency. Though C might be empowered to collect the sums on A's behalf, and therefore give a good discharge to B, in principle, such sums would

[17] Financial Ombudsman Service, 'Dealing with Debt', *Ombudsman News* (Issue 147, February 2019) at www.financial-ombudsman.org.uk/news-events/ombudsman-news-issue-147-dealing-debt (accessed 10 August 2021).

[18] Financial Conduct Authority, 'Debt Purchasers, Debt Collectors and Debt Administrators Portfolio Letter' (2021) at www.fca.org.uk/publication/correspondence/debt-purchasers-collectors-administrators-portfolio-letter.pdf (accessed 10 August 2021).

[19] C would, accordingly, be free to enjoy the fruits of such collection without having to consider A's interests.

[20] Say, by also constituting a trust over the benefit of the debt; but if so, there would arguably have been an equitable assignment (see n 23).

be held by C as a mere agent for A's benefit. Since C acquires no legal or equitable interest in the receivable as a mere agent of A, without more, the collected sums remain A's personal assets, and so remain available for distribution to A's creditors if A were to become insolvent. C would thus remain exposed to the risk of A's insolvency.[21]

If, however, A had employed technique (ii) and constituted itself trustee of the benefit of B's indebtedness for C's benefit, C would acquire an equitable proprietary interest in the debt. Since such asset would no longer be beneficially held by A for A's own self-interest, it would no longer form part of A's assets for purposes of, say, insolvency.[22] But as a mere trust beneficiary, C would have no power to accept any tender of payment by B so as to discharge the debt at law. Nor would C have any power at law to make or to accept offers of variation of the contract of debt by B (say, to repay the sum in instalments). Given the rules of privity of contract, such powers would remain solely A's, with whom the contract of debt had been made.[23]

But suppose A assigned the debt to C.[24] A common law chose in action such as a contractual debt is equitably assigned once the three 'certainties' are manifested. Upon manifestation of the requisite certainty of intention to effect an assignment (as opposed to any other mode of dealing), certainty of subject matter of the assignment (ie the debt accruing due from the A–B contract) and certainty of the objects of the assignment (ie the identity of the assignee, C),[25] A will have validly equitably assigned the benefit of the debt arising from the A–B contract to C. Significantly, it is not required that the debtor be given, or have received, notice of the assignment for it to have arisen[26] – although this will often be done in order to secure priority,[27] to stop 'equities' from 'running' against the assignee,[28] and, of course, to alert the debtor that payment should thereafter be made to the assignee. The better view is also that consideration is not required so long as the debt that has been equitably assigned is in existence (even if it is not yet due to be paid) at the time of the assignment.[29]

[21] Notwithstanding A's having contracted or covenanted that she would release C from having to fulfil its fiduciary duty to account for the recovered sums, without more, that only creates personal obligations. If breached, C would be left to prove as an unsecured creditor for damages in relation to losses caused as a result in A's insolvency.

[22] See *Scott v Surman* (1742) Willes 400; *Winch v Keeley* (1787) 1 TR 619, 623 (Buller J).

[23] A trust for C's benefit could be combined with an authorisation to C to collect the receivable for his own benefit. But A would have effected an equitable assignment by such combination: see CH Tham, *Understanding the Law of Assignment* (Cambridge, Cambridge University Press, 2019) 451–53.

[24] Method (iii).

[25] These may be referred to as the 'three certainties', which are required for there to be a valid equitable assignment of a common law debt. See M Smith and N Leslie, *The Law of Assignment*, 3rd edn (Oxford, Oxford University Press, 2018) para 13.06; and Tham (n 23) 8.

[26] See *Bell v The London & North Western Railway Co* (1852) 15 Beav 548. The law in Scotland is different (see n 4).

[27] Pursuant to the rule in *Dearle v Hall* (1828) 3 Russ 1, 38 ER 475; Tham (n 23) ch 10.

[28] See Tham (n 23) ch 12.

[29] See *Kekewich v Manning* (1851) 1 De GM & G 176, 187–88; 42 ER 519, 524; *Richardson v Richardson* (1867) LR 3 Eq 686. But cf *Re Westerton* [1919] 2 Ch 104, 112. Where a purported assignment has been made of a future debt (ie a debt that was *not* in existence at the time of the purported assignment), such 'assignment' operates in the manner of a *promise* to assign, and such promise will be given effect in equity if supported by consideration, 'equity deeming as done that which ought to be done': *Meek v Kettlewell* (1842) 1 Hare 464; *Re Tilt* (1896) 74 LT 163, 542 (Chitty J); *Re Ellenborough* [1903] 1 Ch 697.

Once the debt is assigned to C, not only would C be vested with an equitable proprietary interest in the debt,[30] rendering C proof against A's insolvency, but C would also be empowered in certain respects to invoke A's powers arising from the A–B contract: it would be as though C had been delegated those powers of A.[31] And so long as the assignment was 'absolute' and not by way of charge, and had been made in writing under the hand of the assignor (A), once notice of the assignment was given to the customer (B), certain entitlements would 'pass and transfer' from A to C by reason of statute, namely:

(a) A's legal right 'to such debt or thing in action';
(b) all of A's 'legal and other remedies for the same'; and
(c) A's power 'to give a good discharge for the same' without need for A's concurrence.[32]

Where (a), (b) and (c) have been fulfilled, the equitable assignment may be said to have 'become' a 'statutory' assignment.

Admittedly, the service contracts under review also reveal terms that grant some service providers the power to novate the contract. Lord Selborne explained the process of a novation as follows:

> [T]here being a contract in existence, some new contract is substituted for it, either between the same parties (for that might be) or between different parties, the consideration mutually being the discharge of the old contract.[33]

Novation entails termination of the A–B contract coupled with formation of an approximately equivalent C–B contract in which C would undertake the obligations formerly undertaken by A, and where B would then be duty-bound to tender payment to C. Novation therefore substitutes the C–B contract for the A–B contract. But unlike assignments, novations cannot be effectively made without all parties to the original contract agreeing that it be discharged.[34]

While the scenarios above do not exhaustively set out every possible way for debt receivables to be 'dealt' with, they probably represent the most common modes of 'dealing' with receivables. But of these, the hypothesis in this chapter is that in most cases, debt collectors like C will take an assignment from service providers like A, and not employ some other form of dealing.

On the one hand, the employment of agency, or trust principles, in isolation, does too little. If agency structures were employed, the collecting agent would not be insulated from the insolvency of its principal. But although such insolvency risk could be

[30] See *Deposit Protection Board v Barclays Bank plc* [1994] 2 AC 367, 381 (Simon Brown LJ) quoting the observations of PO Lawrence J in *In re Steel Wing Co Ltd* [1921] 1 Ch 349, 357.

[31] For example, it should be open to C to make offers to or accept offers from B to vary the A–B debt contract: C should be able to compromise the debt. See, eg, *Heaton v Axa Equity & Law Life Assurance Society Plc* [2002] 2 AC 329 (HL) (where it was accepted that assignees of a claim for damages against a tortfeasor could enter into a compromise agreement to compromise that claim).

[32] See Law of Property Act 1925, s 136(1), re-enacting Supreme Court of Judicature Act 1873, s 25(6).

[33] *Scarf v Jardine* (1882) 7 App Cas 345, 351.

[34] See *The Tychy (No 2)* [2001] 1 Lloyd's Rep 10, [65]; aff'd *The Tychy (No 2)* [2001] 1 Lloyd's Rep 403 (EWCA).

avoided by employing a trust structure, a trust beneficiary will find it difficult to deal 'directly' with the debtor.[35]

On the other hand, novation does too much. As explained, when a contract between A and B is 'novated' to C, C is substituted in place of A as contractual counterparty to B through replacement of the A–B contract with a new contract between C and B. Consequently, C will become liable to B to perform the kinds of duties for which A had previously been responsible under the A–B contract. In many of the scenarios under present investigation, such substitution of C in place of A is not envisaged at all: only the benefit of the accrued debts of B is to 'pass' to C, and A is *still* to be duty-bound to B to provide the requisite services set out in the A–B contract. Thus debt collectors are unlikely to employ novation as a means of acquiring debts from service providers.

In contrast, an assignment will allow the assignee (C) to deal with the customer (B) without the need for further cooperation from the assignor (A). Because of the equitable proprietary interest that arises from the assignment, the assignee, C, is also protected against the insolvency of the assignor, A. Further, unlike novation, assignment does not entail the discharge of the A–B contract and its replacement with an approximately equivalent C–B contract such that C becomes duty-bound to B to provide services that had hitherto been the responsibility of A. In principle, only the 'benefits' of a contract may be assigned from assignor to assignee: the 'burdens' remain with the assignor.[36] Since debt collectors obviously have no capability to provide the services in question, it is improbable that novation would be employed to 'transfer' the debts of the service providers' customers.

III. Complexities

The nature of debt collecting has raised a number of legal and practical complexities. Two specific complexities – when the consumer pays the service provider instead of the debt collector, and the impact of unfair contract terms – will be discussed in this section.

A. Complexity 1: Consumer Pays Service Provider

Either assignor or assignee may give notice of assignment to the debtor. Once notice of assignment is received, it has been said that 'the only safe way for the debtor in such a

[35] Where a trust has been constituted over the benefit of a debt, the trust beneficiary can bring proceedings at law against the debtor only by joining the trustee of the debt as a co-plaintiff or co-defendant: *Vandepitte v Preferred Accident Insurance Corp of New York* [1933] AC 70 (UKPC). As explained in *Harmer v Armstrong* [1934] Ch 65, 84, this joins proceedings and not parties. In *Barbados Trust Co Ltd v Bank of Zambia* [2007] EWCA Civ 148, [2007] 1 Lloyd's Rep 495 [99], it was accepted such joinder may also be applied to cases of equitable assignment. Additionally, unless the terms of the trust reserve a power to the beneficiaries of the trust to vary the trustee's trust duties and powers, trust beneficiaries have no such powers: see *Re Brockbank* [1948] Ch 206. Hence, beneficiaries of a trust over a contract debt have no power to make or accept any offers of composition of that debt with the debtor. See also *Joseph Hayim Hayim v Citibank NA* [1987] 1 AC 730, 748.

[36] See, eg, *Tolhurst v Associated Portland Cement Manufacturers (1900) Ltd* [1902] 2 KB 660 (EWCA), 668 (per Collins MR).

case would be to send at once to the assignee and pay him the debt. That would be a valid discharge.'[37] However, notice notwithstanding, consumers often still tender payment to the service provider. That raises the question of whether the debt is still actionable. Case law tells us that '[o]nce notice of an equitable assignment is given to the debtor, he cannot thereafter deal inconsistently with the assigned interest, for instance by making payment to the assignor';[38] and 'The whole object of the notice to the debtor is to protect the assignee. After receipt of that notice the debtor pays the assignor at his peril …'[39] As to *what* this peril might be, Smith and Leslie posit that 'If the debtor disregards the notice, then he must pay again.'[40]

Despite appearances, the reason for the liability to 'pay again' is not because the assignment has modified the debt contract by substituting the assignee in place of the assignor as creditor, such that tender to the assignor is no longer precise performance of the debtor's payment obligation, so modified. Equitable assignment does not modify the terms of the debt contract, not even the terms as to the identity of the creditor to whom the debtor is indebted.[41]

In tendering payment to the assignor despite knowing of the equitable assignment to the assignee, the debtor may have become liable to the assignee in *equity* for having assisted the assignor in breaching its duties (namely, to invoke its creditor entitlements for the benefit of the assignee).[42] It has been argued that this leads to the equitable wrong of dishonest assistance,[43] as explained in the following illustration.

When A equitably assigns to C the benefit of a debt owed to A by B, C acquires an equitable interest in the debt.[44] In a case where B paid A in ignorance of the assignment, the case law is clear: such payment *will* discharge the debt at law,[45] *and* such payment attracts no liability in equity as the conscience of the debtor would have been unaffected by any knowledge of the assignment. Following such payment, the assignor would then hold the tendered sums on trust for the assignee.[46] However, if the payment was made *with* such knowledge, B's immunity from equitable liability falls away and equitable liability will arise once notice of the assignment is received by the debtor.[47] This may be referred to as a 'substantive' basis for B's liability, since it arises by operation

[37] *Jones v Farrell* (1857) 1 De G & J 208, 218 (Lord Cranworth LC).

[38] *Deposit Protection Board v Dalia* [1994] 2 AC 367 (CA), 381 (Simon Brown LJ).

[39] *Walter & Sullivan Ltd v J Murphy & Sons Ltd* [1955] 2 QB 584 (CA), 588 (Parker LJ).

[40] Smith and Leslie (n 25) para 26.16

[41] *Keighley, Maxsted & Co v Durant* [1901] AC 240 (UKHL), 244: 'The parties to the contract … are just as much part of the contract as any other part of the contractual obligations entered into.'

[42] See, eg, *Jones v Farrell* (1877) 1 De G & J 208, 44 ER 703.

[43] See *Royal Brunei Airlines v Tan* [1995] 2 AC 378, 392; *Ivey v Genting Casinos (UK) Ltd (Trading as Crockfords Club)* [2017 UKSC 67, [2018] AC 391 [74]. For detailed analysis, see Tham (n 23) ch 11.

[44] *Roberts v Gill & Co* [2010] UKSC 22, [2011] 1 AC 240 [68].

[45] *Stocks v Dobson* (1853) 4 De GM & G 11, 15 (Turner LJ): 'The debtor is liable, at law, to the assignor of the debt, and at law must pay the assignor if the assignor sues in respect of it. If so, it follows he may pay without suit. The payment of the debtor to the assignor discharges the debt at law.'

[46] *Fortescue v Barnett* (1834) 3 My & K 36; *Re Patrick* [1891] 1 Ch 82, 87; *Holt v Heatherfield Trust Ltd* [1942] 2 KB 1; *Pharoahs Plywood Co Ltd v Allied Wood Products Co (Pte) Ltd* [1980] LS Gaz R 130.

[47] *Stocks v Dobson* (1853) 4 De GM & G 11, 16 (Turner LJ): 'If a Court of Equity laid down the rule that the debtor is a trustee for the assignee, without having any notice of the assignment, it would be impossible for a debtor safely to pay a debt to his creditor. The law of the Court [of Chancery] has therefore required notice to be given to the debtor of the assignment, in order to perfect the title of the assignee.'

of substantive (equitable) principles. But there is an alternative 'procedural' basis as well, through judicial interference with what may, and may not, be pleaded.

B can be held to be liable *at law*, despite the tender of payment to A, because B can be barred from pleading the facts of such tender to (and acceptance by) A to defend against such action at law as might be brought on the debt. So barred, the action would then succeed in lieu of such pleaded defence, unless some other defence were available to B. These procedural developments have been detailed elsewhere,[48] but the following provides a potted account.

In *Mangles v Dixon*, Lord Cottenham LC observed:

> If there is one rule more perfectly established in a court of equity than another, it is that whoever takes an assignment of a chose in action … takes it subject to all the equities of the person who made the assignment.[49]

By 'equities', inter alia, Lord Cottenham was referring to pleas the debtor might raise by way of defence, for example the defences of set-off or release. Another would be the defence of tender and acceptance, that is, payment. So, if B had tendered payment to A in respect of the debt between them, once accepted by A, ordinarily, B could plead the fact of payment as a defence against any action on that debt. However, B would be barred from asserting such defence if B had tendered payment despite having received notice that A had assigned the benefit of the debt to C.

This was the position in the Court of Chancery, which would issue common injunctions to bar the pleading of such defences in an action at law.[50] These Chancery developments were then emulated by the common law courts pursuant to the so-called 'equitable jurisdiction of the common law courts',[51] under which a common law rule barring the defendant at law from pleading such defence was developed.[52] In time, these developments were extended by statute.[53]

[48] See Tham (n 23) ch 12, especially 292–322, for a discussion of the development of this 'bar' as a matter of case law developments, and by way of statute. Alternatively, see CH Tham, 'Equitable fraud and double liability of a debtor following notice of equitable assignment of the debt' (2019) 13 *Journal of Equity* 237.

[49] *Mangles v Dixon* (1852) 3 HLC 702, 731.

[50] See, eg, *Stewart v The Great Western Railway Company v Saunders* (1865) 3 De GJ & S 319; *Lee v Lancashire and Yorkshire Railway Company* (1871) LR 6 Ch 527.

[51] *Phillips v Clagett* (1843) 11 M & W 84, 91 (Lord Abinger CB): 'It has been the practice of Courts of law (especially in modern times), where they see that justice demands the interference of a Court of equity, and that a Court of equity would interfere – in every such case to save parties the expense of proceeding to a Court of equity, by giving them the aid of the equitable jurisdiction of a Court of common law, to enable them to effect the same purpose.'

[52] See, eg, *Legh v Legh* (1799) 1 Bos & Pul 447: 'The conduct of the Defendant has been against good faith, and the only question is, whether the Plaintiff must not seek relief in a Court of Equity? The Defendant ought either to have paid the person to whom the bond was assigned, or have waited until an action was commenced against him, and then have applied to the Court. Most clearly it was in breach of good faith to pay the money to the assignor of the bond and take a release, and I rather think the Court ought not to allow the Defendant to avail himself of his plea since a Court of Equity would order the Defendant to pay the Plaintiff the amount of his lien on the bond, and probably all the costs of the application.'

[53] Common Law Procedure Act 1854, s 85. The purpose of this provision was 'to enable courts of law to administer equitable relief, without driving the parties to the useless and vexatious expense of proceedings in a court of equity': *Vorley v Barrett* (1856) 1 CB (NS) 225, 240. For an example of the operation of s 85, see *De Pothonier v De Mattos* (1858) El Bl & Bl 461.

This state of affairs was largely preserved when the Supreme Court of Judicature Act 1873 (1873 Act) came into force in 1875.[54] As Jessel MR stated in *Salt v Cooper*:

> It is stated very plainly that the main object of the [1873] Act was to assimilate the transaction of Equity business and Common Law business by different Courts of Judicature. … [The 1873 Act effected] the vesting in one tribunal the administration of Law and Equity in every cause, action, or dispute which should come before that tribunal. That was the meaning of the Act.[55]

Section 16 of the 1873 Act vested the 'new' High Court of the Supreme Court of Judicature with all jurisdiction previously exercised by the Court of Chancery and by the courts of common law. This included the power of pre-Judicature courts of common law to bar pleadings of tender by way of defence because of the 'equitable jurisdiction of the common law courts', or to give effect to 'replications on equitable grounds' pursuant to section 85 of the Common Law Procedure Act 1854. As for the power of the Court of Chancery to enjoin such pleadings, this too was transferred pursuant to section 24(1). And that state of affairs has been left intact in the successive re-enactments of the 1873 provisions dealing with the administrative fusion of the Court of Chancery and the courts of common law.[56]

But what if the equitable assignment had 'become' statutory? Would that make a difference, given that section 136(1)(c) of the Law of Property Act 1925 provides that once an assignment fulfils the requirements of 'absolute, writing and notice', the assignor's 'power to give a good discharge [for the debt assigned] without the concurrence of the assignor' shall 'pass and transfer' from the assignor to the assignee? For example, Smith and Leslie posit that 'Once a [section] 136 assignment has been completed, performance by the debtor to the assignor will not discharge his obligation. Performance must be rendered to the assignee.'[57]

It has been suggested elsewhere that section 136(1)(c) can be read more narrowly, as referring to the power of an assignor-creditor to *give* a good discharge by way of release,[58] without going so far as to encompass the creditor's power to effect discharge by acceptance. In addition, when read in its proper context, the broader construction sketched out above becomes untenable.

Section 136(1) re-enacts section 25(6) of the Judicature Act 1873. Save for trivial formatting and linguistic changes,[59] the two are *in pari materia*. So the legislative intent behind each should be the same. But section 25(6) was enacted as part of a suite of provisions in the 1873 Act to effect administrative fusion of the judicial system. It would be otiose to read section 25(6) expansively as also entailing a 'transfer' of the assignor-creditor's power to accept a conforming tender of payment so as to discharge the debt, since the problem of debtors doing so despite knowledge of assignment would have already been dealt with by sections 16 and 24(1). And if that be the case

[54] Supreme Court of Judicature Act 1875, s 2.

[55] *Salt v Cooper* (1880) 16 Ch D 544, 549. See also *Jospeh v Lyons* (1884) 15 QBD 280, 287.

[56] Sections 16 and 24(1) were re-enacted, *in pari materia*, in the Supreme Court of Judicature (Consolidation) Act 1925 as ss 18 and 37, respectively. Though repealed by the Senior Courts Act 1981 (UK), ss 18 and 37 were re-enacted in the 1981 Act respectively as s 19 (*in pari materia*) and s 37 (in slightly more compressed language). See Tham, 'Equitable fraud and double liability of a debtor' (n 48).

[57] Smith and Leslie (n 25) para 26.09.

[58] Tham (n 23) ch 13, esp at 360.

[59] Principally, substituting 'thing in action' for the French law 'chose in action'.

for section 25(6), the same would hold for its modern-day equivalent in section 136(1), particularly when we can also find modern-day equivalents to sections 16 and 24(1) in the form of sections 19(2) and 49(2)(a), respectively, of the Senior Courts Act 1981.

Whether the equitable assignment from A to C has 'become statutory' or not, B can be made substantively liable in equity to C for having tendered payment to A where such payment was made with knowledge of the assignment to C. Alternatively, B can be held liable to C at law by reason of the procedural rules barring B from pleading the facts pertaining to such payment to A by way of defence. Although such liabilities to C make it seem as though C had replaced A as creditor, both of these forms of liability rest on a different basis: the former on dishonest assistance in equity, and the latter on a procedural bar against adducing evidence of payment in the action at law. Even though the precise performance of B in tendering payment to A had discharged the debt at law, because B is precluded from pleading such facts, the action will succeed in lieu of such defence. This leads to the following points.

First, contrary to common assumption,[60] B arguably does *not* have an unjust enrichment claim against A in relation to the sums paid to A, since such payment arguably *does* discharge the debt at common law. That is, as a matter of *substantive* common law doctrine, B's debt to A *is* discharged given B's precise performance of their contractual duty to A. There is, accordingly, no relevant mistake of law (or, for that matter, failure of basis), the basis for B's seeming continued liability at law on the debt arising for procedural reasons only.

Given this, it is arguable that heed should be paid to the equitable maxim that 'he who comes to equity must do equity'.[61] When C seeks to make B liable to them in equity for dishonest assistance, in 'coming to equity', C 'must do equity'. But the maxim should also be pertinent to B's common law liability, since the procedural 'bars' to the pleas of payment explained above are rooted in the availability of equitable injunctive relief to bar unconscionable pleadings in actions at law: at bottom, these procedural bars are equitable remedies too. Hence, it is arguable that a claimant ought *not* to be entitled to invoke either of these bases for liability against a defendant debtor without having complied with the equitable maxim that 'he who comes to equity must do equity', particularly in circumstances where the party seeking equitable relief (C) knew or ought to have known that the debtor (B) would act as he had done[62] – say, where the language of the notice of assignment is impenetrably obscure (as may often be the case).

[60] *Barclays Bank Ltd v Willowbrook International Ltd* [1987] 1 FTLR 386; *GE Crane Sales Pty Ltd v Commissioner of Taxation* (1971) 46 ALJR 15. Cited by RM Goode, *Legal Problems of Credit and Security*, 3rd edn (London, Sweet & Maxwell, 2003) [3-36]: 'Where the debtor, despite notice of assignment, makes payment of a receivable to the assignor, the latter holds the sum received, whether in cash or in the form of a cheque or other instrument, on trust for the assignee.' But Goode goes on to suggest that '[i]n the latter case, wrongful appropriation of the instrument [by the assignor], eg by paying it into the assignor's bank account, constitutes a conversion, with an alternative liability to account for the proceeds of the instrument in an action for money had and received'. Relying on this, Smith and Leslie (n 25) [26.18] suggest that in the case of an equitable assignment that has not 'become statutory', '[i]f obliged to pay again because he has failed to account to the assignor, the debtor will be able to recover his original payment from the assignor'.

[61] *Comyns Digest of Chancery* 3 F 3; *McDonald v Neilson* 2 Cowp 139; *Farr v Sheriffe* 4 Hare 521; *Hanson v Keating* 4 Hare 4; *Bowser v Colby* 1 Hare 143.

[62] See JD Heydon, MJ Leeming and PJ Turner (eds), *Meagher, Gummow & Lehane: Equity Doctrines and Remedies*, 5th edn (London, LexisNexis Butterworths, 2014) [3-060], which suggests that the operation of the maxim is constrained by reference to the knowledge of the party seeking relief.

If the maxim were applicable, B, arguably, might not pursue A in unjust enrichment for the sums paid to A, but C certainly might (since the sums received by A in discharge of the debt are undoubtedly the traceable substitutes of the debt that had been assigned to C). So the argument may be made that, before being permitted to obtain equitable remedies in light of B's dishonest assistance, or the benefit of the procedural bars against pleas of payment were B to be proceeded against at common law, C should *first* proceed against *A* to recover the sums in question: it is only when C has done such 'equity' that C may *then* proceed to invoke what are, ultimately, doctrines originating from the court's equitable jurisdiction to bar such pleas of payment.[63]

Second, our investigation into debt collection practices reveals that in many cases, the notice of assignment uses ambiguous language that does not clearly set out the basis for the 'change' of payee. The authors reviewed multiple different letters from debt collectors, and the terminology used was uniformly vague and unclear. For example, the consumer was often merely directed to pay the debt collection agency without any explanation as to why, or without specific description of the legal processes utilised. At other times, phrases such as 'collecting on behalf of' or referring to the service provider as 'our client' were used. Such wording seems to indicate that the service provider has just appointed the debt collecting agency as an agent, and therefore makes it seem that the consumer may still pay the outstanding debt directly to the service provider as 'principal' and not to the debt collecting 'agent'.

Where the debtor–creditor relationship has arisen between parties of approximately equal bargaining power, such obscurity as to the relationship between the service provider and the debt collecting agency could be readily resolved by querying the service provider. However, timely response to such inquiries in consumer cases would appear to be improbable.[64] If so, is it truly *unconscionable* for the customer (B) to tender payment to their creditor in light of such obscurities of language? Further, even if the notice used the language of 'assignment', it is also doubtful whether the legal significance of such language would be fully appreciated by the average consumer. Notwithstanding that 'ignorance of the law is no excuse', given the law's complexity in this area, there is the countervailing policy of consumer protection. Thus, even if such payment *were* taken to be unconscionable in light of current case law, it is an open question whether it *should* continue to be so taken in light of consumer protection policy.

B. Complexity 2: Unfair Contract Terms

Contracts between A and B and, if relevant, between B and C, will be subject to the Consumer Rights Act (CRA) 2015.[65] Any unfair terms in these contracts will therefore not be binding on the consumer.[66] Our analysis of the 28 consumer contracts that

[63] While the Supreme Court has clarified in *Marex Financial Ltd v Sevillega* [2020] UKSC 31, [2021] AC 39 [86]–[88] that there is no rule governing the priority of claims by multiple claimants against the *same* entity so as to lead to the possible of double recovery, the scenario set out in the main text is distinct, as it involves a single claimant having multiple claims against *different* entities.

[64] See, eg, the significant number of complaints raised by the FOS on debt-collecting practices.

[65] See definitions in CRA 2015, s 2(2) and (3).

[66] ibid s 62(1).

reference debt collection highlights a number of potential unfair terms. In determining whether a clause would be 'unfair' under the CRA 2015, it needs to be considered whether it causes a significant imbalance in the parties' rights and obligations to the detriment of the consumer.[67] When coming to a decision on this matter, the courts will look at a wide range of factors, including the nature of the subject matter of the contract.[68]

i. Fees and Charges

The fees charged by debt collectors clearly have the potential to be unfair. Of the 28 contracts reviewed, only two contracts specifically stated what fees and charges would apply if the account were to be sent to a debt collector. A further eight contracts did not make any specific references to how much the customer would be charged in the event of non-payment. The remainder of the contracts had general clauses stating that if the consumers did not pay their bills, they would be subjected to a number of financial penalties and/or the service provider would be entitled to pass on any third-party charges to the consumer. Leaving aside the technical difficulties as to how contractual duties arising between debt collector and service provider may be 'passed on' to the service provider's customers,[69] the fees and charges that can be charged by debt collectors are subject to significant regulation. This includes CONC 7.7.2 (discussed in section II.B), the common law on penalty clauses and, potentially, the unfair terms regime in the CRA 2015, with various outcomes.

In *Cavendish v Makdessi*,[70] the Supreme Court expanded the scope of liquidated damages clauses from the previous 'genuine pre-estimate of loss'[71] to the more generous 'legitimate interest in performance' test. Unless the fees are particularly unconscionable or extortionate, it may be difficult to have the fees and charges levied against consumers held to be unfair penalties. That said, while businesses are allowed to 'fund [their] own business activities and make a profit',[72] it could be argued that, as the debt collectors purchase the debts for a fraction of their full value, *any* additional fees and charges levied beyond the principal debt would not meet the 'legitimate interest in performance' test. While detailed analysis of this point is beyond the scope of the current chapter, it is likely that a determination would depend on the circumstances of the specific case and an analysis of the amount of debt, what it had been purchased for and the time/resources spent liaising with the consumer in question. The analysis of these factors creates particular difficulties with consumer debt collection, as the debts are generally combined with many others and sold 'in bulk' by the service providers. It could

[67] ibid s 62(4).
[68] ibid s 62(5).
[69] How these provisions operate as a matter of law is unclear. One possibility could be that these provisions create a contractual obligation by the customer (B) to indemnify the service provider (A) for such charges as a debt collector (C) might impose on B as part of the consideration from A to C in exchange for C's 'purchase' of B's debt, such sum by way of indemnity then being agglomerated into the capital sum owed by B.
[70] *Cavendish v Makdessi* [2015] UKSC 67, [2016] AC 1172.
[71] *Dunlop v New Garage* [1915] AC 79.
[72] *Cavendish v Makdessi* (n 70) [286].

therefore be that the courts instead consider the average costs charged in the industry to determine what is 'fair' – but that is assuming that the industry as a whole is acting fairly and charging reasonably. The experiences of the sale of payment protection insurance (PPI) and payday lending shows that this assumption can often be unfounded.[73]

Alternatively, it could be argued that the fees and charges levied by C on B would be excluded from the fairness analysis of the CRA 2015 as they are the 'price payable under the contract'.[74] This is in line with the wide approach taken by the House of Lords in *Office of Fair Trading v Abbey National Plc*.[75] There are significant similarities between fees for unauthorised overdrafts and debt-collecting fees and charges, such that the decision in *Office of Fair Trading v Abbey National Plc* would arguably also apply to debt-collecting contracts. However, this case was decided under the previous regulatory regime of the Unfair Terms in Consumer Contracts Regulations 1999 (SI 1999/2083). There are potentially additional protections in place under the CRA 2015, which require these terms to be both 'transparent and prominent'.[76] It is possible that the fees and charges clauses under the contracts reviewed would not pass either of these requirements. As discussed previously, the clauses are often expressed in difficult and legally complex language.[77] Moreover, the clauses are sub-clauses in long and complicated standard form contracts, and therefore are not presented in such a way that an average consumer would be aware of the term.[78]

ii. Complexity of Terms Utilised

The complexity of debt collection processes creates significant confusion for the consumer. It is also common for the contract to refer to multiple terms denoting different legal concepts, further adding to the complexities. One contract reviewed utilised eight separate concepts in its debt-collection discussion (agency, assign, transfer by novation, pass, transfer, sub-contract, grant security and declare a trust over). In fact, only 21 per cent of the contracts reviewed specified a single method by which the debt was assigned. One contract did not mention debt collection – which would leave assignment as a possibility, since equitable assignment does not require prior assent from the debtor. But in that case, the consumer-debtor would surely be caught by surprise when told, post-assignment, to pay the assignee debt collector. As discussed in section II.C, the different assignment methods can involve different rights and responsibilities for parties. This lack of clarity creates a confusing state of affairs, which is exacerbated by the nature of consumer-debtors who are, in the main, unlikely to have the benefit of commercial legal advice or experience. Such confusion thus seems ripe for regulation by the unfair terms regime.

[73] See J Gardner, 'High-Cost Credit in the United Kingdom: A Philosophical Justification for Government Intervention' in K Fairweather, P O'Shea and R Grantham (eds), *Credit, Consumers and the Law: After the global storm* (Farnham, Ashgate Publishing, 2016).

[74] CRA 2015, s 64(1).

[75] *Office of Fair Trading v Abbey National Plc*[2009] UKSC 6, [2009] 3 WLR 1215.

[76] CRA 2015, s 64(2).

[77] A term is 'transparent' if 'it is expressed in plain and intelligible language': ibid s 64(3).

[78] A term is 'prominent' if 'it is brought to the consumer's attention in such a way that a reasonably well-informed, observant and circumspect consumer would be aware of the term': CRA 2015, s 64(4) and (5).

iii. Assigning Debts of Consumers in Financial Distress

Under *Aziz v Catalunyacaixa*,[79] when determining whether a clause is unfair, it must be considered if the consumer is being deprived of an advantage that they would have had under national law in the absence of the contractual provision in question.[80] If so, is it ever fair to assign debts of consumers who are in financial distress? Service providers have significant obligations when dealing with vulnerable consumers, with the FCA recently providing additional guidance to firms on how these matters should be dealt with.[81] A vulnerable consumer is defined as 'somebody who, due to their personal circumstances, is especially susceptible to harm, particularly when a firm is not acting with appropriate levels of care'.[82] The FCA states that there are four key drivers that increase consumer vulnerability: (i) health conditions or illnesses; (ii) major life events (such as bereavement, job loss or relationship breakdowns); (iii) the inability to withstand emotional or financial shocks; and (iv) low knowledge of financial matters.[83]

The Office of Fair Trading (OFT) specifically notes that COVID-19 is likely to significantly exacerbate many issues already affecting consumers, such as ill health, bereavement and job loss.[84] A survey of over 16,000 individuals in February 2020 highlighted that approximately 24 million people in the United Kingdom have characteristics of vulnerability, 10.7 million of whom have low financial resilience. Out of these people, 7.2 million are over-indebted and 3.8 million are in severe financial difficulty.[85] There is substantial overlap between individuals in severe financial difficulty and those subject to debt collection processes. People in financial distress are more likely to be constantly or usually overdrawn, have persistent credit-card debt and/or utilise high-cost credit to cover day-to-day expenses. This has only worsened with COVID-19, with an additional 3.5 million adults now having low financial resilience. Despite this, service providers are continuing to use debt collectors for overdue debts, including energy companies.[86]

There are significant legal obligations when dealing with customers who are in financial difficulties.[87] On top of the specific legal obligations, vulnerable consumers must be treated appropriately and with best practice, or service providers risk an adverse finding by the FOS. One of the key advantages of referring an outstanding account to a debt collector is that the service provider can avoid the risk and practical burden of seeking repayment of outstanding amounts. For example, due to the burdensome nature of the

[79] Case C-415/11 *Aziz v Catalunyacaixa* [2013] 3 CMLR 5.

[80] This approach was confirmed by the House of Lords in *OFT v Abbey National* (n 75) [105].

[81] Financial Conduct Authority, *Guidance for firms on the fair treatment of vulnerable customers* (GC20/3, 2020) at www.fca.org.uk/publications/finalised-guidance/guidance-firms-fair-treatment-vulnerable-customers (accessed 11 August 2021).

[82] ibid [1.1].

[83] ibid [2.1].

[84] ibid [1.15b].

[85] Financial Conduct Authority, *Financial Lives 2020 Survey: the impact of coronavirus* (2021) at www.fca.org.uk/publications/research/financial-lives-2020-survey-impact-coronavirus (accessed 11 August 2021).

[86] J Ambrose, 'UK energy firms using debt collectors despite coronavirus agreement' *The Guardian* (London, 26 April 2020) at www.theguardian.com/business/2020/apr/26/uk-energy-firms-using-debt-collectors-despite-coronavirus-agreement (accessed 11 August 2021).

[87] See discussion in Financial Conduct Authority, *FG21/1 Guidance for firms on the fair treatment of vulnerable customers* (2021) at www.fca.org.uk/publication/finalised-guidance/fg21-1.pdf (accessed 11 August 2021).

tasks, in early 2021 certain banks proposed creating an industry-wide debt collection service to chase unpaid COVID-19 support loans.[88] Service providers, understandably, do not want to engage in these types of activities.

Debt collectors do have legal obligations when dealing with vulnerable consumers (as discussed already). It is highly likely, however, that individuals will receive more empathetic and understanding treatment from service providers, who have an ongoing relationship with the consumer. This can be contrasted with debt collectors, which, whilst subject to largely the same regulatory obligations, have a limited relationship and are focused solely on extracting maximum payment from the individual in question. Referring unpaid accounts to a debt collector therefore allows service providers to avoid, or at least pass on, the legal obligations they owe to consumers in financial difficulties. This could arguably contravene the concern emphasised in *Aziz v Catalunyacaixa* that consumers ought not to be denied advantages they would have under national law because of the contractual provision allowing the service provider to assign the debt to another party.

It is therefore worthwhile considering whether debt collection clauses in consumer contracts[89] are, in general, unfair contract terms. They clearly fulfil the criteria of creating a significant imbalance in the parties' rights and obligations to the detriment of the consumer, as the service provider benefits at the disadvantage of the consumer. Since a consumer's inability to pay sums owed is prima facie evidence of financial vulnerability, is it fair to sell such indebtedness (at a fraction of a price) to a business that makes a profit from extracting a maximum level of payment from parties already struggling?[90] The harms of debt collection have been outlined by Montgomerie, who states:

> When lenders decide that an outstanding loan is not going to be paid … they can discharge these debts, and the lender is given a tax break equivalent to the value of the loss against an asset. Lenders have made a practice of selling these loans to debt collection agencies, often for 2 per cent to 10 per cent of their face value. Debt collectors … try to make a profit by extracting payment from the borrowers that lenders have long given up on. Debt collection agencies are well known for causing emotional and even economic and physical harm to people.[91]

In light of these characteristics, it is arguable that terms allowing for consumer debt collection are unfair contract terms. The authors recognise that this is a controversial position, and it would change the landscape of how consumer debts are collected. It is, however, one that is worthy of further consideration. If firms were prevented from referring consumer debts to debt collectors, they would have to consider the approach taken

[88] S Morris and D Thomas, 'Talks stall on shared Covid loan debt collector for UK banks' *Financial Times* (London, 7 February 2021) at www.ft.com/content/ca1c77e1-acc6-4500-b75a-4c0d16870312 (accessed 11 August 2021).

[89] This discussion is limited to debt collection of consumer contracts; the authors recognise that debt collection has a valid and important role in many other scenarios.

[90] It is recognised that there will be some consumers who refuse to pay outstanding amounts but who are not in financial difficulties. As outlined by the recent FCA research discussed above, these people will be in the minority. The service provider will still have significant legal rights to enforce payment of the outstanding amount against these parties and, as they are not financially struggling, it will be a much simpler process.

[91] J Montgomerie, 'Relief from Austerity: The Case for a Targeted Write-off of the UK's Household Debt Stock' in J Gardner, M Gray and K Moser (eds), *Debt and Austerity* (Cheltenham, Edward Elgar, 2020) 280, 286.

to outstanding accounts more broadly and flexibly. This could include processes such as payment holidays, repayment plans, downgrading services to more affordable levels and working closely with consumer welfare organisations, such as StepChange Debt Charity. Considering that debts are sold for such a small fraction of their face value, it is highly likely that these alternative processes will not be excessively financially detrimental to the service provider but will bring significant benefits for the indebted consumer.

IV. Conclusion and Recommendations

The workings of the law of assignment are arcane and convoluted. Though this chapter has engaged with prior work of one of the co-authors in the area, that work runs counter to other academics in the field in many respects. So although assignment is an essential tool of commerce, its workings remain contested and confused. If that be the case for legal experts, then pity the layperson consumer-debtor who has been notified that he must pay a stranger. In many of the instances we have examined, the notice originates from the debt collector, a stranger to the service contract. And even if such notice originates, on its face, from the service provider, is it *really* from them? In a world filled with payment scams and frauds, one can surely sympathise with the consumer-debtor.

In this situation it is entirely understandable that, when reminded that sums are due and outstanding, the consumer does not contest additional fees and charges (even if there may be no legal basis for charging these amounts) and immediately tenders payment to the service provider, and not the debt collector, for fear of incurring further late-payment and other charges. Or the consumer may not contest additional fees and charges added by the debt collector, even though adding these may not be mentioned in the contract or, if mentioned, may constitute an unfair contract term.

Over and beyond the confusing nature of the law, assignments of debts in the present context largely occur by standard-form contracts, with consumers having little, if any, opportunity to analyse their rights. And unfortunately, the nature of consumer debt means that we are generally dealing with vulnerable parties and small amounts of money. This means that questions as to whether such clauses fall foul of relevant consumer protection legislation and the unfair contract terms regime are likely to remain unanswered. These matters are unlikely to be litigated, and there is limited opportunity for case law to develop principles to address the issues discussed and/or clarify some of the uncertainties.

In light of the complexities associated with this area of commercial and consumer life, the authors believe that further research and analysis on the different rights and responsibilities of debt collectors are justified. To ensure that debtors can better understand the nature of their dealings with service providers, and the powers such service providers have reserved in connection with the debts that arise, some form of legislative intervention to standardise the terminology in use may be desirable. We therefore believe that the regulation of consumer debt collection, and the role of debt collectors as commercial law intermediaries, should be referred to the Law Commission for consideration.

15

Financial Wellbeing – The Missing Link in Financial Advice under Private Law and Statute

ANDREW GODWIN, WAI YEE WAN AND QINZHE YAO

I. Introduction

Consumers of financial products such as insurance or investment funds will often be introduced to such products by persons holding themselves out as 'financial advisers'. The term 'financial adviser', and variants of this term, is used worldwide for different classes of person – from persons directly associated with insurance companies who often market their products on an exclusive basis to truly independent professionals who make a living from providing independent and objective financial planning advice.

Financial advisers face significant regulation. Their advice can and does lead to major impacts on the lives of ordinary people, including the loss of their life savings at the extreme end. A global loss of trust in the financial industry has highlighted the role of financial advisers in consumer finance and the frequent conflicts of interests leading to consumer losses. Prompted by the 2008–09 Global Financial Crisis and a number of financial product mis-selling scandals, financial advisers have seen significantly increased regulation and reforms in their industry in recent years.

Such regulation has largely focused on a disclosure-based, process-centric model, with limited attention paid to outcomes. The authors suggest that this approach has achieved all it could possibly achieve. The existing model does not, however, promote financial wellbeing at its heart, and presents significant challenges to individual consumers as they seek to navigate the complicated world of finance despite having the support of an 'adviser'. The increased regulation has also resulted in a significant downsizing of the financial advice profession in Australia and other jurisdictions.

This chapter argues that a return to an outcomes-focused model of regulation is necessary to ensure that the financial adviser industry serves its purpose of providing quality financial advice to the individual consumer or household (as the case may be).[1] The desired outcome is that the consumer is better off, not in the sense that they are wealthier, but in the sense that they receive advice that is appropriate for them and consistent with their financial wellbeing. In order to provide such advice, financial advisers must consider the requirements of the individual customer or household, not by way of checklists or 'safe harbours' but through a systematic 'financial wellbeing framework'.

The concept of financial wellbeing is introduced in section II, which explores how the concept has been adopted by policy-makers and financial institutions. Section III outlines the nature and effect of the 'best interests' duty in private law and statute, and the extent to which it has involved a traditional focus on process and not outcomes. Section IV outlines the trend in jurisdictions such as the United Kingdom towards adopting an outcomes-focused model of regulation and its limitations to date from the perspective of financial wellbeing. Section V examines whether the existing regulatory framework in Australia accommodates financial wellbeing and considers how financial wellbeing might be incorporated into that framework. Through exploring these issues, the authors hope to demonstrate how the incorporation of financial wellbeing into the regulatory framework for financial services is necessary in order to restore trust, increase the professionalism of the financial advice sector and promote positive consumer outcomes.

II. The Concept of Financial Wellbeing

It is widely accepted that there is a causal interrelationship between financial wellbeing and mental/physical health wellbeing. In other words, financial stress leads to mental and physical stress and vice versa.[2] Accordingly, financial wellbeing is increasingly recognised by policy-makers as an integral part of the wellbeing of members of society generally.

The concept of financial wellbeing, however, is not amenable to an easy definition. In part, this is due to the fact that a determination of a person's financial wellbeing inevitably involves a subjective assessment by the person themselves. Although various objective measures can be adopted to determine financial wellbeing, such as the levels of debt and savings, it is necessary to recognise that a person's financial wellbeing is a state or situation that is subjectively perceived or experienced. Indeed, it has been noted that 'two people with objectively similar financial situations may report markedly different assessments of their financial wellbeing'.[3]

[1] By 'household', the authors refer to a unit of persons who manage their finances together to some extent. This can range from cohabiting couples in a relationship to wealthy, multi-generational extended families with significant family assets.

[2] C Breidbach et al, *FinFuture: The Future of Personal Finance in Australia* (Melbourne, The University of Melbourne, 2019) (hereinafter 'FinFuture White Paper') 18.

[3] ibid 22. The FinFuture White Paper notes that 'observed (objective) and reported (subjective) financial wellbeing differ significantly between Australians': ibid 22, citing J Haisek-DeNew et al, *Using Survey and Banking Data to Understand Australians' Financial Wellbeing: Financial Wellbeing Scales Technical Report No 2* (Melbourne, Commonwealth Bank of Australia and Melbourne Institute, 2018).

In addition, it is important to recognise that the concept of financial wellbeing is dynamic and temporal in nature; in other words, it is likely to change over time as a result of a range of factors, including 'the death of a partner, fluctuations in the economy or even as a result of subtle changes in an individual's attitudes and beliefs'.[4]

Despite the challenges associated with defining financial wellbeing, most definitions share common elements, including the ability of a person 'to meet current commitments comfortably and [to] have the financial resilience to maintain this into the future'.[5] For the purposes of our analysis, a useful working definition is that adopted by the Commonwealth Bank of Australia (CBA) as follows:

> [Financial wellbeing is] the extent to which people both perceive and have: (1) financial outcomes in which they meet their financial needs; (2) financial freedom to make choices that allow them to enjoy life; (3) control of their finances; and (4) financial security – now, in the future, and under possible adverse circumstances.[6]

The Bank states that 'financial wellbeing is a state that is best described in degrees or extents, rather than with absolute values or as an "either/or" condition'.[7] It further refers colloquially to the concept of financial wellbeing as having three dimensions in terms of meeting financial situations; namely, 'every day, rainy day, one day':

> 'Every day' financial situations: how well people are meeting their immediate needs, such as mortgage or rent and utilities payments.
>
> 'Rainy day' financial situations: how well prepared people are to deal with unexpected, adverse events such as illness or job loss.
>
> 'One day' financial situations: how well people can achieve long-term goals such as buying an auto-home or a comfortable retirement.[8]

The working definition of financial wellbeing posited by CBA above incorporates both a subjective ('perceive') test and an objective ('have') test and is broadly designed around four elements: financial needs; financial freedom; control over finances; and financial security.

Of these four elements, perhaps the most nebulous is 'financial security' as it requires consideration of both the present and the future.[9] Accordingly, it appears broad enough

[4] FinFuture White Paper (n 2).

[5] ANZ, 'What is financial wellbeing?' at www.anz.com.au/personal/financial-wellbeing/ (accessed 10 March 2022).

[6] CBA, *Improving the Financial Wellbeing of Australians – Toward better outcomes for Australians ... every day, rainy day, one day* (April 2019) 13. See also FinFuture White Paper (n 2) 22. See also ANZ Survey 2018 at www.anz.com/resources/2/f/2f348500-38a2-4cfe-8411-060cb753573d/financial-wellbeing-aus18.pdf.

[7] CBA (n 6) 13.

[8] ibid. Similar elements were identified in a document prepared by the Financial Advice Working Group for HM Treasury and the Financial Conduct Authority in the United Kingdom, entitled *Rules of Thumb and Nudges: Improving the financial wellbeing of UK consumers* (March 2017). This document proposes the following 'Financial Five' rules of thumb, which are designed to help people meet their most common financial needs: '1. Clean up your finances regularly 2. Manage your borrowing, don't let your borrowing manage you 3. Save when you can – even a little helps a lot 4. Pile into your pension – it's your future income 5. Other people get help to make the most of their money, so can you.'

[9] The FinFuture White Paper (n 2) 22 notes that 'In a Norwegian study, considerations regarding long-term financial security were deemed secondary to three core elements of financial wellbeing: financial resilience, ability to meet financial commitments and comfort. This was explained in terms of Norway's world-leading retirement provisions.'

to cover or affect all of these four elements and the three financial situations captured by CBA's 'every day, rainy day, one day' formulation. One financial services firm has suggested that financial security 'encompasses the ability to have income stable enough to cover your expenses and to cover financial emergencies and future goals'.[10]

Despite the challenges of defining financial wellbeing, it is increasingly being incorporated into the discourse of financial institutions and industry associations in policy statements and codes. Indeed, the Chief Executive Officer of CBA, Matt Comyn, has stated that the purpose at CBA is to 'improve the financial wellbeing of our customers and communities'.[11]

Further, although not a substantive part of the Australian Banking Association *Banking Code of Practice*, the concept is referred to by Anna Bligh, its Chief Executive Officer, in her opening statement as follows:

> The new Banking Code of Practice sets a new standard of customer service for Australia's banks. The new Code is part of a significant reform agenda to improve banking services to better meet community standards and expectations. Australians, along with businesses large and small, entrust their *financial security and wellbeing* to one or more of the banks who are signatory to this Code …[12]

The concept of financial wellbeing is sometimes expressed in other terms, including 'financial health', 'financial resilience', 'financial fitness' or an absence of 'financial stress'. The concept has also been the subject of policy at the government level in Australia, with the Federal Government supporting vulnerable individuals and families through the Financial Wellbeing and Capability Activity framework. Services that are available under the framework include crisis support, financial counselling and access to micro-finance products. According to the website, this framework

> supports eligible individuals and families to navigate financial crises and build financial wellbeing, financial capability, and resilience. These activities help vulnerable people and those most at risk of financial and social exclusion and disadvantage.[13]

It is relevant to note that the Government has expressly mentioned the need for this policy to be 'based on a firm legislative footing',[14] highlighting the relevance of incorporating the concept of financial wellbeing into the regulatory framework.

[10] See Invest Blue,' What does it mean to be financially secure?' (4 August 2020) at www.investblue.com.au/knowledge-centre/insights-news/finance/what-does-it-mean-to-be-financially-secure (accessed 10 March 2022).

[11] CBA (n 6) 2.

[12] Australian Banking Association, *Banking Code of Practice* (1 March 2020 revision) 3 at www.ausbanking.org.au/wp-content/uploads/2021/02/2021-Code-A4-Booklet-with-COVID-19-Special-Note-Web.pdf (accessed 10 March 2022) (emphasis added). See also Customer Owned Banking Association, *Customer Owned Banking Code of Practice* (January 2018) at www.customerownedbanking.asn.au/how-it-works/code-of-practice, 1: 'Our Code is an important public expression of the value we place on improving the financial wellbeing of our individual members and their communities.'

[13] Department of Social Services, 'Frequently Asked Questions: Changes to the Financial Wellbeing and Capability (FWC) Activity' at www.dss.gov.au/communities-and-vulnerable-people-programs-services-financial-wellbeing-and-capability/frequently-asked-questions-changes-to-the-financial-wellbeing-and-capability-activity (accessed 10 March 2022).

[14] See Australian Government, Department of Social Services, 'Communities and Vulnerable People' at www.dss.gov.au/communities-and-vulnerable-people/programmes-services/financial-wellbeing-and-capability (accessed 10 March 2022). See also the Financial Capability website managed by the Australian Treasury at www.financialcapability.gov.au/ (accessed 10 March 2022).

The concept is also embraced by the corporate and financial services regulator, the Australian Securities and Investments Commission (ASIC), on its Moneysmart website, which aims to 'help Australians take control of their money and build a better life with free tools, tips and guidance'. The website recognises that '[m]aking informed decisions leads to greater financial wellbeing'.[15]

Given its importance to the wellbeing of members of society generally, it is relevant to consider the extent to which the concept of financial wellbeing should extend beyond the policy and soft law domain to the regulatory and 'hard law' domain, particularly as it relates to financial advice. As the authors argue in section V, the existing regulatory framework in Australia governing financial advisers focuses on process over outcomes and is tied to objective standards that are very difficult to apply in practice. The authors argue that incorporating financial wellbeing into the regulatory framework in Australia would be advantageous for two reasons. First, it would give substance to, and assist to operationalise, the existing duties of financial advisers under private law and statute, such as the 'best interests' duty and the obligation to provide advice that is appropriate to the client. This is because it would enable advice to be tailored to individuals and households by reference to their own financial wellbeing. Second, the inclusion of financial wellbeing as an integral factor in obtaining and providing financial advice would enable consumers to make financial decisions on an informed basis and to assume an appropriate level of responsibility for the financial decisions that they make. The concept of financial wellbeing would, accordingly, act as a yardstick against which the appropriateness of financial advice and the satisfaction of the 'best interests' obligation could be measured.

It might be argued that incorporating financial wellbeing into the regulatory framework overlooks the difficulties of prescribing good financial outcomes and the element of risk-taking that is inherent in many financial decisions. Accordingly, it overlooks the reality that in order to generate a return or benefit from their investments or borrowings (in the case of credit), some consumers are willing to assume a higher degree of risk than might be considered optimal by reference to their own financial wellbeing, whether measured objectively or subjectively. In these circumstances, it might be argued, financial wellbeing is irrelevant because the impact of the financial decision on financial wellbeing is just as likely to be negative as positive. The authors argue, however, that consumers still need to determine and assess the nature and extent of financial risks on an informed basis, and that the concept of financial wellbeing (incorporating the concept of financial security) would act as a yardstick against which financial risks could be properly measured.

In its Regulatory Guide 175, ASIC states that 'when assessing whether an advice provider has complied with the best interests duty, [ASIC] will consider whether a reasonable advice provider would believe that the client is likely to be in a better position if the client follows the advice'.[16] Further, one of the factors that ASIC will take into account in assessing whether an advice provider has complied with the best interests

[15] ASIC, Moneysmart website at moneysmart.gov.au/about-us (accessed 10 March 2022).

[16] ASIC, Licensing: Financial product advisers – Conduct and disclosure (Regulatory Guide 175, November 2017) 175.245 and 175.246 at asic.gov.au/regulatory-resources/find-a-document/regulatory-guides/rg-175-licensing-financial-product-advisers-conduct-and-disclosure/ (accessed 10 March 2022).

duty is 'aligning their [clients'] financial position with their appetite for risk'.[17] It is submitted that the concept of financial wellbeing can act as a yardstick in determining whether a client is likely to be in a better position by following the advice and in aligning the client's financial position with their risk appetite. Indeed, it is difficult to understand how such a determination could be made other than through a consideration of financial wellbeing.

III. The Traditional Focus in Private Law and Statute on Process Over Outcomes

In Australia, the traditional focus of the legal and regulatory framework governing the provision of financial services has been on the *conduct* of the providers of those services and the *process* for complying with the relevant conduct obligations. Relatively little attention has been paid to the *outcomes* from the perspective of consumers. To date, the belief has been that complying with the right process will lead to the right outcomes. The focus on conduct and process can be attributed in part to the difficulties in identifying, and prescribing requirements in respect of, outcomes, as noted in section II.

Under the relevant legislation in Australia, a core obligation to which financial advisers are subject in the provision of personal advice is to 'act in the best interests of the client in relation to the advice'.[18] The imposition of a statutory 'best interests' duty was the subject of debate when it was introduced following the *Future of Financial Advice* (FOFA) reforms in 2012.[19] These reforms sought to 'improve the quality of financial advice while building trust and confidence in the financial advice industry through enhanced standards which align the interests of the adviser with the client and reduce conflicts of interest',[20] as a result of the collapse in trust in the banking sector. This regime is administered by ASIC, which issues licences to financial services providers. One of the questions that continues to be debated in respect of the section imposing the 'best interests' obligation is 'whether the section imports an obligation to act in the best interests of the client [that] in substance replicates the best interests obligation found in equity'.[21]

The 'best interests' duty in equity has often been considered synonymous with a fiduciary relationship, which arises between two persons when one person is 'entitled to expect that the other will act in [the first person's] interests in and for the purposes of the relationship'.[22] It has been noted, however, that 'the general equitable duty to act in

[17] ibid.

[18] Corporations Act 2001 (Cth), s 961B(1).

[19] These reforms were introduced by the Corporations Amendment (Future of Financial Advice) Act 2012 and the Corporations Amendment (Further Future of Financial Advice Measures) Act 2012.

[20] Corporations Amendment (Further Future of Financial Advice Measures) Bill 2012, Revised Explanatory Memorandum, 3.

[21] S Degeling and J Hudson, 'Fiduciary Obligations, Financial Advisers and FOFA' (2014) 32(8) *Company and Securities Law Journal* 527, 538, fn 67.

[22] ibid, citing P Finn 'Fiduciary Reflections' (2014) 88 *ALJ* 127, 137. Degeling and Hudson (n 21) 531 note that '[f]iduciary scholars and judges do not agree exactly when and why a fiduciary relationship arises' (citations excluded). See also S Walpole, MS Donald and RT Langford, 'Regulating for Loyalty in the Financial Services Industry' (2021) 38(5) *Company and Securities Law Journal* 355, 356: 'Precisely which combination

good faith in the best interest of the principal is not properly to be understood as a true fiduciary duty [and that] "while some fiduciaries owe a duty to act in the best interests of their principals, that is not itself a fiduciary duty"'.[23]

Although the question of whether the statutory formulation in Australia replicates the best interests duty in equity remains an open question, there is case law in support of this proposition.[24] Hanrahan has noted that '[t]he policy intention behind the new Div 2 Pt 7.7A appears, initially at least, to have been to incorporate elements of the equitable "best interests" concept … into the law governing the provision of personal advice to retail clients' but that

> [a]s drafted, the statutory best interest provision is a long way from what equity understands the 'best interest' concept to mean … The statutory best interest obligation is expressed as a series of steps to be taken, not as an obligation to prefer the client's interests over the firm's or to avoid the situations of conflict or collateral advantage that fiduciary law proscribes.[25]

One point on which there appears to be general consensus, however, is that irrespective of whether the issue is considered from the perspective of private law or statute, the best interests duty is not about achieving the best outcomes. This has been argued by reference to the anomalies that would arise from a literal interpretation of the best interests duty.[26] Courts in Australia, in relation to the various statutory formulations of the 'best interests' duty, have also accepted that it is not about achieving the best outcomes. In the context of managed investment schemes, for example, the High Court has held that the 'best interests' duty

> is a duty to act in the best interests of the members rather than a duty to secure the best outcome for members. Key factors in ascertaining the best interests of the members are the purpose and terms of the scheme, rather than 'the success or otherwise of a transaction or other course of action'.[27]

of circumstances is required to justify the imposition of fiduciary obligations "on the facts" remains a matter of both curial discussion and academic debate', citing JD Heydon, MJ Leeming and PG Turner, *Meagher, Gummow and Lehane's Equity Doctrines and Remedies*, 5th edn (Chatswood, NSW, LexisNexis Butterworths, 2015) [5-005].

[23] Degeling and Hudson (n 21), fn 67, citing M Conaglen, *Fiduciary Loyalty* (Oxford, Hart Publishing, 2010) 57.

[24] For a discussion of the case law and relevant issues, see Walpole et al (n 22) 357–58.

[25] PF Hanrahan, 'The relationship between equitable and statutory "best interests" obligations in financial services law' (2013) 7 *Journal of Equity* 46. Hanrahan (ibid 73) goes on to note that 'Where both the equitable and statutory obligations apply, the statutory duties do not displace the equitable principles. The equitable principles may well impose different (and more onerous) obligations on financial services firms than the statutory duties; and the kinds of remedies available to clients and the identity of those against whom those remedies may lie are different.'

[26] D Pollard, 'The Shortform "Best Interests Duty": Mad, Bad and Dangerous to Know' (2018) 32(2) *Trust Law International* 106, 176. Pollard continues (ibid 191): 'A literal "best interests" duty would impose an objective standard requiring the trustee or company board to make a decision that had an outcome which, it objectively turns out (in retrospect), to have been in the best interests of the trust or company or beneficiaries. This would clearly impose too great a standard on trustees and directors. It would be fundamentally in conflict with the usual business judgment test.'

[27] *Australian Securities and Investments Commission v Lewski* (2018) 266 CLR 173 [71]; [2018] HCA 63 (citations omitted), as referred to in Walpole et al (n 22) 362; *Australian Securities and Investments Commission v Australian Property Custodian Holdings Limited (Receivers and Managers appointed) (in liquidation) (Controllers appointed) (No 3)* [2013] FCA 1342 [488] (Murphy J): 'I do not though wish to be seen as accepting the proposition that to act in the members' best interests a trustee must actually achieve the best outcome.' See also K Lindgren, 'Fiduciary Duty and the Ripoll Report' (2010) 28(7) *Company and Securities Law Journal* 435, 441–42.

In the context of the statutory provision under section 961B of the Corporations Act 2001 (Cth) (Corporations Act) that imposes a 'best interests' obligation on financial advisers who provide personal advice, it has been noted that '[c]ourts have generally held that s 961B relates to the "process or procedure", whereas s 961G[28] is concerned with the "substance" of the advice'.[29]

The position as outlined above is consistent with the explanatory memorandum in respect of the legislation enacting the 'best interests' duty in Chapter 7 of the Corporations Act, which stated that

> [t]here are steps that providers may prove they have taken to demonstrate that they have acted in the best interests of the client. These steps recognise that the requirement to act in a client's best interests is intended to be about the process of providing advice, reflecting the notion that good processes will improve the quality of the advice provided. The provision is not about justifying the quality of the advice by retrospective testing against financial outcomes.[30]

Although it would be unrealistic and naive to justify the quality of financial advice by retrospective testing against financial outcomes, it is submitted that the stated focus on 'the process of providing advice' is too narrow if it does not incorporate financial wellbeing as a factor in the provision of advice by financial advisers and also in financial decision-making by consumers. Even if the existing legislative framework were wide enough to incorporate consideration of financial wellbeing, which is examined in section V of this chapter, the express inclusion of financial wellbeing would help to direct attention towards outcomes and would enable consumers to make financial decisions on an informed basis. As argued in section II, the concept of financial wellbeing can act as a yardstick in determining whether a client is likely to be in a better position by following the advice and in aligning the client's financial position with their risk appetite. This is particularly relevant in the context of advice on complex financial products and in circumstances involving vulnerable consumers, as section V.D will discuss further.

IV. The Trend Towards an Outcomes-Focused Model of Regulation

In the United Kingdom, a principles-based, outcome-focused framework has been adopted in the financial services legislation – one that is supported by regulatory guidance.[31] The Financial Conduct Authority (FCA) *Handbook* defines principles as

[28] Section 961G provides that the advice must be appropriate to the client.

[29] Walpole et al (n 22) 363, citing *Australian Securities and Investments Commission v Westpac Securities Administration Ltd* (2019) 272 FCR 170 [294]–[301] (Jagot J), [405] (O'Bryan J); *Australian Securities and Investments Commission v Westpac Banking Corporation* [2019] FCA 2147 ('*Westpac Banking Corporation*') [14] (Wigney J); *Australian Securities and Investments Commission v Financial Circle Pty Ltd* (2018) 131 ACSR 484 [129] (O'Callaghan J); *Australian Securities and Investments Commission v NSG Services Pty Ltd* (2017) 122 ACSR 47 [21] (Moshinsky J); cf *Australian Securities and Investments Commission v Westpac Securities Administration Ltd* (2019) 272 FCR 170 [151] (Allsop CJ); *McDonald v AMP Financial Planning Pty Ltd* (2018) 129 ACSR 605 [48] (Douglas J).

[30] Replacement Explanatory Memorandum Corporations Amendment (Further Future of Financial Advice Measures) Bill 2011 (Cth) [1.23].

[31] See Financial Services and Markets Act 2000 (UK). See also the FCA approach to consumers: 'Our regulation is outcomes-focused and is based on a combination of the Principles, other high-level rules and,

'high level statements of the core obligations of firms, [which] act as an overarching framework to govern the actions of firms'. It provides that a 'breach of one or more of the Principles for Businesses will make a firm liable to disciplinary action' and, '[w]here appropriate, a firm can be disciplined on the basis of a breach of the Principles alone'.[32]

The FCA *Handbook* defines outcomes as '[setting] the baseline of our expectations of how firms should treat consumers and … [providing] the basis of what consumers can expect to see when firms are treating them fairly'.[33] An example of the combination of principles, outcomes and regulatory guidance in the context of financial advice is as follows:

> **Principle**
>
> Customers: relationships of trust – a firm must take reasonable care to ensure the suitability of its advice and discretionary decisions for any customer who is entitled to rely upon its judgment.[34]
>
> **Outcome**
>
> Where consumers receive advice, the advice is suitable and takes account of their circumstances.[35]
>
> **Guidance for firms**
>
> We expect firms to pay attention to indicators of potential vulnerability when they arise and to have policies in place to deal with consumers who may be at greater risk of harm.[36]

The outcome that 'advice is suitable and takes account of their circumstances' is logical. It does not explain, however, how to determine the suitability of advice and whether it takes account of the consumer's circumstances. Accordingly, there is a need to consider how this expectation should be operationalised. The 'Consumer Duty', on which the UK FCA issued a Consultation Paper in 2021, is likely in part to be a response to this need. The Consultation Paper states that the FCA is

> proposing to introduce a new 'Consumer Duty', that would set higher expectations for the standard of care that firms provide to consumers. For many firms, this would require a significant shift in culture and behaviour, where they consistently focus on consumer outcomes, and put customers in a position where they can act and make decisions in their interests.[37]

According to the Consultation Paper, the proposed Consumer Duty would require firms to ask themselves what outcomes consumers should be able to expect from their

where necessary, detailed rules and guidance' 12–13 at www.fca.org.uk/publication/corporate/approach-to-consumers.pdf (accessed 10 March 2022); FinFuture White Paper (n 2) 32–34.

[32] FCA approach to consumers (n 31) 13.

[33] ibid. For a general discussion of outcomes-based regulation, see New South Wales Department of Finance, Services and Innovation, *Guidance for regulators to implement outcomes and risk-based regulation* (2016) 8, [2.1]: 'Regulatory outcomes that are clearly defined and achievable are critical to effective outcomes and risk-based regulation. It requires regulators to consider: their legislative mandate; their core purpose to regulated entities, regulation beneficiaries, and the broader strategic context; and the options available to implement regulatory initiatives'.

[34] *Financial Conduct Authority Handbook of Rules and Guidance* (hereinafter *FCA Handbook*) Principle 9 at www.handbook.fca.org.uk/handbook (accessed 10 March 2022).

[35] ibid, Outcome 4.

[36] ibid 25.

[37] FCA, Consultation Paper CP21/13: A New Consumer Duty (May 2021) [1.1].

products and services; act to enable rather than hinder these outcomes; and assess the effectiveness of their actions.[38] The proposed duty would have three elements: (i) a consumer principle; (ii) cross-cutting rules; and (iii) four outcomes.[39] View were sought on two options for the consumer principle:

> Option 1: 'A firm must act to deliver good outcomes for retail clients'
>
> Option 2: 'A firm must act in the best interests of retail clients'[40]

The Consultation Paper makes reference to the concept of financial wellbeing in the following paragraphs:

> 1.14 In summary, we want all firms to be putting consumers at the heart of their businesses, offering products and services that are fit for purpose and which they know represent fair value. We want financial services markets to be consistently effective in supporting the lives of consumers across the UK. Products, services, communications and engagement from firms should instil trust, enabling consumers to make effective and confident choices to advance their *financial wellbeing* and build positive futures for themselves and their families. [emphasis added]
>
> 2.12 To achieve good outcomes and support their *financial wellbeing*, consumers need to be able to trust that the range of products and services they choose from are designed to meet their needs, and offer fair value. They need help to understand products and services, and they need confidence that firms will act in a way that helps, rather than hinders, their ability to make decisions in line with their needs and financial objectives. [emphasis added]
>
> 3.31 The Four Outcomes represent the key elements of the firm-consumer relationship: how firms design, sell and service products and services, and the key contact points along the customer journey. The behaviour and actions of firms for each of these outcomes are instrumental in enabling consumers to meet their financial needs. If done right, they can be drivers of improved *financial wellbeing* … [emphasis added]

Given that improved financial wellbeing is recognised in the Consultation Paper as an objective of the financial services markets in the United Kingdom, it is relevant to consider whether this concept should be incorporated into the regulatory framework and, if so, how this might be done. Otherwise, it is likely that the potential benefits that arise from the proposed reform will be limited. A statutory solution is likely to be necessary for the reason that falling back on private law duties such as the 'duty of care' and 'fiduciary duty' is likely to be ineffective, as noted by Chiu and Brener.[41] Section V examines this issue in the context of the regulatory framework in Australia.

[38] ibid [1.2].

[39] The consumer principle would '[set] a clear tone and [use] language that reflects the overall standards of behaviour we want from firms'. The cross-cutting rules would 'develop our overarching expectations for common themes that apply across all areas of firm conduct'. The four outcomes would '[represent] the key elements of the firm-consumer relationship'. The four outcomes would be 'Communications; Products and Services; Customer Service; and Price and Value': ibid [3.2].

[40] ibid [3.12].

[41] Centre for Ethics and Law at UCL, Response to the FCA's Consultation Paper 21/13 A new Consumer Duty (June 2021) 4 at www.ucl.ac.uk/ethics-law/sites/ethics-law/files/cel_response_to_fcas_consumer_duty_consultation.pdf (accessed 10 March 2022). Chiu and Brener further note (ibid 11) that 'the common law duty of care is nowadays raised in private litigation largely as a fall-back if claimants are not able to benefit from the protection of existing regulatory duties'. See also I Chiu and A Brener, 'Changing Financial Services Firms' Behaviour through a Duty of Care' (2018) 3(1) *Journal of Financial Compliance* 67.

V. Incorporating Financial Wellbeing into the Regulatory Framework

A. The Statutory 'Best Interests' Obligation

Australia serves as a useful case study for assessing the extent to which the concept of financial wellbeing is reflected in, or missing from, the current regulatory framework.

Australia enacted legislative amendments to the Corporations Act in 2012 through the FOFA reforms.[42] These reforms sought to 'improve the quality of financial advice while building trust and confidence in the financial advice industry through enhanced standards which align the interests of the adviser with the client and reduce conflicts of interest'.[43] This regime is administered by ASIC, which issues licences to financial services providers.

The core of these reforms is a 'best interests' obligation imposed on financial advisers. This obligation requires a financial adviser to 'act in the best interests of the client in relation to the advice'.[44] Curiously, this obligation is left undefined. However, a financial adviser is deemed to have complied with this duty if it has satisfied a number of factors, for example identifying the needs of the client that were communicated by that client[45] and making reasonable inquiries where it is reasonably apparent that client information is incomplete.[46] These factors are a 'safe harbour' for an adviser facing accusations of a breach of the best interests duty.[47] Coupled with this is an 'appropriate advice duty', requiring financial advisers to provide advice it is reasonable to conclude is appropriate to that client.[48]

A number of other provisions require financial advisers to prioritise their client's interests in the event of any conflict of interest,[49] and impose liability on financial service licensees who have not adequately ensured that their authorised representatives discharge these duties.

The Australian reforms were perhaps some of the most aggressive interventions worldwide following the Global Financial Crisis of 2008–09. Australia was one of the first jurisdictions to impose a 'best interests' duty on financial advisers. However, it does not appear to have worked as envisioned.

This 'best interests' duty, on its face, provides that financial advisers must act in the best interests of a person. However, it has been interpreted in case law as focusing on procedure instead of substance:

> [S]upport for this way of viewing the focus of s 961B is provided by the context in which it appears, including the language of s 961G, the legislative history, and the legislative materials

[42] See n 20.
[43] Corporations Amendment (Further Future of Financial Advice Measures) Bill 2012, Revised Explanatory Memorandum, 3.
[44] Corporations Act 2001 (Cth), s 961B(1).
[45] ibid s 961B(2)(a).
[46] ibid s 961B(2)(c).
[47] *Australian Securities and Investments Commission, in the matter of NSG Services Pty Ltd v NSG Services Pty Ltd* [2017] FCA 345 (hereinafter 'NSG Case').
[48] Corporations Act 2001 (Cth), s 961G.
[49] ibid s 961J.

> (see, in particular, the revised explanatory memorandum to the Corporations Amendment … It is unnecessary for present purposes to reach a concluded view on this issue.[50]

It appears that industry also treats the 'best interests' obligation in this way. The Final Report of the Royal Commission into Misconduct in the Banking, Superannuation and Financial Services Industry (the 'Financial Services Royal Commission'), released on 1 February 2019, considered the impact of the FOFA reforms on the industry. It agreed that process was emphasised in the treatment of this duty, and that in general no comparisons or evaluations were made as to what the best interests of the client were. As stated by the Final Report:

> In practice this requires the adviser to make little or no independent inquiry into, or assessment of, products. Instead, in most cases, advisers and licensees act on the basis that the obligation to conduct a reasonable investigation is met by choosing a product from the licensee's 'approved products list'.[51]

The Financial Services Royal Commission also found that in a very significant number of cases, even as the law stood, the best interests duty had not been complied with in substance. It was often the case that the adviser had prioritised their personal interests instead – recommending unnecessary products or an in-house product rather than making a proper review of suitable products.[52] It recommended that the safe harbour provision be repealed at some point in the future, though not necessarily immediately.[53]

Leaving the substantive breaches of this provision aside, the best interests duty did not appear to have an effect on how financial advisers actually operated. The FinFuture White Paper describes it as a 'tick-the-box approach to compliance'.[54] Financial advisers appear to have treated this duty as a compliance exercise as opposed to its purpose – to provide added value to the consumer. Statements from regulators have not helped: in the NSG Case, ASIC reinforced this approach in its submission that

> in a 'real world' practical sense, s 961B(2) (ie the safe harbour provision) was likely to cover all the ways of showing that a person had complied with s 961B(1) and, in this way, a failure to satisfy one or more of the limbs of s 961B(2) is highly relevant to the Court's assessment of compliance with the best interests duty.[55]

Australia faces issues with quality of advice, particularly affordable quality advice, and a review of the quality of financial advice will be undertaken by Treasury in 2022.[56] In terms of the quality of advice, ASIC has identified issues with the delivery of scaled or limited-scope advice; namely, advice provided for a particular transaction or issue as distinct from comprehensive advice. Australian consumers report that they believe that financial advice is too expensive for them to afford, resulting in their choosing not

[50] NSG Case (n 47) at 21 (Moshinsky J).
[51] Financial Services Royal Commission, *Final Report* 3.1.1.
[52] ibid, 3.1.2.
[53] ibid, 3.2.4.
[54] FinFuture White Paper (n 2) 32.
[55] NSG Case (n 47) [18].
[56] See Senator The Hon Jane Hume, 'Address to the 12th Annual Financial Services Council's Life Insurance Summit 2021' (21 April 2021).

to engage financial advisers.[57] Although the absolute cost of advice is relevant, with consumer research suggesting that '[m]ost consumers do not want to pay more than $500 for comprehensive, face-to-face advice',[58] research suggests that many consumers do not believe that financial advice is worth the cost.[59] Robo-advice should logically provide a cost-effective alternative, particularly for lower-income consumers, but it has had limited uptake to date.[60]

In addition, the industry has seen significant downsizing in recent years.[61] Around 13 per cent per year of licensed individuals have chosen to leave instead of trying to make do with the new model of financial advice, and financial adviser numbers in the big four Australian banks have shrunk from 4,690 in 2015 to 1,161 in 2020.[62] It is estimated that only AUD $962 billion out of potentially AUD $6.6 trillion investable assets are the subject of financial advice.[63]

If combined with measures to increase financial literacy, the adoption of a financial wellbeing approach is likely to make consumers more aware of the positive outcomes that the regulatory framework is seeking to support, and might encourage them to obtain financial advice. In turn, this is likely to strengthen demand for financial advice and increase tolerance for the costs involved.

B. Outline of the Regulatory Framework in Australia

The framework in respect of financial advice is informed by the general statutory object or purpose, which is to promote:

(a) confident and informed decision making by consumers of financial products and services while facilitating efficiency, flexibility and innovation in the provision of those products and services; and
(aa) the provision of suitable financial products to consumers of financial products; and
(b) fairness, honesty and professionalism by those who provide financial services; and
(c) fair, orderly and transparent markets for financial products; and
(d) the reduction of systemic risk and the provision of fair and effective services by clearing and settlement facilities.[64]

Under the regulatory framework, 'financial product advice' is a subset of the definition of financial service,[65] and is a licensed activity to the extent that such advice is provided in

[57] ASIC, *Promoting access to affordable advice for consumers* (Consultation Paper 332, November 2020) at asic.gov.au/media/5853864/cp332-published-17-november-2020.pdf (accessed 10 March 2022).

[58] R Warner, *Future of Advice* (Report commissioned by the Financial Services Council, 6 August 2020) 11, [2.6.1] at www.ricewarner.com/wp-content/uploads/2020/10/RW-Future-of-Advice-Report.pdf (accessed 10 March 2022).

[59] ASIC, *Financial advice: what consumers really think* (Report 627, August 2019) 31, [80] at download.asic.gov.au/media/5243978/rep627-published-26-august-2019.pdf (accessed 10 March 2022).

[60] See Warner (n 58) [2.4.5]; ASIC (n 59) [51].

[61] Intheblack, 'What's the future for financial services' (1 March 2021) at www.intheblack.com/articles/2021/03/01/future-financial-services (accessed 10 March 2022).

[62] A Sandhu, M Stewart and R Gollakota, *Future of Financial Advice* (Oliver Wyman, 2021) at www.oliverwyman.com/content/dam/oliver-wyman/v2/publications/2021/jan/future-of-financial-advice.pdf (accessed 10 March 2022).

[63] ibid 6.

[64] Corporations Act 2001 (Cth), s 760A.

[65] ibid s 766A(1)(a).

the course of a business. Two types of financial product advice are recognised: personal advice and general advice. This distinction is significant because rigorous conduct and disclosure obligations are triggered in circumstances involving the provision of personal advice, together with the 'best interests' obligation.[66]

An outline of the regulatory framework in Australia that is applicable to personal advice is set out below:

1. A financial adviser must be authorised under an Australian financial services (AFS) licence to provide financial product advice.
2. The term 'financial product advice' is subject to both a subjective and objective test and is defined to mean –

   a recommendation or a statement of opinion, or a report of either of those things, that:

   (a) is intended to influence a person or persons in making a decision in relation to a particular financial product or class of financial products, or an interest in a particular financial product or class of financial products; or
   (b) could reasonably be regarded as being intended to have such an influence.[67]

3. The term 'personal advice' is also subject to both a subjective and objective test and, subject to various exclusions and qualifications, is defined to mean –

   financial product advice that is given or directed to a person (including by electronic means) in circumstances where:

   (a) the provider of the advice has considered one or more of the person's objectives, financial situation and needs (otherwise than for the purposes of compliance with the *Anti-Money Laundering and Counter-Terrorism Financing Act 2006* or with regulations, or AML/CFT Rules, under that Act); or
   (b) a reasonable person might expect the provider to have considered one or more of those matters.[68]

4. A financial adviser must act in the best interests of the client in relation to the advice.[69]
5. A financial adviser enjoys a 'safe harbour', under which the financial adviser will satisfy the duty to act in the best interests of the client if the financial adviser has done each of the following:

   (a) identified the objectives, financial situation and needs of the client that were disclosed to the provider by the client through instructions;
   (b) identified:
      (i) the subject matter of the advice that has been sought by the client (whether explicitly or implicitly); and
      (ii) the objectives, financial situation and needs of the client that would reasonably be considered as relevant to advice sought on that subject matter (the *client's relevant circumstances*);

[66] For a discussion of the differences between the requirements in respect of personal advice and general advice, see *Westpac Securities Administration Ltd v Australian Securities and Investments Commission* [2021] HCA 3 [37]–[40] (Gordon J).
[67] Corporations Act 2001 (Cth), s 766B(1).
[68] ibid s 766B(3).
[69] ibid s 961B(1).

(c) where it was reasonably apparent that information relating to the client's relevant circumstances was incomplete or inaccurate, made reasonable inquiries to obtain complete and accurate information;
(d) assessed whether the provider has the expertise required to provide the client advice on the subject matter sought and, if not, declined to provide the advice;
(e) if, in considering the subject matter of the advice sought, it would be reasonable to consider recommending a financial product:
   (i) conducted a reasonable investigation into the financial products that might achieve those of the objectives and meet those of the needs of the client that would reasonably be considered as relevant to advice on that subject matter; and
   (ii) assessed the information gathered in the investigation;
(f) based all judgements in advising the client on the client's relevant circumstances;
(g) taken any other step that, at the time the advice is provided, would reasonably be regarded as being in the best interests of the client, given the client's relevant circumstances.

Three points are relevant to note in relation to the safe harbour. First, an objective test applies under (b)(ii) and (e)(i) in terms of the identification of, or a recommendation in respect of, the objectives, financial situation and needs of the client on the relevant subject matter. Second, (f) requires the financial adviser to have based all judgements in advising the client on the client's relevant circumstances. Third, a catch-all provision is contained in (g), which imports an objective test. As Liu et al have observed, 'the safe harbour arguably cannot eliminate the legal risk of non-compliance because of the open-ended nature of s 961B(2)(g)'.[70] The repeal of this catch-all provision had previously been proposed in 2014.[71]

6. A financial adviser 'must only provide the advice to the client if it would be reasonable to conclude that the advice is appropriate to the client, had the provider satisfied the duty under section 961B to act in the best interests of the client'.[72]

The regulatory framework as outlined above incorporates two important concepts that are not defined: the client's 'objectives, financial situation and needs' and 'the client's relevant circumstances'. Logically, these are concepts that need to be interpreted by reference to a client's specific circumstances.

The term 'objectives, financial situation and needs' was recently interpreted judicially by Gordon J of the High Court of Australia:

> Fifth, the phrase 'objectives, financial situation and needs' bears its ordinary meaning. As the primary judge held, and as has not been disputed, an objective is an end towards which efforts are directed, a situation is a state of affairs or combination of circumstances and a need is a case or instance in which some necessity or want exists. And the relevant objectives, financial situation and needs referred to must be 'the person's'. They must be personal. That follows linguistically from the words of the provision, including the fact that this kind of advice is described as 'personal advice', and it is also implicit from the obligations that arise in

[70] H Liu et al, 'In Whose Best Interests? Regulating Financial Advisers, the Royal Commission and the Dilemma of Reform' (2020) 41(1) *Sydney Law Review* 37, 49.

[71] See Degeling and Hudson (n 21) 538 and fn 66.

[72] Corporations Act 2001 (Cth), s 961G.

> connection with the giving of personal advice. Those obligations would be unnecessary and nonsensical if the only relevant matters to be considered were universal or generic, and not personal.[73]

In the first instance judgment, the primary judge (Gleeson J) stated that the concepts of 'objectives', 'financial situation' and 'needs' were not mutually exclusive and might contain significant overlap. Gleeson J gave the following example:

> [A] customer with a dependent disabled child may characterise the goal of accumulating sufficient wealth to provide for that child as both an objective and a need. Further, the dependence of the child on the customer may form part of the customer's 'financial situation'.[74]

On appeal to the Full Court of the Federal Court of Australia, O'Bryan J disagreed that the expressions had overlapping meanings, although his Honour recognised that they might often be related and stated the view that each of the expressions had a distinct meaning.[75] The point was not considered by the High Court on appeal.

C. Is the Concept of Financial Wellbeing Reflected in the Existing Framework?

As discussed in section II, the CBA definition of 'financial wellbeing'[76] contains four elements: financial needs; financial freedom; control over finances; and financial security.

One might argue that the terms 'financial situation' and 'needs' – both of which are contained within the phrase 'objectives, financial situation and needs'[77] – are wide enough to embrace all four elements of financial wellbeing, with the possible exception of the dynamic and temporal dimension (ie how financial wellbeing changes over time). It is important to recognise, however, that personal advice arises in circumstances where the financial adviser 'has considered one or more of the person's objectives, financial situation and needs' and that, accordingly, financial advice might be given just in relation to a client's objectives and not in relation to the client's financial situation or needs. In other words, a financial adviser is under no obligation to give financial advice that takes account of the client's objectives, financial situation and needs together. The wording of the safe harbour suggests that one of the elements that must be satisfied is that the financial adviser has identified the objectives, financial situation and needs of the client; however, this is qualified by reference to whatever was 'disclosed to the provider by the client through instructions'. The scope of the advice and the requirement to identify the objectives, financial situation and needs of the client (or 'the client's relevant

[73] *Westpac Securities Administration Ltd v Australian Securities and Investments Commission* (n 66) 63 (footnotes omitted).

[74] *Australian Securities and Investments Commission v Westpac Securities Administration Limited, in the matter of Westpac Securities Administration Limited* [2018] FCA 2078 [120].

[75] *Australian Securities and Investment Commission v Westpac Securities Administration Limited* [2019] FCAFC 187 [368].

[76] See the text accompanying n 6.

[77] Corporations Act 2001 (Cth), s 766B(3). See the discussion in section V.B.

circumstances') are further qualified by reference to 'the subject matter of the advice that has been sought by the client (whether explicitly or implicitly)'.

In short, a financial adviser is not subject to any duty or obligation to consider the client's financial wellbeing, except to the extent that the client expressly instructs the financial adviser to do so.[78] This might not raise any eyebrows; after all, an adviser can (and should) only provide advice to the client within the scope or parameters of the client's instructions. Accordingly, if the client wishes to obtain limited advice that does not cover the client's financial situation or needs in a broad sense, on what basis could (or should) regulation intervene to require otherwise?

As argued in section II, however, the concept of financial wellbeing (incorporating the concept of financial security) can act as a yardstick against which risks can be properly measured and consumers can make informed financial decisions. Indeed, it is difficult to understand how an informed decision could be made other than through a consideration of financial wellbeing. This is not to suggest that all financial decisions should be made for the purpose of enhancing an individual's financial wellbeing. However, there are many circumstances in which an informed financial decision requires an understanding of how the decision might impact financial wellbeing.

D. Reform Proposals

The authors argue that there is merit in the following proposition made by the FinFuture White Paper:

> Financial service providers should be subject to a duty to consider financial wellbeing in performing their functions and providing their services; in particular, they should be required to consider what impact a course of action would have, or would be reasonably likely to have, on the financial wellbeing of an individual.[79]

As noted by the FinFuture White Paper:

> The imposition of the above duty would require financial service providers to consider a broader range of factors in determining concepts such as 'best interests' [in the case of financial advisers] and 'suitability' [in the context of credit providers].[80]

Further, it would help financial services providers such as financial advisers to apply their professional judgment – informed by standards of reasonableness – in place of the existing system, which often encourages a tick-the-box approach as noted in section V.A. It would also help to protect vulnerable people.[81]

[78] In its Regulatory Guide 175, ASIC has provided examples of situations in which a financial adviser provides advice on matters that are related to financial wellbeing.

[79] FinFuture White Paper (n 2) 11, 34. According to the FinFuture White Paper (ibid 11), 'A corollary to this is that financial service providers would be subject to a duty to notify customers of material risks (and ways to address them) where they had the information and technological means to do so.' The example given is the use of pop-up warnings on phones in respect of forthcoming payments due on credit cards.

[80] The test of suitability, or 'not unsuitable', is relevant in the context of consumer credit regulation in Australia.

[81] FinFuture White Paper (n 2) 34, citing the High Court decision in *Australian Securities and Investments Commission v Kobelt* [2019] HCA 18 as an example of a case involving vulnerable people and the complexities surrounding the interpretation of' unconscionable conduct'.

Two threshold questions are relevant in any proposal to impose a duty (statutory or otherwise) to consider financial wellbeing. The first question concerns the definition of financial wellbeing and how its constituent elements should be expressed. The second question concerns the circumstances in which a duty to consider financial wellbeing would arise. In the case of financial advice, for example, would it arise in all circumstances where financial advice is given or only in prescribed circumstances?

In terms of the first question, the authors suggest that the specific definition would need to reflect the general consensus among policy-makers and the community as to the meaning of financial wellbeing and how it should be measured. The FinFuture White Paper calls for Australia 'to develop and widely adopt a National Financial Wellbeing Framework … that defines the aspects of financial wellbeing and how they are measured'.[82] Despite the challenges discussed in section II concerning the definition of financial wellbeing, the various formulations adopted by financial institutions, governments and regulators suggest that consensus is emerging around certain key aspects. These aspects include financial resilience, control of finances and financial security, as measured both at a fixed point in time and also on a dynamic, temporal basis into the future. In particular, the definition should incorporate elements that respond to the causes of financial stress.

In terms of the second question, the authors suggest that the duty should arise in circumstances where the financial decision – or the matter on which the advice is given – involves appreciable risk for the client, whether by reference to the complexity of the advice or the financial product or investment. The duty should not arise in the context of simple financial advice that is structural or general in nature (eg general advice on the different choices for superannuation or pension arrangements) and does not involve a recommendation in respect of complex financial products.[83] In these scenarios, the customer's financial wellbeing is unlikely to be substantially affected as the scope of the financial advice is too narrow to require a consideration of broader financial wellbeing. Consideration should also be given to applying the duty in circumstances involving vulnerable consumers.[84]

A question arises as to whether the duty would be considered to be separate or distinct from the general statutory duties, such as the 'best interests' duty in Australia or the 'Consumer Duty' (if the United Kingdom decided to adopt this), or, instead, whether it would be considered to be part of those general duties. The authors would suggest that the duty to consider financial wellbeing should be treated as part of the general duties. In effect, it would broaden the factors that should be taken into account in satisfying those duties. In this way, it would operationalise the duties and, in doing so, act as a yardstick against which the appropriateness of financial advice and the satisfaction of the 'best interests' obligation could be measured.

[82] FinFuture White Paper (n 2) 5.

[83] For a discussion about complexity and risk in the context of the traditional regulatory distinction between retail investors and sophisticated investors, see WY Wan, A Godwin and Q Yao, 'When is an Individual Investor Not in Need of Consumer Protection? A comparative analysis of Singapore, Hong Kong and Australia' (2020) *Singapore Journal of Legal Studies* 190.

[84] Vulnerable consumers are in an analogous position to patients with pre-existing conditions or vulnerabilities in the medical context.

The authors also suggest that the incorporation of financial wellbeing into the regulatory framework for financial advice (and potential financial services more broadly) would overcome or mitigate many of the problems that the financial advice sector has experienced to date. In particular, it would operationalise duties such as the 'best interest' duty and improve consumer wellbeing and consumers' access to financial advice by increasing the quality of financial advice. In turn, this would result in increased demand for quality financial advice.[85]

Finally, from a regulatory perspective, the imposition of a duty to consider financial wellbeing would require financial institutions and advisers to disclose how they implement the financial wellbeing framework and to satisfy continuous reporting requirements by reference to an agreed set of indices for financial wellbeing. This, the authors suggest, would ultimately support the professionalisation of financial advisers and improve the quality of the financial services industry in general.

[85] As recommended by the FinFuture White Paper (n 2) 5, the authors would also suggest that a financial wellbeing framework be adopted by national governments along similar lines to health care (both physical wellbeing and mental wellbeing).

16

Adjudicating Intermediary-Related Losses

HANS TJIO*

I. Introduction

The commercial landscape would be quite different without intermediaries. For a start, the number of transactions and economic activity would be much lower. But the use of intermediaries comes at a cost, which includes agency costs of monitoring them, information costs for third parties dealing with principals through these intermediaries, and the costs of adjudicating disputes arising between principals and third parties due to the actions of intermediaries. Where possible, we try to avoid the unnecessary use of intermediaries and/or intermediary analysis. Three-party situations complicate things. However, reducing this to two parties can sometimes be artificial, and that leads to its own difficulties.

An example of this is the law of assignment, which in some contract law textbooks[1] comes right before the chapter on agency. Both are meant to be exceptions to privity and focus on the need to bring a third party into the contractual relationship. With assignments, the accepted view is that there is a property transfer of the chose from assignor to assignee and, in equity, involving the obligor is not strictly necessary. In a recent book, however, Tham challenges the neatness of this narrative, which attempts to replicate a principal seller to principal buyer transaction involving tangible property.[2] Instead he sees all parties remaining in the picture, with the assignor becoming a bare trustee and the assignee a limited agent with respect to the entitlements that the assignor has against the obligor. With agency law, the archetypal situation with disclosed agents is that they drop out of the picture once the contract is made. But the three-party picture cannot be avoided with undisclosed principals. It also comes back in disclosed agency once there are any disputes or difficulties arising in the original tripartite relationship. A disclosed agent can also still be liable to a third party even when a contract is properly made with the principal.[3] And apparent authority is always there to haunt us, as

* I would like to thank Professors Paul Davies and Tan Cheng-Han, Kanaga Dharmananda, Kenneth Khoo, Daniel Ang and Selena Chiong for helpful suggestions and constructive comments.

[1] See, eg, E Peel, *Treitel: The Law of Contract*, 15th edn (London, Sweet & Maxwell, 2020).

[2] CH Tham, *Understanding the Law of Assignment* (Cambridge, Cambridge University Press, 2019).

[3] A disclosed agent that drops out of the picture can still be liable to the third party by, eg, assuming personal liability on the contract, D Fox et al, *Commercial Law, Text, Cases and Materials*, 6th edn (Oxford, Oxford University Press, 2020) 175.

'[e]very few years, the vexed question of whether an agent of a company is able to represent his own authority arises before a Commonwealth court'.[4] The answer there, which invariably in practice is in the negative, is a good example of incentivising third parties, especially in their initial transaction with the principal, to seek out the principal or to obtain independent verification as opposed to relying totally on an agent. One should not rely on intermediaries before some contact with, or representation has been made by, the principal.

II. Intermediaries are Unavoidable Even With Aggregated Entities

There is an unavoidable need to use intermediaries in one form or other, and many seemingly two-party situations in fact involve more participants than that. Incorporation creates a separate legal entity that captures the 'web of agency relationships'[5] needed to run a business. This is done to reduce hold-out costs by otherwise outside contracting parties, but it then creates other agency costs.[6] Even if the corporate fund is partitioned separately so that shareholders have no control over it, how it is committed to a person dealing with a company, an 'artificial construct',[7] means that intermediary analysis, usually involving the directors, cannot be avoided. There are many occasions when we have to look within a company even when we try not to.

Attempts have been made to see the shareholders in general meeting or the board of directors not as agents but as organs of the company. It has never been clear whether these organs are the company itself for the purposes of a particular decision but organs were seen to be more than just a discrete part of the company. It has also been cogently argued that the board as a whole should still be seen as an agent of the company.[8] A contextual approach[9] to the attribution of the rogue director's knowledge to the

[4] T Evans-Chan and H Tjio, 'Unusual Apparent Authority and Vicarious Liability' (2012) 128 *LQR* 27.

[5] FH Easterbrook and DR Fischel, 'Corporate Control Transactions' (1982) 91 *Yale Law Journal* 698, 700.

[6] EM Iacobucci and GG Triantis, 'Economic and Legal Boundaries of Firms' (2007) 93 *Virginia Law Review* 515, 517. It 'creates different and more complex problems': GM Cohen, 'The Law and Economics of Agency and Partnership' in F Parisi (ed), *The Oxford Handbook of Law and Economics*, vol 2: *Private and Commercial Law* (Oxford, Oxford University Press, 2017) 399, 402.

[7] *Townsing Henry George v Jenton Overseas Investment Pte Ltd* [2007] SGCA 13, [2007] 2 SLR(R) 597 [77] (Chan CJ).

[8] P Watts, 'Directors as Agents – Some Aspects of Disputed Territory' in D Busch, L Macgregor and P Watts (eds), *Agency Law in Commercial Practice* (Oxford, Oxford University Press, 2016) 97, stating that boards can be considered agents of the company having to serve in the company's interest and not creditors, even in insolvency. Compare, PL Davies, S Worthington and C Hare, *Gower's Principles of Modern Company Law*, 11th edn (London, Sweet & Maxwell, 2021) [8-004].

[9] Ultimately, whether such attribution is made depends on its context and purpose, ie whether the company's responsibility is being apportioned with an agent or with a third party: *Singularis Holdings Ltd (in liq) v Daiwa Capital Markets Europe Ltd* [2019] UKSC 50, [2020] AC 1189 [34] (noted R Leow, 'Attribution and illegality again' (2020) 136 *LQR* 181), citing *Jetivia SA v Bilta (UK) Ltd (in liq)* [2015] UKSC 23, [2016] AC 1 ('*Bilta*') [92] (Lord Sumption). The court disapproved its earlier decision in *Stone & Rolls Ltd (in liq) v Moore Stephens* [2009] UKHL 39, [2009] 1 AC 1391, which held that the wrongdoing of a company's directing mind and will is automatically attributed to the company so that a top management fraud defence was fully available to the defendant auditors on the basis of *ex turpi causa non oritur actio* on the part of the company.

company has also prevented 'absurd extremes'[10] where controlling agents say that the attribution always means that the company approved or ratified their actions.[11]

Outsiders dealing with a company can, however, rely on the 'indoor management' rule,[12] which was an attempt at allowing third parties to use a presumption of regularity to cure any irregularities that may have existed within the corporate structure in terms of the co-ownership of property or co-sharing of power.[13] It is a powerful rule as described by *Boyle & Birds' Company Law*, which states that 'where it applies, the *Turquand* rule is conclusive and does not simply raise a rebuttable presumption'.[14] Similarly, *Ford's Principles of Corporations Law* points out that the evidential presumption of regularity is rebuttable whereas the indoor management rule is not, preferring instead to explain the rule on the basis that third parties have no access to the company's records.[15] On one view, this is a two-party situation between an outsider and a monolithic entity.

The operation of the rule appears to be founded on the fact that despite having undertaken due diligence, third parties might have not been able to determine whether things had in fact been regularised. This is linked to the doctrine of constructive notice, which is often used to decide whether a principal or third party would have to bear the losses in situations occasioned by the wrongdoing of an intermediary. The Privy Council, in the recent decision of *East Asia Company Ltd v PT Satria Tirtatama Energindo*[16] ('*East Asia*'), held that the indoor management rule did not allow a third party to circumvent the normal rules of agency.[17] It referred to Dawson J's judgment in *Northside Developments Pty Ltd v Registrar General*[18] to confirm that the rule only applied where it was already independently established that the person in question had actual or ostensible authority.[19] Relying on Sargant LJ's judgment in *Houghton & Co v Nothard, Lowe & Wills Ltd*,[20] the Privy Council also thought that the indoor management rule was limited in scope, and simply because a company's articles of association contained the *power* of delegation did not necessarily mean that the power was *exercised* in favour of the relevant officer of the company.[21] Something more is required to trigger the application of the rule, which is not a magical elixir protecting outside parties dealing with a company in all circumstances.

[10] PL Davies, *Gower and Davies Principles of Modern Company Law*, 8th edn (London, Sweet & Maxwell, 2008) [7-30]. See also H Tjio and EB Lee, 'Understanding the Company in Context' in HT Chao et al (eds), *The Law in His Hands: A Tribute to Chief Justice Chan Sek Keong* (Singapore, Singapore Academy of Law, 2012) [16]–[17].

[11] Or if the directors raise the illegality defence against the company, which was rejected in *Bilta* (n 9).

[12] *Royal British Bank v Turquand* (1856) 6 E & B 327, 119 ER 886 (QB); *Mahony v East Holyford Mining Co Ltd* (1875) LR 7 HL 869.

[13] J Armour and MJ Whincop, 'The Proprietary Foundations of Corporate Law' (2007) 27 *OJLS* 429, pt C (this could be sequential or joint).

[14] J Birds et al, *Boyle & Birds' Company Law*, 10th edn (Bristol, Jordan Publishing, 2019) 174.

[15] RP Austin and IM Ramsay, *Ford's Principles of Corporations Law*, 17th edn, (Sydney, Butterworths, 2018) [13-160]; preferring this to the evidential presumption of regularity supported by cases like *Morris v Kanssen* [1946] AC 460 (HL) 475 (Lord Simonds); *Northside Developments Pty Ltd v Registrar General* (1990) 170 CLR 146 (HCA) 177 (Brennan J).

[16] *East Asia Company Ltd v PT Satria Tirtatama Energindo* [2019] UKPC 30, [2020] 2 All ER 294.

[17] ibid [63].

[18] *Northside Developments* (n 15).

[19] *East Asia* (n 16) [64].

[20] *Houghton & Co v Nothard, Lowe & Wills Ltd* [1927] 1 KB 246, 266.

[21] *East Asia* (n 16) [63].

On this view, the issue of third-party notice is incorporated into the question of whether the indoor management rule applies in the first place, as is the case with ostensible authority, rather than as a triggering device that causes a transaction to be avoided. The ruling in *East Asia* means that we cannot avoid the involvement of an intermediary, as the need to be informed means that the third party would have had to approach one, rather than just relying on, for example, the corporate constitution without any human interface (which could be a board resolution). Once that happens, issues of agency law and authorisation come into the picture.

East Asia confirms that the burden of proof is on the third party to show that it had acted reasonably (and not just rationally) in relying on any representations made in corporate documents or by individuals in the company. As no agreement has been established yet, it is not about setting aside an existing agreement but asserting that one existed in the first place. As Peter Watts put it:

> At least where an alleged contract is still executory, and arguably even when it is not, the onus lies on the party alleging a contract to prove its existence. While the point is not always appreciated, where such proof requires that an agent has acted on the promisor's behalf, the onus again rests with the promisee to show that it dealt with a person with actual or apparent authority to bind the promisor.[22]

The Privy Council also discussed a contrary view of Lord Neuberger NPJ in the Hong Kong Court of Final Appeal in *Thanakharn Kasikorn Thai Chamkat v Akai Holdings Ltd*[23] ('*Akai*'), that only required the representee to not be irrational or dishonest in order to invoke the operation of apparent authority.[24] The Privy Council rejected Lord Neuberger's view in *Akai* that the third party must take reasonable steps to ascertain relevant facts only when relying on the indoor management rule but not on ostensible authority. Lord Neuberger had expressed concerns that have existed since *Manchester Trust v Furness* about constructive notice disrupting commercial transactions.[25] While the Privy Council appreciated this,[26] in those situations *A* bought goods from *B* honestly believing that *B* was principal and not knowing that *B* was agent for *C*, and so *C* cannot claim for the price and yet assert that *A*'s belief was negligent.[27] But in the *East Asia* type scenarios, it is *A*, not *C*, who claimed that there was a binding agreement, and it bore the burden of showing that, which included dispelling any notice on its part.

[22] P Watts, 'Authority and Mismotivation' (2005) 121 *LQR* 4, 5.

[23] *Thanakharn Kasikorn Thai Chamkat v Akai Holdings Ltd* [2010] HKCFA 63, [2011] 1 HKC 357 [62] (noted Ji Lian Yap, 'Knowing Receipt and Apparent Authority' (2011) 127 *LQR* 350), where the transaction was unusual as Akai did not benefit from it.

[24] *East Asia* (n 16) [83].

[25] ibid [84].

[26] ibid [85]. See, eg, PG Watts and FMB Reynolds, *Bowstead & Reynolds on Agency*, 21st edn (London, Sweet & Maxwell, 2018) [8-049]–[8-050]; P Watts, 'Some Wear and Tear on *Armagas v Mundogas* – The Tension between Having and Wanting in the Law of Agency' (2015) 1 *LMCLQ* 36, 52–53, stating that 'it is at least doubtful whether Lord Neuberger was right to treat the case before him as involving two steps, namely whether there was a holding out and, if so, whether the promise was put on inquiry, rather than a single step, where all the information known to the third party is taken together in considering whether there has been a reliable representation of authority'.

[27] *East Asia* (n 16) [86]. See also I Sin, 'Corporate contracting, ostensible authority and constructive notice: returning to orthodoxy' (2020) 136 *LQR* 364, 367.

On such narrow classifications do such cases turn, as they can lead to different gateways that may have different states of mind triggering liability. The case that perhaps shows this most clearly was *Criterion Properties plc v Stratford UK Properties LLC*.[28] There, the House of Lords doubted the correctness of the decision of the Court of Appeal in *Bank of Credit and Commerce International (Overseas) Ltd v Akindele*,[29] which suggested that cases of knowing receipt and want of authority were both founded on the unconscionability of the recipient third party. The House reclassified the issue in *Criterion* as based solely on whether an agreement could bind a company despite the want of authority on the part of directors, in creating a 'poison pill' to frustrate potential takeover offers, and not the knowing receipt of company property resulting from directors' acting for improper purposes, as had been the case at first instance and in the Court of Appeal.[30] Lord Scott pointed out that the latter presupposes the receipt of assets by one person from another, and this did not include the creation of contractual rights by an executory agreement whose enforceability was in question.[31] The issue of whether the acts were in fact within the directors' powers was sent back to trial. However, indications that restitutionary liability is strict, particularly in Lord Nicholls' speech,[32] do not remove the need for the court to first answer the question whether the agreement should be, in his Lordship's words, '*not* set aside'.[33] As we have seen, as the law stands, the third party has to prove that it reasonably relied on the appearance of authority.

III. Two- versus Three-Party Situations – a Distinction Without a Difference?

Another example of the importance of characterisation is the more recent decision in *Singularis Holdings Limited (in liq) v Daiwa Capital Markets Europe Limited*.[34] The Supreme Court and Court of Appeal focused on corporate attribution, as regards which, as noted in section II, it was said that a contextual approach should be taken, so that the wrong of a sole shareholder who was also a dominant director would not be

[28] *Criterion Properties plc v Stratford UK Properties LLC* [2004] UKHL 28, [2004] 1 WLR 1846, noted Watts (n 22), R Stevens, 'The Proper Scope of Knowing Receipt' [2004] *LMCLQ* 421.

[29] *Bank of Credit and Commerce International (Overseas) Ltd v Akindele* [2001] Ch 437; H Tjio, 'No Stranger to Unconscionability' [2001] *Journal of Business Law* 299; G Virgo, 'Conscience in Equity: a new utopia' (2017) 15 *Otago Law Review* 1.

[30] *Criterion Properties plc v Stratford UK Properties LLC* [2002] EWCA Civ 1883, [2003] 1 WLR 2108.

[31] *Criterion* (HL) (n 28) [27].

[32] ibid [5].

[33] ibid [4]. This appears to suggest that the agreement was only voidable, not void. While this is the case for transactions involving self-dealing by directors, cases of directors acting without actual authority are different: RC Nolan, 'The Proper Purpose Doctrine and Company Directors' in BAK Rider (ed), *The Realm of Company Law* (Alphen aan den Rijn, Kluwer Law International, 1998) 1, 5, 27. In the latter situation, the contracts do not bind the company unless the directors had ostensible authority to do so, in which case they do. It is likely that this is what Lord Nicholls meant in *Criterion* in the context of directors acting for improper purposes. See also *Heinl v Jyske Bank (Gibraltar) Ltd* [1999] Lloyd's Rep Bank 511 (CA). D Fox, 'Overreaching' in P Birks and A Pretto (eds), *Breach of Trust* (Oxford, Hart Publishing, 2002) 95 argues at 98–99 that self-dealing is not an equitable wrong but involves a trustee acting beyond its proper powers, relying on *Tito v Waddell (No 2)* [1977] Ch 106 (Megarry V-C).

[34] *Singularis* (n 9).

attributed to a company.[35] This was to prevent the corporate customer from claiming against its bank for the bank's failure to prevent the defrauding shareholder director's transfer of money out of the corporate customer's bank account to his other business operations, which had succeeded in the High Court.[36] This is possibly the first time that this *Quincecare* duty had been successfully invoked. In that case 25 years ago,[37] Steyn J thought that there was an implied term in the banker/customer relationship that the bank would observe reasonable care and skill in executing its customer's order, which would be breached if it knew that it was 'dishonestly given, shutting its eyes to the obvious fact of the dishonesty or acting recklessly in failing to make such inquiries as an honest and reasonable man would make'.[38] Although the reasoning was in the two-party context, there are signs here of the notice we have seen used in the three-party situation. The bank did not challenge the finding of Rose J at first instance in *Singularis* that it had been negligent, or that *Quincecare* was wrong given the burdens it would impose on a bank that also has to observe its customer's mandate, which Steyn J had stressed in that earlier case.[39] Rose J also dismissed a claim based on dishonest assistance, as the bank had not been wilfully blind in relation to the breaches of fiduciary duty by the director. Again, this shows the fortune in being able to find different pathways, in that even if the test in dishonest assistance is one of objective dishonesty,[40] that is still possibly at least one level higher (using the *Baden Delvaux*[41] classifications) than the kinds of constructive notice/negligence involved in *Quincecare*. In *Singularis*,[42] Rose J also observed that none of the defences raised in relation to the *Quincecare* claim (which was the focus on appeal) applied to the dishonest assistance claim. Put differently, this was a form of negligent assistance at common law.[43]

So a higher standard was imposed on the bank because it was held that the purpose of the *Quincecare* duty was to protect Singularis against the misappropriation of funds by an agent of the company.[44] This, though, is a failure to meet the standards of conduct

[35] ibid [34].

[36] *Singularis Holdings Ltd (in liq) v Daiwa Capital Markets Europe Ltd* [2017] EWHC 257 (Ch), [2017] 2 All ER (Comm) 445.

[37] *Barclays Bank plc v Quincecare Ltd* [1992] 4 All ER 363.

[38] ibid 376.

[39] ibid 376d–f.

[40] Recently, RT Langford, 'Dystopian Accessorial Liability of the End of "Stepping Stones" As We Know It?' (2020) 37 *Company and Securities Law Journal* 362, has highlighted that derivative stepping-stone liability was seen in *Cassimatis v Australian Securities and Investments Commission* [2020] FCAFC 52 as just an application of a direct statutory duty as well.

[41] *Baden v Société Générale pour Favoriser le Developpement du Commerce et de l'Industrie en France* [1983] 1 WLR 509.

[42] *Singularis* (n 36) [115].

[43] *Quincecare* (n 37) 375d.

[44] It was thought that the *Quincecare* duty does not cover individual customers of the bank that have been defrauded by outside third parties, as the instruction given by that customer would validly transfer title to the third party as an authorised push payment: *Philipp v Barclays Bank UK plc* [2021] EWHC 10 (Comm), [2021] Bus LR 451 [161]–[167]. This was reversed by the Court of Appeal: [2022] EWCA Civ 318, [28]–[30] finding that the duty was not restricted to corporate customers defrauded by its own agent, where a constructive trust arises where the agent misappropriates the customer's monies. But the court acknowledged that how a *Quincecare* duty should be balanced with the bank's mandate to comply with the customer's instructions should go to trial. See also *Roberts v Royal Bank of Scotland plc* [2020] EWHC 3141 (Comm).

expected. But that negligence standard was pegged to the fact that the bank was put on inquiry, which is more about a state of mind. There is an elision of the two here, which was fortuitous in a way, as negligence liability then allowed a finding that Singularis had been contributorily negligent to the extent of 25 per cent in not monitoring and controlling what its director was doing. It is harder to balance relative fault in three-party analysis where the focus is on secondary liability and states of mind as opposed to conduct.

Even more recently, however, the duty of care of a director (a corporate services firm) towards the company was framed in terms of third-party liability in *Ciban Management Corporation v Citco (BVI) Ltd*,[45] so that it was entitled to rely on the ostensible authority of a company's agent who was not himself a director. The Privy Council acknowledged that 'there has been considerable difficulty in deciding in this case whether the doctrine of ostensible (or apparent) authority has a pivotal role'.[46] The director was said to have acted reasonably due to the close links between the agent and the company's sole shareholder, who informally consented to the representation by conduct that the agent had authority. The contrast with section 40 of the UK Companies Act 2006 and indoor management is stark, as it is said that insiders like directors usually find it hard to rely on those rules that protect outside third parties to the corporate entity.[47] With *Ciban*, the director was not liable because it was characterised as a third party that was not put on inquiry and so was entitled to rely on the appearance of authority and did not breach its duty of care owed to the company.

The point about achieving the right balance in terms of protecting both principals and third parties, however characterised, will be the focus for the rest of this chapter. That balance must take into account the fact that it has to prevent arbitrage between different causes of action in that they have to be calibrated consistently. We will see that third-party notice may be the tiebreaker most of the time, even in what are ostensibly two-party cases, particularly where relationships are captured within an artificial separate entity. The strategy to be adopted should be disclosure of information rather than mandatory rules, and that seems to be captured in the use of the doctrine of notice. In a world of increasing individual preference, mandatory or property-type rules seldom work given the number of customised intermediary relationships. As Zhang shows,[48] while information costs are negatively correlated with social and political cohesion, the latter is negatively correlated with the diversity of individual preferences. In turn, there is less correlation between information costs and legal standardisation because the latter frustrates preferences. Individual preferences make it very hard to create a mandatory rule giving blanket protection to one party or the other. Intermediaries like agents thus have a great deal of flexibility in terms of what they can or cannot do in their internal arrangements with their principals.

[45] *Ciban Management Corporation v Citco (BVI) Ltd* [2020] UKPC 21, [2021] AC 122.

[46] ibid [6].

[47] Davies, Worthington and Hare (n 8) [8-012]. Compare *Hely Hutchinson v Brayhead Ltd* [1968] 1 QB 549 (CA) (implied actual authority).

[48] Zhang T, 'Beyond Information Costs: Preference Formation and the Architecture of Property Law' (2020) 12 *Journal of Legal Analysis* 1.

IV. Balancing Agency and Information Costs

Sitkoff points out that the goal, then, 'is to design a body of law applicable to agency relationships that minimises agency costs while preserving the benefits of agency'.[49] Armour and Whincop believe that that '[i]t seems likely that the overall costs of the system would perhaps be reduced by a corresponding shift to allocate greater responsibility to third parties'.[50] However, they also say (and this is consistent with the individual preference point noted in section III):

> Reducing the monitoring costs of other shared owners does, however, come at the price of imposing costs on TPs [third parties]. For every 'unauthorized' transaction where P succeeds in asserting their entitlements to an asset against a TP, the latter may suffer a reliance loss of an equivalent or greater amount. If the entitlements of P are completely enforced in every case, then the sum of the costs imposed on TPs may exceed the savings in P's monitoring costs.
>
> The legal system must therefore make a trade-off between maximizing the effectiveness of shared control arrangements for organizational participants, and imposing externalities on third parties. There are also the procedural costs of administering the system. All other things being equal, it would be desirable for the legal system to seek to minimize the *total* costs of shared ownership amongst organizational participants. Property and organizational law employ a mix of 'balancing' strategies, which are not mutually exclusive, to effect this fundamental trade-off. Each has comparative (dis)advantages in relation to some elements of the total cost function, and therefore the selection of the optimal mix of strategies will depend upon the context.[51]

One of the balancing strategies is to use a 'least-cost avoider' approach to determine whether a principal should be bound to a third party despite the agent's wilfulness – the principal should, if it was far easier for him to have policed the agent's actions. But enforcement should be selective, for a blanket rule, such as with overreaching, that always imposes liability on the principal could create incentive problems – this should be used only when it involves certain stylised property substitutions. At the other extreme would be a blanket rule protecting the principal, such as with the old ultra vires doctrine that rendered any transaction with a company beyond its objects void. Here Armour and Whincop thought that it might 'impose disproportionate costs on third parties'.[52]

The balancing strategy today with cases of true ultra vires has been to make it such that it would not affect third parties transacting with the company in good faith by virtue of the Companies Act 1985, section 35 (now section 40 of the UK Companies Act 2006). Together with section 35B (now section 39), this also absolves third parties transacting with the company from having to inquire about the capacity of the company or the authority of its directors.[53] Just prior to this, *Rolled Steel Products (Holdings) Ltd v British Steel Corporation* narrowed the scope of the ultra vires doctrine and shifted

[49] RH Sitkoff, 'An Economic Theory of Fiduciary Law' in AS Gold and P Miller (eds), *Philosophical Foundations of Fiduciary Law* (Oxford, Oxford University Press, 2014) 197, 200.

[50] Armour and Whincop (n 13) 459.

[51] ibid 445 (footnotes omitted).

[52] ibid fn 135.

[53] Introduced by Companies Act 1989, s 108. But see Davies, Worthington and Hare (n 8) [8-010], who say that 'only little need to be added to knowledge of lack of authority to produce bad faith', although good faith is a stricter test than notice and the burden of showing it is on the company: Armour and Whincop (n 13) 458.

the focus onto the authority of the directors of the company to enter into a particular transaction.[54] Put differently, many cases were not in fact about the lack of corporate capacity but about directors' want of authority (where the burden is on the third party to prove an agreement) or breach of duty (where the burden is on the company to set aside a voidable agreement). Although the burden of proof can be crucial, what matters then is whether the third party knew or had been put on inquiry, or, more contentiously, where the cost of determining the extent of the agent's authority was in fact cheaper for the third party to bear (but in many cases some fault may lie on both sides[55]).

Lord Sales has pointed out, however, the thin distinctions that lie between void and voidable contracts outside of ultra vires transactions, and that

> in that exercise of a discretion for an improper purpose is itself an action taken in excess of power … we should treat the basic problem to be confronted – to resolve this tension between competing interests in a principled, coherent and fair way – as the same whether one conceives the relevant legal framework to be the common law or equity or a mixture of both.[56]

While he suggests the consistent use of a *Turquand*-type rule dependent on notice, it is submitted here that there should also be more principled use of notice in terms of where the burden of proof lies (and what parties are expected to do) in that regard, if it is always to be used as a tiebreaker. We should try to provide greater certainty to what has to be done, especially if the burden is on the third party to prove the absence of notice. As we shall see, the problem is also that courts may favour minimising their own administrative costs of adjudication.[57]

V. Notice in the Modern Context

Notice today is a wider concept than that known to conveyancing lawyers.[58] Lord Sales appeared to link notice with priorities between competing interests in a way that some did with *Barclays v O'Brien*.[59] But we saw how that evolved from a duty to make inquiries to one to take reasonable steps to ensure that the surety receives independent advice[60] and then to obtain advice from a solicitor,[61] which may have its basis in an equitable

In the United Kingdom, ss 39 and 40 of the Companies Act 2006 relate to corporate capacity and directors' powers, whereas in some parts of the Commonwealth, constructive notice has been removed in relation to the entire corporate constitution: see New Zealand (Companies Act 1993, s 19) and Singapore (Companies Act (Cap 50, 2006 Rev Ed), s 25A).

[54] *Rolled Steel Products (Holdings) Ltd v British Steel Corporation* [1986] Ch 246. See also Companies Act 1985, s 35A, introduced by Companies Act 1989, s 108.

[55] See section V at text accompanying n 74.

[56] P Sales, 'Use of Powers for Proper Purposes in Private Law' (2020) 136 *LQR* 384, 400.

[57] W Farnsworth, *The Legal Analyst* (Chicago, IL, University of Chicago Press, 2007) ch 6.

[58] *Macmillan Inc v Bishopsgate Investment Trust plc (No 3)* [1995] 1 WLR 978, 1000 (Millett J).

[59] *Barclays Bank plc v O'Brien* [1994] 1 AC 180. See, eg, JRF Lehane (1994) 110 *LQR* 167, relying on *Latec Investments Ltd v Hotel Terrigel Pty Ltd* (1965) 113 CLR 265 (HCA), a true three-party priority case. Compare Sales (n 56). See also A Phang and H Tjio, 'From Mythical Equities to Substantive Doctrines – Yerkey in the Shadow of Notice and Unconscionability' (1999) 14 *Journal of Contract Law* 72.

[60] J Mee, 'Undue Influence, Misrepresentation and the Doctrine of Notice' [1995] *CLJ* 536.

[61] *Royal Bank of Scotland plc v Etridge (No 2)* [2001] UKHL 44, [2002] 2 AC 773.

duty of care.[62] There is an interplay between the state of mind and judgeable conduct, as we saw in *Singularis*, as once a bank takes reasonable steps to advise the surety to seek independent advice or to consult a solicitor, it avoids constructive notice of any possible wrongdoing by the debtor because there is now, on the surface, less likelihood of such.[63] The problem is that this distinction is not always appreciated, but that may also be because we do not always maintain a difference between a state of mind and an assessment of the wrongdoers' actions given what they know against an external benchmark that is often objective in order to lower administrative costs of judicial decision making.[64] What in effect happened with *Etridge* is the creation of a banking code in the particular repeated situation where a weakened surety is asked to provide security or quasi-security for a bank loan to a related borrower. It is actually akin to a due diligence defence for banks, and not dissimilar to the need to be informed before one can rely on the indoor management rule, which we saw in *East Asia*. But because the situation has become so stylised, the solution is mandatory in nature for greater certainty and easy adjudication, even if the burden of proof in *O'Brien* situations is in fact on the surety.[65] But the latter point lessens the criticism of *Etridge*, which is that '[o]ne of the difficulties posed by determinate legal rules is that unscrupulous parties can take advantage of the loopholes that occur when conduct is regulated in blunt terms'.[66]

What needs to be done, where possible, is to create perhaps more stringent *Etridge*-like steps for a third party or counterparty to take in other, more commonly encountered situations, particularly where the burden is on it to show the absence of notice. Aside from apparent authority and indoor management in *East Asia*, the Privy Council in *Credit Agricole v Papadimitriou*[67] also held that in the case of a fraudulent disposal of property, the equity's darling rule applies and the burden is on the bank to show that it was without notice, following *Re Nisbet and Potts Contract*.[68]

In partnerships, the burden of proof is also on the third party to show that a partner's act was carried out in the ordinary course of business in order to be an act of

[62] C Rickett and D McLauchlan, 'Undue Influence, Financiers and Third Parties: A Doctrine in Transition or the Emergence of a New Doctrine?' [1995] *NZ Law Review* 328.

[63] The crucial point is that one only has constructive notice of matters that necessarily affect property and not matters that may or may not: *English and Scottish Mercantile Investment Company, Ltd v Brunton* [1892] 2 QB 700.

[64] Farnsworth (n 57) 60–61.

[65] *Barclays Bank v Boulter* [1994] 4 All ER 513, where Lord Hoffmann overruled the Court of Appeal and held that the bona purchaser for value without notice situation was different as the land was burdened by a prior equitable interest.

[66] E Sherwin, 'Equity and the Modern Mind' in JCP Goldberg, HE Smith and PG Turner (eds), *Equity and Law Fusion and Fission* (Cambridge, Cambridge University Press, 2019) 353, 366.

[67] *Credit Agricole Corp and Investment Bank v Papadimitriou* [2015] UKPC 13, [2015] 1 WLR 4265.

[68] *Re Nisbet and Potts Contract* [1905] 1 Ch 391 (Ch). Some conflicting authorities are set out in JD Heydon, MJ Leeming and PG Turner, *Meagher, Gummow & Lehane's Equity Doctrine and Remedies*, 5th edn (Chatswood, LexisNexis Butterworths, 2015) [8-300], although they conclude that the burden should lie with equity's darling. Compare *Polly Peck International plc v Nadir (No 2)* [1992] 4 All ER 769 (CA), where a claimant had to prove third-party notice even with a proprietary claim at the end of a tracing exercise. In *Papadimitriou* (n 67) [33], Lord Sumption thought that that the 'notice' in equity's darling and knowing receipt were the same. He set it at a lower level than an investigative duty and saw it perhaps more like an inference of knowledge: see n 80.

the partnership.[69] It is particularly hard to prove a negative if notice is left an open-ended question. It may be, however, that there has to be some uncertainty attached to it.

Following on from the discussion in section IV about mandatory rules, *Etridge*-type codes of conduct can only work in common stylised situations. Many other transactions have peculiar characteristics, or there are not enough of them to standardise. There, it is ultimately about *balancing* the needs of flexible internal governance structures of an institution and of protecting external parties dealing with that institution that is required to facilitate any such dealing in the first place.[70] But it may be that co-owners are given too much flexibility today, such that not only has it reached a stage where a mandatory rule is impossible, but using notice as a 'selective strategy' may also still impose too much of an informational cost on the third party. Very often, as in *Rolled Steel*, *Akai* and *Singularis*, the question is whether the court sees the transaction on its face as conferring any benefit on the principal. This may leave the third party with too much to do, as it will have to satisfy itself that there was a proper commercial purpose for the transaction, and then later convince the court that that was the case if, for example, it was decided on the basis of want of authority instead of a breach of fiduciary duty on the part of the agent director. On the other hand, the director treated as a third party in *Ciban Management* was seen as a service provider, which it was, subject to 'execution only'[71] responsibilities, which had acted reasonably in relying on a powerful agent without having to conduct any due diligence itself on the relationship between the agent and principal. Its sphere of responsibility was reduced because it was able to craft the right characterisation for the issues at hand. But the test was still ultimately whether it had been 'put on notice because of the "red flags"'.[72] While that is defendant-sided, and consistent with the burden of proof, it is likely, however, that the examination of the director's state of mind was made in the shadow of the relationship between the agent Mr Costa and the company's controller Mr Byington. In that context, the Privy Council agreed with the trial judge that Mr Byington 'accepted the risk that Mr Costa might one day betray him'.[73]

In many cases, the principal would have contributed in some way to that appearance of authority, and it would have been impossible, or extremely costly, for the third party to have discovered otherwise. There is a balancing of relative fault, even if modern

[69] *Lim Hsi-Wei Marc v Orix Capital* [2010] 3 SLR 1189 (SGCA). It is what is usual for firms in that business rather than the firm itself: *Kotak v Kotak* [2017] EWHC 1821 (Ch) [127]. The UK Partnership Act 1890, s 5, states that any act of a partnership carried out in the usual way business of that kind is carried on by the partnership is binding, unless 'the person with whom he [the partner] is dealing either knows that he [the partner] has no authority, or does not know or believe him to be a partner'. With limited liability partnerships, see Limited Liability Partnerships Act 2000, s 6. See also A Televantos, *Capitalism Before Corporations* (Oxford, Oxford University Press, 2020) 4.2.

[70] Trust Law Committee, *Report: Rights of Creditors against Trustees and Trust Funds* (King's College London, June 1999) [3.7].

[71] *Ciban Management* (n 45) [25].

[72] ibid [23]. The red flags were that the director knew or ought to have known that the agent was acting without authority. In particular, that the agent had sent the e-mail from his personal account, that he asked for the invoice to be sent to him personally and that he settled it out of his son's bank account. However, the Privy Council agreed with the trial judge that none of these things should have been expected to put the corporate director on notice given the totality of the factual matrix.

[73] ibid [22].

courts do not like this because it increases the costs of adjudication. Televantos has argued that earlier on, courts did in fact determine 'who was *more* at fault' as they were suspicious of business in general.[74] Today, the greater focus on commerce and certainty means that it is presently captured by the doctrine of notice where an objective standard is imposed on the third party. Although this area of law can be improved upon, it still cannot be a bright-line rule, in order to provide the correct *ex ante* incentives for contracting parties. There would be too much moral hazard were the costs always to be imposed on third parties, although in many cases they are, perhaps with the advent of the information superhighway. The danger, however, with readily shifting informational costs to third parties is that it could incentivise principals to create agency costs, or at least not minimise them. The case that may have recognised this most clearly is *Ciban*, where the Privy Council thought that the principal and agent simply went too far.[75] A contrast is with the Singapore Court of Appeal decision in *Skandinaviska Enskilda Banken AB v Asia Pacific Breweries (Singapore) Pte Ltd*,[76] where third-party banks were unable to claim on loans made to the company whose financial manager gambled away the monies, even though the company was seen to be 'derelict in its corporate governance duties'[77] by allowing the finance manager to run the entire finance division without much supervision.

In summary, we have seen that if we cannot avoid the use of intermediaries or intermediary analysis, we have to control costs. That is not usually a problem with agency costs as we are quite protective of principals today. But that then shifts informational costs to third parties. There seems to be more of that today, especially as we are seeing objective standards imposed on them when principal–agency relationships are even more fluid. This lowers the administrative costs of adjudication, which 'often explain the large structure of rules'[78] but, if so, we need to get those objective standards right. The problem is that things like notice and recklessness are both about states of mind and standards of behaviour, and at some point they elide with negligence and dishonesty respectively.[79] But the burden of proof may not have been fully worked out in a consistent way, and where it is borne by the third party it could be too onerous. In exceptional cases it can become a set of procedures to be followed, as in *Etridge*. But if notice remains as a tiebreaker, we need to know when it is a synonym for negligence, whether it is purely a defence to a proprietary or restitutionary claim, or allows for the inference of knowledge that is really the test of liability, and, related to this, whether it should ever allow an argument that any inquiries would have been futile in the circumstances.[80] Constructive notice creates difficulties even for equity lawyers[81] and 'leads to loose thinking'.[82]

[74] Televantos (n 69) 70 who also points out (ibid 117) that in *Akai* (n 23), there was discussion about the difference between the common law concept of being put on inquiry and the equitable doctrine of notice, which historically had never been made.

[75] It has been said that the 'primary economic purpose of agency law is to enhance the benefits of agency by deterring such collusion': Cohen (n 6) 401.

[76] *Skandinaviska Enskilda Banken AB v Asia Pacific Breweries (Singapore) Pte Ltd* [2011] SGCA 22, [2011] 3 SLR 540.

[77] ibid [5].

[78] Farnsworth (n 57) 61.

[79] See the criticism of counsel's doing so in *Macmillan Inc v Bishopsgate Investment Trust Plc* (n 58) 1014.

[80] See, eg, *Janvey v GMAG, LLC*, 66 Bankr Ct Dec (CRR) 167 (5th Cir (US), 2019) (rejected argument that inquiries would have been futile due to the complexity of the transferor's scheme). In *Papadimitriou*

VI. Further Balancing Strategies

But notice, even if properly worked out, cannot do all the work alone. What is needed are perhaps greater responsibilities on the part of a principal to disclose its arrangements and more information-creating mechanisms, as Armour and Whincop suggest can happen with electronic notice-filing or registration.[83] Ironically, this may then lessen the need to work out what notice is precisely. But outside of formal registration systems, technology clearly can make the monitoring of agents more effective,[84] and also reduce for third parties the costs of ascertaining the truth behind the appearance of authority.[85] An increasingly connected world is primed for this at a time a leading hedge fund manager has suggested is an opportune juncture for fraud.[86] The abuse of preferences in highly differentiated principal–agent relationships was recognised in *Ciban Management*, where the Privy Council concluded by saying:

> A central message of the decision in this case is that the ultimate beneficial owner who chooses such arrangements takes the risk of being betrayed by an agent who is being used to convey instructions to the director. Although there may be claims by the ultimate beneficial owner against the agent, the ultimate beneficial owner, on facts comparable to this case, cannot throw the risk taken onto the director by instigating an action by the company against the director for breach of the director's duty of care. The courts will treat the ultimate beneficial owner – Mr Byington in this case – as having been hoist by his own petard.[87]

There is some kind of legal realism going on here in terms of disclosure duties[88] and, arguably, the decreased costs of permanent record keeping.[89] While blockchain and decentralised ledgers can be used for this purpose, again, this works best in standardised transactions that are repeatable without too much customisation. But technology does not have to be cutting-edge to help third parties to reach principals or other agents

(n 67) [33], Lord Sumption, while acknowledging this position, thought that 'If even without inquiry or explanation the transaction appears to be a proper one, then there is no justification for requiring the defendants to make inquiries. He is without notice.' See also *Selangor United Rubber Estates Ltd v Cradock (No 3)* [1968] 2 Lloyd's Rep 289, 324, cited with approval in *Yogambikai Nagarajah v Indian Overseas Bank* [1996] 2 SLR(R) 774, [1996] SGCA 45 [60].

[81] See, eg, *Macmillan Inc* v *Bishopsgate Investment Trust Plc* (n 58) 1014–15, criticised by the Privy Council in *Papadimitriou* (n 67) [17] (Lord Clarke).

[82] AW Scott and WF Fratcher, *Scott on Trusts*, 4th edn (New York, Aspen Publishers, 1989) 110, [297]. *Meagher Gummow & Lehane* (n 68) points out that the burden of proof with respect to equity's darling is even more uncertain in the United States.

[83] Armour and Whincop (n 13) fn 148 (with respect to security interests).

[84] One goal of decentralised autonomous organisations is to do away with human management or employees altogether, but decision making may be less efficient and slower than with corporations: Ruo-Ting Sun et al, 'Transformation of the Transaction Cost and the Agency Cost in an Organization and the Applicability of Blockchain – A Case Study of Peer-to-Peer Insurance' (2020) 3 *Frontiers in Blockchain*, available at https://doi.org/10.3389/fbloc.2020.00024, 13, art 24 (accessed 11 March 2022). Human intervention is also required where there are complications, such as when a 'hard fork' is required: C Bruner, 'Distributed Ledgers, Artificial Intelligence and the Purpose of the Corporation' (2020) 79 *CLJ* 431, 441.

[85] While blockchain can improve trust and transparency, it may actually increase bargaining costs if it leads back to the use of markets over aggregated entities: Ruo-Ting Su et al, ibid 10.

[86] H Agnew, 'Jim Chanos: "We are in the Golden Age of Fraud"' *Financial Times* (London, 24 July 2020).

[87] *Ciban Management* (n 45) [54].

[88] Televantos (n 69) 72, points out that for earlier courts, 'the real issue was the actual behavior of A and B.'

[89] Bruner (n 84) 435.

or organs within an organisation as part of its due diligence exercise. It is not about imputing constructive notice on such parties via the use of formal registers but about giving them a better chance at determining what is the actual state of play by improving the quality of information available to them. Even real-time balance-sheet accounting will help. This is to help them overcome the burden of proving the absence of notice or knowledge, if such is to be imposed on them. Greater disclosures would make constructive notice and actual knowledge come together, as closing one's eyes in the face of available facts leads to the inference of something more subjective.

We are not in a position to determine what additional registers or information/data bulletins will come about: that should be driven by market forces. But having more information available may paradoxically reduce the application of doctrines like apparent authority, since that makes it less likely that there can be the appearance of authority on which a third party can safely rely. It could drive apparent authority back to its roots in requiring a clear representation from the principal as to the agent's authority, as opposed to hard modern cases that turn on silence, self-representations, course of dealing or, in effect, some form of estoppel by negligence. Modern law has never really been able to use estoppel by negligence in situations where two innocent parties have been deceived by a rogue middleman, whether with respect to ownership or authority. The statement of Ashurst J in *Lickbarrow v Mason* that 'whenever one of two innocent parties must suffer by the acts of a third, he who has enabled such third person to occasion the loss must sustain it'[90] exemplifies its indeterminacy. It creates too much administrative cost for the courts. Instead, the use of estoppel ends up in the search for a representation by the principal (which in the case of a company is usually proxied) that was relied upon by a third party, and morphs into apparent authority.[91] But not only is that sometimes contrived,[92] it then also leads to the question of notice, which focuses on the third party and at present does not formally take relative fault into account.

We have seen how it was perhaps fortuitous that a negligence claim succeeded in *Singularis* where the dishonest assistance claim failed against the bank, which was in a sense more an outsider to the corporate structure than the director in *Ciban*. However, this allowed a finding of contributory negligence on the part of the company and avoided an all-or-nothing solution that might create moral hazards. Outside of duty of care cases, however, it is not clear how relative fault will be apportioned in situations where most of the time both parties would have been guilty of some wrongdoing and oversight. Again, while this protects the court from having to perhaps make value judgements on relative fault or concern itself with ideas of proportionality, the time may have come for that to be embraced not just in public law but in private law as well, and not just for discrete parts of contract law like the defence of illegality.[93]

[90] *Lickbarrow v Mason* (1787) 2 Term Rep 63 (KB), 70, which 'statement is notorious as having been frequently cited (not least in examination questions!) and rarely, if ever, applied': Fox et al (n 3) 368.

[91] *Farquharson Brothers & Co v King & Co* [1901] 2 KB 697 (CA), noted (1902) 2 *Columbia Law Review* 44 (with traces of ostensible ownership). See also Tan CH, 'Estoppel in the Law of Agency' (2020) 136 *LQR* 315, preferring to see apparent authority as a form of estoppel rather than 'real authority' as in the United States.

[92] See *Ciban Management* (n 45), where it was combined with the *Re Duomatic* unanimous assent principle to find that the company had made the necessary representations of the agent's authority that were made by the sole shareholder.

[93] E Lim and F Urbina, 'Understanding Proportionality in the Illegality Defence' (2020) 136 *LQR* 575; ZX Tan, 'The Proportionality Puzzle in Contract Law: A Challenge for Private Law Theory?' (2020) 33

Contributory negligence was itself an all-or-nothing outcome in the past in the United Kingdom,[94] and this still is the case in some US States (as opposed to comparative fault or negligence).[95] It is also not a defence in intentional torts,[96] nor perhaps in most forms of third party liability.[97] But the need for counterfactuals has been recognised,[98] and at a broader level consideration should be given to how losses are allocated where accepted notions of fault and causation, like the 'but-for' test in negligence, may not serve as well as alternative conceptions of shared risks and responsibility. Such ideas, and even the 'formerly discredited approach'[99] in *McGhee v National Coal Board*,[100] where one 'materially increased the risk of injury',[101] have appeared in causation issues in tort law, although by and large only in hard cases, such as in the mesothelioma cases.[102] Greater use can be made of this with less protected values such as economic loss as opposed to the integrity of person or property. In the English Court of Appeal in *Rubenstein v HSBC Bank plc*,[103] for example, Rix LJ thought that an investment adviser who had been negligent in recommending a specific investment to an investor (as opposed to providing information) 'may well be responsible if some flaw in the investment turns out materially to contribute to some investment loss'.[104] But there should be less concern in correspondingly finding contributory negligence here on the part of an investor. There is consequently enough in the cases that will allow further development of proportionate fault as opposed to an all-or-nothing approach.

In *Singularis*,[105] the Supreme Court acknowledged Lord Hoffmann's concerns, expressed in the earlier House of Lords decision of *Reeves v Commissioner of Police of the Metropolis*,[106] with respect to the incongruity of fully allowing a claim against another for harm the claimant inflicts on itself. But the *Quincecare* duty is seen as a

Canadian Journal of Law & Jurisprudence 215; and ZX Tan, 'Illegality and the promise of universality' [2020] *JBL* 428.

[94] E Dongen and H Verdam, 'The Development of the Concept of Contributory Negligence in English Common Law' (2016) 12 *Utrecht Law Review* 6, arguing that it allowed for apportionment by the late 19th century before it was formalised by the Law Reform (Contributory Negligence) Act of 1945.

[95] GD Hollister, 'Using Comparative Fault to Replace the All-or-Nothing Lottery Imposed in Intentional Torts Suits in Which Both Plaintiff and Defendant Are at Fault' (1993) 46 *Vanderbilt Law Review* 121.

[96] J Goudkamp and D Nolan, *Contributory Negligence Principles and Practice* (Oxford, Oxford University Press, 2018) 2.02.

[97] ibid 2.03, observing that it is not clear that it applies even to the primary breach of fiduciary duty.

[98] N Venkatesan, 'Causation in Misrepresentation: Historical or Counterfactual? And "But For" What?' (2021) 137 *LQR* 503.

[99] K Amirthalingam, 'The Changing Face of the Gist of Negligence' in JW Neyers, E Chamberlain and SGA Pitel (eds), *Emerging Issues in Tort Law* (Portland, OR, Hart Publishing, 2007) 467, 470.

[100] *McGhee v National Coal Board* [1973] 1 WLR 1 (HL).

[101] ibid 5 (Lord Reid); see also Lord Salmon, ibid 12–13.

[102] *Fairchild v Glenhaven Funeral Services Ltd* [2002] UKHL 22, [2003] 1 AC 32. This was confirmed in another decision on asbestos poisoning, *Barker v Corus UK Ltd* [2006] UKHL 20, [2006] 2 AC 572, although the specific effect of this was later reversed by the Compensation Act 2006 (UK). The risk of harm can be seen as a form of damage: G Turton, *Evidential Uncertainty in Causation in Negligence* (Oxford, Hart Publishing, 2018) 182ff ('risk as gist').

[103] *Rubenstein v HSBC Bank plc* [2012] EWCA Civ 1184.

[104] ibid [103]. LK Yang, 'Causation, Remoteness, Scope of Duty and the *Rubenstein* Decision' *Singapore Law Gazette* (February 2013) argues, however, that such an approach towards causation may not be applicable outside the line of medical cases discussed here, and that the focus of *Rubenstein* was on remoteness and the scope of duty, not causation.

[105] *Singularis* (n 9) [22].

[106] *Reeves v Commissioner of Police of the Metropolis* [2000] 1 AC 360 (HL), 368.

'rare case'[107] in which this is permitted. Nonetheless, it does not have to be a binary solution, as there may be a whole spectrum of cases, ranging from such a rare case at one end to the other extreme where claimants 'must look after themselves and take responsibility for their actions'.[108] And yet even in this rare (if not only) instance in which the *Quincecare* duty was breached by the bank, its customer Singularis was found to have been 25 per cent contributorily negligent. This suggests that the *Quincecare*-type situation is only triggered in very narrow circumstances, possibly when the bank is between 50[109] to 75 per cent at fault. This suggests that there are some situations where there is always relative fault involved, and this is invariably intertwined with issues of causation and contributory negligence (where available). It was said in *Philipp v Barclays Bank*,[110] a recent case that had attempted to restrict the bank's *Quincecare* duty of care to corporate customers being defrauded by their officers (and not individual customers):

> A finding that the only duty owed by the Bank (in relation to the two payments and by reference to facts sufficiently incontrovertible to support a summary determination) was the duty to process the payments – unqualified, on those facts, by any meaningful Quincecare duty – will therefore dispense with any further point about causation; just as the finding in *Singularis* of a breach of the duty led to the issue of causation being resolved in favour of the claimant in that case.[111]

There are shades of Lord Hoffmann's 'assumption of responsibility'[112] here, although apportioning losses can be very messy for courts to adjudicate upon. It is true that balancing has been criticised in the context of illegality, but that is because that usually leads to an all-or-nothing outcome. But if the balancing also leads to a proportionate outcome, it could be more acceptable. Principled criticism of proportionate liability as opposed to joint and several liability can be made in the context of joint tortfeasors,[113] but here we are dividing fault or responsibility between two relatively innocent (or not) parties claiming against each other. This does not have to be a common law solution. It could also take into account the different values involved across jurisdictions, and this can be seen in how contributory negligence or comparative fault operates in different US States. The increased costs of adjudication may be counterbalanced by lower informational costs borne by third parties, and also by incentives for principals to lower agency costs themselves *ex ante*. And in the longer term, even the former will decline with use.

[107] ibid.
[108] ibid.
[109] No award below 50% or 51% can be made in some US States adopting 'comparative contributory negligence'.
[110] *Philipp v Barclays Bank* [2021] EWHC 10 (Comm). While the Court of Appeal (n 44) reversed the decision on the basis that a *Quincecare* duty could be owed to individual customers who were victims of authorised push payment fraud, there was no appeal on the issue of causation.
[111] ibid [123].
[112] eg *South Australia Asset Management Corporation v York Montague Ltd* [1997] AC 191 and *Transfield Shipping Inc v Mercator Shipping Inc (The Achilleas)* [2008] UKHL 48, [2009] 1 AC 61 (both applied in *Rubenstein* (n 103) [5], with the former seen to go to the scope of duty and the latter to remoteness of damages).
[113] K Barker and J Steel, 'Drifting towards Proportionate Liability: Ethics and Pragmatics' [2015] *CLJ* 49, 67, see comparative negligence as ethically different from proportionate liability. It is perhaps better called comparative fault here.

VII. Conclusion

It is clear that intermediaries and intermediary analysis cannot be avoided much of the time where the intermediary has caused a loss to be borne by either a principal or a third party. The exceptions are where property-like rules help in avoiding a three-party picture. That seldom occurs, and so the test is whether a third party has been put on notice and made the necessary inquiries. But imposing the burden of proof on the third party means that this is often a due diligence defence in disguise, and it can impose a heavy duty of care, as cases like *East Asia* have in effect raised the standard of proof. It may in fact be better to frame it in such terms, as it is difficult even for equity lawyers to understand what notice is, let alone their clients. But in a world of individualised preferences, principals and agents desire flexible arrangements that may impose too much informational cost on third parties dealing with them. Steps may need to be taken, as was done with *Etridge*, which is like a mandatory rule in a particular context.[114] If that is not possible, as is usually the case, we should also require greater disclosure from principals and use technology for more notice-creating mechanisms, so that an objective standard used to reduce administrative costs of adjudication does not create impossible burdens on third parties. We should, where possible, also apportion responsibility and fault as a starting point rather than as an afterthought. There should be some calibration (even if not perfect) between different causes of action (and comparative fault) that are similar in nature.

Just as important as *ex post* compensation is *ex ante* prevention and, as we have seen, the need to minimise total transactional cost. Certain equitable doctrines create too much uncertainty. But the suggestion here is only that there be some modification with intermediary rules around a settled middle, where third-party notice is applied in a less binary fashion, and not that the rules be thrown out completely. Ideas like the least-cost avoider and proportionality can be used to check on existing rules, much as Lord Hoffmann may have intended concepts he introduced towards the end of his career in relation to the scope of duty, causation and remoteness. Here, these ideas may be used not just to found liability, but to apportion it in an area where notice has tried very hard to be the tiebreaker but has been found slightly wanting.

[114] There is a difference between what is central to the idea of the trust and other mandatory rules that may for policy or other reasons apply to some forms of trusts but not others: J Fee, 'Trust-owned Companies and the Irreducible Core of the Trust' (2021) 26(9) *Trusts & Trustees* 826, discussing *Zhang Hong Li v DBS Bank (Hong Kong) Ltd* [2019] HKCFA 45, which upheld the effectiveness of anti-*Bartlett* clauses. *Bartlett v Barclays Bank Trust Co Ltd* [1980] Ch 515 had held that a trustee of a trust holding controlling shares in a company had a high standard of care in terms of monitoring and supervising its business.

17

Intermediaries as 'Gatekeepers' in International and Domestic Regulation

ALEXANDER LOKE

I. The 'Gatekeeper' in Regulatory Strategy

In legal literature, the term 'gatekeeper' has primarily been used in the capital markets. It refers to intermediaries who play an integral role in the smooth functioning of the capital markets. An intermediary's participation in the fund-raising process may be so critical that, without its involvement, there is no pathway to the desired outcome. In other words, the gatekeeper controls the issuer's access to the desired outcome.[1] This may be due to regulatory requirements or market expectations. The role of intermediaries is not confined to the primary market. To the extent that the value of the securities or financial products relates to the financial health of the issuer, it may speak to the quality of management. Where compensation depends on the issuer's performance, the managers will have an abiding interest in the intermediaries' attesting, whether directly or indirectly, to the performance indicators.

In the capital markets context, the information asymmetry between the entity seeking capital investment and the providers of capital may be regarded as the 'friction' that prevents the capital provider from investing her capital in the company or financial product in question. The issuer may hold great potential, but absent a mechanism that credibly conveys the information to the potential investor, the issuer may not obtain the desired price and may exit the market. What remains on the market are 'lemons', issuers whose products are likely to be overpriced and that investors shy away from – with the resultant market failure.[2] Intermediaries help with conveying credible signals and play a part in solving the lemons problem. Various intermediaries play a part in rendering the capital solicitation process viable. The investment banker investigates the business prospects of the issuer and the viability of the fundraising proposition. In addition to reputational risk, the investment banker risks legal liability *sans* demonstrating

[1] RH Kraakman, 'Gatekeepers: The Anatomy of Third-Party Enforcement Strategy' (1986) 2 *Journal of Law, Economics, and Organization* 53, 53–56, 61–66.

[2] GA Akerlof, 'The Market for "Lemons": Qualitative Uncertainty and the Market Mechanism' (1970) 84 *Quarterly Journal of Economics* 488.

that it has conducted due diligence.[3] The lawyer ensures that the regulatory parameters are complied with; to the extent that public policy imperatives are embedded in the regulatory requirements, the lawyer checks and provides assurance that there is due compliance. Where there are ways around burdensome regulations, the lawyer is valued for his ability to navigate these and plan the most cost-efficient manner for achieving the clients' desired outcomes. There is little market perception that beyond the bright-line compliance requirements, lawyers are gatekeepers for the protection of the investors.[4] Despite relatively less controversy over these intermediaries,[5] one should bear in mind the key roles that they play and consider why they have attracted less attention.

Much of the debate over the last 20 years has focused on the failures of the auditors, the analysts and, arising from the Global Financial Crisis (GFC) of 2008, the credit rating agencies (CRAs). The critical role played by the auditor is self-evident. To the extent that an entity's financial statements provide an indication of its financial health – how profitable it is, the efficiency in the use of its assets, the risk of financial distress – the auditor checks on the company's financial statements and verifies whether they give a 'true and fair' view of its accounts. Where there are hard norms, these form bright-line rules by which the auditor verifies whether they are complied with. The Enron scandal showed up the gaps in the norms, as well as the lapses in the professional judgement of the auditors. Had the auditors in Enron performed their function with greater rigour, the accounting devices used by the Enron management to conceal the amount of debt taken on would have been called to a halt. Auditor lapses similarly contributed to the failure of Worldcom, which had improperly capitalised its line costs instead of expensing them, and conveyed to the outside world an impression of great efficiency.[6]

The gatekeeper failure associated with the CRAs relates to the credit ratings that the CRAs assigned to the structured products issued by special purpose vehicles (SPVs). Typically, these structured products consisted of debt obligations, which source of payment was invariably based, first, on assets transferred to the SPV and, often, on swap arrangements in which the swap provider promised to make payments under the defined conditions. The CRA's role is, at first glance, a pretty prosaic one. The credit rating reflects the CRA's assessment of the likelihood of default on the debt obligation. In the aftermath of the GFC, when many of the structured products went into default or were massively devalued, the CRAs were seen as being too willing to please their clients' demands for the structured products to be assigned an investment grading.

John Coffee has sought to argue that a notion of gatekeeper that focuses on its capacity to withhold consent and control access omits the distinctive characteristics

[3] US Securities Act 1933, s 11.

[4] JC Coffee, *Gatekeepers: The Professions and Corporate Governance* (New York, Oxford University Press, 2006) 318.

[5] Nonetheless, the lawyer's obligations were further tightened under s 307 of the Sarbanes–Oxley Act 2002 (US), Public Law 107–204, 116 Stat 745 (hereinafter 'SOX'). See also Securities Act Release No 33-8185 (6 February 2003) (Implementation of Standards of Professional Conduct for Attorneys). For an argument that lawyers should play a heightened role as gatekeepers, see JC Coffee, 'The Attorney as Gatekeepers: An Agenda for the SEC' (2003) 103 *Columbia Law Review* 1293.

[6] *In re WorldCom, Inc Securities Litigation* [2004] US Dist Lexis 25155 (SDNY, 15 December 2004). The Bankruptcy Examiner found that the auditor, Arthur Andersen, failed to carry out the necessary testing of areas vulnerable to fraud: 'Third and Final Report of Dick Thornburgh, Bankruptcy Court Examiner' (26 January 2004) in *In re WorldCom Inc* (SDNY) Ch 11, Case No 02-13533, 19.

of gatekeepers who serve investors, viz 'an agent who acts as a reputational intermediary to assure investors as to the quality of the "signal" sent by the corporate issuer'.[7] In the words of Jennifer Payne, 'intermediaries will be regarded as gatekeepers if they have significant reputational capital that they can pledge in order to verify or certify information produced by the issuer'.[8] The reputational intermediary acting as a gatekeeper has built up its reputation capital over time; in verifying or certifying the issuer's disclosures, it lends credibility to the issuer's statements and thus promotes investor reliance on them. This broader definition has the merit of including securities analysts who do not gatekeep in the traditional sense of controlling access; rather, they pledge their professional reputation in their assessment of the investment merits of a financial product, and in so doing influence the investors' investment decisions.

This notion of the gatekeeper serves the purpose of analysing the problems that attend such reputational intermediaries. However, insofar as one seeks to go beyond reputational intermediaries to understand why gatekeeping by reputational intermediaries might work less effectively compared to other gatekeepers, it is apposite to return to the access control notion of gatekeeper. For this purpose, we expand the inquiry to encompass the use of intermediaries as gatekeepers in the financial system, where the conflict of interest problem persists. The return from reputational intermediaries to 'access control' notion facilitates a broader inquiry, and helps inform how we should design a regulatory system and what one may fairly expect from a gatekeeper.

II. The Travails of the Reputational Intermediary as a Gatekeeper

The theory underlying the reputational intermediary in the securities market is that the reputational intermediary functions as a credible certifier, and serves to assure investors about the information that the issuer conveys to the market. Whereas the issuer may be a 'one-time player' whose statements might be treated with great scepticism, the reputational intermediary is a repeat player whose certification involves a pledge of its reputation. The premise is that the expected returns from the services provided by the reputational intermediary to any one issuer do not justify putting at risk the goodwill associated with its reputation and the potential legal liability that might arise from being connected with the issuer's fraud. The scandals involving accounting irregularities in the early 2000s demonstrate how the theory of the reputational intermediary is flawed, and reveal the reasons why many of the institutions failed the investors. In the GFC of 2008, the flawed gatekeeper was revealed to be the CRAs, which were accused of giving unduly sanguine ratings to structured products that imploded. In this chapter, we first review why the reputational intermediary failed to function as desired, and the regulatory responses that have been put in place as a result. I argue for downplaying the notion of the reputational intermediary. While market institutions that certify or

[7] Coffee (n 4) 2.

[8] J Payne, 'The Role of Gatekeepers' in N Moloney, E Ferran and J Payne (eds), *Oxford Handbook of Financial Regulation* (Oxford, Oxford University Press, 2015) 254, 257.

verify information relating to issuers and their products do put some store on their reputational capital, it is unrealistic to expect that the concern for market reputation will adequately safeguard pursuit of the public good. Instead, we should revert to the more foundational notion of the gatekeeper as controlling access to particular market outcomes. In so doing, not only do we cast off undue reliance on reputation as the mechanism for desired policy outcomes, we open the inquiry to asking what controls can better bring about the desired outcomes. The failure of gatekeepers should not be a surprise; instead, a realistic appraisal of the incentive structures should give us a clear-eyed view of where the points of failure might be located and enable us to address them before they occasion serious harm. Gatekeepers are thus recognised as useful but inherently flawed institutions. This prompts us to ask more meaningful questions about how their self-interest might be at variance with policy objectives, and the kind of regulatory mechanisms that might be put in place to mitigate potential weak points in the controls.

III. Accounting Irregularities in the 2000s

Perhaps the most salient instance of gatekeeper failure is Enron.[9] A year before its bankruptcy filing on 2 December 2001, Enron was a much-sought-after company. At the end of the calendar year on 31 December 2000, its stock price was $83.13 and reflected a price-earnings ratio of 73.[10] Within a year, the company collapsed into bankruptcy because of accounting irregularities.

Enron traces its beginnings to the merger of two natural gas pipeline companies – Houston Natural Gas and Internorth. With a vast network of inter-State pipelines – the largest in the United States – Enron occupied a tremendously advantageous position when deregulation of natural gas prices occurred in the early 1990s and introduced volatility to the price of natural gas. Ownership of the vast pipeline infrastructure and the diverse points of supply and demand provided Enron with valuable information, which enabled it to offer to utilities and other companies reduced volatility in the form of long-term fixed-price contracts. To manage the risks assumed, Enron would hedge against the volatility of future prices by financial derivatives, of which swaps featured prominently. The astute exploitation of its information advantage meant that its energy-trading operations became a key profit centre.

To further enhance its profitability, its Chief Financial Officer Jeff Skilling set the company on course to embrace an asset-light policy. What prompted this policy were the low returns associated with the ownership of pipelines and production facilities. These weighed down the profitability of the company, and the debt associated with these assets limited the further assumption of debt. If these assets and their associated debts could be moved off Enron's balance sheet, Enron could take on more loans and

[9] For a good account by a journalist, see K Eichenwald, *Conspiracy of Fools: A True Story* (New York, Clown Publishing Group, 2005). For the post-mortem investigative report by the independent directors of Enron, see WC Powers, RS Toroubh and HS Winokur, *Report of Investigation by the Special Investigative Committee of the Board of Directors of Enron Corporation* (1 February 2002). The account that follows draws from them, as well as from Coffee (n 4).

[10] PM Healy and KG Palepu, 'The Fall of Enron' (2003) 17(2) *Journal of Economic Perspectives* 3.

thus exploit more profitable opportunities. Nonetheless, such shedding of heavy assets should not compromise Enron's continued access to the information that underpinned the success of its trading operations. This, together with challenges of finding buyers in sufficient numbers who were willing to pay the prices Enron desired, explains its employment of Special Purpose Entities (SPEs) to achieve its asset-light objective.

Enron was able to do this because there were no clear rules on the nature of an outside investor's involvement in an SPE before non-consolidation with the parent company's accounts was permitted. The two principal bodies responsible for accounting rules in the United States were the Securities and Exchange Commission (SEC) and the Financial Accounting Standards Board (FASB). Neither had taken a definitive position on the issue. Exploiting this, Enron relied on the view expressed by the Emerging Issues Task Force, an advisory arm of the FASB, that non-consolidation was justifiable if an outsider invested a minimum of 3 per cent in the SPE's total debt and equity. However, this was only one of several elements for non-consolidation treatment. Amongst other requirements, the outside investor must also have a controlling voting interest in the SPE.[11] Enron by and large ignored the other substantive conditions.

In the months before its collapse, Enron created hundreds of SPEs to act as unconsolidated affiliates to hold assets and move debt off its balance sheet. It was estimated that in late 2000, 45 per cent of the approximately $60 billion assets that Enron effectively controlled were held through such unconsolidated affiliates.[12] Moving the debt off the balance sheet accomplished the objective of allowing the company to take on more debt that would have been precluded given the debt covenants that served to preserve Enron's 'investment grade' credit rating. The problem was that although the SPEs became the new principal obligors, Enron remained contingently liable in the event that an obligor was unable to pay. This was not properly recognised in the financial statements. When the scale of the off-balance sheet liabilities came to light, the restated balance sheet for the year ending 31 December 2000 reported an increase of $628 million in liabilities. This triggered a loss of Enron's investment grade credit rating and accordingly caused it to default on its loan covenants.

Enron's exploitation of the gaps in the accounting rules was not confined to the use of SPEs as unconsolidated affiliates. One of its aggressive accounting practices involved how the profits from long-term supply contracts were computed. 'Mark-to-market' accounting practice requires such future income and profits to be recognised by their 'present value'. This inevitably involved variables and risks: for example, increased costs, fluctuations in prices and interest rates. Enron took extremely optimistic assumptions, whether in recognising revenues or in making assumptions on when a State would deregulate its energy prices. These and other earnings-related accounting practices resulted in inflated earnings, amounting to a total of $613 million for the period 1996–2000 – about 23 per cent of the reported profits.[13]

[11] Deloitte & Touche, 'Through the SPE Looking Glass: Improving the Transparency of Special Purpose Entities' (*For the Record*, Technology, Media and Telecommunication (TMT) Group Technical Update, April/May 2002) vol 3 at www.iasplus.com/en/binary/dttpubs/spedt.pdf (accessed 18 October 2021).

[12] US Senate Permanent Subcommittee on Investigations of the Committee on Government Affairs, *The Role of the Board of Directors in Enron's Collapse* (107th Congress, 2nd Session, Report 107-70, 8 July 2002) 8.

[13] Healy and Palepu (n 10) 11.

Enron's high stock price and financial numbers were publicly called into question by Jim Chanos, a professional trader, at a national short seller's conference in February 2001.[14] His doubts about Enron's profitability and accounting numbers led Bethany McLean of *Fortune* to write 'Is Enron overpriced?',[15] which was instrumental in triggering market scrutiny of Enron and its price fall. Internal investigations revealed the necessity for the company to restate its accounts, which precipitated its impending loss of investment grade credit rating, a futile attempt at merger with a smaller competitor and, ultimately, to its filing for bankruptcy protection when the credit-rating downgrade meant it was in default of its loan covenants.

There were many potential institutions that should, at an earlier stage, have prevented Enron from exploiting the gaps in the accounting rules: the audit committee that oversaw the internal controls; the in-house counsel and external counsel who have expertise over the disclosure of related party transactions; the auditors who check on the accounting practices of the company; and the securities analysts, whose task it is to analyse the financial information and appraise investment opportunities. For a variety of reasons, these institutions did not prevent the accounting manipulations. The accounting irregularities grew so large that when the market scrutiny finally came about, they caused the demise of the company.

The auditor, Arthur Anderson, was the most salient intermediary at fault. It is true that Arthur Andersen had, in the course of its historical development, built a good reputation for rigour and integrity in its auditing services. It had a substantial store of reputational capital that, importantly, underpinned its audit services, which spanned the globe. According to the reputational intermediary theory, it would not place its goodwill associated with its brand name at risk by reason of one client, albeit a big and important one. And yet, even if it was not a co-conspirator to the accounting manipulations, it is fair to say that it was less than rigorous in its audit work.

A thorough review of Enron's financial statement records, seasoned with a touch of scepticism, would have yielded a very different outcome. This is aptly demonstrated by the due diligence investigation conducted by Dynergy, the competitor to whom a merger proposal was pitched when Enron realised that downgrade of the credit-risk rating was imminent. Dynergy exercised its right to conduct due diligence investigations after the merger agreement was agreed to on 9 November 2001; within three weeks, Dynergy found the financial statements unacceptable and terminated the merger on 28 November 2001. The difference lay in this: whereas it was in Dynergy's self-interest to be sceptical, the same could not be said of Arthur Andersen.

Enron was far from being an isolated instance of accounting irregularities and the failure of auditors as gatekeepers. It was but the most notorious example of accounting manipulation that escaped detection by the auditors. A close competitor for notoriety was Worldcom, where management illegitimately capitalised line-costs totalling $3.8 billion over five quarters – payments to other telecommunication companies

[14] J Laing, 'The Bear that Roared: How short-seller Jim Chanos helped expose Enron' *Barron's* (New York, 28 January 2002) 18. See also Chano's testimony before the House Committee on Energy and Commerce in House of Representatives, 'Hearings before the Committee on Energy and Commerce' (107th Congress, 2nd Session, Serial No 107-83, 6 February 2002) 71–75.

[15] B McLean, 'Is Enron overpriced?' *Fortune* (New York, 5 March 2001) 122.

for rights to use their telecommunication lines – which should have been treated as expenses. Arthur Andersen was again the auditor. The Bankruptcy Examiner investigating the collapse of Worldcom found that management had deceived the auditor 'on a number of occasions'; however, he found lapses in the auditor's approach to testing the areas where there existed the risk of fraud.[16] The post-mortem report of the independent directors similarly concluded that while the auditors identified areas of risk and assessed the adequacy of controls, they did not sufficiently carry out the 'traditional substantive testing of information maintained in the accounting records and financial statements'.[17]

IV. What Went Wrong?

First, the origins of the accounting irregularities lie with the accounting rules and the process. If the accounting rules specified strict rules on what counted as 'unconsolidated affiliates', and had required consolidation of all affiliates that Enron effectively owned or controlled, they would have precluded the entire scheme to obtain off-balance sheet treatment of Enron's debts. But more than the gaps in the accounting rules, the auditor was very much answerable for why the egregiously misleading presentation of liabilities came to be. The view that an independent investor holding a minimum of 3 per cent in the debt and equity of the SPE was sufficient to count as an unconsolidated affiliate was merely a position on a matter that was in flux. Moreover, it was invariably paired with the requirement that control resided with the independent investor. A prudent auditor would first test whether there was in fact such control by the independent investor. But more than that, the exercise of professional judgement would require it to make an assessment whether non-consolidation was justified, given that Enron remained contingently liable even if the SPE assumed primary obligation for the debts associated with the 'heavy assets'.

This leads to the second point – why did the auditor let matters slip? A common phrase used to capture the problem is 'conflict of interest', though the problem is better viewed as professionalism-distorting incentives. Arthur Andersen was not conflicted merely because Enron paid for it to audit its accounts. The problem was more serious. Arthur Andersen was offering more than auditing services; its auditing services were merely an entry point for Arthur Andersen's provision of more lucrative consultancy services. And the firm culture had developed accordingly. The performance of audit partners was judged by more than the revenues from the auditing work carried out; they were expected to create new streams of revenue by selling consultancy services. If the pressure on retaining an audit client placed pressure on the professional judgement expected of auditors, judging audit partners by the additional revenues from consultancy work increased that pressure. The pressures might have been resisted if the firm had retained the former workings of the Professional Standards Group (PSG), the firm's

[16] 'Third and Final Report of Dick Thornburgh' (n 6).

[17] DR Beresford, N deB Katzenbach and CB Rogers, *Report of Investigation by Special Investigative Committee of the Board of Directors of Worldcom, Inc* (31 March 2003) 19.

internal professional setting mechanism. There was a time when the auditing standards of the firm were determined by this central body – what it determined governed how the local partners carried out their work. But in the period leading up to the Enron implosion, the PSG no longer carried the authority of the past. Local partners were given the authority to make the final decision after considering the position of the PSG. This is not to say that all were swayed in their professional judgement because of the hold that an important client had over the firm. The local PSG representative in Houston – Carl Bass – did raise concerns regarding Enron's aggressive accounting policies behind the scenes. Enron came to learn of his views and insisted that Andersen made arrangements to ensure that Bass cease any further involvement with Enron matters. Despite some misgivings, Andersen gave in to Enron's demand. Apparently, this was driven by the fear that the lucrative consulting work would be moved to other firms.[18]

This leads one to a third insight. While professionalism and professional reputation is important – as exemplified by Carl Bass and other individuals who played their part to signal their concerns with Enron's accounts – the reputational capital has a number of facets. Apart from mastery over one's tools of trade, the reputation extends to how one deals with clients. The audit practice is, after all, a business. A reputation for being difficult can drive away clients. At the level of client interaction, bounded rationality invariably operates. Faced with an irate client and the very real prospect of losing lucrative work, the risk of aggressive accounting positions causing severe damage to one's reputation would tend to be downplayed. Especially so if the account is one's responsibility and the downside reputational risk is borne by the whole firm. Given this, it is far too optimistic to expect that reputational capital by itself will be a reliable guardrail for ensuring that the individuals who operate the gatekeeping services will provide the verification or certification of consistent quality. One has to keep constant watch over the professionalism-distorting incentives and ensure that there are sufficient rules and institutions in place to check on problem areas. Gatekeepers operate in an eco-system. It is necessary to keep constant watch over the factors that undermine the integrity of the gatekeeping task.

V. Reforms in the Aftermath of the Enron and Other Accounting Scandals

Predictably, a slew of changes took place in response to Enron. On 22 January 2002, the SEC responded to a petition by accounting firms to provide interpretative guidance on disclosures in the Management Discussion & Analysis (MD&A),[19] on three areas of particular concern:

- liquidity and capital resources, including off-balance sheet arrangements;
- certain trading activities involving non-exchange traded contracts accounted for at fair value; and

[18] Eichenwald (n 9) 426.

[19] Item 303 of Regulation S-K; item 303 of Regulation S-B; Item 5 of Form 20-F, Operating and Financial Review and Prospects.

- relationships and transactions with persons or entities that derive benefits from their non-independent relationship with the registrant or the registrant's related parties.[20]

In the guidance on disclosures relating to off-balance arrangements, the SEC advised that where the 'registrant may be economically or legally required or reasonably likely to fund losses of an unconsolidated, limited purpose entity … or may be financially affected by the performance or non-performance of [the entity]', the MD&A was expected to provide information so that investors have 'a clear understanding of the registrant's business activities, financial arrangements, and financial statements'.[21]

On the accounting front, the FASB issued FIN 46 on 17 January 2003, which was an interpretation of Accounting Rule Bulletin 51 (ARB 51) relating to Consolidated Financial Statements.[22] For investments in an SPE that amounts to a Variable Interest Entity (VIE), FIN 46 shifted the focus from the criteria of control indicated by majority voting interest, to identification of the primary beneficiary through examining who has a majority of the risk and rewards in the undertakings of the SPE. Upon being identified as the primary beneficiary, its accounts must consolidate the accounts of the SPE–VIE. The Interpretation fixes the gap that Enron exploited; but more than this, it addressed the increasing problem related to VIEs, that is, entities where the legal holdings in shares do not adequately reveal the risk and rewards assumed by other stakeholders in the company.[23] The accounting scandals (of which Enron was the most salient and emblematic) gave momentum to resolution of a matter that had reached stalemate in the FASB.

In the meantime, the US Congress enacted SOX 2002.[24] Apart from requiring the SEC to create final rules relating to the disclosure of all material off-balance sheet transactions with unconsolidated entities, the Act created new institutions and put in place a number of mandatory institutional arrangements and obligations to deal with the lapses revealed by the accounting scandals.

A new institution – the Public Company Accounting Oversight Board (PCAOB) – was created to oversee the audit of public companies subject to securities laws. The PCAOB was also given the mandate to register and thus regulate all public accounting firms that sought to provide auditing services to public companies. Amongst other matters, the creation of this public body having oversight of accounting standards of public companies places front and centre the element of public interest in the integrity

[20] SEC, 'Commission Statement about Management's Discussion and Analysis of Financial Condition and Results of Operations' (Release Nos 33-8056; 34-45321; FR-61) at www.sec.gov/rules/other/33-8056.htm (accessed 24 May 2021).

[21] ibid. Following the mandate in SOX 2002, s 401(a), the SEC on 28 January 2003 issued rules on 'Disclosure in Management's Discussion and Analysis about Off-Balance Sheet Arrangements and Aggregate Contractual Obligations' (Release Nos 33-8182; 34-47264; FR-67) at www.sec.gov/rules/final/33-8182.htm#P76_4771 (accessed 24 May 2021).

[22] Financial Accounting Standards Board (FASB), 'FIN 46' (17 January 2003) at www.fasb.org/summary/finsum46.shtml (accessed 24 May 2021).

[23] FIN 46 was revised in December of the same year to provide further guidance on how to calculate the economic risk and rewards: FASB, 'FASB Interpretation No 46 (revised December 2003) Consolidation of Variable Interest Entities; an interpretation of ARB No 51' (December 2003) at www.fasb.org/jsp/FASB/Document_C/DocumentPage?cid=1175801627792&acceptedDisclaimer=true (accessed 24 May 2021). This was, in turn, replaced by FASB Statement 167 in June 2009, which addressed the new issues presented by the GFC of 2008.

[24] SOX 2002 (n 5).

and transparency of financial statements. Whereas such an objective was an outworking of professionalism of the accounting firms in the FASB, the creation of a public institution having oversight of both the accounting-auditing standards and the accounting firms servicing public companies served to mitigate the latent tensions that subsist when the profession is considering creating rules and issuing interpretations that may incur the displeasure of its clients.

Given the professionalism-distorting incentives resulting from auditors' use of auditing services as a portal for obtaining more lucrative consultancy work, SOX 2002 imposed a wide-ranging prohibition against auditors' providing non-audit services, which extend to 'expert services' unrelated to audit and any other service determined impermissible by the Board.[25] The prohibition is not absolute, however, as the audit committee of the issuer is empowered to authorise such non-audit-related service engagements.[26] Thus, whereas management previously had untrammelled authority to decide on engaging auditors for other services, the change requires such decisions to be channelled through the audit committee. To mitigate client capture of an audit partner, SOX 2002 stipulates that an audit partner having primary responsibility for the audit or with responsibility for reviewing the audit cannot hold that role for more than five years.[27]

The audit committee is not a new institution, but its significance has grown over time.[28] Under SOX 2002, the audit committee assumed significantly heightened responsibilities to safeguard the integrity of the auditing process and, consequently, the reliability of the accounts and audited financial statements. The Act stipulates that the audit committee of the public company hold the authority to decide on the appointment and compensation of auditors.[29] As a corollary to this, the audit committee exercises oversight of the auditing process, and the auditor is obliged to report, inter alia, all critical accounting policies and practices adopted, and alternative treatment of financial information. Where there are differences between management and the auditor,

[25] Securities Exchange Act 1944, s 10A(g), introduced by SOX 2002, s 201.

[26] Securities Exchange Act 1944, s 10A(h), introduced by SOX 2002, s 201.

[27] Securities Exchange Act 1944, s 10A(j) introduced by SOX 2002, s 203. The related idea of mandatory audit firm rotation has been explored from time to time. SOX 2002, s 207 required the US Comptroller General to study and review the potential effects of such an initiative; the resultant GAO Report to the Senate Committee on Banking, Housing, and Urban Affairs and the House Committee on Financial Services advised that mandatory audit firm rotation 'may not be the most efficient way to strengthen auditor independence and improve audit quality': 'Required Study on the Potential Effects of Mandatory Audit Firm Rotation' (GAO-04-216, November 2003) 8 at www.gao.gov/assets/gao-04-216.pdf (accessed on 25 May 2021). In 2011, the PCAOB revisited the idea of mandatory audit firm rotation when it released a concept paper for public comment: 'PCAOB Issues Concept Release on Auditor Independence and Audit Firm Rotation' (*PCAOB*, 16 August 2011) at pcaobus.org/news-events/news-releases/news-release-detail/pcaob-issues-concept-release-on-auditor-independence-and-audit-firm-rotation_348 (accessed 19 October 2021). After some exploration, the matter was finally dropped in 2014: C Posner, 'PCAOB Nixes Mandatory Auditor Rotation' (*Cooley*, 6 February 2014) at www.cooley.com/news/insight/2014/pcaob-nixes-mandatory-auditor-rotation (accessed 19 October 2021).

[28] Blue Ribbon Committee on Improving the Effectiveness of Corporate Audit Committees, 'Report and Recommendations of the Blue Ribbon Committee on Improving the Effectiveness of Corporate Audit Committees' (1999) 54 *The Business Lawyer* 1067; SD Buchalter and KL Yokomoto, 'Audit Committees' Responsibilities and Liability' (2003) 73(3) *The CPA Journal* 18.

[29] Securities Exchange Act 1934, s 10A(m)(2), inserted by SOX 2002, s 301.

the audit committee is expected to superintend the resolution of such differences.[30] It is also required to institute procedures for dealing with complaints relating to accounting, auditing and internal controls, as well as employee submissions regarding questionable accounting or auditing matters.[31] Coffee views this as a realignment of the principal–agent relationship, viz prescribing an organ within the public company whose members are independent and sufficiently removed from managerial interest and that is charged with the responsibility of ensuring the integrity of the accounts and the audit process.[32] As we shall see, the better view is to view the regulatory response as creating robust institutions with healthy lines of accountability – a dynamic eco-system that needs to be monitored for professionalism-distorting influences.

Another noteworthy regulatory response that needs to be mentioned is the strategy of senior management responsibility. The 2002 Act prescribes that the equivalent of the chief executive officer (CEO) and the chief financial officer (CFO) must sign off on the annual or quarterly reports to be filed with the SEC. This involves the designated senior managers certifying that they have reviewed the reports to be filed and that, based on their knowledge, the reports do not contain any untrue statement and fairly present the financial condition and operations of the issuer.[33] Designated senior management are also responsible for establishing and maintaining robust internal controls, and making an assessment of the internal controls.[34] This focuses the attention of individuals within the firm on the substance of what they are responsible for – and saliently warns that there are real regulatory consequences for the individual.[35]

VI. The Global Financial Crisis of 2007–08 and Credit Rating Agencies

The credit rating agencies counted as one of the gatekeepers that failed to safeguard the interest of Enron investors.[36] Up until four days before Enron filed for bankruptcy, its

[30] ibid.

[31] Securities Exchange Act 1934, s 10A(m)(4), inserted by SOX 2002, s 301.

[32] Coffee (n 4) 340.

[33] SOX 2002, s 302 and Securities Exchange Act 1934 Rules 13a-14 and 15d-14, 17 CFR § 240.13a-14 and 17 CFR § 240.15d-14 respectively. See also SEC, 'Certification of Disclosure in Companies' Quarterly and Annual Reports' (Release No 33-8124) at www.sec.gov/rules/final/33-8124.htm (accessed 25 May 2021).

[34] SOX 2002, s 404; and SEC, 'Management's Report on Internal Control Over Financial Reporting and Certification of Disclosure in Exchange Act Periodic Reports' (Release Nos 33-8238; 34-47986) at www.sec.gov/rules/final/33-8238.htm (accessed 25 May 2021).

[35] In some contexts, it may be possible to regulate the remuneration structures to safeguard against problematic incentives. See, eg, Monetary Authority of Singapore, 'Consultation Paper on Proposals to Refine the Tier Structure Requirements and to Introduce New Requirements Relating to Remuneration' (12 July 2021) at www.mas.gov.sg/publications/consultations/2021/cp-on-proposals-to-refine-the-tier-structure-requirements-and-to-introduce-new-requirements-relating-to-remuneration (accessed 23 September 2021).

[36] There remain those with faith in market institutions. See, eg, SL Schwarcz, 'Private Ordering of Public Markets: The Rating Agency Paradox' [2002] *University of Illinois Law Review* 1. Cf F Partnoy, 'The Siskel and Ebert of Financial Markets? Two Thumbs Down for the Credit Rating Agencies' (1999) 77 *Washington University Law Quarterly* 619 (asserting that the demand for CRA ratings is driven by the lower regulatory burdens (regulatory licence) associated with holding 'investment grade' securities). Hunt argues for a liability scheme based on the limitations of reputation and other controls over novel and complex financial

credit rating had not changed.[37] The aftermath of the accounting irregularity scandals of the early 2000s saw the enactment of the Credit Rating Agency Reform Act (CRARA) 2006. The inadequacies of credit rating agencies as gatekeepers were further revealed in the GFC of 2007–08, where the CRAs were regarded as one of the major contributors to facilitating the issue of structured financial products that triggered the crisis.

Structured financial products have certain characteristics in common with corporate bonds – but other features render their nature much more complex and their credit rating more challenging. Structured financial products are invariably issued by SPVs, into which assets are transferred. Structured products typically take the form of bonds; investors are promised a fixed return on their investments. The returns to the investors depend on the revenue generated by the assets. In order to generate investment grade bonds, different tranches of securities are issued by the SPV. The higher tranches have priority over the lower tranches, and thereby provide greater assurance of payment. Tranching is therefore key to generating 'investment grade' bonds, even if the underlying assets are not of high quality. The SPV will also enter into swap arrangements with service providers in order to ensure that there are no liquidity problems arising from the mismatch between the revenues and obligations.

An incentive problem inhabits the creation of structured financial products. The underlying assets tend to be debt claims, for example property mortgages and student loans. As the underlying assets will be taken off the books of the originators and transferred to the SPV, the originators do not have the same incentive to scrutinise the creditworthiness of the debtor and, hence, the quality of the debt claims they create. In the case of mortgage-backed securities, the incentive problem resulted in banks' providing loans to home buyers whose credit-risk profiles would not ordinarily qualify them for housing loans. This carried implications for the quality of the underlying assets, even as the credit ratings were based on historical default rates drawn from data relating to assets of different quality.

The CRAs were tasked with rating structured finance products that had bond-like features, but for which there were inadequate data to support sound mathematical models, especially given the complexity of the structured finance products. There was considerable pressure for the products to be accorded investment grade. For the originators and investment bankers, it was imperative that the top tranche be of investment grade; more than this, successful fundraising required this tranche to be as large as possible. As the credit rating of the structured finance products was lucrative and the investment banks providing this kind of work constituted a concentrated circle of retainers, the investment banks could credibly threaten a CRA that it would shop for another agency more amenable to its demands. This even if the credit rating market was dominated by Moody's, Standard & Poor's, and Fitch.[38] The demand for investment grade 'bonds' was also driven by institutional investors.

products: JP Hunt, 'Credit Rating Agencies and the "Worldwide Credit Crisis": The Limits of Reputation, the Insufficiency of Reform and a Proposal for Improvement' [2009] *Columbia Business Law Review* 109.

[37] Committee on Government Affairs of the US Senate, 'Financial Oversight of Enron: The SEC and Private-Sector Watchdogs' (7 October 2002) 84–85.

[38] A Senate report on Dodd-Frank Act attributed the CRAs' errors to conflicts of interest in the rating process and flawed mathematical models based on inadequate data: 'The Restoring American Financial Stability Act of 2010' (Senate Report No 111-176, 2010) 36.

In the global financial crisis, many structured products went into default. And the CRAs were blamed for providing erroneous ratings or giving investment grade credit ratings when they were not deserved.[39]

VII. Reforms Relating to Credit Rating Agencies

Regulatory initiatives relating to the CRAs began soon after the revelation of the accounting scandals. In 2006, the CRARA was passed.[40] The Act firmly established the SEC's regulatory powers over CRAs, which had hitherto been somewhat uncertain. The Net Capital Rule issued in 1975 distinguished between 'investment grade' assets and non-investment grade assets, and how they count toward the capital requirements of broker dealers.[41] The credit rating depended critically on whether it was assessed by a Nationally Recognized Statistical Rating Organization (NRSRO). What constituted an NRSRO was defined neither by statute nor by regulations. Instead, whether an organisation was regarded as an NRSRO depended on the SEC's willingness to issue a 'no action' letter in response to a rating agency's application to be so regarded.[42] Despite attempts by the SEC to define the NRSRO, the attempts did not bear fruit. One of the concerns was whether the SEC had a sound statutory basis for assuming regulation of NRSROs. The CRARA 2006 put the matter beyond doubt by making it clear that the SEC has the authority to provide such recognition and require applicants to furnish substantial information in support of their application. Amongst other matters, this includes statistics relating to credit ratings performance, and the procedures and methodologies used to determine credit ratings. By introducing objective criteria for qualifying as NRSRO, the CRARA 2006 sought to facilitate new entrants seeking to enter the market; at the same time, the measures introduced a formal accountability framework for NRSROs. Although the SEC was invested with increased regulatory powers – including the power to regulate conflicts of interest[43] – it did not have the power to 'regulate the substance

[39] Suits for civil liability have, by and large, been unsuccessful. In the United States, the CRAs have been able to defend themselves by reason of the rights under the First Amendment. See C Picciau, 'The Evolution of the Liability of Credit Rating Agencies in the United States and in the European Union: Regulation after the Crisis' (2018) 15 *European Company and Financial Law Review* 339. An exceptional case is *ABN Amro Bank NV v Bathurst Regional Council* [2014] FCAFC 65, where, on appeal, Standard & Poor's accepted that the rating of the 'Rembrandt notes' was not done with due care. The Full Federal Court rejected Standard & Poor's argument that it did not owe a duty of care to the investors with whom it did not have a contractual relationship. See further A Sahore, '*ABN Amro Bank NV v Bathurst Regional Council*: Credit Rating Agencies and Liability to Investors' (2015) 37(3) *Sydney Law Review* 43.

[40] Credit Rating Agency Reform Act 2006 (CRARA) (US), Public Law 109–291, 120 Stat 1327.

[41] Securities Exchange Act 1934 Rule 15c3-1, 17 CFR § 240.15c3-1. See further CRS Report for Congress, 'Credit Rating Agency Reform Act of 2006' (11 October 2006) at www.everycrsreport.com/files/20061011_RS22519_5c843e84ccf35bd2c2e9d17a9a059a84b380c341.pdf (accessed 19 October 2021).

[42] Staff of Senate Committee on Governmental Affairs, 'Financial Oversight of Enron: The SEC and Private Sector Watchdogs' (107th Congress, S Prt 107-75, 2002) 80: '[A] credit rating agency initiates the no-action letter process by requesting a no-action letter that will state that the Commission staff will not recommend enforcement action against persons who use the firm's credit ratings for purposes of the Commission's net capital rule'. See further, CM Mulligan, 'From AAA to F: How the Credit Rating Agencies Failed America and What can be Done to Protect Investors' (2009) 50 *Boston College Law Review* 1275, 1280.

[43] See Securities Exchange Act 1934 Rule 17g-5, 17 CFR § 240.17g-5. See further, L Bai, 'On Regulating Conflicts of Interests in the Credit Rating Industry' (2010) 13 *NYU Journal of Legislation and Public Policy* 253.

of credit ratings, or the procedures or methodologies by which an NRSRO determines credit ratings'.[44]

The Dodd-Frank Act enacted in the aftermath of the GFC of 2007–08 sought to address many perceived shortcomings in the financial system. As regards CRAs, a number of initiatives were taken. Congress noted the conflict of interest that especially confronted CRAs in the rating of structured financial products, and instructed the SEC to come up with rules to prevent sales and marketing considerations from influencing ratings.[45] Together with the 'look-back requirement'[46] – which entailed examining whether an ex-employee who has joined the subject of a credit rating has influenced the rating – the conflict-of-interest rules were made more comprehensive. Credit rating agencies were also made more accountable for internal controls, to ensure that ratings were carried out in accordance with the policies, procedures and methodologies determined by the CRA; the CEO is required to attest to the report on internal controls to the SEC.[47] To bolster the internal controls for compliance with the rating policies, procedures and methodologies adopted by the board of the CRA, the SEC is empowered to prescribe rules that secure the fidelity of the rating process to these policies, procedures and methodologies.[48] An Office of Credit Rating (OCR) was also set up, inter alia to conduct an annual examination of each NRSRO.[49] Transparency in ratings was promoted by the requirement to disclose detailed information, including the methodology used for the credit rating, the data used to generate the rating, an assessment of the quality of information considered, the potential volatility of the rating and the sensitivity of the rating to the NRSRO's assumptions.[50]

VIII. Financial Intermediaries as Gatekeepers in the International Financial System

In the international financial system, financial intermediaries are designated gatekeepers against money laundering and terrorism financing. Despite criticisms of the effectiveness of the global anti-money laundering (AML) and counter-terrorism financing (CFT) system,[51] it is still remarkable that norms formulated by the Financial Action Task Force (FATF) – whose members currently consist of 37 jurisdictions and two regional groupings – are able to be disseminated globally. These norms do not

[44] Securities Exchange Act 1934, s 15E(c)(2).
[45] ibid s 15E(h)(3), added by Dodd-Frank Act, s 932.
[46] Securities Exchange Act 1934, s 15E(h)(4), added by Dodd-Frank Act, s 932.
[47] Securities Exchange Act 1934, s 15E(c)(3), added by Dodd-Frank Act, s 932.
[48] Securities Exchange Act 1934, s 15E(r), added by Dodd-Frank Act, s 932.
[49] Securities Exchange Act 1934, s 15E(p), added by Dodd-Frank Act, s 932.
[50] Securities Exchange Act 1934 Rule 17g-7(a), 17 CFR § 240.17g-7(a), in accordance with s 15E(q), added by the Dodd-Frank Act, s 932.
[51] RF Pol, 'Anti-money laundering: The world's least effective policy experiment? Together, we can fix it' (2020) 3 *Policy Design and Practice* 73 (estimating that AML measures have less than 0.1% impact on criminal finances, and that compliance costs exceed recovered criminal funds more than a hundred times); J Cusack, 'Global Threat Assessment' (*Financial Crime News*, November 2019) at thefinancialcrimenews.com/global-threat-assessment-to-download-read (accessed 19 October 2021) (estimating that financial crimes amounting to $5.8 trillion were perpetrated; this is approximately 6.7% of global GDP).

form part of a treaty. They do not have the status of hard law in international law. They are merely soft norms. Yet they are sufficient to induce jurisdictions in which significant financial centres are located to enact legislation giving effect to them. More than that, jurisdictions are willing to subject themselves to the mutual evaluation process, in which assessors carry out fairly intrusive inquiries into the effectiveness of a jurisdiction's laws and the enforcement of the norms. Functionally, these jurisdictions have become gatekeepers against money laundering and terrorism financing in the international financial system.

To understand why this has happened, one needs to understand the eco-system. Specifically, the eco-system to which the AML and CFT norms are attached, and the disincentives regarding non-compliance. At the centre of the measures is the flow of funds. This, in turn, is intimately connected with the business activity and reasons for the movement of funds. If a jurisdiction is perceived to be an attractive refuge for illegal activity or the proceeds of crime, its reputation will be affected accordingly. The taint to its reputation has tangible consequences for its economic well-being. This is saliently illustrated by two instances of blacklisting by international organisations, which can be held up as lessons for other jurisdictions considering a departure from international soft norms.

Liechtenstein was blacklisted by the FATF in mid-2000 for deficiencies in its AML regulation, and by the OECD as a tax haven.[52] After the blacklisting, a number of unfavourable developments took place. First, it was found that formation of new trusts (*Anstalt*) declined significantly.[53] This despite the fact that the Government of Liechtenstein worked with the FATF to address the deficiencies identified by the FATF. Second, the blacklisting had a very tangible impact on the finances of Liechtenstein and its banks. In the period 2000 to 2002, taxes paid by banks declined from SFR 64 million to SFR 27 million.[54] This reflected the decline in assets managed by banks from SFR 112 billion to SFR 96 billion, and the fall in net income from SFR 548 million to SFR 251 million.[55] The reputational damage to Liechtenstein impacted on the willingness of existing and potential clients to have associations with Liechtenstein.

Vanuatu was blacklisted by the OECD as a tax haven in 2000 and as an uncooperative tax haven in 2002.[56] As regards money laundering, it took sufficient measures to avoid being placed on the FATF blacklist. The reputational damage nevertheless brought in its wake a few unpleasant consequences. In early 2002, certain banks refused transactions from Vanuatu; these included Barclays Bank, HSBC and Chase Manhattan Bank.[57] Transactions with other banks that did not cease relationships were 'intermittent'.[58]

[52] 'Liechtenstein blacklisted over money laundering' (*swissinfo*, 22 June 2000) at www.swissinfo.ch/eng/liechtenstein-blacklisted-over-money-laundering/1535350 (accessed 19 October 2021). At the same time, the Financial Stability Forum (FSB, renamed the Financial Stability Board in 2009) regarded it as a vulnerable financial system by placing it in Category 3. See further JC Sharman, 'The bark is the bite: International organizations and blacklisting' (2009) 16 *Review of International Political Economy* 573, 589–91.

[53] Sharman (n 52) 590.

[54] ibid.

[55] ibid.

[56] OECD, 'The OECD Issues The List of Unco-operative Tax Havens' (18 April 2002) at www.oecd.org/ctp/harmful/theoecdissuesthelistofunco-operativetaxhavens.htm (accessed 23 September 2021).

[57] Sharman (n 52) 587–88.

[58] ibid.

More significantly, the National Bank of Vanuatu was unable to obtain US dollars on the international foreign exchange market. Instead, it had to obtain US dollars from the local branches of Australian banks; foreign currency transactions became more costly and were subject to delays as the transactions were subject to increased scrutiny.[59]

The *FATF Recommendations* have developed in sophistication and detail. In addition to the reputational damage caused by a country's being designated a 'higher risk country', the FATF may call upon countries to apply 'enhanced due diligence measures to business relationships and transactions with natural and legal persons, and financial institutions' from such a country.[60] The FATF may also require countries to apply more serious countermeasures.[61] The initiative to apply particular countermeasures does not have to emanate from the FATF; as long as a countermeasure is effective and proportionate to the identified risk, a country is entitled to apply the countermeasure independently. An Interpretative Note sets out examples of the countermeasures that might be applied. Amongst the most damaging countermeasures are:

- prohibiting or refusing permission to financial institutions from the blacklisted country to set up subsidiaries, branches or representative offices;[62]
- limiting business relationships or financial transactions with the blacklisted country and/or persons in the country;[63]
- requiring financial institutions to terminate correspondent relationships with financial institutions in the blacklisted country.[64]

This is not to say that enhanced due diligence measures do not hold much threat. The enhanced due diligence measures may sound prosaic, with many of them involving 'obtaining additional information' on a variety of subjects, ranging from customer-related information, to the intended purpose and the nature of the business relationship, to the source of funds.[65] These portend delays and increased costs. For business that rely on timely payment, the enhanced due diligence measures are more than an inconvenience; they can be highly damaging to business relationships and sap the willingness of counterparties to enter into deals with the affected entities.

Reputational damage, together with the threat of countermeasures and the call for enhanced due diligence measures against businesses associated with a country, goes a long way towards nudging a country to create an AML/CFT system that passes muster according to the FATF standards. This explains the widespread adoption of AML/CFT legislation globally and, materially, the imposition of obligations on financial institutions that reflect the demands of the *FATF Recommendations*.

[59] ibid.

[60] Recommendation 19 of *FATF Recommendations: International Standards on Combating Money Laundering and the Financing of Terrorism & Proliferation* (2012–2020) (hereinafter *FATF Recommendations*). The black list and grey list jurisdictions are referred to as 'high-risk jurisdictions subject to a call for action' and 'jurisdictions under increased monitoring', respectively: see FATF, 'FATF Recommendations' (as amended June 2021) at www.fatf-gafi.org/publications/?hf=10&b=0&s=desc(fatf_releasedate) (accessed 19 October 2021).

[61] *FATF Recommendations* (n 60).

[62] Interpretative Note to Recommendation 19 para 2(c) and (d), *FATF Recommendations* (n 60).

[63] Interpretative Note to Recommendation 19 para 2(e), *FATF Recommendations* (n 60).

[64] Interpretative Note to Recommendation 19 para 2(g), *FATF Recommendations* (n 60).

[65] Interpretative Note to Recommendation 10, *FATF Recommendations* (n 60).

The financial institutions that have to implement compliance measures for AML and CFT are 'gatekeepers' in the original sense of the term. They control a person's access to funds and control over funds: from account opening, to the outward transfer of funds, to the receipt of funds. To the extent that a person wishes to invest in financial products available from a financial institution, it is a checkpoint as regards the person's access to the financial product. And to the extent that a person wishes a fund transfer to accomplish other business purposes, the due diligence measures might check the legitimacy of those purposes. The measures cannot be expected to be fail-safe, and they should be viewed as a first line of checks against ready use of the international financial system for money laundering and terrorism financing.

In common with the other gatekeepers, a financial institution that performs frontline gatekeeping functions against money laundering and terrorism financing may encounter conflicts of interest. Its drive for profits means that it is in its interest to take on customers who place a significant amount of funds with it; the corollary to this is the desire to earn fees by providing customers with the services they desire, whether these consist of fund transfers, investments or other financial services. That will explain why the media periodically report on large fines imposed on banks that have been lax in their AML/CFT compliance.

Some of the triggers are fairly straightforward, for example the reporting of transactions above designated thresholds. Others require the exercise of some judgement, for example whether the circumstances of the transaction raise a suspicion that money laundering or terrorism financing is involved, or whether the beneficial owner of the funds is identified to the satisfaction of the banker. To ensure the robustness of the AML/CFT regime, the FATF carries out periodic 'Mutual Evaluations'. Assessors from the FATF evaluate submissions from the subject jurisdiction, and carry out an on-the-ground assessment of whether the implementation and enforcement accord with the norms that have been created. This, in turn, puts pressure on the national regulators to ensure that the financial institutions within their jurisdiction are duly carrying out their compliance operations, and that the regulators themselves are carrying out their functions with competence and diligence.

IX. What Lessons for the Notion of Gatekeepers and Reputational Intermediaries?

The theory of the reputational intermediary should be recognised as an aspiration built on a hope. Reputations are valuable to businesses, but a moment's thought will reveal that it is far too simplistic to posit that a business's concern for its reputation will be sufficient to prevent its representatives from seeking increased earnings, even if the latter is not commensurate with the reputational capital. The risk undertaken may be under-appreciated, as was the case with Andersen's removal of Carl Bass from any further involvement in the audit of Enron. Moreover, reputations have different facets. Given the pressures on revenue growth placed on the local partners of Andersen in Houston, it is inevitable that their judgements would be affected more by growing the business than by the seemingly remote reputational risk. A reputation for upholding standards in the best traditions of professionalism is good, but pushed too far, one might be perceived as being unreasonably demanding and finicky. Consequently, clients may prefer another professional who is more accommodating of the positions taken by the client. Reputation alone cannot ensure professionalism that inures to the public good.

The eco-system matters. One needs to discern the parameters that determine rules or norms by which professionals do their work, the incentives that drive changes and the institutions that are involved in the change. The largely self-regulatory nature of the accounting profession and the interest of the profession not to antagonise its clients explain the lack of progress over the consolidation rules with SPEs; it took the heavy price of the accounting scandals borne by diverse investors to further move the FASB to issuing new rules on VIEs. The PCAOB, with regulatory oversight of accountants servicing public companies, is thus a useful institution to deal with the conflict-of-interest issues that inhibit the professionals from developing rules and norms in the public interest. It also builds in an additional dimension of accountability, which potentially checks on self-interested considerations that are at variance with what public interest demands. A healthy regulatory eco-system requires institutions that focus on what the public interest requires. While the SEC had regulatory competence to deal with accounting rules, the creation of the PCAOB probably better fulfils the function of engaging with the accounting profession and giving the necessary special attention to matters dealing with accounting and audit.

From an eco-system perspective, the creation of the OCR signals the creation of an institution that enhances the system for accountability of CRAs. The rules on the separation of sales from the credit rating personnel go some way towards addressing the conflict-of-interest issues that might skew the ratings assessment. Similarly, the requirement in statute for a majority of the board of directors to consist of independent directors. However, insofar as the rating process involves judgements relating to the creation of mathematical models and determination of what kind of data are suitable, these are matters of professional judgement as regards which the OCR and the SEC are precluded from having substantive input. And perhaps the complexity of creating new ratings models is a matter best left to professional judgement. But that reveals a gap: what is there to constrain revenue or business development considerations from skewing the judgement of the professionals working on ratings models? Despite the separation of the sales and marketing team from the ratings team, and the creation of a board constituted by a majority of independent directors, considerations of revenue and business development might nonetheless be transmitted under the guise of competitive pressure or client engagement. Accountability in the form of requirements to submit to the regulators information relating to the rating model and the data relied on might go some way toward mitigating actions that might betray the public trust on the credit ratings. The current model of dealing with the problems with CRAs revealed in the GFC does not provide a complete solution. Alternatives suggested thus far have not held the promise of a necessarily better solution. One can only hope that the eco-system that has been created after the GFC has engendered sufficient accountability and controls to prevent inaccurate ratings swayed by professionalism distorting considerations. The reputation of the CRA doing a rating still matters, but the GFC holds the lesson that reputation alone cannot ensure that the ratings evaluation can withstand professionalism-distorting influences.

By comparison, the AML/CFT eco-system as regards financial intermediaries as gatekeepers is more tractable. The inter-connectedness of finance means that the influential jurisdictions have the levers to require other jurisdictions that want to plug into the international financial system to play by the rules that they create through the FATF. There is very real economic pain to be expected from being placed on the list of Non-cooperative Countries and Territories. And to the extent that financial institutions need to be plugged into the international financial system to be of value to the clients they serve, they too need to play along. Reputational harm would visit financial institutions that blatantly violate or negligently fail to comply with the AML/CFT norms. Yet there is little mention of financial intermediaries as driven by reputation. Perhaps everyone knows deep down that the banks are driven to increase their revenues, and that reputation is not infrequently put at risk through bankers who are amenable to doing their clients' bidding. Such healthy scepticism should similarly arise when engaging with the notion of the reputational intermediary. And it would usefully highlight why an accountability system constantly updated to ensured its continued robustness is critical to any eco-system that involves actions for the public good.

Conflict of interest is a phrase that features frequently in the literature on gatekeepers. Indeed, it is also found in the legislation. The fundamental problem with the phrase is that it is a problem that never goes away. It is inherent in the nature of how the relationships are set up. The gatekeeper is paid by the client. Yet one seems to expect the gatekeeper to uphold the public expectations unaffected by the demands of the client. Many of the measures dealing with conflict of interest can only mitigate the inherent problem: the drive for business and taking care of the client relationship on the one hand, and the social/public good that results from one's professionalism on the other hand. China walls and independent boards do not fully resolve this tension. This is not to say that they are useless. What is important is to recognise the prevalence of professionalism-distorting incentives, and the limitations of market institutions in dealing with this tension. Astute regulatory oversight and robust accountability requirements help safeguard the public interest. Properly employed, they help maintain balance in the eco-system. Improperly used, they impose undue burdens and exact unnecessary costs.

18

A Fine Balance: Insolvency Practitioners and the Leveraging of Intermediary Power

SARAH PATERSON

I. Introduction

This chapter is concerned with the role that insolvency practitioners have played in the development of so-called landlord Company Voluntary Arrangements (landlord CVAs). As we shall see, insolvency practitioners have a statutory role in Company Voluntary Arrangements (CVAs), which is described in this chapter as a gatekeeper intermediary role between the company and its creditors. However, the argument is made that insolvency practitioners have adapted the CVA to meet a specific demand of companies that have approached them for advice, and in the process have come to be seen by certain creditors and stakeholders as performing an advisory role for what insolvency practitioners loosely see as their client (the company in financial distress) rather than a gatekeeper intermediary role between the company and its creditors. The specific demand is for a solution to the problem of rental liabilities on over-rented leasehold estates, and the innovation that has emerged is the landlord CVA.

The chapter locates this narrative in the theoretical literature on the battle for work between, and within, professions. It argues that the battle for work became heightened for insolvency practitioners in the last decade because of changes in the finance and corporate markets, leading insolvency practitioners to leverage procedures where they have an advantage as the statutorily appointed intermediary, to win appointments. However, it also suggests that insolvency practitioners only occupy this privileged position because they are mandated to fulfil the gatekeeper role. Thus, it suggests that if creditors and stakeholders come to see the balance tipped too far in favour of the advisory role then insolvency practitioners will face ever-increasing difficulties in defending work as specialised insolvency practitioner work in an increasingly crowded market. As a result, the chapter argues that insolvency practitioners must take care to balance the two roles, and some suggestions as to how this might be achieved are advanced.

II. The CVA and the Role of the Insolvency Practitioner

The CVA was first proposed by the Cork Committee when it reported on reform to English corporate insolvency law in 1982,[1] and was introduced in the Insolvency Act 1986.[2] Only seven, relatively brief sections set out the procedure, and even with later amendments, the entire procedure is contained in sections 1–7B of part 1 of the Insolvency Act 1986. Some further, limited guidance is given by the Insolvency Rules[3] but, as we shall see, the rather skeletal nature of the legislation has provided ample ground for interpretation and adaptation of the procedure.

The CVA is available for a company to make a proposal to its shareholders and its creditors for composition in satisfaction of its debts or a scheme of arrangement of its affairs.[4] We know, from case law in the context of schemes of arrangement proposed under a different statutory procedure (now contained in part 26 of the Companies Act 2006), that 'arrangement' is to be interpreted broadly and goes wider than a compromise.[5] The crucial element is that there is some 'give and take' between the company and those to be bound by the arrangement.[6] In a classic trading CVA, outstanding liabilities to unsecured creditors are compromised and the company is provided with a period (typically one to five years) after the CVA is approved in which it makes regular contributions to the insolvency practitioner (who acts as supervisor of the arrangement after it is approved), to facilitate dividends to pay down the CVA liabilities. If contributions are missed then usually the CVA is terminated and the company is placed into an insolvency procedure. Company Voluntary Arrangements may also be used to affect a more orderly wind-down than a liquidation, perhaps by allowing contracts to complete.[7] And they may even be used simply to create a longer runway for payments to be made.[8]

An administrator or a liquidator of the company may propose a CVA,[9] but it is primarily conceived of as a debtor in possession procedure.[10] Indeed, the Cork Committee envisaged that the CVA was 'only likely to be used … where for some reason it is not appropriate to appoint an Administrator'.[11] The statute envisages that, unless the company is in administration or liquidation, the directors of the company will make the proposal. Two roles are seen for the insolvency practitioner. First, before the CVA

[1] *Insolvency Law and Practice: Report of the Review Committee* (Cmnd 8558, 1982) (hereinafter the Review Committee is referred to as the 'Cork Committee' or the 'Committee', and the Report is referred to as the 'Cork Report').

[2] Insolvency Act 1986, pt 1.

[3] Insolvency (England and Wales) Rules 2016 (SI 2016/1024).

[4] Insolvency Act 1986, s 1.

[5] *Re Guardian Assurance Co* [1917] 1 Ch 431 (CA).

[6] *Re NFU Development Trust Ltd* [1972] 1 WLR 1548 (Ch); *Re Uniq plc* [2011] EWCH 749 (Ch).

[7] P Walton, C Umfreville and L Jacobs, 'Company Voluntary Arrangements: Evaluating Success and Failure' (R3 and ICAEW, May 2018) 12; S Frisby, 'Insolvency Law and Practice: Principles and Pragmatism Diverge?' (2011) 64 *Current Legal Problems* 349, 374.

[8] See, eg, the R3 Standard Form COVID 19 CVA Proposal at www.r3.org.uk/technical-library/england-wales/technical-guidance/r3-standard-form-covid-19-cva-proposal/ (accessed 28 April 2021).

[9] Insolvency Act 1986, s 1(3).

[10] ibid s 1(1).

[11] Cork Report (n 1) [430].

is approved, the insolvency practitioner acts as the 'nominee'.[12] The legislation contemplates that the directors will provide the nominee with a document setting out the terms of the proposed voluntary arrangement and a statement of the company's affairs.[13] The nominee's principal role is then to report to the court (within 28 days of receiving notice of the proposal or such longer period as the court may allow) on whether, in the nominee's opinion, the proposed voluntary arrangement has a reasonable prospect of being approved, and whether it should be put to the company's shareholders and creditors for approval. As already touched on, if the CVA is approved, the insolvency practitioner acts as supervisor of the arrangement. The precise nature of the supervisor's role will depend on the terms of the proposal and what it is that needs to be done to implement it.

Thus, the role envisaged for the insolvency practitioner is as a gatekeeper intermediary between the company and the creditors. It is worth noting that although the nominee submits 'a report to the court', this is merely a paper filing. No court hearing is held in a CVA, unless the CVA is challenged by a shareholder, or a creditor after it has been approved. This provides considerable explanatory power for the role of the insolvency practitioner who, in preparing his report, acts as an officer of the court. Looking solely at the statutory provisions, we might anticipate a relatively narrow role in which the insolvency practitioner preserves a rigidly independent position to provide an objective view on the fairness of the proposal the company has developed.

The reality, however, is different. In practice, the company will approach an insolvency practitioner with details of its financial difficulties, and the insolvency practitioner will be intimately involved in determining how best to address those difficulties and whether the CVA might offer a solution. As Peter Walton, Chris Umfreville and Lézelle Jacobs have noted, this advisory role is now explicitly recognised in Statement of Insolvency Practice (SIP) 3.2, which deals with practice guidance for CVAs:

> An insolvency practitioner should differentiate clearly between the stages and roles that are associated with a CVA (these being, the provision of initial advice, assisting in the preparation of the proposal, acting as the nominee, and acting as the supervisor) and ensure that they are explained to the company's directors (where they are making the proposal), shareholders and creditors.[14]

Yet it seems unlikely that an insolvency practitioner who has been intimately involved in advising the company on crafting the CVA would decide, as nominee, not to recommend it for a vote. In their 2018 report into CVAs, Walton, Umfreville and Jacobs conducted an interview of R3's members (the trade association for UK insolvency practitioners) and some semi-structured stakeholder interviews. They report concerns that 'scrutiny by the nominee of the CVA proposal may be limited'[15] and that '[s]ome practitioners felt that nominees may have a self-interest in recommending a CVA'.[16] This latter concern arises, of course, because the insolvency practitioner stands to earn fees from the CVA – a point made by Ian Fletcher in a slightly different context.[17] Indeed, as we

[12] Insolvency Act 1986, s 1(2).
[13] ibid s 2(3).
[14] Statement of Insolvency Practice 3.2, cited in Walton, Umfreville and Jacobs (n 7) 11.
[15] Walton, Umfreville and Jacobs (n 7) 57.
[16] ibid.
[17] I Fletcher, 'UK Corporate Rescue: Recent Developments – Changes to Administrative Receivership, Administration, and Company Voluntary Arrangements – the Insolvency Act 2000, the White Paper 2001, and the Enterprise Act 2002' (2004) 5 *European Business Organization Law Review* 119, 131–32.

shall see, some stakeholders have called for a new, independent party to be introduced into the process: what emerges is an example of the familiar problem, '*Quis custodet ipsos custodes?*'

A specific aspect of this problem is the concern that the insolvency practitioner's role is, in practice, more closely aligned with that of adviser for a client (the company in financial distress) than that of the neutral gatekeeper intermediary that appears to be envisaged by the statute. We have already mentioned Ian Fletcher's perceptive insights into the role of the insolvency practitioner in a specific aspect of the CVA process. And other scholars have investigated the incentives of insolvency practitioners in other processes,[18] given their repeat-player status. In an excellent book chapter, Sally Wheeler considers the way in which insolvency practitioners have leveraged their intermediary role to shape the way retention of title claims are dealt with in administration, reducing the power of ordinary unsecured trade suppliers in the process.[19] Yet overall, the way in which insolvency practitioners leverage their intermediary power in the interests of the party whom they see as controlling their access to work is under-theorised in the literature. The development of a specific adaptation, the landlord CVA, offers a fascinating lens through which to view the issue. Before we turn to the theoretical framing of the problem, it is necessary to understand something of the evolutionary history of these so-called landlord CVAs.

III. The Development of the Landlord CVA

As we have seen, the introduction of the CVA procedure was first recommended in the Cork Report. Chapter 7 of the Cork Report suggested the development of out-of-court, voluntary arrangements for individuals, and the Committee suggested that these could be adapted for use by companies.[20] The proposal was not discussed in any depth, but the Committee did provide its view of when such a voluntary arrangement for a company might be used, that is,

> where the scheme is a simple one involving a composition or moratorium or both for the general body of creditors which can be formulated and presented speedily … [W]e are convinced that the facility to promote such arrangements without the obligation to go to the Court will prove of value to small companies urgently seeking a straightforward composition or moratorium.[21]

The CVA was introduced in the Insolvency Act 1986, based on these recommendations. All creditors, secured and unsecured, receive notice of, and are entitled to vote on, the

[18] V Finch and D Milman, *Corporate Insolvency Law: Perspectives and Principles*, 3rd edn (Cambridge, Cambridge University Press, 2017) 320–21; J Armour and R Mokal, 'Reforming the Governance of Corporate Rescue: The Enterprise Act 2002' [2003] *LMCLQ* 28, 36–37; V Finch. 'Insolvency Practitioners: the Avenues of Accountability' (2012) 8 *Journal of Business Law* 645; R Stevens, 'Security after the Enterprise Act' in J Getzler and J Payne (eds), *Company Charges: Spectrum and Beyond* (Oxford, Oxford University Press, 2006) 160.

[19] S Wheeler, 'Capital fractionalized: the Role of Insolvency Practitioners in Asset Distribution' in M Cain and CB Harrington (eds), *Lawyers in a Postmodern World* (Oxford, Oxford University Press, 1994) 85.

[20] Cork Report (n 1) [428]–[430].

[21] ibid [430].

CVA proposal.[22] In order for the CVA to be approved, a majority of 75 per cent by value of voting creditors is needed[23] (of whom at least 50 per cent must be unconnected creditors).[24] And all creditors vote together in a single meeting. This contrasts with the position in a part 26 scheme of arrangement[25] and the new part 26A restructuring plan procedure introduced by the Corporate Insolvency and Governance Act 2020.[26] In these procedures, creditors are divided into classes for the purposes of voting. The starting point is found in *Sovereign Life Assurance Co v Dodd*, in which it was stated that a class 'must be confined to those persons whose rights are not so dissimilar to make it impossible for them to consult together with a view to their common interest'.[27] In practice, when applying this test, it is necessary to consider both creditor rights that are released and varied under the compromise or arrangement, and the rights creditors are to be granted pursuant to it. If those rights are so dissimilar that the creditors cannot be expected to consult together with a view to a common interest then a separate class will be formed. Moreover, the company is not required to put a scheme to all its creditors, and if a creditor's rights are untouched by the scheme, they will be left outside it.[28] Thus, the approach to the CVA is different on two counts: all creditors are invited and entitled to vote on the CVA; and all creditors vote together without separate class meetings.

This is perhaps not surprising if we return to the Cork Committee's vision for the procedure. If the Committee envisaged the promotion of 'a straightforward composition or moratorium' for 'the general body of creditors', little purpose would be served by inquiries into class voting. Furthermore, given that the Cork Committee envisaged that the procedure would be of utility for 'small companies', it is not surprising to find a simple procedure. In section II of this chapter, we briefly explored two types of CVA: the trading-based CVA and the orderly wind down. Both of these broadly conform to the Cork Committee's vision of a 'straightforward arrangement' for 'the general body of creditors'.

More difficult questions began to emerge as companies reached out to insolvency practitioners and the insolvency practitioners identified that a major cause of companies' financial difficulties was rental liabilities on leasehold estates. The question here was whether the CVA could be used to compromise *future* rental liabilities. This posed a quite different issue from compromising liabilities that had accrued due before the vote on the CVA was taken. Enterprising insolvency practitioners began to develop CVAs in which landlords' entitlements to future rent were compromised by the terms of the arrangement. As we have seen, while both part 26 schemes of arrangement and part 26A restructuring plan procedures require two court hearings, a CVA proceeds entirely out of court, unless a creditor raises a challenge. A creditor is entitled to raise a challenge on two grounds: that the voluntary arrangement unfairly prejudices their interests, or that

[22] Insolvency Rules 2016 (n 3) r 15.28(5), although secured creditors only vote the unsecured portion of their claim: r 15.31(4) and (5).

[23] ibid r 15.34.

[24] ibid.

[25] Companies Act 2006, ss 895–901.

[26] ibid ss 901A–901L.

[27] *Sovereign Life Assurance Co (in liq) v Dodd* [1892] 2 QB 573 (CA).

[28] *Sea Assets Limited v Perusahaan Perseroan (Persero) PT Perusahaan Penerhangan Garuda Indonesia* [2001] EWCA Civ 1696.

there has been a material irregularity in the shareholder meeting to approve the CVA or the decision procedure by which creditors voted.[29] In *Cancol*, a landlord did challenge a CVA on the basis that the CVA could not affect the landlord's entitlement to future rent.[30] Knox J was not persuaded. He had already concluded that future rent could be included in a voluntary arrangement for an individual.[31] He had based that decision on the breadth of the words 'a scheme of arrangement of his affairs' in the relevant section of the Insolvency Act 1986, and on the fact that the statutory definition of 'creditor' was wide enough to include future payment of rents. Knox J noted that in the context of a CVA, section 1(1) of the Insolvency Act provided:

> The directors of a company … may make a proposal under this Part to the company and to its creditors for a composition or satisfaction of its debts or a scheme of arrangement of its affairs (from here on referred to, in either case, as a 'voluntary arrangement').[32]

Considering the breadth of this description, and that the definition of 'creditor' was wide enough to include future payment of rents, Knox J was content that it was possible to include future rent in CVAs. In *March Estates*, Lightman J agreed, saying:

> A voluntary arrangement may postpone, modify or extinguish the lessor's right as a creditor of the company to the reserved rent whether past or future (see *Re Cancol Ltd* [1995] BCC 1133) and excuse the company (whether original lessee or assignee) personally from performance. The voluntary arrangement in such a case by operation of law absolves the lessee from, or limits or postpones, his personal liability.[33]

At the end of the day, while the Cork Report used qualified descriptions of a 'straightforward arrangement' intended for 'the general body of creditors' and for use by 'small companies', none of these qualifications appear in the legislation, which is drawn in rather broad terms. Thus, a decisive first step was taken along the road to developing the landlord CVA.

However, the Court of Appeal in *Thomas v Ken Thomas* potentially threw something of a spanner in the works.[34] That case concerned the landlord's right to forfeit the lease. In an important, obiter passage Neuberger LJ observed:

> There is no doubt that the rent which accrued due but was not paid, before the CVA was proposed in this case, would be expected to be caught, at least in its capacity as debt, within the CVA. As at present advised, it appears to me that the rent falling due after the CVA should by no means necessarily be expected to be caught by the terms of the CVA, even if it is capable of being so caught (as was held at first instance in *In re Cancol Ltd* [1996] 1 All ER 37). It strikes me that, at least normally, it would seem wrong in principle that a tenant should be able to trade under a CVA for the benefit of its past creditors, at the present and future expense of its landlord. If the tenant is to continue occupying the landlord's property for the purposes of trading under the CVA (and hopefully trading out of the CVA) he should normally, as it currently appears to me, expect to pay the full rent to which the landlord is contractually

[29] Insolvency Act 1986, s 6.
[30] *Re Cancol Ltd* [1995] BCC 1133 (Ch).
[31] *Doorbar v Alltime Securities Ltd* [1994] BCC 994.
[32] Isolvency Act 1986, s 1(1), cited in *Re Cancol* (n 30) 1137.
[33] *March Estates plc v Gunmark* [1996] 2 BCLC 1 (Ch).
[34] *Thomas v Ken Thomas Ltd* [2006] EWCA Civ 1504, [2007] Bus LR 429.

> entitled – see by analogy, in the administration context, *In re Atlantic Computer Systems plc* [1992] Ch 505, 542–543 and, in a liquidation context, *In re ABC Coupler & Engineering Co Ltd (No 3)* [1970] 1 WLR 702. Therefore as at present advised, I consider that a CVA should so provide, or if it does not provide, in the absence of special circumstances the landlord may well be entitled to object to the proposals as unreasonable.[35]

Notwithstanding that the passage is obiter, it is, nonetheless, from the Court of Appeal and might have been expected to give insolvency practitioners pause for thought. The passage does not suggest that Neuberger LJ thought that *Cancol* was wrong, and that future rent could not be included in a CVA. Rather, it suggests that it would generally be unfair to include it. Yet insolvency practitioners clearly did not agree, and CVAs continued to be proposed in which future rent was compromised.

This resulted in two rather notorious cases: *Powerhouse*[36] and *Miss Sixty*.[37] In the *Powerhouse* case, the directors proposed to close 35 underperforming electrical retail sites and to continue trading out of 53 more profitable sites. The landlords of the closed stores had the benefit of a guarantee from Powerhouse's parent company, but the CVA sought to 'strip' the landlords of the benefit of this guarantee. Perhaps unsurprisingly, the landlords raised a challenge, and Etherton J held the arrangement to be unfairly prejudicial, given that the landlords were worse off in the CVA than they would have been in a winding up.[38] Yet he did not cast doubt on the jurisdiction to include future rent in the CVA. The facts of *Miss Sixty* were similar, and Henderson J found the arrangement to be unfairly prejudicial on similar grounds.

In the *Powerhouse* judgment, Etherton J compared the position in the CVA with what would have happened if a part 26 scheme of arrangement had been used instead. He noted that in a scheme of arrangement, the landlords would have been a class of their own and would have vetoed any scheme; and the scheme would not have included creditors who were to be paid in full. The result was only different under the CVA because the creditors formed a single class, including those creditors who were to be paid in full, outvoting the relevant landlords. This could have been another vital turning point for the development of landlord CVAs. Insolvency practitioners might have interpreted Etherton J's comments as meaning that, even though separate class meetings did not need to be held, the courts would look at the result that would have been achieved if the arrangement had proceeded as a part 26 scheme of arrangement rather than a CVA. Indeed, there are some signs of concern for this in the cases immediately after the *Powerhouse* and *Miss Sixty* judgments. Thus, in the Schefenacker proposal, not only was the CVA conditional on the statutory majority at the creditors' meeting but it also required the support of more than 75 per cent of the bondholders.[39]

Yet Schefenacker remained an outlier. It was crucial to the success of many landlord CVAs that all creditors voted together in a single class, because this enabled the votes of unimpaired or barely impaired creditors to push the CVA through if the landlords did

[35] Ibid [34].

[36] *Prudential Assurance Co Ltd v PRG Powerhouse Ltd* [2007] EWHC 1002 (Ch), [2007] Bus LR 1771.

[37] *Mourant & Co Trustees Ltd v Sixty UK Ltd (in admin)* [2010] EWHC 1890 (Ch), [2010] BCC 882.

[38] *Powerhouse* (n 36) [81].

[39] K Baird and LK Ho, 'Company Voluntary Arrangement: the Restructuring Trends' (2007) 20(8) *Insolvency Intelligence* 124.

not achieve the statutory majority as a group. Moreover, landlord CVA technology was becoming increasingly sophisticated. As we have seen, the Powerhouse and Miss Sixty CVAs divided stores into those that were to be closed and those that were to be retained. Increasingly, however, leases were divided into three or more categories: sites that were to be retained, where rent would be paid in full; sites that would be closed; and sites where landlords were asked to accept a compromise on the full rent. If class constitution principles from schemes of arrangement had been followed, this would, in many cases, have resulted in multiple classes of landlords, each with a veto right over the scheme (the ability to cram down a dissenting class has only recently been introduced in the new part 26A restructuring plan procedure inserted into the Insolvency Act 1986 by the Corporate Insolvency and Governance Act 2020). Thus, landlord CVAs continued to be developed in the retail, hotel and casual dining sectors in ever greater numbers, with creditors voting as a single class. Inga West has estimated that, from 2009 to 2017, somewhere around 35 landlord CVAs were approved.[40]

A vital question with which these CVAs grappled was the value to be put on the landlord's claim for the purposes of voting. Even with all unimpaired creditors voting for the full amount of their claims, in many cases, if the aggregate future rental stream determined the size of the landlords' vote they could be expected to outvote the other creditors. The Insolvency Rules provide that if a debt is of an unliquidated or unascertained amount it shall be valued at £1 for the purpose of voting on a CVA proposal, unless the chair of the meeting or the convenor of the vote puts a higher amount on it.[41] Insolvency practitioners and their lawyers treated future rent as unliquidated and unascertained because the landlord had the right to terminate the lease at some point in the future. In *Re Park Air Services Plc*,[42] the court had been required to determine the value of the landlord's claim for loss following disclaimer of a lease. The House of Lords decided that the landlord's claim for future rent should be discounted following a relatively complex formula. Insolvency practitioners began to apply the formula across the portfolio of properties. Yet they did not stop there. A further 75 per cent discount was then typically applied for voting purposes. The justification for this discount was that it represented the uncertainty of the landlords' losses – although, of course, this is also part of the motivation for the *Park Air Services* formula.[43] Crucially, however, no challenge was brought, and the approach rapidly became relatively standard in the market. Of course, it reduced still further the relative weight of the landlord vote when

[40] I West, 'The Evolution of Landlord CVAs: At A Tipping Point?' (Insolvency Lawyers' Association Conference, 23 April 2021, on file with the author).

[41] Insolvency Rules 2016 (n 3) r 15.31(3). Note that before the Small Business, Enterprise and Employment Act 2015 (the 'SBEE Act'), creditors voted on a CVA proposal at a physical meeting. The SBEE Act largely abolished compulsory meetings in English corporate insolvency and replaced them with various decision-making procedures. A CVA cannot be approved by deemed consent. Instead it must be made by a qualifying decision procedure: correspondence; electronic voting; a virtual meeting; or, if one is requisitioned, a physical meeting. A physical meeting can be requisitioned within 5 business days' notice of the decision-making procedure by 10% of creditors by number, 10% of creditors by value or 10 individual creditors. Thus, the reference is to chairman (where there is a meeting) or convenor (where an alternative decision-making procedure is used).

[42] *In re Park Air Services Plc* [2000] 2 AC 172 (HL).

[43] L Raeburn-Smith, 'CVA Briefing 2019' (*British Property Federation*, 2019) at https://bpf-stage.wearewattle.com/media/2630/bpf-cva-briefing-2019.pdf (accessed 22 April 2021) (hereinafter BPF CVA Briefing).

compared with the vote of other creditors, and further facilitated the development of the landlord CVA.

Many of the CVAs in the 2009–17 period subsequently failed, and the company was placed into administration. However, as Walton, Umfreville and Jacobs have noted, this does not necessarily mean that they were not a success of sorts for the landlord creditors.[44] It is possible that the CVA period gave the landlords time to re-let their premises while avoiding paying business rates on an unoccupied property. Similarly, and following the line of argument in Walton, Umfreville and Jacobs again, trade suppliers may have benefitted from a continuing business relationship while having a breathing space in which to reduce reliance on the company as a customer. Whether the CVAs were in the interests of employees poses particularly difficult questions. On the one hand, employees also kept their jobs for a period of time while, as Walton and others put it, being 'on notice' of the company's financial difficulties, so that they may have been more inclined to search for other work or consider other ways of protecting themselves.[45] Yet on the other hand, CVAs give rise to a specific problem for employees, who may find that they lose the right to claim for certain payments from a state fund in the ensuing administration or liquidation because the administration or liquidation was preceded by a CVA.[46] Overall, it is difficult to know what 'success' looks like. Yet one thing stands out: throughout this entire period there was no significant court challenge to the emerging landlord CVA.

In 2018–19, the number of landlord CVAs rose dramatically: Inga West has estimated that there were around 33 cases in a two-year period.[47] And there were changes to the typical terms during this period. Both the rise in cases and the change in terms were prompted by changing commercial conditions. By this time, the rise of online shopping, increases in business rates and Brexit were all putting considerable pressure on the high street. Landlord CVAs began to include more aggressive rent reductions and a larger proportion of compromised leases.[48] Yet the commercial proposition may have begun to change for landlords too. In the 2009–17 period it was tentatively suggested that landlords may have seen some benefit in having a period in which the premises were still occupied, so that the landlord did not become liable for business rates, but during which the landlord could search for a new tenant. By 2018–19 conditions on the high street were such that the search for a new tenant was, in many cases, extremely challenging. Coupled with the more aggressive terms that were emerging in CVA proposals, landlords became increasingly unhappy with the development of what practitioners began to see as a 'product'. Indeed, the British Property Federation (BPF) published a paper containing a series of swingeing criticisms of the development of the landlord CVA.[49] The briefing alleged that landlord CVAs amounted at an abuse of the CVA process.[50]

[44] Walton, Umfreville and Jacobs (n 7) 50.
[45] ibid.
[46] D French, 'Something a bit Niffy – the ERA, the RPO and a failed CVA' (2013) 26(4) *Insolvency Intelligence* 60
[47] West (n 40).
[48] ibid.
[49] BPF CVA Briefing (n 43).
[50] ibid [4].

The BPF raised five specific criticisms: lack of transparency; manipulation of the vote; lack of effective restructuring; lack of oversight; and lack of legislative clarity. All of these implicated the insolvency practitioners who were devising and promoting the landlord CVA. Insofar as transparency was concerned, the BPF alleged:

> A CVA proposal document typically runs in excess of 200 pages, yet, there is almost always a lack of quality financial information regarding the company's financial status, the basis for future funding to support a successful restructuring and the assessment of profitability applied to the properties in its property portfolio. All of this information is available to the company, and often made available to secured creditors, but is not given to the unsecured landlord creditors being asked to vote and support turnaround.[51]

The BPF alleged that landlords had every right to be suspicious of the CVA proposal in the absence of this financial information. Indeed, it suggested that many of its members had decided to exercise a right offered in a CVA to break the lease, rather than accept the compromised rent, only to be offered a higher rent than that payable under the original lease.[52] Of course, one of the principal roles of the insolvency practitioner, as nominee, is to opine on whether the proposal should be considered at a meeting of shareholders and by the company's creditors.[53] For this purpose he is provided with a copy of the CVA proposal and a statement of the company's affairs.[54] We would expect that the insolvency practitioner would be paying close attention to disclosure and transparency: ensuring that creditors are provided with sufficient information to decide whether they should support the proposal or not. And, as we have seen, in practice the insolvency practitioner is likely to have a more significant advisory role than the legislation might imply and will be closely involved in negotiations with creditors. Overall, then, the BPF's criticisms are criticisms of the role of the insolvency practitioner. Later, the BPF makes the point explicitly:

> Some [insolvency practitioners (IPs)] working on CVAs for major retailers still though do not engage with us, or even individual property owners effected, or seem to believe that one can be substituted for the other. Even those IPs we consider to be relatively good at engaging often only bring proposals to property owners a matter of days before launch, even though we know they work on these proposals for months in advance.[55]

The BPF next alleges that the way in which the landlords' vote is calculated for the purposes of the CVA amounts to a 'manipulation of the vote'.[56] The focus of the complaint is on legislative reform. Yet, once again, as we have seen, the legislation provides considerable discretion to the chairman or convenor in deciding how to calculate votes for unascertained or unliquidated claims.[57] It is insolvency practitioners, and their advisers, who have developed the voting mechanics in landlord CVAs. If the BPF considers that the mechanism that has emerged is blatantly unfair then, once again, this is a criticism of the insolvency practitioner profession in promoting it. The BPF moves on to

[51] ibid [13].
[52] ibid [16].
[53] Insolvency Act 1986, s 2(2)(b).
[54] ibid s 2(3).
[55] BPF CVA Briefing (n 43) [23].
[56] ibid [25]–[32].
[57] Above n 41 and accompanying text.

consider the fact that many CVAs do not result in an effective restructuring. Indeed, we have already seen that many of the landlord CVAs have subsequently failed. The BPF notes that 'CVAs do not require firms, or indeed their IPs, to adequately assess why they are failing'.[58] It is true that this is not an explicit requirement in the somewhat skeletal legislative provisions for CVAs. Nonetheless, it is reasonable to assume that a nominee should only recommend a proposal if he is confident that it is in the interests of creditors to support it. However, in this context we have seen that more nuanced responses might be made to the BPF's arguments. Indeed, it has been tentatively suggested that many of the CVAs in the 2009–17 period may have been in the interests of landlords, who had a period to re-let without responsibility for unpaid business rates. It may be that it was only as market conditions deteriorated, and prospects of re-letting diminished, that this no longer suited a landlord's commercial demands. This might explain why no challenges were raised during this period, and why many landlords did vote in favour of the early landlord CVAs. We will return to this point later because, if it is right, landlords arguably only have themselves to blame for the development of the 'product': by supporting its development at a stage when it met their commercial needs, they allowed practices to become entrenched that they wished to walk away from later. For the moment, however, the central point is that the BPF's criticisms firmly implicate the insolvency practitioner in developing what it sees as an abusive and unfair process.

The BPF then squarely attacks the intermediary role of the insolvency practitioner in the CVA process. Paragraph 38 of its briefing goes to the heart of the matter:

> In many cases, IPs … abdicate … responsibility and claim that CVAs are a company led process and it is not for them to assess fairness or scrutinise the terms of the proposal, or indeed, the financial information upon which CVAs are based. This is deeply concerning. As an out of court process, creditors rely on the IP to be the 'honest broker' and provide independent oversight of the CVA in the interests of creditors, as is the case in other insolvency situations. This is not happening.[59]

This, then, is the issue with which this chapter is concerned. The insolvency practitioner is conceived of in the legislation as the intermediary between the company and the creditors in the absence of the court. The nominee acts as the gatekeeper, determining that the proposal is one the shareholders and creditors should vote on. It seems somewhat extraordinary if insolvency practitioners are denying this aspect of their role. Yet, as the developing argument in this chapter is beginning to show, in practice the insolvency practitioner fulfils a role that is closer to that of adviser for his client (the company) than a neutral intermediary between the company and the creditors. Companies approach insolvency practitioners with a specific problem: the need to reduce rents on their commercial property sites. Insolvency practitioners act as advisers to the company in crafting a response to the problem. Starting in earnest in 2009, they adapt the CVA for this purpose. They take what was intended to be a procedurally straightforward tool for small companies and adapt it to solve a relatively complex problem for some very large companies. Initially, this is supported by many in the landlord community, but as conditions in the market worsen, cases rise and terms move against landlords,

[58] BPF CVA Briefing (n 43) [33].
[59] ibid [38].

landlords' views against landlord CVAs harden. Unsurprisingly, perhaps, the next thing that happens in our story is that a significant legal challenge to landlord CVAs is finally launched.

The challenge arose in the context of the Debenhams CVA in 2019.[60] The first ground of challenge revisited the question of whether future rent could be included in a CVA. Norris J noted the obiter remarks in *Thomas*, but also noted that *Cancol* had not been overruled so that he should, as a matter of precedent, follow it unless it was wrong.[61] Norris J was at pains to make clear that he thought *Cancol* was right. He concluded:

> 'Future rent' is a pecuniary liability (although not a presently provable debt) to which the company may become subject by reason of the covenant to pay rent in the existing lease: whilst the term endures the company is 'liable' for the rent, and the fact that in future the landlord may bring the term to an end by forfeiture does not mean that there is no present 'liability' … As a matter of jurisdiction, 'future rent' can be included in a CVA.[62]

For reasons that are not clear from the judgment, no argument seems to have been raised in *Debenhams* about either the practice of voting as a single class or the discount that was applied to the landlords' vote. Yet challenges were raised on the fairness of compromising the landlords' liability when other general, unsecured creditors were unimpaired. This is, indeed, perhaps closer to Neuberger LJ's observation in *Thomas*, in which he doubted the fairness of trading from the premises at a discounted rent for the benefit of other, general, unsecured creditors.

Earlier cases had concluded that a CVA was not unfair simply because it differentiated between creditors. In *Cancol*, Knox J said 'I do not consider that it is unfair within the meaning of the section to make a differentiation between members of the class of creditors with future claims on the basis proposed'.[63] At first instance in *Wimbledon Football Club*, Lightman J stated that the 'existence of unequal or differential treatment of creditors of the same class will not constitute unfairness'.[64] In *Powerhouse*, Etherton J stated that 'the fact that a CVA involves differential treatment of creditors will not necessarily be sufficient to establish unfair prejudice'.[65] Norris J agreed that a CVA that differentiated between creditors was not automatically unfair, stating that 'the CVA was introduced to provide greater flexibility for companies in financial difficulty'.[66] He thus added his voice to the chorus proclaiming that the relevant issue was not whether a CVA that differentiated between creditors was automatically unfair, but rather whether the differentiation was substantively fair on the facts.

Setting this conclusion against the long line of cases with which it agrees, it is tempting to see this as an obvious conclusion. Yet returning to the Cork Report gives pause for thought. As already discussed, the bulk of chapter 7 of the Cork Report is concerned with individual voluntary arrangements. It is quite true that the Cork Committee advocated for flexibility in that context – particularly the flexibility for friends or relatives

[60] *Discovery (Northampton) Ltd v Debenhams Retail Ltd* [2019] EWHC 2441 (Ch), [2020] BCC 9.
[61] ibid [60].
[62] ibid [60]–[61].
[63] *Cancol* (n 30).
[64] *Inland Revenue Commissioners v The Wimbledon Football Club Ltd* [2004] EWHC 1020 (Ch) [18].
[65] *Powerhouse* (n 36) [88].
[66] ibid [65].

of the debtor to provide funds for the creditors if bankruptcy can be avoided.[67] In a paragraph referred to in the Court of Appeal by Neuberger LJ in *Wimbledon Football Club*,[68] the Cork Committee said that its proposal for an individual voluntary arrangement offered

> far more flexibility than is available in a creditors' voluntary winding up with regard to the type of proposal capable of being submitted to and accepted by the creditors or some of them: for example, a basis of distribution other than *pari passu* may be adopted.[69]

Neuberger LJ appears to have read across from this paragraph, which relates to individual voluntary arrangements, to the proposal, later in the Cork Report, to adapt the procedure for companies.[70] Yet it is not at all clear from the Report that the Cork Committee intended to read across from one application of the voluntary arrangement to the other in this way. Indeed, the comments in the Report that the Committee saw the company adaptation as being used 'where the scheme is a simple one involving a composition or moratorium or both for the general body of creditors'[71] suggests that perhaps it did not see the company adaptation of the individual voluntary arrangement as being used where the composition differentiated between creditors. For that purpose, a company could turn to the scheme of arrangement. Thus, it is suggested here that what was crucial was the interpretation put on the legislation by the insolvency practitioner community and its legal advisers. The exceptional brevity of the statutory provisions left significant room for professional interpretation. Insolvency practitioners, approached by companies facing the specific difficulty of over-renting, saw a chance to adapt the CVA to address the problem. The structure of the CVA means that challenges were few and far between. And no one appears to have challenged the read across from part of the Cork Report addressing individual voluntary arrangements to the three, extraordinarily brief paragraphs on adapting them for companies. By the time Norris J considered the case for automatic unfairness in *Debenhams*, the narrative that the CVA provides flexibility and the interpretation that the statute permits differential treatment, notwithstanding that all creditors vote as a single class, had firmly taken hold.

Thus, Norris J moved on to what he saw as the relevant question: whether the offer to landlords in the *Debenhams* case was substantively unfair. Three reasons led him to conclude that it was not. The first reason is evidence that the offer reflected the market rent for the premises (which no one appears to have disputed). Norris J drew a contrast between the compromise offered to landlords and the position of other suppliers, 'who provided goods under "one-off" contracts or "short-term" supply deals that would naturally reflect the current market price for such supplies'.[72] Second, and importantly, he noted that all of the landlords had been provided with the opportunity to break the lease and exercise a right of re-entry if they did not like the terms. There was some debate around the notice period and terms set if a landlord exercised such a right to determine the lease, and once again Norris J emphasised the concept of a market rent. Norris J also

[67] Cork Report (n 1) [351].
[68] *Wimbledon Football Club* (n 64) [52].
[69] Cork Report (n 1) [364(2)].
[70] ibid [429].
[71] ibid [430].
[72] *Debenhams* (n 60) [66].

applied the 'vertical comparator' used by Etherton J in *Powerhouse*:[73] he compared the position of the landlords under the CVA with their position in administration. The analysis was somewhat complicated by the requirement for landlords to pay rates on empty properties, but Norris J referred to 'the unchallenged evidence of Mr Tucker that … the "vertical comparator" is satisfied'.[74]

Later in the judgment Norris J returned to the 'horizontal comparator' to which Etherton J referred in *Powerhouse*:[75] this exercise involves comparing what the landlords are receiving with what other, unsecured creditors are receiving. Norris J was unconvinced of the case of unfairness because the landlords had suffered a compromise but trade creditors were unimpaired. In its evidence, the company focused on 'contagion risk'. 'Contagion risk', in this context, means the risk that once trade creditors are concerned that they may be compromised, they will take steps to protect themselves such as refusing supply or tightening credit terms. This will lead, in turn, to poor customer experience and brand damage.[76] Counsel for the landlords argued that the company was trying to sweep too many creditors within this 'contagion risk' justification. He highlighted that there were other unsecured creditors, such as a minicab firm, a firm of accountants and a firm of solicitors, who could scarcely be said to pose this risk.[77] Norris J dealt with this in a passage that is worth quoting at length:

> [I]n my judgment both the directors and the nominees were entitled to look at the matter in the round having regard to the likely reaction of the 1600 suppliers of goods and services, rather than to single out a small number of individual suppliers for separate treatment where such separate treatment would make a wholly immaterial contribution to the outcome. As Mr Haskell indicated in cross-examination, the question was not whether their supplies were critical to the business but whether their treatment was critical to the success of the CVA.[78]

Thus, Norris J was content that there was no substantive unfairness in the proposal, particularly having regard to the right for landlords to break the lease and re-enter, and that there was no substantive unfairness in the differential treatment between landlords and other, general unsecured creditors. This left just one important argument: whether the CVA could remove a landlord's right of forfeiture. Norris J held that it could not, as this was a proprietary right.[79]

The *Debenhams* decision did have an impact on the market, and on the terms proposed for landlord CVAs. It had made clear that the landlords' right to break the lease and re-enter if they did not like the terms on offer was important for the finding on substantive fairness. After *Debenhams*, therefore, it became usual to include a break clause in the CVA terms. *Debenhams* had also established that a CVA could not remove a right of forfeiture, so that this term was no longer included in post-*Debenhams* CVAs. In *Thomas*, Neuberger LJ had expressed the view that where rent is compromised by the CVA, the right of forfeiture can only be exercised if the compromised rent is not

[73] *Powerhouse* (n 36) [75]–[85].
[74] *Debenhams* (n 60) [72].
[75] *Powerhouse* (n 36) [75], [86]–[96].
[76] *Debenhams* (n 60) [106].
[77] ibid [107].
[78] ibid.
[79] ibid [91]

paid, rather than if the full rent is not paid.[80] And Norris J agreed with this assessment in *Debenhams*, saying '[t]he CVA can modify any pecuniary obligations upon breach of which the right of re-entry may be exercised; and the right will then be exercisable only in relation to the pecuniary obligation as so modified'.[81] Nonetheless, the bargaining landscape shifted slightly after *Debenhams*, as a company must now take the risk in the CVA that landlords will either exercise their break rights or exercise their rights of forfeiture, so that the business may be left with insufficient sites. At around the same time, Zacaroli J decided, in a scheme of arrangement case, that it was not possible for a tenant to terminate a lease and force a surrender.[82] We might wonder why a landlord would not accept a surrender if a tenant stopped paying rent. The answer is that the landlord becomes liable for business rates on the unoccupied property and so, if it considers that it will have difficulty re-letting the premises, may prefer to leave the tenant in occupation. Once again, insolvency practitioners and their advisers found a route through: it now became common for CVAs to provide that certain premises would be closed, and no rent would be paid, but that the lease was not surrendered.

Just as this chapter was being written, Zacaroli J delivered important judgments in response to challenges to the New Look and Regis CVAs.[83] The *New Look* challenge engaged, for the first time, with legislative intent and the comments in the Cork Report. Zacaroli J could find nothing to justify reading the legislation down to small companies and 'simple' compromises: a CVA could differentiate between creditors. And, in common with other post-*Debenhams* CVAs, landlords were offered a break right in the New Look CVA that prevented the proposal from being automatically unfair. Thus, *New Look* may be seen as a vindication of the landlord CVA. Yet in *New Look*, the statutory majority was secured by the votes of holders of senior secured notes (SSNs) – which Zacaroli J found to have been compromised by a related scheme of arrangement, with nothing offered in respect of the unsecured portion of the debt. In short, this was not a case in which the statutory majority was achieved through the votes of a class that was unimpaired or barely impaired. Thus, there are reasons to suspect *New Look* is not the end of the story, and it will be interesting to see how, if at all, it influences subsequent landlord CVAs. *Regis* sheds light on two issues we have discussed in this chapter. First, Zacaroli J held that one of the joint supervisors of the arrangement had paid inadequate attention to the justification for treating a connected creditor as a crucial and, therefore, unimpaired creditor. This was not only unfairly prejudicial to those creditors whose rights were impaired;[84] it also amounted to a breach of duty.[85] Second, while he did not find that any consequences flowed from the decision, Zacaroli J found that a blanket discount of 75 per cent applied to landlords' claims for the purposes of voting was not justified.[86] We will return to both aspects of the *Regis* decision when we consider the implications of our account.

[80] *Thomas* (n 34) [39]–[47].
[81] *Debenhams* (n 60) [99].
[82] *Re Instant Cash Loans Ltd* [2019] EWHC 2795 (Ch).
[83] *Lazari Properties 2 Ltd v New Look Retailers Ltd* [2021] EWHC 1209 (Ch); *Carraway Guildford (Nominee A) Ltd v Regis UK Limited* [2021] EWHC 1294 (Ch).
[84] *Regis* (n 83) [160].
[85] ibid [206]–[207].
[86] ibid [166].

What is important, for the purposes of the argument developed in this chapter, is the evolutionary history of the landlord CVA and the role the insolvency practitioners have played in its development. If we date the recent trend for landlord CVAs to 2009,[87] over 20 years elapsed during which the 'product' was developed with very little judicial review. The question that arises is whether insolvency practitioners have leveraged their gatekeeper intermediary role to shape the CVA in the interests of companies in financial distress that have approached them for advice – and the implications if they have.

IV. The Insolvency Practitioner as Gatekeeper Intermediary versus Company Adviser

The first thing to note is that the requirement to appoint an insolvency practitioner as a nominee in a CVA already defines the CVA as an insolvency process, requiring the insolvency practitioner's expertise. This contrasts with some other restructuring procedures in English law that are frequently used to restructure the liabilities of financially distressed companies. Neither the part 26 scheme of arrangement,[88] nor the part 26A restructuring plan procedure[89] requires the appointment of an insolvency practitioner. Insolvency practitioners are appointed in these procedures in practice. This occurs particularly where an operational restructuring is contemplated, and an estimated outcome statement is required for the court to show what creditors would be expected to receive by way of distribution in an insolvency process if the scheme or restructuring plan were not to be sanctioned.[90] Yet as there is no formal role for insolvency practitioners, these procedures are not exclusively their domain. Indeed, schemes and restructuring plan procedures may be driven by investment banks and lawyers, rather than by insolvency practitioners, particularly if the restructuring is limited to financial, rather than operational, liabilities. The CVA, in contrast, offers what Larson calls a 'structural position' that 'allows a group of experts to define and construct particular areas of social reality, under the guise of universal validity conferred on them by their expertise'.[91]

This is particularly potent for insolvency practitioners, because they face increasing competition for work. Until comparatively recently, insolvency practitioners enjoyed a virtual monopoly over advice to financially distressed firms in the United Kingdom. If we were to turn the clock back to the 1990s, banks were the dominant lenders to UK industry, and if a borrower faced financial difficulties, the bank would typically turn to an insolvency practitioner with whom it had a relationship for advice. Most restructurings

[87] West (n 40).

[88] Companies Act 2006, pt 26, ss 895–901.

[89] ibid pt 26A, ss 901A–901L.

[90] See, eg, the role of Deloitte in the Virgin Active pt 26A restructuring plan procedure: *Re Virgin Active Holdings Ltd* [2021] EWHC 814 (Ch).

[91] MS Larson, *The Rise of Professionalism: A Sociological Analysis* (Berkley and Los Angeles, CA, University of California Press, 1977), cited in CB Harrington, 'Outlining a Theory of Legal Practice' in Cain and Harrington (eds) (n 19) 49, 57.

occurred out of court; but if a restructuring could not be agreed, the insolvency practitioner would be appointed as administrative receiver to sell the business and assets, or assets, and distribute the proceeds. In short, the insolvency practitioner's place in the firmament was secure.[92] However, changes in the financial and corporate markets have altered the nature of the corporate reorganisation landscape,[93] with the result that insolvency practitioners face much greater competition for work. We have already touched on the point that investment banks have been an important force in schemes of arrangement and part 26A restructuring plan procedures in the financial reorganisations of the last decade. At the same time, because these procedures do not require a practitioner to be licensed, a number of boutique and other advisory firms and individuals have sprung up, styled 'turnaround specialists'.[94]

In this context, it is unsurprising that insolvency practitioners increasingly focus on what Harrington calls 'market sources of power'.[95] In other words, as the boundaries between professionals shift, insolvency practitioners have an interest in developing tools in which they have a statutory intermediary role. At the same time, like the lawyers Cain writes about, insolvency practitioners face 'persistent demands for assistance, coupled with (later) threats [from clients] of taking their business elsewhere'.[96] Thus, reflecting both Harrington's and Cain's accounts of the reasons motivating lawyers' development of the law, we can situate the evolutionary history of the development of the landlord CVA within the struggle between insolvency practitioners and non-insolvency practitioners, and between the insolvency practitioners themselves, for work. The insolvency practitioner emerges from this account in a role more closely aligned with an adviser for a client than a gatekeeper intermediary. The question is, of course, does it matter?

It matters profoundly if this turn has caused insolvency practitioners to slough off their independence entirely, translating the objectives and demands of the company into adaptations of insolvency procedures that may never have been in the contemplation of the legislature and that are not in the interests of the creditors. Walton, Umfreville and Jacobs' survey results suggest that many stakeholders feel that this is, indeed, what has happened. As we have seen, they report that '[s]ome practitioners felt that nominees may have a self-interest in recommending a CVA';[97] '[t]he problem identified was that stakeholders do not always have full confidence in the recommendations of the nominee';[98] '[s]ome unsecured creditors felt that not all nominees were sufficiently rigorous in assessing the rights of some (often unconnected) creditors to vote on CVA proposals with the result that potentially fictitious debts were allowed';[99] and '[t]here was often a lack of confidence in the judgment of the IP when providing an opinion on

[92] For a more detailed description of the role of the insolvency practitioner in England at this time, see S Paterson, *Corporate Reorganization Law and Forces of Change* (Oxford, Oxford University Press, 2020) esp ch 2, 33–45.

[93] ibid, in the sections of the book dealing with England.

[94] Finch and Milman (n 18) 247.

[95] Harrington (n 91) 62.

[96] M Cain, 'The Symbol Traders' in Cain and Harrington (eds) (n 19) 36.

[97] Walton, Umfreville and Jacobs (n 7) 56.

[98] ibid.

[99] ibid 63.

the validity of the company in the CVA'.[100] The concept of the insolvency practitioner seeking remunerative work is captured in serious complaints about fees:

> It was commented that IP fees are often seen as high. In addition, such fees are usually fully payable before any dividends to unsecured creditors. The effect of this is that creditors often see no dividend or a much reduced dividend even when the IP may receive full payment or close to it.[101]

And, as we have seen, the BPF report into landlord CVAs was damning in its conclusions and in its assessment of the role that insolvency practitioners have played.[102]

Yet at the same time, insolvency practitioners would vigorously defend the adaptation of the CVA to address the specific problem of over-renting, in a way that saves the company for the employees, trade suppliers and those landlords whose sites remain in use, albeit potentially at a compromised rent. They would point to the now entrenched right of landlords to take back the property and attempt to re-let it if they do not like the terms of the proposal. And they would argue that including a wider group of unsecured creditors in the case will simply increase cost and time, potentially risking the rescue, without materially affecting the result for landlords.[103] We have not particularly focused on the outcome for shareholders in this chapter: there are issues to be explored that will need to wait for another day. Yet, overall, insolvency practitioners would argue that the landlord CVA produces a fair result. To the extent that the landlord gets a tough deal, that is a consequence of the realities of the marketplace. This perspective is clearly reflected in Zacaroli J's 2021 *New Look* judgment, in which he expressly recognises that it is the insolvency of the company that means that rent cannot be paid, and that landlords who do not like the terms on offer can exercise their break rights and try their luck in the market.[104] It is certainly the case that one is hard-pressed to find a wealth of examples of businesses shrugging off leasehold liabilities and performing spectacularly in their post-CVA life. A far more common story has been the ultimate failure of the CVA and an insolvency proceeding. As Sandra Frisby puts it, 'principle must give way to pragmatism'.[105] And, as we have seen, there is a hint that in the early years of the development of the landlord CVA, many landlords supported the innovation that provided them with breathing space to find a new tenant without paying rates. If this account is right, it was only as market conditions hardened that landlord attitudes to the CVA also hardened, by which time the landlord CVA had become a developed technique. Thus, we can distinguish the account in this chapter from Alexander Loke's account of intermediaries as gatekeepers in chapter 17. Loke's account relates to intermediaries who fail in their gatekeeping role with obviously deleterious outcomes. In the account in this chapter, there is a question mark as to whether the insolvency practitioner has fulfilled his gatekeeping intermediary role. Yet even if he has not done so, it is not obvious that the outcome has harmed the intended beneficiaries of that role.

[100] ibid.
[101] ibid.
[102] BPF CVA Briefing (n 43) and accompanying text.
[103] For a more detailed analysis of this point, see S Paterson and A Walters, 'Selective Corporate Restructuring Strategy' (2021) at https://papers.ssrn.com/sol3/papers.cfm?abstract_id=3924225 (accessed 16 September 2021).
[104] *New Look* (n 83) [215]–[220].
[105] Frisby (n 7) 362.

But that may not be the important point. If the insolvency practitioner comes to be seen as an adviser to the company, and if creditors (or a significant class of them) are of the view that the gatekeeper intermediary role has been abandoned, there will almost inevitably be calls for a new intermediary to be inserted into the process. This has already occurred in the related area of pre-packaged administration sales, where new regulations demand that a sale of a financially distressed business by an insolvency practitioner acting as administrator must, in certain defined circumstances, be reviewed by an 'evaluator'.[106] And we have seen calls for similar regulation in the CVA field, with Walton, Umfreville and Jacobs reporting stakeholders' questions as to whether some other form of independent assessment of the CVA would be 'useful',[107] and the BPF demanding a second opinion on large CVAs.[108] Ironically, then, if insolvency practitioners exploit their sources of power in a way the stakeholder community regards as an abdication of the statutory gatekeeping role, there is a risk that they will increasingly have to work harder to defend their work as insolvency practitioner work. Indeed, if new gatekeepers are then inserted into the process, insolvency practitioners risk losing their privileged access to this work. Thus, it is suggested, the advisory role cannot entirely usurp the gatekeeper intermediary role, and principle cannot be sacrificed entirely for pragmatism, if insolvency practitioners are to maintain professional boundaries around their specialised work. A fine balance is required.

Ultimately, then, the message of this chapter is for insolvency practitioners. The argument is that insolvency practitioners must take their statutory gatekeeper intermediary role seriously if they wish to retain their privileged status in the fight for insolvency work, and that this is not dependent on their view of the legitimacy of the outcome of the restructuring process. Four specific lessons emerge from our account. First, insolvency practitioners must foster an environment of transparency and engagement with the creditor body, ensuring adequate disclosure of financial information to facilitate assessment of the proposal. Second, they should be seen to be taking the viability of the restructuring promoted in the CVA seriously. Third, they should ensure that creditors have time to consider the proposal. And, finally, they should consider carefully how far to push the boundaries of the legislative scheme, mindful always of the fine balance between their role as advisers for companies in financial distress and their role as gatekeeper intermediaries between companies and their creditors. In this context, a specific area of focus comes into view. It is now well-established in the case law that uneven treatment of otherwise equally ranking creditors does not automatically render a CVA unfair. Yet this is not a passport for insolvency practitioners to abandon any attempt at even-handedness. Insolvency practitioners must be able to justify why certain creditors have been left unimpaired in the proposal: failure to adequately consider this issue will amount to a breach of duty. Although creditors vote as a single class in a CVA, insolvency practitioners must consider whether the votes of unimpaired creditors are being used unfairly to swamp the votes of impaired creditors, notwithstanding their very different interests. And insolvency practitioners must not use arbitrarily high discounts to claims for voting simply to achieve what they may see as their 'client's' objectives.

[106] Administration (Restrictions on Disposal etc to Connected Persons) Regulations 2021 (SI 2021/427).
[107] Walton, Umfreville and Jacobs (n 7) 57.
[108] BPF CVA Briefing (n 43) [40].

Failings in any of these areas are likely to give rise to serious doubts as to the independence and integrity of the insolvency practitioner: core characteristics of any gatekeeping intermediary.

V. Conclusion

The argument has been made in this chapter that the insolvency practitioner is firmly conceived of in the legislation governing CVAs as a gatekeeper intermediary. However, in practice, an insolvency practitioner must also perform an advisory role: advising companies in financial distress on whether the CVA offers a solution to their problems; helping them to develop a proposal; and attempting to broker a negotiation among creditors to secure approval. Thus, a tension emerges between the insolvency practitioner as adviser and the insolvency practitioner as gatekeeper intermediary: it seems unlikely that an insolvency practitioner who has been intimately involved in developing a proposal will decide not to propose it to shareholders and creditors for a vote.

The question the chapter has explored is whether this tension has become particularly strained as insolvency practitioners have developed landlord CVAs. We have seen multiple decision points at which insolvency practitioners could have pulled back from innovations, but it is suggested that in the battle for work in an increasingly crowded advisory market, they have seen real benefit in leveraging the CVA, which is defined as insolvency practitioner work by their statutory role in it, in the interests of winning work from financially distressed companies hoping to address over-rented rental estates. In contrast with Loke's account in chapter 17, it is not obvious that even if this does amount to gatekeeper failure, anyone has been harmed by it. This is because the legitimacy of the landlord CVA is contestable and contested. However, it is suggested that perception may be as important as the reality. Indeed, it suggested that if insolvency practitioners are widely regarded as having abandoned their gatekeeper intermediary role, this may ironically intensify their battle for work rather than soften it. Ultimately, then, the suggestion is that a fine balance must be maintained between the 'useful' insolvency practitioner as adviser and the independent insolvency practitioner as gatekeeper intermediary. Four specific ways in which this balance can be maintained have been suggested: developing an environment of transparency and disclosure; focusing on the viability of the restructuring; ensuring creditors have time to consider the restructuring proposal; and considering carefully how far to push the flexible legislative boundaries.

INDEX

Introductory Note

References such as '178–79' indicate (not necessarily continuous) discussion of a topic across a range of pages. Wherever possible in the case of topics with many references, these have either been divided into sub-topics or only the most significant discussions of the topic are listed. Because the entire work is about 'intermediaries', the use of this term (and certain others which occur constantly throughout the book) as an entry point has been restricted. Information will be found under the corresponding detailed topics.

www.ingramcontent.com/pod-product-compliance
Ingram Content Group UK Ltd.
Pitfield, Milton Keynes, MK11 3LW, UK
UKHW020230290926
15470UKWH00002B/458

9 781509 949090